IBM

AND THE U.S. DATA PROCESSING INDUSTRY

An Economic History

Franklin M. Fisher
James W. McKie
Richard B. Mancke

PRAEGER STUDIES IN
SELECT BASIC INDUSTRIES

PRAEGER SPECIAL STUDIES • PRAEGER SCIENTIFIC

Library of Congress Cataloging in Publication Data

Fisher, Franklin M.
    IBM and the U.S. data processing industry.

    Includes index.
    1. International Business Machines Corporation
—History. 2. Computer industry—United States—History.
I. McKie, James W. II. Mancke, Richard B., 1943-
III. Title. IV. Title: I.B.M. and the United States
data processing industry.
HD9696.C64I4843 1983 338.7'62138195'0973 83-3988
ISBN 0-03-063059-2

Published in 1983 by Praeger Publishers
CBS Educational and Professional Publishing
A Division of CBS, Inc.
521 Fifth Avenue, New York, New York 10175 U.S.A.

456789 052 98765432

Printed in the United States of America
on acid-free paper

ACKNOWLEDGMENTS

As discussed in the introduction, this book is closely based on the "Historical Narrative" that we jointly wrote as part of our testimony in *U.S.* v. *IBM*. As in that testimony, each of us has authored a different part of the book (although we have exchanged comments). In particular, the section on the 1950s was written by Mancke, that on the 1960s by Fisher, and that on the 1970s by McKie.

Our involvement in the IBM antitrust litigation began in 1970 (Fisher) and 1974 (McKie and Mancke) and lasted for many years, the government suit finally being dismissed in January 1982. In the course of that lengthy involvement, we were aided by a great many people. It is impossible to thank all of them in detail, and unfortunately, over so long a time, we cannot recall all the names. We apologize for omissions in what follows, and, of course, the responsibility for errors is ours.

The research here reported is directly based on the very extensive trial record of *U.S.* v. *IBM*, but background preparation was important and extensive. Among those within IBM who assisted us were John F. Akers, Charles J. Bashe, George B. Beitzel, Richard M. Bennett, Jack Bertram, Erich Bloch, Manson Drummond, Richard M. DuBois, Nicholas deB. Katzenbach, Warren Lynde, Thomas F. Mierswa, Earl Orchard, Paul F. Rizzo, Michael deV. Roberts, Nathan Rochester, Francis G. Rodgers, L. I. Spector, Gene J. Takahashi, and Ace W. Vanderwinckel. B. O. Evans was especially helpful as regards the section on the 1970s.

Others in the industry or involved with computers who spoke with us included H. Dean Brown (Zilog), Fred C. Buelow (Microtechnology), James Burkhard (Ball Computer Products), Lou Geiger (Lockheed), Ed Gelbach (Intel), Cuthbert C. Hurd (Cuthbert C. Hurd Associates), Scotty Maxwell (Rockwell), Thomas J. Perkins (Tandem), Neil Peterman (Systems Enhancement Associates), Mel Shader (TRW), Bud Sprague (Applied Magnetics), Paul Teicholz (Guy F. Atkinson), William Terry (Hewlett-Packard), and Leland H. Williams (Triangle Universities Computation Center). Of course, many, many other industry participants and IBM employees testified at the trial or in the private litigation.

Attorneys who guided our preparation, shepherded us on visits to IBM, various other computer companies and to national computer conferences, and who forced us to formulate our ideas clearly included Thomas D. Barr, David Boies, R. John Cooper III, Arnold Messing, and Frederick A. O. Schwartz, Jr. In addition, we owe special thanks to the following, who, in addition to performing some or all of the above functions, were of enormous help in organizing and providing access to the trial record for us: for the section on the 1950s, Roger Cummings; for the 1960s, John E. Beerbower and Morris Waisbrot; for parts of both of these sections, Howard Weber; and, for the 1970s,

Evan Chesler and Richard L. Hoffman. It is impossible adequately to acknowledge the help given by Ronald S. Rolfe in all aspects.

The assistance given by members of the research staff of Charles River Associates was invaluable. Led by Joen E. Greenwood, they provided very considerable assistance in facilitating access to the trial record, particularly in 1980-81. Ms. Greenwood, herself, the late John J. McGowan, and — in the early days — William R. Hughes participated in much of our preparation and contributed to our understanding. Members of the staff who contributed included Stephen Anderson, Jeffrey Ashford, Peter Ashton, Janis Bowersox, Carin Boyer, David Howe, Andrew Kaufman, Rhona Mahoney, Paul Mangano, A. J. Matsuura, Kathleen Moore, Kenneth Morrison, George Newman, Elizabeth Ryan, Patrice San Souci, Joy Sargent, Alice Thompson, Susan Vitka, Scott Williamson, and Robert York. We are especially grateful to Victoria Hamilton, Thomas Reindel, Stephen Kalos, and Roy Marden.

Typing of the book itself was principally done by Paul Church, Barbara Davis, Jane Ann Jones, Bernadette Kelley, Carol McIntire, Elizabeth Walb, and Jean Zafiris. Proofreading assistance was provided by Ruth Pelizzon and Julia Stiffler, and by Ellen and Naomi Fisher.

Proofreading assistance, however, was far from the most important kind of assistance provided by family members. For example, the demands of preparing the testimony on which Mancke's contribution is based caused him to be a frequent absentee father during the first year and one half of his son Max's life. Both Max and his mother, Barbara Hobbie, deserve special thanks for enduring this unplanned dislocation with both grace and good humor. Such dislocations, indeed, were a common experience for all three of us during our involvement in the case, and we are very conscious of the sacrifices made, not only by the Mancke family, but also by Ellen, Abraham, Abigail, and Naomi Fisher, and by Catherine and Ellen McKie. Neither they nor we realized what would be involved when we began this enterprise.

January 1983   **Franklin M. Fisher**
                                                                      Richard B. Mancke
                                                                      James W. McKie

CONTENTS

INTRODUCTION

In its short history of approximately thirty years, the computer industry has become a major feature of the modern economy. Yet that development was not originally foreseen. While the earliest computers provided computational abilities and speeds that seemed remarkable in their day, they were, by today's standards, cumbersome and slow. In addition, early computers were physically large and very expensive, so that it seemed doubtful in the earliest days that more than a handful would ever be used. It was expected that only large universities, defense contractors, and government laboratories and agencies would ever use the strange new device. Indeed, in the early days, many computers were built as one-of-a-kind machines by such users, with only a few companies producing them as commercial ventures.

From such relatively modest beginnings, computers have become increasingly important, pervading every facet of business and scientific activity in what has been termed a new industrial revolution. Indeed, in recent years computers have expanded into use in the home. Modern computer usage far exceeds anything thought possible thirty years ago; indeed, it far exceeds all projections of twenty or even ten years ago. The growth of the computer industry has been nothing short of phenomenal.

This explosion of computer use has not, of course, been an explosion of demand for the relatively cumbersome and expensive machines of the early days. Rather, the history of computers and of the computer industry has been one of continual, rapid, often unanticipated technical change. That change has involved both vast improvements in computer hardware and software and innovation in the ways in which computers can be used. Machines that only fifteen years ago were considered powerful are now obsolete, while computers that equal or surpass them in computing power are now considered small and are cheap enough to be afforded by households.

The computer industry has changed as well. While some of the early manufacturers have exited in whole or in part, a flood of other companies have entered, offering an often bewildering variety of hardware, software, and associated services. Where early computers seemed a venture of doubtful profitability, today the computer industry is very big business indeed – and big business for firms of many different sizes and approaches. The largest of those firms is, of course, IBM; but, while much of the history of the computer industry is the history of IBM, IBM is not, and has never been alone. Only a very myopic view of the computer industry sees its activities, history, and competition as involving only IBM and a handful of others.

The very important role of IBM has been subject to more than one interpretation. In fact, more than one-third of the history of the computer industry occurred while IBM was defending itself in enormously protracted antitrust litigation. That litigation involved both private suits brought by such competitors as Control Data Corporation (CDC), Telex, and Memorex and a vast public antitrust suit brought under Section Two of the Sherman Act by the Antitrust Division of the United States Department of Justice.

U.S. v. *IBM*[1] was brought by the Justice Department in January 1969, in what were literally the waning hours of the Johnson Administration. It ended on January 8, 1982 when William Baxter, the Assistant Attorney General in charge of antitrust stipulated that the case was "without merit." By that time, the suit had been in trial since May 1975, setting an unenviable record for length. Meanwhile, IBM had settled a few of the private suits and won the others, sometimes by directed verdicts.

The IBM antitrust litigation may have been an enormous waste of resources and an exercise in futility so far as any outcome was concerned, but it provided an unparalleled opportunity for research into the economics and history of the computer industry. The record of the government case, which drew upon the private cases, provides a particularly rich source of material. Part of the reason for this is the exhaustive length of the trial record, which reflects the exhaustive (and exhausting) length of the case itself. The trial transcript contains over 104,400 pages, and the parties — with the government often drawing on the results of discovery in the private suits — introduced tens of thousands of documents. Further, that testimony and those documents do not merely concern IBM. Every aspect of the computer industry was involved in one way or another, with witnesses from many different companies. The documents introduced came from an immense variety of sources, including the subpoenaed files of IBM, its competitors and customers, government departments, laboratories, and agencies. It is no exaggeration to say that the trial record is a veritable treasure-trove of material, of a type rarely available to, and still more rarely fully utilized by economists. It is made all the richer by the fact that it comes from an adversary proceeding with each party introducing material to buttress its case and cross-examining witnesses put forward by the other side.

The richness of the trial record is no accident. Following the doctrine laid down in the cases of *Alcoa* and *United Shoe Machinery*, monopolization under Section Two of the Sherman Act can involve acts that, while not wrong in themselves, are deliberately undertaken to achieve or maintain monopoly power.[2] This can lead, as in the IBM case, to a situation in which the plaintiff calls into question every significant act of the defendant as part of a pattern of conduct designed to monopolize, while the defendant seeks to show that the same acts were the natural result of competitive pressures. Since such questions can only be analyzed when viewed against the backdrop of the entire industry, trials that involve them are likely to explore matters quite widely. Where a trial is not tightly controlled by the judge (as the IBM trial certainly was not), and where the plaintiff's allegations are relatively unfocused (as those of the government in *U.S.* v. *IBM* certainly were), it is not surprising that the result, however appalling in terms of the judicial process itself, can produce a record of unparalleled richness for research.[3]

The use of that record, however, is no simple matter. The task involved is an enormous one, and researchers starting afresh may find it overwhelming. Fortunately, the three authors of this book did not have to undertake such a project *de novo*. All three of us were involved in *U.S.* v. *IBM* for many years, and the current book is an edited version of a major piece of testimony that we produced jointly — our "Historical Narrative."[4]

In more detail, the genesis of this book was as follows. All three of us appeared as expert economist witnesses for IBM, and our involvement in the case and study of the industry lasted for many years, with Fisher beginning in 1970 and Mancke and McKie in 1974. In addition, both Fisher and McKie testified on behalf of IBM in the private antitrust litigation that accompanied the government case. When the time came (in 1979-80) for us to prepare our direct testimony for *U.S.* v. *IBM* — testimony that, by agreement between the parties, was to be in written form — it became apparent both that a very considerable amount of factual, historical material would have to be included as the basis for any serious economic analysis and that for each of us separately to attempt to summarize the incredibly voluminous trial record to provide the necessary background would lead to an intolerable duplication (or triplication) of effort. We therefore agreed to divide the labor and jointly produced the "Historical Narrative" from which this book derives. In so doing, we adopted the same division of responsibility which has persisted into the present work: Mancke wrote the history of the 1950s, Fisher the 1960s, and McKie the 1970s.

With this account of its origin in mind as background, it is important to understand what the present book is and what it is not. This is not a book about the IBM case itself. Further, it is not a book that analyzes the economic issues that that case presented. Such analysis was the subject matter of our individual testimonies for which the "Historical Narrative" served as background; a volume based on Fisher's testimony has already been published elsewhere.[5] Rather, this book is our distillation of the source material that must underly any such analysis. It represents our best effort to present the material in the trial record in an organized and chronological fashion so that analysis of the facts can take place.

That is not to say that the present book contains no analysis whatever. It is commonplace that selection and presentation of material involves judgment, and, we hope in our case, analytic judgment. The focus, however, is on the story itself rather than on the issues of economics or public policy that may derive from it. Accordingly, in choosing from the wealth of material that both parties placed in the trial record, we have tried to organize our presentation as objectively as possible.

For of course it has not escaped our attention that our involvement in IBM's defense must make the objectivity of this book open to question. Such involvement is not the typical fashion in which academic economists do research. In this regard, we can say the following. First, each of us has a reputation and an active professional life that stretches well beyond the IBM case; the preservation and enhancement of those reputations provides a consideration greater than any monetary emolument received from IBM. Second, the case is now over. Our involvement in it has terminated. We have recevied no payment from IBM, directly or indirectly, for the writing of this book. Hence, even had we been inclined to shade our testimonial opinions for the sake of our client, we have no monetary reason to continue to do so.

To leave it at that, however, would be to ignore the deeper issue involved. We must recognize the danger that our involvement with the case has led, not to a deliberate departure from objectivity, but to a more subtle process in which we no longer know where objectivity lies. In one sense, of course, we ourselves can never give a fully satisfactory answer to this. We point out, however, that the process that led to the writing of the "Historical Narrative" and hence to the writing of this book was one in which we had complete and untrammeled access to the trial record. Further, as already observed, that record was created by the interaction of both sides, not by IBM alone. This book represents our best attempt objectively to draw on that record.

Whether we have succeeded in that endeavor is not for us to say. In the last analysis this book must speak for itself. We hope, however, that our involvement in IBM's defense will not mean that the book is automatically judged to be partisan. While its origins are unconventional, to condemn this mode of doing research would be to ensure that research of this kind is never done at all, that the kind of treasure represented by the trial record of the IBM case remains forever hidden from view, at the bottom of a sea of litigation.

NOTES

1. *United States* v. *International Business Machines Corporation*, Docket number 69 Civ. (DNE) Southern District of New York.
2. *United States* v. *Aluminum Company of America, et al.*, 149 F. 2d 416 (1945); *United States* v. *United Shoe Machinery Corporation*, 110 F. Supp. 295 (1953).
3. See Steven Brill, "What to Tell Your Friends About *IBM.*" *The American Lawyer*, April 1982, pp. 1, 11-14, 16-17.
4. DX 14971.
5. Franklin M. Fisher, John J. McGowan, and Joen E. Greenwood, *Folded, Spindled, and Mutilated: Economic Analysis and U.S. v. IBM.* Cambridge, MIT Press, 1983.

PART I
THE 1950s

1

FIRST ATTEMPTS TO COMMERCIALIZE COMPUTER SYSTEMS: THE EARLY 1950s

PRECURSORS OF A COMMERCIAL EDP BUSINESS

The first large electronic digital computer, the ENIAC, was developed during World War II at the University of Pennsylvania's Moore School of Electrical Engineering under a contract with the U.S. Army. The team of scientists, mathematicians, and engineers that created the ENIAC was led by J. Presper Eckert and Dr. John W. Mauchly. Their original purpose was to develop an electronic computational machine that could be used by the army's Ballistics Research Laboratory to calculate trajectories for field artillery and bombing tables, a tedious job previously performed by large numbers of mathematicians using desk calculators.[1]

The ENIAC was a physically enormous machine (measuring 100 feet long, 10 feet high, and 3 feet wide, and containing about 18,000 vacuum tubes) thought to be one of the most complicated devices in the world. Indeed, it was so complicated that Enrico Fermi reportedly doubted whether it would run for more than five minutes at a time. In fact, according to one of ENIAC's principal creators, Eckert, the giant computer broke down only about once a day.[2]

The ENIAC differed from prior, sophisticated computational machines that were electromechanical — that is, they performed arithmetical calculations by using electricity to close mechanical relays. ENIAC's use of vacuum tubes rather than electromechanical relays made it faster than its electromechanical predecessors by a factor of at least 100 and, more likely, about 500.[3] In consequence, with ENIAC it was possible to perform a wide range of previously impracticable or impossible calculations.[4]

The ENIAC was programmed by setting switches; whenever its program needed to be changed, the switches, numbering in the thousands, all had to be reset by hand.[5] This limitation was removed by the next major step forward in computing — the development of electronic stored-program digital computers.

A stored program is a series of instructions telling the computer what to do, depending either on the results previously calculated or on the conditions existing at the time the computations are made. In computers based on the stored-program concept, instructions are stored within the machine in the same

3

form as data. The programmed instructions are capable of being stored any-where in the system, of being recalled with the same ease, or of being modified to the extent of the capability of the system.[6] In 1944, while the ENIAC was still under construction, a group based at the Moore School, including Eckert and Mauchly, Dr. Arthur W. Burks, Dr. Herman Goldstine, Adele Goldstine, and, after August 1944, Dr. John von Neumann, began to meet regularly to develop the conceptual design of an internally modifiable, stored-program, digital computer that became known as the EDVAC.[7] The stored-program capability would result in far more computational flexibility than had been known before.

The EDVAC's stored-program concept was developed in detail in a series of papers written by, among others, von Neumann and Herman Goldstine.[8] These papers circulated widely after the war and were the subject of extensive and intense discussion among the close fraternity of people in universities, industry, and government who were working on designing and developing computers.[9] These people communicated with each other about new circuits, new devices, and new computing machines.[10] In 1948 they formed the Association for Computing Machinery to provide a professional organization, as well as an associated scientific publication, to promote and describe the scholarly and pioneering work in computing.[11]

In the late 1940s, following the initial scientific/technical discussion of the EDVAC stored-program concept, many universities, government-related labora-tories, and private firms began to design and develop their own stored-program computers, frequently with government funding. Table 1.1, which does not purport to be all-inclusive, lists 20 nonprofit organizations designing and devel-oping prototype stored-program digital computers in this period. Among the profit-seeking firms pursuing similar activities (often in connection with military or intelligence-gathering and -analyzing projects) were American Telephone and Telegraph (AT&T), Eckert-Mauchly Computer Corporation, Engineering Research Associates, and Raytheon.[12]

POTENTIAL EARLY ENTRANTS INTO THE EDP INDUSTRY

Because of the Great Depression and then World War II, spending by Ameri-cans on consumer durables (including housing) and nonmilitary capital goods was at low levels between 1930 and 1945. As the United States emerged from the war with its capital stock and consumer durables worn out, and a populace that was both eager and able to make up for past economic deprivations, there was a surging demand for those products for which the nation was famous — automobiles, appliances, steel, food, oil, and new construction. Led by surging production in these traditional, prewar basic industries, the U.S. economy experienced rapid economic growth in the decade following World War II.

During World War II the requirements for such important efforts as the development of radar and jet aircraft, as well as the Manhattan Project, had stimulated the growth of firms capable of providing the U.S. government with

Table 1.1. Twenty Nonprofit Organizations Designing and Developing Prototype Stored-Program Digital Computers in the Late 1940s

---

University of Amsterdam
University of California at Berkeley (CALDIC)
University of California at Los Angeles (as operating agency; SWAC)
Cambridge University (EDSAC)
University of Frankfurt
Harvard University (Mark III)
University of Illinois (ORDVAC, ILLIAC)
Institute for Advanced Study at Princeton (IAC computer)
University of Manchester
University of Michigan (MIDAC)
Massachusetts Institute of Technology (Whirlwind)
University of Pennsylvania (EDVAC)
University of Rome
University of Vienna
Federal Polytechnical School in Zurich
Los Alamos Scientific Laboratory (MANIAC)
Patrick Air Force Base (FLAC)
RAND Corporation (JOHNIAC)
National Bureau of Standards (SEAC)
U.S. Naval Research Laboratory

Source: Hurd, Tr. 86, 324-26; Smagorinsky Deposition, pp. 11-13; Plaintiff's Admissions, set II, para. 558.-0-.6; Plaintiff's Admissions, set IV, paras. 48, 121.

complicated, high-technology products incorporating state-of-the-art scientific knowledge. With the rapid demobilization following the war, the markets for most of these products went into eclipse, compelling their manufacturers to shift most of their resources to providing the relatively simple products demanded by the private sector. Nevertheless, the usefulness of high-technology products had been demonstrated during the war and, as the years passed and the Cold War worsened, markets for such products gradually emerged.

By the early 1950s the knowledge and resources necessary to build primitive, stored-program, electronic digital computer systems were widely held, and several firms were in a position to begin developing and supplying these products commercially. The most likely early entrants into the computer business possessed one or more of three attributes: (1) expertise in the electronic and electromechanical technologies necessary to build computers (for instance, vacuum tubes, relays, and transistors); (2) experience in obtaining federal research and development contracts to design and build one-of-a-kind data-processing and/or control systems; and (3) expertise in selling complicated and expensive products to the rather small number of sophisticated organizations thought likely to purchase a computer system.

Categories of firms possessing these attributes included the following: (1) high-technology defense contractors with expertise in designing and building sophisticated electronic control systems who also possessed large, in-house

the Electronic Control Company's products were far beyond their capabilities. They then established a new company, the Eckert-Mauchly Computer Corporation. After doing preliminary design work on what became the UNIVAC, Eckert-Mauchly contracted with Northrop Aviation (which had a contract with the U.S. government) to build a one-of-a-kind computer called the BINAC, to be used for missile navigation. Eckert described the BINAC as "sort of an experimental venture" and, in fact, Northrop ultimately chose to solve its missile navigational problems with gyroscopes.[19]

Eckert-Mauchly made computer history in 1948 by contracting with the Bureau of Standards to build a large-scale, fully automatic, general-purpose computer system called the UNIVAC (Universal Automatic Computer), which was based on the ENIAC and EDVAC development. UNIVAC was intended to be used by the Bureau of the Census to process data collected in the 1950 census.[20] Eckert and Mauchly intended UNIVAC to be the first electronic stored-program computer system commercially available — that is, a standard rather than one-of-a-kind machine, and a product available for sale to anyone desiring to acquire it.[21] The first UNIVACs were beginning to be manufactured at the time of Eckert-Mauchly's acquisition by Remington Rand in 1950. The first delivery was in 1951, to the Bureau of the Census, at a purchase price of about $1 million.[22]

In testifying about the UNIVAC (subsequently called UNIVAC I), Alan Perlis described it as a "creative masterpiece" because it demonstrated the "extraordinarily important recognition" that "The computer which had been born to carry out ballistics calculations for the Army was adaptable and economically useful in the commercial fabric of the nation."[23] According to UNIVAC's cocreator, Eckert:

> What we attempted to build in the first UNIVAC was a machine which within the limitations of cost and speed and memory size could be used universally, that is to say, could be used for scientific problems or could be used for statistical problems such as the Bureau of Census had, or could be used for business problems, such as a company or insurance company might have.[24]

Remington Rand and Eckert-Mauchly initially intended to build six of the UNIVAC I.[25] Mauchly testified that he recalled a forecast on "the order of 12 of these systems, arrived at ostensibly [by considering] the cost of the system, and the number of companies in the U.S. who could afford to buy a system at that cost."[26] The handful of customers who installed UNIVACs between 1951 and 1953 were all government or government-related organizations.[27] (The first five UNIVACs were delivered to the Bureau of the Census, the air force, the army, the navy, and the Atomic Energy Commission's Lawrence Livermore Laboratory.[28]) Indeed, Mauchly thought in 1951-53 that it was "a gamble . . . whether any UNIVAC system would be sold to a commercial customer."[29] However, in 1954 GE became the first private firm to acquire a UNIVAC for explicitly nongovernment-related applications when it installed one at its Louisville appliance park. After the GE installation demand picked up, and approximately 40 of the UNIVAC I were eventually installed.[30]

It does not diminish Eckert and Mauchly's contribution to stress that the UNIVAC I was a primitive computer. According to one early user, John Jones, it required rather extensive maintenance; initially it could be programmed only in machine language, and while "It was staggering in speed relative to what we knew at that time, . . . it was, indeed, a very slow machine."[31]

Engineering Research Associates

Engineering Research Associates (ERA) was formed in 1946 by a group of former naval officers, including William Norris, who did extensive work on communications and computing techniques during World War II. Much of this group's research was classified and was directed toward military intelligence rather than more orthodox naval applications.[32] At the end of the war some of the intelligence agencies of the U.S. government became concerned that the naval communications group might be disbanded. To prevent this, they indicated to some of its members that if they could find sufficient private capital to set up a company to carry on classified EDP work, the government would consider contracting with them in the area of computer research and development.[33] The necessary financing was obtained (primarily from John Parker, a wartime manufacturer of plywood gliders), and ERA was established with the objective of serving navy requirements for special-purpose computing machinery in a highly classified environment — these included providing devices not only for military purposes but also for deciphering secret information.[34]

In 1946 ERA contracted with the navy to design, develop, and deliver a complete stored-program computer system.[35] In fulfillment of that contract ERA produced a computer system called the ATLAS I.[36] The government then permitted ERA to seek other customers for ATLAS-type computers. According to Henry Forrest, who marketed ERA's computers from 1948 to 1958, "There never was any attitude by the Government that that which we developed in full or in part through government sponsorship could not be put out commercially."[37] The ATLAS I, renamed the 1101, became ERA's first commercially available computer system. The first unit was delivered in December 1950, several months before the first UNIVAC I was installed at the Bureau of the Census.[38] It used vacuum tubes and had a rotating magnetic drum for its main memory.[39]

As an offshoot of the 1101, ERA also developed the 1102 computer system.[40] The 1102 was a general-purpose computer with features allowing it to be used in instrumentation activities. It sold for about $575,000 upon its introduction in 1952 and included, as peripherals, products made by other companies, including teletype punches from AT&T, a Ferranti paper tape reader, Friden Flexowriters, and an FAI digital plotter.[41]

Approximately three 1101s and three 1102s were sold.[42] According to Forrest, ERA did not find a large number of customers interested in acquiring the 1101:

> We felt we didn't have the right assemblage of components arranged in the right configuration and this was evident from the customer response, that for those dollars and for the kinds of things the customer wanted, they just weren't going to buy the things. Technology and machine architecture and organization development was [*sic*] proceeding so fast and so much progress was being made . . . that we withdrew [the 1101].[43]

As early as 1949 ERA began designing a new computer system, the 1103. Forrest testified that the 1103 was markedly superior to the 1101 "in terms of organization, what it would do for the customer and on a price performance basis."[44] The first 1103 was delivered in 1953, following ERA's acquisition by Remington Rand. Approximately 20 1103s were eventually delivered, and they were used in both scientific and business applications.[45] Although some of the features of the 1103 were derived from the 1101, the machines were not compatible.[46]

According to Eckert, Remington Rand's 1952 acquisition of ERA, with its approximately 500 employees, "represented a substantial increase in the electronic or computer ability for the organization."[47] Indeed, ERA had more people involved with computers at the time of the acquisition than did Remington Rand (including Eckert-Mauchly).[48] Moreover, ERA sources "estimated that by the end of 1952 ERA had built and delivered more than 80 percent of the value of electronic computers in existence in the United States at that time."[49]

The Leadership Position of the Merged Companies

Both the recollections of computer pioneers and contemporaneous documents agree that Remington Rand's acquisition of Eckert-Mauchly and ERA, coupled with its own corporate resources, gave it initial leadership in the emerging EDP field.[50] Cuthbert Hurd, IBM's director of applied sciences in the early 1950s, testified that "Remington Rand was the leading company in the EDP industry in the early 1950s" with the acquisition of ERA and Eckert-Mauchly, and with the delivery of the UNIVAC; indeed, "IBM's first computers were popularly referred to as 'IBM's UNIVACs.' "[51] Henry Forrest testified that he stayed on when ERA was acquired by Remington Rand in 1952 because "It was a technically exciting company . . . probably the leader in digital system technology in the country at that time over any other company."[52] In John Mauchly's view, Remington Rand had an "immense advantage," a "five-year lead," over IBM in 1951. "Of course, at that time we did not know that we had a five-year lead, but assumed that we had at least a two- or three-year lead."[53] William Norris testified that he viewed Remington Rand as facing "emerging competition" from IBM in the early 1950s, but believed that at that time Remington Rand "had a chance to take over the computer market."[54]

IBM'S EARLY EDP INVOLVEMENT

IBM was built by Thomas J. Watson, Sr., from a small, struggling manufacturer of punch-card products and time-recording equipment (primarily punch clocks) in 1914 to a firm with U.S. revenues of approximately $180 million in 1949.[55] In the 1930s IBM entered the typewriter business and began producing the first electric typewriter.

In the 1930s and 1940s IBM began sponsoring research in the techniques of electromechanical computation, including the MARK I, a project initiated by Harvard's Howard Aiken and on which Aiken and IBM personnel worked together between 1937 and 1944.[56] In addition, in 1944-47 IBM developed and built a one-of-a-kind, partially electronic and partially electromechanical, stored-program digital computer, called the SSEC (Selective Sequence Electronic Calculator), that used relays, punched paper tape, and electronic registers for storing a program. The SSEC, which occupied about 1,500 square feet at IBM's New York world headquarters, was demonstrated to the public in 1948. At that time no other manufacturer had installed and demonstrated a stored-program computer system, and the designers of the SSEC received a significant patent, including a claim covering the stored program.[57]

In the late 1940s IBM established its Applied Science Group to probe possible business applications of the evolving electronics technology. Applied Sciences was headed by Cuthbert Hurd, who was one of IBM's first Ph.D.s when he was hired in 1949. Nevertheless, IBM's initial interest in electronics was tentative; other than a limited amount of electronic circuitry incorporated in its unit record (punch-card) equipment, little else was done with this new technology.[58]

Events related to the outbreak of the Korean War in 1950 led to IBM's entry into the manufacture and marketing of electronic digital computer systems. At the war's beginning IBM's chairman, Thomas J. Watson, Sr., wrote to President Harry Truman, offering IBM's services to aid in the war effort. Thomas Watson, Jr., who had rejoined IBM in the late 1940s after his discharge from the armed services, and who was his father's heir apparent, made it clear to IBM's management that the "offer was not limited to IBM's existing products or services and was to be a priority undertaking."[59]

During the second half of 1950, James Birkenstock, special assistant to the younger Watson, and Cuthbert Hurd "visited government contractors and spent many days in the Pentagon, knocking on doors to ask in what fashion IBM's abilities and resources might best be utilized" to aid the war effort.[60] These visits "verified [Hurd's] view that government agencies had problems whose solution required large amounts of processing and calculations." Birkenstock and Hurd concluded that all these problems could be solved better on the type of general-purpose computer then being discussed within the scientific and academic communities.[61]

Within IBM, however, there developed substantial internal resistance to the idea of building such a computer. The elder Watson and high-level executives in engineering and sales initially opposed such an effort. They questioned whether there would be a demand for computer systems, and feared that the effort would divert funds from research and development for IBM's profitable unit record products.[62] Accordng to W. W. McDowell, who was IBM's director of engineering at that time, the dispute as to the wisdom of developing a computer system arose because:

> The large majority of our people were not knowledgeable in the field of large computers. . . . It required that we train and hire people who did have these kind [sic] of abilities.
>
> We had to get that know-how and this meant that we had to spend considerably more money, for instance, in research and development, and that was not an easy decision to make.
>
> There were not unlimited funds within the IBM Company.[63]

Steven Dunwell, then in IBM's Future Demands Department, described how the development of computer systems technology required skills different from those previously present at IBM. According to Dunwell, the developers of IBM's unit record equipment were "Edisonian" engineers who solved problems "by trial and error rather than by understanding the underlying physical nature of the problem."[64] This group foundered when confronted with electronic rather than electromechanical technology, forcing IBM to seek a remedy. Dunwell testified:

> Between 1949 and 1951 a new group of approximately thirty electrical and electronic engineers was hired. I know of none of those who had past experience in punch card equipment. Of those thirty, approximately eighty percent were hired directly out of college. Included in that group were Gene Amdahl, Charles J. Bashe, Erich Bloch, Werner Buchholz, Robert Crago and Lawrence Kanter. In fact, the engineers from Endicott were discouraged from transferring to the Poughkeepsie electronic group for fear that they might dishearten the young electronic engineers.[65]

The differences between IBM's traditional unit record products and the proposed general-purpose computer were significant. Hurd testified:

> Compared with IBM's punched card equipment . . . general purpose computers differed in terms of components, method of control, amount of human intervention required, and the problems which could be solved.
>
> The components of punched card equipment included brushes which would detect the presence of a hole in a punched card and which then produced an electrical signal, commutators which divided an electrical signal into a number of timing intervals, relays which opened and closed — much like a light switch but which were actuated by magnets, mechanical devices for punching holes in cards and mechanical printers. Relays could be opened and closed a few dozen times a second

and were subject to unreliable operation because they were mechanical and because of dust particles, for example. IBM had built a variety of machines using these components, including a key punch, verifier, interpreter, reproducer, gangpunch, collator, tabulator, sorter and calculator.

These devices were controlled by control panels or "plug boards". . . . Such a control panel might measure three feet by two feet and contain perhaps a thousand holes. Each machine type had a different control panel. . . .

In the use of punched card equipment, manual intervention . . . was the key and because of manual intervention and because of the mechanical nature of the devices, the results were slow and unreliable. Consequently, there was a sharp limit on the size and kind of applications or tasks that could be performed. . . .

By comparison, general purpose computers relied on electronic technology. This technology utilized vacuum tubes and diodes which . . . were thousands of times faster than the electromechanical components then being used in punched card equipment. Moreover, the electronic technology permitted high speed random access storage on cathode ray tubes and high speed magnetic recording on media such as tapes and drums and high speed communication between various portions of the machine.

Not only were the components different, but the method of control was also completely different. The concept of a modifiable stored program meant that a completely automatic machine could be built. For example, a general purpose computer when . . . fed a few instructions, can call for more instructions and for data from input devices, can assign addresses for such instructions and data, can consider a number of sub-programs which have been written independently and assign addresses for each and assemble them into a single program, and can then generate new instructions and new data as the processing proceeds, while at the same time discarding instructions and data which are no longer needed — An Automation![66]

Faced with such significant differences between its traditional, very profitable line of unit record products and the new computers, IBM found the decision to develop computers difficult. McDowell testified:

Many people disagreed with this direction of developing a large scale computer. They felt strongly that we were — we would be foolish to spend the time and the money on that kind of effort as compared to our more — the field in which we were primarily competent, the punched card equipment.

This feeling was from the highest level . . . on down within the organization.

And what I am trying to emphasize by this is that it was a tough decision to make, and required — I have often used the term "guts" — to say we were going to move ahead with a significant, expensive . . . computer. . . .[67]

Another source of uncertainty troubling many within IBM was whether there really was likely to be a demand for a computer. According to Hurd, the elder Watson told him during that period that IBM's single SSEC "could solve all of the important scientific problems in the world involving calculations."[68] He summarized the skeptical views of others within IBM as follows:

> They told me that they believed that general purpose computers would not be used in great numbers by IBM's customers and would not contribute significantly to IBM's profitability. They also told me that, in their opinion, general purpose computers had nothing whatsoever to do with IBM or IBM's main line of equipment and profitability, IBM's customers or the problems those customers wished to solve. They told me that they could not imagine that enough problems or applications could ever be prepared by IBM's potential customers to keep a computer busy because such machines were to have the capability of performing several thousand operations a second. . . .[69]

Moreover, many within IBM questioned whether customers would be willing to pay the high price — "not just the cost of the machine itself, but the cost of reorienting the customers use of the machine."[70] Dunwell testified, "There was little evidence that more than a few government agencies and aircraft manufacturers would ever consider their computing work important enough to justify the expenditures involved in such a machine."[71]

By mid-1950, while the debate within IBM was under way, Eckert-Mauchly, ERA, and Raytheon had each announced the intention to build commercially available, general-purpose computers, but none had yet been delivered. In addition, none of the one-of-a-kind computers being developed by universities and research organizations were operational on a regular basis.[72] Thus, according to Dunwell, there was

> . . . no evidence that a machine of such complexity could be made to work reliably or could be maintained in working condition. . . . No one had ever programmed a machine of that kind except on paper, and even such questions as how to get the machine started taxed our imagination. Every single instruction used by the machine had to be written by hand and an error of a single bit in a program was sufficient to make the entire process inoperative.[73]

Finally, IBM hesitated about making a decision to build a commercial computer because the construction of a computer required "the development of high-speed circuitry, a new form of high-speed storage, and major sub-systems such as magnetic drums and magnetic tapes which IBM had not delivered in any machine."[74]

The Defense Calculator or IBM 701

After substantial internal debate the younger Watson, who was then 36 years old, eventually authorized the development of a high-performance computer initially called the Defense Calculator (later renamed the IBM 701). The name Defense Calculator was deliberately chosen because it "helped to ease some of the internal IBM opposition to it since it could be viewed as a special project (like the bombsights, rifles, etc., which IBM had built during World War II) that was not intended to threaten IBM's main product line."[75]

The initial paper design for the Defense Calculator called for a machine that would rent for \$8,000/month; 30 letters of intent were received from defense and related agencies and companies. However, after completing the detailed design work, IBM realized that although its computer system would be substantially more powerful than that initially proposed, it would also be much more costly to manufacture than had been anticipated. When in March 1951 IBM raised the Defense Calculator's proposed price to \$15,000/month, all but six letters of intent were withdrawn. Nevertheless, IBM's management made the decision to build 19 of these expensive products.[76] The first customer installation was made in the spring of 1953, and thereafter IBM began shipping one per month, a production record unmatched at that time by any other company. Indeed, the Defense Calculator or 701 was the first computer to be manufactured on a multiple, identical, assembly-line basis.[77]

In a May 1952 announcement IBM described the 701 as an "Electronic Data Processing Machine," a term coined by IBM's James Birkenstock.[78] The term "electronic data processing" (EDP) has since been used by industry participants to mean the same thing as processing with computers or computer systems.

The IBM 701, like the UNIVAC I, was a stored-program, general-purpose, digital computer system between 10 and 100 times faster than the ENIAC.[79] It included a central processing unit (CPU), card reader, card punch, magnetic tape unit, and magnetic drum. The 701's basic circuitry was an "eight-tube pluggable unit" that "eliminated a lot of wiring on the back panels of the computers, and . . . led to more efficient and lower cost manufacturing techniques and provided for easier maintenance or replacement of failing components in the field."[80] The 701 was the first computer to be packaged "in boxes in such fashion that any box would fit in a standard size elevator and go through a standard size door and fit on a standard size dolly".[81] Thus, it was the first general-purpose computer that did not have to be built, or rebuilt, in the customer's computer room.

In certain respects the 701 was initially less capable than the UNIVAC I. For example, the UNIVAC I hardware had the ability to handle directly both numeric and alphabetic characters, whereas the 701 hardware could not handle alphabetic characters directly. In 1953, however, after first delivery of the 701, IBM provided utility programs or software that allowed the 701 to handle alphabetic characters by conversion under the program's control.[82]

On the other hand, the 701 was superior to the UNIVAC I in a number of respects. For example, the IBM 726 tape drive, a peripheral used to input and output data for the 701, used plastic tape and a vacuum column drive. In contrast, the UNIVAC I's tape drive used metal tape and mechanical rollers. The introduction of plastic tape enabled the IBM tape drive to operate much more rapidly. In addition, the 701 used a Williams tube random-access main memory with a capacity of 1,024 bits. The UNIVAC I's main memory was an acoustic delay line that allowed only serial (or nonrandom) access.[83] From the beginning, peripheral devices intended to facilitate data input, output, and storage played a significant role in customer procurements. For example, in 1953 a joint effort of the Weather Bureau, air force, and navy selected an IBM 701 in preference to an ERA 1103 "because [the 701's] input/output devices were more effective in meeting . . . operating requirements."[84]

As initially designed, the 701 was thought to be oriented more toward performing scientific applications involving the complex numerical calculations required by defense contractors. However, the types of uses and users quickly multiplied, and included programs to assemble financial data and prepare quarterly financial reports (Monsanto Chemical), statistical analyses of seismic and well logging data for oil companies, analysis of returns during the 1956 presidential election, actuarial reports, and payrolls.[85] Some users of the 701 reportedly used it for business applications as much as 50 percent of the time; and at least one of the defense contractors initially targeted by IBM for a 701 sale (Lockheed) chose it rather than a UNIVAC I after concluding that the 701 would better handle "both our scientific and our business work loads."[86]

The IBM 650

By the late fall of 1952, prior to the first customer delivery of the 701, IBM's Applied Science Group began pushing for a corporate commitment to manufacture a second, smaller computer system subsequently called the 650. According to Hurd, the number of firm 701 orders was increasing at that time from a low of six, and Applied Science began to feel that "There was a need for a medium-priced general purpose computer . . . in the rental range of $3,000 to $4,000 a month."[87] Applied Science projected that such a computer could be marketed in substantially greater numbers than the 701, and it strove to make it "so easy to use that individuals from many different departments of a customer's organization would begin to wish to apply such a machine to the solution of their problems."[88]

The proposal to build the 650 provoked great controversy within IBM — "even stronger than the opposition prior to the decision to build the 701."[89] The momentum generated by a desire to aid the Korean War effort had passed by this time, and the large-scale commercial feasibility of computers still remained to be demonstrated. According to Hurd, IBM's heads of product planning and sales

. . . continued to make statements such as "You can never sell a machine except to scientists which rents for more than $1,000 a month."

Individuals from the Engineering Department . . . were arguing for the development of more powerful punched card machines. At a week-long engineering meeting at the Harriman estate, the debate continued without resolution twenty hours a day.[90]

Nevertheless, in the spring of 1953, Thomas J. Watson, Jr., at the urging of McDowell and Hurd, approved a plan for announcing the IBM 650.[91] The forecasts developed by the Sales and Product Planning groups were pessimistic — no 650s would be sold because it "could not be produced for $1,000 a month and, therefore, in their opinion, no customers would buy it."[92] On the other hand, Applied Science forecast "200 machines at $3,500 a month with the bulk of the machines to be used by scientists and engineers."[93] Sales of an additional 50 machines were forecast by IBM's Washington, D.C., office, which had exclusive responsibility within IBM for servicing U.S. government accounts, and thought that the 650 would be useful for defense supply-related applications. Based on projections of 250 installations, a rental price of $3,250/month was set for the 650 Model 1 with 1,000 words of storage; a price of $3,750/month was set for the 650 Model 2 with 2,000 words of storage.[94]

The IBM 650 magnetic drum calculator was announced to the public in early 1953 and first delivered in 1954 with two models of a rotating magnetic-drum main memory having a capacity of either 10,000 or 20,000 decimal digits. The 650 announcement stated that the "flexibility inherent in its stored program control makes [the 650] adaptable to both commercial and scientific applications."[95]

The 650 proved to be a great commercial success. Approximately 1,800 were produced and delivered to customers.[96] No other computer system at that time was produced in anything like that quantity. Accordingly the 650 was described by Hurd as computing's Model-T because it was the first general-purpose computer system to be mass-produced on such a scale.[97]

In addition to underestimating the demand for the 650, IBM's planners were wrong in projecting that its principal use would be for scientific applications. Although used extensively in scientific work, the high performance of its input/output peripherals resulted in the 650's being used extensively for business applications.[98] Chrysler's use of the 650 illustrates its versatility. Chrysler installed three 650s — two in its Research Department and one in its Accounting Department. The two Research Department 650s were used to support the engineers in calculations involving the design of a gas turbine engine and the modeling of suspension systems, engine mounting systems, and drive shaft systems. Chrysler's Accounting Department used its 650 to perform payroll and cost accounting.[99] Other customers used the 650 to do inventory control (Caterpillar Tractor), statistical applications (Stanford University), college admissions (MIT), and scientific applications (Purdue University).[100]

In addition to the 650's flexibility in performing both scientific and commercial applications, its unexpected success derived from its reliability, ease of installation and operation, compact size, and relatively low price.[101] Moreover, after making initial deliveries IBM began introducing several improvements, including the addition of alphabetical capabilities, a printer, tape drives, the RAMAC disk drive (described subsequently), and the SOAP assembly program, which increased programmer productivity by allowing the programmer to use a symbolic language rather than actual machine instructions.[102] As a result of the 650's flexibility and the introduction of many product enhancements, customers added more and more applications to their 650 systems.

The IBM 702

The 702, IBM's next general-purpose computer, was announced in September 1953 and first delivered in early 1955. Fourteen were installed during the mid-1950s.[103]

The 702 utilized the same type of circuit components, memory, pluggable unit design, and input/output as the 701. However, it was organized differently at the character level. Specifically, the 702's designers believed that by putting into the hardware of the computer itself, in contrast with the software, "a facility for representing decimal digits . . . and alphabetical characters . . . the machine would be much more useful to businessmen."[104]

The 702 was used for a variety of commercial and scientific applications. For example, the Atomic Energy Commission's Hanford facility used a 702 for inventory control as well as for designing new equipment; Chrysler used a 702 primarily to keep track of spare parts but also for vibration analysis in designing new cars; Prudential's primary 702 application was maintaining life insurance policy files, but the computer was also used for actuarial calculations; Commonwealth Edison used its 702 primarily to prepare bills and do associated accounting, but its Engineering Department also used the 702 as an aid in designing power plants; and General Electric used a 702 both for inventory control and for the design of turbine generators.[105]

OTHER EARLY ENTRANTS INTO THE COMPUTER FIELD

Although Remington Rand and IBM were the two most active participants in the business of producing and marketing computers in the early 1950s, they did face other competitors. In May 1954 John Mauchly responded to Remington Rand personnel who had requested "a list of companies in the electronic computer field, arranged in rough order of probable importance with regard to patent matters" by listing 23 firms: AT&T, IBM, RCA, GE, International Telemeter Corp., National Cash Register and Computer Research Corp., Raytheon, Underwood and Electronic Computer Corp., Ferranti, IT&T, Burroughs, Hughes, Logistic Research Corp., Consolidated Engineering Corp. and Electro Data, Bendix, Northrup, Librascope and Minnesota Electronic Corp., Jacobs Instrument Company, Monroe Calculator, Marchant Calculator, Clary Multiplier Corp., Friden Calculator, and General Mills.[106]

Mauchly added that the names of aircraft companies, such as Boeing, Lockheed, Douglas, and Consolidated Vultee, should possibly be included, and that patents might show up from such research centers as the Rand Corporation, MIT, the University of Michigan, or wherever computers were being built under government contract, and that other companies might well be quite important, including Westinghouse, Telecomputing Corp., Potter Instrument, MacDonald Electronic, Intelligent Machines Research Corp., and Federal Telephone and Telegraph. Finally, Mauchly noted that foreign companies (in addition to Ferranti) were working on computers, and that Remington Rand might be interested in components or devices emanating from smaller firms such as Reeves Instrument.[107]

In sum, there were a large number of firms either in the commercial computer business or on its fringes. (We profile the most important of these in Chapter 4.) However, it is important to emphasize that of all the companies active in computers in the early 1950s, none made investments to develop and market computers commercially that were comparable in scope with those of Remington Rand and IBM.

CUSTOMER IGNORANCE AND UNCERTAINTY

In the early and mid-1950s potential EDP customers (with the exception of certain research or defense-oriented departments in the government, large industrial corporations, universities, and national laboratories) had little knowledge of what computers were, how they worked, and what applications they could usefully perform. As UNIVAC's codesigner, J. Presper Eckert, expressed it, businessmen were "afraid of this strange new beast."[108] For the computer industry to achieve substantial commercial success, it would be necessary to reduce these fears.

Early customers for computer systems faced at least five types of uncertainty: (1) almost every customer was a first-time user, and for most of them the computer was an unknown and exotic tool; (2) acquisition of a computer entailed an investment several times larger than that for the most expensive electromechanical business machine; (3) there was doubt as to whether the computer could perform reliably and over an extended period of time the applications for which it was being acquired; (4) there was uncertainty as to the types of operations the computer could perform; and (5) there was a shortage of people qualified to program and operate computers.

Donald Hart, who first became involved with computers in 1951, when he helped General Motors (GM) Research develop a one-of-a-kind computer dubbed the SAMJAC (Slow as Molasses in January Automatic Computer), described the ignorance of computers that pervaded GM in the early 1950s:

There was very little knowledge of computers anywhere within General Motors. I would say in 1952 there were perhaps three or four smaller groups within General Motors who really knew anything about computers other than what one might find in the newspapers at that period of time.[109]

One of Hart's responsibilities as a member of GM's Research Department was to make presentations throughout the corporation designed "to explain what a computer was, and how a computer was used for the solution of engineering and scientific problems, and to give some feeling for the way in which computers might be used by these various industries within the corporation for the solution of their engineering and scientific problems."[110] Hart characterized his listeners' reactions as ranging "from general interest to great skepticism to an occasional reaction of enthusiasm."[111] When asked to explain the reasons for the skeptical reaction, he replied:

> Well, this was a new kind of device, a new approach to problem-solving, and many of the engineering groups that we talked to felt quite competent to deal with their jobs in the manner that they had been doing without these computers. And they failed to believe that computers were going to be of any value to them in carrying out their work, and to some extent I think it was looked upon as a scientific curiosity and perhaps a passing fad. . . .
>
> [M]ost of us who were working in the computer field, particularly within an industrial environment, were in about the same boat; namely, that we were a small island of expertise in a large organization that knew very little, if anything, about this field. So we all tended to look upon ourselves as missionaries.[112]

Most potential or first-time users of computer equipment had to address a fundamental question: was there any reason for them to use a computer? In the words of Richard Bloch, head of Raytheon's computer efforts in the early 1950s:

> [I]t had not been demonstrated . . . that what we now know today as being an obvious major element in our society would ever even come to fruition, and that is the use of these machines to do all aspects . . . of business processing and more.[113]

Lawrence Welke, who was an IBM systems engineer in the 1950s, described the uncertainty facing first-time computer users as follows:

> I think for some people, if not all of them, getting their first computer was a rather traumatic experience. . . . It was the first time that they had ever been doing anything like this. And it was a large financial commitment on their part as well, not just for the equipment but to change all of their procedures in order to accommodate the equipment.
>
> So, yes, there was a lot of uncertainty, a lot of apprehension, a lot of nervousness. Certainly much more so then . . . than now. . . .
>
> [T]he second, third or fourth computer is no longer that much of a trauma.[114]

EXPANDING THE MARKET FOR EDP PRODUCTS AND SERVICES

To spur use of computers by technically unsophisticated customers, it was necessary to reduce customers' risks and to provide them with support and education.

Short-Term Leases

IBM and several other early entrants into the computer business used short-term leases to market computer systems. Short-term leasing shifted to the manufacturer/vendor a large portion of the economic risk of investment in computer equipment at a time when computer technology was both new and rapidly changing. It offered the great majority of customers three benefits. First, short-term leases helped customers avoid the risks of acquiring a computer system that did not satisfy their needs either because it did not work properly or because it did not meet the operational needs of the business. Specifically, short-term leasing offered customers the flexibility of disposing of or reconfiguring their computer systems. "[I]f the user was not satisfied with the equipment or services provided by the vendor, he could demand that the equipment be removed at once."[115] One result was that leasing "fostered a relationship" in which a supplier "was required to respond rapidly to user needs" and was under constant pressure to keep its users satisfied.[116] Second, short-term leases reduced the magnitude of the initial investment necessary to acquire the computer system and shifted that capital requirement to the manufacturer.[117] Third, short-term leases helped customers avoid the risks of technological obsolescence and enabled them to take full advantage of technological improvements in computer systems.[118] This was especially valuable because the EDP industry was experiencing rapid technological change.[119]

Many early customers benefited from the availability of short-term leasing. For example, H. Dean Brown testified that "[W]ith the option to lease [the customer] may acquire a machine that he would not otherwise acquire under any terms." Brown also believed that leasing "increased the use of computer systems [because it] has made computers available to users who would not otherwise acquire them."[120] Similarly, John L. Jones remembered that in the 1950s "Leasing was considered to be a good way of acquiring equipment because it did not represent the long-term commitment that was implied by a purchase."[121] In addition, one of Jones's government employers always leased its computer systems because "there was [*sic*] no capital dollars available to purchase this equipment."[122]

Customer Support

During the 1950s, users and potential users demanded that manufacturers and vendors of computer systems provide certain software, as well as customer education and training, and systems engineering support.[123] For example, a UNIVAC employee, Edwin McCollister, recalled that suppliers of computer equipment had to offer services and software support if they were to market their products successfully:

> My recollection is that in the early installations of computers, which would have been the UNIVAC I and the IBM 701, that both of these manufacturers offered support to one degree or another to the users of these equipments, and both of these manufacturers offered what software was available at that time, which would have been such basic items of software as assemblers, utility routines, sort routines, and so on.
>
> I think that this was a matter of necessity and that both of these manufacturers did this at that point in time.[124]

IBM's Cuthbert Hurd testified about the same period:

> At the time IBM delivered the 701 in 1953, very few people in the United States had any experience with general purpose computers. The Applied Science Department therefore began a program of educating customers on how to use the 701 hardware and software and how to recruit and train personnel in-house.[125]

John Mauchly, writing in approximately 1954 and 1955, expressed his concern about the shortage of people knowledgeable in computers:

> [M]y conviction [is] that the market for large electronic office equipment is limited chiefly by the lack of education and information as to how such equipment could be used. There is lack of that information and experience within our company as well as among potential customers.
>
> It is everywhere recognized that there is a shortage of trained personnel for the application of electronic computers to the problems of business and industry. . . .
>
> Everyone [sic] of us who has any contact with this situation is all too familiar with the distressing results of such a personnel shortage. The operating history of some of our [Remington Rand's] industrial installations might have been quite different, had there been a better supply of properly trained people.[126]

Richard Bloch testified that users in the 1950s and early 1960s demanded that manufacturers provide "total competence" — a "total data processing system," including the mainframe, the peripherals, "system support, software, and even assistance in applied programming": "It was at that time a total competence that had to be offered."[127] According to Bloch, users demanded total competence because "They were taking quite a risk in picking up equipment in the first place. . . . And these customers . . . were pioneers and they had to have these elements to have any chance whatsoever of even doing their pioneering in the early days."[128] Since the elements "were not available elsewhere . . . they had better be available from the manufacturer of the central equipment, otherwise the application would be doomed to failure."[129]

In addition to meeting user demand, computer manufacturers found it to be in their interest to provide technical assistance and support for their users. By doing so, they could enable customers to use their equipment properly, and to make more effective use of that equipment, which led to enhanced user satisfaction and more rapid growth in the use of electronic data processing. Mauchly wrote in 1955:

> [I]t is a well-recognized principle, followed by Remington Rand as well as IBM, that expert assistance must be given to any customer to assure that his equipment is properly utilized.[130]

Martin Goetz, who set up one of the first independent software companies (Applied Data Research) in the late 1950s, testified at length on the importance of providing customer service if a computer company were to persuade customers to acquire its wares:

> Manufacturers made a concentrated effort to hire and train programmers beginning as early as 1953. When a computer sale was made, the computer manufacturer would 1) initially train the customer's own personnel in programming, and 2) provide continuing on-site programming assistance after delivery of the computer. The sale itself, however, was considered the "computer hardware," while all other services provided were specified simply as support for the "sale." The computer hardware business which emerged during the 1950's and gained momentum in the 1960's was soon recognized as a major and growing industry. IBM acquired a reputation as a marketing-oriented firm which wouldn't desert a customer after a sale was finalized. Thus "providing programming assistance" became an important sales asset to IBM as well as all other manufacturers. Another fact which fostered customer assistance was that many companies frequently would not pay rent on their equipment until their particular applications were programmed. The capability for providing extensive "programming assistance," therefore, became a significant criterion for evaluating competitive computer manufacturers' proposals.[131]

Bundling

During the 1950s most computer vendors provided customers with education, support, and certain software at no separate charge from their equipment. This practice came to be called bundling. It began at the dawn of the computer industry: the UNIVAC I included the cost of software, systems engineering, and customer education in its hardware price.[132] During the remainder of the decade virtually all of the computer manufacturers, including Remington Rand, IBM, Honeywell, RCA, and Control Data, marketed most of their computer systems on a bundled basis.[133]

The provision of necessary support at no additional charge beyond the price of the hardware was in response to customers' demands. Specifically, most customers were not interested in acquiring computer hardware alone, but in acquiring a data-processing capability. Thus, users were less interested in the price of the hardware than in the total cost of getting their jobs done reliably and consistently.[134] Hence, according to Welke, bundling offered users two kinds of advantages:

> On the one hand, it gave the users a predictable cost that they could budget against. They knew that their system would cost them "X" number of dollars a year or per month, and they could budget that amount and predict it. And by the same token, they also knew that the undefined problems that existed in data processing, in their computing world, would be covered as well.[135]

Welke explained how bundling made a user's costs more predictable:

> [I] f I know that education, maintenance, the various support services are mine for the asking . . . that in whatever quantity I might need them they will be made available, then I have a predictable cost that I can allocate to computing. I can say that . . . my installation, my computer is going to cost me . . . $15,000 a month or whatever it might be . . . and all of these things are included. It will be an operating system. [I] t will do my job for me. It is the solution to that data processing problem.[136]

The provision of assistance without separate charge contributed to the rapid growth of the computer industry.[137] According to Arthur D. Little consultant Frederic Withington:

> Users, knowing they would have to pay for any and all assistance they received, would probably have been significantly more reluctant to undertake their initial experiment with data processing system, general purpose ones, than they were, because as things stood at the time, they could all be sure of obtaining whatever support they needed or at least have a hope of doing so without having an unknown liability for future costs.[138]

More than Remington Rand or any other supplier of computer systems in the early 1950s, IBM committed itself to stimulating the EDP market by educating customers and potential customers about the capabilities of computers. Thus, for example, Remington Rand's John Mauchly wrote in 1954 that his firm was not "matching the manpower which IBM is putting in the field to help their customers program problems and study applications of their equipment."[139]

IBM's relatively greater emphasis on customer education and support was an important reason for the subsequent commercial success of its EDP business. According to Jacqueline Johnson, an employee of Sperry Rand and

GE during the 1950s and 1960s:

> The difference in IBM's marketing approach and those of competing vendors could be correlated to that of the chicken and the egg. The two critical aspects of success were sale of the equipment and support of the equipment. Most vendors sold the equipment and then attempted to support it. IBM took the approach that they supported the equipment and then attempted to sell it. IBM created a strong customer following by doing so and a greater sense of customer loyalty than other vendors.[140]

2

IBM AND
SPERRY RAND IN
THE MID-1950s

SAGE

In 1952, shortly after the Soviet Union successfully demonstrated its first nuclear weapon, the U.S. Air Force moved to develop and implement a computer-based air defense system for the continental United States. That system, called SAGE (Semi-Automatic Ground Environment), was intended to provide early warning of a Soviet air attack by tracking airplanes automatically as they traveled across North America and dispatching fighters in case of unauthorized entry. SAGE was called semiautomatic because the design left to human operators certain tasks, such as tactical decisions about weapons deployment and commitment.[1]

Under the SAGE plan the United States was to be divided into 24 radar-monitored sectors. Each sector contained a SAGE direction center with a computer installation capable of monitoring that sector's air space by processing radar input. The computers at each direction center, together with input-output equipment, were to be part of the larger system, which included additional SAGE computers and input-output equipment at three central combat centers. Implementation of the SAGE plan required the development of a large number of highly complex, interrelated devices including sensors, communication links, displays, consoles, and computers.[2]

The SAGE concept grew out of work performed from 1945 through 1951 by MIT's Lincoln Laboratory under an air force contract. A Lincoln Laboratory team, headed by MIT professor Jay Forrester, designed and built the Whirlwind, a one-of-a-kind experimental digital computer system that used magnetic core memory (for the first time) and was intended to be a real-time digital computer system capable of receiving and transmitting data over telephone lines for instantaneous display on monitors. In 1951 the Whirlwind was tested in an experimental air defense system.[3]

In 1952 the air force authorized Lincoln Laboratory to discuss proposals from a number of companies to design and implement the SAGE computer system. To develop and manufacture the actual SAGE computers, it would be necessary to move from the Whirlwind prototype, which had been designed so that it could be experimented with, changed, and modified, "to a reliable, repeatable, practical design and to manufacture, install and maintain several dozens of the systems — systems of unprecedented complexity which employed heretofore unproved technologies."[4] MIT recognized that the talents of a major industrial company were required for this transition from the prototype Whirlwind computer to the complete, operational system. After initiating inquiries with several firms, MIT chose to pursue discussion with a smaller group that included RCA, Raytheon, Remington Rand, Sylvania, and IBM.[5]

In October 1952, after conducting detailed discussions with each of these firms, MIT selected IBM to work with Lincoln Laboratory on the preliminary design specification of the digital computer for the SAGE system. In April 1953 the air force awarded IBM a prime contract to develop more detailed design specifications for SAGE's digital computers. Shortly thereafter IBM began an intensive collaboration with MIT's engineers, who commuted by air on a daily basis between Poughkeepsie, New York, and the Lincoln Laboratory, near Boston.[6]

In September 1953 the air force asked IBM to design, fabricate, support, and maintain two prototype computers for the SAGE system. MIT had the responsibility for the overall systems design, and Western Electric had the responsibility for coordinating the activities of the prime contractors, as well as for designing and building the SAGE centers and scheduling, budgeting, and testing the various parts of the SAGE system.[7] According to Jay Forrester, the primary reason for IBM's selection was that MIT believed "IBM could massproduce a high-quality reliable system."[8] According to Hurd, IBM's selection "was based primarily on [the] assembly line kind of concept for quantity production and [on] the quality of [IBM's] people."[9]

IBM had three principal responsibilities in regard to SAGE: (1) to design, engineer, and manufacture the SAGE computer systems; (2) to install those computer systems and maintain them for round-the-clock operation at SAGE sites throughout the United States; (3) to provide air force personnel with the training and manuals they needed to operate the SAGE computer systems. In February 1954, immediately after being awarded the contract to massproduce the SAGE computers, IBM purchased 200 acres of land in Kingston, New York, and began construction of the necessary facility. Many engineers working on the IBM 701 and 702 were transferred to work on SAGE. Also, a field engineering training course of approximately six months' duration was set up to facilitate SAGE's eventual installation and maintenance. The first trainees were some of IBM's most experienced customer engineers, who then became instructors for newly hired employees and transferees from other IBM customer engineering assignments. At the peak of its involvement IBM employed 7,000 to 8,000 people on the SAGE project.[10]

SAGE was an enormous undertaking, involving numerous subcontractors in addition to IBM. As finally installed, each of the 24 SAGE direction centers contained two IBM-manufactured AN/FSQ-7 SAGE computers and related input-output equipment. The central computer of the AN/FSQ-7 was a general-purpose, binary, parallel, single-address machine with 32-bit word length and a magnetic core memory of 8,192 words. Each of these SAGE processors "was capable of simultaneously driving over 100 display consoles, accepting data from over 100 on-line operators and 12 remote sites, and providing output data to the same sites plus 25 Teletypes."[11]

Each of the three combat centers contained two IBM-manufactured AN/FSQ-8 SAGE computers and related input-output equipment. "The function of the combat centers was to combine, summarize and display air defense information supplied to them by the direction centers over which they had supervisory control."[12] The two computers at each combat center had far fewer display consoles and much less input processing equipment than did the direction center computers because they received data previously processed and transmitted by the direction center.

SAGE represented IBM's largest undertaking through the mid-1950s.[13] Hurd described the substantial risks IBM incurred by undertaking SAGE:

> Many of the concepts had been tried only in a laboratory. There was no guarantee IBM could hire the numbers of people that would be needed to carry out its responsibilities. Failure to deliver the computers successfully, because the project was so massive, could have led to adverse financial repercussions and damage to IBM's reputation. . . . All of us were concerned in 1953 about the diversion of key engineering and systems persons and Applied Science persons who were barely completing the design of the 650, 701, and 702. Moreover, IBM would need to construct a completely new factory to build the SAGE computers and all of us in the highest management group wondered what would happen if the contract were cancelled in midstream.[14]

Despite these risks, IBM expected to obtain substantial benefits from its involvement in the SAGE program, and therefore undertook the commitment. The manager of IBM's SAGE program concluded in a 1954 analysis that the benefits to IBM were of three principal types: (1) SAGE would contribute directly to IBM's current and planned commercial computer products; (2) SAGE would obviate or reduce IBM's future expenditure on research and design work for its commercial computer products; and (3) because of research and development done for SAGE, IBM would gain an economic advantage over competitors in marketing its commercial computer products.[15] Indeed, the 1954 report predicted that as a result of its SAGE involvement:

> IBM will be recognized as the undisputed leader in the large scale, high speed, general purpose, digital computer field. If a competitor were performing on this contract, that competitor might gain enough advantage to force IBM into a relatively secondary position.[16]

In fact, SAGE did yield substantial technical, manufacturing, and educational benefits to IBM by allowing it to place into actual production large computers possessing many of the most advanced concepts, designs, and technologies known at that time.[17] Three of these advances merit brief description.

SAGE was the first production-line computer to incorporate core memory. This represented a major advance because core memories provided a highly reliable and inexpensive means of high-speed storage. According to Erich Bloch, who worked on IBM's commercial core-memory program at the time of the SAGE program:

> Cores could be inexpensively fabricated, tested and assembled into core arrays, and the ability to access cores in multiple dimensions permitted a relatively small number of devices to access a large capacity memory thereby reducing costs and increasing reliability. The speed of magnetic core memories was much faster than the speed of Williams tube and magnetic drum memories. . . . Magnetic core memories also consumed less power and were more reliable than Williams tube and magnetic drum memories and could be assembled in larger capacities than Williams tube memories.[18]

Credit for recognizing the value of core memory and for its early development belongs largely to Jay Forrester and his Lincoln Laboratory colleagues. However, IBM was the first to commercialize core memory by developing and manufacturing a uniform, high-speed, reliable, and inexpensive product. Its manufacturing techniques allowed it to make millions of cores with uniform electronic characteristics. IBM developed devices that partially automated the stringing of core planes, and it developed semiautomatic core testing equipment.[19] Core memories proved so successful that they were used in virtually every computer system manufactured after SAGE until they were replaced by semiconductor memories in the 1970s.

Because of the importance of its air defense mission, the SAGE system was designed to be extremely reliable. According to Robert Crago, one of the managers of IBM's SAGE activities:

> IBM took many new measures to assure that the extreme reliability and continuous operation requirements for SAGE were met. To assure continuous operation, any part of the computer system whose failure might bring down the system was duplexed. Every SAGE direction center was equipped with two complete computers. At all times, one of the computers was active in air defense surveillance while the other was in a standby mode ready to be switched over into the active mode within seconds. The active computer continuously transmitted changes in the air situation data to the stand-by computer . . . so that the air situation picture would not have to be regenerated when switchover occurred.[20]

Real-time computer systems implemented after SAGE frequently used the duplexing technique to guard against system failure.

SAGE was the first large, geographically dispersed, real-time computer system. Because of the military's concern with controlling certain types of external events, the stimulus for developing real-time computing capabilities was derived from the need to satisfy military applications. However, as will be discussed later, as the real-time technology developed, it became apparent that it would have widespread use for applications such as reservation systems for airlines and hotels, transactions processing, and process control. Thus, SAGE was the precursor of those systems where immediate response to the waiting customer was vital.[21]

IBM realized significant technical and production advances from its SAGE involvement. However, at least as important were the financial and personnel resources that IBM reaped. According to Hurd:

> The several thousand engineering and programming and maintenance personnel who were hired to work on SAGE added greatly to the company's store of technical knowledge and expertise. These persons worked on developing and maintaining many of IBM's subsequent general purpose computer systems.[22]

During the 1950s more than half of IBM's domestic EDP revenues came from its work on SAGE and a B-52 program undertaken during the Korean War.[23] Without the stimulus provided by these large federal contracts, the early growth of IBM's EDP business would have been significantly slower.

THE IBM 704 AND 705

In 1954, building on its work on SAGE, IBM announced the 704 and 705, substantially improved successors to the 701 and 702, respectively. At that time, although several 701s had been built and installed, deliveries of the 702 (announced in September 1953) had not yet begun. The IBM 704, announced in May 1954 and first delivered in 1955, was two to three times faster than the 701 and offered an approximately 20-1 speed improvement over Remington Rand's principal challenger, the UNIVAC I. The 705, announced in October 1954 and first delivered in 1956, was two to three times as fast as the 702, depending on the application.[24]

Taking advantage of its work on SAGE, IBM used magnetic core memories in both the 704 and the 705.[25] In announcing the 704, IBM described it as the first large-scale, commercially available computer to employ a magnetic-core main memory.[26] At that time there were other computer manufacturers offering core memories. However, their core memories were much smaller than IBM's, containing a few tens of thousands of bits of storage rather than the 1 million bits of core storage eventually available on the IBM 704.[27]

Alan Perlis characterized the 704 as a creative masterpiece:

> The 704 welded together some separate technologies, magnetic core tecynology [sic], vacuum tube technology [and] mechanical hardware for peripherals into one very excellent computer that in effect brought several important segments of American industry into the computer world: the aircraft industry, the oil producers, some of the chemical

firms all came into computing at about the same time via the 704, and they all developed together, they developed . . . certain standard approaches to using computers together that had an enormous impact on the entire field.[28]

According to Perlis, the 704

represented the first introduction of magnetic core technology into a commercial machine, to the best of my knowledge anyhow, and it provided a machine for that time of great speed that could be used in science and engineering problems. It seems to fit very nicely into the use patterns and needs of an extremely large segment of the user population at that time and in effect, it defined pretty well what one meant by scientific and engineering computation in the United States in the period of years when it came out. . . .[29]

The 704 and 705 continued a bifurcation in IBM's 700 series product line, with the 701 and 704 thought to be oriented more toward scientific applications and the 702 and 705 more toward business applications. Regardless of their orientation, however, both the 704 and the 705 could handle both business and scientific applications, and were used for both by customers. Indeed, Arthur D. Little's Frederic Withington estimated that despite its scientific orientation, some customers used the 704 for business applications up to 50 percent of the time.[30]

The IBM 704 and 705, like other computers marketed in the mid-1950s, did not have operating systems. Donald Hart of General Motors described the problem of using computers before operating systems were developed:

With the 701 it was necessary to schedule people to the computer one at a time to read in the cards at the card reader, wait for the computation to compute, print out the results, and then log off and let the next person approach the machine to repeat that process.

There was an inefficiency involved in that because the speed of the machine far exceeded the speed of the person who was trying to use it.[31]

To deal with this problem, efforts were undertaken to develop an operating system that would provide "an automatic mechanism via software for executing one job after another without operator intervention."[32] GM and North American Aviation jointly developed one of the first operating systems for use on their IBM 704s. Hart testified that use of their operating system "quadrupled the throughput of the 704 computer by eliminating several steps of manual handling."[33]

In the mid-1950s users of IBM's 704 computers formed one of the first computer user groups, SHARE. According to Hart, SHARE's goal was "to provide a forum by which their people could get together and engage in joint planning and to share the process of preparing for this new equipment."[34]

Through SHARE, IBM users influenced IBM's product development. For example, in the late 1950s SHARE members began jointly to develop the SHARE Operating System (SOS). At SHARE's request, IBM took over further development of SOS and in the early 1960s released IBSYS, an SOS derivative provided as an operating system for the 7090/7094 series of computer systems.[35]

FORTRAN AND COBOL

There are three levels of programming languages: machine level, assembly level, and higher level. Machine-level language is the basic language of the computer, ones and zeroes, and it is the instruction level of the computer when it executes programs. There is a one-to-one relationship between machine level and assembly level, but the assembly language is a mnemonic language that is more convenient for programmers. A higher-level language is a programming language that is more like English than machine language but is not directly executable by a computer. A program written in a higher-level language is translated into machine language by a special program called a compiler. Higher-level languages are also called machine-independent languages since, given suitable compilers, programs written in those languages can be run on machines of different designs and different architectures, and built by different manufacturers.[36]

John Backus of IBM was responsible for the development of FORTRAN, an algebraic, higher-level programming language intended initially for use with the IBM 704 and aimed at the solution of engineering and scientific problems. FORTRAN was the first higher-level language compiler to be provided commercially, and its introduction in 1957 marked an important advance that spurred the growth of the computer business.[37]

By making programming much easier, FORTRAN enabled many more people to use computers. For example, according to Hart, prior to FORTRAN, GM Research

> . . . had been attempting to have engineers and scientists learn to write programs . . . on the computer. With the types of programs that were available on the 701 and initially on the 704, this was difficult. We [were] dealing with some form of an Assembly language or an interpretative system which required a great deal of attention to detail, it required pretty much that the person writing the program become a computer expert.
>
> A few of our users managed to do this, but many others found that this was too difficult a hurdle to get over and required the services of a professional programmer to write their programs.
>
> We were looking for a way by which we could in fact move this program development process more out into the hands of the users and FORTRAN provided us with the potential opportunity to do this.[38]

By simplifying programming, FORTRAN made it much faster, easier, and less expensive. At GM, for example, FORTRAN decreased programming time by a factor of five.[39] The development of FORTRAN, as well as subsequent programming languages, also increased manyfold the size of the population competent to use computers. Alan Perlis testified that FORTRAN provided engineers and scientists "with a language that was directly attuned to their abilities in the way they thought about problem-solving"; "they found FORTRAN to be just what they wanted for expressing the problems that they had in mind."[40] FORTRAN, together with early operating systems, facilitated the development of an open shop, where a computer user could do his or her own programming independent of the professional programmers associated with the computer center. In short, the user could "begin using computer services without the necessity of becoming a trained computer programmer."[41]

The introduction of FORTRAN also facilitated cooperation and information exchange among computer users. Perlis testified:

> [FORTRAN] formed a kind of glue that brought together large numbers of people from different industries who used the computer for different purposes, who now in a sense could almost speak to each other in common language.
>
> Although they didn't speak to each other in FORTRAN, they spoke to each other about what they did in FORTRAN, and also, I think, FORTRAN . . . gave an enormous impetus to IBM, because FORTRAN, when it came out in 1956 was associated with IBM and with IBM computers.[42]

FORTRAN was initially intended for scientists and engineers. However, it simplified programming so much that it was quickly adopted by other users. IBM's Richard Case testified:

> Other people . . . used the FORTRAN language for a wide variety of applications. There are payroll programs written in FORTRAN, there are accounts receivable programs written in FORTRAN, there are process control programs written in FORTRAN, indeed, I am not aware of any major application or any significant application area which has not had application programs for that area written in the FORTRAN language. . . . [T]oday more FORTRAN programs are written for business-oriented applications than are written for science and engineering kinds of applications.[43]

FORTRAN was widely accepted by users, and beginning around 1958 other computer manufacturers began to develop their own FORTRAN compilers.[44] That development had a further benefit for users, in that they could take a FORTRAN program running on an IBM 704, for example, and transfer it to a different computer (made either by IBM or by one of its competitors) with, in many cases, very little difficulty.[45] In consequence, the substitutability between different kinds of computers was increased significantly.

Following its development of FORTRAN, IBM began to develop COM-TRAN, a higher-level language oriented toward business rather than scientific applications.[46] At about the same time, however, a group of users decided to develop a problem-oriented, but machine-independent, common language for business problems. The project was sponsored by the Department of Defense, which in May 1959 convened a conference to develop such a language. Although many manufacturers attended that conference, more than half of those attending were users or consultants. The group adopted a name, CODASYL (Committee on Data Systems Languages), and developed a higher-level language called COBOL (Common Business Oriented Language). COBOL specifications were published by the Department of Defense in 1960 and again, with clarifications and corrections, in 1961.[47] As with FORTRAN, COBOL specifications could be used by any user to write programs for his applications and by vendors to develop compilers that would translate common language programs into the specific machine language for the various classes of machines.

IBM's 1956 Consent Decree

In January 1952, more than a year before IBM was to begin delivering its first computer, the 701, the Justice Department's Antitrust Division commenced an action against various practices used by IBM in connection with marketing its electromechanical unit record equipment. On January 25, 1956, IBM consented to the entry of a final judgment on this proceeding before any testimony had been taken and without trial or adjudication of any issues of fact or law. Because of their impact on IBM's subsequent marketing practices, several provisions of the 1956 consent decree merit brief review.

1. Users and prospective users of tabulating and EDP products offered by IBM for lease and sale were to be given "an opportunity to purchase and own such machines at prices and upon terms and conditions which shall not be substantially more advantageous to IBM than the lease charges, terms and conditions for such machines."[48]

2. IBM was enjoined from acquiring any used IBM tabulating or EDP machine except as a trade-in or as a credit against an account receivable, and was ordered "to solicit . . . from dealers in second-hand business machines orders for the purchase of any used IBM" machines so acquired, subject to a price limitation.[49]

3. IBM was (a) "to offer to render, without separate charge, to purchasers from it of tabulating or electronic data processing machines the same type of services, other than maintenance and repair services, which it renders without separate charge to lessees of the same types of machines";[50] (b) "to offer . . . to maintain and repair at reasonable and nondiscriminatory prices and terms IBM tabulating and electronic data processing machines for the owners of such machines";[51] and (c) to offer to sell repair and replacement parts to owners of, or persons engaged in maintaining and repairing, IBM tabulating or EDP machines.[52]

4. IBM was enjoined for 10 years from entering into any lease for a standard tabulating or EDP machine for a period longer than one year, unless the lease was terminable after one year by the lessee upon no more than three months' notice.[53]

5. IBM was enjoined from "requiring any purchaser of any IBM tabulating or electronic data processing machine to have it repaired or maintained by IBM or to purchase parts and subassemblies from IBM."[54]

6. IBM was to grant "unrestricted, non-exclusive license [s] to make, have made, use and vend tabulating cards, tabulating card machinery, tabulating machines or systems, or electronic data processing machines or systems under, and for the full unexpired term of, any, some or all IBM existing and future patents."[55]

Two provisions of the 1956 consent decree are of particular interest. First, apparently recognizing the value of customer education, software, and related support that IBM provided without separate charge to lessees of its products, the Department of Justice required IBM to provide the same types of services, also without separate charge, to purchasers. Second, the requirement that IBM sell its EDP products as well as lease them led to the growth of the computer leasing companies.[56]

OTHER IBM COMPUTERS

With the development and installation of the 650, 704, and 705, "the IBM debate . . . as to whether IBM should enter the computer business" finally ended.[57] The corporation implemented several managerial changes assuring that thereafter computers would be its principal focus.[58] Specifically, T. Vincent Learson, who was named IBM's first director of EDP machines in 1954 to coordinate the development of the 705, was appointed IBM vice-president of sales in 1955. Cuthbert Hurd replaced Learson as director of EDP machines. In 1956 Thomas J. Watson, Jr., who had become IBM's president in 1952, assumed the responsibilities of chief executive officer. Thus, by 1955-57 IBM was well on the way to transforming itself from a manufacturer and vendor of unit record equipment to a manufacturer and vendor of computer products and services.

The IBM 305 RAMAC

In September 1956, IBM announced the 305 RAMAC, which it characterized as "a revolutionary new 'in-line' data processing system."[59] The 305 RAMAC was first delivered in 1957. It was the first computer system to incorporate a disk drive, the 350, which could store a total of 5 million alphanumeric characters.[60]

The disk drive was one of the most significant technical innovations in the EDP industry because it allowed rapid, random access to relatively large amounts of data, thereby making the computer a more effective tool for performing a wide variety of customer applications requiring immediate access.[61] Prior to the introduction of the disk drive, tape drives and magnetic drums had been the two principal methods of electromechanical data storage.

Tape drives, while capable of storing large amounts of data, permit only sequential access. Hence, to the extent that an application requires data in an order different from the sequence in which it was placed on the tape, the time necessary to access that data is increased. Drums permit random access to data — that is, just as the user of a phone book does not need to pass over all entries prior to finding the one desired, use of a drum allowed the computer to access, almost directly, the particular data record desired. However, because data could be stored only on the outer surface of the drum's cylinder, the amount of storage was severely limited. By contrast, disk drives substantially increased the volumetric efficiency of data storage because data could be stored on the many disks that were, in effect, slices of a drum.

The 350 disk drive's average access time when performing applications in which the desired data were not demanded sequentially was 200 times faster than the average access time of tape drives available at that time. Thus, where a tape drive would take perhaps a minute to find some particular data record, IBM's 350 disk file would access it in a fraction of a second.[62] The fact that disk drives allowed much more rapid access to nonsequentially stored data proved to be especially valuable to businesses maintaining records for individual customers. Led by the airlines, which soon introduced real-time passenger reservation systems, disk drives made transaction processing economically feasible.

The 350 disk file recorded and read data from 50 disks that were not removable except by a customer engineer. Each disk measured two feet in diameter and the whole stack of disks stood two feet high. Recording and reading were performed by two heads, one for either side of one disk. Because the RAMAC disk revolved so fast, the heads would damage the disk media if disks and head came in contact. To prevent this, IBM successfully reduced to practice an innovative scheme by which air pressure from a compressor was pumped into the space between the heads and the disk to maintain a constant distance ("flying height") between the two. The two heads were moved from disk to disk by retracting them outside the array of disks and moving them linearly along the array until reaching the disk containing the desired data and then inserting the heads into the disk stack.[63] In short, both in appearance and in operation the 350 RAMAC disk drive resembled a jukebox.

The development of the disk drive was widely recognized as one of IBM's major contributions to the computer field. For example, Nicholas Metropolis, then director of the University of Chicago's Institute for Computer Research, wrote to IBM in 1963 that the

> . . . development of disk files represents a real triumph for IBM in the computer field. By solving the problem of very large storage capacity with fast access times, IBM has succeeded in combining the virtues of

both magnetic tapes and drums and has thus provided a new dimension of possibilities in coping with the ever increasing demands in modern computing.[64]

It was not until several years after the RAMAC was first delivered to customers that IBM's competitors provided disk drives of comparable performance and reliability.[65] However, by that time (as will be discussed later) IBM had introduced additional major improvements to the disk drive. IBM's disk efforts gave it an advantage over its competitors. Withington testified:

> Prior to 1965, alternatives to disks were being experimented with, such as particularly magnetic card devices, and also I think no one realized the degree to which the transaction processing mode of use was going to prove popular. I believe only IBM among the major competitors at the time offered an alternative between magnetic card devices and disk drives, with developments proceeding along both lines. A number of the other manufacturers committed themselves almost entirely to the magnetic card devices, sometimes also using magnetic drums.
>
> When it became apparent that the class of magnetic card devices was not going to be successful in the marketplace, for reasons of reliability, and that the disk drives was [*sic*] critical product, many of IBM's competitors were left for a while without a satisfactory option.[66]

Prior to IBM's introduction of the disk drive, real-time applications were feasible only on computer systems such as SAGE, which were far too large and expensive for the ordinary user. The disk drive made transaction and other types of on-line processing feasible for EDP customers, thereby broadening and expanding the EDP marketplace.[67]

The IBM 709

The IBM 709 EDP system was announced on January 2, 1957, and first delivered to customers in 1958. The announcement described the 709 as having sufficient speed and flexibility to make it "outstanding in the processing of large-scale scientific, engineering, management, and business problems."[68] The 709 was approximately three times faster than its predecessor, the 704. It was also program-compatible with the 704; "existing 704 programs" could "be run on the 709 without alteration, except for changes in input-output routines and floating point overflow-underflow." In addition, the 709 offered magnetic tape interchangeability with the tape equipment used on the 704.[69]

The 709 was the first computer to use a channel, a device IBM patented.[70] Channels allowed input-output and computing to proceed in parallel. According to Richard Case,

> [A] channel, together with the main memory that it works with, is something like a staging device that enables the relatively slower peripheral

personnel in Remington Rand's computer division, Mauchly wrote in approximately 1954:

> Back of almost any superficial reason seems to be the fundamental one that Remington Rand has not been willing to pay sufficient expenditure for any phase of the electronic computer sales program.
>
> Month after month, from 1950 up to the present, there have been countless problems which have reinforced the basic theme, that we are suffering serious losses of efficiency and consequently not giving IBM all the competition we should give them, as a result of all sorts of efforts which try to save a dollar and result in wasting a hundred dollars.[88]

As to whether there was a commitment by Remington Rand to expanding the marketing of computers, Mauchly later testified:

> I think I saw a lot of effort from time to time, but I'm not sure I could describe them as a commitment. In other words, the efforts were not well coordinated or definitely stated as the goal which was being pursued in a rather sensible way, instead it seemed as if they were random thrusts.[89]

Examples of the ways in which Remington Rand's lack of commitment to support its EDP operations restricted its growth include its failure to support the marketing of its EDP products, its failure to support adequately the development of new products, and its failure to hire and retain qualified employees.

Inadequate Marketing

Just after Remington Rand bought Eckert-Mauchly, a small group that included John Mauchly drew up a plan for training sales personnel in electronic computer equipment. Mauchly described the subsequent events as follows:

> We wanted to have about a dozen persons with sales and business systems background selected and trained . . . as a nucleus for an expanding sales program. If this had been done, then we would have been ready in 1951, when the Census Brueau UNIVAC was in operation and others were being made ready for delivery, to capitalize on the five-year lead which we then had over IBM. . . . However, our plan for training a sales staff at that time was brushed aside with one comment — this would be entirely too expensive.[90]

Mauchly estimated that Remington Rand might have been able to sell an additional 15 UNIVAC I units (at approximately $1 million each) if it had spent the $300,000 necessary to implement this training program — "a quite reasonable price to pay for the immense lead which this would represent over our competitor."[91]

Remington Rand also faild to retrain its punch card salesmen to market UNIVACs. Instead, the firm set up a marketing force that Mauchly thought was neither proper nor effective, and that was understaffed.[92] A minor example of the firm's marketing shortcomings is that after UNIVAC I passed the Census Bureau's acceptance test, no advertising campaign took advantage of that fact. Instead, the company took an ad in the *Scientific American* that told (presumably scientific readers) "how wonderful the UNIVAC was for commercial business problems."[93] A more serious marketing shortcoming was that Remington Rand's punch card salesmen got no remuneration if they somehow sold a UNIVAC. Indeed, they would lose commissions if a UNIVAC displaced Remington Rand's unit record equipment. In short, Remington Rand's punch card salesmen were given negative incentives to sell UNIVACs, thereby dissipating a potentially valuable marketing resource.[94]

Mauchly testified about Remington Rand's management:

I didn't feel that the Remington Rand management . . . had a very good understanding of what kind of a business they had acquired and . . . of how to market any product which might emmanate [*sic*] from that business, nor now to manage the business most effectively so as to cause it to answer the needs of a market even if they identified that market.

. . .

[T]he IBM Company was doing what I would call an aggressive job, both in marketing and in development of the things to market, and I felt that the Remington Rand Company was losing a position which was in their favor by being unwilling to do some of the things which seemed obvious to us should be done, and sometime [*sic*] doing things which seemed obvious to us should not be done. . . .[95]

John Jones, a UNIVAC I customer, testified in a similar vein:

[T]here was not, in my view and the view of many others at that time, a strong marketing effort put on by UNIVAC to try and expand and increase this market.[96]

Remington Rand also failed to support education of both its own employees and its customers in the application of EDP products. This led Mauchly to lament in 1955:

The immense advantage which Remington Rand had over IBM in 1951 has gradually been lost. We are not losing the battle of hardware but the battle of applications research and education.[97]

Mauchly was especially critical of Remington Rand's efforts to train its own employees, and said a conspicuous difference between the IBM training plans and those of Remington Rand had long been evident:

IBM has tried to train people in all its branches by sending them to their courses at Poughkeepsie along with customers. We occasionally have representatives from branches attend initial seminars, but . . . have done almost nothing to provide a large staff of branch-based people who are familiar with UNIVAC applications and able to advise potential customers, or help actual customers. We have considered this "too expensive" or "impractical." During the last few years IBM has made an effort to provide not one but several representatives in each of their major branches, and they are, in general, requiring persons of mathematics or engineering background, preferring people with advanced degrees.[98]

Elsewhere Mauchly elaborated on the theme that Remington Rand was losing out to IBM in promoting new applications for computers:

While we look with a somewhat vacant stare at a mathematician and wonder whether or not he would be useful to us, IBM is hiring mathematicians and scientists . . . and giving them carte blanche to work on anything they find interesting. When an engineer at MIT does a master's thesis on a problem involving engineering computations, IBM hires him. We don't even know the computational application exists.[99]

Mauchly was also critical of Remington Rand's lack of efforts to expand the computer market by educating potential customers. He made the following comments about a speech by IBM's Cuthbert Hurd in approximately 1954:

[Dr Hurd said that] IBM recognizes the need for them to contribute funds toward educational programs in the computer field. . . .

He went on to say that universities should be trusted to run their training in the best interests of all. . . . He spoke against too much pressure from the industry for vocational courses and in favor of a broad liberal education.

[S]uch words mean nothing if not followed up by deeds. However, we know that IBM *does* follow such words by deeds. . . . I reported to you . . . the talk now going on between the University of Pennsylvania and IBM, aimed at providing better University training in Applied Mathematics. . . . IBM would not expect any specific commitment from the University in return. The graduates of this Applied Mathematics Department would not be required to do anything for IBM. . . . However, a greater demand for computing equipment and a corps of enthusiastic exponents for enlarging the scope for computing activities would automatically be built up. It will make little difference whether all of these graduates insist on using IBM equipment. The main thing is to swell the number of persons who are not only active in the use of computers, but who in turn infect others with the possibilities of application and hence enlarge the computer market.[100]

Inadequate Product Development

Remington Rand's failure to commit adequate resources to its computer business manifested itself in its slowness in developing new and improved EDP products. In consequence, by no later than 1954-55 technological leadership of the EDP industry had passed to IBM. An example of Remington Rand's product shortcomings was its delay in providing a successor to the UNIVAC I.

Soon after first delivery of the UNIVAC I, it became clear to Remington Rand's engineers that this computer would be greatly speeded up if it had a faster memory. However, although the UNIVAC I began to face competitive pressures from IBM computers, Remington Rand felt that it could not spare the resources necessary to develop enhancements. Instead, it directed all of its efforts toward developing a successor system.[101] As described by John Jones, "It was a long time [1957] before the UNIVAC II came out. By that time . . . more advanced machines were on the arket, such as . . . initial models of the [IBM] 705 and 704." The "initial year to two-year lead UNIVAC had by having a machine that was available and operational before other machines began to appear no longer was a lead . . . it was many years before UNIVAC really again caught up in the sense of having machines which were of comparable power available to the competition."[102]

In addition to a successor for the UNIVAC I, the Eckert-Mauchly Division wanted to produce a small computer aimed at a larger number of customers. According to Mauchly, "A lot of the effort . . . was occupied in trying to get a recognition of the fact that a smaller computer meeting a larger market was a very important endeavor for the Remington Rand organization."[103] Remington Rand's management did not strongly support this request.[104] This hesitation contrasts unfavorably with IBM's decision to back development of the 650 even before the first 701 had been delivered.

In 1956 — two years after first delivery of the IBM 650 — Sperry Rand did begin delivering a small computer, called the File Computer, about which Mauchly testified:

> [N]o one in Philadelphia had either proposed such a device, or was asked whether such a device should be built, but there were elements in the Remington Rand management who decided that the device was something that they would like to have for the punch card sales people to sell because they were not allowed to sell UNIVAC equipment.[105]

The File Computer, developed by Remington Rand's ERA group in Minneapolis/ St. Paul, was a medium-priced magnetic drum machine generally comparable with the IBM 650. According to Withington, the File Computer was a "major product failure" because it was "deficient in price performance . . . partly because its primary file storage device was . . . [a] magnetic drum" and "also because at least part of its programs . . . had to be on external plug boards, which was inconvenient for the users."[106] A third shortcoming was that, like the UNIVAC I, the File Computer's tape drives used metal rather than plastic tape.[107] Only about 100 File Computers were delivered.[108]

Loss of Employees

It was widely recognized in 1954-55 that because of the complexity of the early computers, the "market for computers [was] limited more by the inability to get trained people than it [was] by the inability to manufacture the equipment."[109] Yet, throughout the mid-1950s, key Sperry Rand employees were leaving to start their own companies or to join competitors or users. Managerial infighting and heedless budget-cutting forced many of these key employees to leave.

William Norris testified that Sperry Rand's failure to focus its concentration and efforts on the EDP business was one of the reasons he left in 1957 to form Control Data Corporation (CDC). Norris believed that a firm was more likely to be successful in the computer business if it concentrated its resources in that business. Norris had other reasons for leaving Sperry, arising in part out of the persistent conflict and lack of coordination among the Eckert-Mauchly group in Philadelphia, the ERA group in Minneapolis/St. Paul, and top management.[110]

Norris was not alone in leaving Sperry Rand because of dissatisfaction with the management of its EDP business. Describing this period severl years later, John Lacey wrote:

> The creative and scientific people of ERA . . . became extremely frustrated. After five years with Remington Rand and Sperry Rand and after giving it every bit of professional and management effort that they could muster during that entire period, Norris, Mullaney, Cray, Keye, et al. decided to leave Sperry Rand and started Control Data Corporation.[111]

Henry Forrest, who also left Sperry Rand to join CDC, recalled that around this time, people he worked with at Sperry "were talking about trying to still seize an opportunity in the computer business, and when I heard this opportunity talked about, I expressed interest in it."[112] Indeed, he said, the idea of seizing such an opportunity "was a common thought of anybody who was concerned about Remington Rand's lack of forceful position and approach to the computer business."[113]

The problem of qualified people leaving Sperry Rand's computer business extended to levels beneath its senior management. John Mauchly complained to his superiors about his inability to retain qualified people responsible for pioneer developments in automatic programming envied by competitors. In 1954 he wrote:

> [S]ome of the members of [Dr. Grace Hopper's] staff have already left for positions with users of IBM equipment, and those of her staff who

still remain are now expecting attractive offers from outside sources.
. . . The Eckert-Mauchly Division has not, however, been able to make
offers sufficiently soon enough, or good enough, to prevent the deple-
tion of her staff, because there is no budget allowance in the Eckert-
Mauchly Division for such personnel.[114]

Mauchly recognized that in comparison with industry standards, the persons
in his division were not adequately compensated, making it difficult to recruit
and keep personnel. In 1955 he wrote:

It is a well-recognized principle . . . that expert assistance must be given
to any customer to ensure that his equipment is properly utilized.
Remington Rand's . . . ability to do so has been seriously hampered by
the lack of well-trained and very experienced personnel.[115]

Conflict Among Sperry Rand's Divisions

Throughout the 1950s Sperry Rand failed to integrate its two principal
computer efforts — Eckert-Mauchly and ERA. (Indeed, it maintained a third,
smaller computer effort at Norwalk, Connecticut, that was an outgrowth of
Remington Rand's business machine operations.) The Eckert-Mauchly and
ERA divisions both attempted to pursue the same areas and develop similar
(hence competing) but incompatible products. This resulted in unnecessary
duplication of research, engineering, product development, manufacturing,
and marketing expenditures that, in turn, raised EDP's demands on the corporation's financial and technical resources.[116] Mauchly spoke about the
lack of interaction between Sperry Rand's Philadelphia and Minneapolis/St. Paul
computer groups:

From our point of view . . . we would have helped them more than they
could have helped us, but I'm afraid they had the same type point of
view. They . . . didn't want to pay much attention to what we had to
say.[117]

Norris recalled a similar situation when describing the situation leading to
his 1957 departure:

I left Sperry-Rand because of turmoil. This turmoil was made up of
confusion, indecision, conflicting orders, organization line breaches,
constant organizational change, fighting and unbridled competition
between divisions.[118]

CDC's Lacey stated:

Rand now had three laboratories in Norwalk, Philadelphia and St. Paul
all attempting, essentially, to pursue the same markets and develop

similar products. . . . And throughout the years 1953, 1954 and part of 1955 the whole activity with respect to computing in Remington Rand was extremely uncoordinated.

During this period . . . [c]onstant battles ensued between Philadelphia and St. Paul and these were never really adequately solved.[119]

Sperry Rand's turf struggles continued even after Norris and his associates departed to form CDC. Indeed, Eckert believed that as late as 1963 "different diverse groups of UNIVAC acting to protect their own political interests" prevented UNIVAC from developing its product line effectively.[120]

As *Business Week* subsequently wrote when describing this unfortunate period of Sperry Rand's EDP history, Sperry "snatched defeat from the jaws of victory."[121]

OTHER COMPANIES

As Chapter 4 describes in more detail, in the early to mid-1950s no other computer company made a commitment to the EDP business that was even close to that made by either Sperry Rand or, especially, IBM. For example, Honeywell's Datamatic Division designed and delivered only one computer system prior to 1958; approximately ten of these systems were sold. GE had only one major involvement in the EDP business prior to 1960 — ERMA, commissioned in 1956 by the Bank of America to perform a variety of retail banking applications. National Cash Register acquired a small computer manufacturer in 1953 but failed to deliver a new computer system between 1954 and 1959. RCA's first digital computer, the BIZMAC, was first delivered in 1956; only six were installed, and RCA did not deliver another computer system until 1959. Philco delivered several one-of-a-kind computer systems during 1955-57, but failed to announce a commercial computer until 1958. Burroughs acquired Electrodata in 1956, and by 1957 cumulative installation of Burroughs' small computers approximated 200. In sum, the breadth and depth of IBM's early commitment to the EDP business was unique. The historical record confirms that IBM recognized the enormous commercial potential of computers and decided to concentrate principally on them roughly ten years before any of the other firms that had been similarly situated in the early 1950s.

3

THE SECOND-GENERATION
COMPUTERS OF IBM AND
SPERRY RAND

IBM'S STRETCH

In 1954 the Atomic Energy Commission's (AEC) Lawrence Livermore Laboratory requested bids to build an advanced, high-speed computer. IBM and Remington Rand were the only firms to submit proposals. IBM was interested in winning the contract because, with Livermore's financial and technical assistance, it hoped to develop a state-of-the-art, large computer that would enhance the company's technical capabilities and ultimately result in more advanced commercial computer products. However, the Remington Rand proposal was chosen, primarily because it promised an earlier delivery date. To satisfy this contract Remington Rand ultimately built its LARC (Livermore Advanced Research Computer); delivery was 27 months late.[1]

In 1955 the AEC's Los Alamos Laboratory expressed an interest in acquiring a high-speed computer. IBM responded by offering essentially the same computer it had proposed for Livermore. Los Alamos accepted IBM's proposal in November 1956. The contract called for IBM and Los Alamos to share in the design of the computer, which became known as STRETCH and subsequently was renamed the IBM 7030.[2]

The STRETCH acronym reflected IBM's goal of stretching the state of the computer art by producing the fastest and most versatile computer possible, employing the leading-edge technology and knowledge then available.[3] According to Stephen Dunwell, head of IBM's STRETCH design team: "The STRETCH Project involved exploring the unknown and rethinking and redesigning almost every aspect of earlier IBM computer systems."[4] Among the specific objectives that had never before been achieved in a general-purpose computer were offering performance 100 times faster than IBM's then most powerful commercially available computer, the 704; being equally capable of both data manipulation and computation; using transistors rather than vacuum tubes; and utilizing computer-aided design as a development tool.[5]

The shift from vacuum tubes to transistors marked the beginning of the second generation of computer products. This transition was expected to be especially difficult because engineers would be forced to redirect their thinking

47

away from the more traditional vacuum tube technology.[6] Nevertheless, IBM (along with several other companies at about the same time) thought it was essential to make the switch to transistors because, according to Dunwell:

> [T]he development of vacuum tube machines [had been carried] about as far as it could go. . . . [L]arger and more complex machines were required for the solution of the problems presented to IBM by its customers, but . . . those machines could not be built at a cost that was acceptable to those customers using vacuum tube machines. . . . IBM laboratory leaders . . . recognized that the transistor was faster, smaller, used less power, avoided problems, was more reliable and was inherently less costly.[7]

Even though the transistor promised to yield significant advantages, IBM recognized that the cost of developing computers with the still-emerging transistor technology would be enormous. It chose to enter into contracts with Los Alamos and (subsequently) the National Security Agency in part to receive some independent financing for these high costs, and in part to work with partners who, as Hurd testified, would help "define the characteristics for a high-speed general purpose computer based on the problems which that partner wished to solve."[8] In fact, as discussed below, STRETCH did set the standard for IBM's transistorized 7000 series of commercial computers announced in late 1958, and also contributed to the 360 family of computers announced in 1964.

IBM accepted significant risks when it signed the STRETCH contract. Specifically, the Los Alamos contract was for only $3.5 million, whereas the projected engineering cost of STRETCH was $15 million and the estimated cost of building the first STRETCH was an additional $4.5 million.[9] Faced with these cost projections, IBM senior management initially objected to the idea of making STRETCH for Los Alamos at a $3.5 million price. Nevertheless, Hurd, who favored acceptance of the Los Alamos contract because he believed IBM would ultimately make a profit by selling between 20 and 30 of these machines, obtained authorization to proceed after pointing out that:

> Livermore had entered into a contract with UNIVAC . . . for . . . LARC and that machine, although in my opinion [it] would not be as powerful as STRETCH, was priced at $3.5 million. And I thought it would be extremely difficult, since Livermore and Los Alamos were two sister laboratories within the AEC, to obtain much more than the $3.5 million and [I] also reminded [IBM management] that . . . I had had preliminary discussions with Los Alamos about the $3.5 million.[10]

IBM delivered its first STRETCH computer system to Los Alamos in April 1961. STRETCH was subject to various criticisms after its first delivery. Some IBM employees thought the machine failed to meet its design goals; in particular, there was dispute as to whether STRETCH met its goal of being 100 times faster than the IBM 704.[11] Another criticism of STRETCH from within IBM was that it cost too much to build. A 1959 estimate indicates that STRETCH cost $25.4 million to develop, and another IBM source suggests that IBM's financial losses on the whole STRETCH program totaled $40.7 million.[12] According to Dunwell, such losses arose in part from the fact that:

> IBM was developing componentry that had not previously been used in IBM computers, and at the same time IBM was developing a system design that was different from those of earlier IBM computers. Good system design requires a thorough knowledge of the components which will be used. . . . As [the STRETCH] engineers . . . got into the STRETCH system design [they realized] that the performance of the transistor components would fall below their expectations. That was eventually overcome by modifications to the system design, but those modifications made the system design more complex than had originally been anticipated.[13]

At the Western Joint Computer Conference in 1961, Thomas J. Watson, Jr., publicly criticized STRETCH for not meeting its specification targets, as well as for its high costs. He announced that because STRETCH did not meet all of its performance targets, its price would be cut nearly in half. In addition, IBM would build machines only for committed orders. He set a cutoff date after which no further orders for STRETCH would be taken.[14]

Eight STRETCH computer systems were ultimately manufactured and installed. According to Frederic Withington, the problems with STRETCH taught the computer industry that the complexity of components "was becoming so great as the computers evolved that it was necessary to be more cautious than had been necessary in earlier years in designing and delivering complex central processing units."[15]

As the years passed, the criticisms of STRETCH were muted, and it was gradually recognized both within and outside IBM that the intangible benefits flowing from IBM's STRETCH involvement far exceeded the costs.[16] STRETCH was responsible for many advances in the state of the art of computer technology. Sidney Fernbach, who was at Livermore in the early 1950s, testified about STRETCH:

> It was highly parallel in structure, in architecture, so that many operations could be performed simultaneously, thus speeding up the machine.
> It set a standard for the entire 7000 series of computers for memory. It had a disk that was extraordinary, that was a very high performance disk drive. The peripherals were far advanced over what had been available at the time.[17]

IBM reaped substantial technological fallout from STRETCH, both in terms of both how to organize large-scale computing machines and how to develop components and incorporate new manufacturing techniques.[18] Among STRETCH developments incorporated subsequently in IBM's second-generation computer systems were standard modular systems (SMS) component technology, printed circuit cards, and improved back panel wiring. Erich Bloch, one of the members of the STRETCH design team, described in detail IBM's efforts to understand and manufacture semiconductor components:

> Second-generation EDP equipment manufactured by IBM utilized packaging for discrete components (i.e., transistors, diodes, resistors and capacitors) called Standard Modular Systems ("SMS"). A complete circuit consisted of discrete components packaged together on standardized cards ("SMS cards"). SMS cards were manufactured by IBM in a standard size and had printed circuit patterns on which the discrete components were mounted. . . .
>
> SMS packaging was . . . designed at IBM. . . . Discrete component packaging available from other suppliers . . . at the time was not as satisfactory because it had not been optimized for use in EDP equipment. EDP equipment required higher reliability than consumer products using similar or the same components. It required a high rate of production with exact replication and tolerances. . . .
>
> Among the improvements which resulted from IBM's development and use of SMS packaging were in the areas of uniformity, reliability, serviceability and ease of manufacture. Uniformity of SMS components resulted in savings in engineering design, recordkeeping, cost of purchased and manufactured components and cost of stocking spare parts. Reliability improvements resulted from controlling the manufacturing process for individual SMS circuits, the manufacturing process of assembly and the precise use of the components. Serviceability improvements came about because service personnel were able to become familiar quickly with the limited number of SMS circuits. During the period 1957 to 1960, IBM's SMS innovations in automation of manufacture included the ability to put printed wiring on the circuit card (fully automated by photograph and chemical steps), automatically to insert components into holes in the card, automatically to solder components to printed wiring . . . and automatically to interconnect socket pins on back panels (by the then recently developed Bell Laboratories technique known as wire-wrap).[19]

In addition to improved componentry, STRETCH contained architectural features that were forerunners of features included in the System 360: eight-bit byte, emphasis on alphabetic characters, a combination of fixed and variable word-length operation, a common method of attaching peripherals, and advances in magnetic tape recording and handling technology.[20]

IBM'S COMMERCIALLY AVAILABLE SECOND-GENERATION COMPUTER SYSTEMS

In the late 1950s IBM and its competitors began introducing their second-generation, or transistorized, commercial computers. There is considerable dispute as to who was first. William Norris testified that Control Data's 1604 was the "first solid-state, large-scale computer" when it was announced in

April 1958.[21] He agreed, however, that IBM delivered its transistorized 7090 computer before CDC's first delivery of the 1604. Philco announced a large-scale transistorized computer, the TRANSAC 2000, in 1958, claiming that it was the first transistorized computer.[22] RCA announced its transistorized 501 computer system in December 1958, proclaiming it to be the "first completely transistorized" computer.[23] NCR announced its 304 (manufactured by General Electric) and called it the "industry's first all-solid-state system."[24] And Honeywell announced its transistorized 800 computer system in late 1958, followed by its smaller 400 in 1960.[25]

A March 1963 report to Congress by the General Accounting Office described the many virtues of transistors:

> Transistors are but a fraction of the size of vacuum tubes, require much less power, generate less heat, and are generally more reliable. The diminutive size of transistors has led to miniaturization of circuitry so that whole circuits can be placed on small card forms. In contrast to the vacuum tube systems, the solid-state systems are more compact, require less floor space and reinforced flooring, require less special power and air conditioning facilities, are more easily maintained, and operate at faster speeds and with greater versatility.[26]

As a result of these advantages, transistorized computers rapidly replaced their vacuum tube predecessors. As Withington testified, the Burroughs Datatron 220, "the last vacuum tube computer ever announced . . . came to a sudden and permanent end" with the introduction of transistorized computers that offered "sharply superior" price/performance.[27]

7000 Series

The 7070 and 7090, announced in September and December 1958, respectively, were IBM's first commercially available second-generation computers.[28]

The 7090 was developed initially in response to an air force request for computers to be used in the DEWLINE air defense system. Four 7090s were delivered to the air force in November and December 1959, making the 7090 the first large transistorized computer system to be delivered commercially.[29] The 7090 provided the vehicle by which the componentry of the STRETCH system (including transistors, circuits, pluggable units, cards, frames, power supplies, and memories) became a part of IBM's commercial product line. In fact, most of the components used in the first 7090s came directly from the supply of parts being collected to produce the first STRETCH, and engineers working on STRETCH were diverted to the 7090 development program.[30]

The 7090 used the system design of the 709 and was program-compatible with it; it also had a compatibility feature for the 704. The 7090 offered five times the computing speed of the 709, eight input-output data channels, automatic priority processing, new high-speed core storage, and FORTRAN. Because of these improvements, the 709 was rendered obsolete almost immediately.[31]

The 7090 was described by IBM as a scientific computer. However, its use was not limited to scientific or military applications. One of its most important commercial applications was shown in 1963, when American Airlines used two 7090s to implement the first on-line, passenger-name reservation system.[32] That system, developed jointly by American Airlines and IBM, was called SABRE (for semi-automatic business research environment). According to James O'Neill, at the time director of American Airlines' computer operations, the SABRE system was one of the first real-time commercial computer applications with terminals spread across the nation; "the term SABRE became generic with . . . real time processing."[33] Development of SABRE was an extensive effort involving an estimated 1,000 man-years.[34] SABRE was derivative from SAGE "in the sense that each used remote terminals and telephone wires to communicate from those remote terminals to the central processor which did its processing and then sent back the results over the telephone wires"; both systems had a general system design referred to as "Command and Control"; and the SABRE software was similar to that used in SAGE.[35]

Although announced first, the IBM 7070 was the second IBM second-generation computer system to be delivered. The 7070 offered both variable and fixed-word logic as well as automatic floating-decimal arithmetic. Like the 7090 it used STRETCH components. The 7070 was considered to be "business oriented."[36] The IBM 7074, announced in 1960, was intended to be an improvement on the 7070. Compared with the 7070, it had six times faster internal processing speeds, two times faster through-put for most applications, and ten to twenty times faster scientific computing. The 7074 was a modular system that offered complete compatibility with the 7070 — that is, every application program written for a 7070 could be used on a 7074 without reprogramming and without any loss of efficiency.[37]

IBM also introduced the 7080 (delivered in 1961), a transistorized version of the 705 and compatible with it. Like the 705, the 7080 was thought to have a business orientation.[38]

Two other 7000 series computers were the 7040 and 7044, both delivered in 1963. Although intended to have a scientific orientation, these systems came with an excellent COBOL compiler, prompting many customers to use them exclusively for business applications. The 7040 and 7044 were hardware- and program-compatible, so that a user desiring more computing capacity could move readily from the 7040 to the larger 7044.[39]

In 1962 IBM introduced the 7094 and, later, the 7094 II as compatible upgrades to the 7090. According to GE's Weil, these large systems were "at the time by far the leading scientific and engineering computer[s] in the field."[40]

1400 Series

The IBM 1401, announced in October 1959, proved to be an extremely successful computer. The total number of 1401 installations, between 15,000 and 20,000, dwarfed that of all earlier computers (only about 6,000 general-purpose computers had been installed in the United States through the end of 1960).[41]

The 1401 was intended to be the successor to IBM's popular 650, although the two machines were not program-compatible. According to Jack James of Telex, an IBM salesman in the late 1950s, the 1401

> . . . provided a major breakthrough, from a price/performance standpoint, in that it brought the entry point . . . I mean the lowest [priced] configuration that a customer [could] order and practically install . . . down significantly lower than had existed in prior systems that were available. . . .[42]

The 1401's lower price, coupled with its substantial improvements in speed, reliability, and peripherals, caused it to sweep the market. It could execute seven times as many instructions per second as the 650 and, as it evolved in the marketplace, "became available in at least dozens of different models with at least dozens of different peripheral equipment options."[43] IBM subsequently introduced a number of CPUs compatible with the 1401 CPU, thereby enabling users to upgrade their 1400 systems without changing their peripheral equipment. Such modularity had not been possible with the 650.[44]

One reason for the 1401's popularity was the 1403 printer introduced with it. The 1403 was a high-speed chain printer that operated at 600 lines per minute (compared with a typical speed of 150 lines per minute for earlier machines), and for many years stood out as the highest-quality printer in the computer industry.[45] Withington testified that the 1403 "represented a very large step forward in the functionality and price/performance of high speed printers available for computer systems."[46] He believed that this printer gave IBM a tremendous advantage that began to diminish only in 1963 or 1964, as competitors began to offer alternatives to it. Withington described the advantages of the 1403 as follows:

> [It] introduced a new basic printing technology, that of the chain printer, in which the characters move laterally across the line of print on a chain. This proved markedly superior to the other technologies in use at the time in that higher quality print was produced [by eliminating the wavy line associated with prior printers] and the cost of printing at what was then considered a high speed was lower using this technology.
>
> In addition, the 1403 also had some attractive features in terms of carriage control, forms feeding and the like.[47]

The 1403 made IBM the technological leader in impact printer products. It was so successful that it proved to be a major factor causing sales of 1400 computer systems to far exceed even IBM's expectations.[48]

The 1401 was used in numerous applications — both as a stand-alone computer system and as a part of much larger computer systems centered on IBM's

700 and 7000 series central processing units. For example, when Livermore acquired its first 7090, it also purchased two 1401s. One of these was used as a card-to-tape converter, a peripheral device to the 7090. After several years this 1401 was no longer needed to perform that task, so it was used by Livermore's Data Processing Services Group primarily as a printer controller.[49] In another example, the Southern Railway did its revenue and accounting work on an IBM 705, with two 1401s doing peripheral processing — card-to-tape and tape-to-print operations. The Southern Railway used a third 1401 in stand-alone mode, with six associated tape drives, to perform accounting work, and a fourth to do peripheral work for an IBM 7074.[50]

IBM's competitors recognized that, because of its versatility, the 1401 offered competition to most of their computer systems, both large and small. For example, a December 1959 business review prepared by RCA's EDP Division stated:

> A major competitive move developed in the announcement by IBM of their 1401. This low level system was announced as an independent low-cost system as well as a direct coupled adjunct to the IBM 7070. . . .
>
> Early reaction to the IBM 7070 was not as favorable as originally anticipated. However, the range of this system was substantially enhanced by the . . . announcement of the IBM 1401. The 1401 as an adjuct to the 7070 permits both a price reduction and an increase in performance. The IBM 7070 with the 1401 is now offering a stronger level of competition in the $20,000 to $25,000 monthly rental range.
>
> The 1401 standing alone is also a stronger competitor in the $3,000 to $10,000 range and competes with the Rem-Rand Solid State 8090 as well as the RCA 502. Competitive marketing strategy calling for "doubling up" on these systems at a single site is noted. In other words, an IBM proposal to use two 1401's presents a problem in the low end of our 500 series.[51]

Sperry Rand's larger computer systems also faced competition from IBM's much smaller 1400 series machines. According to Presper Eckert, the UNIVAC III faced competition from IBM 1400s because a customer "could . . . use several of these 1400 machines to do the work of a UNIVAC III, and if this was the choice of a customer to do it that way, it could be regarded as a competitor."[52]

The 1401 proved so successful that it prompted some of IBM's competitors to attempt to develop program-compatible products (see Chapter 4). Most notably, Honeywell introduced the Honeywell 200 computer system, which was incompatible with its earlier computer products but, with the assistance of a conversion program called LIBERATOR, provided users with the ability to convert 1401 programs automatically so that they could run on the 200.[53] Similarly, GE targeted its 400 series at IBM's 1400 family because it was the most widely installed small computer system and thus offered the largest customer base for an attempt to convert. GE provided a 1401 simulator (a combination of hardware and software) intended to permit programs written for the IBM 1401 "either to be run or to be converted easily to the 400."[54]

Second-Generation Disk Drives

IBM introduced two new disk drives with its second-generation computer systems – the 1301 and the 1311. These embodied fundamental innovations that maintained, and indeed enhanced, IBM's previous superiority in direct-access storage technology, a superiority that greatly contributed to the competitiveness of IBM's second-generation computer systems in the early 1960s and that laid the foundation for the critical contribution of disk storage to the success of System 360 in the mid- to late 1960s.

IBM announced the 1301 disk file in June 1961. In comparison with its predecessor, the 350 RAMAC disk file, the 1301 had four times faster access speed, five times greater bit density, two and a half times greater track density, ten times greater total storage capacity, and more than seven times faster data transfer rates.[55] The 1301 had two principal innovations that were largely responsible for these improvements.

The 1301 was the first commercially available disk file using hydrodynamic slider bearings to maintain the spacing between the head and the disk recording medium. This innovation eliminated the need for the external air supply used in the 350 RAMAC disk file to maintain the spacing between the two disk heads and the recording media of 50 disks. In contrast, the 1301 disk drive had one head per recording surface, 100 heads in all.[56] Not only did the slider-bearing technology make practical having one head per recording surface, it also permitted a nearly fourfold reduction in the height at which the disk head "flew" over the disk recording surface. This was important because "The key to dense magnetic recording is to get the magnetic recording element . . . as close as possible to the media that you want to record on or retrieve data from."[57] Thus, the engineering advances that precipitated lowering the disk head's flying height on the 1301 led directly to its greater disk and track densities and increased disk capacity.

The 1301's second major innovation was that it was the first commercially available disk file with a hydraulic actuator. The RAMAC had a mechanical actuator that was designed to retract the head from one disk, move along the axis of the disks, and go in on another of the 50 disks. In contrast, because the 1301 had a disk head for every recording surface, its hydraulic actuator only needed to move the arms holding the heads in and out. As a result, the access speed of the 1301 was many times faster than that of the RAMAC.[58]

Announced in October 1962, IBM's second new disk drive, the 1311, was a smaller-capacity, lower-entry-cost device than previous disk drive products, and featured the first removable as well as interchangeable disk pack. Providing disk pack removability required IBM to solve many substantial engineering and manufacturing problems arising from increased contamination exposure, increased spindle precision requirements, increased pack precision requirements, aggravated thermal expansion problems, actuator accuracy, increased head alignment problems, and increased vibration tolerances.[59]

The 1311 disk drive proved to be of great commercial value, both because it was affordable for use on IBM's smaller second-generation computer systems, including the 1400 series and the 1620, and because of the advantages inherent in a removable disk pack. According to IBM's Richard Case:

> [T] he value of [the removable disk pack] was that the cost of storage was substantially reduced because just the disk pack could be removed and put on a shelf for long-term storage; whereas, in prior devices since the disks could not be removed if the information was going to stay there a long time, it was associated also with the electrical and mechanical parts of the disk drive.[60]

The 1311 combined the disk drive's fast random-access capability with the tape drive's advantage of permitting data to be transported from one system to another and extra packs to be stored on the shelf, resulting in lower-cost storage.

Summary

The preceding discussion of IBM's second-generation computer products is not intended to be all-inclusive. Nevertheless, it shows that IBM steadily and quickly introduced new computer products and systems that were far superior to their immediate predecessors. In comparison with IBM's first-generation computers, its second-generation products occupied less space, required less air conditioning, consumed less power, and offered greatly improved price/performance, speed, and through-put, and more functions.[61] Moreover, by the early 1960s IBM had started to introduce modular peripherals and CPUs, allowing the customer to configure a substantial number of different computer systems out of the different products supplied by IBM.[62]

Some of IBM's second-generation computers were compatible with a corresponding first-generation product and with some of the other second-generation computers. Nevertheless, as the 1960s progressed, one deficiency became increasingly apparent: IBM's computer systems were not compatible over a broad range of size and speed categories. Remedying this deficiency would be one of the goals of the designers of IBM's System 360.

SPERRY RAND: THE PROBLEMS CONTINUE

In the late 1950s and early 1960s, Sperry Rand participated in the remarkable growth of the computer business, but it continued to suffer from many of the managerial and organizational difficulties described in Chapter 2. Thus, even though Sperry expanded its product line to include smaller computers, introduced new UNIVAC and 1100 series computer systems, produced a new real-time computer system, and produced several special-bid computer systems for government agencies and the military, its relative standing among EDP companies continued to deteriorate. As Withington testified, despite the expansion of Sperry Rand's product line between 1955 and 1963, the company was "slow to introduce successor or improved models" at the time technology was changing fastest, and "middle-range UNIVAC customers" left UNIVAC "for IBM or some other supplier offering substantially more modern products."[63]

Sperry Rand was one of the first conglomerate firms in the United States. Conglomerates have had a mixed record of business performance. Virtually all of them have discovered that the only way to manage organizations that engage in highly disparate and dynamically changing businesses is to set up individual profit centers. Sperry Rand, however, had no computer-related profit centers from approximately 1959 through 1964. Instead, the principal line components of the corporation were divided according to function (marketing, finance, and production) rather than product segments or profit centers such as computers.[64] For example, the person within Sperry who was in charge of manufacturing computers also had responsibility for "office products such as typewriters and equipment, filing cabinets and general business products"; a different person "headed up all of the marketing activities for computers and office equipment."[65] As described by Robert McDonald, who was general manager of the UNIVAC Military Department in the early 1960s and became president of a consolidated UNIVAC Division in 1966, "The corporation was set up on an engineering basis with a manufacturing head in charge of the marketing activities. Now, that is not a computer company."[66]

Throughout the early 1960s Sperry Rand's computer operations experienced rapid turnover in senior management.[67] According to Withington, UNIVAC's historically high turnover, with its consequent "inability to assemble a smoothly working, reasonably permanent management team," was one of Sperry's greatest drawbacks.[68] High turnover also exacerbated UNIVAC's lack of a consistent product policy.

LARC

As previously discussed, in 1954-55 Remington Rand won a competition with IBM to obtain a contract with the AEC's Lawrence Livermore Laboratory to "make a leap ahead in using advanced components," to build a computer with "as much power as possible."[69] The purchase price of that first LARC was $3.5 million. LARC was later offered to other potential customers at a price as high as $7 million.[70]

Sperry Rand did not deliver LARC until 1960, approximately 27 months behind schedule. One reason for the delay was that in 1956-57 engineers were transferred off LARC to help solve problems that were delaying the design and manufacture of the UNIVAC II, Sperry's rather tardy successor to the UNIVAC I. According to Eckert:

> There had been some difficulty with UNIVAC II, and we had to make a decision as to whether to delay LARC and put the manpower we had on LARC over to correct the problem of UNIVAC II, or . . . whether to

leave [*sic*] the manpower remain on LARC so it wouldn't be delayed and let the UNIVAC II schedule be delayed.

Dr. Fry made a decision to delay LARC, and push harder on UNIVAC II.[71]

However, in dealing with the AEC, Sperry did not mention this source of LARC's 27-month delay. Instead, it listed the causes as the following:

1. disappointment by Sperry Rand in the performance of production run components furnished by its suppliers, which in many cases failed to meet the exacting requirements of LARC;

2. underestimation by Sperry Rand of the engineering and other technical complexities involved; and

3. the institution by Sperry Rand of a budgetary curtailment on LARC which was imposed as a result of impairment of working capital, the 1957-58 recession and the large monthly losses incurred on the LARC project.[72]

Apparently only two LARCs were produced.[73] In Eckert's view, LARC's 27-month delay cost Sperry Rand several sales. Writing in 1961 about the lack of LARC sales, he stated:

We had no nerve on this. After the great setbacks due to Fry's dragout policy and Dr. [Edward] Teller's anger at the delays produced, plus no guts on the corporation's part, we flunked.[74]

Sperry Rand lost several million dollars on LARC.[75] Withington testified that LARC "developed a very poor reputation for reliability" and classified it as a major product failure, adding that LARC's "concentration on magnetic drums, after it had become apparent to the rest of the industry that magnetic disks were superior," contributed to its failure.[76] Nevertheless, like its IBM counterpart, STRETCH, LARC did advance the state of the computing art. Fernbach described some of these advances:

[LARC] had parallel features. It was not quite as advanced in that respect as the STRETCH was. But it did have some very fine features other than that. It really consisted of two processors. One, the central processor, operated on the arithmetic portion of the problem, whereas the I/O processor took care of all the requirements for input and output while the operations were going on in the central processor, so in a sense it was a dual machine using a common memory to carry out its work. . . .

It also had some advanced peripheral devices such as its drums, which were designed in such a way there was essentially no lost time in accessing information on a drum that had to be fed into central memory.[77]

The LARC project concentrated on developing better computer hardware. Sperry Rand did write certain input-output processor software for LARC, but the AEC was not satisfied, and chose to rewrite it. In fact, the Livermore Laboratory wrote all of LARC's applications software as well as much of its systems software.[78] Some of LARC's hardware advances benefited Sperry Rand's subsequent EDP products. Eckert testified:

> The circuit development ideas of LARC found their way into a machine called the UNIVAC III, which followed LARC. Not only just the circuits themselves, which were improved somewhat, with somewhat better transistors, but the modular board construction and the sockets and plugs, and many of the things that we learned about LARC enabled us to build a much better UNIVAC III than we would have been able to construct.
>
> Also some of the things that we learned about improving tape units went into even further improvements in the tape units for UNIVAC III.[79]

The Solid-State Computer

As described in Chapter 2, it was not until 1956 that Sperry Rand first delivered a low-cost computer aimed at competing with IBM's extremely successful 650. Known as the File Computer, this product was developed by the Minneapolis/St. Paul group. About the same time the Philadelphia group was developing its own low-cost computer, called the Solid State Computer although it was not, in fact, fully transistorized. Instead, its circuits were made from a combination of transistors and magnetic core amplifiers.[80]

Beginning in 1957-58, the Solid State Computer was marketed commercially in Europe. However, even though many American customers were aware of the Solid State Computer and sought to acquire it, Sperry Rand withheld it from the U.S. market for more than a year in order to protect its existing base of installed unit record equipment that used a 90-column punch card incompatible with the 80-column punch card used on the Solid State Computer.[81] Withington testified: "I can remember users explicitly saying that they wanted it, and that the Company refused to give it to them."[82]

The Solid State Computer was superior to Sperry Rand's File Computer and, in 1957-58, also offered a better value than the IBM 650, which had been on the market since 1954. Although IBM had introduced enchanced peripherals for 650 attachment, the CPU had not been modernized and had become nearly obsolete.[83] However, by the time Sperry Rand finally started marketing the Solid State Computer in the United States (where it was known as the SS-80), the computer had lost its competitive advantage because its principal competition was no longer the 650, but the IBM 1401 (announced in 1959). Withington believed that because of the delay, most of the people who earlier would have been customers for the Solid State Computer ordered the IBM 1401 instead.

Nevertheless, the SS-80 was still, according to Withington, Sperry Rand's "most successful computer" in the late 1950s and early 1960s, with "about 600 installations at one time."[84]

In 1960 and 1961 Sperry tried or considered various means of making the Solid State Computer more competitive with the superior IBM 1401. One effort was to enhance the SS-80 by attaching a random-access storage device called the RANDEX II. Unfortunately, the attachment was done so ineptly that Eckert was moved to comment caustically in 1961:

> RANDEX II stores 200,000,000 pulses. We ineptly hooked it to [the UNIVAC Solid State Computer] and lost 75,000,000 of the 200,000,000 pulses. No accessor speed improvement in the last 20 months. No cost reduction, thus high rent. Result — almost no sales. IBM now is cheaper, faster, for same storage. A lead was possible but we dropped the ball.[85]

UNIVAC also considered speeding up the memory available for the Solid State Computer but, as Eckert lamented, this had not been done by April 1961:

> Core Memory for [the Solid State Computer]. This was investigated at least three times in the last 1-1/2 years, by Sales, Engineering, and Product Planning. Now at this late date, we have decided to do something. We now face whether at this late date it is worth doing. . . .
>
> There is [also] no adequate tape speed up program to match the core memory speed up for the Solid State Computer. I have been scrambling around this last two weeks trying to make up for this failure of Engineering and Product Planning. I have found some very good things that can be done in time and at rather low engineering cost. . . . This is, however, the "last drop" that can be squeezed from the [Solid State Computer] and we must not lose sight of this.[86]

As late as 1964, Sperry Rand remained committed to its aging SS-80, prompting Withington to write that Sperry "did not and still has not . . . provide[d] successors to the SS-80 convenient in both programming compatibility and price," with the result that "The number of SS-80 installations must have shrunk considerably, with most lost to competitors."[87]

New Large-Scale Computers and Related Peripherals

In comparison with IBM, a principal shortcoming of Sperry Rand's EDP business during the 1950s was its delay in introducing either enhancements or improved successors to its existing product line. It was not until 1959 that Sperry Rand's Minneapolis/St. Paul organization first delivered the 1105 Scientific model, a computer expected to be used in engineering and scientific applications involving large-volume data-handling problems and intended to be the successor to the 1103-A first delivered in 1953.[88] Similarly, the successor to the UNIVAC I, the UNIVAC II, was not delivered until 1957; and its solid-state successor, the UNIVAC III, was not delivered until 1962, three years after IBM introduced its transistorized 7090.

As early as 1955, individuals within Remington Rand recognized that:

[C]ustomers for electronic data-processing equipment are interested in what is loosely known as "compatibility." As time goes on we are going to get more and more pointed questions regarding the compatibility of various units in our UNIVAC line. Even though compatibility is not well defined, we should, as a part of our long-range planning, strive toward more compatibility of our various units.[89]

A second major shortcoming of Sperry Rand was its failure to act effectively on this advice.

In 1958-59 Eckert unsuccessfully attempted to get Sperry Rand to consolidate its overlapping, noncompatible product lines by developing only one large-scale computer system. According to Eckert:

Back when Mr. Schnackel was president of UNIVAC in 1958-59, it was proposed that we build a 490, a UNIVAC III and an 1107. I strongly opposed this idea and told Mr. Schnackel that I didn't care which of the three we built (although the UNIVAC III was my proposal), but that a real time I-O system and floating point should be available on whatever we built and that because of the engineering and software problems, we should certainly build no more than one large scale computer. My feelings of course, were the same as those that must have developed later in IBM and produced for IBM a more or less unified 360-370 line. Unfortunately, the political nature of UNIVAC prevented a resolution of this problem and we went ahead and built three logically unrelated machines.[90]

As Eckert indicates, Sperry Rand's management did not choose to follow his advice. In 1960 Sperry Rand announced three large, new, and incompatible computers: the UNIVAC III, the UNIVAC 1107, and the 490 Real-Time System. In early 1961 a disgruntled Eckert described some of the adverse consequences of that decision:

[We are building] [t]hree machines where one (with a choice of two arithmetic units) would have done the job. . . .

A single "speed up" of circuits would have later been possible for LARC, UNIVAC III, and its variations. The way things have been managed, four projects would be needed to up date [*sic*] these machines. . . .

1. Three 4 microsecond memories have been designed, a 27 bit (UNIVAC III), a 32 bit (490), and a 36 bit (1107). The last two have no checking — a horrible omission.

2. We have three types of new circuits and circuit cards, all uselessly different from LARC. This means different card testers, production

set ups [*sic*], backboard wiring routines, and all the rest.

3. We have three different casework designs . . . in spite of Philadelphia using a former St. Paul man to do the work.

4. We have two complete sets of synchronizers for all the peripheral equipment under way.

5. We have three complete sets of "software" under way.

A loss of 10 months in UNIVAC III delivery — three months due to foolish redesign of the LARC circuits — 7 months due to trying for final test at the factory. . . . In any case 4 microsecond memories are obsolete before we deliver anything . . . IBM already had 2 microsecond memories.[91]

In discussing other avoidable engineering shortcomings, mostly incurred in 1959-61, Eckert described the "Horrible Peripheral Mess at Norwalk" as causing Sperry to have five printers where "one printer frame and case, with 2 actuator assemblies would have handled all this at half or less of the cost of what we have and are doing."[92] A similar situation existed for card readers and punches.[93]

With respect to disk drives, Eckert described how Sperry had started to develop a "disc unit, much like IBM's RAMAC," that had "[w]orked but was given up as too intricate in comparison to present drum approach."[94] In 1959-61 St. Paul made several more attempts, but finally dropped much of its disk work. Beginning in 1960, and for four or five years thereafter, Sperry Rand marketed its large FASTRAND drum memory in competition with the disk drives offered by IBM and other manufacturers. Sperry's marketing of computer systems was substantially and adversely affected by its lack of competitive disk drives.[95]

Eckert also described how little real exploratory work was being pushed at Sperry in 1961, with the exception of thin-film memory, and even that was being done in "a crazy hap-hazard [*sic*] way": there were five groups working on thin-film memory at Minneapolis/St. Paul and two more at Philadelphia, but they "usually don't believe each other and will not usually use same design test equipment."[96] With respect to circuitry, no real progress was being made, and manufacturing costs were not being controlled.[97] Eckert wrote:

This is really sad since three-fourths of our large machines and almost one-half of our small machines costs are in logic circuits, etc. We have the people but no overall guidance, no program. We just do the simple next obvious step stuff the whole way and never really get ahead.[98]

Eckert also blamed Sperry's expensive components on "a rush ill considered standardization and partly due to poor lay technicians at both Norwalk and St. Paul."[99] These problems persisted well into the 1960s. In 1965 Sperry's Product Line Task Force reported: "UNIVAC cannot manufacture equipment at costs as low as can be achieved by IBM. . . . Our manufacturing cost situation is in bad shape compared to IBM."[100]

Sperry Rand began to deliver its three new commercial computer systems in 1962 and 1963. It compared the UNIVAC III with the UNIVAC I as follows:

> The first UNIVAC III System, a large solid-state computer . . . will be 60 times as fast as the UNIVAC I System and will have 32 times as much memory. But so rapidly has the computer art advanced, that the UNIVAC III System rents for less than the early machines.[101]

However, unlike IBM's 7000 series computers, the UNIVAC III was not compatible with its vacuum tube predecessors, the UNIVAC II and the UNIVAC I, nor with any of the 1100 series computers or the new 490. Customers ultimately installed approximately 100 UNIVAC IIIs.[102]

Sperry described the UNIVAC 1107 thin-film memory computer, first delivered in 1963, as "the first commercially available EDP system utilizing magnetic thin-film memory," with "one of the largest total memory capacities ever delivered to a commercial user."[103] As with previous 1100 series computers, much of the 1107's development expense was paid by the government.[104] Although Sperry's 1100 series computers were described as scientific, in its 1962 annual report the firm added:

> Computer programming techniques − characterized as software − have made significant advances in keeping pace with the technological improvements in computer hardware. . . . [B]y utilizing sophisticated programming in the new computers, interchangeability between scientific and business type computers may be achieved.[105]

Eckert testified that with the passage of time, the "natural evolution of hardware developments were [*sic*] such as to blunt some of the differences that we saw historically," with respect to computers oriented toward business or scientific applications:

> We began to see lower costs and more reliable forms of logic which came about through solid state device[s], magnetic amplifiers, transistors, and so on. That meant that one could afford more logic in the machine, at a given price level, so that the question of whether we had a little extra logic in there to be able to do both the things you like for business and . . . for scientific and . . . for statistical purposes, for all these different purposes, it became possible to put enough in there to perhaps satisfy everybody.[106]

Sperry Rand's UNIVAC 490 real-time system was based on what Sperry described as its military counterpart, the UNIVAC 1206 military real-time computer. According to Sperry, the 1206 and the 490 were developed "to meet the needs of industry and government for a computer that can solve problems or answer questions virtually as soon as they are posed, or in 'real time.' "[107] The UNIVAC 1206, for example, was intended to be used (among other things) to "record all the information that is sent from a rocket in flight and to send guidance signals back to the rocket."[108] Its commercially available counterpart, the 490, performed both business and scientific applications. Eastern Airlines, for example, used the 490 to perform an early reservations application, and Westinghouse used it to perform message switching.[109]

Sperry Rand supplied many computers to the military, including both its commercially available computers and a number of computers made more rugged or radiation-resistant in accordance with military needs. Two important examples were a ground-based system developed for the army, in conjunction with Bell Laboratories, to be used in the Nike-Zeus antimissile program, and the UNIVAC 1218, described by Sperry as "a medium-scale, general purpose unit, designed to meet stringent land-based and shipborne military specifications."[110]

In the early 1960s Sperry Rand's EDP business was plagued by the proliferation of noncompatible and overlapping product lines.[111] In 1963 Eckert became chairman of Sperry's Gemini Committee, and once more tried unsuccessfully to get the firm to begin finding a remedy for burgeoning problems:

> Again the groups from the different diverse groups of UNIVAC acted to protect their own political interests and the only thing that really happened was that no successor to the UNIVAC III was developed. . . .[112]

By contrast, as early as March 1961 IBM began a corporation-wide attempt to address, head-on, the problem of proliferating, noncompatible computer product lines. As described in Chapter 5, the result was the December 28, 1961, SPREAD Report, which led to the announcement of System 360.

4

OTHER
EARLY PARTICIPANTS IN
THE EDP BUSINESS

Although IBM and Sperry Rand were the most active firms in the EDP industry during its first decade (see Table 4.1), the industry had several other significant participants. Contracts with departments and agencies of the U.S. government often provided the principal stimulus for entering the EDP business. However, unlike Sperry Rand and, especially, IBM, until the late 1950s no other firms made substantial commitments of their own resources to EDP. Thus, during most of the 1950s none of these firms was able to project itself as a major EDP supplier on a sustained basis.

Beginning in the late 1950s and early 1960s, however, the importance of other firms in the EDP industry began to change rapidly. Some large, established firms chose to limit or reduce their fledgling EDP activities; others finally made the decision to commit sufficient resources to establish a sustained presence in

Table 4.1. U.S. EDP Revenues of Major Computer Manufacturers, 1963
(in rank order)

Firm	1963 Revenues
International Business Machines (IBM)	$ 1,244,161,000
Sperry Rand (SR)	145,480,000
American Telephone & Telegraph (AT&T)	97 million-plus
Control Data (CD)	84,610,000
Philco (P)	73.9 million
Burroughs (B)	42,145,000
General Electric (GE)	38.6 million
National Cash Register (NCR)	30,718,000
Honeywell (H)	27 million
Radio Corporation of America	not available

Sources: IBM, DX 3811; SR, DX 8224, p. 624; AT&T, DX 8224, p. 133; CD, DX 298; P, DX 8387, pp. 1, 6; B, DX 8224, p. 1; GE, DX 8224, p. 6; NCR, DX 8224, p. 3; H, DX 8631, pp. 31, 37; DX 14484, p. R.1.

the market; and a few newly formed, small firms dedicated to the computer business laid the foundation necessary to become successful computer companies.

AMERICAN TELEPHONE AND TELEGRAPH

In 1950 American Telephone and Telegraph Company (AT&T) had assets exceeding $11 billion and was the largest firm in the United States.[1] In addition to its enormous size and financial resources, AT&T owned the Western Electric Company and Bell Telephone Laboratories. Western Electric was the manufacturer of most of the telephone equipment used by the Bell System's operating companies, as well as of communications and electromechanical equipment sold to other organizations, including the U.S. government. With sales in 1950 of over $758 million, Western Electric was, in its own right, one of the largest industrial companies in the United States, and significantly larger than IBM.[2] Bell Telephone Laboratories was the premier privately owned scientific organization in the United States, with an unrivaled commitment to basic research in the physical, mathematical, and behavioral sciences to support its extensive applied development efforts.

AT&T had long been involved in the development of electromechanical computing equipment, and in the course of that work had made important contributions to the computer field. According to the company:

> The earliest large electrical computers were built at Bell Telephone Laboratories. The first large digital computer, for example, was completed in 1940 from components and techniques normally used in dial switching systems. It was demonstrated that year to mathematicians at Dartmouth College using a data communications link between Hanover, New Hampshire and the computer located in New York City. Analog computers designed by Bell Telephone Laboratories were used to control and direct the fire of anti-aircraft batteries early in World War II. During the 1943-47 period, the Bell System supplied several digital computers to various agencies of the Federal Government.[3]

Known to possess the greatest expertise on the reliability of relays, plugs, and connectors, AT&T was consulted by Eckert and Mauchly in connection with the design of the ENIAC.[4] In addition, AT&T did substantial early research in electronic logic, and claimed to have produced more than half of all the large electrically operated digital computers made prior to 1950.[5]

AT&T's dial system has many of the features of a giant computer. According to the company:

> [C]ircuit switching is a technique that has been used practically since the beginning of telephone. . . . The nationwide Direct Distance Dialing (DDD) network is made up of all of the existing dialing systems, long distance and exchange, forming a huge circuit switching network. It is,

in effect, a giant computer, containing all of the elements of a computer, i.e., control, processing, memory, input and output units.[6]

And, when describing AT&T's dialing system, a former AT&T chairman stated: "Our common control switching systems, in big cities, nearly 40 years ago, were probably the first exemplars of real-time data processing."[7]

In 1954, when John Mauchly was asked by his Remington Rand managers to list those companies (excluding Remington Rand) with a significant patent position in the EDP field, he responded with a list of over 20 in which he ranked AT&T first and IBM second.[8] Three examples of AT&T's pioneering work in EDP-related electronics are (1) in 1947 Bell Telephone Laboratories' employees invented the transistor (for which three later received the Nobel Prize), and Bell began producing transistors on a production line basis in 1952;[9] (2) about 1950 AT&T operated the first time-sharing computer system;[10] and (3) in 1954 AT&T demonstrated TRADIC, which it described as the first general-purpose transistorized digital computer.[11]

In the early and mid-1950s AT&T had the potential to become one of the principal manufacturers and vendors of computer equipment. That prospect diminished sharply in 1956, when Bell agreed to enter into a final judgment to settle an antitrust suit that the U.S. government had brought against it in 1949. The decree provided, in part:

> The defendants [AT&T and Western Electric] are each enjoined . . . from commencing [or] continuing, directly or indirectly, to manufacture for sale or lease any equipment which is of a type not sold or leased or intended to be sold or leased to Companies of the Bell System, for use in furnishing common carrier communications services. . . .
> . . . Western [Electric] is enjoined . . . from engaging, either directly or indirectly, in any business not of a character or type engaged in by Western or its subsidiaries for Companies of the Bell System. . . .
> . . . AT&T is enjoined . . . from engaging, either directly, or indirectly through its subsidiaries other than Western and Western's subsidiaries, in any business other than the furnishing of common carrier communications services. . . .[12]

The prohibitions of the consent decree had one important exception: both AT&T and Western Electric could manufacture and sell the prohibited classes of products (noncommunications products) to the U.S. government and its contractors. This exemption reflects AT&T's vital role in providing the U.S. government with electronic goods and services intended to advance national security interests.

The 1956 consent decree limited AT&T's ability to compete in large parts of the computer business. However, AT&T continued to manufacture computer products for the U.S. government, for the Bell operating companies, which used them in providing common carrier services, and, through its Teletype subsidiary, for commercial customers. Its post-1956 EDP products included computer systems, terminals, modems, and data sets.[13]

By the early 1960s AT&T had announced the development of its Number 1 electronic switching system (ESS), which it described as "a stored program control system . . . developed to handle a variety of switching jobs."[14] The Number 1 electronic switching system was in fact a computer dedicated to performing real-time, telephone-switching applications. It had "primary inputs from telephone lines and trunks via scanners, and outputs to the network and signal distributor, with teletypewriters as administrative input-output devices and with a magnetic tape for automatic message accounting . . . output."[15] The memory units in the No. 1 ESS could be expanded over a wide range to accommodate the largest office. The first No. 1 ESS was installed in 1965.[16]

That AT&T continued to have a significant presence in the EDP business even after the 1956 consent decree is confirmed by the fact that its U.S. EDP revenues rose from $770,000 in 1952 to more than $97 million in 1963.[17] More than $61 million of AT&T's 1963 U.S. EDP sales were products sold by its Teletype subsidiary, and nearly $32 million were from the sale of computer products manufactured by either AT&T or its subsidiaries to the U.S. government.[18] AT&T's 1963 U.S. EDP revenues were higher than those of all other companies except Sperry Rand and IBM.

RAYTHEON AND HONEYWELL

Raytheon rose to prominence during World War II primarily as a manufacturer of radar and other electronic equipment for the military. It was involved in developing and producing computers as early as 1947, when it began work on the RAYDAC (Raytheon Digital Automatic Computer) under the sponsorship of the Bureau of Standards and, later, the Office of Naval Research. The RAYDAC was first delivered about 1951.[19] In the late 1940s and early 1950s Raytheon also developed other computers that went to classified, national security-related users.[20] In the early 1950s it manufactured electronic components including transistors, triodes, rectifiers, and Klystron tubes.[21]

During the late 1940s and early 1950s, Raytheon's extensive EDP operations were funded entirely by government contracts, and its computers were used exclusively by U.S. government agencies.[22] Richard Bloch, who joined Raytheon in 1947 as head of its Analytical Department and later became general manager of its Computer Division, described Raytheon's EDP activities in the early 1950s as "one of the prime centers of technological development at that time, and probably [a] leader roughly parallel with the UNIVAC Operation in terms of scope of competence."[23] In 1952 Raytheon was one of the select set of companies with which MIT's Lincoln Laboratory conducted detailed discussions concerning proposals for designing the SAGE computer system.[24]

About 1953-54 Raytheon began developing a computer known as the RAYCOM, a "general purpose commercially oriented . . . digital computer, which was a takeoff of work [Raytheon] had done on the RAYDAC."[25]

However, Raytheon ultimately decided not to pursue a commercially oriented computer. According to Bloch:

> The primary reason was that Raytheon at that time was primarily a Government-funded corporation, very heavily so; they did not attack commercial activities in other fields very effectively, and had no desire to make a move into this commercial field. Furthermore, and probably most importantly, they did not have the funds that would be required. They were accustomed to being funded by Government contract, and this required funding from the [corporate] exchequer.[26]

Nevertheless, Raytheon had in its employ an extremely capable group working on computers. Rather than disperse them, in 1955 Raytheon entered into a joint venture, called the Datamatic Corporation, with the Minneapolis-Honeywell Regulator Company (hereafter Honeywell). The purpose of the joint venture was to design, develop, and produce large-scale computer systems for business data processing based on Raytheon's work on the RAYCOM.[27] At the time of the joint venture, Honeywell was one of the largest U.S. manufacturers of automatic control equipment for home, commercial, military, and industrial applications.[28]

Raytheon, with a 40 percent interest in Datamatic, contributed essentially all of the computer know-how. Indeed, Bloch testified that the group he headed at Raytheon, which had designed the RAYDAC and worked on the RAYCOM, was subsequently responsible for developing the Datamatic-1000 (based on the RAYCOM), as well as the later Honeywell 800 and 400 computer systems, and had an important role in developing the Honeywell 200 computer system. Honeywell's major contribution was said to be money and management.[29]

Bloch thought that Raytheon missed a magnificent opportunity when it cautiously decided not to pursue the RAYCOM development:

> Some of this I must say is a question of an immodest belief that we would marshal the necessary forces to do the job, but remembering that we had a strong technical group, I feel that we would have developed, with time, the necessary marketing force, and so on.
> This was an early time in the field. The most important thing at this time, certainly, was technical competence in terms of being able to develop any product that made sense. And that we had.[30]

From Honeywell's point of view, the purpose of the Datamatic joint venture was to bring it overnight into an important position, certainly technologically, in the then infant computer field. According to James Binger, Honeywell's chairman, Honeywell "looked upon the move as a very natural extension of [its] existing automation business."[31]

In 1955, when the Datamatic joint venture began, Honeywell had sales of $244 million, net income before taxes of $40 million, and total assets of $164 million; Raytheon had sales of $182 million (fiscal year ending May 31, 1955), net earnings before taxes of $9 million, and total assets exceeding $82 million.[32]

Combined, the two firms were rougly comparable in size with IBM and Sperry Rand.

Datamatic's first product was the D-1000, a large-scale, first-generation, vacuum tube computer system first shipped in late 1957 at a price of approximately $2 million. Honeywell manufactured the D-1000's CPU and tape drives, but obtained other peripheral products from several suppliers, including printers from Analex, card readers and various tabulating equipment from IBM, and large magnetic rotary files from a machine tool business located in New England. Honeywell had eight or ten customers for its D-1000 and, even though this computer system had its origins in the computer work Raytheon had done for the military, the D-1000 was used primarily for processing business data, generally of an accounting nature.[33]

In 1957 Honeywell acquired Raytheon's 40 percent share of Datamatic for about $4 million.[34] Raytheon reported on its reasons for exiting from the computer business:

> Substantial additional investments will be required to develop Datamatic's full potential. In view of Raytheon's growing cash requirements, it was decided to dispose of our interest in Datamatic and to concentrate all available funds on our own business.[35]

Prior to selling its Datamatic equity to Honeywell, Raytheon had approached Lockheed. According to Norman Ream, Lockheed's corporate director of systems planning from 1953 to 1965, Lockheed was initially interested because "In the 1956-57 era . . . the aerospace companies were branching out into electronics and . . . [Lockheed] looked upon this as a possibility of getting some advanced electronic techniques — or technical knowledge."[36] Ream testified that in 1957 Datamatic was estimating the sale of a very large number of its D-1000 systems. However, after studying Datamatic, Ream did not believe its sales projections. His own study suggested that Datamatic, which had already delivered about nine D-1000s, would not "sell another machine — and they did not" — because Datamatic "had not advanced the state of the art."[37] Lockheed, accordingly, decided not to acquire Raytheon's interest in Datamatic.[38]

At the end of 1958, Honeywell announced its second computer system, the transistorized Honeywell 800, which it marketed as its first medium-scale computer. Honeywell described the 800 as a fully transistorized, small, but extremely high-speed and efficient computer that could "be expanded in small economical increments to meet a growing data processing requirement — business and scientific."[39] First delivery was anticipated in the third quarter of 1960.

In 1959 Honeywell's Datamatic Division announced another new product, the H-290, a digital computer developed "for use in the public utility field and to control continuous processes in the chemical, petroleum and other industries."[40]

In December 1960, Honeywell announced the H-400 — a computer system fully compatible with the Honeywell 800 at half the price. The first 400 was delivered in late 1961. Taken together, the Honeywell 400 and 800 covered a large size range with prices ranging from approximately $400,000 to several million dollars. Honeywell described the 400 as a full-scale data-processing system that included magnetic tape and diverse input-output capabilities that could be used independently or in conjunction with the 800.[41]

In 1961 Honeywell introduced the FACT compiler for use on its 800 computer systems. Like IBM's COMTRAN, (see Chapter 2), FACT was a programming language based on English and a compiler to develop machine programs from programs written in the FACT language. Honeywell described FACT as perhaps "the most complete and powerful program for compiling business applications." Although Honeywell maintained that its FACT programming language was superior to both COMTRAN and COBOL, it ultimately abandoned FACT in favor of COBOL, just as IBM had been forced to abandon COMTRAN.[42]

In 1962 Honeywell announced the H-1800, describing it as "an extremely powerful computer capable of handling both business and scientific applications."[43] Honeywell also concluded an agreement with Japan's Nippon Electric Company under which Nippon, on a royalty basis, would "produce and market, in the Far East, computers incorporating Honeywell designs and features."[44]

In 1963 Honeywell announced the 1400 as providing "a ready means of expansion to Honeywell 400 customers who desire to move to a larger system without reprogramming" and as having "unique real time capability in the field of computer-communication systems."[45] Honeywell also announced its H-200 system in December 1963. The 200 was directed at the same customer base as IBM's extremely successful 1400, and contained an "automatic program conversion package, called 'Liberator,'" designed to automatically convert "instruction programs written for three competitive systems, thus eliminating major reprogramming costs."[46]

Thus, in the late 1950s and early 1960s Honeywell began to strive to establish a presence in the computer business. It introduced several product lines, and its U.S. EDP revenues rose from $1 million in 1958 to $27 million in 1963.[47] Nevertheless, Honeywell had yet to make a corporate commitment to EDP of the same scope as either IBM or Sperry Rand: its 1963 U.S. EDP revenues accounted for less than 5 percent of its total corporate revenues and were less than one-fortieth of IBM's corresponding revenues.[48]

RCA

Radio Corporation of America (RCA), with 1952 revenues of nearly $694 million, was another large, technically sophisticated company well situated to enter the computer business during the early 1950s. In the 1940s and early 1950s it gained experience in computer-related activities in three areas: computing devices, vacuum tubes and transistors, and core memories.

Scientists at RCA Laboratories began a study of electronic computing devices as far back as 1945, and the firm claimed that in the early 1940s RCA pioneered in EDP with its systems for antiaircraft fire control.[49] RCA produced its first computer in 1947 at the request of the U.S. Navy. This computer, the

Typhoon, was a very large analog computer used primarily for simulation studies.[50]

By 1950 RCA had undertaken exploratory investigations of a digital computer for commercial applications.[51] Moreover, in 1952 the firm reported that a "substantial part of [its] Laboratories Division activity . . . was devoted to research on classified Government projects in such fields as electronic computers."[52] Because of RCA's skills in electronics, it was selected by MIT as one of the finalists in the competition to produce SAGE computer systems.[53]

In the 1940s and early 1950s, as an outgrowth of manufacturing radios and television sets, RCA was a large manufacturer of vacuum tubes. Indeed, the designers of the ENIAC consulted with RCA's engineers in an effort to develop ultrareliable tubes for their computer.[54] Following the invention of the transistor, RCA began research on possible transistor applications. As early as 1952 it recognized that substitution of transistors for vacuum tubes would permit the construction of computers of greater versatility and utility, as well as reduce their size and power consumption.[55] RCA also pursued the development of core memory during the early 1950s. An RCA employee wrote in 1953: "Recently ferrite materials have been developed which are suitable for use as memory elements for large-scale electronic computers. A memory unit capable of storing ten thousand bits of information has been developed by RCA."[56]

Although RCA had the financial and technical capabilities for developing, manufacturing, and marketing digital computers, it did not deliver its first digital computer until 1956. In that year RCA delivered the BIZMAC, a large computer with a purchase price of $4 million that contained a small amount of core memory, approximately 28,000 cores.[57] Developed for the army, BIZMAC was intended to be used for business-type applications: "stock control of replacement parts for military combat and transport vehicles."[58] The army hoped to use BIZMAC to "provide speedy and accurate information on inventories, to determine in minutes the current supply of any item at any Ordnance depot in the nation, and to compute forecasts of future requirements."[59]

RCA spent a lot of time and committed substantial monies to developing BIZMAC. However, it shipped only about six BIZMAC systems. Frederic Withington testified that the BIZMAC worked relatively poorly, and classified the product as a failure. Because of its size, the BIZMAC program kept RCA's EDP personnel fully occupied until 1956 or 1957.[60] In 1958 RCA began work on the 501, described by its management as the first completely transistorized, general-purpose EDP system. RCA announced the 501 in December 1958, and made its first delivery in mid- to late 1959. Apparently only three 501s were delivered to customers outside of RCA prior to 1960.[61]

Edwin McCollister, an RCA employee in the 1950s, described the 501 as a competitive system well designed by the standards of the time. However, RCA did experience difficulties with some of its peripherals. In particular, the card reader and card punch equipment were slow and unreliable, and the line printer required a lot of maintenance; its print quality wasn't particularly good.[62] As of December 1959, RCA reported commitments for 41 of its 501 systems.[63] Nevertheless, because the Computer Division had "optimistically scheduled production in excess of what they were able to sell," more 501s were built than were marketed.[64]

To provide its computer customers with random-access auxiliary storage, RCA manufactured a device called RACE that stored data on numerous short strips of magnetic tape. As with similar products from Sperry Rand (FAST–RAND) and National Cash Register (CRAM), RACE proved unreliable and was regarded by customers as a poor alternative to the disk drive. Withington classified RACE as a major product failure.[65]

In the late 1950s RCA was chosen program manager for the BMEWS project, a computer system commissioned by the North American Air Defense Command to provide early warning of any ballistic missile attack. Among RCA's BMEWS subcontractors were IBM (which provided the main CPUs, IBM 7090s), GE, and Sylvania. RCA also developed computers for use on the BMEWS system, and its subsequent commercial EDP products incorporated the improved electrical circuitry and packaging of the BMEWS.[66]

Despite its substantial technological capabilities at the beginning of the 1950s, RCA had not succeeded in establishing a significant presence in the computer industry by the end of the 1950s. Thus, in a December 1959 business review of RCA's EDP Division, the company stated that it was just "beginning to overcome the major obstacle which plagued us previously; namely, doubts as to RCA's seriousness in the EDP business."[67]

In the late 1950s RCA's management was faced with a decision as to what it should do about the firm's future involvement in the EDP business. Expressing one point of view was RCA President John Burns, who felt that in view of RCA's technical capabilities and what appeared to be great growth opportunities in the computer field, this was a business in which RCA should be.[68] Pushing in the other direction was RCA's desire to develop and commercialize color television. The resultant intracorporate battle for investment monies continued throughout the 1960s, to the detriment of RCA's computer-related activities. As Arthur Beard testified concerning the allocation of RCA's total corporate resources throughout the 1950s, there was a "greater total effort in television from the engineering point of view than there was in the computer."[69]

In April 1960, RCA announced two new computer systems, the 601 and the 301. It described the 601 as "an ultra-high speed, general purpose EDP system . . . equally efficient for massive business data processing *and* complex scientific computation"; the 301 was described as a small- to medium-size computer.[79]

Unfortunately, according to McCollister, RCA's 601 was a disaster. First, its manufacturing cost turned out to be substantially higher than the original cost estimates upon which the pricing had been predicated, and if RCA had raised the 601's price to cover its costs, the product would have been uncompetitive. Second, RCA had difficulty in providing some of the functional capabilities that had originally been announced and specified. For example, RCA intended the 601 to be an on-line and multiprogramming type of system. Its attempt to make the system operate that way proved economically impractical. Furthermore, "There was a big slowdown in being able to accomplish these functions in a technical sense." Third, RCA used coaxial cable to improve the performance of the CPU. However, so many cables were used that it proved virtually impossible to make all of the necessary interconnections.[71] John Jones, then employed at the Air Force Logistics Command, described the 601's problems from a customer's perspective:

> It required a large amount of special wiring and the wiring got so thick on the back board, the back plane of the machine, that they could no longer get down to the pins to attach more wires through this layer of wiring and there was still a large number of wire connections that needed to be placed, and at that point they gave up on delivering the RCA 601 on its original schedule and, of course, that impacted the decision as far as the Logistics Command was concerned. And, in fact, what they had to do was to go back and redesign a new type of very thin coaxial cable in order to again come forward with the RCA 601.[72]

Thus, after marketing the 601 for a short time, RCA realized that

> There were severe technical problems, both in a functional and in a manufacturing sense, and there were also severe financial problems, so much so that the company began to look for a way out of the program.[73]

In 1962 RCA stopped marketing the 601. At that time it decided to honor the existing commitments but not to sell any more. Of the five 601s RCA manufactured, only four were delivered.[74]

The aborted 601 program hurt RCA's computer business in several respects. McCollister testified:

> [The 601] cost [RCA] money, from which we received no worthwhile return, both from the manufacture and the development expense, which was quite substantial, and it also lost us time of engineering people because, while they were working on that product, trying to salvage it within the limits that had been established, they were unable to put their efforts into the design of products that might have had a more important business future.[75]

The failure of the 601 also embarrassed RCA and "hurt RCA's reputation very badly, because we had placed great public emphasis upon the 601 as a product and its capabilities, and it hurt us with several important customers."[76] Another adverse consequence of the 601's failure was that it hurt RCA's ability to market other products because the 601 had been counted on to fill the upper end of the computer systems market. Thus, the absence of the 601 left a void for firms owning the 301 that wanted to move to a larger system.[77] In sum, the failure of the 601 cost RCA about three of four years in development of its computer business.[78]

RCA intended the 301 for regular data-processing work loads. The 301 achieved sufficient sales to be considered a success by RCA.[79] However, it did suffer some problems, particularly with some of its peripheral products. In the late 1950s and early 1960s RCA's Computer Division had decided to curtail the development of peripherals in order

> . . . [t]o concentrate RCA's investments in areas where they felt they would get the most return and where it would be possible to procure such things as printers, card readers, and punches from other manufacturers who were making them available directly to other manufacturers.[80]

RCA used a Bryant disk file on the 301. When it failed, "It took a long time to get the necessary part in to get the equipment back on the air, as much as six or twelve hours."[81] Withington regarded the RCA 361 disk, used on the 301, as a major product failure because of reliability problems.[82] Another problem area was the printer, obtained from Analex, which had insufficient print quality for certain applications.[83]

By the end of 1961 RCA's EDP Division "was in considerable trouble. It had grown rapidly and it was incurring a substantial operating loss and, worst of all, it was in severe technical difficulties."[84] In 1962 RCA decided to resume developing and manufacturing its own peripherals. According to Beard, this was done for two reasons:

> The first was that our experience with some of our suppliers had not been entirely satisfactory. Secondly, it was felt that resources were available to expand the product development to include more in the peripheral area and that as a consequence of this we would have control over the product characteristics, such things as reliability, and certainly would be able to enjoy a greater contributed value in the product, and our manufacturing costs we expected to be less than the purchase price we were paying to other people.[85]

Stopping and then restarting its development of peripheral products hurt RCA's product line:

> It certainly had an effect on how far forward RCA was able to move in the development of peripheral products. . . .
> But when RCA decided to redevelop its products, it had lost the continuity of the engineering effort that had been going on in such things as printers and essentially had to reestablish its engineering skills and manufacturing skills in those areas. So in that sense time was lost by the early decision to abandon these peripheral developments.[86]

By the end of 1963 RCA's computer business had not made up for its arrested development during the 1950s. McCollister testified that IBM made "greater strides" than RCA during the 1950s "in the sense of a wider range of products and a larger quantity of products delivered to customers."[87]

GENERAL ELECTRIC

During the 1950s General Electric (GE) was a large, diversified manufacturer of industrial and consumer products including electrical generating and transmission equipment, turbines, transformers, jet engines, nuclear power apparatus, process control systems, television sets, radios, and home appliances. In 1952 GE was several times larger than IBM, with corporate revenues approximating $2.6 billion.[88]

GE's first computers were specialized systems directed to ordnance and military applications, and included the OARAC (Office of Air Research Automatic Computer), installed in 1953 at Wright Patterson Air Base. The air force described OARAC, a one-of-a-kind computer, as "quite slow, limited in input/output capability, and very unreliable."[89]

ERMA (Electronic Recording Method of Accounting), announced in 1956, was GE's first commercially available computer. According to John Weil, ERMA was developed "on an opportunistic basis" under a large contract with the Bank of America that called for GE to produce "a system basically for reading checks and for doing the accounting within the bank associated with those checks."[90] Valued at $60 million, ERMA was the largest nongovernmental computer contract awarded to that time. GE produced 30 ERMA systems under the contract for installation, beginning in 1958, at 13 Bank of America branches.[91]

ERMA gave GE a head start in the application of EDP technology to the banking industry.[92] According to Weil, however, within GE it "was generally regarded and often voiced that [ERMA] was an opportunity that had not been capitalized on," and "that was voiced with some regret."[93] Weil's experience in GE's Computer Division, which he joined from another division of GE, was consistent with that conclusion:

> [A]s of that time General Electric had become more interested in those markets which were normal to it, the kind of businesses which were typical of General Electric and in which General Electric had user's experience.
>
> So it was interested in serving business and technical computations of a kind that were more familiar than banking was. GE is not in the banking business.[94]

It was later widely believed within GE that failure to capitalize on its ERMA involvement resulted in potential customers' perceiving that GE had an image of failing to follow through in EDP. In a 1970 advanced product line master plan, GE's Advanced Systems Division concluded:

> An enviable image in the banking industry was built through the success of the ERMA project and GE's leadership in development of Magnetic Ink Character Recognition standards. This image was subsequently lost due to neglect.[95]

While building ERMA, GE also began to manufacture, under contract with National Cash Register (NCR), an NCR-designed processor. NCR marketed that processor to end users as part of its 304 computer system. Weil described the 304 as "a minor offering for [GE] . . . intended primarily for use in business data processing, in commercial applications."[96] Only 29 of the NCR 304s were installed by customers; four others were used internally by GE.[97]

In the late 1950s GE also developed the GE 312, a computer intended to perform process control applications.[98] Using the 312 as the starting point, in 1961 GE delivered the GE 225, which was based on the design features of the 312, including circuit components, word length, a similar input-output structure, and a similar instruction repertory. The 225 was initially intended as a small, scientifically oriented machine. However, once shipments began, it was used increasingly for nonscientific commercial and business applications. Business users were attracted to the 225 by its software, especially the GECOM business compiler, a COBOL precursor. The 225 never sold strongly to the scientific market that was its original target.[99]

In the first half of 1963, GE introduced the 215 and the 235. The 215 was smaller, slower, and cheaper than the 225; and, compared with the 225, the 235 employed more advanced electronic circuits and was designed to be higher-performance and more cost-effective.[100] According to Weil, the features of the GE 235 made it suitable for both scientific and business applications:

> First of all, since it was an upward compatible machine with the GE 225 . . . it did all the things that the 225 would do. In addition, it had a special high performance floating point . . . particularly suited for scientific applications. I believe the only way in which the 235 would be more appealing to business data processing than the 225 may have been in the additional peripheral capability that comes from the additional speed of the circuits, and the Dual Controller Selector.[101]

In 1963 GE also announced the DATANET-30 computer, which Richard Bloch described as "a superb machine meant for [a] communication environment"; IBM, he said, had nothing comparable.[102] GE believed that it "assumed a leadership position in the area of communication systems and communications control concepts" with the introduction of this product.[103]

GE also offered data-processing services to customers as early as 1963, using GE-manufactured computer equipment. A forerunner of the computer service bureau, these were computer installations to which people could bring their problems for the computer to provide batch processing servicing.[104]

The principal shortcoming of GE's EDP activities during the 1950s and early 1960s was its failure to devote the resources necessary to develop a significant corporate presence in the EDP market. Thus, by 1963 GE's Computer Department accounted for less than 1 percent of total corporate revenues. In retrospect, many of GE's senior managers lamented their firms's delay in investing substantial resources in EDP. GE's chief executive officer during the 1970s, Reginald Jones, testified that the firm did not "make the allocation of resources to the [EDP] business that were warranted."[105] He added:

> I can only say that as early as the 1950's, if we had increased substantially the technical manpower assigned to the business, if we had

increased at that time the financial resources required for the business, they would have been much smaller in terms of absolute numbers than they would have been . . . some fifteen years later.[106]

Ralph Cordiner, GE's chief executive from the mid-1950s through 1963, shared Jones's view. Jones testified that Cordiner was once asked to identify the most important mistakes GE had made in managing its computer systems business, and Cordiner was quoted publicly as having said:

> General Electric's mistake was that it failed to realize the opportunity and therefore made an inadequate allocation of resources, both human and physical, to the business.[107]

GE's hesitation to commit resources to EDP was also recognized by more junior officers. Weil reported at a 1964 GE meeting that the firm's mistake was its failure "to bring its corporate strength behind its entry into the information business."[108] Similarly, Richard Bloch, who joined GE in 1968, testified that in the 1950s and early 1960s it had been his feeling that GE's commitment to the EDP business was

> . . . tainted with some tentativeness or speculativeness . . . as a long-term commitment to the field. My feeling was that if it turned out to be a great success, the company would be delighted; if it turned out not to be a great success, the company could extinguish parts or all of its activity in the field without necessarily any great remorse.[109]

And in a 1964 report to GE's executive office, the general manager of its Computer Department confessed:

> As a result [of GE's] late start and limited product coverage, General Electric did not participate to any great extent in the expansion period of 1960-64.[110]

GE's commitment to those businesses emerging from activities that it regarded as part of the firm's main line differed sharply from its relative lack of commitment to EDP. For example, Weil contrasted GE's interests in the emerging commercial nuclear power industry with its interest in EDP during the early 1960s:

> General Electric was then . . . a very strong supplier of major equipment to the power generating industry, turbines and generators and the like.
>   Nuclear power, which was a set of equipment that went to the same customers and into the same plant, was regarded as, first of all, an adjunct to the core business of the company and, second of all, that if someone should get in the business of supplying central station

nuclear power on a turnkey basis, that perhaps GE would lose some of the business it enjoyed in turbines and generators, so that was regarded as a threat to a strong existing business.

It was clear that the mission of the nuclear power business was: We don't know whether there is a business, but if there will be a nuclear power business, you will be one of the leading competitors.

That was the charge as I interpreted it to the Atomic Power Equipment Department.

The computer business I don't believe was ever viewed as a threat in any strong sense to other businesses that General Electric was in. And the equivalent charge might be: We are sure there will be a computer business, now you must demonstrate that you can compete.[111]

Although GE failed to commit adequate resources to EDP during Cordiner's years as its chief executive, Weil testified that it possessed several major advantages that could make it a serious factor in the computer business. He described them as follows:

It had a very broad technical basis in the many different businesses in which General Electric participated at that time. Many of these technologies would be applicable to the computer business.

Second . . . General Electric used computers very broadly. They were in fact one of the pioneering users in the commercial world of computers and as such probably understood how to use the then existing computer technology as well as anyone.

Thirdly, because of the capital resources of General Electric, it could devote, if it wished, enough effort to put all this together and become a significant competitor.[112]

Weil believed that if GE had a potential shortcoming in EDP, it resulted from being "relatively naive when it came to the discipline of manufacturing large electronic systems or designing them or bringing them to market."[113]

ELECTRODATA/BURROUGHS

Electrodata began as a division of Consolidated Engineering Corporation (CEC), a small company with 1952 revenues of $8 million. CEC was engaged in the technical data recording and acquisition field, and made mass spectrometers as well as a line of scientific instruments used "to sense physical phenomena and data and to record them in one form or another during the testing of physical devices such as aircraft."[114]

Edwin McCollister, who left IBM in 1954 to become head of Electrodata's marketing, testified that in the early 1950s the tiny firm's parent, CEC, viewed computers as a new business opportunity and a logical addition to their product line:

If you could sense data and record data, the final link in the chain was to process data. So, with the aid of a consultant or two, CEC undertook the development of a digital data processor, the CEC . . . Model 202 or 203 . . . and this is what became the Electrodata Corporation DATA-TRON 203/204.[115]

CEC spun off Electrodata in the early part of 1954. Electrodata's initial capitalization was between $1 and $2 million, and McCollister estimated that its first computer system, the DATATRON, cost in the neighborhood of $300,000 to $500,000 to develop.[116]

The first DATATRON, with a selling price of about $120,000 was shipped to the Jet Propulsion Laboratory in June 1954; six additional DATATRONS were installed that year by the U.S. Navy Ordnance Laboratory, Socony-Vacuum Oil Company (now Mobil), Purdue University, Allstate Insurance, American Bosch Arma, and Land-Air (located at Wright-Patterson Air Base). Electrodata's revenues were just under $1 million in 1954.[117]

McCollister testified that the DATATRON

. . . [i]nitially . . . was sold largely to the engineering scientific market-place. Subsequently it was offered to the commercial marketplace due in part to the fact that the All State [sic] Insurance Company became a major customer and this led to our going into the commercial marketplace or so-called data processing marketplace as well as the scientific. . . .

We were a small company. The potential business with All State [sic] Insurance was so important to us that we really couldn't ignore it.

We needed the business. We had to get it wherever we could. This led to our seeking opportunities in the commercial marketplace as well as in the scientific, engineering marketplace.[118]

In its 1954 annual report Electrodata stated:

As a result of the operating success of the installed DATATRON systems and the apparent potentialities for future sales, we have more than doubled our personnel, begun work on a new plant with twice our present production capacity, and undertaken development of auxiliary and accessory products to broaden our potential market. . . . Development of a general-purpose computer opened up a broader potential market than was originally anticipated.[119]

According to McCollister, the initial competition for DATATRON computer systems was "in the scientific marketplace . . . almost entirely IBM [the 650]. In the commercial marketplace we encountered IBM and very, very occasionally the UNIVAC file computer."[120] Withington, who was employed in Electrodata's marketing support group, also testified that the IBM 650 was the DATATRON's primary competitor.[121]

By March 1956, Electrodata had installed 24 DATATRON systems and had unfilled orders for 19 additional systems.[122] In addition, the firm introduced two new peripheral products in 1956, the Cardatron and the Datafile. The Cardatron used individual magnetic storage drums as buffers, and controlled the operation of as many as seven card readers as inputs, and punches or printers as outputs. Electrodata claimed that with the Cardatron, all of that input-output equipment could operate simultaneously at maximum speed, enabling the computer to do computation continuously.[123] The Datafile was an auxiliary storage, random-access device, described by Electrodata as using "short, 250-foot, disconnected lengths of magnetic tape housed in static-free metal bins, rather than conventional tape reels, which substantially shortens the time required to locate any record."[124] Withington described the Datafile as a major product failure because it was "insufficiently reliable, or, put another way, they never worked for very long."[125]

Electrodata was acquired by Burroughs on June 29, 1956, in return for 475,465 shares of Burroughs stock, valued at $20,504,000.[126]

At the onset of World War II, Burroughs was a manufacturer of adding machines, accounting and bookkeeping machines, and cash registers. During the war Burroughs placed its facilities and know-how in precision fabrication at the disposal of the U.S. government and produced, among other things, the Norden bombsight on a large-scale basis. Virtually all of Burroughs' wartime business was for the military.[127]

At the end of World War II, Burroughs mounted a substantial effort to return to its more traditional businesses; however, as Burroughs President Ray Eppert recollected in a 1959 speech:

> World War II propelled Burroughs into other fields which ended our preoccupation with purely mechanical equipment. Experience with military contracts, and management awareness of the new era which technology had ushered in caused the company to move into electronics and thence into automation and data processing.[128]

In 1947 Burroughs decided to begin its own electronics research. According to Ray MacDonald, who joined Burroughs in 1935 and became its president in 1966 and chief executive officer in 1967:

> The decision to begin electronics research, which may have been the most important decision to Burroughs in the past 30 years, was made by John Coleman, who was then our President. He determined that our company should develop its own scientific capability and development program in close association with the great technical universities.
>
> That decision represented courage and foresight, because in the 1946/1948 period, our revenue averaged less than $100 million a year and our net profit was as low as $1.9 million, in 1946. Yet Coleman began the electronic research and development program in excess of $1 million per year, rapidly expanding to $3 million, because he recognized

the importance of electronics and of establishing our own capability. A
significant portion of our R and D budget was allocated to the critical
area of applied research.

The early research performed under Coleman's direction, and continued and expanded by his successor, Ray Eppert — who increased the
R and D budget to four percent of revenues in spite of modest profit —
produced substantial invention and design. By the early 1960s, we
already had introduced significant early data processing systems.[129]

According to MacDonald, the postwar years also marked the end of the
"era of traditional management by the founders of Burroughs" with the selection of Coleman, "a university-trained manager and career manager," as president.[130] In MacDonald's view:

> Professional management of our company was given strong impetus
> during Coleman's administration, with the introduction of a program to
> attract young university-trained people from many of the country's
> leading schools of engineering, science, and business administration.
> Many of these new people, entering our company in the late 1940's
> and in the 1950's, reached the early levels of management and inter-
> mediate levels by the late 1950's. By the early 1960's, they had ma-
> tured in responsiblity and some had reached the level of senior man-
> agement.
>
> Our company was fortunate in developing this professional man-
> agement, because we were required [in the 1960s] to bring about a
> major transformation of our business.[131]

The preceding suggests that Burroughs was well positioned to enter the EDP
business in the early 1950s. Nevertheless, its early efforts were modest. In 1953
the firm reported that its Philadelphia Research Center had completed a static
magnetic memory to be used with the U.S. Army's ENIAC, and that this memory basically increased ENIAC's memory sixfold. However, in the same report
Burroughs downplayed the immediate significance of computers to its office
equipment business:

> [D]espite extraordinary advances in new fields of technology, the
> automatic office cannot be expected in the near future.

New Technologies Not Yet Practical

> While a few electronic devices have been applied to highly special-
> ized office problems, the majority of electronic computers now in
> operation were designed for scientific use. In this field the input and
> output problem is relatively simple. The core of the job is rather the
> complex and vast work of computation. But in business the arithmetic
> is usually not difficult. It is the feeding of the business machine, item
> by item, and the printing of the result which is both time consuming
> and costly. It would be no advantage to speed up the rate of figuring,

if input, output and other peripheral operations did not keep pace.

Other Difficulties

There are other difficulties, too, which will delay the practical application of electronics to the office, not the least of which is the major obstacle of cost. The outlook for electronics in business, then, must be summed up in the words "not yet."[132]

In the early 1950s Burroughs built two models of an experimental computer called the UDEC (Unitized Digital Electronic Computer), one of which was installed at Wayne State University in Detroit as part of its Computation Laboratory. Burroughs stated that the "[p] rimary purpose of UDEC in Wayne's educational program is to help train urgently needed personnel for the operation of the country's growing number of electronic computers and to seek new developments in the field of automatic data processing equipment."[133] In 1955 a redesigned and reassembled UDEC, called UDEC II, was used to solve complex problems in such fields as design analysis, production scheduling, cost analysis, inventory control, and market forecasting.[134]

Burroughs introduced its first commercial computer, the E-101, in 1954. It described the E-101 as follows:

. . . the first of a series of low-cost electronic digital computers for scientific and business use . . . designed for the large volume of computations between the problems adaptable to mechanical devices and the highly complex problems requiring large-scale electronic computers.[135]

The E-101 was desk size and "employed a modified accounting machine for input from the keyboard and output to the printer, and its program was provided through an external plug board."[136] It cost about $35,000, and Burroughs hoped that the combination of its low cost, small size, and versatility would make it attractive to a wide range of users.[137]

Withington testified that the E-101 was "perhaps the very first of the small scientific computers," though he also testified that it was intended for use both by "actuaries and other business mathematicians, and also by scientists having problems small enough to be able to fit within the limitations of this external plug board."[138] Burroughs shipped the first E-101s in 1955.[139]

According to Withington, the E-101 was a major product failure:

[The] business market for it never developed, perhaps because the things it could do were too limited, and the scientific market proved to be of limited size for the same reason. The basic reason for its failure, then, was that the external plug board program provided insufficient versatility to handle the problems of users.[140]

In 1954 Burroughs reported that it also was developing computers for the military and that it had integrated that defense work with its commercial research, development, and production activities:

> Because of its strong position in electronics, electronmechanics and magnetics, Burroughs has been given responsibility for highly specialized work for the armed forces. . . . Several extensive long-range projects are being carried on, including the development of general-purpose and special-purpose computers for data-handling systems. Involving as it does techniques closely associated with the Corporation's work in new type equipment for business and industry, the defense program has been integrated with Burroughs' commercial research, development and production activities.[141]

Burroughs used its defense work to bolster its efforts to market computer equipment to commercial customers. The firm began to seek out defense contracts for which its facilities and capabilities were best suited and that had the greatest potential for commercial systems development. According to a Burroughs vice-president, Kenneth Tiffany, the firm

> . . . did not, however, break into electronics with a San Juan charge . . . rather, we insinuated ourselves into a field that was still unknown and unpredictable, testing every step of the way. A major stimulus was our receipt of government contracts involving precision computational and data processing equipment in the area of fire control, navigation, anti-aircraft battery evaluation, and ultimately, the guidance computer for the Atlas ballistic missile and the data processing systems for the SAGE intercontinental air defense network.[142]

During 1955 Burroughs received contracts to build hard-wired computers to process data collected by radar units for transmission over phone lines to SAGE direction center computers. Deliveries of these large-scale computers began in 1956.[143] Burroughs also received an air force contract giving it complete responsibility for the concept, design, and production of computers for the Atlas ballistic missile's ground guidance system.[144] By the end of 1957 Burroughs had received a cumulative total of nearly $40 million for its SAGE computers and $37 million on its Atlas contracts.[145]

In a 1956 speech to security analysts, Tiffany discussed the linkage between Burroughs' defense work and its commercial EDP business:

> The knowledge gained from our research, the development of original concepts and design ideas, and the experience in high precision volume production are also invaluable in the design and production of our commercial line.
> [T]his reasoning — that our defense experience will help to accelerate the Company's plans for automatic business systems of the future — lies behind most of our defense work. . . .[146]

As noted, Burroughs acquired Electrodata in 1956 with the intention of greatly strengthening the corporation's competitive position in electronics.

Indeed, Burroughs' president maintained that the acquisition made Burroughs one of the world's three major producers of EDP systems.[147]

Burroughs' Electrodata Division began preparations in 1957 to develop the DATATRON 220 for delivery in December 1958. Unfortunately, the 220 was a vacuum tube machine that soon faced competition from far superior transistorized computers such as the IBM 7070 and 1401. According to Withington, the DATATRON 220 was

> . . . the last vacuum tube computer ever announced. It was superseded within two years by [the] 7070, which was both a second-generation machine of much better price/performance, but also offered the beginning of improved programming tools, and the DATATRON line came to a sudden and permanent end.[148]

Because the 220 was "wrong in establishing a set of standards and ways of designing a machine," Withington testified that Burroughs "effectively left the [computer] business and re-entered only later."[149]

In 1958-59 Burroughs was, in fact, working on developing new computers. The company maintained a high level of research and development expenditures and continued to pursue defense contracts, at least in part because it believed the "cross fertilization between our military and commercial development activities has important implications for the future."[150] According to Ray Eppert, "The knowledge gained by organizations involved in research for new military techniques is helping to strengthen total competency on commercial products."[151]

In the early 1960s Burroughs introduced several new data-processing systems, helping its U.S. EDP revenues to reach $42 million in 1963. However, it still had not made the major transformation from electromechanical office equipment to electronic computer technology that it would ultimately have to make if it were to survive, much less prosper.[152] Ray MacDonald wrote:

> The survival of Burroughs required that we supplement the precision mechanical technology of the earlier office machine industry — at which we excelled — and establish ourselves as a major force within the new, electronic, data processing industry, which embraced an entirely new technology. These two technologies — and the new and the old "breeds" of people who represented them — had to be reconciled and coordinated, and an entirely new range of products had to be developed which would make use of the best of both technologies.[153]

NATIONAL CASH REGISTER

From the 1880s until the early 1920s NCR was a single-product company — the cash register. In the 1920s the company entered the accounting machine market, and it purchased the Allen-Wales Adding Machine Company in 1943.[154] In the late 1930s NCR began experimenting with electronics and "formed a very small electronics engineering group of only two men who . . . did build a device which through vacuum tubes performed all the normal arithmetic functions."[155] During World War II, NCR suspended its commercial electronics research, but its electronics division did some secret work for the government.[156] From the end of World War II until 1952, NCR resumed research in electronics on a small scale. During that period it produced an electromechanical bombing navigational computer that it described as "in effect, a giant brain which calculated at such speed that its answers are practically continuous."[157]

In 1953, when NCR's total revenues approximated $260 million, it acquired the Computer Research Corporation (CRC), a spin-off of Northrop Aviation, "to expand substantially [NCR's] efforts in electronic research and development."[158] CRC, a small producer of computers for the military, had been founded in 1950 by five missile-guidance systems electronic engineers. CRC was one of the earliest manufacturers of medium-priced, general-purpose systems. A 1952 ad listed three CRC digital computers available to perform engineering, science, and business applications.[159] According to Robert Oelman, who subsequently became NCR's chairman, the ad exaggerated the capabilities of CRC's products. He testified that at the time of CRC's acquisition by NCR, the firm "was engaged in the business of building a very few scientific computers, which they sold some to the military branches of the government and some to air frame companies" to solve, for example, "very complicated differential equations" or to "determine the location of an airplace in flight."[160]

NCR paid approximately $1 million to acquire CRC, and within two or three years had invested an additional $4-5 million.[161] Oelman described NCR's reasons for acquiring CRC:

> [I] t was becoming quite clear . . . that the mechanical state of the art . . . had just about reached its zenith . . . and we could see that through electronic technology, you would have a product, the computer, which could be sold for general business purposes, and we could also see that our traditional products, the cash register, the accounting machine, that you could apply electronic principles to those products and achieve results . . . far better than we were able to get through mechanical methods and at considerably lower costs.
>
> Also, . . . at that period of time . . . there was a movement throughout the business equipment industry of some of the major companies acquiring smaller electronic companies. . . . Burroughs . . . acquired one, Underwood did, Marchant did, and NCR did, so it was kind of a general movement of recognition of what the state of the art could do for business equipment.[162]

Shortly after the CRC acquisition, NCR introduced the CRC 102D computer, primarily for scientific applications. However, NCR chose not to pursue production of CRC's existing product line, noting in its 1953 annual report:

We have always been associated with recordkeeping in the average business up and down Main Street: the retail store, the bank, the department store and many others. In this field lies our greatest experience . . . and our first responsibility for the development of new methods. We have, therefore, devoted our efforts to applying the advantages of electronics to the fields we have always served.[163]

In 1954-55 NCR worked on the development of a computer system called the 303. However, the system was never fully developed, manufactured, or delivered. Development was discontinued around 1955-56 because the 303 "used an earlier technology vacuum tubes and . . . in our judgement [*sic*] it would not meet the marketplace in an early enough time frame to make it a viable system."[164] NCR redirected its efforts toward designing a transistorized computer called the 304.[165] The modest level of NCR's commitment to EDP in the mid-1950s is demonstrated by the fact that the firm's U.S. EDP revenues fell from $3.1 million in 1954 to $211,000 in 1955 and $308,000 in 1958.[166]

In 1957 NCR announced a solid-state computer, the 304, scheduled for delivery in late 1959. It cost "between five to 10 million" dollars to develop, and was priced between $750,000 and $1.25 million, depending on the peripherals selected. The 304 CPU was designed by NCR, but was production-engineered and manufactured by GE, using transistorized computer circuits GE had developed. NCR also obtained certain peripherals from GE.[167] NCR chose to enter into this arrangement because it "thought that General Electric was more experienced in the art at that time than NCR was, and that a joint relationship would be helpful and profitable to NCR."[168]

Although senior NCR managers testified that the 304 was NCR's "major entry into general purpose computing systems," its "[m]arketing strategy was to sell [the 304] to selected customers only since this product was considered as an experimental entry into the EDP marketplace."[169] NCR's original plan projected installation of 25 systems; actual installations totalled 33, of which four were used by GE for internal purposes. Typical 304 applications were order processing, customer billing, inventory control, actuarial studies, and personnel records.[170]

In 1960 NCR began marketing the small 310 computer manufactured by Control Data. The basic computer hardware was the CDC 160, which NCR did not modify. NCR had an exclusive right to sell this CDC equipment in the U.S. financial and retail markets. The 310, which NCR viewed as a rather minor computer line, was sold by NCR's accounting machine salesmen rather than by its EDP salesmen.[171] Withington classified it as a major product failure, in part because it was one of the last vacuum tube machines.[172]

NCR began operating computer data centers in 1960, using first the 310 and later the NCR 315. The data centers sold their computing services primarily to small retailers, who furnished NCR with information on their sales breakdown; NCR then provided merchandise reports, inventory control reports, and so on.[173] By 1962 NCR's Dayton data center was processing several million items monthly.[174]

NCR introduced the 390 computer in 1960. This computer was intended to offer moderate-cost data processing for small business firms.[175] NCR also announced the 315 computer system, first shipped in early 1962 and intended as a greatly improved successor to the 304. When NCR priced the 315 in late 1960, it estimated it could secure 200 orders for delivery over the next three to four years. In fact, 315 sales proved to be substantially stronger than initially projected. NCR obtained orders for 135 systems by 1962 and delivered approximately 700 by the program's end.[176]

NCR developed CRAM (Card Random Access Memory) in connection with the 315. It described CRAM as a revolutionary electronic filing unit and claimed:

> CRAM . . . was a magnetic storage device which operated on the basis of 256 magnetic cards that were available from memory for the recovery of information stored on those cards and rewriting of fresh information. In provided a capability of being able to access the information at a faster speed than that which would be available under your normal magnetic tape device, since you could randomly select the cards, but on a magnetic storage device, you had to sequentially search for the information.[177]

Nevertheless, Withington classified CRAM as a major product failure because, like RACE and FASTRAND, it required replacement by disk drives.[178]

NCR's 315 system was developed as a family of products giving NCR a range of computer systems renting from approximately $5,000 per month to $12,000 per month. The 315 had both COBOL and FORTRAN compilers. NCR advertised the 315 with CRAM as a "general-purpose computer to handle both your business and scientific problems."[179] NCR's strategy was "to sell our traditional customers and our traditional equipment in conjunction with the delivery of 315 computers in order to satisfy the customer's total systems requirements."[180] Thus, NCR "developed cash registers which would produce as a by-product of the clerk's recording of the transaction, either a punch paper tape or sales journal . . . which then could be used to provide input to the computer system."[181]

Largely as a result of the success of the 315, NCR's U.S. EDP revenues rose from $308,000 in 1958 to $30.7 million in 1963.[182]

PHILCO

Philco was a manufacturer of industrial, military, and consumer electronics with 1952 revenues of $366 million.[183] In approximately 1955, based on its work to develop a surface barrier transistor, Philco won a competition to develop an airborne computer for the U.S. Air Force.[184] In 1955-56 Philco developed three one-of-a-kind transistorized computers, the C-1000 (described by Philco as an airborne real-time, general-purpose, parallel computer using surface barrier transistors), the C-1100 (a general-purpose, stored-program digital computer occupying only five cubic feet), and the C-1102 (an advanced version of the C-1100). During 1955-56 Philco also began developing what it described as "the world's first all-transistorized computer" for the National Security Agency. That work then led Philco to develop the TRANSAC S-2000 as the "first large-scale transistorized EDP system."[185]

The initial TRANSAC S-2000 was the model 210; significantly faster follow-on models were developed in 1960 and 1961. Philco advertised that TRANSAC could be "selected for commercial, scientific, real-time, and military applications."[186] Customers included the Atomic Energy Commission, GE (which converted applications from an IBM 704 and an IBM 7090), the California Department of Motor Vehicles, United Aircraft, Chrysler, System Development Corporation, Ampex, the government of Israel, the University of Wyoming, and the Defense Communications Agency.[187] Philco obtained core memory for the S-2000 from Ampex, and contracted with Applied Data Research to develop software, including sort programs and a simulator that permitted programs written for an IBM 705 to run on the S-2000.[188]

Philco's TRANSAC computers were among the most powerful computers of their time, in some ways comparable with LARC and STRETCH.[189] Further evidence of the sophistication of Philco's EDP products is provided by the fact that it was one of only four manufacturers (the others were IBM, Burroughs, and Control Data) that, in 1962, bid a large computer of their own manufacture for installation by NASA for use in the Gemini Program.[190]

The public record of Philco's EDP involvement is sketchy — in large part because much of its work was classified. That it was a significant participant in the U.S. market is confirmed by the fact that Philco's U.S. EDP revenues were $19.8 million in 1955 and $73.9 million in 1963 — greater than the U.S. EDP revenues of Burroughs, GE, Honeywell, and NCR.[191] Nevertheless, shortly after bidding on the Gemini Project, Philco chose to exit from the EDP business. This decision was apparently an outgrowth of its acquisition by Ford Motor Company in December 1961. According to Arjay Miller, at the time a Ford vice-president, Ford's interest in acquiring Philco was to get into the space and defense business.

[I] n the 1960s we were generating excess cash, we wanted to get into space and defense. We had a small space and defense business of our own that was not growing fast enough. We saw in the purchase of Philco an opportunity to grow in that particular area. It had a significant position. It was producing other products, and we decided to get out of the other products of which the computer business was one.

It was a phase process that as soon as we could, we moved the resources, the computer resources we had, into space and defense.[192]

CONTROL DATA CORPORATION

Control Data Corporation (CDC) was formed in mid-1957 by William Norris, along with two former colleagues who had left Sperry Rand, and a Minneapolis attorney. CDC's initial capitalization was approximately $600,000, of which Norris contributed $70,000 in return for slightly more than 10 percent of the total equity.[193] Norris testified that CDC initially contemplated doing "[p]rimarily consulting business and research and development work, principally for the Government, the plan being that out of the research and development work, and possibly the consulting work for business, would come ideas for products which we could later put on the market."[194]

Shortly after its formation CDC hired other employees who had previously worked for Sperry Rand, including Seymour Cray. Led by Cray, CDC (with only 12 employees) started working in a Minneapolis warehouse to design what became the 1604 computer system. A 1/10-scale prototype was in operation by April 1958, when the 1604 was announced.[195] According to Norris, the 1604 was the first solid-state, large-scale computer announced.[196] In early 1958 CDC also began producing missile and aircraft components for the military and developing a special air traffic control inquiry-keyboard-display unit for the Civil Aeronautics Authority.[197] In May 1958 CDC received $500,000 in military orders, including its first computer research and development contract. The following month CDC obtained additional financing from the navy for developing and manufacturing the 1604.[198]

When first delivered in January 1960, the 1604 computer system sold for slightly less than $1 million. CDC did not initially manufacture the peripheral products; instead, it obtained magnetic tape units from Ampex, printers from Analex and IBM, card readers from IBM, and paper tape readers from Ferranti, an English firm. CDC marketed the 1604 primarily to government laboratories and agencies doing a large amount of scientific work, and to large companies doing military, space, and nuclear work.[199] In 1962 CDC offered the 1604-A computer with COBOL capabilities "[b]ecause there were customers who wanted to use the machine also for some business data processing requirements that fitted with his total business aspect and he wanted to get those done on the same computer."[200]

In Norris' view, at the time CDC began marketing the 1604, it competed with Philco, UNIVAC, and IBM.[201] The 1604 was initially very successful. Because of this success, Norris anticipated that other firms would offer a product competitive with the 1604. Subsequently the 1604 did meet very severe competition from IBM computers, including the IBM 7090 (announced after the 1604 but delivered one month before it), the 7044 and 7040, and, somewhat later, the 7094.[202]

CDC announced its second computer, the 160, in December 1959. The 160 was first delivered in May 1960. It was a small computer that CDC marketed primarily for engineering work. CDC also sold the 160 computer to NCR.[203] Norris described that arrangement:

> The sales of the 160 through our own marketing organization are augmented through an arrangement we negotiated with the National Cash Register Company. The arrangement between Control Data and NCR provides that . . . [NCR] has exclusive marketing rights to the Model 160 Computer within the United States for the banking and retail trade areas, and can sell it world-wide on a non-exclusive basis in all other fields.[204]

CDC said that the 160s could be used as input-output data processors for the 1604 computer; they could also be used in a satellite system with a 1604, communicating directly with the 1604's magnetic core memory and all of the 1604's peripheral equipment.[205] In 1961 CDC announced a follow-on computer, the 160A, with twice the memory capacity of the 160, that sold for approximately $90,000. CDC ultimately sold more than 275 of its 160As.[206]

Norris testified that CDC was very successful initially because "We picked out a particular niche in the market" — the "scientific and engineering part of the market" — and "met the needs of the particular part very proficiently and much more so than any computer then available."[207] He described CDC's initial strategy as being

> . . . to build large, scientific computers with a lot more bang for the buck.
> This was achieved primarily by very high performance hardware with a relatively small amount of software with the customer doing most of his own software. Our business took off like a rocket to the moon as our large computers made rapid and significant penetration in the education, aerospace and large government laboratories markets.
> . . . With the success of the initial strategy there was also early recognition in Control Data that we would need to broaden our product line and markets to sustain growth.[208]

CDC's first product diversification, in 1960, was to begin manufacturing peripheral equipment. Its first product was a magnetic tape handler. Shortly thereafter it also started to offer data services, at first using a CDC 1604.[209] The company entered the data services business because it believed "There would develop an important market consisting of organizations that could benefit from the power of a large computer to solve large scale problems," but that lacked "either capital or technical resources to afford such a system."[210] CDC sold time on a service bureau basis primarily to universities and scientific and business organizations; it also used its data center facilities to perform in-house engineering design and accounting applications. By 1965 CDC had data centers in seven large U.S. cities.[211]

Almost from the beginning CDC also undertook to speed up its expansion by making acquisitions. Its intent in making acquisitions was not to broaden its "base as . . . a conglomerate, but rather to buy new computer products and services and markets to spread development costs and gain economies of scale as rapidly as possible."[212] CDC's acquisitions were facilitiated by the high price/ earnings ratio of its common stock. According to Norris, "[O]ur high P/E ratio stock, or Chinese money . . . was used to acquire companies with complementary technology, products, services and markets."[213]

CDC's first acquisition, of Cedar Engineering for $428,200, was made just four months after CDC's formation. At the time of the acquisition, Cedar Engineering did not manufacture computer-related products, but had the basic skills and facilities to manufacture high-performance peripheral products at very competitive costs.[214]

In 1960 CDC delivered to the Defense Department a large-scale, special-purpose, solid-state digital computer, several times larger than the 1604, that used a 1604 for input-output purposes.[215] That year CDC also acquired the Control Corporation for $2,274,814 of CDC stock. This acquisition allowed CDC "to implement a decision to enter the industrial market area of computers for automatic control purposes . . . for electric utilities and gas and oil pipeline companies."[216]

CDC enjoyed rapid growth during its first years. Employment grew from about 250 people in June 1958, of which approximately 40 were scientists and engineers, to more than 1,000 in March 1961. Over the same period sales rose from about $600,000 to $8 million. Moreover, as of 1961 CDC had reported a profit for every year except the year it incorporated.[217]

In 1961 Norris delivered an address to the Twin Cities Security Analysts. He described CDC's products as being

> . . . at the forefront of computer technology. Through aggressive research and engineering we intend to have our products in front tomorrow. Control Data is the smallest company in the industry today selling complete computer systems; however, mere numbers don't precisely determine the effectiveness of research and engineering. Significant technical innovations still spring from the flash of genius and again it's — "Not how many, it's who." Millions of dollars and massive engineering effort without those sparks produce only mediocre results. Unfortunately, the number of creative engineers in the computer industry is woefully small.
>
> Thus, if a small company has creative talent and since it has access to the general store of scientific knowledge, it can spark computer technology. The hugh [*sic*] government expenditures for research and development is [*sic*] the equalizer between large and small companies. Approximately 70% of all basic research done in the United States is financed by the government. This means that most of the new additions to scientific knowledge are just as available to the little company as to the large company. Furthermore, there is no company today with resources sufficiently large that it alone can significantly alter the state of the computer art.[218]

In the same speech Norris also described CDC's efforts to design a computer many times more powerful than either its 1604 or IBM's 7090.[219] Indeed, prior to the time of Norris' speech, CDC was discussing this new computer with MITRE Corporation and the Lawrence Radiation Lab, as well as many other users or potential users.[220]

In July 1962 CDC formally announced its new large-scale computer, the CDC 6600, stating that the first one had been ordered by Lawrence Livermore at a sales price of approximately $7 million. CDC delivered its first 6600 in September 1964.[221] Norris testified that CDC had substantially more difficulty designing and building its 6600 system than it had anticipated when it began its marketing. These problems took long periods of time to solve, causing delays in delivery schedules and entailing additional expenditures of funds and efforts by CDC employees.[222]

In May 1962 CDC announced the first of its 3000 series computers, the model 3600. The first 3600 was delivered to Lawrence Livermore in 1963 as an interim system prior to its acquisition of the first CDC 6600.[223] Norris testified that CDC developed the 3600 because "[W]e were under severe competition — competitive pressure from IBM computers" — the 7044, the 7040, and the 7094.[224] In 1962 CDC also began a joint venture with the Holley Carburetor Company to develop and manufacture medium-speed printers. CDC acquired 100 percent ownership of this joint venture in 1964.[225]

CDC made seven acquisitions in 1963, principally in exchange for its common stock. The most significant of these was Bendix's computer business. In 1952 Bendix was a diversified high-technology firm producing aviation, automotive, marine, radio and television, and other products, many of which were incorporated in military systems. Its revenues exceeded $508 million. In that year Bendix announced it was applying its "years of Electronic Leadership" to the development of digital computers. Bendix built two commercially available general-purpose computer systems, the G-15 and G-20, and was also involved in the SAGE Project. Its 1963 U.S. EDP revenues were nearly $13 million.[226]

CDC's other 1963 acquisitions were MEISCON, a company developing techniques for employing computers to automate industrial and highway design procedures; Beck's, a designer and manufacturer of unique embedded printed circuits; Electrofact, a manufacturer and vendor of a broad line of measuring, recording, and control devices as well as systems for use in industrial processes; the Digigraphic system business of Itek, a researcher and developer of a cathode ray tube/photoelectric pen system for conversion of graphic documents stored in a digital computer; the Control System Division of Daystrom, a leader in the development and installation of advanced electronic digital computers for use in power, chemical, and petroleum industries; and Bridge, a designer and manufacturer of card punch and reader systems and other computer peripheral devices.[227]

A central tenet of Norris' business philosophy was that there is a relationship between a company's "determining to focus all of its resources and concentration on the computer business as such . . . and success in that business."[228] He also believed that one of the key factors in CDC's record of business success was being willing to take risks:

> Our willingness to take risks was in reality probably the safest course for a small company with limited resources competing in the high and

fast-moving technology of computers. Now not every risk can pay off — nor did they all. To have played if [sic] safe would have meant one of two things: 1) being too late in the marketplace with a new product; or 2) having a good marketable new product but being unable to capitalize on the demand before our giant competitors moved in with a similar product. Therefore, Control Data, while still in the conceptual stage of designing a large computer made commitments on production for inventory, before the development and testing was complete. In those early years this is what is correctly called "total commitment" — i.e., failure of the product for some reason meant bankruptcy for the company. Some of our people called it a "you bet your company strategy." Control Data made a total commitment three times, once for the 1604, then the 3600 computer and the third time the 6600 computer. Fortunately all three were very successful — particularly the 6600.[229]

Control Data was one of the great successes in American business in the late 1950s and early 1960s. Its total assets grew from $1,223,311 in 1958 (its first full year of business) to $71,338,765 as of June 1963.[230]

REASONS FOR IBM'S EDP SUCCESS THROUGH THE EARLY 1960s

Although other firms enjoyed some individual successes from their early involvement in the EDP business, the revenue data summarized in Table 4.1 confirm that IBM's total set of computer offerings enjoyed unrivaled customer acceptance. With the benefit of hindsight, it is easy to see that IBM's initial successes in the EDP marketplace were the product of its making an early, large, effective, and sustained commitment to the business that became the most dynamic of the 1950s. It is necessary to examine the combined effects of many factors to explain why IBM proved to be far and away the most successful of the many established firms well positioned to enter the commercial EDP business at its birth.

Unlike many of its competitors, IBM did not obtain its EDP expertise by acquisition. In the early 1950s computer products were so unique and the technical, manufacturing, and marketing uncertainty so pervasive that it was especially vital for a firm's EDP operations to be well integrated into the corporate chain of command reporting to top management. Because EDP was so different from IBM's traditional unit record business, IBM's decision to develop its first computer system aroused considerable corporate opposition. Nevertheless, because IBM chose to rely on internal corporate resources to develop its computer business, and because of Thomas J. Watson, Jr.'s, personal involvement in that business, EDP never became isolated either from the rest of the corporation or from top management. Remington Rand's problems in integrating Eckert-Mauchly and ERA into its mainstream business, NCR's long delay in introducing successors to the CRC product line, and Burroughs' failure to introduce a successor to Electrodata's DATATRON 220 contrast unfavorably with IBM's accomplishments.

In the first years of the computer business, there was enormous uncertainty as to whether it was either technically or economically feasible to manufacture and market a computer system that would be of value to a sufficient number and range of customers. In addition, as Stephen Dunwell put it, there was "no evidence that a machine could be made to work reliably or could be maintained in working condition."[231] Yet IBM chose to commit far more of its corporate resources to this risky business venture than any other firm.

Richard Bloch summarized the reasons why IBM acquired technical leadership of the EDP business from Remington Rand between 1953 and 1955:

> [IBM] made a sustained effort to be a paramount element in the business equipment field, and they showed at that time strong determination to do so, allocated the necessary resources to begin to exert their power — or attempt to exert their power in the field and did a very fine job of it in the beginning in that era.[232]

When asked to explain, Bloch continued:

> The dedication of the company was, to my view, greater than the dedication of [Sperry Rand or General Electric]. And I would say that the organization of the resources, aside from the size of the resources, which at one time were no greater than these others, if not smaller — the organization power of the resources was what I felt was a forte of IBM management.[233]

IBM's senior management consistently demonstrated a willingness to commit substantial corporate resources to uncertain, risky EDP investments. As GE's Joseph Rooney testified, IBM "had excellent and aggressive management willing to take risks at the right time."[234] Most of these investments proved successful and, as a result, IBM reaped economic profits. Indeed, Thomas J. Watson, Jr.'s, foresight in deciding to risk investing IBM's corporate resources to develop the 701 and the 650 must be recognized as one of the most profitable decisions in the history of American business.

At approximately the time of Thomas J. Watson, Jr.'s, appointment as chief executive officer in the mid-1950s, IBM became the first large, established firm to conclude that its principal business should be EDP. Because of this early commitment, EDP accounted for a much larger fraction of IBM's total business than it did for competitors such as GE, Sperry Rand, Burroughs, NCR, RCA, and Honeywell. Since the EDP business subsequently grew much more rapidly than other businesses, this meant that even if IBM's EDP business only expanded at the same rate as the total market, its total revenues and profits would grow disproportionately as compared with these firms.

IBM management recognized that for the EDP market to grow rapidly, it was essential both to increase the range of applications that could be performed cost-effectively on a computer system and to reduce customer uncertainty. IBM achieved these results by offering its equipment on short-term leases, working closely with customers, educating them and providing them with programming aids (such as FORTRAN), and introducing a steady stream of more versatile, reliable, and maintainable products offering substantial improvements in price/performance and spanning a large size and price range. Withington testified:

> I think one of the major factors [that led to the current size of IBM's installed base] was IBM's rate of innovation during the first decade. The series of machines 701, 704, 709, 7090, 7094, appeared within a ten-year period for a significant part of the market, and with these as leaders, IBM innovated almost as rapidly in its larger volume business machines. No other vendor was willing or perhaps able to obsolete its own products and innovate at that rate in those days.[235]

It is now evident that such a strong commitment to innovation was essential for any firm to have a sustained record of success in a market as technically dynamic as EDP. However, in EDP's early years IBM's managers faced a nearly overwhelming temptation to stick with the proven technology already embodied in its successful unit record and early EDP products. W. W. McDowell testified about IBM in the early 1950s: "[T]he large majority of our people were not knowledgeable in the field of large computers," and getting that know-how meant spending considerably more money.[236] He observed that the decision to do so was "not an easy decision to make. There were not unlimited funds within the IBM Company."[237] The fact that IBM, like no other computer vendor, resisted the temptation to maximize short-term profits and instead consistently introduced new products making its still profitable lines obsolete, contributed greatly to the firm's becoming the world's largest EDP company.

More quickly than any of its competitors, IBM recognized that EDP customers were not really interested in acquiring computer hardware but, rather, data-processing capabilities.[238] To perform data processing efficiently requires access to a well-balanced computer system — not just a high-performance CPU. From the beginning of its involvement in EDP, IBM consistently responded to customers' data-processing needs by emphasizing the provision of generalized, highly functional software and high-quality peripherals.[239] Indeed, in the 1950s and 1960s many IBM-manufactured peripherals were so well regarded that several IBM competitors (including Honeywell, RCA, Burroughs, and UNIVAC) offered them as part of their computer systems.[240]

IBM was the first company to reap sizable production economies and reliability gains from producing its computers in high volume and on a production line rather than individually. Throughout its involvement with EDP, IBM management pushed efforts to mechanize production and cut costs.[241] IBM became the first EDP firm to reap "experience curve" economies when it began high-volume production of the 650.

The ultimate orientation of IBM's EDP business, however, has always been toward the marketplace. As an IBM chairman, Frank Cary, described it, the

> . . . orientation of always keeping the customer in mind, as I call it, "[t]he customer is king," kind of idea . . . has been a very, very

important element in the success of the IBM Company. It's something that the founder of the company drilled into everybody. . . .[242]

Jacqueline Johnson, an employee of Sperry Rand and GE in the 1950s and 1960s, testified in a similar vein about the reasons why IBM achieved its position of leadership in the EDP industry:

> . . . through the excellence of its management and marketing. IBM marketing is the best in the world. With respect to IBM management decisions, IBM supported what they sold. They enhanced their product lines. They introduced new products. They kept the state of the art and advanced technology well ahead of all vendors. They poured large amounts of money into research and development, and they developed a marketing arm that supported what they manufactured.[243]

Combining the varied resources and skills needed for success in the EDP business required systematic attention to the business of management. Speedy resolution of conflicts is an obvious principle of good management. IBM's principal EDP competitor during the early and mid-1950s, Sperry Rand, was unable to resolve the managerial disagreements between the two warring camps based in Philadelphia and Minneapolis/St. Paul, as well as between each of these camps and corporate management. By contrast, IBM set in place a contention system for dispute resolution. Whenever two parties or organizations within IBM disagreed on an issue, it was escalated for resolution to the next highest level. IBM management strove to resolve conflicts speedily rather than allow them to fester and breed disharmony.[244]

Paul Knaplund described how IBM's contention system worked in the late 1950s:

> It was the responsibility of the product divisions to respond to marketing requests wherever it was practical and economic to do so, but to resist those requests and provide acceptable alternatives where necessary in order to assure profitable results. . . . It is my understanding that IBM top management, that is, Mr. Watson, Jr., and Mr. Williams, deliberately established the responsibilities of the product and marketing divisions . . . to insert conflict in the IBM organization structure between the product divisions, on the one hand, and the marketing division, on the other, so as to ensure that the IBM Corporation would maintain its vitality and responsiveness to the competitive requirements of the marketplace. . . . [T]his conflict in the IBM organization structure was sometimes referred to by me and others as the "contention system."[245]

Throughout the 1950s and early 1960s, IBM chose to invest far greater resources in what was becoming the most important new market of the post-World War II period, and it organized these resources more effectively than any of its large competitors. As Burroughs' chief executive officer, Ray MacDonald, testified, IBM

. . . has been an extremely well managed company and not only has it been extremely well managed but this has been over a very long period of time in a rather continuous experience which someone remarked doesn't allow much room for error on the part of their competitors.[246]

PART II
THE 1960s

IBM AND SYSTEM/360

For IBM the 1960s constituted an era of great change, of great risk and difficulty, and, most of all, a decade marked by the phenomenal success of its System/360. The 360 story begins in 1960-61. As we have seen, by that time IBM was marketing more than 15 different processors and at least seven separate lines of second-generation computer systems. The architecture of those systems was quite dissimilar, as was their programming.[1] Whatever software compatibility there was existed only over a narrow range of processor performance.

In addition, different input-output equipment had been developed for each processor in order to optimize the performance of each of the different system types. Because peripheral equipment differed for different families or attached in different ways to different processors, customers "had great difficulty in moving even from one member of a processor in one family to another, let alone moving from one family type to another." In this regard IBM's computer systems were no different from the computer systems of its competitors. The result of this situation was that customers generally acquired set systems and had little flexibility to change their configurations as business demands changed.[2]

THE 8000 SERIES AND THE SPREAD COMMITTEE

In the early 1960s IBM's General Products Division (GPD) was responsible for the development and manufacture of IBM's small and intermediate systems, such as the 1401 and 1620, as well as IBM's disk drives.[3] IBM's Data Systems Division (DSD) was developing and manufacturing IBM's larger systems, the 7000 series, as well as IBM's tape drives.[4] DSD and GPD were achieving great success in the marketplace with their current lines — particularly with the 7090 and 1401.[5] In fact, as we have seen, the 1401, which had been announced in October 1959, was the most successful computer system that IBM or anyone else had ever introduced, with domestic shipments of more than 1,600 by the end of 1961.[6]

Nevertheless, neither of the divisions was resting on its laurels; they were planning for the future. If IBM was to continue to compete successfully, it would have to commit itself to the development of even better products. Such a commitment would require the firm to make large financial investments. Thomas J. Watson, Jr., IBM's chairman, fully understood this requirement and reported the following in an April 24, 1961 management briefing:

> [O] ur competition is getting stiffer all the time. . . . The best way to meet this competition is to keep our prices competitive. Prices involve costs and earnings. . . . We need constantly to spend large sums in research and development of new products which will not produce revenue for some years to come. Without funds for this vital expense, competition would eventually surpass IBM.[7]

Thus, within both divisions, improvements and extensions to the then current product lines were being developed. GPD had set up two groups of engineers — one to pursue improvements to the 1400 family and another to outline and define a replacement for that family.[8] At DSD development was even further along. A machine, the 8106 (which was an outgrowth of the STRETCH program), had been under design for some years and was already under construction within DSD in 1960. Thereafter, IBM began to develop the 8106 into a series of machines called the 8000 series. By 1961 IBM had spent many millions of dollars on the 8000 series development.[9]

Despite the relatively advanced state of the 8000 project and the money IBM had already invested in it, there was vigorous debate within the company over whether the 8000 was the right way to proceed.[10] With the first elements of the 8000 nearing announcement, B. O. Evans, who at that time was director of systems development and planning for DSD, was charged with evaluating the 8000 to determine whether it was a "leadership" program. Evans was charged by DSD's group executive, T. V. Learson, to get the 8000 into production if it was the right thing to do or, if Evans thought the 8000 series was the wrong approach, to do what was right.[11]

Evans concluded that the 8000 series was "wrong" for a variety of reasons:

1. The family was based on "contemporary transistor technology" and would not be "far-reaching enough." In Evans's view it would have been a "terrible mistake" to build a new family of machines that could be rendered obsolete by competitive products incorporating much better transistor technology that would soon be available.

2. The 8000 had a "lackluster" plan with respect to peripherals.

3. The 8000 series was planned to be "a range of five different machines: a small scientific machine, a small business machine, a medium to high performance business machine, a higher speed scientific machine . . . [and a] superspeed scientific machine." Evans thought that offering this "collection of differing machines with kind of loose ties . . . in their structure" was a "basic mistake from the user's standpoint."[12]

Although Evans believed that the 8000 series would be an improvement over IBM's existing product line and might give IBM a "momentary advantage" over competition, he recommended its cancellation.[13]

In late 1961 T. V. Learson, then IBM vice-president and group executive, appointed a task force called the SPREAD Committee to develop a new plan for IBM's data-processing products during the 1960s.[14] Its chairman was J. W. Haanstra, vice-president of development for GPD, and its vice-chairman was Evans.[15] Other members of the SPREAD Committee included Frederick Brooks, systems planning manager of DSD, and J. W. Fairclough, manager of product development at IBM's Hursley Laboratory in England, who had been in charge of yet another processor development, the SCAMP, an experimental computer whose innovative use of microprogramming was later embodied in System/360.[16]

The SPREAD Committee issued a report of its recommendations in December 1961. It called for "termination of the proliferation of IBM products and the development of a family of compatible processors which would employ a common technology (Solid Logic Technology or SLT), a compatible set of peripherals and a compatible program operating system." The report and recommendations of the SPREAD Committee were accepted by IBM management, and the development of the New Product Line (NPL), which ultimately became System/360, began in 1962.[17]

The principal alternative course of action, which the SPREAD Committee considered and rejected, was the addition of improved successors to the existing product lines, rather than development of an entirely new line.[18] The one course of action that IBM could not afford to take was simply to maintain the status quo and continue marketing its current products. That much was plain from the "product survival charts" incorporated in the SPREAD Report.[19] Those charts "showed that all of the existing products in the IBM product line were estimated to have very short lives, that they would be very quickly coming out of users' installations . . . [b]ecause other systems manufacturers were developing new and better products and that the evaluation was that all of the existing product line was very rapidly heading toward being non-competitive."[20]

The survival chart for the 1401 made the point graphically.[21] This most successful of IBM's systems, announced only two years earlier, was projected to reach a peak of installations by 1965, the number declining rapidly thereafter. Projections for the rest of the product line were similar. In the face of these projections, the SPREAD Committee clearly saw the need for new products to be developed and delivered by 1965. Accordingly, it recommended announcement of the first processors in the line during the first quarter of 1964.[22]

The SPREAD Report, and the Systems Architecture Group that was responsible for implementing its recommendations, created a product plan that went far beyond the recognized competitive need for new and improved products and set forth a revolutionary concept of a future product family. The concept, subsequently embodied in IBM's System/360, held the potential for enormous business success for IBM and also for revolutionizing the EDP industry. It sought not just competitive success with existing users but also a vast expansion of the number and types of EDP users and uses. At the same time, the magnitude of the commitment — the devotion of virtually the entire business to that concept — carried with it a risk of staggering proportions. Both internally and externally the IBM System/360 program came to be referred to as a "you bet your company" undertaking.[23]

THE SPREAD REPORT AND SYSTEM/360

The concept for the NPL that became 360 embodied a number of objectives, including the following:

1. The clear assertion of price/performance and technological leadership

2. The merger of business and scientific capabilities in a single family of systems (in fact, the attainment of a series of computer systems that would be an industry leader in the performance of all applications, hence the origin of the name "System/360" to denote the full 360 degrees of the circle)[24]

3. Upward and downward compatibility across the broad family of processors

4. A comprehensive set of systems software

5. Compatibility of a wide range of peripherals across the entire family of CPUs

6. The substantial user flexibility attainable from the resulting modularity of the boxes constituting a 360 computer system.

Each of the objectives held the promise of greater customer acceptance and a substantial broadening of the demand for and use of computers, and each raised its own particular challenges and risks. The attainment of each objective posed obstacles in development, design, and manufacturing, each of which carried with it the possibility of failure.

Price/Performance and Technological Leadership — Generally

The 8000 series was canceled because it would not have been a "leadership" product for a significant period of time, either technologically or in a price/performance sense. System/360 was intended to be both. In December 1962 Learson write to Evans that IBM's aim was to make the new line "economical as hell, simple to operate and the best on the market."[25] IBM's Chairman Watson wrote in June 1963 that it was important for IBM to "make these machines good enough so they will not be just equal to competition," because IBM expected that once they were announced, its competitors would "immediately try to better them" and "I [Watson] want our new line to last long enough so we do not go in the red."[26]

The price/performance of System/360 turned out to be a spectacular improvement over IBM's earlier product line.[27] In particular the Model 30 had "six times greater internal speed" than the 1401, which it was largely intended to replace.[28]

The following comparisons at the time of announcement illustrate these improvements:

	1401	*Model 30*
Rental price (with maximum memory)[29]	$ 2,680	$ 3,875
Maximum main memory capacity (characters)[30]	4,000	65,536
Speed (instructions per second)[31]	5,000	30,000
Speed/rental price	1.87	7.74

	7090	*Model 75*
Rental price (with maximum memory)[32]	$43,500	$60,300
Maximum main memory capacity[33]	196,608 (6-bit characters)	1,048,576 (8-bit characters)
Speed (multiplications/second)[34]	38,200	366,000
Speed/rental price	.88	6.07

By the time of its announcement in April 1964, it was apparent within IBM that System/360 would achieve price/performance superiority not just over IBM's own existing lines but, more important, over the systems of competitors.[35] The manager of market analysis wrote: "It is difficult to estimate the competitive jolt NPL will create. Never before has a single announcement obsoleted [sic] so much existing equipment at one time," since "NPL will have an advantage over all existing systems offered by major competitors."[36] Moreover, the analytical methods used at the time to predict price/performance understated the comparative advantages of System/360 by failing to take into account the benefits to the user stemming from the use of disks, the advantages of compatibility, the system's improved reliability, the advantages expected to come from its software, and the availability of large memories.[37]

The price/performance and other advantages of System/360 were recognized outside of IBM as well. For example, the government's industry expert witness, Frederic G. Withington of Arthur D. Little, reported in October 1964 that "With the introduction of their System 360 equipment, IBM established the new price-performance standard for equipment within the computer industry for the next several years," an opinion he reiterated during his testimony.[38] Similarly, in a June 1964 presentation to General Electric's Executive Office, John Weil called System/360 an "excellent product line with outstanding peripheral offerings," and stated that it was "no longer possible to offer equipment with a significant advantage over IBM."[39] RCA's June 1964 "Five Year

Plan" noted that System/360 "has and will have a significant impact on the marketplace and other suppliers are obliged to meet its capabilities."[40]

System/360 Component Technology

In explaining his recommendation to cancel the 8000 series, Evans had written, "New technology is essential to a new IBM machine family. Committing a new family's lot to current technology is opening IBM to a major competitive coup."[41] The improvements in price/performance offered by 360 could not have been achieved without the superior circuit technology that Evans had envisioned.[42] Development of such technology (called solid logic technology or SLT) had already begun in IBM when the SPREAD Committee met. The committee recommended the use of SLT as processor componentry because it "promised improved cost/performance and reliability,"[43] and "[T]he entire System/360 line . . . was predicated on the availability of the new SLT technology."[44]

SLT development, which had begun prior to 1961, was accelerated in April of that year on the recommendation of IBM's Advanced Technology Study Committee that a "high priority SLT program" be established.[45] According to Erich Bloch, who headed that committee until September 1964, the committee had been charged with recommending the logic component technology that IBM should use in its future EDP equipment and with establishing the schedule and cost objectives for its implementation.[46]

The committee decided that the new technology had to be producible at half the cost of the then current SMS (standard modular system) technology and be four times as fast.[47] These performance goals were influenced by both the technology performance and the computer performance that could be achieved by IBM's competitors, including both computer manufacturers and component manufacturers.[48] Because of such competitive pressures, the committee decided that the development of the new technology had to be accomplished within 18 months and the delivery of machines incorporating the technology to customers begun within three years.[49]

The committee considered three courses of action: improvement of the existing technology, development of monolithic technology, and further development of a hybrid technology (SLT) with discrete semiconductor components combined with screened circuit elements.[50] SMS was the packaging for discrete components used by IBM in its second-generation equipment. It had been designed and developed by IBM for Project STRETCH, and was superior to the discrete component packaging available from outside suppliers because it was optimized for use in EDP equipment.[51] Despite this, the committee concluded that SMS technology had apparently been pushed close to its limits in terms of cost, performance, and reliability, and would not yield the desired performance improvements.[52]

In order to gain additional information about the feasibility of going directly to monolithic circuitry ("the total integration of all devices . . . and interconnecting wiring in a single piece of semiconductor material"),[53] IBM was advised by other companies, including Fairchild, Texas Instruments, and Motorola, as to their development activity with monolithic technologies.[54] The committee concluded that, while monolithics could meet the performance requirements laid down, they could not be produced in the time or at the cost desired.[55] The committee therefore recommended moving part, but not all, the way to monolithics: the continued development of the "hybrid (SLT) configuration."[56]

That recommendation was based on several advantages possessed by the SLT technology: (1) it would lend itself well to automation and to a fast production buildup; (2) it would lend itself "to a product spectrum of applications" in processors of all sizes as well as input-output devices; (3) it would be capable of providing the necessary speeds or performance ranges; (4) the semiconductor packaging would accommodate the semiconductor well, provide the needed electrical characteristics, and give the desired packaging densities.[57]

These anticipated advantages were in fact realized, and SLT became a high-performance technology for its day, offering a substantial increase in speed at a substantial reduction in size.[58] SLT was a significant advance in other ways as well: it required less space, power, and cooling per circuit than SMS; it had higher performance and "ten times the reliability" of the earlier technology — all at a reduced cost.[59] Thus, SLT enabled IBM to offer very substantial gains in price/performance.[60] Further, SLT lent itself to automation,[61] and IBM took advantage of that fact by investing heavily in the development of automatic tools. "IBM coordinated the development of tools, the development of a design automation system and the production and testing of components with the development of the components themselves. Each of the parts of the technology took into account the other parts."[62]

Such automation enabled IBM to reduce production costs and improve the reliability of its circuits. Its substantial investment in automatic manufacturing techniques was a very important factor in allowing IBM to make System/360 much more powerful for the same price or to be a lot less costly for the same power.[63] From 1965 to 1969 SLT technology and the automation that accompanied it gave IBM a cost advantage over other component manufacturers who moved their assembly outside the United States in order to get a cheaper labor source for their relatively labor-intensive production processes.[64] No other computer manufacturer had the equivalent of SLT technology at the time of System/360's announcement and delivery, despite the substantial benefits that SLT held and despite the fact that SLT was an extension of the existing transistor technology that was readily available to everyone.[65]

Only with the benefit of hindsight, however, was it obvious that the SLT decision was the correct one. During the mid-1960s, up to about the beginning of 1966, criticism of the decision was expressed within IBM. Critics thought that SLT had been the wrong choice, that by being more aggressive IBM could have gone to monolithic circuits and taken a larger jump forward.[66] Implicit in that criticism was the apprehension that IBM would be the victim of a "competitive coup" by other companies moving beyond IBM in circuit development.

This failed to happen. On the basis of a comparison of the cost and capabilities of IBM's SLT circuits with competitive monolithic circuits that became available from the mid-1960s on, Bloch concluded that SLT had as good a performance as those later-developed products, was "much denser," and was produced at lower cost than the products that IBM's competitors acquired from outside vendors.[67] Moreover, when IBM did convert to monolithic circuits in 1968-70, it was able to use a great deal of what had been done in SLT to ease the transition.[68] This planning for the future had been taken into account by the Advanced Technology Study Committee, and for that reason IBM designed techniques and tools during the SLT development that could be adapted to the manufacture of monolithic circuitry.[69] SLT was still being used by IBM in secondary circuit functions of newer products in the late 1970s.[70]

The advantages of automation, of taking an intermediate step toward monolithics, and of coordinating circuitry, component, and product development could be fully realized only through in-house development and manufacture. Accordingly, the Advanced Technology Study Committee recommended the establishment of a Components Division that would be able to manufacture SLT on a large scale.[71]

Looking back, Richard Case, who had been involved in the development and design of System/360, called IBM's decision to develop and build its own new circuitry "perhaps the riskiest single decision that had to be made by IBM in the development of System/360."[72] It required a substantial capital investment in a new business — developing and manufacturing transistor components — in which IBM had had little prior experience. Not surprisingly, there was considerable debate within IBM over whether components was an "appropriate business" for IBM to get into, and the decision to establish the Components Division in 1961 continued to be second-guessed well into the 1960s — long after IBM had committed itself to the point at which there was no turning back.[73] In short, as T. V. Learson put it in 1966: IBM "had to become, in a very short time, the largest component manufacturer in the world."[74] If IBM were successful, the potential benefits overrode those risks:

1.   In-house manufacture could help IBM reduce its total costs by eliminating middleman profits.

2.   By designing the new circuitry and the new machines simultaneously, IBM could get the best new circuitry earliest because it would not have to wait for another firm to finish its circuit development process and make the circuit available in order to explore the circuit's potential characteristics and use in a computer system.

3.   Unlike other manufacturers who were less integrated and who would have to adapt generalized circuitry to their particular needs, IBM would be able to enhance the price/performance of its computer systems by tailoring its own circuitry to the requirements of System/360.[75]

In-house manufacture would also permit IBM to accelerate the training of computer engineers in both the characteristics and the use of the new circuit technology. According to Case, it was believed that IBM "could synchronize the development activities between the circuit development organizations and the computer development organizations more effectively if they were in one corporation rather than if they were in two or more corporations."[76]

Such synchronization was to grow increasingly important. Bloch testified that as the integration level of components increases, "more and more of a machine is on a single component. And therefore when one has in mind the designing of a new computer one can learn a lot by just looking at the individual components that go into it."[77] As the degree of component integration increased during the 1960s, both symbiosis in development and confidentiality became increasingly more important reasons for in-house development.

IBM's Advanced Technology Study Committee took the long view in 1961,[78] and its long-range planning paid off handsomely. IBM achieved the objectives that it set with respect to the design, development, and manufacture of SLT, and the ultimate success of System/360 was "in large measure" dependent on the success of that circuit development activity.[79]

A Single Family for All Applications

The SPREAD Committee recommended development of a single line of processors to "meet the needs of the commercial, scientific, and communications and control markets."[80] That objective called for a "fundamental change" in IBM's design emphasis, but one that was thought to be necessary for developing user requirements.[81] At the time of the SPREAD Report, IBM's product lines were "distinctly either commercial or scientific in their emphasis."[82] This was true of other vendors' product lines as well. Up to that time customers who wanted to do what had traditionally been considered both "scientific applications" and "business applications" often acquired two computers.[83]

By the end of the 1950s, however, the distinctions between business and scientific applications were beginning to blur, and "customers themselves were not observing [the] lines between scientific and business machines in actual practice."[84] Evans testified that "more and more" often the "scientific side" of a user's operation needed the data-handling capabilities associated with business data processors, and the "business side" needed the arithmetic and logic capabilities associated with scientific systems.[85] As we have seen, the history of the 1950s and early 1960s is full of examples of "business" computers doing "scientific" applications and vice versa.

That user need for "dual use" was a major factor in the SPREAD Committee's thinking. According to Evans, "One of the premises from the beginning was [that] there would be great savings to the users if we could combine in the single machine the ability to cover the full range of business applications and scientific applications as well. So our concept was a single machine that would be equally able in either of those areas."[86]

Although the committee did foresee a need for separate development of ruggedized products for military purposes, it stated that "standard products will satisfy about 32 percent of the available military market" and that a basic objective should be "to further penetrate the ultrareliable portion of the military market with the SPREAD family."[87]

Thus it became an objective to design the NPL architecture for the "broadest possible range of applications . . . equally well suited" to what had previously been considered scientific or business computing. An instruction set and processing capabilities were to be designed to be "equally suitable to both of those classes of applications and indeed well suited to the broadest possible range of applications that one could think of," including process control applications and communications control applications.[88] The name "System/360" was chosen for the new line to indicate the "full circle of the applications ability of the machine."[89]

The combining of capability to do the whole range of applications in a single machine promised great savings to users and great returns to IBM. It was far from clear, however, that the objective of designing "dual purpose" computers could be accomplished without a degradation of either performance in business applications or performance in scientific applications — or, indeed, in all the application areas. Evans testified that this risk was perceived by IBM management and "haunted" them:

> The question was whether we could build machines that in their own right as a scientific performer would be the best and also had the ability to do the business kind of a problem, or in so doing would we really be building mediocrity and someone could come along and optimize as the industry had done before and build better scientific machines, better business data processors, and in the process negate our plans and our aspirations.[90]

Moreover, even if 360 was as powerful as more specialized competitive machines in their specialties, there was a risk that customers might reject System/360 because they just "might not see it that way."[91] In the face of these risks, some people in IBM became proponents of continuing work on the preexisting "scientific" and "business" product lines. During 1962 and 1963 a project to build a scientific computer compatible with and as a successor to the 7094 was continued;[92] and as late as December 1963-January 1964, a group in the General Products Division led by John Haanstra (who had been the chairman of the SPREAD Committee) opposed development of the 360/30 in favor of extending the 1401 line instead.[93]

Such fears were not unfounded. As we shall see, competitors did attempt to offer more specialized systems to meet the needs of certain users and were successful in competing against System/360 where customers wanted such relative specialization rather than the more generalized range of functions that

System/360 offered. Some of the history of the later 1960s is the history of IBM's attempts to respond to such competition.

Despite the risks, the concept proposed by SPREAD was pursued. System/360 was designed to be a machine equally powerful in scientific and business applications and with facilities for real-time applications, which "machines of that age had not been able to address before System/360 with real power and versatility."[94]

IBM's achievement in this regard was immediately recognized. Within General Electric, John Weil wrote in June 1964:

> . . . System/360 integrates into a single set of equipment the capability for business data processing, scientific calculations, data communications, and process control. It seems clear that all of these are now but facets of the basic information handling and processing system.[95]

Testifying at the trial, Weil stated that the distinction between scientific and commercial processing was "erased" "[i]n a practical sense, with the announcement of the IBM 360."[96] Moreover, "[s]ince the early sixties, it really hasn't been economically important to design a computer system only for business or only for scientific applications, except at the extreme ends of this spectrum, where you are trying to do as much scientific calculation as you possibly can within the limits of the technology."[97]

System/360's ability to "do the 360 degrees of the circle" resulted in acceptance by users who could not get the same range of performance from other architectures.[98] Its broad range of applications helped simplify customers' acquisition decisions, enabled them to achieve economies of scale by acquiring one large-capacity, rather than two smaller-capacity machines, and permitted them to reduce the required training and improve the efficiency of their EDP staffs.[99] The combination of business, scientific, and other applications in the same line also helped reduce IBM's costs. It enabled IBM to concentrate on a single machine type with fewer sets of program support and software, and with a single program of training and education for customers and IBM personnel.[100]

System/360 Compatibility

Some of the benefits associated with the "erasure" of the business-scientific distinction and some of the techniques used to effect it were also associated with the achievement of another objective of the SPREAD Committee: having a single compatible line of processors extending over a wide performance range. "Compatibility" in this sense meant that programs written for one processor in the line could be run on a second processor, provided the second processor had at least the minimum memory capacity and complement of input-output and auxiliary storage devices required by the program, and that successful execution of the program did not depend on the speed of the CPU.[101]

The SPREAD Committee stated:

> IBM customers' needs for general-purpose processors can be most profitably met by a single compatible family extending from the smallest stored-program core-memory machine to the machine for customers growing beyond the 7094 and 7030. There are processor needs above and below this range — it is not yet evident that these can be compatible with the new processor family.[102]

The new family was to consist of at least five CPUs — those five to be upward- and downward-compatible with one another.[103]

According to Evans, this concept of compatibility envisaged by the SPREAD Committee and implemented in System/360 was "just a mile apart from the rest of the world."[104] Prior to the introduction of System/360, it was generally the case that the computer lines of a particular manufacturer were not compatible with one another. Although both IBM and a number of its competitors had achieved upward compatibility over a very narrow performance range covered by two or three machines, no one had achieved full upward and downward compatibility over the very substantial systems performance range of System/360.[105]

The SPREAD Committee viewed compatibility for an entire family as a "major advance" that would appeal to customers and "sell more processors." From the customer's perspective, the committee regarded compatibility as a "powerful selling tool" because it would:

1. Protect programming investment

2. Permit phased growth

3. Minimize investment in personnel training

4. Expand the available labor market of personnel trained to operate in the customer's environment

5. Simplify the adaptation of the customer's applications to several processors

6. Permit the customer to transfer applications among installations

7. Thus provide an incentive for the customer to convert to System/360 from noncompatible families.[106]

Such benefits did, in fact, accrue to customers. Indeed, since System/360 was compatible over a far broader range of processor capacities than any previous EDP line, the advantages of compatibility were made available to a great many users of all sizes — from the large, multiple-location user who was able to reduce training, system development, and programming costs to the small, first-time user who could plan to grow rapidly without incurring reprogramming costs. Of course, this meant that a great many users would be attracted to System/360.[107]

Joseph Rooney, who held a position as an IBM branch manager and later became the president of RCA's Data Processing Division, testified that the "high degree of program compatibility" within System/360 provided an advantage to IBM in that

> Their clients could grow from a smaller system to a larger system, or if the economic situations were such that they wanted to go to a lower system, they could do so without having to reinvest in their software. It also was an advantage if you had a multi-faceted organization that had large computers and small computers, and some commonality of applications that they wanted to use on both types of systems. It gave the client the advantage of not having to modify his software to do so.[108]

In addition to the tremendous competitive advantage that IBM would derive from offering users a compatible family, the SPREAD Committee recognized that compatibility was "clearly advantageous to [IBM's] development and manufacturing."[109] Commonality in processor logic and programming was anticipated to provide IBM with economies in training of field personnel, development of programming, and standardization of installation and maintenance procedures. Competitors were not expected to be able to overcome such advantages during the rest of the decade unless they adopted new approaches to the achievement of compatibility,[110] which (as we discuss below) a number of IBM's competitors did, albeit several years later.

In the event, System/360 compatibility permitted IBM to realize these and other benefits. Training of programmers, salesmen, and systems engineers was made considerably easier because they had to be trained for one group of machines instead of for different, incompatible machines. IBM achieved cost reductions in manufacturing because of the ability to share parts among the various models of System/360 and to provide common training to manufacturing personnel. Finally, IBM had to develop fewer operating systems than it would have for incompatible processors, and the design of the individual models was facilitated because commonality of design permitted the various engineering groups to communicate effectively and assist in one another's design efforts.[111]

The decision to provide a compatible line over a large performance range was recognized within IBM as a risky one. Thus, the SPREAD Committee anticipated that competitors' salesmen could market against a single compatible line by developing "knock-offs" applicable to the entire family. That family would also provide a more nearly unitary target toward which competitors might aim more effectively with their own product and price moves. Perhaps most important, it would "encourage competition to be compatible with [IBM] in order to tap [IBM's] support efforts."[112] That latter possibility was one that IBM plainly foresaw throughout the 1960s and that came to fruition in different ways in the latter half of the decade and in the 1970s with the explosive growth of leasing companies and the advent of suppliers of plug-compatible peripherals and IBM-compatible CPUs.

The compatibility objective presented technical risks as well. Just as the attempt to combine business, scientific, and other applications in the same line raised the possibility that the new system would do none of them as well as a more specialized machine, so the attempt to achieve compatibility between very fast processors and relatively slower ones raised the possibility that none of them would be truly optimal. As Case stated:

> It was thought prior to System/360 that having one machine architecture for both the fastest and the slowest machines in a product line and, in fact, all places in between, could not be right because either the fast machines would be unnecessarily restricted in the amount of function and capability that they could provide . . . or alternatively, that the slowest and cheapest machines would be far too expensive by virtue of having to provide the richness of the instruction set that was provided by the larger and more expensive machines in the product line.[113]

The difficulty of the compatibility undertaking was clearly recognized by the SPREAD Committee, and its success required a "technological change in the way computer systems were built . . . in IBM."[114] That technological change was the introduction of microprogramming or "firmware."

Microprogramming was invented by M. V. Wilkes of Cambridge University in 1951, but IBM was the first computer manufacturer to use firmware in the building of computers, starting with the experimental SCAMP and continuing with System/360 (and, later, the invention of the floppy disk).[115] Firmware permitted the behavior of a machine to be altered semipermanently through the use of replaceable or reprogrammable parts. Its use required the development and application by IBM of "new technical components" (such as transformer and capacitor read-only storage) and a new design "discipline."[116] Through the use of firmware (rather than hardware or software) IBM was able to achieve a number of the design trade-offs that System/360 required. It was the "technical device . . . most responsible" for the fact that IBM System/360 computers were able to be designed efficiently for both business and scientific applications, as well as the method by which IBM was able to achieve full upward and downward compatibility and to emulate earlier IBM computers on System/360 (as explained below).[117] So important was microprogramming that the 360/40 — the lead system in development — was assigned to Hursley because of that laboratory's experience with microprogramming in SCAMP.[118]

Some measure of the success that IBM achieved in implementing the architectural objectives laid down for System/360 may be gleaned from the longevity of that architecture. Compatibility and suitability for a wide range of applications were characteristics (assuming that they were effectively implemented) that would undoubtedly be desirable in future systems. Accordingly, Case testified:

> We tried to develop the computer architecture which would be extendable, which would be useful not only for the machines that were going

to be announced in 1964, but also for subsequent machines as far into the future as we could plan for. . . . We were thinking in terms of 15-20 years . . . and we would like to have had that last even longer if that were possible.[119]

The architecture of System/360 lasted through the 370 into the 303X and 43XX lines, and continues to the present time.[120]

Incompatibility and Emulation

Withington called IBM's introduction of the System/360 "a substantial risk" for two main reasons:

> One, IBM adopted a new machine architecture and a dependence on systems programs to cause the machine to be usable to the users. This was a large step in terms of the evolution of machine architecture and design, and it was not immediately certain either whether it would work well or whether the users would accept it.
>
> The second primary area of risk was the lack of compatibility between the 360s as announced and the predecessor IBM machines.
>
> It was immediately obvious that the willingness of the customers to reprogram from the older machines to the 360s was a major question relating to its probable degree of success.[121]

The disadvantage of offering a new, incompatible line was clearly recognized by the SPREAD Committee. It was, however, a disadvantage that had to be overcome rather than avoided if the committee's concept for the new line was to be instituted. As the SPREAD Report noted, "Since [the new] processors must have capabilities not now present in any IBM processor product, the new family of products will *not* be compatible with our existing processors."[122]

The SPREAD Committee anticipated that the new capabilities provided by System/360 would induce many users to switch to that family despite the need to convert their programming. Indeed, for many of these users, the very fact that they wanted to implement new functions rendered the entire question of conversion moot:

> . . . While incompatibilities are a marketing disadvantage, it should be noted that systems reprogramming will, in many cases, be required, independent of the processor used. This will occur whenever the user wishes to obtain the benefits of any of the following:
>
> a. Random access rather than batch processing
> b. The integration of communication facilities
> c. The simultaneous operation of multiple processors
> d. Multiprogramming to achieve efficient on-line operation.[123]

The committee also recognized, however, that "Some customers [would] be dissatisfied unless an alternative [was] provided to permit utilization of [their] prior machine investment."[124] IBM provided customers with that alternative in the form of emulators — combinations of hardware and software that permit one computer system to execute programs written for another system.

Other manufacturers of computer systems also recognized the desirability of facilitating conversion and provided users a number of aids, such as simulators and translators, to ease the transition between incompatible systems. (A simulator performs the same function as an emulator, but is implemented entirely in software. A translator is a computer program that takes as input the source programs of a particular computer and translates them as closely as possible into an equal program in the same or a different language that will run on the equipment to which conversion is desired.) Thus, GE offered a 1401 simulator that permitted programs written for a 1401 to be run on its 400 line and a 7090 simulator that permitted programs written for the 7090 or 7094 to be run on GE's 600 line.[125] RCA developed a simulator that allowed programs written for IBM's 650 computer to run unchanged on the RCA 301.[126] Honeywell offered a LIBERATOR program that translated IBM 1400 series programs into programs usable on the Honeywell 200.[127]

As late as August 1963, IBM was still working on software simulation as a means of providing System/360 compatibility with prior systems. However, work on providing conversion through emulation had commenced within IBM prior to that time.[128] On August 1, 1963, D. H. Furth, corporate director of programming, sent a memorandum to Evans expressing the view that it was "feasible" to use read-only memory control (microprogramming) to achieve compatibility. He wrote:

> Since such a hardware simulation would appear to be very economical from the customer's point of view and since it would eliminate some half dozen simulators from an already mountainous Programming Systems load, it would appear reasonable to pursue the realization of this feasibility as part of the overall NPL program.[129]

By October that recommendation had been accepted, and Brooks (who had become the manager of the NPL project and was to go on to be the manager of OS/360) wrote that "We are hopeful that microprogrammed simulation can add substantially to the bag of tools for aiding conversion."[130]

During 1964 IBM announced microprogram-based compatibility features on System/360 for the 1401, 1410, 1440, 1460, 1620, 709, 7010, 7040, 7044, 7070, 7074, 7080, 7090, 7094, and 7094 II processors.[131]

Case estimated IBM's cost of developing the 1401 compatibility feature on the Model 30 as $200,000 and the cost of developing the 7090 emulator on the Model 65 as $500,000.[132] Withington testified that System/360 was "the first major use of microprogramming for purposes of establishing backward compatibility."[133] He also testified that implementation of emulation using control store and microprograms, while it is more expensive [than software emulation], is regarded by users as preferable in most cases because it is so much faster.[134]

The provision of emulators on System/360 afforded users an alternative to conversion.[135] It permitted them to transfer jobs to System/360 and to concentrate on new application areas without immediately having to convert their existing applications. Although programs run in emulation mode generally ran more slowly than they would have if rewritten to run in native mode on the new systems, they could be run effectively enough to permit users to forgo reprogramming if they chose to do so.[136]

Nevertheless, because 360 was incompatible with IBM's second-generation equipment, the conversion from that equipment to 360 involved as large a task for users as would converting to another vendor's systems.[137] Indeed, in some instances conversion to non-IBM equipment would have been easier than conversion to 360. Weil of GE testified that GE was initially "overjoyed" with the announcement of System/360 because GE had introduced a system "designed to displace" IBM's 7090s and 7094s and believed that "it would be easier . . . to convert from the 7090/7094 to . . . [GE's] 600 series" than to 360.[138] Southern Railway ran benchmarks that showed that conversion from an IBM 7000 series system to an IBM 360 was "about equal in difficulty" to conversion to an RCA or Burroughs machine, but not as easy as conversion to a UNIVAC 1108.[139]

Despite this, IBM was successful in getting users to convert to System/360 from IBM second-generation systems. One reason for that success was, undoubtedly, the benefits that users were able to derive from System/360's improved price/performance and new capabilities.[140] Thus, for example, Donald Hart, head of the Computer Science Department of the General Motors Research Laboratories, testified that his department went from a 701 to a 704 to a 7090/94 to a System/360.[141] Several years after these changes, Hart wrote that "conversion costs must be taken into account when changing computers; however, in retrospect, the value of each of the above changes far exceeded the costs incurred."[142] He explained that improvements in sheer computer speed, reduced computation costs, and the availability of "new kinds of capabilities" were all reasons for changing computer systems. To decide whether conversion is justified, "you take into account the costs of making the change, the benefits which are going to result from the change, [and] determine whether the benefits exceed the costs."[143]

A similar cost/benefit analysis was performed by the National Aeronautics and Space Administration (NASA) about 1965. NASA had just made a large purchase of second-generation machines to lower its operating costs when a "new series of equipments" including IBM 360s, Univac, CDC, and GE computers became available with multiprogramming capabilities, I-O flexibility, different memory sizes, program logic, and the ability to use remote I-O devices. NASA decided to convert "at the earliest possible time."[144] Its analysis of the conversion difficulties was that

> This conversion has created a considerable workload and has resulted in overlapping of older and newer equipments with its attendant increased rental costs during the conversion period.

NASA concluded, however:

> The benefits from the more complex software and the flexibility of the new machines far outweigh any conversion cost we may incur.[145]

Despite the powerful incentives that users had to incorporate System/360's new capabilities, it seems clear that 360 would have been far less successful without emulators. Xerox's Competitive Reference Manual noted the success of IBM's emulation approach to converting second-generation users to 360,[146] and Edwin McCollister of RCA testified that it was a "very widespread practice" in the late 1960s for IBM users to choose the option of emulation on 360.[147] An IBM corporate programming study based on a November 1967 customer survey estimated that "more than half of the systems hours now being used by our Models 30, 40, 50 and 65 are being used in emulator mode."[148]

System/360 Software

As computer systems became faster and more complex, it became increasingly important to manage efficiently the resources they provided. Operating system software relieved programmers of the need to incorporate instructions scheduling different tasks and controlling different pieces of equipment in each program they wrote. In effect, such scheduling and control jobs were turned over to the computer itself. Operating systems enabled users to take advantage of a computer's total processing power, including its multiprogramming and multiprocessing capabilities.[149]

Given the complex new applications and modes of use at which System/360 was being aimed — "multi-terminal, on-line, real-time, multiprogramming operation"[150] — it was imperative that IBM automate the system's resource management task as much as possible. IBM embarked on the creation of a set of operating systems of varying complexity. The most complex of these, OS/360, was particularly ambitious.

OS/360 was designed to let customers "make the maximum possible use of the relatively greater speed of the . . . System/360 central processing units." Since multiprogramming was anticipated to be a "normal" mode of use, facilities (such as an interruption mechanism) were to be included to make multiprogramming "easier, straight forward [*sic*] and efficient." In addition, OS/360 was to contain facilities that would permit programmers to develop applications more efficiently, optimize the utilization of peripherals, and simplify maintenance.[151] OS/360 was a generalization of "every aspect of operating systems known at the time."[152] Within IBM it was recognized that "no one [had] ever undertaken a programming task of [OS/360's] magnitude."[153] This recognition was shared by later outside observers.[154]

So ambitious an undertaking entailed significant risk. Apart from the difficulty of constructing the operating system, there was the additional risk that users would reject the unusual multiprogramming environment.[155] That would mean that IBM's investment in the hardware and software needed for multi-programming, when reflected in System/360's prices, would make the systems less competitive. In addition, OS/360's "extensive" resource management, data management, languages, aids to program development, and error recovery techniques did not come "without a price." The use of those capabilities would take up auxiliary storage space, main memory space, and time on the CPU – an "operating system overhead." There was a significant risk that users would be unwilling to accept such "overhead" for the richness of function provided by OS/360.[156]

As discussed below, OS/360 did, in fact, run into "difficulties in design, in correctness [and] in completion"[157] (as did the complex operating systems of many other suppliers during the 1960s). However, "when the system finally worked it had properties that were beyond about any other operating system around."[158] Meanwhile, OS/360 was only one of five general programming packages that IBM announced in 1964 for use with System/360. The others – Basic Programming Support (BPS), Basic Operating System (BOS), Disk Operating System (DOS), and Tape Operating System (TOS) – were less complex sets of systems software. These operating systems "worked reasonably well from the start" and were well accepted by customers.[159] DOS in particular, which was less complex than OS/360 but still 25 to 50 times as complex as the systems software provided with the 1401, was highly rated by users and widely used.[160]

System/360 Peripherals

One of the design objectives for System/360 was to provide "a wide variety of peripheral equipment that could be combined in a very wide range of configurations."[161] Prior to announcement, the breadth of 360's peripherals was viewed within IBM as a prime motivation for users to reorganize their applications and convert to 360. In January 1964 Frederick Brooks wrote:

> Even though present applications can be simply mapped onto System/360, many new system concepts will offer substantial incentive for the customer to re-plan his application. These include file orientation, communication facilities, large memories, bulk stores, etc.[162]

The April 7, 1964 announcement of 360 contained "many features different from those previously offered by IBM." Included in the announcement were "direct access storage devices (including the 2311 disk drive, the 2321 data cell and the 2301 drum storage device); control units; high performance tape drives (including the 2400 series and the 7340 Hypertape drive Model 3); visual display units (including the 2250); 7770/7772 audio response units; communication and data acquisition equipment (including the 1070 process communication system); and a printer, the 1403-N1." After April 7 IBM also announced numerous additional peripheral devices for use with System/360 — including the 2314 disk drive, new terminals, additional models of the 2400 tape drive, the 2420 tape drives, and optical character recognition equipment.[163]

The combination of the peripheral product announcements and the announcement of so many CPUs with a wide range of memory options was "unprecedented in the industry."[164] This range of peripherals was important to customers when considering System/360 against competitive systems because it greatly expanded their ability to change or add to their systems as their requirements changed. While specific peripherals such as the 2321 data cell or Hypertape turned out to be failures,[165] as a whole the peripherals offered with System/360 "played a large part" in customer decisions to go to that system.[166]

The broad range of peripherals announced with 360 promoted two of the SPREAD Committee's primary objectives: the creation of a single system able to perform all applications and one that would address increasingly important new applications (multiterminal, on-line, real-time applications). The announcement of new disk drives, tape drives, communication controllers, card and printer I-O, terminals, audio response equipment, magnetic and optical character readers, and paper tape and process control units meant that users could build configurations specifically tailored to their application requirements — whatever those requirements happened to be. One of the features of 360 that permitted it to be used for both scientific and business applications and to "erase the previous distinction" was "the very wide range of input/output equipment easily attachable through a common interface, . . . [which] made it relatively simple to configure a commercial system . . . or one optimized for scientific computing."[167]

In addition, the variety of remote I-O and communications equipment offered with System/360 underscored 360's emphasis on new applications. Weil of GE wrote that System/360 "has major strength in a variety of new mass storage devices and a whole new array of remote terminal equipment. . . . It has many of the features which will make possible its application in direct access systems."[168] Displays, remote data-collection equipment, remote process-control equipment, communications controllers, data communications equipment, and on-line banking equipment were all made available to permit users to bring the power of 360 to bear at the point of transaction — in real time. The ability of System/360 to communicate with other computers or terminals "opened up a whole new gamut of applications in industries, airline reservations industries, modern business, so that remote stations could have access to the enormous data in a central computer and do so in real time."[169] The ability to do such applications resulted in placement of systems that otherwise would not have been placed.[170]

The importance of System/360's peripherals to the success of the product line cannot be overestimated. Even a single peripheral device — such as a disk drive, terminal, or printer — that is sufficiently better than competitive offerings can swing the total system decision.[171] In this respect, of all the peripherals offered with System/360, the 1403 N1 printer and the 2311 and 2314 disk drives were most critical to 360's success.

The 1403 N1 Printer

We discussed earlier the importance of the 1403 printer to the success of IBM's 1401 computer system and how that printer gave IBM a tremendous advantage in the marketing of systems until competitors began to offer satisfactory alternatives by 1963 or 1964. In 1964 IBM announced the 1403 N1 printer for use with System/360. The 1403 N1 ran at almost twice the speed of its predecessor (1,100 lines per minute, compared with 600 for the 1403) and cost only about 15 percent more than the 1403.[172] At the time of its introduction IBM's competitors did not offer a printer that matched the 1403 N1 in print quality, price, and speed.[173] Arthur Beard (former chief engineer of RCA's Computer Systems Division) testified that RCA began offering the 1403 N1 with its Spectra series because there were applications for which customers desired print quality "of a very high standard." Such customers "insisted" on "1403 chain printer type quality," and "after resisting these requests some period of time," RCA acquiesced and "put the 1403 into the RCA computer line."[174]

The 1403 N1 was particularly important to System/360's ability to perform certain business applications, such as payroll, billing, accounts receivable, and inventory control. F. Rigdon Currie of Xerox testified that Xerox Data Systems (XDS) was at a "disadvantage" relative to IBM with respect to its line printer for customers who wanted to do "any significant amount of buiness data processing."[175] As late as 1969, XDS was only "marginally competitive" in peripherals, and its line printers "were not acceptable to some of our users." Those printers lacked the range of "speed/performance" that some customers wanted and did not produce as high a quality print as a chain printer or a train printer.[176]

CDC also experienced "substantial problems" in marketing some of its computer systems because they incorporated printers that "lacked sufficient reliability to meet normal customer expectations" and had "a poor print quality, in terms of wavy print." To help solve these problems, CDC acquired the Printer Division of Holly Carburetor in 1966.[177] CDC ultimately developed a 1403 N1-type printer of its own, but it had to be "reworked and re-developed" around 1969-70 in order to effect reliability improvements. The changes resulted in a design that was "more like the original IBM design."[178]

While CDC attempted to copy the 1403 N1 design and RCA simply incorporated it into its product line, Grumman Data Systems took advantage of the 1403 N1's superiority by offering to attach it to a number of non-IBM computer systems. As late as 1975, an advertisement for Grumman Data systems stated:

> For years people have been trying to imitate the IBM 1403. Unsuccess-
> fully. Now, with the Grumman Printer Controller you can connect
> your present computer to an IBM 1403 and give yourself the best
> printing in the business.
>
> The IBM 1403 has built an extraordinary record. Highly reliable,
> high speed operation. Unusually consistent, clearly readable printouts.
> (No wavy lines so typical of drum printers.) Type fonts your operator
> can readily interchange. And, of course, it handles form changes easily.
>
> . . . .
>
> With our printer controller you can connect the IBM 1403 to your
> present DEC, Xerox, GE, or CDC computer. We'd like to hear from
> Burroughs, Univac and the other computer users, too.[179]

Grumman later offered the 1403 N1 for attachment to Burroughs, Data General,
Digital Scientific, and Univac computers.[180]

System/360 Disk Drives

IBM maintained its superiority in direct-access storage technology with the
disk drives introduced for use with System/360. Both the 2311 and 2314 were
substantial improvements over IBM's earlier disk drives, and both proved crit-
ically important to the success of System/360. These disk drives were unique in
the industry: there were no similar competitive offerings for several years after
their introduction. They gave IBM an advantage in the marketing of 360 systems
that competitors were unable to match until the late 1960s, when they adopted
IBM's disk technology in one way or another.

IBM announced the Model 2311 disk drive on April 7, 1964. The 2311
had approximately twice the access speed, twice the data rate, and two and one-
half times the storage capacity of the 1311.[181] The 2314 disk drive, announced
on April 22, 1965, had a faster access speed, double the data rate, and almost
four times the storage capacity per spindle of the 2311.[182] Further, the two
drives provided "for the first time, the degree of reliability that was required
of random access devices."[183]

IBM foresaw and depended upon the widespread acceptance of disk drives
as a key factor in the ultimate success of System/360. IBM Vice-President Paul
Knaplund testified:

> An important element of the System 360 forecast was the anticipation
> that disk files would be used extensively, both in applications that had
> historically utilized magnetic tape or punched card storage and in the
> development of new communications oriented — or "teleprocessing" —
> applications.[184]

It is important to note that the use of disk drives was not common on second-
generation computing systems.[185] Nevertheless, IBM gambled that System/360
would be widely used in "operational-type" applications (as opposed to batch-
type applications) and that disks would play a pivotal role in such use.[186]

System/360's more advanced operating systems were designed in a way that required a direct-access storage device for their successful operation.[187] IBM was therefore betting that users would be willing to trade off the expense of disk drives for the increased efficiency of operation and the additional capabilities that a disk-based system would be able to provide. It gambled that users would widely accept an approach to computing that had not been widely accepted before and that they would make heavy use of the capability that disk drives offered for having on-line information readily available — a capability particularly important in real-time applications such as those performed by banks and airlines.[188]

In hindsight, that bet was a good one. Indeed, IBM "totally underestimated the demand for such devices": "we [in IBM] found ourselves hard pressed to deliver the devices as fast as customers were demanding them."[189] Today, "nobody thinks of developing a wide range of computing equipment or a family of computer systems without having a direct access storage device as a prerequisite for the operating systems."[190] Back in 1964, however, nobody but IBM had that thought or acted upon it as forcefully. As a consequence, the tremendous acceptance of IBM's disk drives swept before it all of the other approaches to random-access storage then being offered. As Withington testified:

> During that period the entire industry and the users began to appreciate the importance that disk drives were going to play in the great majority of general purpose computer systems. . . . A number of the other manufacturers committed themselves almost entirely to the magnetic card devices, sometimes also using magnetic drums.
>
> When it became apparent that the class of magnetic card devices was not going to be successful in the marketplace, for reasons of reliability, and that the disk drive was a critical product, many of IBM's competitors were left for a while without a satisfactory option.[191]

Both the level of performance and the attractiveness of System/360 were substantially dependent on the 2311 and 2314 disk drives.[192] The 2311 was far more important to the marketing of System/360 than the 1311 had been for IBM's earlier systems,[193] and the 2314 was, if anything, even more important. It provided "a functional capability very much needed in terms of price/performance in the competitive marketplace and without that capability you were in a weak competitive situation against IBM."[194] Within IBM the 2314 was recognized as a "catalyst to make many systems sales for previously undeveloped application use of computers" and as a "door opener that beats competition."[195] IBM's emphasis on the use of disk drives with System/360 contributed to the objective of increasing the market for IBM products in particular and computer system products in general.[196]

Not surprisingly, other systems suppliers wanted the kind of sales catalyst that IBM already had. Eventually, they either acquired them from others or from IBM itself, or they undertook to manufacture them themselves. As we discuss in detail in Chapter 10, the acceptance of 360 spurred the growth of peripheral equipment manufacturers, some of whom supplied IBM 2311- and 2314-type disk drives directly to IBM end users. During the later 1960s, however, these manufacturers served as a prime source of disk drives for many systems suppliers.

In 1968 Memorex became the first of the plug-compatible manufacturers (PCMs) to offer IBM plug-compatible disk drives. During the period 1967-70 Memorex hired almost 600 former IBM employees, three of whom became Memorex vice-presidents.[197] In 1967 it hired a number of disk drive engineers from IBM, including Roy Applequist, who had designed IBM's voice coil actuator.[198] Applequist designed the voice coil actuator for Memorex's 630 disk drive, which, according to an independent engineering assessment, was "directly derived" from IBM's 2314B (3330) and "not the result of coincidence."[199] D. J. Guzy, former executive vice-president of Memorex, testified that the hiring of Applequist and other IBM engineers was important to the success that Memorex achieved with the 630, and that the 630 and the later 660 were styled and intended to be, respectively, 2311-type and 2314-type disk drives.[200] Memorex marketed the 630 and 660 not only directly to IBM end users, but also to a number of systems manufacturers, including RCA, Univac, DEC, Burroughs, Honeywell, SEL, Hewlett-Packard, Siemens, Phillips, and ICL.[201]

Information Storage Systems (ISS) was formed in December 1967 by 12 former IBM employees who had resigned from the firm's San Jose laboratory, where they were responsible for disk drive development. A number of them had worked on IBM's Merlin (3330) program.[202] Like Memorex, ISS manufactured 2311-type disk drives, the 701 and 714, which were marketed by Telex to IBM end users beginning in 1969.[203] ISS also marketed disks to Hewlett-Packard, Itel, and Storage Technology Corporation.[204] The ISS 2311-type drive was similar to IBM's 2311 except for the addition of a voice coil actuator, and the ISS 2314-type drive was functionally equivalent to IBM's 2314, again except for the addition of a voice coil actuator.[205] ISS was acquired by Sperry Rand in 1973.[206] It then became the developer and manufacturer of disk subsystems for use in Univac systems, but continued marketing 2314-type disk drives to IBM users and to original equipment manufacturer (OEM) customers.[207]

CalComp also offered 2311-type and 2314-type disk drives, manufactured by Century Data Systems, to end users and on an OEM basis.[208] It shipped its first plug-compatible (2311-type) disk drive in June 1969,[209] and later became the "first company to produce and ship a 2314 equivalent."[210] Century Data marketed these disk drives to leasing companies such as Randolph and to other systems suppliers such as Nixdorf, Burroughs, and Univac.[211]

CDC manufactured and marketed 2311- and 2314-type disk drives, both to end users and to OEM customers. CDC's OEM customers included Honeywell, GE, Siemens, RCA, XDS, ICL, SAAB, CII, Burroughs, and Telex.[212]

RCA did not even wait for PCMs to copy IBM's technology, but went directly to the source. "It was apparent [to RCA] that this capability which was offered by IBM was going to be required by RCA in order to successfully market its products."

This capability at the time was not available from any other source. So, therefore, when we announced the Spectra 70 family or series, which came out about eight months after the IBM 360 announcement, we announced as a part of the RCA product line this particular Model 2311 disk pack file capability and we obtained these files by buying them from IBM, the same as any other customer would buy them from IBM.[213]

RCA subsequently contracted with Memorex to supply disk drives for use with RCA computer systems because Memorex's development program was further ahead than RCA's. RCA went to Memorex because RCA was "under a handicap in selling the Spectra 70 Systems" because of a lack of a "comparable product to the IBM 2314 at the time." RCA "couldn't afford in the marketplace to wait that additional year" necessary for RCA's development program to produce the required disk drives "[b]ecause we were losing too many sales for the lack of it" to IBM.[214]

GE, on the other hand, attempted to build an IBM plug-compatible 2311-type drive.[215] But "it met with limited success and arrived to the marketplace much too late to meet market, or customer requirements."[216] GE entered into an exclusive contract with Greyhound Computer Corporation to sell the device, but Greyhound ended up having to take a significant write-off on its investment in the GE equipment and even sued GE.[217]

Not until the very end of the 1960s had disk technology been sufficiently spread around the industry for some of IBM's systems competitors to have pulled even, and by then IBM was getting ready to announce its new disk drive, the 3330 or Merlin, putting it back in the lead.[218]

The Standard Interface and Modularity

IBM adopted a "standard interface" for the peripherals in the compatible 360 line. This meant that (with some exceptions) the same peripherals would attach to all processors in the line and would do so in the same way. The standard interface helped maximize the benefits that customers could derive from the broad range of peripherals offered with 360 and the compatibility across the entire line. It helped give System/360 a configurability that was unmatched by competitors and permitted customers the utmost flexibility to optimize their data-processing systems by piecemeal or modular changes. At the same time it enabled IBM to reduce costs through economies in development and manufacturing. Others undoubtedly recognized these benefits and also moved toward more modular product lines — but not until well after IBM had done so.[219]

The interface that was standardized was that between the System/360 channel and the control units of the various peripheral devices. The control-unit-to-peripheral-device interface was not standardized, however, which meant that each device required its own control unit. That requirement would persist until the 1970s when IBM's "New Attachment Strategy" would standardize the device-to-control-unit-level interface and thereby achieve benefits similar to those obtained with the standardization of the control-unit-to-channel interface in System/360.[220]

Those benefits were substantial. The standard interface, together with compatibility, provided IBM with a number of development and manufacturing advantages. "It reduced the design time of many groups" that would otherwise have spent time designing their "own pet means of attachments."[221] Instead, the CPU and peripherals designers were able to concentrate on building "the best products they knew how" and on "advancing the state of their art as far as possible."[222]

The standard interface, together with compatibility, also helped IBM reduce development costs by reducing the number of circuits that had to be designed to permit each peripheral to attach to each CPU. Prior to System/360, peripherals that attached to the CPU did so by means of a unique interface. As a result, a separate design effort and set of circuitry was required for each such attachment. With much of System/360, only a single design effort and set of circuits were required because of the standardization of the interface betweeen the control unit and the channel of the CPU.[223]

The standard interface and compatibility helped simplify IBM's manufacturing process and reduce its costs. "[I]t led to higher quantity production runs of the peripheral devices since the same peripheral device and the same attachment, or plug-in circuitry, was associated with the interface to any of the CPU models."[224] Because of this commonality, similar economies were achieved in the testing process. That was particularly important to IBM in getting 360 ready for announcement. Ernest Hughes, who had held responsibility for development of the 360/30, testified that

> [S]ince we had a multitude of I/O devices and a prescribed time to get it done, [compatibility and the standard interface] helped us a great deal in both our engineering and all aspects of testing . . . to get the total job done.[225]

A related objective of the 360 Advanced Systems Group was to develop "elements of a computer system which could be put together, or configured in a wide variety of ways."[226] That objective, called modularity, was promoted by the standard interface because it allowed users to plug any peripheral device into different 360 CPUs "without changes in the central processing unit."[227]

Not only did IBM achieve the modularity objective set for System/360, but it did so to an extent that other manufacturers were unable to match for almost a decade. Withington testified that among the manufacturers and marketers of computer systems from 1964 to 1972:

> IBM was the leader in providing . . . modularity. With the announcement of the System/360, IBM provided the first line offering anything like the the degree of modularity which has since become available from all the major manufacturers.

During the 1960's, all of the manufacturers, including IBM, evolved their product lines further in the direction of making them more modular, but . . . it is fair to say that throughout the period . . . IBM's product line remained the most modular of all the general purpose product lines available.[228]

Case testified:

The achievement of the modularity objective was . . . very helpful to IBM in enabling the computer products produced by IBM to be chosen by customers in a way that would optimize the price/performance of their installation, and in a way which would provide for convenience and small accepted changes in the installation as the requirements of the enterprise changed.

That is an important benefit to customers for two reasons:

First, . . . they can most accurately adjust the capabilities of their computing installation and, hence, the cost to them of their computing installation to their real needs.

Second, . . . they are able to change the performance or the capabilities of their configuration to match their changing requirements . . . without changing the entire installation, but just adding or subtracting parts, or boxes from the installation.[229]

There were, however, risks associated with modularity and the standard interface. The design trade-offs necessary to create a system that could be assembled in a wide range of configurations might have resulted in a design that was not optimal for any particular configuration, at a cost higher than need otherwise have been. Development of the standard interface entailed a similar risk "that no one attachment or no one plug-in capability [would be] optimal for the particular device involved."[230] Thus, the question of separate control units versus native attachment of peripherals (that is, direct attachment to CPUs) became a matter of some controversy within IBM, with important figures (such as Haanstra) disagreeing with the stand-alone control unit method of attachment that was finally adopted for most of 360.[231]

There was risk to IBM of another type as well. The 360's standard interface and modularity of design, together with its wide-ranging compatibility, presented an attractive target for competitors. The new, modular environment in which 360 would be offered created the prospect that other manufacturers would produce "modules" that would be marketed in direct competition with comparable IBM products. The standard interface of System/360 offered others the same advantages it gave IBM.[232] Moreover, such competitors would have the further advantage of being able to copy IBM's designs and use IBM's software without having to invest in developing either. As a consequence they could be expected to have lower costs than IBM and to offer their products at lower prices than IBM initially charged.[233] IBM's own manuals facilitated the design of such products.[234]

The prospect that others would be able to "tap" IBM's support and offer compatible products in competition with IBM was foreseen by the SPREAD Committee and others within IBM prior to 360's announcement.[235] That prospect became a reality in the late 1960s and in the 1970s — with many competitors offering replacements for each and every box (such as disk drives, tape drives, or CPUs) in IBM's systems. IBM could not keep to itself the advantages of compatibility, modularity, and the standard interface. On the other hand, it had little alternative but to provide such features if 360 was to succeed. As Withington testified, because of user demand, "the manufacturers attempting to compete were forced to maintain continuous developments of different modular types of equipment that could be configured together."[236]

The great modularity of System/360, however, meant that IBM would have to price each and every box in the system carefully. As had always been true, there was no system price as such, the "price" of a system merely being the sum of the prices of the boxes comprising it.[237] IBM thus had to make its prices attractive on a box-by-box basis because users made box-by-box performance comparisons between IBM and its competitors; because System/360 was susceptible to such a wide range of configurations that a single box price that was out of line could make the whole system unattractive; and because competition was anticipated from suppliers of plug-compatible peripherals and CPUs who would attempt to replace IBM's products on a box-by-box basis. The last reason, in particular, made competitive box prices for System/360 "critical."[238]

THE SYSTEM/360 COMMITMENT

System/360 was a "fantastic undertaking" involving "fantastic risks."[239] The 360 was "vastly different" from anything IBM had previously undertaken in terms of "magnitude, complexity and functional characteristics," and was "fundamentally new and different" compared with competitors' EDP offerings.[240] It was clear from the outset that no halfway measures would suffice to carry out the SPREAD Committee's plans — and none were taken. IBM committed more skill, energy, and corporate resources to the successful implementation of System/360 than to any previous undertaking in its history.[241]

Virtually IBM's entire EDP operations were involved in the development and manufacture of System/360. The scope and magnitude of the undertaking required a worldwide, interdivisional effort by IBM.[242] Thus, the 360/30 was developed in Endicott, New York, and was manufactured in Endicott and Sindelfingen and Mainz, Germany. The 360/40 was developed in Hursley, England, and manufactured in Poughkeepsie, New York, and Essonnes and Montpellier, France. The 360/50 was developed in Poughkeepsie and manufactured (assembled) in Poughkeepsie, Essonnes, and Montpellier. The 360/20 was developed in Boeblingen, Germany, and manufactured (assembled) in Sindelfingen, Vimercate, Italy, San Jose, California, and Boca Raton, Florida. System/360's SLT circuit packaging was designed in Endicott and East Fishkill, New York, and manufactured in East Fishkill, Endicott, Essonnes, and Sindelfingen.

The 2401 tape subsystem was developed in Poughkeepsie and manufactured (assembled) in Poughkeepsie, Essonnes, Montpellier, and Boulder, Colorado. The 1403 N1 printer was developed in Endicott and manufactured in Endicott, Raleigh, North Carolina, Sindelfingen and Valligby, Sweden. The 2311 disk drive was developed in San Jose and manufactured in San Jose and Sindelfingen. The 2671 paper tape recorder was developed in LaGaude, France, and manufactured in Essonnes and Montpellier.[243]

Within IBM it was recognized that achievement of SPREAD's recommendations would require "great effort" to "control and coordinate the work of several divisions and that of the IBM World Trade Corporation."[244] At the time of SPREAD there were 15 to 20 engineering groups generating processor products in IBM. These groups were in four principal areas – DSD, GPD, FSD (Federal Systems Division), and WTC (World Trade Corporation). If a single compatible line of processors was to be achieved, design control had to be centralized in a single location. Accordingly, the SPREAD Committee recommended the establishment of a systems architecture group that would be charged with formalizing the design objectives for NPL and providing logical specifications for the hardware and software.[245] Such a group – the NPL Architecture Committee – was formed in early 1962 and served as "advisor" to the various NPL engineering groups. It held "dozens if not a hundred or more meetings" relating to NPL.[246]

On the manufacturing side, too, a number of disciplines were imposed to assure that there were no major discrepancies among the products produced on either side of the Atlantic. IBM's plants worked very closely to develop "world-wide manufacture plans" and employee training plans.[247] IBM also introduced with System/360 the system of "single engineering control." Under this concept any laboratory responsible for designing a part, component, or product was also responsible for releasing that design to all the plants, worldwide, that were going to manufacture that part, component, or product.[248] By introducing this system, IBM was able to do the following:

1. Achieve a high level of confidence that all parts, wherever produced, would perform in a comparable fashion

2. Achieve the ability to exchange parts or assemblies or products among manufacturing locations in times of technological difficulty or great demand

3. Avoid duplication of engineering effort, since there was no need to design the same product or component twice in two different places.[249]

Apart from the need to impose new disciplines, it was apparent that a substantial segment of IBM's "new product development resources in the electronic data processing (EDP) area" would be required to announce the NPL in the first quarter of 1964.[250] Brooks (who was manager of the NPL project from 1961 to 1964) testified that the original estimate for 360 programming was between $100 and $200 million. That estimate was exceeded by better than $25 million.[251] Brooks's staff in DSD alone grew from "20 or 30" in June 1961 to "several hundred" by February 1964.[252] A presentation made to IBM Chairman Thomas J. Watson, Jr., in November 1964 showed that IBM's annual research and development expenditure rose from approximately $175 million per year in 1961 to $275 million per year in 1964.[253]

Indeed, in 1959-64, IBM's research and development (R&D) expenses were not only absolutely higher than those of some of its major competitors (Burroughs, NCR, Sperry Rand, and CDC), but also more than double those of Burroughs, NCR, or Sperry Rand as a percentage of revenue. Each of the latter firms' ratios of R&D to revenue remained about level over that period. Among the four, only CDC, which was developing the highly successful 6600, showed an increasing R&D-to-revenue ratio.[254]

Still more investment was needed to meet the requirements for SLT components. The 1961 decision to manufacture SLT in-house required a rapid buildup in manufacturing facilities and resources.[255] To meet the projected volumes for 360, IBM had to become "in a very short time, the largest component manufacturer in the world."[256] In 1961 it established a Components Division to "focus all of its resources in terms of both manufacturing and development on that goal of making SLT components." In 1963 the Components Division opened a new plant in East Fishkill, New York, as a manufacturing development site for System/360 components. Prior to the 360 announcement, IBM hired a large number of people and started to construct additional buildings in order to meet the anticipated SLT requirements. In addition, IBM's Endicott, New York, facility was enlarged to help produce packages for mounting SLT modules, and part of a plant in Essonnes, France, was converted into a component facility to help meet worldwide requirements.[257]

Perhaps as significant as the magnitude of IBM's investment in 360 was the fact that all of those resources were being put into a single project: IBM was "putting a lot of eggs in one basket . . . and the success of the company was in many ways to be determined by the success of that one project."[258] If 360 were rejected by customers, there would be few alternatives around for IBM to offer, and none that was thoroughly funded or covered a very large part of the product line. Thus, once the die had been cast and the decision made to go forward with the SPREAD Committee's recommendations, IBM's fortunes became "inextricably tied up with the NPL project."[259] Within IBM and without, the 360 project came to be known as the "you bet your company" venture.[260] As Evans stated, if that venture had failed, IBM would have become a "radically different company, if even in the computer business."[261]

Despite the risk, IBM decided to develop the 360 line because "[we] thought that the System/360 development was the best way to more rapidly grow the market, more rapidly expand demand for our products."[262] It was the sort of risk that IBM was forced to take by competition if it was to succeed. Seemingly safer alternatives to 360 continued to be advanced within IBM right up to the time that 360 was announced.[263] As they had rejected the 8000 series, IBM management rejected those alternatives because they would not have given the firm the kind of long-range solutions that it needed in the competitive environment of the day.[264] Thus, despite the fact that it was recognized that no "single announcement" had ever "obsoleted [*sic*] so much existing equipment at one time,"[265] IBM had to make its own line obsolete or stand by and watch others do so.

In an effort to blunt the impact of System/360 on IBM's existing product line, IBM Treasurer K. N. Davis recommended that 360 be offered for sale only. He made the suggestion because technology and price/performance were "changing and improving so rapidly" that he believed it might be in IBM's interest to transfer some of the risk of technological obsolescence to customers. In addition, System/360's price/performance was so superior to that of existing IBM systems on rent that customers would rapidly replace those systems with 360s. The recommendation was rejected because, as Knaplund stated, "IBM had to continue to offer a rental option in order to remain competitive": competitors offered that option and customers found it desirable.[266] In this respect IBM's experience was no different from that of its competitors.[267] Indeed, customers as well as IBM could perceive that technology was changing and would not have been willing to accept the risk of obsolescence. Competition ensured that they did not have to do so.

The fact that IBM had to introduce a product line comparable in performance and function to System/360 if it wanted to stay in business[268] was not an easy pill for the developers of the firm's existing very successful systems to swallow. Learson wrote to C. J. Bashe, manager of technical development, GPD, and T. C. Papes, manager of systems development, GPD, in July 1963:

> The 101 [announced as the System/360 Model 30] must be engineered and planned to impact solidly the 1401.
> I know your reluctance to do this, but corporate policy is that you do it. It is obvious that in 1967 the 1401 will be as dead as a Dodo bird. Let's stop fighting this.[269]

This letter was passed down through the management chain to emphasize the importance of the 360/30 program and the company's policy with respect to that program. It was understood that the 360/30 would make the 1400 family obsolete — and had to do so. Despite the fact that by 1964 IBM had shipped thousands of 1401 systems, of which 75-80 percent were still owned by IBM and on lease to customers, it was perceived that "[i]f we didn't obsolete [*sic*] it and replace it, someone else would."[270] That same view was echoed outside IBM in a letter written by a staff vice-president to the president of Southern Railway in April 1964, recommending the acquisition of 360/30s to replace Southern's 1404s:

> This will reduce the IBM rentals by $4,000 a month in Atlanta. There is also a good possibility that we will be able to eliminate the 1401 computer in Washington, using computers in Atlanta by tape to tape control from Washington. This would also save us $4,000 to $5,000 per

month rental in Washington. Prices of computers have been coming down while the computer capacities are being increased tremendously. If IBM does not bring out new computers at reduced prices, their competitors take the business.[271]

This was a view of life in the computer industry that was shared by IBM's competitors as well. As three of them testified:

There is no looking backward in our industry [the computer business] as you undoubtedly know. If one stops to ponder the past and be self-satisfied, the more aggressive competitors will quickly charge past. (W. Hindle [Digital Equipment Corporation – DEC])[272]

It was our finding that the life of a family of computers was quite limited . . . and that you did not bring out a family of products that simply met the price/performance characteristics of the then existing competition. You had to bring out something that would exceed the price/performance of the existing competition because you knew full well that they were going to be moving ahead of you. It is a constant leap frogging game. (R. Jones [GE])[273]

[One gets] to a point in which the price/performance is so improved over equipment of days of yore that it is clear that . . . users are going to move to new equipment, and either [one is] going to provide that new equipment or [one's] competitors are going to provide it. (R. Bloch [Honeywell/GE])[274]

Similar views were expressed by many other witnesses.[275]

Such views were realistic and applied to IBM as well as to its competitors. The SPREAD Committee's prediction that, starting about 1965, IBM's highly successful second-generation line would be superseded by competition turned out to be accurate as to substance, but overly optimistic as to time. In July 1963 Learson could write that "in 1967 the 1401 will be as dead as a Dodo bird" because it was already being surpassed by newer models of computer systems.[276]

Indeed, at the highest level within IBM there was concern that the System/360 might not be enough of an improvement to recover its costs. Thus Watson, writing to Learson in June 1963, stated concerning the NPL:

I think it important to note, however, since we seem to have suffered for a few months or even years because our machines predated the effective competitive machines now in the marketplace, that we now make these [System/360] machines good enough so they will not be just equal to competition, for I am sure that once they are announced our competitors will immediately try to better them. This is all to the good and I am for competition, but I want our new line to last long enough so we do not go into the red.[277]

Similarly, writing in November 1963 to a group of IBM executives, Watson said:

There is a great deal of running about and extra effort being expended in all areas of the IBM company now because once again we have allowed ourselves to become somewhat non-competitive without recognizing one simple obvious fact. In bringing new machines and devices to the marketplace, our competitors in today's market are simply not going to stand still. We should recognize that in every area, they will take the best we have and immediately start working in a tough, hard-minded fashion to produce something better.

We find ourselves in our present position because we seem to assume our competitors will stand still in certain areas after we announce a superior product. . . .

I believe that whenever we make a new machine announcement, we should set up a future date at which point we can reasonably assume that a competitor's article of greater capability will be announced. We should then target our own development program to produce a better machine on or before that date.[278]

Charts prepared in February 1964 by DSD Market Evaluation Manager J. C. Wick, comparing the price/performance of the NPL with that of competitive products, showed that 360's price/performance was superior to that of recently announced machines from RCA, Burroughs, CDC, Honeywell, Univac, and GE, but also showed quite clearly that those competitive machines had a price/performance advantage over the earlier announced IBM machines of the 1400 and 7000 series.[279] We discuss some of the competitors' announcements that created this situation in describing the histories of these competitors during the early 1960s in Chapters 8 and 9. Some of the announcements merit particular attention here, however, especially in terms of perceptions within IBM.

In October 1963 DSD President G. F. Kennard wrote to Thomas J. Watson, Jr., and IBM President A. L. Williams: "RCA has recently announced the 3301. . . . Initial performance specifications indicate that the 3301 has about 50 percent better processing capabilities than the IBM 7010" at a comparable price.[280] In November 1963 it was reported within IBM that GE was discussing in public a new series of machines planned for announcement before the end of the year. "In one case GE stated, system cost would be approximately the same as the IBM 1410 but would be 40% faster."[281] GE announced the 400 series in December 1963 and at the same press conference revealed the future availability of its 600 family, which was aimed at IBM 7090 and 7094 users.[282] The 400 series offered a 1401 simulator that permitted IBM 1401 programs to be run on or converted "easily" to the 400. It was aimed at 1401 users.[283]

The CDC 6600, which CDC began discussing with customers before announcement in 1962,[284] caused IBM Chairman Watson to ask "why we have lost our industry leadership position by letting someone else offer the world's most powerful computer."[285] CDC's 3600, which had been announced in May 1962, was viewed within IBM as "technically superior to the 7094."[286] By April 1963, O. M. Scott, IBM vice-president and group executive, was reporting to Watson and others that "3600-type competition" was creating a "serious situation" and that such competition (from CDC's 3600 and 6600 and from

Philco's 212) was able to offer "one-and-a-half to two times the performance of the 7094 at a lower price." Scott added that the 501 (360/70), as planned, would enable IBM "to favorably compete with the CDC 3600."[287] On April 23, 1963, Watson determined to "just sit tight" and stay with the 501 approach "unless the roof falls in," but noted that IBM had an active program in DSD called the "7094 B prime" that was sufficiently advanced to be announced in June 1963.[288] Within two weeks, cascading losses to CDC's 3600 caused a reevaluation of that decision, and Watson asked Scott to advise him when the situation got "out of control."[289] One week later, Scott reported back that IBM was repeatedly "being beaten" by CDC's 3600, 6600, and 1604, Philco's 212, and Univac's 1107. He recommended announcement of the 7094-B' "at the earliest possible date."[290] IBM announced the 7094 Mod. II on May 16, 1963,[291] but this extension of the 7090 series still "could not meet either the performance level or the price of a comparable CDC 3600." As a result, CDC's success with the 3600 continued unabated.[292]

With virtually all of IBM's development resources tied up in 360, the firm was unable to respond effectively at that time,[293] a fact that did not escape attention at CDC. The latter firm's chief development engineer for the 6000 series, Vice-President Seymour Cray, urged at CDC's June 1963 corporate planning meeting that CDC announce the 6600 and a successor in order to "slug" IBM because, he speculated, IBM had "made a mistake in putting all [its] eggs in an integrated circuit basket."[294] Until 360 became available, CDC was able to achieve success "by concentrating on an area of IBM price weakness, and by showing a major price performance advantage to potential customers," an advantage that would not persist after the announcement of 360.[295]

Perhaps most important of all the competitors' announcements during the period was that of the Honeywell 200 in early December 1963.[296] This machine offered substantially improved price/performance over the 1401.[297] It also offered a conversion program called LIBERATOR that made the H-200 compatible with IBM's 1401 to a considerable degree.[298]

Within IBM the H-200 announcement was viewed as "even more difficult than we anticipated." Within two days of the announcement, Learson wrote to T. J. Watson and A. L. Williams that the 101 (360/30) would have to be announced "as soon as possible" and priced at its "lowest projection" in order to be competitive.[299] IBM's marketing force regarded the H-200 as a real challenge, and at least one person in IBM called it "the most severe threat to IBM in our history."[300] By February 1964 the Sales Division was "reeling from losses" to the Honeywell 200 and "wanting a more competitive answer."[301] Because of the H-200, IBM's Data Processing Division continued and intensified its pressure for the earliest possible announcement of System/360, still earlier than even the then-planned mid-March announcement date.[302]

As competitive pressure mounted, the debate whether to go forward with 360 as planned or to announce extensions to the existing product lines was rekindled. The latter approach would be safer and easier: it would not be as revolutionary as 360, and would therefore run a lower risk of user rejection.[303] Moreover, it would not require users to convert their existing applications programs. In November 1963, IBM's corporate staff advanced the position that "new marketing developments" required a change in IBM's processor strategies. These new developments included the announcement of competitors' processors offering easy conversion to IBM customers and other new offerings with improved price/performance. The corporate staff recommended the announcement in May-June 1964 of "several improved current line systems – such as the 7074X, 7010X and 7094X." In their scheme of things the NPL announcement was to be put off for 6 to 12 months.[304]

The Honeywell 200 announcement provided perhaps the sharpest temptation to depart from the System/360 plan. In early 1963 IBM had a 1401 built out of SLT circuitry to establish the feasibility of using SLT in the new line.[305] The Honeywell 200 prompted sharp debate within IBM whether a new technology (SLT) version of the 1401 (called the 1401S) should be brought out and the 360/30 announcement delayed or canceled.[306] The chief proponent of this new plan was GPD President John Haanstra, who had been chairman of the SPREAD Committee. Haanstra believed that the 1401 was a "fundamentally sound" approach to meeting user needs, and that the 360/30 approach was "improper" because it required customers to convert.[307] The Data Processing Division, on the other hand, regarded the 1401S as only a fallback position in the event that the 360/30 was not ready soon enough or was not good enough.[308]

Evans was sure that it was a mistake to produce the 1401S instead of the 360/30 and that it would not make sense to do both. As early as September 1963 he had inveighed against "continual competition with temporary machines" because they would "only dilute [IBM's] already overcommitted resources and ability to meet the NPL challenge."[309] In his view, if the 1401S had proceeded, it would have "delayed if not killed" the 360/30 and "wreaked havoc with the costs of the rest of the System/360 line."[310] In addition, Evans regarded a decision to produce the 1401S as relegating the NPL more to the scientific area and signaling "a discrete scientific line, probably along the 7090 philosophy particularly if competition does the H-200 type of thing to the 7090 family." He felt this would erode the basis for NPL and lead to a processor policy of "discrete 1400-type commercial, discrete 7090-type scientific, plus various custom units for new application areas" as "the inevitable conclusion."[311] (As we shall see in Chapters 6 and 8, GE was in fact attempting to do "the H-200 type of thing to the 7090 family." Evans was right.)

Although contingency plans were laid for a possible February 1964 announcement, IBM decided not to proceed with the 1401S. Evans testified that the 1401S was ultimately rejected

[b]ecause the evaluations and conclusions of senior management were that it was not an advanced system that would solve the applications of the future as we then saw them – that . . . it was a machine that would not have long life and would not be competitive for more than a short period, and that the 360 family plan with all of its advanced features and functions and capability and the unusual power it brought the users was a substantially better plan.[312]

In short, the 360/30 was expected to be "a better overall performing system than the 1401 had been or could have been, had we extended its life."[313]

Preparation for Announcement

It was clear by the end of 1963 that announcement of System/360 was required for IBM to remain competitive. System/360 was nearly ready. We have already discussed how, beginning in 1961, IBM started applying massive resources to the NPL project. The "whole 360 program had been on a crash basis . . . since almost inception," and by the latter part of 1963 it had become an "enormous program with its own inertia."[314] In December 1963 development of the line was "on or ahead of the schedule called for two years earlier in the SPREAD report."[315]

By the time 360 was announced in April 1964, engineering models of all the processors had been built;[316] full instruction-set compatibility across the five processors had been achieved;[317] a complete processor using SLT technology had been built and demonstrated to establish the feasibility of the new circuitry;[318] many thousands of SLT modules had already been produced; most of the processors and some of the peripheral equipment were in the early stage of product test;[319] all, or almost all, the memories had undergone technical evaluation testing;[320] microprogramming and multiprogramming had been tested on the Model 40;[321] and four estimating, forecasting, and pricing cycles had been completed.[322] By the time of the announcement thousands of tests had been made, and "literally hundreds of problems and potential problems" had been identified and resolved. The componentry, systems, and product testing program already completed was more extensive than the entire program IBM had previously undertaken for any system.[323]

By industry standards System/360 was very far along. RCA, Honeywell, and GE all announced systems that were, by comparison, in an embryonic stage of development.[324] No wonder that by late 1963 two of the prime movers of the project, Evans and Brooks, were recommending announcement of the entire family in the first part of 1964.[325]

Although the SPREAD Report had not recommended announcing the entire NPL family at once, by December 1963 it was plain that there were powerful reasons for doing so. On December 27, 1963, Evans proposed that the NPL family be announced as a group in March 1964:

> [T]he customers must better understand the abilities of the architecture and conversions necessary. It would be unwise of us to announce systems sporadically in an effort to optimize market penetration or profit. It is proper that IBM announce all the systems in a group so that our customers have the benefit of the family and can properly plan.[326]

Less than one month later, Brooks wrote to John W. Gibson, Haanstra, and Kennard, stating that the equipment was "technically ready for announcement" and recommending announcement on April 7. He emphasized that System/360 "*must* be announced at one time":

> Piecemeal announcement would utterly confuse and misguide the customer in his planning. He could not make the best selection from the available models until all the models are announced.[327]

Knaplund "understood that simultaneous announcement . . . would place an unprecedented load on the development of manufacturing resources of the product divisions." The advantages outweighed the risks, however. "It was my business judgment that partial announcement by IBM would result in customer confusion, superseding orders following subsequent IBM announcements, and churning of the order backlog in IBM's production schedules."[328]

The March or April announcement dates recommended by Evans and Brooks were virtually mandated by the first shipment dates planned for the 360 processors, which ranged from June 1965 for the 2030 (the processor for the 360/30 system) to January 1966 for the 2070 (the processor for the 360/70 system).[329] It was "generally industry practice on most computer systems at that time to announce a system at least a year, and frequently as much as two years, ahead of the actual first delivery."[330] There were well-recognized practical reasons for this procedure from the viewpoint of both manufacturers and customers, each of whom needed time to prepare for delivery and installation.[331]

As Brooks wrote in January 1964, such lead time was particularly important in the case of System/360 with its many innovations.[332] That time would be necessary to do the following:

1. Permit customers to replan their applications and take advantage of 360's new concepts, such as disk file orientation, communications facilities, and large memories

2. Permit customers to assimilate the "sheer amount of new abilities, new options, new specifications, and new prices" that 360 would provide, and select the best configurations of equipment to perform their applications

3. Permit IBM and customers to educate their personnel and prepare them for proper installation and maintenance of the 360

4. Permit IBM to avoid deferred installations and consequent inventory build-ups

5. Permit customers to determine the need for and to submit RPQs (requests for price quotation) for special requirements

6. Permit customers to prepare their physical sites for 360 installation.[333]

In December 1963 Knaplund was assigned responsibility for assembling the technical evaluations, forecasts, cost analyses, and profit projections that IBM top management would need to address the 360 announcement decision.

Beginning in January 1964, he conducted weekly meetings with IBM line and staff management to identify and assess the magnitude of outstanding problems and to outline programs to solve those problems, so that he and they would be prepared to make judgments and advise top management on whether to proceed with the 360 announcement.[334]

On March 18, 1964, IBM Chairman Thomas J. Watson, Jr., made the final decision to announce all of the models of the new line simultaneously on April 7. IBM's Product Test Department did not support the April 7 announcement; all other departments whose effort was required to provide the products, features, and services offered in the System/360 announcement supported it.[335] To understand the significance of the Product Test Department's lack of support, it is necessary to understand the role of the Product Test Department in the IBM management system.

In addition to all the other testing that was done within IBM, the firm's management used the Product Test Department to isolate problems and to challenge the product development personnel to determine how they would solve those problems. Thus, in IBM's contention system, nonsupport by Product Test did not mean that products were untested; rather, it meant that problems had been identified. Announcement without the support of Product Test could take place only if a satisfactory plan to solve such problems had been agreed on. As a result, Product Test, after it took its nonsupport position regarding announcement, later supported the shipment of System/360 to IBM's customers.[336] G. B. McCarter, the head of Product Test, testified:

> It did not follow from Product Test's non-support of March 16, 1964, that IBM could not or would not deliver what it committed to customers. . . . To the contrary, Product Test's input was one of the mechanisms, like internal targets, designed to ensure that it would.[337]

Prior to 360 there had been numerous occasions on which IBM announced products without Product Test support, including the 1403 printer; 1302 disk file; the 709, 7090, and 7074 systems; and more than two dozen software programs.[338]

In the case of 360, the processors announced on April 7, 1964, were all shipped on or before the shipment dates estimated at announcement, except that the 2060 and 2062, on the one hand, and the 2070, on the other, were superseded by faster memory versions called the 2065 and 2075, respectively, which were delivered on or before the dates planned for their predecessor processors in April 1964.[339] Those first-shipped systems, as planned, were made available with the simpler operating systems offered with 360.[340]

There were, however, "significant schedule slippages in OS/360 software" (the most advanced operating system for 360), which meant that some customers "received the full announced capabilities later than originally planned."[341] The problems with OS/360 occurred even though Product Test "cumulatively did more testing of OS/360 than we ever had before for any set of programs for a particular system," and despite the fact that IBM's programmers believed prior to April 7, 1964, that they could produce OS/360 "in the way that it was originally intended."[342] IBM misjudged the "enormous complexity" of developing complex operating systems — a mistake also made by the rest of the industry. Burroughs, Univac, Xerox, GE, Honeywell, and RCA all experienced similar problems and delays of considerable magnitude.[343]

In a way, the modularity and standard interface of the System/360, which made hardware testing easier, made software testing harder. It allowed customers great flexibility in the range of configurations they chould choose, and that, coupled with the wide variety of ways in which OS/360 could be used, led to "a very complex hardware-software system" that was literally impossible to test adequately.[344]

> If you were to take the various permutations of the options available to the user, the number of different tests that would have to be performed [in testing systems software] would exceed the time available for testing. I am talking about millions of different permutations and combinations of features that can be selected by the users. To test in each of those environments would preclude the issuance of first release of any operating system. . . . [b]ecause as soon as you got around to testing the 999,000 somebody would come out with another option and you'd have to go all the way through it again.[345]

Only by expending "considerable internal efforts" was IBM able to remedy the problems with OS/360 — but IBM did so, and provided customers with an operating system widely recognized as a "very sophisticated, very complex software system, a software system that permitted the customer a great deal of flexibility . . . [so that the] customer could do a great deal with a minimum amount of effort," which in turn caused System/360 "to show steadily increasing performance relative to competition and remain saleable longer."[346]

The 360's Success and Its Impact on IBM

System/360 was launched on April 7, 1964, and the internal doubts about its reception were soon dispelled.[347] As seen in Table 5.1, orders for the systems far exceeded IBM's forecasts and the associated production plans.[348] By October 1966, IBM's 360 order backlog represented an income of "almost three times . . . [its] worldwide, annual sales of *all* products."[349]

As discussed earlier, prior to 360's announcement IBM management had authorized substantial increases in plant capacity, including the establishment of an SLT manufacturing plant in East Fishkill, New York, and the addition of a new building at IBM's Endicott, New York, plant site for the manufacture of SLT cards and boards. Management believed that these manufacturing capacity increases "adequately provided for the component and box production volumes required to support the System/360 announcement together with planned future announcements."[350] Because the total orders were far beyond

Table 5.1. Estimated and Actual Production Versus Gross Orders Booked for System/360 Models Announced on April 7, 1964

	Estimated	Actual	Gross Orders Booked
1965	589	668	4,487
1966	2,897	3,132	4,526
1965 & 1966 (combined)	3,486	3,800	9,013

Source: JX 38, para. 28.

what was forecast, however, and because larger processors and more memory and peripherals than anticipated were being ordered, the demand for SLT modules also far exceeded IBM's expectations.[351] By May 1964, a little more than one month after announcement, the projected "maximum annual module requirements" had increased from 70-90 million to 130-190 million.[352]

It was plain that the manufacturing capacity planned at announcement would be insufficient, and IBM began moving to meet the increased demand. By the third quarter of 1964, additional component production capacity was approved at the Burlington, Vermont, plant site, and plans were initiated for additional assembly plant locations. By the end of 1964, IBM top management had approved expansion of the Owego, New York, plant "to increase manufacturing capacity for SLT cards and boards"; and in early 1965 two new plant sites in Boulder, Colorado, and Raleigh, North Carolina, were approved "to increase IBM's overall EDP manufacturing capacity."[353] In addition, IBM provided special tools and training to Texas Instruments employees so that Texas Instruments might serve as an additional source for SLT components.[354] By October 1965, IBM announced that it was "completing more than three million square feet of new manufacturing space" to meet requirements for System/360 — including plants in Boulder, Colorado; Raleigh, North Carolina; Montpellier, France; and Vimercate, Italy; and expansion of existing facilities in Owego, East Fishkill, and Endicott, New York; Burlington, Vermont; and San Jose, California.[355] New plants were later added in Boca Raton, Florida, and Brooklyn, New York.[356]

IBM also began hiring substantial numbers of new employees. Between the end of 1964 and the end of 1967, IBM increased its work force by approximately 50 percent — adding more than 70,000 new employees.[357] Evans testified that it was "an enormous job" to get the supply of parts flowing, hire the people, and train them in order to meet System/360 commitments. At one point IBM "even rented a circus tent to temporarily store parts" until more permanent facilities could be secured.[358] In January 1965, IBM combined all product division manufacturing functions in a new Systems Manufacturing Division (SMD), with former GPD President C. E. Frizzell at its head. By June 1965, Frizzell reported to IBM management that the production buildup would enable IBM to meet product shipments committed to customers.[359]

Within a few months, however, an unforeseen technical difficulty developed in the production of SLT technology.[360] The problem took about three months to solve, despite intensive efforts by IBM to do so, and the delay put the firm several months behind the schedule for SLT production needed to satisfy existing customer commitments.[361] This was reported to IBM Chairman Watson, who immediately informed IBM's board of directors and issued a public statement advising that "during 1966 most System/360's will be delivered 60 to 120 days later than originally scheduled."[362] Despite the problem, IBM's SLT output for 1965 was higher than that planned in April 1964, and there was a 74 percent increase of production in 1966 over 1965.[363] Knaplund testified that, but for the unanticipated production problems, System/360 shipments at that point "would have continued on the committed plan."[364] Indeed, in May 1966 the two thousandth System/360 was shipped.[365] In the end, although many 360 hardware deliveries were made as scheduled and committed, there were some significant schedule slippages despite all of IBM's efforts to prevent them.[366]

The production, delivery, and installation of System/360 — "almost a complete replacement of our principal product line"[367] — required a massive effort on IBM's part and placed a severe strain on the corporation.[368] It was a task that some in IBM likened to "trying to swallow an elephant."[369] The size of the job was compounded by the software difficulties with OS/360. IBM placed a "top priority" on the solution of those problems and, at its peak, had over 1,000 people working on OS/360. Some 5,000 man-years went into its design, construction, and documentation between 1963 and 1966.[370]

All of this, plus the need to provide customers more assistance than ever in installing, understanding, and applying 360 and all its revolutionary new concepts,[371] placed "tremendous capital demands" on IBM.[372] During 1964 the firm had prepaid $160 million in debentures and promissory notes.[373] As a result, when the partially unforeseen expansion required an investment of approximately $1.1 billion in 1965 and $1.6 billion in 1966, IBM did not have sufficient money on hand. In 1966 IBM raised approximately $371 million through an equity offering, the first such offering since 1957.[374] Further, largely in order to increase cash flow, in 1966 IBM raised its lease prices and decreased purchase prices by 3 percent (the "3 x 3" price change).[375]

IBM's multibillion-dollar investment yielded fantastic rewards, changing the face of IBM and of the computer industry for all time. System/360 was a "phenomenal success," perhaps the greatest "in the history of American industry."[376] At the end of 1965, before volume shipment of 360 had begun, IBM had worldwide revenues of $3,572,824,719;[377] by the end of 1970, those revenues had increased to $7,503,959,690.[378] Just prior to the 360 announcement, IBM had approximately 11,000 computer systems installed in the United States. By the time System/360's successor, System/370, was announced in 1970, that number had tripled to approximately 35,000. In the interim, IBM's corporate growth, revenue, and profits were "way beyond anything that [IBM] had anticipated."[379]

T. V. Learson wrote in October 1966:

Observers have characterized the 360 decision as perhaps the biggest, in its impact on a company, ever made in American industry — far bigger even than Boeing's decision to go into jets, bigger than Ford's decision to build several million Mustangs.

IBM has certainly not been the same since, and never will be again.[380]

6

IBM AFTER SYSTEM/360: COMPETITIVE RESPONSE AND COUNTERRESPONSE

INITIAL COMPETITIVE RESPONSES TO SYSTEM/360

System/360's announcement and subsequent success evoked a large number of competitive responses from a variety of different sources, including systems suppliers, leasing companies, peripherals manufacturers, and software houses. The latter three kinds of competitors, in particular, grew in importance as the repercussions of System/360 were felt in the industry. We begin, however, by reviewing the immediate actions taken by a number of systems suppliers as they were perceived by and affected IBM. (These actions are discussed in more detail when we discuss the history of the companies involved in Chapters 8 and 9).

As discussed above, System/360 gave IBM a price/performance advantage over competitive machines, which had themselves "leapfrogged" over IBM's earlier lines. The System/360 announcement, therefore, forced IBM's competitors to reduce prices or increase performance in order to remain competitive. John Weil of GE said in June 1964:

> The entire competitive picture in the information processing business at this time in 1964 is characterized by the impact of the IBM System/ 360 . . . announcement and by the reaction to this announcement of our competitors.[1]

In July 1964, T. V. Learson reviewed the price reductions in the industry that had taken place since the introduction of System/360 (called NPL, for "new product line," within IBM). He wrote:

> There can be only one conclusion; namely, the cost/performance of computers today is less than it has been and . . . the price structure surrounding the main body of our line is threatened by: (a) Present day cost[,] (b) New technologies, as typified by NPL[.] Perhaps what we are missing is that NPL was a price reduction of 30-50%, so that competition is forced to come along with us.[2]

143

RCA

RCA both reduced prices on its current products and shaped its planned new announcements in reaction to System/360. In approximately May 1964, RCA reduced the price of its 3301 between 20 and 35 percent.[3] Within IBM the price reductions were seen as "drastic," as "the first significant competitive reaction to System/360," and as making "the 3301 very competitive in the model 40/50 area."[4] Arthur D. Little's Frederic Withington wrote that the "primary reason for the price reduction . . . would seem to be a requirement for a competitive product during the interim until RCA announces its 'counter-360' efforts."[5]

Soon afterward RCA announced the Spectra 70 series, which was designed to be compatible with the 360 line. The preliminary design of that series had started in 1963, with "[m]ajor design efforts. . . . under way by the latter half of '64."[6] The strategy of compatibility with IBM equipment had been considered prior to the 360 announcement,[7] and was firmly decided "within two weeks, three weeks at the most, after the announcement."[8] By making its Spectra 70 compatible with IBM's System/360, RCA hoped to be able to persuade 360 users to move to Spectra: it was "aimed primarily at the IBM 360 series range of computers."[9]

Within IBM, C. E. Frizzell, president of the General Products Division (GPD), wrote that the Spectra series offered better price/performance than IBM in CPU-memory speed, magnetic tapes, and high-speed printing, but assured Thomas J. Watson, Jr., that he was "moving rapidly to meet this challenge and expect[ed] to respond effectively in the very near future."[10]

GE

John Weil's assessment in 1964 was that it was "no longer possible to offer equipment with a significant advantage over IBM."[11] Price reductions were called for, and GE planned to announce a new series of magnetic tape units "which will permit adjustment of our 400 line system prices to increase our competitiveness."[12]

Such price reductions began quickly and were noticed within IBM. Learson wrote in July 1964:

> GE has not officially reduced prices, but they are selling their 400 line at 18% off. They have also reduced their extra shift to a 10% charge.
>
> Further, GE is selling their 635, a competitor to the 7094, at no extra shift charge.[13]

A September 1964 competitive news release from the Data Processing Division's (DSD) Commercial Analysis Department confirmed GE price reductions of 8-15 percent and went on to say, "The price reduction gives the GE 400 a price/performance advantage over comparable Sytem/360 configurations."[14] However, a subsequent price/performance evaluation made within IBM concluded: "While the recent price reductions have improved GE's position, the System/360 Model 30 retains its price/performance superiority."[15] Statistical analysis confirms that the price reductions pulled the 400 line to about the price/performance level of System/360.[16]

GE announced its 600 series in the summer of 1964. That series had been planned, long before the 360 announcement, to displace IBM's 7090 and 7094 computer systems. Weil had compared the 600 series against the 360 line in a June 23, 1964 internal GE presentation and concluded that the 600 is "either just a little more favorable or just a little less favorable than comparable members of the 360 series. We are, however, able to deliver our equipment a year earlier than IBM."[17]

GE saw itself as being able to capitalize on one of the risks IBM had taken with the 360 — the risk involved in making the older lines obsolete. Weil testified that the computer group at GE was

> initially at least overjoyed with what had occurred because it meant right at the time we were introducing a system designed to displace 7090s and 7094s, IBM had itself abandoned the 7094 and 7090 computer series and brought out an entirely different computer series, and it was our belief at that time that it would be easier, if you were a user, to convert from the 7090-7094 to the 600 series than it would be to convert to IBM's new 360 series.[18]

The user of the 7094 was "forced . . . to either go to a 360 or to some other competitive system, and we were sitting there with a system designed to make that conversion as easy as possible."[19]

Control Data Corporation (CDC)

CDC also reduced prices in response to System/360.[20] At IBM, Learson analyzed CDC's behavior as follows:

> CDC followed [360's pricing] with a price reduction of their 3600, which was no longer competitive with the 360-Model 70. In dropping the price of the 3600, they had to keep their deck of cards in order and so moved the 3200 and 3400 downward. Reductions of 20-40% were made.[21]

And Withington wrote:

> Control Data's main reliance is on price; apparently its intention is to provide a lower cost answer to every System 360 model. After the System 360 announcement, the price of every existing Control Data computer was reduced, and the prices of the later models are still lower. . . . This should unquestionably help Control Data's position because . . . the market is becoming increasingly price-conscious.[22]

Several months later CDC announced new members of its current product lines — the 6000 and 3000 series. The formal announcement of the 6400 (a "scaled down" 6600) and the (never delivered) 6800, to go with the existing 6600, was made in mid-December 1964.[23] The 3300 and 3500 were announced in 1965.[24]

Sperry Rand

Two weeks after the 360 announcement, Univac management met to consider the Univac product line strategy. They decided to enhance and expand the 1050 program to provide a compatible line of systems from the 1004 through the 1050 Mod V.[25] Learson reported in July that Sperry was "announcing new models of 1050 and 1004 where the price/performance ratio is not following the historical trend in the original announcement, so they are, in effect, using this as a method of price reduction."[26] Univac management also decided to extend the 1107 program to the 1108 and 1109, which were to be program-compatible upward with the 1107, for large-scale users.[27] In mid-1964 Sperry Rand announced its 1108 at a price that Withington described as "impressive when compared to that of the System 360."[28] Withington wrote that, in terms of price/performance, "IBM's initial offerings in the 360 line were inferior to it."[29] (Later we shall see IBM's response to this rather quick "leapfrogging.")

By 1965, Univac's Product Line Task Force was contemplating the introduction of an entirely new line in reaction to System/360. It faced a dilemma in that two of the three models under development were likely to benefit from technological improvements if they could be delayed, but waiting would have meant that a full family could not be announced at one time.[30] Univac finally compromised and announced the 9200 and 9300 (rather than an entire family).[31] These systems "aimed at compatibility" with 360 but achieved it only in part.[32]

Burroughs

Burroughs also responded with a new product introduction. In August 1964 it announced the B5500,[33] "a more powerful successor to the earlier B5000" and what was to become the first member of the 500 System family. Withington described the B5000 family as "incorporat[ing] very advanced design features, facilitating the use of compilers and executive programs," but concluded that "Burroughs apparently has not attempted to answer the System 360 across the board."[34] By 1966 Burroughs had turned the 500 family into "a major new product line,"[35] adding the B6500, B2500, and B3500 to the B5500 and the very large (and never delivered) B8500.[36]

Honeywell

After the 360 announcement, Honeywell took its successful 200 system and turned it into a compatible "family of computer systems": the 120, the 1200, the 2200, the 4200, and the 8200.[37] After the introduction of IBM's 2311 disk drive, Honeywell abandoned its attempts to develop a mass storage system and began buying disks from other manufacturers.

Scientific Data Systems (SDS)

SDS announced successive new products beginning in 1964 with what it termed "the first computer to use monolithic integrated circuits, the SDS 92,"[38] and eventually the Sigma series, which was announced beginning in 1966.[39] A press release at announcement stated that "Sigma . . . represents the first family of computers with an entirely new design since the IBM 360 announcement." As IBM had done with 360, SDS stressed the new line's universal applicability.[40]

IBM's INITIAL RESPONSES (1964-66)

With competitors responding rapidly to the initial System/360 announcements, IBM was soon faced with the need to respond in turn or lose the competitive advantage it had obtained by the introduction of System/360. We now discuss IBM's initial responses, particularly its reduction of extra shift charges, improvement of memory speeds, announcement of improved tapes and disks, and the introduction of the Model 20.

Reduction of Extra Shift Usage Charges

At the time of the System/360 announcement, IBM was charging its rental customers a flat rate for 176 hours of computer use per month — the monthly availability charge (MAC). For use beyond that number of hours, an additional charge was billed at a rate of 40 percent of the per-hour MAC rates.[41]

One of the ways that competitors responded to 360 was by reducing or eliminating extra shift charges. An IBM Wins and Loss Report for June 1964 cited "erosion of extra shift" as one of the most significant aspects of competitive announcements since System/360.[42] On July 29, 1964, Learson wrote that GE had reduced its extra shift on the 400 line to 10 percent and was offering its newly introduced 635, "a competitor of the 7094," with no extra shift charge.[43]

IBM reduced its additional use charge from 40 percent to 30 percent on August 11, 1964, effective retroactively to July 1.[44] It was not enough, and

IBM received pressure for additional reductions. On August 13, 1964, B. O. Evans and others in IBM were notified by DSD's Advanced Systems Group that:

> We are currently facing severe competition in the medium and large scale scientific areas from such machines as the GE 625, GE 635, [the DEC] PDP-6, etc. A goodly part of this problem is due to our additional use charges. GE, particularly, is offering their 600 series on a 24-hour basis. Even in cases where we are price competitive on a single shift basis, we rapidly become noncompetitive when additional use is involved. The 30% extra shift charge is good but not nearly enough.[45]

In addition, IBM was losing orders to the Honeywell 200, particularly at service bureaus. In October DPD "fought" for a reduction in extra use charges to 10 percent, this being, Frank Cary wrote to Thomas J. Watson, Jr., at the beginning of December, one of "the instances where we have 'screamed' for action."[46] On October 14, 1964, IBM announced a further reduction in its extra shift charge for System/360 to 10 percent.[47]

Memory Improvements

Within two months after System/360 was announced, it became clear that the memory speed of certain IBM systems had been surpassed by newly announced competitors' machines. A June 1964 Wins and Loss Report cited "the fast memory speeds of [competitors'] new systems" as one of the "three most significant aspects of competitive announcements" (the others being price cuts and the "erosion of extra shift"). In particular, the memory speeds of the Honeywell H-2200, the NCR 315 RMC, the Univac 1108, the GE 635, and the CDC 3800 were mentioned.[48]

J. A. Haddad, director of technology and engineering, addressed this problem further in a July 28, 1964 letter to Vice-President and Group Executive John W. Gibson:

> I am becoming increasingly concerned over the possibility that some of the 360 machines will be technically obsolete before they are delivered. With the recent round of price-cutting by some of our competitors, it is even more important that our machines remain technically superior.
>
> There is obviously a strong trend toward the use of faster memories across the board. This is exemplified by the Univac 1108 . . . the NCR 315 . . . the CDC 3800 . . . the H2200 . . . and the RCA 3301. . . . All of these examples appear to give the competitor a memory speed advantage at an equivalent 360 machine level.[49]

The need to improve memory speed, and with it processor price/performance, was particularly acute for the larger models of the 360 line: the 60, 62, and 70. An IBM Wins and Loss Report for August 1964 reported that "there have been no credited orders for Models 60, 62 and 70 since June. . . ."[50]

Within IBM it was believed that those models compared particularly poorly with CDC's new entries. On October 19, 1964, Ralph A. Pfeiffer, Jr., vice-president and federal regional manager for DPD, wrote to Cary, recommending "that DPD request a 100% performance improvement in the Model 70 with no increase in rental price and not more than a 20% increase in purchase price" in order to compete with the larger CDC machines.[51] On December 1, Cary recommended that the price of the one-microsecond memory on both the Model 70 and the Model 91 (discussed below) be reduced "in order to make our bids . . . more competitive from a price/performance standpoint."[52] Those price reductions (which reflected a redesign of the memory) were announced on December 23.[53]

These price reductions were not enough, however. In December 1964, DSD President George Kennard wrote to Watson and IBM President A. L. Williams that the performance of the 6400, as indicated by CDC, would place it between Models 62 and 70, while "[f]ield reports indicate a price somewhat above our Model 50." He reported that steps were being taken to improve the competitiveness of the larger IBM machines, including an increase in the memory speed from one microsecond to three-quarters of a microsecond for Models 62 and 70.[54] Such memories had been in development before April 1964, but had not been far enough along to be announced at that time.[55]

The improvements were needed. On March 10, 1965, C. B. Rogers, Jr., director of product programs for DPD, wrote to Learson:

> The CDC 6600 overpowers our 70 . . . for approximately the same rental. . . . The new entry of the CDC 6400 . . . clearly out-performs our Model 62 by a factor of 2 at a substantially lower price for both purchase and rental. . . . It is accurate to say we are in trouble.[56]

On April 22, IBM announced the Model 65 and Model 75, each having a memory speed of three-quarters of a microsecond. The faster Model 65 superseded Models 60 and 62, and Model 75 superseded Model 70.[57] (A faster memory for the smaller Model 30 — 1.5 microseconds compared with 2 microseconds — had already been announced in January.)[58]

Tape Drive Improvements

On August 21, 1964, the System/360 Compatibility Committee reported that because of the nature of 360, manufacturers of peripherals could be expected to market compatible replacements for IBM's peripherals:

> (1) I/O [input/output] manufacturers, whether independent or divisions of computer manufacturers, are in a position to market devices of comparable IBM capacities at approximately 20% less price.
>
> (2) It appears that I/O manufacturers will attempt to sell tape drives and terminals to System/360 customers.

(3) There will probably be concerted activity from competitors in marketing I/O devices on System/360 in the Federal Government.[59]

Further, they stated:

> The heretofore heavy emphasis on processor planning as the criterion for improved price/performance should be re-oriented towards I/O developments. The across-the-board improvements in price/performance which will be required in the 1967-68 time period will probably be brought about more by improved I/O capability than by CPU and memory improvements. As part of the regular development effort, such activity will be necessary in any event to keep System/360 a viable product line. . . .[60]

Tape drives, in particular, needed improvement. A presentation to the DP group staff in November 1964 by a group headed by C. J. Bashe, entitled "Group Staff Review of IBM's Technological Position in the Marketplace," recommended attention to "box-by-box superiority" and concluded that half-inch compatible tape drives constituted an area in which IBM was "inferior."[61] That assessment was echoed in the call for a general managers' meeting on action plans for technical problem areas, scheduled by Paul Knaplund for December 4, 1964:

> We're outclassed in half-inch tape and apparently can't sell one-inch tape equipment. We need a tape drive that is superior in performance and acceptable.[62]

The problem was felt to be particularly acute for small systems used to control peripherals, as in tape-to-printer or card-to-tape applications, a common use of 1400 series computers.[63]

IBM's fears about its lack of technological superiority in tapes were made even more immediate by additional actions of its competitors. On December 11, 1964, C. E. Frizzell, president of GPD, reported to Thomas J. Watson, Jr., on the recent RCA Spectra 70 announcement. He listed among the "significant advantages" of the Spectra 70:

> One-third higher speed magnetic tape drives at equivalent rentals compared to IBM. . . . Availability of magnetic tapes on the Model 15 gives them a magnetic tape system in a price range where we have no current entry.[64]

Honeywell, CDC, and GE tape drives were also a problem.[65]

IBM improved its tape drives in two steps. The first step was the announcement of the 2415 tape drive and control unit on April 5, 1965. The 2415, a lower-cost unit for Models 20 and 30, solved the tape drive needs of users of those models. The second and more important step was the announcement on August 9, 1965, of the 2401 Models 4, 5, and 6 tape drives and control units. These 2401s incorporated several advantages in tape technology: 1,600-bit-per-inch density, phase encoding recording, and twice the data transfer rate of IBM's earlier models.[66] For the time being these announcements appeared to have solved the tape problems.[67] Soon, however, competition, particularly from plug-compatible manufacturers (PCMs), would push IBM to improve its tape drives even more.

Disk Drive Improvements

For several years prior to making disk drives an integral part of System/360 with the 2311, IBM had marketed the 2302, a drumlike file with very high capacity. The 2302 was larger but less versatile than the 2311. Soon after System/360 was announced, IBM found that

> It was beginning to be apparent that customers had a far greater need for data stored in disk drives than we had anticipated a year or two earlier when System/360 was under development and when the 2311 disk drive was first introduced.[68]

IBM introduced its 2314 (announced April 22, 1965) for two reasons. First, since the 2314 would be larger than the 2311, it would "provide a better relation to competition than the 2302 files." Second, because the improved price/performance of the 2314 would improve the overall system performance of 360 systems on which it was used, "the 2314 was announced . . . to sell more 360 systems."[69]

The 2314 represented a considerable advance over prior disk drives. Compared with the 2311, it provided a fourfold increase in capacity per spindle, a twofold improvement in data rate, and the ability to operate on-line.[70] Arthur Beard, chief engineer of RCA's computer division, testified that while "the 2311 demonstrated the reliability" of random access devices, "[t]he 2314 not only offered the reliability but also a practical cost for the random access user."[71]

The superiority of the 2314 provided substantial benefits to IBM. IBM "totally underestimated the demand for such devices" and was "hard pressed to deliver the devices as fast as customers were demanding them."[72] It also had the desired effect on systems sales:

> The availability of the 2314 has been the catalyst to make many systems sales for previously undeveloped application use of computers.[73]

> The 2314 is an example of where the product developed a market beyond our initial forecast expectations. Every company should have a door-opener that beats competition — the 2314 is such a product and will continue to be only if our pricing policy can stand the challenge of competition.[74]

Introduction of the Model 20

IBM's success with its 650 and 1401 had shown that small, low-cost computers were important because they helped increase the market by permitting users who otherwise might have been unable to afford them to obtain computer systems. In the face of that experience, the SPREAD Committee had recommended that IBM develop a "very small" processor, even though such a processor might not be fully compatible with the rest of the 360 line.[75] The development of such a small processor was assigned to the IBM World Trade Corporation's laboratory in Stuttgart, Germany.[76] In early 1964 that small processor was judged "not to be as far advanced in development as the Models 30 through 70," and it was therefore not announced with the rest of the 360 line in April 1964.[77]

The need for a low-cost computer was evident within IBM. A document of April 15, 1964, entitled "Forecast Assumptions for the 1430N Data Processing System" (360/20), stated:

> This system will bring the world of the System/360 down to the price range the small user can afford.
>
> For the first time a new technological breakthrough, like the one realized with SLT for the System/360, will be made available at lower cost to the small customer at the same time as to the larger user.
>
> The 1430N system offers growth within the system and upward growth into the System/360, Model 30.[78]

Even though the 360/20 was in large part expected to be acquired by new users, it was anticipated that a variety of customers would find it attractive. Such customers included users replacing old unit record equipment used to support larger systems and those with "a number of branch locations requiring frequent and/or prolonged contact with the central data processing center or among each other."[79]

After the announcement of System/360, the need for the Model 20 increased. On July 20, 1964, John Opel, vice-president of marketing in the Data Processing Division, wrote to Learson concerning banking-product deficiencies and stated that "we need to have a more competitive response to the [Univac] 1004 and other competitive small card processing systems."[80] Writing after the announcement of the Model 20, Withington observed that IBM had to announce "such a computer to protect its position" from "the Univac 1004 and 1005, the Honeywell 120 and the GE 115."[81]

IBM announced the Model 20 on November 18, 1964. Because of the need to keep its cost down, the processor did not share all the features of the 360 line. First, the Model 20 contained only a subset of the 360 instruction set and, hence, was not compatible with the rest of System/360 to the extent that the other members of the System/360 line were compatible with each other.[82] Second, the 360/20 did not use the System/360 standard interface for attaching peripherals and instead used "native attachment." This was done to lower costs so that IBM could offer the 360/20 at a more competitive price.[83]

The 360/20 was used in a variety of ways by a variety of users, not all of them small. For example, an IBM Competitive Daily Report stated that "[t]here are about 600 Model 20's installed with communications equipment and 700 installed in large customer accounts."[84] A memorandum on the GUIDE Project on remote batch computing of February 1966 contemplated a large 360 as "the central facility" of a system in which "[t]he remote terminals may be small typewriter keyboards, but, more likely, will be Model 20 360's, Model 30's, or even larger machines with their own operating systems." "The bulk of the terminals planned for use would be small computers[,] mostly 360's Model 20 or 30."[85]

As it turned out, the 360/20 was more than merely a good competitive response; as had the 1401 in its day, the 360/20 became the largest-selling of IBM systems, with more than 7,400 installed in the United States by 1970.[86]

In December 1965, Withington summarized the effect of IBM's competitive responses:

> Soon after the System 360 line of computers was announced, it became apparent that despite the basic soundness in the line there were a few deficiencies and weak points. IBM, apparently desiring to establish a product position now that will remain sound for a number of years, has moved very vigorously to remedy the deficiencies. It has announced new products to add to the line, improved the price-performance of the initially announced products, and adjusted marketing policy in certain respects.
>
> . . . .
>
> The 360/20 extends the line downward in price, while still retaining most of the features of a full-scale computer system. Considering the appearance of the Univac 1004 and 1005, the Honeywell 120 and the GE 115, one had to expect IBM to announce such a computer to protect its position in a market area representing important dollar volume. It should be effective protection; the 360/20 offers very competitive price-performance characteristics. . . .
>
> . . . .
>
> The 360/65 appeared when it was clear that the initial 360's at the "top of the line" could be bested by the competition. The 360/65 cannot, at present; it offers price-performance as good as anything on the market. . . .
>
> . . . .
>
> When pressed by competition, IBM has also made significant improvements in the previously announced products — even before delivery of the first models. The 360/30 initially showed a price-performance characteristic inferior to those of some of its competitors, so IBM increased its speed sharply by substituting a faster memory at no increase in price. The initial terminals and control devices for remote input-output were too expensive, so IBM has supplemented the initial offering with a number of lower-cost devices. Perhaps most important overall, IBM increased the packing density of all its magnetic tape units from 800 characters per inch to 1600, at a small increase in price, by using a new recording technique. This factor is important

to the overall productivity of most computer installations, so the entire 360 line benefited considerably. The competitors will be able to match this improvement, but for the time being IBM's position is improved.[87]

MORE SPECIALIZED COMPUTERS: MODELS 90, 44, AND 67

The Model 90 Program

As already discussed, during the 1950s IBM undertook a number of leading-edge development projects designed to advance the computing state of the art. Each of those programs (such as the 701, SAGE, NORC, STRETCH, and various projects for the National Security Agency[88]) was a response to the needs and demands of users (predominantly government agencies) who required computing capabilities beyond the most advanced then available. In addition to advancing the computing state of the art, benefiting computer users, and serving the nation, such projects proved extremely valuable to IBM. They served as training grounds for future IBM managers and engineers, and as proving grounds for important new concepts that were incorporated into subsequent IBM computer products. With the first STRETCH computers commencing shipment in 1961, IBM began work on its next "super computer."[89] As Frederick Brooks testified: "at any point in time there was somebody working on a machine beyond the fastest one we had; in any project there should be somebody looking for a successor to it."[90]

The SPREAD Report contemplated the development of a "very large processor" beyond one that could easily be made compatible with the rest of the line.[91] Work on the "high end" was under way even as the SPREAD Committee was meeting, with the project, begun in January 1961, designated "Project X" (ten times STRETCH) in August.

A general timetable for development was decided upon, and deliveries projected for 1966 or 1967. Responsibility for Project X was given to the Data Systems Division in October 1961. Development of the Project X computer, which ultimately became the 360/90 program, proceeded throughout 1961-63.[92] The Model 90 program was an effort to "push technology" and build "the most powerful computer" possible at the time.[93] It consisted of the System/360 processor Models 2092 I, 2092 J, 2091, and 2095.

The impetus for the Model 90 program was much the same as the impetus for IBM's earlier efforts to "stretch" the state of the art. Beginning in 1961 and carrying through the Model 90 announcements in 1964 and 1965, an increasing number of "leading-edge" customers requiring advanced solutions to complex computing problems began pressing IBM for systems with higher performance than IBM then had available. Such customers included the Atomic Energy Commission facilities, the U.S. Weather Bureau, various universities, and the National Security Agency, as well as private research organizations.[94] Not surprisingly, as it had in the 1950s, a good deal of this pressure came from the federal government.[95]

In the early 1960s such demands were not taken lightly. As Dr. Louis Robinson, IBM's director of scientific computing, testified:

> At that time in history, the President of the United States and the people at large had dedicated themselves towards a substantially higher level of scientific and engineering and technological achievement than the country had experienced prior to that time due to a variety of considerations, including the Russian success in areas of technology and science, and a national goal had been stated relative to the need for the country to achieve great leaps forward in various areas of science and technology.[96]

In August-September 1963, "IBM top management was deeply concerned that IBM's efforts had not yet developed a competitive offering for a number of very large and influential users, especially the federal government laboratories for atomic energy research, weapons development, space exploration and weather research, and defense contractors to the government."[97] "Mr. T. J. Watson, Jr., and others expressed concern that IBM was not responding adequately to the needs of the United States Government for advanced EDP systems in connection with the Government's high priority defense and related programs." Thereafter, Watson ordered that IBM inquire of government users directly, to make certain that their needs were being taken into account in IBM's "super computer" (Model 90) development, and ordered acceleration of development efforts on a computer more powerful than even the Project X computer.[98]

Development of advanced, state-of-the-art computers was not only in the nation's interest, but in IBM's self-interest as well.

First, as demand for such capabilities increased, so did the potential business opportunity in meeting those demands. In August 1963, T. V. Learson wrote:

> I am informed that a machine 10 times 7090 has a market of some 53 machines. If the market is anywhere near this number we will be committing a very serious crime in not moving Project X . . . at a more rapid pace.[99]

Second, there was considerable promotional value in being able to offer the world's most powerful computing capabilities to solve the problems of highly advanced users.[100]

Third, the opportunity to work on projects at the technological leading edge of the industry offered a powerful incentive for the best young talent to work for companies that undertook such projects. These projects therefore served as important training grounds for future employees. IBM's experience on SAGE and STRETCH had provided ample proof of the benefits to be gained in that respect.[101]

Fourth, "super machine" development held the promise of substantial future value that would be realized through the incorporation of new learning in later products.[102] IBM's experience on STRETCH had shown that although high-technology projects might lose money when all the costs of research were allocated to them, they could still turn out to be very profitable in terms of "technological fallout."[103] Thomas J. Watson, Jr., writing to IBM President A. L. Williams in May 1965, stated:

> Although four or five years ago there was some doubt as to whether or not we should continue to try to lead in this area because of expense and other considerations, at some point between two and three years ago, it became evident that the fallout from the building of such large-scale machines was so great as to justify their continuance at almost any cost. Therefore, for the past two years, under Vin Learson and Dick Watson, this subject has had the highest priority, at least in the upper areas of the management of the corporation.[104]

There were many others within IBM who felt the same way. Dr. Charles DeCarlo, IBM director of systems research and development, wrote in June 1964 concerning the Model 90 program:

> We can be intuitively sure that the technological benefits which will flow from this commitment will filter through the rest of the product line. Surely there can be no doubt the STRETCH program spawned highly successful financial programs.[105]

Although these reasons for embarking on the Model 90 program antedated the public announcement of the CDC 6600 (CDC discussed the 6600 with customers earlier[106]), CDC's announcement brought the importance of that program home to IBM management with greater force. Within IBM the CDC 6600 caused concern about IBM's industry leadership in state-of-the-art computing and about the perception of IBM's role by its customers. In August 1963, Thomas J. Watson, Jr., wrote:

> Last week CDC had a press conference during which they officially announced their 6600 system. I understand that in the laboratory developing this system there are only 34 people, "including the janitor." . . .
> Contrasting this modest effort with our own vast development activities, I fail to understand why we have lost our industry leadership position by letting someone else offer the world's most powerful computer.[107].

The matter of computers having very advanced capabilities had a top priority among the subjects discussed at the September 5, 1963 IBM Executive Conference in Jenny Lake, Wyoming.[108] IBM Research was instructed by Chairman Watson:

> to ensure that IBM does have clear leadership in the computer field — meaning a computer which is sufficiently far ahead of any other computer — that it will maintain that position of leadership and prestige for at least three or four years after announcement.[109]

DSD was instructed to move ahead "as fast as possible" with Project X (which was already planned to have twice the capability of the CDC 6600), and Research was instructed to accelerate its work toward a machine with ten times the capability of Project X.[110]

Thus, the many reasons for undertaking the Model 90 program were reinforced by CDC's growing success. IBM was spurred to advance the pace of the program by increasing the time and resources allocated to it.[111] Nevertheless, the Model 90 was not announced with the rest of the 360 series on April 7, 1964, because Paul Knaplund (who was responsible for bringing before IBM management recommendations concerning the number of processors to be announced with System/360) "did not feel that the Model 90 had progressed far enough to warrant a general announcement."[112] Customers were informed, however, "that the Model 90 development effort was under way. That information was supplied in a footnote to the System 360 announcement."[113]

Between April and August 1964, IBM management received information from the National Security Agency that the ASLT (advanced solid logic technology — also called ACPX) circuitry on which the Model 90s depended was in fact feasible.[114] Relying on this and the judgments of its top technical people, IBM announced the first Model 90 processors — the 2092 I and 2092 J (superseded before delivery by Models 91 and 95, which had improved memories) — on August 17.[115] Model 2091 was announced in November 1964. Product Test did not support these announcements because it could not perform its standard "announcement testing" on a product where "it was necessary to work closely with individual customers to understand their needs."[116] Each of the Model 90 systems delivered to customers performed well and to customers' satisfaction and passed acceptance tests imposed by the government where such testing was performed.[117]

The first Model 90 computer was delivered nine months late because, despite the results of the NSA tests, IBM encountered unexpected, substantial, and critical problems in its circuitry (ACPX) in 1965.[118] The principal problem, known as the "cracked stripe problem," could not have been foreseen because it appeared only when a sufficiently large number of components had been put together in an operating machine.[119] That problem, which was also potentially present in other computers, was discovered much earlier than it would otherwise have been because of the high current densities in the Model 90 circuits. As a result, IBM was able to correct the problem on the rest of the 360 line before most machines had been built and to inform others in the industry about the problem before they ran into similar difficulties.[120]

Discovery and solution of the cracked stripes problem was an example of the kind of technological fallout that had been expected from the Model 90 program. As that program proceeded, additional fallout resulted from developments in thin-film technology, monolithic circuitry, transistor technology, packaging technology, interconnection technology, memory technology, and machine organization.[121]

Although the anticipated technological fallout from the Model 90 program was realized, the 90 series did not fare well competitively. Only 15 Model 91s were manufactured (four for internal use), and two Model 95s were specially manufactured for NASA.[122] By contrast, CDC manufactured 94 Model 6600/ 6700 computers and 121 additional Series 6000 computers.[123] Indeed, CDC's revenues and gross profits between 1964 and 1972 from the sale and lease of 6600s exceeded its targets.[124]

The 360/44

As discussed in Chapter 5, one of the risks in providing a line of computers like System/360, intended to do all applications equally well, was that, at least for some applications, the machines of the family would be less suitable for some customers than competitors' machines, optimized in their design for such particular applications. In addition there was a risk that not all customers would be willing to accept the "overhead" associated with System/360's highly functional systems software — that a certain number would attempt to locate alternatives with less function and better price/performance in terms of throughput per dollar. For some (certainly not all) users in such areas, this turned out to be true.

> In the months following the System 360 announcement, marketing personnel began to report that, although many users found the System 360 products adequate for data acquisition and data reduction, some felt that a general purpose processor more tailored to those specific applications would be required. The Data Processing Division urgently requested that the Product Group undertake development of a system to meet these needs.[125]

The need for a competitive response became increasingly apparent during the latter part of 1964 and into 1965. Learson wrote to Watson in December 1964 concerning the acceptance of the Models 40 and 50 in the "Intermediate Scientific Area": "Our position here since announcement in April, 1964 is that we have won 44, lost 44, and have 172 doubtful situations. CDC and SDS have a total of five machines which out-price, out-perform us by a good margin."[126] This was just one of many cries for a competitive answer.[127]

In August 1964, DSD began a program the objective of which was to develop a processor (eventually the 360/44) "within the general architecture of the System 360 family" but with better price/performance than the Models 40 and 50 for "data acquisition, data reduction and certain scientific calculations."[128] In April 1965, Knaplund wrote that "[t]he performance needed [in the Model 44] approaches the Model 50. The system price required is close to that of the Model 30." He went on to say:

> Wherever possible within the framework of our main thrust price/ performance curve . . . we must and will bend every effort to preserve complete compatibility for marketing, as well as programming reasons. But when an anomalous performer is required, we must be prepared at

all times to offer lean, hard systems with slight incompatibilities, if these incompatibilities help mitigate impact and/or cost.

Such is the case with the Model 44. . . .[129]

The Model 44 was announced in August 1965, being described as "a powerful computer . . . designed specifically for the small to medium-sized scientific user . . . ideally suited for customers and prospects who want raw binary speed and high throughput to solve a wide range of scientific problems, including high speed data acquisition jobs."[130] To reduce costs and achieve the "raw binary speed and high throughput" needed for this "lean, hard system," some sacrifice in compatibility with the rest of System/360 had to be made.[131] The required cost savings were achieved "by eliminating read-only storage [firmware] through the utilization of hard-wired logic for the interpretation and execution of stored program instructions, by reducing the number of instructions executed directly by this hard-wired logic, by simplifying the checking logic and by taking advantage of lower component costs." The required performance increase was achieved "by using hard-wired logic in place of read-only storage and by including within the processor a single disk storage device known as RAMKIT for program residence."[132]

Apart from its inability to execute the complete System/360 instruction repertoire, the 360 Model 44 was "basically the same" as the other 360 processors.[133] Indeed, it was initially expected that the 44 would be manufactured in the same facility as the Model 40, and that schedule restraints would require the substitution of Model 44s for production of Model 40s "on a one-for-one-basis."[134] This substitution never happened because additional manufacturing capacity sufficient to meet the demand for both Model 40s and Model 44s was authorized prior to the Model 44 announcement.[135]

The Model 44 was not particularly successful. It failed by a wide margin to meet the level of acceptance forecast at the time of its announcement.[136] To at least some in IBM, it appeared that this was because IBM had learned to meet customer needs generally, but had not successfully learned to specialize within that talent.[137]

In part, however, the Model 44 was unsuccessful because it was relatively quickly outperformed by later systems of competitors. By the end of 1967, at least some in IBM believed that "hardware performance was excellent at announcement time, but recent competitive announcements have now bypassed the Model 44."[138] That situation continued to worsen, so that by 1970 one group in the company wrote: "As a result of being consistently outperformed by the XDS Sigma 5, PDP 10 or CDC 3300, the Model 44 is seldom proposed."[139]

The 360/67

Time-sharing is "the use of a computer by many people at once with each user having the illusion that he is the sole user of the computer."[140] IBM was involved in a number of time-sharing development efforts before System/360 —

in particular the joint development with MIT of CTSS, "the first example . . . of a general purpose time sharing system," described by Alan Perlis of Carnegie Tech and Yale as "a creative masterpiece."[141] The SPREAD Report called for the New Product Line to be communications-oriented, multiprogramming systems that would be capable of performing time-sharing.[142] That objective was met, and 360 as announced included time-sharing capability.[143] A number of highly sophisticated customers with advanced requirements, however, rejected 360's particular approach to time-sharing and demanded time-sharing facilities not available with System/360. Specifically, they wanted dynamic relocation hardware, which provided a "means for interrupting a program at an arbitrary point, moving it out of core, proceeding with the interruption, bringing the interrupted program back into memory at a new location, and starting it again."[144] Such hardware was being developed within IBM but was not considered necessary for time-sharing in System/360.[145]

In early 1964, MIT's Project MAC — an advanced research project in time-sharing funded by the Advanced Research Projects Agency (ARPA) of the Department of Defense — sought proposals for the development of "an extremely advanced timesharing system."[146] IBM proposed a multicomputer configuration of a System/360 Model 50; CDC proposed a 6600; RCA proposed its 3301; GE proposed a 635; and Univac proposed "a complex multiprocessor system" then being designed for a classified military weapons system. Digital Equipment Corporation proposed a multiprocessor version of its PDP 6 computer and was "in among the finishers." The winner was GE and, in addition, "a $1 million PDP-6 was purchased by MAC as a peripheral processor."[147] GE won with a "modified" version of the 635 and "proposed working jointly with [MIT] in the development of the software that would reside on that hardware."[148] MIT "had determined that System 360 would not satisfy its needs and that it would accept only a system incorporating some form of dynamic relocation hardware."[149] Shortly thereafter, Bell Labs also ordered a time-sharing system from GE.[150]

In mid-August 1964, IBM formed the Time Shared Task Force

> to develop an IBM plan for time shared systems . . . because of the loss of the MAC account at MIT and other critical customer situations in the area of real time, time shared systems requirements.[151]

The task force was composed of individuals in IBM "most knowledgeable" about remote computing and time-sharing; they scheduled meetings with a number of the leading experts in the field, such as Prof. F. J. Corbato of Project MAC, Dr. J. C. R. Licklider of ARPA, Mr. J. Schwartz of Systems Development Corporation, and Dr. B. Galler of the University of Michigan.[152]

In early September, Nat Rochester, a member of the task force, wrote to C. H. Reynolds, the chairman:

> System/360 has been almost universally rejected by the leading time sharing investigators. Time sharing systems are likely to render obsolete systems that are not based on time sharing. Therefore, there is a legitimate worry that System/360 may not be a resounding success unless proper steps are taken.[153]

He stated that "the commonest reason the customers give for rejecting System/360 for time-sharing is that there is not adequate hardware support for dynamic relocation."[154] IBM was being told that

> Customers want dynamic relocation. It may be unnecessary and undesirable but we have not yet proved that this is so. The technical situation is very unclear and is changing rapidly on a month by month basis as technology advances.[155]

Reviewing the "rejection of System/360" by those desiring time-sharing, Rochester concluded:

> There is much more at stake than these few prestige accounts. What is at stake is essentially all computing business, scientific and commercial. . . . [W]e may find eventually that many of the best programmers will refuse to work at an installation that does not offer timesharing or offers inferior time sharing.[156]

He recommended that IBM "proceed with the design, construction and release of an advanced timesharing system," and that the work be done in public, "so as to benefit from external criticism and so as to have a favorable sales effect."[157]

Two days later the Research Group of the task force reached the same conclusion: "System/360 has been rejected or is about to be rejected by many of the important large-scale scientific users who are pioneering novel ways of using computers such as the 'computer utility.' This has been accompanied by a shift of attention to competitive equipment like the GE 635."[158] They also believed there was "a great deal more at stake":

> The earlier concept of "time-sharing" has now naturally led to the "computing utility" concept. This means that computing capacity should be available right at the working place of the computer user by means of a terminal linked to a powerful central computer. . . . There is a very strong probability that the "computing utility" will be *the* way of all scientific computing in a few years, and a good possibility that it will capture a substantial part of the commercial market as well. IBM cannot afford to overlook a development of this scope. *We are currently in danger of losing all contact with the leading developers of this concept.*[159]

Immediate action, including the announcement of "hardware-aided dynamic core relocation capability *at once* for Models 60, 62 and 70" was called for if IBM were to retain its "position of leadership which threatens to slip from us as a result of the independent development of the utility concept to which we have only belatedly directed our attention."[160]

In mid-September 1964, IBM's Scientific Computing Department reported on "remote scientific computing" to the task force:

There exists in the market place a set of key leader accounts representative of the scientific market segment. These accounts are invariably the innovative and experimentally-oriented accounts. They are the industry's spokesmen on the advanced state-of-the-art computing. They materially affect computer acquisition decisions in a variety of smaller establishments — both scientific and commercially oriented. . . .

. . . .

Today, a subset of this market, led by key university and certain closely related laboratories, has taken a fancy to the so-called area of remote computing. . . .

. . . .

Our time-sharing prospects require responses to the specific functions they have posed as requirements. The balance of the remote scientific community needs to know our responses in this regard as well as more detailed information about operating System/360.

Certain accounts have already been lost. A small set of key accounts are right now in the process of evaluations leading to computer acquisition decisions. For every such case, decisions disadvantageous to IBM appear to be in the offering [sic]. In quantity, such losses do not appear to be large. In quality, they will have a tremendous impact upon a very large market segment. . . .

If we do not respond on the time-sharing requirements in the near future, the time-sharing market will be largely lost to GE who has responded to this requirement. A large part of the balance of the remote scientific market will also be in jeopardy. . . .[161]

The report foresaw that the competitive threat would not be limited to GE:

We can expect similar emphasis on time-sharing system design from the other competitors. The experience of Burroughs with the D 825 and of Remington Rand with the M 490, 1218, and other special forms of real-time computers designed primarily for the military, have provided them with the experience necessary to develop well-honed second generation systems designed for general-purpose use. CDC has also had experience in the design of real-time systems. Furthermore, the system study efforts being conducted by CDC and ITEK at McDonnell Aircraft, General Dynamics and Lockheed, in the area of computer-aided design, will ultimately result in the announcement [sic] generally marketable equipment to compete . . . . The Digital Equipment Corporation is actively marketing the PDP-6 as a time-sharing system at extremely competitive prices. Although no real manifestation of intent has been made by RCA and Honeywell, the ultimate gravitation of the market toward general-purpose time-sharing systems will encourage all manufacturers to develop a product and support plan.

. . . The growing emphasis in the scientific and engineering market must ultimately effect [sic] the system selection process among so-called commercial users. . . .

. . . .

The advent of cost-justified, time-sharing business on centrally located systems should have an explosive effect on the service bureau business. This business is characterized today by the presence of a great many users located remotely from [a] central facility. To some extent, the current business in service bureaus is limited by turnaround time. Most service bureau customers who install their own equipment do so because of the delays introduced by access to a centralized location and service.[162]

In sum, the whole market, in all its dimensions, would be affected by the need for advanced time-sharing capability. This was a judgment widely shared outside of IBM at the time[163] and one reinforced by feedback from important customers.[164]

In late 1964 or early 1965, Dr. Ivan Sutherland, director of information processing techniques for ARPA, contacted V. O. Wright of IBM "eight to twelve" times to discuss time-sharing:

> He spoke words of encouragement, encouragement in the fact that he believed that IBM should pursue development of the timesharing concept in products and software as a matter of not only great importance to the United States government, but also of great importance to IBM and he simply encouraged and wanted to be kept aware, sort of as an insider, of how things were going on the project.
>
> . . . .
>
> [I]t was clear that he felt that two large companies, such as GE and IBM, pursuing developments in time sharing, was beneficial to the government, was beneficial to industry and, therefore, that he thought that was a good situation.[165]

That was indeed Sutherland's view. On September 4, 1964, shortly after GE had been selected over IBM for Project MAC, he had written:

> Project MAC's decision in favor of GE has generated a very healthy spirit of competition between MIT/GE and IBM. In effect, Project MAC has stated publicly that the IBM product is inadequate and that MIT/GE can do better. MIT/GE must produce the best system they can in order to make good their claim. IBM must expend its best effort to show that its product can serve the needs of time-sharing. In fact, IBM has been slow in responding to the needs of interactive computer users; now we *can* expect IBM to show more interest in this field. Competition between IBM and MIT/GE is a good thing; it will stimulate rapid progress in the time-shared use of computers.
>
> . . . .
>
> ARPA must support Project MAC fully. The MIT personnel responsible for choosing GE equipment have made their best technical judgment. They are staking their professional reputations on their choice. In making a decision against IBM, they have stimulated IBM to new efforts. Were ARPA to reject the MIT decision, Project MAC would suffer a blow from which it might never recover, and IBM would be able to relax.[166]

IBM marketing people, too, were "raising an increasing amount of clamour, putting an increasing amount of pressure on the marketing management of IBM" to provide "a product response that would let us be more responsive to our customers' requirements and to our customers' demand."[167] By November 1964, Wright and others within IBM became concerned that the time-sharing movement would build "to a great ground swell," "impact" IBM's installed base of equipment, and result in "a great deal of churning of the installed base, that is, the return of products that IBM had installed because of the requirement for a new capability in a computing system."[168] A response was needed, and it was clear that others would provide that response if IBM did not.[169]

One of the catalysts for such response was MIT's Lincoln Laboratory's request for proposal (RFP), which came in November 1964.[170] At the same time an RFP was received from the University of Michigan for a "central, time-sharing facility."[171] Watts Humphrey, IBM director of time-sharing systems, wrote to T. V. Learson on November 15: "The list of accounts who have interest in Time Sharing is growing daily. . . . By the end of the year, I expect that this number will exceed thirty."[172] Company prestige, as well as current and future business, was on the line.[173] IBM Chairman Frank Cary (DPD president in 1964) testified concerning the Model 67 and time-sharing:

> [S]ome of our very, very best customers wanted it. . . .
>
> . . . .
>
> . . . . I can just tell you that when customers . . . like AT&T and the Federal Government and the universities and General Motors Research . . . ask us to respond, we certainly at least try to respond to them. And we didn't undertake that with any thought that we weren't going to be able to do it.[174]

In November a group reporting directly to T. V. Learson and A. K. Watson was set up under the leadership of Watts Humphrey to try to respond to the time-sharing requirement. V. O. Wright (who was made director of time-sharing marketing) was called to Learson's home on the Saturday after Thanksgiving Day in 1964 and told to begin work that afternoon. According to Wright, Learson said that "the resources of the company were available to us for whatever we needed in order to move this development forward."[175]

Starting in December 1964, IBM made time-sharing proposals to Lincoln Laboratory and "a limited number of other users in order to enhance our ability to learn and understand time sharing."[176] IBM looked at this development "as a learning process for IBM to understand what really a time sharing system ought to be, what the facilities and capabilities should be, both in hardware and in software."[177]

IBM delivered its system to Lincoln Lab four to five months later than originally proposed. Although it did not have all the functions originally proposed and did not perform as rapidly as had been anticipated, Lincoln Lab was able to use it as a time-sharing system. Wright believed, considering the fact that it was the "first of a development program," that Lincoln Lab was "reasonably satisfied with the product."[178]

After the Lincoln Lab proposal, there was a "great deal of demand" for IBM to propose similar products to others.[179] Perlis testified that he and others at Carnegie Tech pressed IBM to provide "the same kind of time sharing service that MAC was developing," and were telling IBM that time-sharing was "important" and "that what MIT and General Electric had joined together to do was the wave of the future."[180] Others in the ARPA community did the same.[181]

IBM selected certain users who were believed to have "the capability of using a development system," and agreed to propose such a system to a limited number in order to enhance its time-sharing knowledge.[182] From January 1965 on, IBM worked with a group of customers nicknamed the "inner six" — the University of Michigan, Lincoln Lab, Bell Labs, SDC, Carnegie-Mellon University, and General Motors. These institutions were selected to act as "consultant or adviser to the group developing the 67" because they were "the most knowledgeable and could make the greatest contribution to [IBM's] designing a product that would fit the requirements of [the] user community."[183]

Although IBM had originally intended to propose the system under development to only six to eight customers, "to enhance [its] experience base in the use of the product," that number was increased "because of the great pressure that built up in demand from users and from the IBM marketing organization." By October 1965, 63 proposals had been made,[184] and the pressure continued:

[A] great many users . . . felt that time sharing offered them some additional capability that they needed. . . .

In some instances they would contact or write a letter to one of the IBM top senior executives. In other instances they would talk to their salesmen in their facilities, and so on, wanting a proposal, wanting to understand what IBM could do to satisfy this requirement.

And all during this period of time, in general, the industry was in a state of agitation because time sharing appeared that it might indeed be a new wave of the future from the standpoint of computing facilities for a company or an institution.

. . . .

[T] here was clearly . . . an understanding that if IBM for some reason did not respond to this particular requirement of customers' need, . . . it was very likely that those customers might very well buy such capability from somebody else.

. . . .

[T] he significance would be that IBM would lose business and that part of the installed base that IBM had at that point in time would disappear.[185]

In March 1965, IBM announced the System/360 Models 64 and 66 "for limited bidding."[186] With the availability of improved memory for the Model 65 in April, the Models 64 and 66 were withdrawn and replaced by Model 67 — essentially a Model 65 with a "Blaauw Box" (dynamic relocation hardware).[187] The Model 67 was also released "for limited bidding."[188] Every time-sharing system proposal made by IBM from November 1964 to the autumn of 1965 was very closely examined to ensure that IBM could deliver what it proposed.[189]

IBM was "very careful to be sure that all of our customers, the people who had orders, knew in fact the status of the program, what might be a problem, if it existed at that time, and how we were progressing." Moreover, because the customers involved were among the most sophisticated users, they "were able to understand the technical problems associated with the development effort."[190] The customers "understood that the Model 67 was a research and development project, and that things would change as they went along," but they were "willing to compromise on some of the things that we said would be included in the product and give them up if we could not produce them."[191]

In August 1965 the Model 67 had its special bidding restrictions removed and was announced for delivery in 1966, with the associated TSS operating system scheduled for delivery beginning in June 1967.[192] The problems of developing TSS, however, were substantially greater than IBM or the customers had foreseen.[193] By July 1966 the number of lines of TSS code had "approximately doubled," largely because of "the fact that the degree of automatic operation of the system and particularly its ability to protect users from each other and from system failures is a great deal more complex than had been anticipated." However, the first release was still expected to be "relatively solid in terms of schedule."[194]

Problems continued to develop. In August 1966, IBM announced a delay of 45 days in the release of the initial TSS package.[195] Further, in the autumn of 1966, shortly after learning of performance difficulties with the TSS software, IBM made calls on its 360/67 customers to explain the situation and to inform them that certain functions were being decommitted and schedules delayed.[196] Wright testified that everybody had been informed, and understood that this might occur:

> All the customers understood that it was a development type of a project, it was a development of a system that was to some extent breaking new ground, . . . and everybody understood that there might be changes. . . .[197]

In the meantime, GE was experiencing similar problems. Its efforts on Project MAC were aimed at developing a software system called MULTICS, which was to be implemented on an advanced version of the 635, called the 645.[198] GE announced the 645 to the public in the autumn of 1965, when neither the machine nor the software was in existence.[199] Before the end of 1966, GE withdrew the 645 from marketing because it

> began to realize that what we had on our hands was a research project and not a product. . . . We were attempting to do something that had never been done before, and, in principle, we might end up discovering that it was not feasible. As it turned out, it was hard and slow, but it was feasible.[200]

The GE 645 was "in the research project stage" until 1969 or 1970.[201] In fact, the GE-MIT MULTICS operating system was never delivered by GE;

Honeywell, after the merger with GE, completed development of the software three years behind the original schedule.[202] These problems arose because "the participants in the Project MAC effort underestimated the difficulty of successfully developing MULTICS."[203] GE's Weil testified:

> The technical task that was being attempted was extremely sophisticated and many of the subjects were at the state of the art as it was then known, and it took a long time to iron out the details of implementing some of these important features.[204]

The 645 was never delivered, and Project MAC received, instead, a system designated the 636.[205] Rather than providing GE with the "top-of-the-line prestige lustre" that had been expected, the 645 provided "very little to General Electric except a drain on its resources."[206]

IBM did not give up on TSS or the Model 67 (although at one point it did consider withdrawing the latter).[207] The initial version of TSS was made available by IBM in October 1967.[208] By April 1969, IBM had delivered a "substantially improved" version of TSS that was generally, but not universally, "considered to be an excellent software programming system."[209]

The Model 67 was not widely accepted, and by the end of 1970, only 52 had been installed by customers.[210] The experience that IBM gained with the Model 67 and TSS proved invaluable, however. As we shall see in Chapter 11, B. O. Evans (who believed that he was sent to the Federal Systems Division in some measure as a punishment for failing to have dynamic address translation hardware incorporated into the design of System/360 from the start[211]) launched an effort, on his return in 1969, to get dynamic address translation hardware put into the 370 plan.[212] He did so because that hardware was crucial for virtual memory (or virtual storage) — a combination of hardware and software that allocates to the machine itself the task of moving data into and out of main storage from auxiliary storage. Virtual storage greatly simplifies the programmer's task because it relieves him or her of the burden of having to make sure that the data will fit into available main memory space at all times. For programming purposes, virtual storage gives auxiliary storage the appearance of being main memory.[213]

Evans was successful, and virtual storage capability became a staple of all 370 systems announced after August 2, 1972.[214] Moreover, the virtual memory function was incorporated in 370 "in almost exactly the same way as the Model 67."[215] Thus, the Model 67 development produced hardware and software that became important elements of IBM's computer systems for the next ten years.

7

CHANGING POLICIES IN
A GROWING MARKET:
EDUCATIONAL ALLOWANCES AND
UNBUNDLING

One of the major obstacles that the early commercial entrants into the EDP industry had to overcome was the newness and unfamiliarity of computers. Until a large group of potential customers had learned how to use this new, and sometimes frightening, device, there could not be a large market for it. The manufacturer who offered principally hardware without much assistance and software would find that the number of people who could be attracted was severely limited, no matter how good the hardware was. (As we shall see, Digital Equipment Corporation [DEC] and Control Data Corporation [CDC], which began by offering relatively little support with their systems, came to offer increasing amounts.)

If the market were to grow to a large size and the uses of computers were to expand, manufacturers had to educate their customers and assist them in the use of the product. From the earliest days of the industry they did so. Led by IBM, they offered support and software to customers at no separately stated charge — a practice called "bundling" — and also subsidized education about computers and in computer use by offering computers at reduced rates to educational institutions — the "educational discount."

As the industry grew and the population of educated users increased, the need for such practices diminished. In the 1960s the policies changed, with the most dramatic change being IBM's unbundling announcement of 1969. This chapter discusses such changes.

EDUCATIONAL ALLOWANCES

Universities had played a key role in the beginnings of EDP in the 1940s and 1950s, and a close working relationship had arisen between academicians and EDP manufacturers. During the 1950s and 1960s many colleges and universities, supported in part by the Atomic Energy Commission, the National Science Foundation, and other government agencies, greatly expanded their utilization of computers.[1] The number of campus computing centers grew from 40 in 1957 to 400 in 1964.[2] A 1966 report of the National Academy of Sciences ad hoc Committee on the Uses of Computers (the Rosser Report) estimated that in 1964, colleges and universities had about $250 million worth of computer equipment installed in those 400 centers. Universities' annual EDP budgets were comparable with the costs of running their libraries.[3] In 1957 computer costs represented only 3 percent of all university research and development costs, but by 1963 those costs had more than tripled to 10.04 percent.[4]

Government funding was insufficient to support that growth in computing. In 1963, for example, about half of the $97 million spent on computers by colleges and universities came from federal sources; colleges and universities themselves were able to pay for about 34 percent; a shortfall of 16 percent remained to be provided from other sources,[5] and this meant computer equipment manufacturers.[6] A National Science Foundation compilation lists 366 proposals from 175 educational institutions between 1957 and 1967 asking computer manufacturers for free or discounted equipment.[7] The business equipment manufacturers had historically offered special discounts to universities, and that practice was continued into the computer era.[8]

Helping universities acquire and use computers was in the enlightened self-interest of computer manufacturers.[9] The use of computers at universities was an important means of gaining the widespread acceptance of the new technology. It offered the promise of overcoming some of the ignorance, fear, and uncertainty about computers by training the new generation in their use.

There were more direct potential impacts. The infant industry was suffering from an acute shortage of people who were trained in computing; educational discounts would help alleviate that shortage. According to the Rosser Report:

> [Educational discounts were] first instituted because the manufacturers realized that they would have trouble selling computers unless people capable of using them were available. To encourage the training of such people, manufacturers gave discounts to schools offering courses related to computers; the more courses, the greater the discount.[10]

Also, as more and more people became knowledgeable about computing, additional applications for computers would inevitably be created, and the market would grow.[11]

In addition, some people believed that computer manufacturers would derive a positive "public relations return" from an active program in support of higher education.[12] Indeed, some thought that such a return would include students who, having been trained on computer equipment of a particular vendor, would later be inclined to favor that vendor.[13] Other evidence, however, suggests that any such advantage was more apparent than real, particularly as computer systems and higher-level programming languages developed.[14]

For these reasons, IBM and other vendors offered a variety of support to educational institutions. Vendors offered educational allowances of varying percentages, depending on whether the equipment was to be used for administrative or instructional purposes. IBM also donated computer time to universities under circumstances that would ensure that the time would be made available to a wide variety of students, establishing regional computing centers at MIT and UCLA in the mid-1950s.[15] In addition to discounts, manufacturers, especially CDC, offered research grants, "buybacks" of computer time, and large cash contributions.[16] Larger discounts for academic or instructional use than for administrative use were not uncommon, and were consistent with the desire of manufacturers to encourage the training of people knowledgeable in computing.[17]

In retrospect, the educational allowance plainly accomplished the goal of supporting the growth of the industry, as well as benefiting society in general. In a draft report prepared for the National Science Foundation, W. F. Miller of Stanford University concluded that the educational allowance

> was a very important form of support in the early years. It contributed immensely to the growth of the computing industry in the country. The computing industry grew in its most spectacular growth from the ground up. When the colleges and universities began to graduate engineers, scientists, business school graduates, etc., who had been introduced to computing through introductory courses and often had taken advanced courses in computing, they began to introduce computer methods into their respective businesses. This in turn stimulated the great demand for computers and the spectacular growth of the computer industry in the early and mid-1960s. There is no doubt that the colleges and universities who first introduced large teaching programs in computing would not have been able to support these educational courses on such an extensive scale without the benefit of the [educational allowance].[18]

Similarly, the President's Science Advisory Committee, in a 1966 report titled "Computers in Higher Education," observed that:

> Great good has been done through donated computers, obsolescent computers, huge educational discounts, grants for the purchase of computers and the struggles of enthusiastic men with inadequate machines.[19]

IBM's Educational Support Programs

IBM's support of education started with the beginnings of the company, and was originated and directed to a large degree by Thomas J. Watson, Sr.[20] That support continued as the company began to move into the computer era.[21] When IBM's SSEC became operational in 1948, Watson dedicated it to science, and IBM allowed educational and research institutions to use the machine without charge.[22]

In October 1955, IBM announced an educational allowance program for the 650 computer. An allowance of 60 percent off the rental price was made available to educational institutions that offered courses in both scientific computing and data processing. This discount provided a great benefit to universities. Alan Perlis of Yale (formerly of Carnegie Tech) testified:

> The 60 per cent discount that IBM made available to universities opened up digital computing in the universities in the sense that almost no university was able to afford or at least thought they could find funds of the kind required to establish a digital computer laboratory until that discount became available, after which there were just a very large number of IBM computers, in particular IBM 650's finding their way into the universities and forming the focus of university computer centers.

That educational allowance policy was "absolutely" one of the "principal forces which enabled universities to become competent in computing as soon as they did."[23]

In May 1960, IBM announced that a 20 percent allowance would be offered on all of its leased or purchased EDP machines, systems, and features used for administrative purposes, and that a 60 percent allowance would be available if the equipment was used for instructional purposes.[24] Allowances were forecast to total $24 million in 1962.[25] The allowance program remained relatively unchanged until February 1963, when IBM abandoned the administrative use/instructional use distinction and reduced the 60 percent allowance to 20 percent on all new orders.[26]

When System/360 was announced in 1964, IBM left the percentage of the educational allowance unchanged (at 20 percent) and made it available on System/360 equipment to colleges, universities, and junior colleges.[27] It soon became apparent, however, that educational users who had second-generation equipment installed under the 60 percent allowance could not afford to take advantage of the price/performance improvement that System/360 offered because the educational allowance on System/360 was so much less.[28]

In addition, competition for the business of educational institutions was especially severe during the mid-1960s; most of IBM's competition offered high educational discounts and other special arrangements, such as lucrative research contracts.[29] CDC, in particular, frequently offered combinations of discounts, research contracts, and buybacks in certain competitive situations.[30] Other computer manufacturers, such as DEC, Scientific Data Systems (SDS), and Hewlett-Packard, were successfully marketing computers to universities.[31] As a result IBM and its competitors frequently became involved in highly competitive situations at universities.[32]

In 1965 IBM raised the educational allowance on System/360 computer equipment and created a sliding scale of discounts ranging from 20 percent on the Model 30 CPU to 45 percent on the larger CPUs. A great debate ensued within IBM, however, as to whether high educational discounts were the most appropriate way for the firm to support education. That debate was fueled by a ruling of the Armed Services Board of Contract Appeals (the *Carnegie* decision) that had the effect of passing the manufacturer's discounts on to the government, a result that manufacturers had not intended.[33] Within IBM some favored continuing the discounts; some favored raising them; others favored lowering or even eliminating them. Still others favored massive efforts in support of education.[34]

The result of the debate was a corporate decision gradually to reduce the allowance to 10 percent.[35] In 1966 the educational allowances on most equipment were reduced by about 10 percent of the price of the equipment. In 1969 the allowance was reduced to 10 percent as planned, and remained at that figure on most products.[36]

IBM'S UNBUNDLING DECISION

Introduction

In the EDP industry bundling is "the offering of a number of elements that are considered to be interrelated and necessary from a customer's point of view, in the computer field, under a single pricing plan, without detailing the pricing of the component elements themselves."[37] The elements that were offered without a separate price were nonhardware items such as education, software, systems design, and maintenance (for lease customers). As described in Chapter 1, the provision of such support services by manufacturers greatly facilitated the marketing of their equipment to users by reducing the users' risks in installing that new, unfamiliar, and expensive object, the computer.[38] As a consequence virtually "[a]ll the computer manufacturers marketed on a bundled basis" during the 1950s from the UNIVAC I on.[39]

At IBM the provision of bundled support began before the installation or even the acquisition of a computer by the customer. Such support was viewed both inside and outside IBM as an essential part of the marketing effort. The IBM systems engineer was "part of the marketing team" and would assist in the preparation of the proposal made to the customer.[40] It was the systems engineers who "had the implied responsibility of . . . developing systems to make sure that the machine was put to good use."[41] They worked with customers to define requirements; in system design, developing approaches to problems; they also engaged in customer education and training, and in programming. Such work would sometimes continue after installation.[42] In short, the systems engineers were responsible for "making sure that the customer was indeed implementing the targeted applications, the business applications, and doing the job properly and being of whatever assistance we could to make sure that the machine was . . . performing properly."[43]

Other firms in the industry also provided those types of services as part of their marketing efforts. RCA's Edwin McCollister testified that it was "normal for some fraction of the time of the [RCA] marketing force" to be dedicated to, for example, "[a]ssisting the customer with applications design and development, training . . . helping the customer plan expanded use of the system."[44] McCollister regarded all the elements of the RCA "field organization," including "salespeople, maintenance people and systems analysts and programmers, technical people," as "a normal and as a necessary part of the successful sale and installation of computer equipment." Similar views were expressed at other companies.[45]

Obviously, the amount of systems engineer services needed by a particular account varied, and not in any simple way. As John Akers, IBM's vice-president and group executive of the Data Processing Marketing group, testified, systems engineers at IBM "were a scarce resource within the branch office," so there was an attempt to "manage the technical talent in a way that was most beneficial in [IBM's] sales efforts and installation efforts with our customers." Systems engineers "were allocated on the basis of how much assistance a particular customer needed at a particular time; the degree of experience that the customer had; whether or not that customer perhaps required additional educational effort because he or she was installing a new computer system or [installing a] computer system for the first time. It was an effort to try to use that resource as productively as possible in pursuing the quota objectives that the branch office had."[46]

Systems engineering services were provided to familiarize users with computers and to ensure that the user, if he or she chose to acquire a computer, used it properly to solve his or her problems. Such services relieved users from some of the risk of acquiring a computer, and thus could induce them to obtain one. But, in relieving customers of such risks, IBM, like other manufacturers, assumed them. By giving users "a predictable cost that they could budget against,"[47] the manufacturer took over the uncertainty of cost resulting from unforeseen variation in user needs.

Plainly, manufacturers stood to gain (by lower costs) if over time the customer required less or no assistance. In the long run the reduction in customer needs would be accomplished in part, as it turned out, by the provision of increasingly sophisticated operating systems relieving customers' programmers of a number of complex tasks, but it could also be accomplished in the short run by training customers' personnel. Thus, according to the IBM "guidelines" concerning programming, "Systems Engineering personnel were to clearly encourage self-sufficiency among the customer [*sic*] in his programming capabilities with regard to application programs."[48] Such self-sufficiency "was a self-serving objective. The objective to enable the user to provide more of his own support would enable an SE [systems engineer] to perform less of those functions," freeing the systems engineer for other assignments. The customer would also be more efficient if he or she did not have to depend on others.[49]

Ralph A. Pfeiffer, Jr., described IBM's philosophy as follows:

> What we were trying to do was to insure customer's profitable use of the equipment. The Manager [had] a certain stable of talents; he had a customer set that he had to support and he tried to make the most productive, efficient use of that cadre of personnel.
>
> We are trying to supply a service to a customer. We are trying to have that customer make profitable use of his equipment. And if he is

unable for some lack of whatever it might be, education in a certain area or a certain person who he relied on left and he was caught short, we try to supply that missing ingredient until he is able to handle it himself. We tried to train him.

We certainly were interested in having him be capable of running his own installation in a profitable way. Whatever that required in the way of training somebody or supplying that piece of education that was missing, I hope I operated accordingly.[50]

The policy of building self-sufficiency in customers, however, carried with it an end to the practice of not charging separately for such services. When enough customers became self-sufficient and when changes in hardware and software ceased to require them to be taught very new ways of operating, it would no longer make sense to bundle. By increasing self-sufficiency in customers, IBM created a growing group who did not require the bundle. The exact date on which that group was sufficiently large that it made sense to unbundle and to provide the formerly bundled services at separate charges for those who wanted them is a matter of judgment. As we shall see, in IBM's judgment it came in 1969.

The Continued Demand for Bundling in the 1960s

During the 1960s most users continued to prefer the bundled offering.[51] The demand for such support was not restricted to new customers unfamiliar with computers. Even in selling to "the large, established user," such services would be required "to some degree." "[T]here would always be areas which are unfamiliar to even a relatively sophisticated customer. The fact that he was graduating from some smaller system to say, a larger . . . system which might involve communications, this communications area would be the first time for that large customer. . . . So even with sophisticated customers these kinds of support were required."[52]

The demand for support services continued in the 1960s as users rapidly explored new computer uses and as software improvements and architecture changes occurred at a rapid rate. RCA's Arthur Beard testified:

[M]ost of the customers we were dealing with in the time frame of 1960 to 1970 were not thoroughly experienced in the use of data processing equipment. The field had gone through a very dynamic growth. It faced new technology, a new set of programs imposed upon the business organizations that used computers. So a lot of people felt they were on very shaky grounds. They were not sure of themselves.[53]

New products and new ways of doing things were being introduced. This required customer training, programming, and systems design services, and imposed additional demands on the manufacturers.[54]

Thus, although users would eventually become familiar with the architecture of System/360, the sharp increase in complexity as users moved from second-generation equipment to System/360 tended to offset the gains from previous experience. Users were being trained and retrained to use more complex equipment in increasingly sophisticated ways, and the bundled IBM offerings were all the more important to the System/360 user, a need that had been foreseen within IBM.[55]

As other third-generation equipment began to appear, other manufacturers found requirements for support services growing as well, for programmers, and especially systems analysts, were in short supply.[56] Scientific Data Systems told its stockholders in its 1965 Annual Report that

> The character of the computer market changed substantially last year as the result of advances in both the understanding of the technology and in the manner in which computers should be employed. . . . During the past year increasing emphasis has been placed by management on providing complete service to SDS customers both before and after installation. To this end, technical staffs and applications programming, systems engineering, customer training and maintenance have more than doubled in size and in the scope of their activities.[57]

Such increases continued for the next few years.[58] Similarly, RCA found that the introduction and installation of its new Spectra series created large user demands for assistance.[59] National Cash Register and Sperry Rand encountered similar needs.[60]

IBM's Unbundling Announcement

On December 6, 1968, IBM announced that it expected "to make changes in the way it charge[d] for and support[ed] its data processing equipment" during the following year.[61] It announced its decision in detail on June 23, 1969, with the changes effective immediately for new orders and effective January 1, 1970, for customers with machines installed or on order.[62] Basically, the announcement instituted charges for systems engineering services and education and for new "program products, as distinct from system control programming." Programs then available from IBM's library continued to be available at no separate charge. IBM also offered to engage in contracts assuming "responsibility for the performance of specified tasks in the areas of systems design and analysis, application and program development and systems installation and evaluation."[63] No change was made in the way in which maintenance was provided, maintenance on purchased equipment continuing to be available for a fee and maintenance on IBM-owned equipment leased to users available without a separately stated charge.[64] IBM also reduced its prices by 3 percent, stating that this reflected its "best approximation" of the expenses that would "no longer be provided for in prices of currently announced equipment."[65]

There were a number of reasons for the announcement. First, IBM, like others, was feeling the strain of standing ready to supply services on demand without an extra charge in an increasingly complex environment. IBM "stated that — as a result of fast-changing data processing market conditions — the need for increasingly complex and comprehensive systems support is growing more rapidly than anticipated. In addition, new support requirements are arising from leasing companies and other owners of IBM equipment as they relocate and reapply their systems." Such demands for "new and additional forms of support services" were expected to continue to grow.[66] During the early and mid-1960s, persons within IBM observed that programming expenditures were "skyrocketing" and "increasing dramatically,"[67] and attempts were made in 1966 to quantify the return to IBM on programming expenditures.[68] IBM's Chairman Frank Cary testified that increasing demands of customers for education led to separate pricing of certain education offerings and that IBM was "always looking for ways of reducing the cost of systems engineering."[69]

The general problem of cost escalation was magnified by the special problems associated with installation of System/360. The training of the enlarged marketing staff, the support required by users to effect their conversion to the new and sophisticated operating system software associated with System/360, and the problems that IBM encountered with some of the 360 software caused the firm to devote an enormous portion of its resources to supporting the installation of System/360. The result of this, however, was that levels of support far greater than ever before required were demanded of IBM. The cost of providing such support had to be borne directly by IBM, but in the long run, of course, it would have to be absorbed by the firm's data-processing users.

At the same time, by 1969, in part as a result of IBM's policy of encouraging self-sufficiency, there had developed a group of relatively efficient and sophisticated users who would accept many of the risks of computers and were willing to do much of the support in-house. Thomas J. Watson, Jr., testified:

> We had some very sophisticated customers by this time, Lockheed, Boeing and others, who felt that they were better at performing some of these services than we were. They felt it onerous to pay for them when they, themselves, could do it in their opinion better.[70]

Another reason for IBM's decision to unbundle in 1969 was that, by that time, the notion of charging for software and services had become relatively accepted because of the entry and success of software houses (as discussed in Chapter 10). That had not always been true, however. From the early days of the computer industry, ". . . computer programs were looked upon as an intellectual product, but not necessarily having proprietary value."[71] This led many people to believe that most users were not willing to accept the notion of software as a "product" in the 1960s.[72] This view was both illustrated and reinforced by the free interchange of software that was characteristic of this period. But during the 1960s software houses began to charge for software products that competed with IBM's unpriced offerings, and by 1969 "the industry had developed to a point where many of those services were available, separately, and outside."[73] In particular, some assurance of protection of proprietary programs against plagiarism was now available.[74] As a result, IBM began to believe that, for the first time, there might be business opportunities in selling software and services separately.[75] Under such circumstances it was possible for IBM to stop offering such services, which it was finding onerous under the bundled system.[76]

Thus it was natural for IBM to consider unbundling in the late 1960s, but not before. The view that such consideration was hastened by the onset of *United States* v. *IBM* (with the Antitrust Division's charge that bundling was anticompetitive) is, so far as we know, only unsupported (if natural) speculation. IBM's announcement on December 6, 1968, of its intention to unbundle came before the filing of the government complaint in early 1969, but after the Antitrust Division's investigation had been under way for some time, as had the consideration of unbundling. No evidence in the trial record suggests that the two events were related.

Not surprisingly, customer reaction to IBM's unbundling announcement varied. Some relatively more sophisticated customers welcomed it; others, generally the relatively unsophisticated, were less happy.[77]

> [U]sers, even in 1969, when they heard about unbundling, were reluctant to accept it or were hesitant and in some cases even hostile to the idea. At that point in time users were beginning to get a pretty good idea of what some of their cost elements were and the more sophisticated, more advanced users had a way of breaking out cost elements in their total computer operation, identifying them, and controlling them.
>
> But for a lot of users, there were still many, many unknowns in their data processing operation, things that they didn't know could happen, they had no way of anticipating, and I think they wanted the assurance that bundling, in effect, offered them, that one way or another, if and when the unknown occurred, they'd be covered. It was an insurance policy in many respects.[78]

As might be expected, reactions of other manufacturers varied. Bundling had been a practice desired by users. Users' needs changed over time as customers became more sophisticated and self-sufficient, but this was a continuous rather than a discrete process, and opinions, even in 1969, could very well differ as to whether the time had come to make the changeover. For many companies the decision whether to unbundle was not entirely a foregone conclusion. Robert McDonald of Univac testified:

> Actually, we felt that there would be considerable anxiety in the marketplace as the result of IBM's decision and announcement to unbundle, and we felt it would be to our competitive advantage to maintain our previous pricing policy so that we could go to the customers, potential customers of IBM, and say to them that we would offer

you these services which we have in the past under the same pricing policy, and you know what you will be getting from us, and under the IBM unbundled pricing policy, only time will tell what your real prices will be; and I think this was effective, at least for a period of time.

.....

[W]e did see some increase in bookings over what we expected our bookings would have been had IBM not changed their policy . . . which we attributed to IBM's unbundling.[79]

Honeywell and RCA also hoped to gain by remaining bundled.[80]

National Cash Register (NCR) went some distance in the direction of unbundling. On October 1, 1969, it stated its belief "that each user of its computer systems must be provided with a certain essential amount of software, systems support, and educational services if he is to successfully install the system and begin to benefit from his investment. NCR believes that this *basic* package of supporting services must be the responsiblity of the equipment manufacturer."[81] NCR stated that "it will continue to be NCR's policy to provide, as part of the basic hardware price, that amount of software and support which will realistically insure that a prudent user will be able to install and successfully utilize his NCR computer system." An allowance based on the size of the system and amounting to "approximately 30 man-days of support for each $1,000 of monthly rental" was to be provided, with support above that level billed separately. The same principle was to apply to educational support and software, "including both applied programs and computer languages."[82]

On January 1, 1970, however, NCR announced a change in its policy:

After further evaluation, it has been decided *not* to price all basic and applied software and *not* to establish an allowance against which such chargeable software would be applied. The NCR software pricing plan will be to continue to establish pricing for software products on a *selective* basis, considering the value to the customer, uniqueness, and other factors.[83]

There was much less disagreement in 1969 and 1970 on the question of whether operating systems or systems control programming should be unbundled, and by the early 1970s only CDC had unbundled its operating system.[84] IBM did not unbundle such programming, stating: "System control programming is an essential part of a data processing system. It is fundamental to the operation and maintenance of the system and will be made available as part of the system."[85]

Such views were widely shared, for it was recognized that hardware and software "are now necessarily designed as one, designed to execute from the same architecture."[86] Indeed, Frederic Withington of Arthur D. Little wrote in June 1969, shortly before IBM's June 23 unbundling announcement, that systems software was "essential to the operation of modern computers and is designed contemporaneously with the machines. It is not possible to separate its development costs from those of the computers themselves, nor is it possible for the machine to operate without some version of the operating system." He concluded that this was a "complex area" and that "basic skeletons of the operating systems" were, at that time, "likely to be provided free with every machine . . . because there is no rational way to separate them."[87] Such views changed gradually during the 1970s and, as we shall see, IBM continued on the course it had set in 1968-69, separately pricing increasing amounts of its software and services in response to rapidly changing market requirements and technological advances.

8

LOST OPPORTUNITIES: THE EXITS OF GE AND RCA

GENERAL ELECTRIC

At the time of IBM's announcement of System/360, General Electric (GE) was (as it still is) a large corporation. From that time to the end of the 1960s, it was always in the top six of the *Fortune* 500. Its corporation-wide revenue grew from $5.1 billion in 1964 to $8.4 billion in 1969.[1] By contrast, IBM's corporate revenue was $3.2 billion in 1964 and $7.2 billion in 1969.[2] However, whereas most of IBM's domestic revenue during the period 1964-69 came from its EDP business,[3] virtually none of GE's did. At no time during that period was GE's U.S. EDP revenue more than 3.5 percent of its total U.S. revenue.[4]

In 1963 computers were a part of GE's "industrial components and materials area," which accounted for 28 percent of the firm's revenues. That area also included advanced controls for machine tools, Lexan plastics, silicone chemicals, component motors, appliance controls, and lamp ballasts. The remainder of GE's business was derived from consumer goods (26 percent of revenue), including appliances, television sets, and lamps; heavy capital goods (24 percent), including diesel electric locomotives and power-generating and -transmitting equipment; and defense sales (22 percent), including jet engines and missile guidance systems.[5]

Despite this, GE was potentially one of the most significant of IBM's competitors in the computer industry in the 1960s. Richard M. Bloch, who joined GE in 1968 as manager of the Advanced Systems Division, testified that GE "was probably the greatest electrical and electronic technical organization, technically oriented organization in the world, and with very strong financial resources."[6] John W. Weil, who was the manager of engineering for GE's Computer Department from 1964 to 1966, and thereafter the manager of its Advanced Systems and Technology Operation until 1970, testified that he believed that "GE had the resources and technological capability to become a major force in the computer industry."[7] That assessment was shared outside of GE.[8] With all that technological potential and financial power, GE was called the "sleeping giant."[9]

But, in the computer field at least, the "sleeping giant" never woke up. Its efforts in computers in the 1960s ended with the sale of most of its computer business to Honeywell in the merger that created Honeywell Information Systems. The story of how GE failed to capitalize on its advantages and succeed is a story of lack of corporate commitment, inadequate management, and a failure to keep up with the demands of the market as technology and competition advanced.

The 400 Series

During 1963, GE was marketing the GE 100 and 210 computers for banking applications (they were derived from the ERMA machine), the 304 (under license from NCR), and the 225.[10] In December 1963, GE announced its 400 series,[11] called the "GE line of the future which would be compatible throughout."[12] Among other potential customers, the 400 line was aimed at IBM 1401 users, for whom GE offered conversion aids.[13] According to Weil, the GE 400 series (which was not compatible with the 200 series) "was intended primarily for business data processing users, although it did have some features that could support engineering and scientific calculations, but strictly as a secondary objective."[14]

Within a few years after the announcement of IBM's System/360, however, "the distinction between a scientific computer and a business computer . . . had been erased."[15] As a result GE marketed the 400 for both scientific and business applications: "Can scientists and businessmen be happy with the same computer? Ask about a GE-400. Many installations have proved the GE-400 can handle engineering and scientific problems as easily as business problems." "So you see the GE-400's don't *just* mean business. They now offer you the broadest capabilities available today on a medium scale information system — all the way from everyday business runs to complex scientific problems."[16]

As we have seen, GE also reacted to IBM's 360 announcement by reducing prices on the 400 systems by 8-15 percent and abandoning extra shift charges, bringing the price/performance of those systems (roughly measured) into line with that of System/360.[17]

GE initially announced four models in its 400 line of "compatibles"; in fact, however, only two were ever delivered. Subsequent GE product announcements (the 600 and 100 series) were not compatible with the 400 series. In 1970, GE's Advanced Product Line Master Plan cited the failure to deliver all the 400 models that had been announced, as well as the incompatibility between 400 and 600 series computers, as one of the reasons why GE developed an "image of failing to follow through" in EDP.[18]

The 600 Series

GE announced its 600 series in July 1964, after the announcement of System/360.[19] At that time the 600 series consisted of the GE 625 and 635, which differed only in memory speed. Later, GE announced the 615, a "special configuration, slower memory speed version of the same 625/635 system"; the 645, associated with MIT in Project MAC; and, eventually, the 655, which reimplemented the 625/635 in higher-speed integrated circuits.[20] There were also "several compatible but physically different military versions."[21] When GE compared the 600 line against the IBM 360 as announced, it concluded that "depending upon exactly which model and details of usage and configuration, the 600 is either just a little more favorable or just a little less favorable than comparable members of the 360 series."[22] (As we have seen, IBM had made its own analyses of the competitive reactions to System/360 and improved its price/performance with the 360/65 and 360/75 before delivery.)

The 600 line was not as technically advanced as the System/360, however. Weil classified the 600 series as a "second generation solid-state computer."[23] Frederic Withington of Arthur D. Little wrote that the 600 series (and the 400) show "the same design emphasis on well-balanced, practical, but unspectacular systems. There are no technological innovations, and their basic speeds and specifications are no more than comparable to those of their competitors."[24]

> At present, GE's systems are somewhat handicapped because their peripheral equipment (particularly random-access file storage devices) is in some respects inferior to IBM's. GE says it is moving actively to remedy this and to equal IBM's peripheral equipment with products of its own manufacture.[25]

Nevertheless, according to Weil, the initial customer acceptance of the 625 and 635 was "extremely good, well beyond our expectations."[26]

One of the reasons for this was GE's success with users of the IBM 7090/7094 computers. GE had "carefully targeted as one of the markets for the GE 600 system the installed base of IBM's 7090's and 7094's" because the 7090/7094 "was at that time by far the leading scientific and engineering computer in the field, it had the largest number of such systems, so it was a large enough target." Further, since GE was itself a large user of the 7090/7094, the "members of these computer installations played a leading role among the user community of the 7090s and 7094s, so that . . . we had an enormous resource to draw on who understood that and the needs of that user very well."[27]

GE "designed the 600 system to feel as familiar as possible to a 7090 or 7094 user." Among other things, its peripheral equipment could accept both media and format from such users, and its software represented "a compatible superset, a software that would include the capabilities of what the user already had but would give him further extensions."[28] To aid conversion, GE provided a piece of hardware "called a 7090 Simulator, so that a user who purchased this piece of hardware and put it in his system could in fact run programs from the 7090 or 7094 without modification, or at least that was the hope. Most of the time it succeeded."[29] Conversion from the IBM 1401 was also assisted by a compatibility feature. This was done in order to enable users who had previously used 1401s as off-line devices in conjunction with the 7090 or 7094 (for example, tape-to-printer peripheral operations) to move both the applications previously done on the 7090/94 and the off-line functions run on the 1401 onto a single computer in the 600 line.[30]

As a consequence, when IBM announced its 360 line as incompatible with its own earlier series, the computer group at GE was

> initially at least overjoyed with what had occurred because it meant right at the time we were introducing a system designed to displace 7090's and 7094's, IBM had itself abandoned the 7094 and 7090 computer series and brought out an entirely different computer series, and it was our belief at that time that it would be easier, if you were a user, to convert from the 7090/7094 to the 600 series than it would be to convert to IBM's new 360 series. We regarded that as a fortuitous occurrence and potentially to our advantage.[31]

The user of the 7094 was "forced . . . to either go to a 360 or to some other competitive system, and we were sitting there with a system designed to make that conversion as easy as possible."[32] That, of course, was one of the risks that IBM was taking with the 360, and by 1964 GE, with its 400 and 600, and Honeywell, with its 200, were attempting to take advantage of the 360's incompatibility with previous IBM lines.

The GE 600 series marketing strategy probably was based in part on the ability of the 7090 users who leased the 7090 to terminate their leases in a relatively short time and send the IBM equipment back to IBM.[33] In Weil's judgment, "the GE 600 competed well with the IBM 7094."[34] He estimated that GE acquired between 10 and 20 percent of the IBM 7090/94 base.[35]

Naturally, in competing for conversion of the 7090/94 customer as well as for other business, GE was competing against the larger of the newer System/360 IBM computers as well, primarily the 360/65 and 360/67. (Later, about 1970, the 600 series competed against the 370/145, the 155, and — less frequently — the 165.)[36] Thus, in "targeting" the 600 line against the 7090/94, GE in part paid a price for its success. Weil testified that the GE 600 competed with the 360/65 "perhaps less well" than with the 7094 "because it was very specifically targeted at the 7090/7094."[37]

Weil testified that the 600 line was originally intended "primarily for engineering and scientific computation, but with specific features that would make it attractive as well for business and commercial application, but that in this case was the secondary market."[38] GE "had the ability to use the growing low cost of logic to provide a number of features aimed at these several markets,"[39] however, reflecting the fact that "since the early sixties it really hasn't been economically important to design a computer system only for business or only for scientific applications, except at the extreme ends of this spectrum, where you were trying to do as much scientific calculation as you possibly can within the limits of the technology."[40] As a result, GE also included business-oriented features in its 600 line and marketed it for business as well as scientific applications.[41] In fact, "the customer base that we built up became more and more business-oriented with time."[42]

Examining the GE product line, Withington wrote in 1964: "GE also believes (and we agree) that in the large-computer area there are no longer significant distinctions between scientific and business machines, so the potential market for the 600 series and its successors is very large."[43]

GE's product line, then, is more analagous [*sic*] to IBM's than that of any other competitor. GE hopes to compete not by being different, but by doing the same things better: by providing a combination of hardware, software, price, and customer service which will appear superior. No competitor desiring a rapid increase in market share and profitability could afford to follow this approach. However, GE has repeatedly stated that its intention is to build a solid and major position in the computer industry: its approach is consonant with this goal.[44]

In part because it drew on GE's previous work with military computers, the 600 also had capabilities for real-time applications, although those capabilities "were used by very few of the actual users that we sold the machine to."[45] Among the real-time uses of the GE 600 were the data reduction and monitoring done in connection with the Apollo launch system.[46] The principal importance of the 600's real-time capabilities, however, was that they later proved very useful for time-sharing (discussed below), an area the importance of which GE was already thinking about at the time of announcement of the 600 series in July 1964.[47]

GE encountered difficulties in delivering the 625 and 635. Weil testified that:

We were attempting to bring to market simultaneously a new central hardware system, a new processor system, a new set of peripherals, and an entire new set of software.

On top of that this was the first time that General Electric had ever attempted to put together and market so large a system, and as a result of all of those factors at once, we had a great deal of difficulty making the systems perform to our customer's [*sic*] and our own satisfaction in the field. A combined set of hardware difficulties and software difficulties . . .

including

. . . a lot of difficulty with the magnetic tape units, we had some unreliability in the memories we were using . . .

and, because of the size and complexity of the system,

[O]ne of the difficulties we had was when something went wrong we had the problem of telling just what had gone wrong in this roomful of equipment, so diagnosis was a problem for us as well.[48]

The difficulty with the software "centered around the operating system called GECOS, which was . . . a comprehensive operating supervisor," among the first of such systems. "[I] t was ambitious in its design. We had a great deal of difficulty in getting it built, made reliable and made efficient."[49]

There were three versions of GECOS. GECOS I, which had originally been intended for the 625 and 635, was never brought to the field.

It died in our test rooms because it was clear that it was sufficiently scrambled up internally that it would not make a good product, and so GECOS II was constructed to take its place using the lessons that we had learned on GECOS I.

GECOS II was the first version of GECOS that was sent to the field, and while it had a good deal of difficulty when it went to the field, eventually, with much patching and baling wire, was made to operate satisfactorily.

GECOS III was initiated at that same time — at the time period that GECOS II was in the field again to make use of the lessons we had in bringing GECOS II to the field, to reflect them back in what we hoped then would be a clean design and a clean product, so that GECOS III would incorporate the lessons of our field experience.

It was started and it was brought to the field much later, I believe around 1968. . . .[50]

Weil echoed the theme of many computer people during the 1960s when he said that GE's problems resulted at least in part because it was attempting to develop a state-of-the-art software system.[51] (We have already discussed the similar problems faced by IBM.)

There were, however, two important differences between IBM's and GE's reaction to developing problems. First, the difficulties GE encountered with the 625 and the 635 did not result in delays of delivery dates, although Weil testified that "perhaps they should have. The difficulties occurred much too often out in the customers' installations." Second, in late 1966 or early 1967, the 600 series systems were withdrawn from the market and "put into . . . hibernation." GE continued to support the systems already sold but did not actively seek new sales. That hibernation period lasted for at least a year or two, and the systems were not marketed again until 1968.[52]

In the fast-moving computer business, withdrawal is a mistake. Whereas IBM, when confronted with similar difficulties, put all of its effort into solving them and keeping its customers satisfied, GE withdrew. Weil said "the hibernation of the 600 was a mistake"; "it led to a considerable undermining in the confidence of General Electric's offering of this class of system" and adversely affected GE's image in the computer industry.

When you buy a computer system, you are expecting a great deal from the man who — the company that supplies it to you. You want to make sure that they will still be in business; that they will stand behind any difficulties that your system has had, and that they will make it do what they told you it was going to do. And any indications that people were backing away from such a full commitment would surely reduce a customer's confidence in that particular vendor.[53]

There were direct financial consequences as well. In 1966 GE reported that "in the information systems business, current operating losses were higher than projected because of difficulties involved in meeting a very sharp increase in shipments, and because of expenses in integrating worldwide product offerings. Substantially increased costs were also encountered in getting some new systems into operation."[54] John L. Ingersoll, who had been financial manager of GE's information systems business in the late 1960s, testified that from 1965 to 1968 GE's difficulties with the 625 and 635 "were a major element in the financial results experienced by that segment of GE."[55]

Such difficulties, experienced with the first computers and software of the 600 line, were aggravated when it came to the development of time-sharing.

Time-Sharing

GE was involved in "two somewhat separate threads" in the development of time-sharing. The first of these, developed by Dartmouth with some help from GE, was

> a very effective small time sharing system which we then brought into our engineering organization and eventually modified, documented and offered as a product . . . initially on a system derived from the 225, later on a system derived from the 235, and eventually, very related, conceptually related systems were offered on the 400 line and on the 600 line.

Weil believed that this was the first commercial time-sharing offering.[56]

That system was "independent of the separate path which involved the more ambitious, technically, time sharing system based upon the 645 and the MULTICS software." That more ambitious development involved Bell Labs and MIT.[57] We have already considered how that development bore on IBM in our discussion of the 360/67 in Chapter 6. Now we examine it as it relates to the history of GE.

Early in 1964 the Project MAC organization at MIT, which had already developed a time-sharing system (CTSS) on a pair of IBM 7090s,[58] was "interested in developing an extremely advanced time sharing system." It approached a number of manufacturers "for a cooperative effort in that development."[59] GE proposed to Project MAC a version of the 635 system that "would be modified in accordance with some of the discussions we had had with them, and . . . would provide then a hardware base for the advanced time sharing system they wished to develop." In addition, GE "proposed working jointly with them in the development of the software that would reside on that hardware."[60]

In the summer of 1964, Project MAC selected GE over bids from IBM, Digital Equipment Corporation (which did place a $1 million peripheral processor, however), and others.[61] As we have seen, IBM believed that its rejection was due, at least in part, to the fact that it had proposed to implement time-sharing without dynamic relocation hardware. Weil confirmed that GE believed that "certain aspects of the 600 architesture [sic], the 600 system, as laid out, were more amenable to some of the things that MIT wanted to do than were either the 7094 based system or the 360 based system." "[W]e had a good meeting of minds, a good agreement on philosphy with the Project MAC team."[62] Project MAC and GE — and others in the industry — believed that computer systems were evolving toward "an information utility," based on the time-sharing concept, that would be of crucial importance to the future of computing.[63] That view, as we have seen, was also being brought home to IBM very strongly.

In addition to being in the forefront of the new wave, GE expected two additional benefits from its work with Project MAC. First,

> it was an opportunity for us to work with one of the organizations that was widely regarded as an advanced thought leader in the field, hence, we hoped to benefit technically from that work, but also because it was based upon 600 line hardware, even though it was largely incompatible with the 625/635, it would nonetheless provide a reflection on the 635 and 625 hardware in the minds of our prospective customers, so that the customers would feel that the machines they were buying were related to and that he might someday look forward to growing into the kind of applications that MIT and GE were developing on the 645.

Second, "it lent an aura of advancement to the rest of our commercial offerings."[64]

GE and MIT were not the only participants in Project MAC. Bell Labs was also to be involved in the development of the MULTICS system, "a system, hardware and software together, for carrying out a very advanced form of time sharing, a multiple access to extensive system facilities."[65]

The first GE system installed at MIT was a 635, which was "used as a development facility, but the project was aimed . . . at developing the MULTICS system, and a part of the MULTICS system was a special expanded version of the 635, which was later termed the 645." The 645 involved "major extensions to the central processor, primarily having to do with the way in which memory was addressed and accessed." "[T]here were hardware protection features" and a "high capacity input/output controller." "A very advanced form of dynamic relocation was included in the 645."[66]

In the fall of 1965, GE announced the 645 as a product at the Fall Joint Computer Conference.[67] In December it announced that it was working toward the "broad commercial availability" of the 645 system.[68] At the time of the public announcement of the 645, the software had not been developed and the 645 itself was not in existence. Within a year the 645 was withdrawn "because we began to realize that what we had on our hands was a research project and not a product."[69] GE never again offered the 645 as a product.[70]

While the 645 was intended "to provide a top-of-the-line prestige luster to the 600 line and to our other products, and also to be a prototype for future sophisticated time sharing systems," as it turned out, "because of its lateness and its difficulty, it represented very little to General Electric except a drain on its resources," although "some of the features that were pioneered in the 645 have since appeared elsewhere."[71] Despite its potential for future success, GE never put its principal marketing thrust on the 645.[72] The 645 was never delivered, and Project MAC received a system designated 636.[73]

Although Weil and others believed in 1964 and 1965 that the MULTICS system "could be technically feasibly designed," the participants in the Project MAC effort "underestimated the difficulty of successfully developing MULTICS."[74] "[T]he system operated in the way that [it] was originally intended about three years behind its own schedule." Weil testified that this was because of the difficulties of cooperation among MIT, Bell Labs, and GE, and because "the technical task that was being attempted was extremely sophisticated and many of the subjects were at the state of the art as it was then known, and it took a long time to iron out the details of implementing some of these important features."[75] Such problems occurred in other state-of-the-art software efforts, including those of IBM.[76]

False Starts

On a number of other occasions during the 1960s, GE began development of product lines that were canceled or greatly reduced. In the early 1960s a series known as WXYZ was in development at Phoenix. "WXYZ was a series of four systems of which the Z was to be the most powerful." By the time Weil became familiar with it, "only the X and the Y were under serious development." After "considerable evolution" the X eventually became the GE 400. "The Y was to be a rather sophisticated, larger system, but it was cancelled at the end of 1962 and its place in the market spectrum was eventually covered by the beginning of the 600 project." Neither the W nor the Z was ever delivered.[77]

Following the announcement of the 600 series of computers, GE considered a series of new product lines. An important event that led to such consideration was the acquisition of overseas affiliates, the Bull Company in France and the Olivetti Electronics Division (later known as GE Information Systems Italia) in Italy.[78] GE at that time was interested in producing "a world-wide product line which would cover the main portions of the product spectrum" and, as a result, a series of product lines was conceived.[79]

The first such line, the GE 100 line, was conceived during the tenure of Dr. Louis Rader. Rader joined GE in 1964 as vice-president and general manager of the Industrial Electronics Division and took over the GE Information Systems Division, which was formed in 1965.[80] The GE 100 line consisted primarily of three sets of processors that were to be manufactured in Italy, France, and the United States, and that GE intended to market throughout the world.[81] In 1966 Rader was transferred from the Information Systems Division to become general manager of a new division, the Industrial Process Control Division.[82] Despite the fact that several study groups recommended proceeding with the 100 line, Hershner Cross, who took over from Rader as general manager of the Information Systems Division in 1966, "overruled all the study groups and decided that the 100 line would be abandoned." (The GE Italian operation pursued the 100 line despite Cross's edict, however, because "they had a strong general manager.") Cross abandoned the 100 line "at the same time that he put the 600 into hibernation."[83]

After cancellation of the 100 line, GE began to consider different new product lines.

> Upon cancellation of the 100 line, one of the measures that was taken was to initiate a study centered in France, but with worldwide participation, to spec out a more advanced line than the 100 line that would serve the same general purpose.
>
> This project, known as Project Charley, met in Paris for a period of a number of months, but nothing broader came out of that beyond a book of proposed specifications.
>
> At that point there were some management and personnel changes in General Electric and it was about at this juncture that John Haanstra came to General Electric [from IBM], and he initiated the development of another line of computers, again to be worldwide and again to serve a broad spectrum.
>
> Eventually this line of machines was known as the ERW line. . . .[84]

The ERW line began in late 1966 and "lingered on for a while after that, but its principal effort was for eight or nine months, beginning in the fall of '66, into the spring of '67." After that,

> John Haanstra's responsibilities were changed and he was put in charge of the Phoenix operation. He lost his personal identification with this worldwide product line and instead became a champion of what was going on in Phoenix, which of course was very heavily the 600.
>
> The ERW line was largely leaderless for a period of time. . . .
>
> Then Dick Bloch came to General Electric and he instituted a line, I believe initially called the 700 line and eventually called APL, which was his conception of a worldwide, broad spectrum computer line.[85]

This was in 1968.[86] Haanstra, who had been recruited from IBM to lead the GE computer operations in 1968, was moved to Phoenix less than a year later, then was killed in a plane crash in 1969. None of these projects ever resulted in delivered products.[87]

Bloch, who came to General Electric from Honeywell via Auerbach Corporation and succeeded Haanstra as general manager of the Advanced Development and Resources Planning Division, testified that when he arrived, there had been "several starts in the direction of an advanced product line."[88] According to Bloch, while there were "some very, very excellent developments afoot," the operation was poorly organized, and "one would have wondered how this would ever be put together into a line." One problem was that there were various development activities under way under different auspices throughout the company.[89]

> GE previously was typified to me as a company of great potential in terms of spot accomplishments in various areas — software, hardware, new attacks, in concept and in hardware too. But the real question was, how was it all going to be put together? That was one side of it. The other side of it was that nobody thought about the total plan, the total objective, what this business data processing world was all about.[90]

Bloch believed "the decentralized organizational approach of General Electric adversely affected their attempt to develop an integrated line of computer products," and individual departments took over responsibilities for obsolescent lines, promoting their own interests.[91] The problem was that GE, unlike IBM, was unable to tie together under central control this disparate collection of products in several different lines produced and marketed throughout the world.[92] What Bloch called GE's "decentralized organizational approach" was a substantial part of its downfall.

The Management of GE's Computer Operation

General Electric encountered substantial difficulties in managing its computer operation. It had a constant turnover of management personnel running its computer business during 1964-70. During that time GE ran through a series of managers and other key personnel whose jobs constantly changed and who were succeeded by people with little computer experience.[93] The result was that projects begun were abandoned, and no continuity of purpose or product development existed. But the problems went deeper than that.

According to Weil, one of the "major mistakes" that GE made in managing its computer business stemmed from its "very strong" belief

> in the philosophy of professional management. This basically is that management is a profession and a good manager can manage any kind of business.
> This in fact works quite well for a mature or gradually declining business, where a man put into a business can model his behavior upon that of his predecessor's [*sic*] and then make adjustments as he learns what's really going on. In a rapidly evolving business, however, his predecessor's behavior, especially if it was unsuccessful, is a very poor model. And since he knows nothing about the business, he is a professional manager and came from Toaster or Welding, or whatever it may be, elsewhere in the General Electric Company, he really could not understand what he was managing.
> . . . .
> But if you have a series of these managers above each other they feel they are in trouble, they now must do something. What can they

do? They do not understand the business well. So the only thing they can do is to replace the man working for them.

So the net result of this was, as we got into difficulties, especially in bringing the 600 to market thereafter, we had a sequence of people running General Electric's computer business, none of whom, except when we come to Dick Bloch and John Haanstra — and, again, they were not in charge of the computer business but were key people — none of whom were experts in the computer business. Furthermore, we had a new one every eighteen months or so.

So that General Electric never developed experienced management that understood the computer business, and I believe this was a major part of why General Electric never learned how to manage the business properly.[94]

This philosophy led to GE's having "a great deal of difficulty . . . in entering dramatically new fields," although it was "extremely successful in managing mature businesses and declining business [es] ."[95] This was undoubtedly associated with GE's decision, discussed below, to remain with its "core" businesses rather than continuing in computers.

GE's management problems were perceived outside of GE as well.[96] In 1970 GE's plan for its future product (then known as Advanced Product Line, APL) recognized that among the "negative factors" affecting GE's image in the computer industry were (1) GE's "management indecision and replacement," (2) GE's "professional manager" image, (3) GE's "lack of long-term commitment," and (4) GE's "loss of key personnel."[97] At Southern Railway, John Jones, vice-president of management information services, reached the conclusion "that General Electric was not a viable competitor, not one that I would consider selecting in the environment that I was in at Southern Railway Company and with the project that I had before me to complete." He testified:

> [T] hrough personal knowledge at several levels in the company, I was at least to some extent aware of the activities of the Computer Division of General Electric, and it was my view that there were some serious problems in terms of how they were managing that function, and it was my concern that I would not be able to obtain the support and continuing responsiveness from General Electric that I would judge to be critical in the system that we were considering installing.
>
> As a result of those concerns, despite the fact that we had been a large customer of General Electric in other areas, it was my conclusion that I did not want to take on the risk of, or what I perceived to be a risk, of considering installing General Electric equipment.[98]

Jones's views crystallized in 1967, about the same time that GE's difficulties were being made public in the form of the "hibernation" of the 600 system.

Rotation of management meant a lack of continuity in decision making, and another difficulty, as already observed, was a decentralization of decision-making responsibility. Bloch testified that

GE operated in a decentralized fashion, with profit centers usually at the departmental level, and for reasons which I do not pretend to comprehend, the top management of the company allowed these growths to occur of quite competent, in their own right, groups, both here and overseas.

Overseas, of course, one can understand some of that, because there was outright acquisition. But even here there were [*sic*] a multiplicity of centers and there was a proliferation of activity; multiple peripheral devices of the same general character being developed at different places at the same time; a lack of coordination from any central area whatsoever.

Our plan was, indeed, to make use of the facilities worldwide but to have it completely controlled and specified, all standards set, from the central operation in New York. And this was a new philosophy to them entirely. And if this was indeed a new philosophy to them, then I can understand why they had problems earlier.[99]

Bloch had "no question" in his mind but that "the decentralized organizational approach of General Electric adversely affected their attempt to develop an integrated line of computer products." He encountered "substantial resistance" to his attempt to limit the decentralization, which reflected GE's general management philosophy.[100]

The Computer Department was always buried deep in the organizational structure. In 1963 it had been within the Industrial Electronics Division, which in turn was part of the Industrial Group.[101] In 1968 GE formed the Information Systems Group, one of ten groups containing 50 to 60 divisions and, in turn, 130 or 140 separate departments.[102]

Because computers were so far down in its organizational structure and because it had so many other products to attend to, GE failed to mobilize its resources in computers to the extent necessary. Weil testified that among the "major mistakes which GE made in the management of its computer business" were two related to this. First,

a lot of ambitious and difficult tasks were attempted which turned out to be more difficult and more ambitious perhaps than was appreciated when we started.

Secondly, General Electric was never fully committed to its computer business. It was always a business . . . that General Electric could live without. So that if troubles came or budgets were suddenly bigger than had been expected, there was always this reconsideration of "Is this really a business we want to be in? And how do we prevent this from draining the profits of our other businesses?" It was not the strong commitment felt by those of us actually in the computer business of General Electric.[103]

He testified that there were differences, for example, between GE's commitment to the computer industry and its commitment to the atomic power business, to which it "manifested a greater commitment to success." Nuclear power was regarded as "an adjunct to that core of business of the company" consisting of the supplying of power generation equipment. "It was clear that the mission of the nuclear power business was: We don't know whether there is a business, but if there will be a nuclear power business, you will be one of the leading competitors." On the other hand, the "equivalent charge" for the computer business would have been "We are sure there will be a computer business, now you must demonstrate that you can compete."[104]

Similarly, Bloch testified that, when he joined GE in 1968:

> They were in the business. They had been in for some period of time furnishing general purpose computing equipment. My feeling was, however, that it was always tainted with some tentativeness or speculativeness on the part of the company as a long term commitment to the field. My feeling was that if it turned out to be a great success, the company would be delighted; if it turned out not to be a great success, the company could extinguish parts or all of its activity in the field without necessarily any great remorse.[105]

GE's lack of full commitment was not seen merely in the eyes of those who worked in its computer activities. Reginald H. Jones, chairman of the board and chief executive officer of GE at the time of his testimony, and a member of the Ventures Task Force that recommended GE's exit (as described below), testified that he and his predecessor, Fred J. Borch, had both agreed with their predecessor, GE's former chairman, Ralph Cordiner, who said about GE's computer business: "General Electric's mistake was that it failed to realize the opportunity and therefore made an inadequate allocation of resources, both human and physical, to the business."[106]

Jones testified that "as early as the 1950's, if we had increased substantially the technical manpower assigned to the business, if we had increased at that time the financial resources required for the business, they would have been much smaller in terms of absolute numbers than they would have been, let's say, some fifteen years later."[107] "We never did make the allocation of resources to the business that were warranted."[108] The contrast with IBM is striking.

GE's Position in the Late 1960s

By 1968 GE had computer research, engineering, and manufacturing facilities at 13 locations in 5 countries with a worldwide sales and service organization of 8,000 employees.[109] It reported that "the company's investments in computer technology have given us an expanded worldwide base in what has been characterized as the world's fastest growing business. Again, our developing capability to serve this industry is leading to further new opportunities."[110] In 1968 GE also broadened its line of input-output and storage devices and extended its time-sharing services. By the end of that year, more than 50 GE time-sharing systems were in place, serving about 100,000 customers in 17 countries around the world. GE reported that this area of the business was "growing even faster than the computer equipment sector."[111]

GE's 1968 sales of information systems were "well above those of 1967 and with operating losses substantially reduced."[112] In 1969 GE announced the GE-655, "the most powerful member of the large-scale GE 600 line," which "had its best year in shipments and orders." According to the GE 1969 Annual Report, the GE-400 line also had a successful year.[113] For the year ended December 31, 1969, the GE computer operations that Honeywell acquired showed a profit.[114] Those operations continued to show a profit for Honeywell in 1970.[115]

Despite these improvements, GE was still in trouble. Yet if, as its later chairman, Reginald Jones, testified, GE "did not appreciate the problem that was building in the late Sixties,"[116] others did. Withington wrote in 1969:

> During 1968, General Electric was able to demonstrate completely successful operation of its GECOS-III operating system for the 625 and 635 computers. . . . The 625 and 635 (recently joined by a smaller 615) are continuing to sell largely because of the success of GECOS-III, but the machines themselves are obsolescent from the point of view of cost-effectiveness. It is to be presumed that General Electric has in development compatible successor machines which can capitalize on GECOS-III, but which will show better performance. When this new line is announced, General Electric will be in a position to make a strong resurgence in the large machine area.

Withington judged the GE-400 line "obsolescent" as well, and said, "General Electric's future position is dependent on the timing and success of the new line."[117] As we have seen, GE had made several false starts in the development of "compatible successor machines" and was not, in fact, "in a position to make a strong resurgence."

As of 1969 GE had several incompatible lines, which had been "developed at different times in different places, and to a great extent under different management."[118] Bloch, who came to GE in 1968, concluded that the large 600 series was of diminishing importance for the future because of a trend toward decentralized computing and smaller processors.[119] GE's smaller processors, the 100, 200, and 400 series, however,

> were beyond their useful time in terms of state of the art. They were in place doing their work, except that we were simply facing the natural problem of the field, and that is with time. You get to a point in which the price/performance is so improved over equipment of days of yore that it is clear that those users are going to move to new equipment, and either you are going to provide that new equipment or your competitors are going to provide it.[120]

The Ventures Task Force, organized in late 1969 to consider GE's future in the computer business and other fields, reported in April 1970 that "most current product lines are obsolete" and that GE had a "lagging technical position in mainframes, peripherals and manufacturing process technology."[121]

This was not a secret held within GE. GE's reputation in the computer industry had suffered badly from its management failures and product obsolescence. Thus, in January 1970 the Advanced Product Line Master Plan recognized that GE's image in the computer industry was poor:

General Electric has the reputation of the "sleeping giant" of the information systems industry, with vast capabilities and resources which have yet to be marshalled for a determined attack on IBM.

GE's image is one of failure to follow through, as characterized by:

- An enviable image in the banking industry was built through the success of the ERMA project and GE's leadership in development of Magnetic Ink Character Recognition standards. This image was subsequently lost due to neglect.
- In 1963, GE assumed a leadership position in the area of communication systems and communications control concepts with the announcement of the DATANET-30. Subsequently, GE has lost its leadership in the field by not following up with any improvements until recent announcements in 1969.
- In the area of system capability, GE coined the phrase, "The Compatibles". When the GE-400 line was introduced, it was characterized as the GE line of the future which would be compatible throughout. Although GE announced four members (GE-425, GE-435, GE-455, GE-465) of this line, it delivered only two.
- Since announcement of the GE-400 line, GE has made two other major line announcements: the GE-600 line, which is not compatible with the GE-400 line; and the GE-100 line, which is compatible with neither. In fact, GE currently supports seven mutually incompatible product lines.
- In 1964, GE recognized the way of the future by an aggressive advertising and promotional campaign with regard to direct access. It indicated that direct access was the way of the future and announced a line of disc storage devices to support this assertion. Since then GE has not followed through on this commitment even though the initial prognostications proved to be accurate.

A brief summary of GE's image with respect to the various product lines includes:

GAMMA 10 — an ideal model for a beginner.
GE-50 — excellent for new users, but no compatible upgrade.
GAMMA 30 — an obsolete machine with no compatible upgrade.
GE-200 — an obsolete line with no compatible upgrade.
GE-100 — a good family of products.
GE-400 — a relatively obsolete line with no compatible upgrade.

GE-600 — a reasonably good line with a need for a higher member (a la the GE-655). Good operating system software — among the best in the industry.

As long as the user is able to remain within a given one of the seven product lines, he is reasonably satisfied.

Measures of customer loyalty appear to fluctuate from year to year, but are generally below IBM and appear to be consistently below the industry average. This loyalty is understandably low when customers must move up from the product line which they are currently utilizing.[122]

By contrast, IBM had integrated its product line in 1964 and was about to introduce System/370, the compatible successor to System/360.

The Advanced Product Line

Plainly, if GE was to overcome its problems, it needed a new product line. This was to be Bloch's task when he joined the company in 1968.[123] This new line was to be "a single integrated line to be marketed on a worldwide basis."[124] GE's plan was to achieve the "number two position" in the field:

We could not also see a company such as GE being satisfied with a $50,000,000 business, say, in some convenient corner of the field, even if it were able to make a profit there, which might indeed happen, because a business that size is insignificant in the GE scheme of things.[125]

As a result of this goal, GE's advanced product line (APL) was to "attack" everything from the $500-a-month rental to the $70,000- or $80,000-a-month rental, which, as Bloch put it, "is a tremendous range." Of course, GE was attacking IBM and "in particular attacking the IBM 360 series, and not only the 360 series, but what we surmised was coming soon, and which became the 370 series."[126] Bloch testified that had the APL line ever been completed, it would have been a "more ambitious . . . or broader, more comprehensive, line than any that was in existence in the year 1970 — or '69 . . . with the exception of IBM."[127]

Bloch felt the situation was urgent:

The importance was simply that of time costing the company its future position in the field. By delaying the time at which we could announce and ship these systems, we would be, it was my feeling and generally agreed, losing some of our current base.

Secondly, IBM was, I thought, much more vulnerable at the earlier time within this period, that is, in the earlier seventies, and that every month that could be compressed with respect to the schedule meant an ability to tackle IBM more readily and to preserve our customers

. . . the present GE CPL [current product line] customers who had obsoleting [*sic*] equipment. And there was the danger, thus, of their moving elsewhere.[128]

The APL line was not to be compatible with the earlier GE lines, nor with System/360.[129] Nevertheless, it was planned that about 35 percent of anticipated worldwide shipments would be made to users of earlier GE lines, with another 35 percent to be shipped to users of competitors' systems, chiefly IBM. The remainder was to go to new users.[130] To effect the necessary conversions, GE planned to offer various emulation and conversion aids.[131]

The APL line had as primary targets "the 360/20, 25 and, to some extent, the 30 and, to still a lesser extent, the higher level machines in the IBM line, and also another IBM line."[132] GE targeted these users because of the difficulties that the users of the lower machines in the IBM line would have in converting from DOS to OS/360[133] and the fact that most of the programs written for such systems were written in higher-level languages.[134] To induce IBM's users to move to the new GE systems, a price/performance advantage of 20 to 40 percent against the 360 was thought to be required, and Bloch believed that it would be necessary for GE to match IBM's peripherals as well.[135] Basically, what GE was intending to do was to duplicate IBM's 360 plan of attack some five or more years after 360's announcement.

The strategy for APL preferred by the GE Information Systems Group called for the offering of the entire line at once, with shipments beginning in early 1973. This was estimated to require an $858 million expenditure before taxes, with an after-tax investment of $429 million for the years 1970-75.[136] Roughly half of the required investment was the financing that would be required for the 80 percent of a presumed successful APL line that was expected to be leased by customers. "It is one of the prices you pay for success."[137]

Ingersoll testified that it was "a general assumption" that the announcement of APL would have the overall effect of increasing revenue and income from GE's current product line, with an increase of $177 million from the combined product lines in 1970-75,[138] a positive effect not taken into account in the $858 million investment estimate.[139] Substantial net profits were expected to be earned in the late 1970s, after which a successor to the APL was contemplated.[140]

The APL plan, then, was an ambitious one, requiring large expenditures. It contemplated an across-the-board attack, even though profits might have been made in a "$50 million business" without such an attack. Further, it had to be pursued immediately. As it turned out, it became just another false start.

The Ventures Task Force and the Decision to Disengage

The Ventures Task Force was formed by GE Chairman Fred J. Borch in the last quarter of 1969. It was asked to review GE's computer business, commercial jet engine business, and nuclear energy business.[141] In particular, the task force stated in its report that Borch "specifically impressed upon us the urgency of our finding some way to arrest the heavy continuing drain on our assets resulting from these major new ventures" (as distinguished from GE's "core" busnesses).[142] The task force "adopted two broad criteria as the bases for our efforts to evaluate each available strategy; the risks and potential rewards inherent in each strategy and impact of each strategy on corporate earnings."[143]

Corporate earnings were a problem. GE's earnings per share had "plateaued" from 1965 to 1969, creating "a dismal record."[144] In 1969 earnings had declined because of an extensive strike.[145] As a result GE's stock price had declined 34 percent from 1965 through 1969, a poor performance compared either with the stock market averages or with Westinghouse. As the task force put it: "Stockholder impatience is indeed understandable."[146]

The members of the Ventures Task Force — Reginald Jones, Jack McKitterick, and Robert Estes — were corporate officers, but not one of them had any responsibility for the computer business or the GE Information Systems Group.[147] Their work on the task force was a part-time assignment, and they studied the EDP companies that GE met in the marketplace only "in a superficial way," in order to understand the strategy, the types of equipment, and the "markets" to be served by "each of the major entrants in the business."[148] Jones testified that "it was not an exhaustive analysis of the computer business. It was an analysis that I think developed a fair comprehension of General Electric's position in the computer business, but I wouldn't characterize it as an in-depth study."[149]

Of the three new "ventures" — computers, jet engines, and nuclear energy — the Ventures Task Force studied computers first. This was because the computer business "did not have long-range, long-standing contractual commitments to deliver product[s] over an extended period of years," as did the nuclear energy, and to a lesser extent the jet engine, business.[150]

The task force ultimately reached the conclusion that GE should "disengage by combining its computer business with that of some other computer manufacturer,"[151] despite the fact that it found that in the computer market "great size and very rapid growth make for a challenging opportunity," with the U.S. and European businesses projected to double in the next five years.[152] It listed a number of negative factors affecting GE: "substantial operating losses," "heavy debt obligations and interest burden," "obsolete product lines," and "poor reputation and image."[153] It stated that GE had

> Limited technical strength other than in data management and multiprocessing software and communication equipment.
>
> Major product lines obsolete, complete but incompatible. Not vertically integrated. Weak in peripherals, mass storage and terminals.[154]

Among listed "Critical Future Problems" were

Across the board system obsolescence.

Vulnerability of PARC [installed base] to competition — lack of specialization. Customer loyalty now under 80%, lowest of any competitor.

Lagging technical position in main frames, peripherals, and manufacturing process technology.[155]

GE's installed base was termed "already obsolete and vulnerable," with the following conclusion: "Time is not on our side."[156] The task force stated that "we need to be realistic about the relatively poor reputation and image we enjoy as a computer equipment manufacturer."[157] Jones testified: "[W]e were not doing the job that was satisfying the customer to the extent that certain competitors were."[158]

The task force "attempted to evaluate the risks associated with the APL plans . . . from a broad business standpoint. . . . [It] did not undertake to verify the accuracy of specific details of the cost estimates, for example."[159] It concluded that the plan

> *conceptually* recognizes the current needs of the business and presents a goal that, if realized, would indeed place the company in a strong position in the business computer field. It is our conclusion, however, that the APL entails very high risks, and that it is doubtful that it could be kept to time, cost and system performance schedules. Even if General Electric were in a position to undertake such an ambitious program, we would not recommend that it invest the requested sums in such a hazardous project predicated on an all-out attack on IBM, one of the world's strongest corporations.
>
> Faced with the lack of earnings growth, but seeking to retain its image as a growth company, General Electric cannot, in our opinion, undertake *any* half-billion dollar venture, such as APL that produces substantial immediate net income losses.[160]

The APL plan, according to the task force, called for a fourfold expansion in GE total shipments in six years, with an expansion of 60 percent to 70 percent per year of its sales force, and "even so, productivity of GE['s] sales force must be twice as great per man as that of IBM."[161] The plan called for technology beyond the current state of the art, which required "invention by schedule in order to achieve its objectives."[162]

In fact, by late 1969 APL was not "well along" in its design and development, and "the software was still in fairly early specification form."[163] At the time of the Ventures Task Force, "detailed engineering specifications" and "firm cost estimates" were not available.[164]

Yet the world would not wait for GE to come up with its 360. The Ventures Task Force called IBM "a moving target," which Ingersoll interpreted to mean that "we at General Electric should assume that IBM would not be a stationary object, it would be a dynamic situation, and the conditions . . . might well change." "[I] t was in effect a high risk to assume that the conditions and evaluations . . . would remain constant, that is, that the comparisions would be subject to change as IBM made plans and introduced its own products."[165] Similarly, the Ventures Task Force and its support staff felt that "it was a high risk assumption" to assume that competitors other than IBM "would stand still with respect to market share."[166]

Jones testified that, as a result, the Ventures Task Force concluded "that the life of a family of computers was quite limited," something in the range of four to six years, "and that you did not bring out a family of products that simply met the price/performance characteristics of the then existing competition. You had to bring out something that would exceed the price/performance of the existing competition because you knew full well that they were going to be moving ahead of you. It is a constant leap frogging game."[167] It was a lesson that GE learned too late and IBM had learned well before.

The Ventures Task Force, of course, had not been called together simply to consider computers. GE's management was concerned with improving the profitability of the company as a whole. It was therefore concerned with the immediate impact of APL on GE's earnings — which impact, from 1970 to 1975, the APL plan had projected to be negative.[168] The Ventures Task Force concluded that "General Electric can ill afford the financial resources needed for an all-out drive for position in this industry, basically because of the needs of other businesses within its scope."[169] The "core" businesses needed "more rather than less support, and the company's immediate earnings goals can only be met from these businesses."[170]

The Ventures Task Force concluded that:

> For the first time in our generation, at least, we face the necessity for an allocation of corporate resources which are not adequate to meet all of our readily identifiable needs — during a period when the company is under special pressure to demonstrate its ability to grow earnings. The general economic climate is not favorable; the capital markets are severely depressed; credit is costly and may be assumed to become progressively less available; inflation has forced higher labor costs on the company following the longest strike in the company's history.[171]

Disengagement in nuclear energy and jet engines was "not an available option" because of GE's contractual commitments.[172] While nuclear reactors, where 20 years of investment had yet to bring a profit,[173] were considered part of GE's "core business" ("essentially those [businesses] that dealt with the generation, transmission, and distribution of the electrical energy in terms of the equipment to do all those jobs, plus the equipment that would utilize electrical energy"), and jet engines were considered "a spin-off of the core, but . . . very closely related," GE never "viewed the computer business as being part of its basic core."[174]

The decision was made to merge a large part of the business with Honeywell, both companies transferring their business computer operations to a new

Honeywell subsidiary. GE retained an interest in the new company and successfully continued its "own independent development of businesses in the promising areas of process computers, computer time-sharing and data communications equipment."[175] It would have liked to take a controlling interest in the new venture, but feared the disapproval of the Antitrust Division.[176]

Did GE Lose Money?

It is questionable whether GE lost much, if any, money in the course of its computer operations or, at least, whether it would have lost money thenceforward had it not sold part of its operations to Honeywell.

A report by Peat, Marwick & Mitchell, GE's outside auditors, showed that GE's domestic business-computer operations lost approximately $163 million in the period 1957 through September 1970.[177] About 10-15 percent of this figure was an allocation of corporate overhead expense to GE's domestic business-computer operation.[178]

Moreover, the $163 million included "the cost of developing the equipment incurred by the Domestic Business Computer Operations that were subsequently transferred to Honeywell — the development, that is, through the date of the transfer."[179] Hence, in order to evaluate whether GE would have ultimately suffered losses had it not sold part of its operations to Honeywell, one must consider the profit stream that would have resulted from those sunk expenses.

According to GE's proxy statement, the portion of GE's computer operations that was sold to Honeywell had an after-tax profit for 1969.[180] Further, in December 1969, GE's Information Systems Group estimated that the net income from its current computer product lines for 1970-75 would be $173 million (this estimate also included a positive impact of APL on current products).[181] The Ventures Task Force in April 1970 estimated that the current product line would bring in $821 million in revenue and $164 million in net income in the years following 1969, regardless of APL (it was evaluating the business from the point of view of a prospective buyer).[182]

The terms of the sale, which was announced on May 20, 1970, were as follows. The two companies formed Honeywell Information Systems (HIS), and GE received an 18.5 percent interest in it. In addition, GE received 1.5 million shares of Honeywell common stock and $110 million of Honeywell subordinated notes (later converted to additional shares of Honeywell common).[183] At the time GE recorded a profit of $1.7 million on the transaction. That amount was quite conservative, GE having undervalued its Honeywell stock, which had a market value of about $120 million.[184] Further, Ingersoll testified that GE valued its minority interest in HIS at "approximately $32 million," "substantially less than the net book value of that minority interest as determined by Honeywell," which valued it at "at least a hundred million dollars."[185] In 1971 GE received 1,025,432 shares of Honeywell stock in exchange for the $110 million in notes.[186] Those shares had an average market value of about

$113.2 million in 1971.[187] In 1976 GE exchanged about one-third of its interest in HIS for 800,000 shares of Honeywell stock and, in 1977, the remaining two-thirds for another 1,400,000 shares.[188] The Honeywell stock received in 1976 had an average market value in that year of about $35.6 million; the stock received in 1977 had an average market value in that year of about $68.5 million. GE sold the Honeywell stock over the years, disposing of the last in 1978.[189]

Taking all these things into account, even allowing for the difference in timing and inflation between the expenditures made in the early 1960s and the returns received from the Honeywell sale, GE appears to have been a net gainer in the computer industry.

RCA

As we have seen, the 1950s were a stagnant period for RCA's computer business. During the early 1960s the firm experienced several problems that continued to retard its growth in computers, in particular the failure of the 601 and its on-again, off-again peripherals development. Toward the middle of 1963, RCA had stopped marketing the failed 601; the 501 was "starting to decline"; and RCA was marketing only one computer model, the 301.[190]

The 3301

The RCA 3301 was announced on August 20, 1963.[191] Edwin S. McCollister, who joined RCA in 1961 as vice-president of marketing for the Computer Division and remained in a similar position until leaving at the end of 1971, called the 3301 an "interim product," designed and marketed by RCA "to round out our overall product program . . . [by] tak[ing] the place of the 601."[192] The 3301

> was not a new design. It wasn't intended to be the foundation of a future line of products; rather, it was a product that we could develop relatively quickly, at relatively low engineering expense, that would give us an additional offering to take the place of the 601, and that in a sense would give us time to get on with a complete new product program in the longer range future.[193]

RCA described the 3301 as an "all purpose computer" that "features advanced communications devices and arithmetic circuitry to make it equally powerful for scientific equation solving, super fast business data processing, instantaneous (real-time) management control, and high-speed data communications."[194] Although a more successful product than the 601, the 3301's success was limited for two reasons: poor peripherals and its "eclipse" by the announcement of the Spectra 70 series less than a year and a half later.[195]

RCA had been beset by problems with the peripherals used on its 501 and 301 systems. According to Arthur D. Beard, chief engineer of RCA's Computer Division from 1962 to 1970, the peripherals on the 3301 "prevented the computer system from achieving its full throughput capabilities."[196] Although RCA had resumed manufacturing its own peripherals in 1962, time and continuity of effort had been lost, and the firm was largely "constrained to live with the peripherals that were then existing on the 301 or which could be made available from outside suppliers."[197]

RCA also experienced problems with a peripheral unit of its own manufacture, the RACE mass storage unit. The RACE unit was a storage device that used magnetic cards. Each card

> had to be extracted from a magazine, put in a channel that carried it to a revolving drum, held on the drum while it rotated past a reading head, where the information was read or reported, and then the card had to be returned to the magazine from whence it came.
>
> And this was a very, very complex mechanism and a very difficult technical task.[198]

RACE was designed to provide random-access storage for the 3301, for RCA had no disk drive of its own to offer with that computer.[199] Compared with IBM's 2311 disk drive, announced with System/360 in April 1964, RACE was "much smaller" in terms of storage, but "considerably faster" in terms of access time. Thus, for the application mix of some users, RACE, when operating properly, was superior to a disk drive, while under other circumstances, the disk drive was superior.[200]

The major problem with RACE was that it was not reliable. Withington classified RACE as "a major product failure."[201] McCollister explained why:

> [T]he cards wore out . . . the cards were damaged in transit . . . sometimes there was a failure to select the proper card . . . it was a tedious process to replace a card in the file when it was beginning to wear out and, indeed, to detect when it was beginning to wear out.

Moreover, even when operational, the RACE unit was "unable to meet the speed of accessibility that had originally been specified in the product."[202]

The success of the 3301 was also limited by RCA's introduction of a new series only a little more than a year after the 3301 was announced. The announcement of the Spectra 70 series in December 1964 "eclipsed" and "superseded" the 3301.[203] Potential customers of the 3301 were encouraged to obtain Spectra 70 computers rather than the 3301. For example, RCA provided emulation of the 301 on the Spectra 70 but not on the 3301.[204] Further, because RCA provided no emulation from the 3301 to Spectra 70 or to any other system, 3301 users had nowhere to go in the RCA line without converting their programs. The 3301 was a dead end.[205]

The Spectra 70 Series

IBM announced its System/360 on April 7, 1964. Beginning "shortly" after the announcement, RCA formulated the "design specifications" for its Spectra series. Those specifications were done "in [a] preliminary fashion" around July or August 1964.[206]

The Spectra 70 series eventually comprised eight models — the 70/15, 70/25, 70/35, 70/45, 70/46, 70/55, 70/60, and 70/61. The sizes of the processors increased in numerical order, and the 70/46 and 70/61 were intended to offer time-sharing capabilities. In December 1964, RCA announced the 70/15, 70/25, 70/45, and 70/55.[207] The 70/35 was announced in September 1965; the 70/46 was announced in 1967; the 70/60 and 70/61 were not announced until 1969.[208]

The status of development of the Spectra 70 series at the time of announcement was in sharp contrast with that of System/360 in April 1964 (as described in Chapter 5). At RCA, at the time of announcement, no prototype of any of the systems was in existence. A prototype of the first machine was not built until the middle of 1965, at which time prototypes of most of the control units were also built.[209] Deliveries of the "small systems" began in 1965 and those of the "larger systems" in 1966.[210]

Four aspects of the Spectra 70 series are particularly important: its attempt at compatibility with System/360, its ability to perform commercial and scientific applications, the problems RCA encountered, and its success.

Compatibility with System/360

In a decision that affected both the Spectra 70 and its successor, the RCA series, RCA decided to make its Spectra 70 series compatible (that is, able to use the same application programs with little or no modification) with IBM's System/360. By doing so, RCA hoped to be able to persuade substantial numbers of 360 users to move to the Spectra series.[211] In particular, RCA expected to aim its marketing efforts at those 360 users who wanted to obtain larger or more functional equipment.[212] Moreover, it was expected that many IBM users with equipment on short-term lease could be induced to return that equipment and move to RCA's compatible machines for a price/performance advantage.[213] Hence, RCA wanted to offer a 15-20 percent better price/performance on its Spectra 70 equipment than IBM did on its 360 equipment.[214]

The pricing of the Spectra series was based upon two assumptions: (1) RCA assumed that in many cases Spectra would be offered to displace existing IBM computers and that some inducement would have to be given to persuade the IBM user to go to the trouble of replacing existing IBM computers and installing Spectras;[215] and (2) Spectra was delivered one to two years after IBM's System/360, and customers expected a new offering to have a price/performance advantage over older computers in terms of raw hardware performance.[216] This was particularly true in the case of Spectra because of the compatibility strategy, which meant that the Spectra series did not offer its own unique characteristics and functional capabilities.[217]

RCA employed the technique of "straddling" — placing its machines in terms of performance "approximately midway between a pair of IBM machines," using "what appeared to be the most commonly used configuration of equipments" for purposes of comparison.[218] Thus, the Spectra 45 was placed between the System/360 Model 40 and the Model 50, and the Spectra enjoyed a price/performance advantage over the 360 Model 40. The 360/50 was superior to the Spectra 45, however. A similar relation held with respect to the comparison between the Spectra 55 and the System/360 Models 50 and 65.[219] A later study showed that in general the roughly measured price/performances of CPU-memory combinations in the Spectra line were somewhat better than estimates for System/360 obtained by interpolation between IBM machines using multiple regression.[220]

A number of arguments against the compatibility strategy were raised at RCA: First, if IBM customers could switch easily to RCA machines, then RCA customers could also switch easily to IBM machines. RCA felt that it "had more to gain . . . than to lose," however, because IBM had many more existing customers than did RCA.[221]

Second, the similarity between Spectra and 360 "sharpened the comparisons" between RCA and IBM, making it "easier for the customer to analyze and quantify the differences" and putting "RCA in a position where its products could easily be criticized versus what IBM was offering. . . . If there were any deficiencies on RCA's part they would probably stand out as weaknesses."[222]

Third, RCA could have chosen "the most natural alternative . . . an extension of the 301, 3301 systems." This would have provided two advantages to RCA: First, it would have given it "a certain advantage" in marketing to the existing 3301 user base, because of the "software investment that [the users] had made in those machines." And it might have enabled RCA to provide a "superior architecture to what IBM had chosen."[223] In fact, RCA did not even provide emulation of the 3301 and, as we shall see, emulation of the 301 on the 70/35 was not attractive to 301 users.

RCA considered this important decision only briefly. McCollister testified that "because of the press of time in this case, I am not even sure that there was a formal product proposal."[224] The compatibility arguments prevailed, and two or three weeks after the announcement of System/360, RCA decided to make its Spectra series "as compatible with the 360 as the circumstances permitted."[225]

With the compatibility approach that RCA chose, its Spectra series had the same instruction set, instruction format, and word length as the 360. However, "in terms of the engineering implementation of this architecture, it was quite different between RCA and IBM. . . . If you took these machines apart, they were totally different machines . . . RCA used a completely different set of components."[226]

The Commercial and Scientific Abilities of the Spectra 70 Series

IBM's System/360 was aimed at all users, regardless of application. RCA, however, initially planned to market the Spectra systems for "commercial as distinct from scientific purposes . . . it was a stated strategy to all of our marketing people that we were selling to the business environment and precisely said that we did not have a computer to compete in the scientific arena."[227] Nevertheless, the design of the Spectra, as with IBM's 360, was flexible enough to be used for many purposes. Beard wrote in 1965 that among the "salient points" incorporated in the "basic design philosphy of the RCA Spectra 70 Series" was a "versatility for handling data processing, real time, and scientific applications from the small user to the very large."[228] Beard testified that the "primary reason" for making that a "salient feature of the design philosophy of the Spectra 70" was the following:

> We felt that as the customer world became more sophisticated that there would be a consolidation in the computer type operations of more than one type of function and therefore this versatility, which allowed for engineering and scientific type problems, communications problems, data processing, batch problems, information control systems . . . could be merged into one computer complex.[229]

Very soon after the initial delivery of the Spectra, the consolidation of the various types of functions that was anticipated in "the design philosophy of the Spectra 70" had come to pass with "some of the more advanced customers . . . ready for these types of systems in the latter half of the sixties, and certainly that trend has continued into the seventies."[230] By 1970 RCA was offering "Systems Scientific Services" for software support for the scientific user and was advertising the versatility of the Spectra 70:

> The emergence of third generation equipment with increased speed and storage capacity has brought us to the realization that scientific applications are within reach of almost every computer user. In the past these applications were confined to the big and expensive machines.
>
> . . . .
>
> For all your data problems — from simple accounting to management science programs — Spectra 70 offers a complete systems approach.
>
> Linear programming . . . statistical analysis . . . simulation . . . automatic machine tool control . . . all are key elements of management science operations. Spectra 70 handles these applications *and* your normal data processing at the same time.[231]

Problems with the Spectra 70 Series

The Spectra 70 series suffered from various problems that hurt its performance in the marketplace. Much of the equipment had reliability problems, which users took into account in choosing between RCA and IBM computers.[232] Joseph W. Rooney, who joined RCA as vice-president for marketing operations in 1969 and was president of the Computer Systems Division from 1970 to 1972,[233] complained about RCA's equipment as late as June 1970:

> RCA equipment apparently requires larger amounts of dedicated preventive maintenance time than that of our main competitor, IBM. Customers that have both our equipment and IBM equipment are aware of this, and this works to our detriment in the marketplace.

Moreover, according to Rooney, RCA's equipment was

> apparently more sensitive to environmental fluctuations than that of competition, particularly . . . IBM. This makes our customers somewhat sensitive to the differences between our maintenance policies and theirs. I am told, for example, the 360/30's can be left without any maintenance whatsoever for weeks on end. Yet, most of our systems require that we take the system from the customer for periods of time every day.[234]

For example, RCA's disks were "more sensitive to air conditioning" than those of IBM, "so, if you did not have the adequate amount of air conditioning, that could lead to the need for more preventive maintenance."[235]

RCA also encountered problems during the installation of the Spectras. In that regard Rooney testified that:

> RCA equipment was more difficult to install because of certain environmental factors. I remember the RCA equipment required more air-conditioning and power and I remember a problem of size, physical size of the units being involved, in terms of: if we replaced IBM, certain of our units would require more physical floor size than IBM equipment.[236]

These problems made it harder for RCA than for IBM to install its equipment.[237] It was reported to Rooney in 1970 that:

> In the area of installation, the RCA-IBM comparison is not restricted to just power and air-conditioning requirements. The problems are more profound, and bear directly on the equipment designed.
>
> The installation of RCA data processing equipment has historically been more difficult and more time consuming than that of our competition, particularly IBM's. Since the RCA marketing strategy is to sell to the IBM replacement market, the installation of RCA equipment is constantly being compared against IBM in an unfavorable light.[238]

During 1968 a portion of RCA's marketing force was diverted from seeking new business to coping with problems of installation. At that time the marketing force was very, very heavily occupied in working with existing customers on the installation of equipments which has [*sic*] been ordered at an earlier time. . . . [D]uring the year 1968 about 75 percent of [the time of] the marketing organization . . . was devoted to working with existing customers as opposed to seeking new business. . . . And this made very heavy demands upon the time and capabilities of our field marketing organization, and this impacted to some degree our ability to get new orders.[239]

RCA also found that its marketing force had to take time out from its normal selling efforts to deal with "[t]he problems of training customers in the programming of the equipment, in working with the customer in the installation of the equipment and the conversion of his system of processing work to this new method."[240]

In addition to the problems that pervaded the entire Spectra line, RCA experienced problems that were uniquely associated with particular models. Those problems caused the Spectra product line to vary greatly in its degree of success.

The Spectra 70/15 and 70/25. First deliveries of the smallest computers in the Spectra series, the 70/15 and 70/25, were made toward the end of 1965.[241] The 70/15 and 70/25 did not use integrated circuits and offered fewer functions than the rest of the Spectra line. This permitted them to be brought out earlier.[242]

The 70/15 and 70/25 were "relatively poor competitors," and thus not very successful.[243] The lack of a complete instruction set and the limited capability of the systems were liabilities.

It turned out that most customers wanted the systems which had the more complete capabilities, and also the 70/15 and 70/25 did not have the communications capabilities that the larger systems had and they did not have the programming language capabilities that the larger systems had.[244]

In addition, there was no COBOL capability provided on the 70/15 and 70/25;[245] this was an anomaly, since the 70/15 and 70/25 processors "in general left out the scientific type of instructions, and concentrated primarily on the data processing instructions."[246]

The 70/15s and 70/25s were also hurt by RCA's absence of "marketing emphasis."[247] McCollister testified that the competitive position of these two systems "really wasn't that important to the RCA computer division." They were "insurance policies" using "existing technology that we could bring to market, deliver to customers before we could deliver the larger systems."[248] As a result RCA put little effort into marketing the "relatively low cost, low margin" 70/15s and 70/25s.[249]

The shipments of 70/15s and 70/25s turned out to be "trivial." And RCA produced the 70/15s and 70/25s "only during part of the total life cycle of the Spectra 70 family."[250]

The Spectra 70/35, 70/45, and 70/55. The Spectra 70/35, 70/45, and 70/55 were larger processors than the 70/15 and 70/25. Deliveries of those systems were about "fifteen months or so behind IBM."[251] The 70/45 turned out to be the "most successful" of RCA's Spectra series.[252]

The 70/55 was less successful than the 70/45. It suffered from several problems:

1. The 70/55 "had serious memory problems. . . . We would get repeated errors in memory due to technical failure in the memory itself and this would bring the system down. [We] had a great deal of difficulty in maintaining the gear and keeping it up."[253] In fact, "there was some exchange of memories . . . some early number of the first machines had to have their memories replaced."[254]

2. RCA experienced "manufacturing problems with the [70/]55s, which gave us an unusual amount of field maintenance attention during the first year."[255]

3. The 70/55 was difficult to install and relocate.[256]

4. The 70/55 came out approximately a year after the 70/45 and tended to be "eclipsed" by the 70/60 and 70/61, which RCA brought out shortly thereafter.[257]

5. The 70/55 was hurt because it did not offer any emulation capability. Notwithstanding the fact that emulation capability was important to the success of the 70/45 system, the 70/55 did not emulate anything.[258]

The result of these failures of the 70/55 had a "dampening effect on the [RCA] sales force" and led to customer cancellations.[259]

As for the 70/35, it was priced too high to attract at least one important group of potential users. While it provided for emulation of the 301, that emulation "did not work successfully because the Spectra 35 was priced at such a high price that it was not a logical move for the 301 user to move up to the Spectra 35 system. . . . [Thus,] 301 users did not move up to the Spectra 35."[260]

The Spectra 70/46, 70/60, and 70/61. RCA's 1969 Annual Report described the 70/60 as a

[l]arge-scale . . . batch processor, which is designed to handle retail credit and reservation systems, automate production control, and service government and industry data banks.[261]

The 70/46 and 70/61 were time-sharing systems.

RCA began its work on time-sharing during 1967 (well after GE and IBM) by attempting with the 70/46 "an expansion of the 70/45."[262] McCollister testified that the hardware for the 70/46 was "in its elements identical" with that of the 70/45, with "the addition of some faster registers in the machine."

He estimated the hardware development effort of the 70/46 was "in the order of $2 million . . . because we made use of what was already existing in the 70/45."[263] The Spectra 70/61 had a relationship to the 70/60 in terms of design approach comparable with that of the 70/46 to the 70/45.[264]

As a result of "[t]he growing acceptance of remote computing" (timesharing), RCA foresaw "excellent potential for sales of data communications terminals and other peripheral equipment as well as for computer hardware" and expanded its manufacturing capabilities for peripheral computer equipment.[265] Orders for the 70/46 and 70/61 during 1969-71, however, were "less than had been projected in the forecasts because . . . the 70/46 had originally been planned as a system from which to gain experience with this class of product."[266] The marketing forecast was "excessively optimistic."[267]

RCA, like GE and IBM, ran into substantial difficulties developing its time-sharing software, called the Time Sharing Operating System (TSOS). The development of TSOS was "[b]y far the largest software development or largest programming system" that RCA had undertaken.[268] Despite this effort RCA had

> [i]mportant difficulties with . . . TSOS-VMOS which substantially impaired, certainly in early installations, the performance of the system as a whole, which includes both hardware and software.[269]

The problem with TSOS was that "there were bugs in it, which took time to get rid of, and it was late, as far as providing functions specified were concerned."[270] Rooney testified that:

> The Time Sharing Operating System was a form of virtual memory system that had a great deal of functional capability to offer, that was new and unique in the marketplace, but its reliability in performance was extremely poor and we had not achieved a high degree of reliability with that system while I was at RCA.
>
> . . . .
>
> The system was referred to as bombed out. There would be a problem. It would essentially go down. There had been a malfunction in the hardware, but in essence it was what was referred to as a bug in the program of the operating system, but it was not able to cope with handling certain data, as it was specified to handle it.

As a result,

> It was available to the user, but there were a great many periods of down time and, also, if you were operating with terminals, the response of the system would be very slow in a timesharing mode.[271]

While the performance of TSOS and its successor, VMOS, improved "as time went on," development work continued until RCA left the computer business.[272]

Other Product Problems. In addition to problems with its processing units, RCA experienced problems with the operating software (in addition to time-sharing software), random-access memory units, card readers, and memory stacks on Spectra 70. These problems created substantial difficulties for RCA in its marketing of Spectra, particularly in comparison with System/360.

For its Spectra systems from the Spectra 45 up, RCA had an operating system called TDOS. Rooney testified:

> When it was announced it was a good system, but RCA did not con-
> tinue to improve upon it at the same pace as IBM improved upon their
> OS. Our system, while performing satisfactorily in terms of reliability,
> did call for a lot more operator intervention in terms of performing
> the work than the OS system.
>
> I made a strong plea for an improved system called OS 70, which
> was under development, to be used on the RCA 6. That system was
> decommitted in the early part of 1971.
>
> By "decommitted" I mean it was never brought to the market.
>
>   . . . .
>
> The people responsible for putting the system together felt that
> they couldn't do it in the time frame that had been asked for.[273]

As discussed, in 1964 RCA introduced its RACE file, which suffered from various problems. RCA marketed the RACE with its Spectra series and continued to market it actively into 1968, at which time it

> was impacted by the progressive development of disk file technol-
> ogy. Disk files were more reliable devices. There were fewer things
> to make mechanical trouble in them. They had a faster access time and
> a faster transfer rate of information from the medium into the proces-
> sor, and as the cost performance characteristics of disk files improved,
> the relative advantage and cost performance of the so-called RACE
> unit was [*sic*] reduced, until you reached the point where, for most
> applications, a disk file, as illustrated by the 2314, was a preferred
> approach.[274]

During the mid-1960s RCA still was not producing disk drives. To meet users' demand for such drives, RCA purchased IBM 2311 and then CDC 2311-type disk drives for use with the early deliveries of the Spectra 45 and 55 in 1967.[275] RCA did not deliver its own 2311-type disk drive until the end of 1967 or beginning of 1968, a year and a half after its first Spectra deliveries.[276] When IBM began deliveries of its 2314 disk drive, RCA found that its marketing people "were under a handicap in selling the Spectra 70 Systems. We did not have a comparable product to the IBM 2314 at the time."[277]

RCA's development of a 2314 equivalent was hampered by the departure of the group that had worked on development of its 2311-type disk drive in 1967-68 to form an IBM-compatible disk manufacturing company, Linnell

Electronics.[278] Partly as a result, RCA determined in 1968 that Memorex was ahead of it in disk drive technology and contracted to have Memorex supply it with its "first year or year and a half supply of disks." Obtaining disk drives from Memorex "cost additional money" because RCA "had in parallel [its] own development going on which was going to be about a year later than Memorex's." Nevertheless, RCA could not afford to wait the additional year to obtain a 2314 equivalent because it was "losing too many sales" to IBM "for the lack of it."[279]

RCA supplied its own controller for the Memorex 2314-type drives, developing it at an engineering cost of about $500,000.[280] RCA started to work on a 2314-type product as a "full design project" in 1968 and delivered the first units to customers "around the latter part of 1969 to perhaps mid-1970."[281] Rooney testified that RCA was hurt by the fact that it "was not able to produce on its own or to duplicate the 2311 or the 2314 disk drives until very much after the IBM delivery."[282] Disk drives offered "a functional capability very much needed in terms of price/performance in the competitive market-place and without that capability you were in a weak competitive situation against IBM."[283] In July 1971, Rooney wrote that "the lack of a 2314 competitive device until later in the product life" was one of the "many functional capabilities which detracted from [Spectra's] ability to meet its product objectives."[284]

RCA also had initial difficulties with the card reader on its Spectra series. The difficulties were corrected only at the cost of making it a "very high cost product."[285]

Finally, one of the most severe problems faced by RCA in 1967 and 1968 was that of providing reliable memory stacks. This problem cost RCA as much as $10 million, and caused J. R. Bradburn, executive vice-president of the Computer Division, to write to Robert W. Sarnoff, president and chief executive officer of RCA,[286] in December 1968, recommending that the Memory Products Division be transferred to his division:

> Modern computing and data processing systems consist in essence of input/output peripheral equipment, control, and memory. Development of complete competitive systems involve [*sic*] simultaneous, continuous, and coordinated development of all components. The single most important element of this overall development is memory.
>
> Development processes must involve more than theoretical analysis and its immediate physical embodiment. A thorough understanding and consideration of mechanical design, reliability, manufacturability, and maintainability of a complete memory system is required. Nothing less can meet competition today. . . .
>
> The present organizational structure within RCA is not conducive to efficient operation or to meeting these requirements. It does not bring to bear upon the decision making process the needed emphasis or the proper sense of order of importance adequate to meet the needs both in the short and long runs.
>
> . . . [This] is what has been demonstrated by the inordinate difficulties encountered in trying to provide reliable memory stacks for our computer shipments in 1967 and 1968. Poor stacks may have

cost us as much as $10,000,000 in those two years. Additionally, our problem is portrayed by what has been inadequate provisioning in the engineering budgets of Memory Products.[287]

RCA's Success with the Spectra 70 Series

Despite the numerous problems experienced by the Spectra 70 series, during the period of its life (1965-69) RCA enjoyed considerable success with its computer business. McCollister testified:

> But I would say that beginning in 1965 through the year 1969 we were making what appeared to be encouraging progress. We did have an ability to compete within our particular scope of operations and the corporation was encouraged about the long term outlook for the Division.[288]

In 1964 RCA reported that its "gross computer sales and rentals" were higher than $100 million, having grown from $14.6 million in 1960. "RCA's total data processing business earned a profit for the full year."[289] In 1965 those profits continued, and "the potential for future profits was enhanced by the booking in 1965 of orders for 92 percent more computer systems than in the preceding year. By 1970, profits from the data processing business . . . are expected to become a highly significant factor in RCA's total earnings."[290]

In 1966 RCA reported that "domestic orders for RCA computers and their associated equipment rose by 53 percent over the 1965 level." With Spectra deliveries beginning, RCA enlarged its field marketing force by 45 percent, planned for another 35 percent increase in 1967, and "boosted production capacity by 75 percent to fulfill the growing demand for Spectra 70 computers and other data processing equipment."[291] RCA reported that a loss in its computer business in 1966 was caused by an increase in leasing as opposed to purchasing by customers, a situation that continued in 1967.[292] Nevertheless, "we look upon this as an investment in future profits and look forward with confidence to the period when our data processing activity will become one of the most important parts of our business, surpassing even color television."[293] By 1969, although losses continued, RCA regarded them as "largely the result of expenditures aimed at future growth, which include the building up of our marketing forces and expansion of software and other aspects of the business." It saw a considerable present and future expansion in shipments.[294] During 1965-69, RCA's U.S. EDP revenue rose from about $89 million to approximately $211 million.[295]

RCA's Computer Systems Division in 1969-71

The story of RCA's involvement in computers at the end of the 1960s and the early 1970s has three parts: (1) the change in personnel at the corporate level and in the computer division, with resulting changes in goals of the computer business; (2) the decision to develop the RCA series and its consequences; (3) the problems that resulted.

Changes in Management Personnel and Goals

On January 1, 1968, Robert Sarnoff became chief executive officer of RCA while continuing as president, replacing his father, David Sarnoff, as chairman of the board in 1970.[296] During 1968 Chase Morsey, Jr., left Ford and joined RCA as vice-president of marketing and the next year became an executive vice-president of RCA.[297] In 1971, A. L. Conrad became president and chief operating officer.[298] Conrad had worked his way up through the RCA Service Company, which, "[i]n addition to its work for the government and in education, . . . install[ed] and maintain[ed] home-entertainment products, commercial electronic systems, and business and industrial equipment."[299]

At the time Robert Sarnoff became RCA's chief executive officer, RCA underwent a change in its corporate philosophy. In its 1968 Annual Report RCA stated: "In its formative years RCA's growth depended primarily on a single product or service. . . . The word that best characterizes the modern RCA is diversity."[300] Starting in 1966, RCA acquired many different and unrelated businesses, and by 1971 it was a conglomerate engaged in a large number of different fields, including home appliances, television sets, radios, recording devices, federal defense contracts, communications services, broadcasting, automobile rentals, food, carpets, books, records, and real estate — and computers.[301]

During 1966-76 the chief executive officers of various RCA divisions and subsidiaries, including Banquet Foods, Coronet, Hertz, Random House, and Global Communications, were directors of the RCA Corporation. No officer of the Computer Division was a member of the RCA board of directors during this period.[302] In 1971 revenues from the operations of the RCA Computer Division represented less than 10 percent of RCA's corporate revenues — $270 million out of $3 billion.[303]

At this time changes were also occurring in the personnel and goals of RCA's Computer Division. During 1969 and 1970 RCA hired people from IBM to manage parts of the Computer Division. For example, L. Edwin Donegan, Jr., became vice-president of sales in 1969 and general manager in 1970.[304] Rooney came from IBM in 1969 and after a brief corporate staff job became vice-president of marketing; in 1971 he was president of the Computer Systems Division.[305] V. Orville Wright was hired in 1970 and the next year was head of Systems Development.[306] Samuel Adams was responsible for business planning. William Acker was put in charge of the financial operation.[307]

The goals of the Computer Division changed with the new corporate and Computer Division management. Until Robert Sarnoff took over in 1968, the RCA Computer Division had placed its emphasis on accomplishing its business plans and obtaining moderate growth.[308] In 1968 RCA changed that emphasis to one of quickly obtaining a larger market share. (McCollister attributed this change to newly arrived Chase Morsey, who he thought gave an exaggerated importance to share figures as "a legacy from his experience in the automobile industry" [he had been at Ford].)[309] In its 1970 Annual Report, RCA stated:

Our highest priorities today are the establishment of a profitable computer business and the capture of the domestic industry's No. 2 position. RCA has made a greater investment in this effort than in any prior venture in its history, and we are convinced that the returns will be substantial.[310]

McCollister testified that the change was not beneficial to the Computer Division:

> It tended to place the emphasis upon increasing market share and relatively deemphasize control of expenses and achieving a profit, and the end result is that the expenses in the RCA Computer Division mounted to the point where they contributed significantly to RCA's withdrawal from the business.
>
> In other words, you place the emphasis upon share of market and you tend to deemphasize some of the other important market aspects of running a successful business, and share of market is only one consideration.[311]

It was this change in strategy that led directly to the ill-fated RCA series.

The RCA Series

During 1968 RCA realized that if it was to achieve its new growth objectives, it would need successor systems to the Spectra series. Unfortunately, RCA was undecided about what successor products to develop, and a lengthy debate ensued.[312]

RCA made two starts at developing a successor product line. The first attempt, referred to at the trial as the X series (because its correct name had been forgotten), was decommitted in 1969 for two reasons: (1) RCA felt that it could not meet what it predicted to be IBM's announcement of System/370; (2) the series included

> [a]n architectural problem [in] that they doubted they would ever be able to complete the product line without a major restructuring of their whole development program. . . . [Rooney's] understanding at the time was that they could not build it at all if they had developed it or had set up the architecture.[313]

The second attempt at a successor to the Spectra was the New Technology System (NTS). The NTS was originally scheduled for announcement in early 1971. However, "[t]here was a slippage in that program and it was subsequently put off for announcement for approximately 18 months as a result of development problems within RCA itself."[314]

RCA made only "marginally small" investments in NTS.[315] It appeared that NTS, if announced as it was being developed, would have encountered competitive difficulties. Withington, who had advised RCA concerning its marketing strategies,[316] testified:

The basic reason for my concern was that I believed at the time that IBM would introduce a new family of general purpose computer systems in the time frame 1973 to 1977, which was the time frame in which RCA's NTS computer systems were to be shipped.

I believed that the nature and functionality of the NTS line would be inadequate to meet the needs of customers who were IBM users or who would otherwise consider IBM systems during that time frame.[317]

Withington told RCA that "a revision and acceleration of the product plan would be necessary if RCA would have . . . '[a] good chance of attaining the desired market share.' "[318]

At this point, during 1970, RCA had several alternative ways it could proceed in the computer business: it could continue to market the Spectra 70 series until NTS, or some other more advanced product line, was developed; it could specialize in particular customer industries or a particular product area;[319] or it could market what became the RCA series. The RCA series was chosen for several reasons:

1. The new management of the RCA Computer Systems Division wanted to stop marketing the Spectra and to market its own line of products:
    The then management of the Division wanted to have a product line that would be associated with their management era or period, as opposed to a product line which was associated with an earlier management era.[320]
    It also thought that a new product line would have a "psychological influence" on the "marketplace."[321]

2. RCA also believed that it could not continue to sell the Spectra series in the face of the price/performance improvements offered by IBM with its System/370. According to Rooney, if RCA had not been "selling against IBM," it could have continued to offer the Spectra series.[322]

3. Because of its desire for a large market share, RCA rejected the idea of focusing on particular product areas:
    [A]t a meeting I attended, [representatives of Arthur D. Little] presented the concept that you had to have a broad product line because you could not possibly sell enough share of any particular product category to achieve this goal and that strategy was accepted as being valid [by] [t]he management of the Computer Systems Group as well as corporate management.[323]

4. RCA believed that it could equal or better the price/performance of the IBM 370 systems and take away IBM users by introducing the RCA series:
    We were faced with a pending IBM announcement; we knew that the IBM announcement would offer their clients improved price/performance; we had just had the X series decommitted; and our objective was to grow to 10 percent share of the market. And we felt that we had to therefore maintain our original strategy of going after the IBM base. And after many discussions, it was concluded that by putting in the

new memory capability we would be able to bring the cost of these systems down, so that we could offer a price competitive system — price/performance competitive system with IBM's 370. And since it was following the Spectra architecture, conceptually it would be the same strategy as IBM was employing, that is, utilizing the existing software for the next generation of equipment.[324]

The RCA series was announced on September 15, 1970, three months after the first announcements of IBM's System/370.[325] The RCA series consisted of four models "of small-to-medium-class computers — RCA 2, 3, 6 and 7."[326] RCA described the RCA series as "offering more power and memory for the dollar than present third-generation systems."[327] Despite this, while the RCA series had new memories, "under the covers, the RCA Series was essentially the Spectra 70."[328]

McCollister described the RCA series thus:

[I]t was a restyled product line. There was a new set of covers, the frames were the same, and it was essentially a cosmetic treatment of the existing Spectra 70 Series with new model numbers and new pricing.

There may have been some minor improvements. But fundamentally the product was not changed from the Spectra 70.[329]

RCA's Computer Division management devised "an elaborate strategy" to make the RCA series succeed:

There was a very elaborate strategy at the time as to where these units of the RCA series would fall against the IBM either 360 or 370, either as it had been announced or was expected to be announced, and I think there was a fallacious expectation . . . in this elaborate strategy that the RCA series would fall at a certain point within the IBM product line spectrum and that IBM would be unwilling to disturb the equilibrium of that product spectrum and, therefore, negate the rationale of the RCA product concept.[330]

Under this "elaborate strategy" the RCA series would "intercept" the System/370. Rooney testified that in 1969-71 "we had a term called intercept strategy, which implied intercepting the upward migration of the IBM client base with RCA equipment."[331]

The "elaborate strategy" failed. The RCA series was a "major product failure" and "a mistake."[332] It failed in two respects: (1) as Withington had warned was likely to happen,[333] instead of "intercepting" System/370, it "intercepted" RCA's own Spectra 70 series; and (2) it had substantial technological problems.

Interception of the Spectra 70. Different witnesses used different words, but all said the same thing: By introducing the RCA series, RCA "obsoleted," "intercepted," and "blew . . . out of the water" its own Spectra 70 series.[334]

[A] customer had everything to gain by ordering an RCA series and returning the Spectra 70. He got a brand new machine. It cost him maybe 15 percent less or so and why not?[335]

The interception of the Spectra by the RCA series seriously hurt RCA in several respects. First, it reduced RCA's rental income because rents for the RCA series were lower than for the Spectra.[336] Second, RCA was forced to buld more RCA series machines while it built up an inventory of returned RCA Spectra 70s. McCollister testified that RCA found itself with

[o]rders for the RCA Series which required a manufacturing investment, in the product being placed out on rental for the most part, which drew capital from the corporation to do this, and it resulted in the displacement of existing Spectra 70 processors in many cases before they had been fully depreciated.[337]

He added:

This tended to build up an inventory of the equipment which was returned by the customers, the rental income from that equipment ceased and the company was faced with the requirement to invest money in new equipment to place in the customer's office to take the place of that which was sent back or returned.[338]

In addition, the early returns of the Spectra 70s

[h]ad serious adverse financial effect upon the Division because it did not permit us to follow a plan or have a strategy which would maximize the return from the investment in Spectra 70 equipments.[339]

The problems of returned Spectra 70 systems were such that RCA established a Returns Task Force, which made its presentation in early August 1971 and, considering both returns experienced to date and those forecast, concluded that "approximately 70 percent of the returns were being caused by RCA's replacement of Spectra series with RCA equipment." Approximately 18 percent were losses to competition and about 12 percent were due to economic problems.[340]

These early returns particularly hurt RCA's profit-and-loss statements by forcing the firm to write off the undepreciated asset value of its "accrued equity contracts."[341] These contracts were arrangements in which the customer leased the equipment for five years, making equal monthly payments over that period, but RCA took 70 percent of the revenue that it expected to achieve into its profit-and-loss statement in the first year of the contract.[342] When the RCA series was announced, some equipment under accrued equity contracts was returned prematurely (according to McCollister) because the manager of the division "was anxious to make a showing with respect to the success of this new product line" and had "an inclination to allow customers to return Spectra 70 equipments prematurely for the sake of being able to cite an order for a machine in the new product line."[343] This meant that debits against current revenue had to be recognized when machines were returned before earning the revenue already reported in prior years.

Technological Problems of the RCA Series. The RCA series suffered from technological deficiencies that hampered its success:

> Because you were in a sense perpetuating technology that was five years old, you were making a new investment in five-year old technology, and the pace of technology in the industry, in it [sic] cost effectiveness characteristics, is such that when you bring out a product line you cannot afford not to take advantage of improvements in cost performance and capabilities up to the time that you bring out that equipment.[344]

In addition, particular products were deficient in various ways. Peripherals continued to be a problem. By 1970 RCA was "[t]wo to three years" behind IBM in the development of peripherals, having fallen into a pattern of producing or buying essentially carbon copies of IBM peripherals two, three, or more years late.[345] Specifically, RCA was hindered by its failure to have a disk drive competitive with the new IBM 3330, which had been announced in June 1970 with System/370. In 1971 Rooney reported that RCA still suffered from its

> [i]nability to provide a 3330 competitive device until some 19 months after IBM's delivery of its 3330 unit. I feel . . . [this is] of major importance to the success of our RCA series marketing efforts and should be resolved.[346]

And in July 1971, RCA's Computer Division monthly report stated that "sales of the RCA 6 and 7 have been and will continue to be hampered by the large delivery differential between the RCA 8580 [disk drive] (March 1973) and the IBM 3330 (August 1971)."[347] By then RCA was arranging to purchase the 3330 from IBM.[348] Keeping up with IBM in tape drives was also a problem.[349]

RCA's problems with software also continued into the RCA series. VMOS 4, an operating system to be used with the RCA 3 and RCA 7, was announced in September 1970.[350] By December 1970 it appeared that there would be a slippage of six to nine months in the delivery of VMOS 4. According to A. L. Fazio, RCA's manager of virtual memory systems, such slippage would be a "product disaster" causing RCA to lose about $3.5 million from delayed installations and approximately 2.1 million points (dollars of monthly rental) from current and future prospects.[351] The slippage occurred and was "significant."[352] Because of that slippage RCA lost $3.5 million in revenue and marketed about 40 systems — 20 RCA 3s and 20 RCA 7s — less than it otherwise would have during 1971 through 1973.[353]

The Computer Systems Division's Problems – Early 1970s

The year 1970 was "essentially" a break-even one for the RCA Computer Systems Division. At the time RCA projected that 1971 would also be "break-even," with 1972 showing a $25 million and 1973 a $50 million "pre-tax operating profit."[354] A five-year business plan drawn up by the Computer Systems Division in late 1970 provided for "a breakeven position in 1971."[355] In its 1970 Annual Report RCA painted a similar picture for its share holders.[356] During the beginning and middle of 1971, however, it was becoming apparent that those plans for the Computer Systems Division would not be met and that the division would be far less successful than had been expected.

In late January 1971, Robert Sarnoff was informed by RCA's auditors, Arthur Young & Co., of a "major . . . change in operating results of the Computer Systems Division in the 1971 business plan," and he asked for an analysis of the problem. Arthur Young responded in a letter dated February 24, 1971.[357]

In April 1971, RCA revised its business plan for the Computer Systems Division. That plan reduced the prediction of revenue for the division set forth in the December 1970 plan from $323 million to $261 million. The revised plan predicted an anticipated pretax loss in 1971 of $37 million.[358]

On April 23, 1971, H. L. Letts, RCA's senior financial officer, wrote to Sarnoff that the magnitude of the division's problems raised serious long-term concern about the business, and suggested reappraisal of the division's objectives. He suggested that a task force be set up to study the division and its objectives.[359]

By June 1971 a task force comprising six persons from Arthur Young and the RCA auditing staff had reported on the problems of the Computer Systems Division. Morsey sent this report to Sarnoff and Conrad with a cover memorandum stating that "the Computer Systems 1971 loss could deteriorate significantly from Business Plan levels."[360]

During 1971

> it became apparent that there would be a loss in magnitude of $30 million or $35 million, a loss that eventually rose to the area of $50 million or $60 million, and this of course was an enormous difference from what had been anticipated at the beginning of that year.[361]

By the middle of 1971 problems at RCA "put in question the anticipated revenue, and in turn opened the question in my [Conrad's] mind as to . . . profitability . . . in the remainder of 1971."[362]

Participants in or observers of RCA's computer business pointed to many problems in its Computer Systems Division that would cause its anticipated losses.

Declining Revenues. The higher-than-anticipated returns of Spectra equipment ($155 million as opposed to $90 million) resulted in a reduction of expected net shipments (even though there was an increase in gross shipments) from $230 million to $186 million. RCA's 1971 Business Plan stated:

The returns implications of RCA's first introduction of . . . the RCA series compatible with the Spectra series . . . were not fully reflected in the first plan. . . . There has also been greater migration than expected from the old to the new series. . . . The increased dependence on the RCA series has a profound impact on revenue projections and attendant risk, since product will not be available until second half of 1971.[363]

Expenses Too High. McCollister attributed RCA's losses to the fact that "there was a substantial increase in expense, and that revenues were not increasing, and that revenues had been seriously overforecast." An example was the construction of the Marlboro, Massachusetts, facility in 1971. "The relocation of the offices, the executive office and the construction of the office building under the circumstances was . . . a mistake. . . . [It] was an expenditure which could have been deferred."[364] Such deferral was suggested in the revised plan of April 1971.[365]

RCA also "had a very serious problem relative to manufacturing costs." According to Wright:

It stemmed from several sources. One was the fact that the manufacturing process in RCA was not as fully automated as I had seen it automated in IBM manufacturing.

RCA was not devoting sufficient attention in engineering a product to the matter of cost. They tended to engineer the product to get it built, but ignored what it might cost to build it after it was engineered.

There was no value engineering work going on after the product was developed to reduce its cost within the manufacturing organization. Those types of things.

The cost, as I recall it, when I first got involved in that, which would have been early in 1971 . . . was running at that point in time about 42 percent of revenue.[366]

Wright recalled the comparable figure for IBM's manufacturing cost as a percent of revenue as "on the order of 14 to 15 percent," and "in certain other products, such as the CPU alone . . . substantially under that." RCA looked at other companies besides IBM and concluded that Sperry Rand's manufacturing cost "was running about 24 percent of revenue," and Burroughs' "was about 21 percent of revenue."[367] Wright "took several steps to reduce those manufacturing costs," but succeeded in reducing them by only eight percentage points of revenue, leaving RCA still a very high-cost producer.[368]

Poor Organization and Unreliable Information. RCA's computer operation was not being well managed in other ways. The Arthur Young report to Robert Sarnoff in February 1971 stated:

The basic failure to develop acceptable planning information in the division involved the lack of a reliable information base, principally relating to revenues, from which plans could be developed and current performance measured. This situation was aggravated by communications gaps which developed in a period of organizational change. Planning responsibilities and assignments were not clearly defined. As an example, the financial group was divided early in 1970; moves to upgrade the remaining group were less than successful. Preparing for the move to Marlboro was probably a further complication.[369]

In 1971 the Returns Task Force reported that the Computer Systems Division suffered from the inadequate tracking of computer equipment:

1. No single, reputable data base for customer/equipment information.
2. No two data sources agree.
3. Regular field inputs to data bases are clearly modulated by quota objectives bias.
4. Recourse to the field for instant surveys leaves them short on time, us long on dependence — in our survey we check out at about 85% accuracy.

Conclusions: Forecast based upon CS [Computer Systems] Data and field surveys inherit a built in error factor of ± 20%.[370]

Inadequate Financial Controls. A study of the Computer Systems Division (CSD) in the summer of 1971 reported:

It has become apparent that CSD has not had adequate financial controls and analytical capability. Because of the complexity of the computer business in terms of revenue and cost forecasting, the interaction between generations of equipment, and the requirement for large, direct sales force, the control and analytical needs are greater in CSD than in most other businesses. . . . If some of these problems had been made clearer earlier, the business might have been conducted in a different manner.[371]

The lack of financial controls resulted in RCA's inventory being overvalued, past-due accounts receivable with significant amounts being prematurely written off, and questionable orders being booked.[372]

Product Deliveries. Because of product problems, forecasts of RCA series shipments were not met. For example:

In the June 2 presentation, the 1971 business plan assumed shipment of sixty RCA 6 series in 1971. As of mid-July, Computer Systems indicated that the best estimate of RCA 6 shipments for 1971 was fifteen. A similar decline has occurred in the case of the RCA 7.

Despite assurances that time-sharing software problems had been solved last fall, software availability continues to be a severe problem. . . .[373]

The Impact of the NTS Series. Just as the RCA series adversely affected the Spectra series, the NTS series appeared to be likely to have an adverse effect on the RCA series:

> Based on expected introduction dates for the NTS series, it appears possible that a six-year life for the RCA series will not be achieved. A shorter system life would result in significantly greater write-downs in 1971 and future years. This impact could be anticipated by increasing the obsolescence reserve or accelerating depreciation but either of these actions would cause additional losses in the shorter term.[374]

Changes in Accounting Procedures. As noted above, premature returns of products placed under "accrued equity" contracts forced RCA to take debits against current revenue.[375] A draft release of the Accounting Principles Board "put in question the accounting practices being applied within RCA to the Accrued Equity lease."[376] This ruling (which also affected Telex and Memorex) would have required RCA to treat such transactions as leases rather than sales, thereby halting its practice of taking 70 percent of the revenues to be received over five years as revenues received in the initial year of the contract.[377] The effect of a retroactive change in accounting practice would be large, involving a $53.6 million reduction in revenue for 1971 and a $104 million reduction in 1972, with a "substantial negative effect on the P&L [profit and loss] performance of Computer Systems in 1971 . . . and even greater negative effect in 1972."[378]

The Economy. RCA's computer business was hurt by the poor state of the economy in 1970 and 1971. "The economic situation for the computer business in 1970 was quite bad. . . . Shipments that year were down some 20 percent from the previous year."[379] The economic situation increased the number of returns of computer equipment that RCA experienced.[380] The Returns Task Force estimated that 12 percent of the returns of the Spectra in 1971 were due to the poor state of the economy.[381]

Increased Competition. During the late 1960s and early 1970s, increased competition hurt RCA's computer business. While RCA was putting out its old-technology RCA series, IBM was introducing System/370, a series based on new technology. As discussed above, prior to the announcement of that new IBM series, RCA had attempted to predict the price/performance of IBM's anticipated new line in setting up its strategy. When the 370 systems were announced in mid-1970, RCA found that its predictions for the 370/155, 370/165, and 3330 disk drive were "accurate." Its predictions for the 370/135 and 370/145, however, were "off target." RCA had anticipated that the price of the 370/145 would be 5 to 10 percent higher than the RCA 6 price; as announced in September 1970, however, the 145 was priced approximately the same as the RCA 6. The 370/135 also came out with better price/performance than RCA had anticipated. The result of the inaccurate predictions was fewer placements for the RCA 6 and 2 because those systems were not as price/performance-competitive as RCA believed they would be.[382]

Moreover, Rooney testified that all of the significant technological innovations in 1970 were achieved by IBM. Those included the 3330 disk drive, which "brought to users significantly improved price/performance, capability of storing and retrieving data on disks at much faster speeds than [previously]"; semiconductor memory, which "reduce[d] the cost to the user in terms of the amount of money he would have to pay for memory . . . [and gave] the ability to have potentially much higher speed"; microprogramming, which allowed the user to "improve the speed" with which he would process different applications, and made it possible for computers to more readily perform the instruction sets of other computers; and the 3211 high-speed printer. Rooney agreed that each of the "significant innovations" attributable to IBM gave IBM "a competitive advantage in marketing commercial data processing systems."[383]

RCA's competition was not limited to IBM, however.[384] In particular, RCA was experiencing increased competition from peripheral manufacturers. Wright, who was chairman of RCA's Peripheral Task Force in 1970, testified that the task force was "surprised" and "shocked" by the number of users employing, or intending to acquire, non-RCA equipment as part of RCA systems. This indicated to him that users "had learned that it was possible for them to achieve certain benefits by procuring and mixing boxes from different manufacturers in the same system."[385] By July 1971, RCA's Data Processing Division monthly report listed "significant problem areas":

> Independent peripheral manufacturers, i.e., Potter, Singer, have been waging extensive sales campaigns at selected customer sites. For example, Singer/Frieden [sic] has proposed a plug to plug capability for replacement of the 70/564 Discs at California Dept. of Justice.[386]

Leasing company competition was also important. It had given a "considerable measure" of "impetus" to RCA's use of the accrued equity contract.[387] Now such competition was increasing. The same July 1971 monthly report said that "discounts being offered on 360 systems by third party leasing companies have [among other things] accounted for the slowdown on the demand for RCA Series systems."[388]

RCA's Decision To Sell Its Computer Business to Sperry Rand

It was clear by the middle of 1971 that RCA's computer business had been hurt substantially by management errors, particularly by the introduction of the RCA series. Yet it was not clear that RCA needed, or even wished, to sell its computer business. In 1971, according to Conrad, RCA's management had "a very strong commitment" to its computer business. Indeed, in July 1971, Conrad, who had recently become RCA's president, spoke by videotape to a Computer Systems Division marketing management meeting and tried to dispel rumors that RCA would exit the business, stating: "We are making a greater investment in the computer business than in any prior venture in our history. This is a measure of our confidence that RCA systems and products will effectively meet competitive challenges in the decade ahead."[389]

By September, however, RCA's view of its participation in the computer industry had changed. On August 27, Conrad and Sarnoff received reports on the status of RCA's computer business, and discussions as to whether to exit were under way in RCA's management.[390] A group of executives consisting of Conrad, Sarnoff, Morsey, and General Counsel R. L. Werner[391] met on September 16, 1971 for an hour and a half, and decided to recommend to the RCA board of directors that RCA exit from the business. None of these four had ever had direct responsibility for the RCA Computer Division or had even worked in it. The board of directors adopted their recommendation on the following day.[392]

The decision to sell the computer business came as a "surprise" to persons working in the Computer Systems Division.[393] RCA's management had not consulted with Wright, Donegan (vice-president and general manager of the division), Rooney, or, to Rooney's knowledge, anyone else in the Computer Systems Division.[394]

The basis for the board's decision to sell the computer business was that if anticipated losses of $137 million to $187 million in the Computer Systems Division over the period 1971-76 materialized, there would be a need for a greater investment in computers than RCA chose to make. According to the memorandum Morsey read to the board of directors, the amount of investment required over the 1971-76 period was estimated to be $702 million.[395] The amount was disputed, however, even within RCA; Julius Koppelman, the financial vice-president of the Computer Systems Group, believed that the $702 million dollar figure was in error by an overstatement of $100 to $200 million.[396] (He, of course, had not been consulted before September 17.)

Competing with the Computer Division for investment funds were the many other divisions in the RCA Corporation. The needs of those other divisions for investment funds also were greater than had been expected. According to the memorandum read to the board, a "preliminary evaluation" showed that "new funds required" during 1971-76 "may exceed $1 billion" for the corporation as a whole.[397]

It was against that background that RCA made its decision. It considered whether to proceed with the magnitude of investments contemplated both in computers and in other areas and believed that "if earnings growth can be maintained at an annual rate of 10%-15%, the Company can raise needed funds." If RCA earnings were to grow only "at a rate similar to GNP (7%)," however, or if a recession were to occur, "the resulting reduction in RCA's overall profit position could bring considerable pressure on obtaining the $1 billion outside financing required." There could be "severe financing problems." Major losses in computers would add to the difficulties.[398]

Conrad testified that he believed that RCA could have raised the necessary capital to finance the projects that the Computer Systems Division had in mind at the time, could have reached its goal of achieving 10 percent of some defined market, and would at some point in time have been profitable.[399] Similarly, Rooney — who as a member of the Computer Systems Division had not been consulted prior to the decision — testified that he believed that RCA could have been successful in displacing IBM products in the 1970s had it been allowed to continue in the business.[400] Withington, who had advised RCA's Computer Systems Division a year earlier, believed that RCA could have been successful in the computer business had it chosen a different, less adventurous strategy and could have remained profitable while growing more slowly.[401]

RCA did consider changing its strategy by keeping the computer business but substantially reducing its size and scope through limiting it to certain narrow market areas. According to the memorandum read to the board of directors, however, it was believed that this would reduce revenue as well as expenses, and "while cash requirements would be reduced substantially, it is questionable whether the business would ever attain economic viability."[402] As a result, "the additional investment required in CSD no longer appears to be a prudent financial risk."[403]

In addition, the memorandum said that, given RCA's position in the computer business, "[t]he manpower and financial resources of IBM, including the size and strength of the marketing, research and development organizations, are such that achieving market share growth as well as acceptable profitability, is extremely difficult."[404]

Thus:

> In summary, the computer business currently accounts for about 6 percent of RCA's total revenues. While it could represent a growing segment of the Company's operations, it is unlikely to ever exceed perhaps 10-15 percent of total RCA volume. Continued commitment to computers, however, could lead to severe financing problems for the Company and may contribute to restricted growth in other operations. On balance, it is believed that the risk does not justify the potential reward. Therefore, withdrawal from the mainframe computer and peripheral equipment business is recommended.[405]

After September 17, 1971, RCA negotiated with Sperry Rand and with Mohawk Data Sciences concerning the sale of its computer business and also had meetings with several other companies, including Burroughs, Xerox, and Memorex. It sold the division to Sperry Rand.[406] In its presentations to prospective purchasers, RCA estimated that the "After Tax Cash Contribution" of its lease base for 1972 through 1974 would be $193 million, assuming no residual value.[407] It sold its computer division to Sperry for approximately $137 million.[408]

RCA reported that it lost approximately $241 million before taxes on its computer systems operations in 1958-71.[409] In September 1971 it set up a reserve of $490 million before taxes, $250 million after taxes, to cover prospective losses in connection with the sale of its Computer Division. The losses that were anticipated related to disposition of assets "such as inventory, receivables, plant," "discharge of claims and obligations for commitments to employees for severance and release," and other purposes. In December 1973 a review indicated that the disposition was going better than expected, and the reserve was reduced by $78 million, leaving a pretax reserve of $412 million.[410]

After the Sale to Sperry Rand

RCA's Activities

RCA's sale of its computer operation was only one part of a continued pattern of withdrawal from some businesses and investment in others believed to be more profitable.[411] That sale did not end its involvement in computer-related businesses. In the mid-1970s RCA made microprocessor chips, offered service on a variety of data-processing or reservation system terminals owned by others, and designed and produced special processors sold to the government in conjunction with tracking devices.[412]

Sperry Rand's Success with RCA's Computer Systems Division

Sperry believed that its acquisition of RCA's Computer Systems Division was "sound business" and a "wise" decision.[413] In its 1973 Annual Report Sperry stated:

> More than 90% of these RCA customers remained with us, and more than $130 million in new equipment was shipped to these users during calendar year 1972. We are continuing to build "bridges" between the RCA systems and Sperry Univac's line, and we are confident that many of these customers will eventually convert to Sperry Univac's systems.[414]

In December 1974, 77 percent of the original RCA customers acquired by Univac were still using their RCA equipment, and 5 percent had moved to Univac systems. The RCA equipment had yielded a "revenue stream (sales, rentals and maintenance) for 3 years of approximately $370 million." Univac believed that "these benefits will certainly not end at this point."[415] By May 1975 approximately 76 percent of the RCA equipment acquired by Univac was still on rent.[416]

Conclusion

Like GE, RCA was a large company with a small computer business. In the last full year before its sale of the Computer Systems Division to Sperry Rand, RCA's U.S. EDP revenue was $226 million.[417] Its venture into computers was a failure; but it need not have been. As we have seen, despite RCA's great technological capability in the 1950s, it placed only nine computers in that decade. RCA's inactivity in the 1950s and early 1960s cost it dearly, but did not stop it. The Spectra, patterned after IBM's 360, was a mixed success. Reliability problems and inadequate peripherals limited the acceptance of the systems. But even then, had RCA understood the need to push ahead with technological development, to commit its ample resources to new, more advanced follow-on systems, it could have succeeded.

Instead, RCA introduced the RCA series — yesterday's technology at lower prices — and chose that vehicle to spearhead its drive to "gain market share" and "become number 2 in the industry." But the RCA series could not compete with the more advanced products of IBM and others, and was a "major product failure," blowing the Spectra series "out of the water."

At the same time, the management of RCA changed hands, and the company sought to transform itself into a conglomerate. The result was that all the various corporate mouths needed feeding at once, and as the company entered the recession of the early 1970s, it found itself stretched too thin to pay adequate attention or commit sufficient resources to save the computer business from the RCA series debacle.

In sum, the story of RCA, like the story of GE, is a story of missed opportunity, bad management, and product failures.

SUCCESSFUL
SYSTEM COMPETITORS

SPERRY RAND/UNIVAC

Not all systems manufacturers failed in the 1960s. Some of them changed relative failure to success. Although Sperry Rand's Univac Division entered the second half of the 1960s lagging substantially behind the industry leaders in the areas of product compatibility and storage technology, it was able to reestablish itself as a major force in EDP by the end of the decade, logging substantial gains in revenues, organization, and technology.

Univac's Problems in 1964

In 1964 Univac was in a state of some disarray. It was in the midst of a succession of presidents[1] and was "still suffering" from the "great drawback" of its "inability to assemble a smoothly working, reasonably permanent management team."[2] In addition, despite the suggestion of J. Presper Eckert that Univac, like IBM, should concentrate on a single product line, it had manufactured, and was still marketing, several incompatible product lines (represented in 1964 by the 490, the UNIVAC III, and the 1107), each requiring different software.[3] Moreover, Univac had failed to provide successors to its obsolete products.[4]

In 1964, "after it had become apparent to the rest of the industry that magnetic disks were superior," Sperry was still marketing its FASTRAND drum instead of quickly proceeding with disk development, a delay that had a substantial adverse effect on the marketing of its computer systems.[5] Consequently, Univac was compelled to purchase disks from other suppliers and did so through the end of the decade.[6]

Univac's financial results during the first half of the 1960s were not particularly encouraging. In 1962 the corporation found that "the rate of technological obsolescence" required it to write down the value of its older EDP equipment by more than $50 million and to accelerate the depreciation of its newer models.[7] In 1964 Univac was "losing money" and experiencing a relatively slow rate of revenue growth (14.8 percent compound growth rate from 1960 to 1964, compared with 27.4 percent from 1956 to 1960).[8]

Notwithstanding its limited success, Sperry reported to its shareholders in its 1965 Annual Report:

> Data processing is a dynamic industry, having great growth potential. It has established a place in the world's economy that is essential and will continue to grow. Such dependence upon any industry in the past has not only led to growth but also profitability. Therefore, we have determined that we will remain in and grow with the data processing business.[9]

According to R. E. McDonald, president of the Univac Division from 1966 to 1971 and later president and chief operating officer of Sperry Rand, from 1963 to 1971 Univac concentrated its marketing efforts on the federal government and airline reservations users.[10] The federal government was a very important customer for Univac in the 1960s, as it was for most of the industry. Military orders were particularly large; in 1964 the U.S. Air Force "ordered more than 150 UNIVAC 1050-II systems, as well as three UNIVAC 1107's for logistic control purposes," which, as Frederic Withington of Arthur D. Little noted at the time, was an order "large enough to cause a bulge in shipment statistics."[11] Indeed, during the 1960s Univac claimed to supply "a complete array of computers" for the military, contending that "no other company in the industry [could] match this range."[12]

Several computer systems were offered to satisfy shipboard, airborne, van-mounted, and military and space requirements. In particular, Univac was the prime supplier of the militarized AN/UYK-5 and 7, which were the standard military specification computers for the U.S. Navy. Univac also had a broad range of computers oriented to navy requirements in wide use aboard navy vessels, performing a wide variety of applications.[13] At the White Sands Missile Range in New Mexico, the Sperry Rand 1218 (identical in design to the commercial Univac 418) was used for a variety of applications, including missile guidance and tracking, data reduction and analysis, simulation, communications, logistics management, and satellite tracking.[14]

In the area of airline reservations, British European Airways ordered a 490 in 1964;[15] two years later, in fiscal 1966, Univac reported that it had won the "biggest commercial computer contract ever awarded," a $39 million contract from United Airlines, "to design and build a computerized information system that [would] handle United's needs through 1975."[16] Univac was in fact unsuccessful in its efforts to meet United's requirements, and the effort was aborted in 1970, with United moving to an IBM system.[17]

The 1108

The United Airlines system was to have been based on Univac 1108s.[18] This computer, introduced in 1964, was compatible with the thin-film 1107 and was intended for Univac's "large-scale users."[19] Withington viewed the 1108 as "technically impressive," claiming that its "very fast control memory" marked "the first significant appearance of integrated circuits in commercial computers. . . ."[20] The 1108-II, a "time-shared version" of the 1108, was introduced in 1965, but the 1108 was not delivered in volume until late 1966.[21] By 1967 the 1108 "accounted for about half the value of Sperry Rand's shipments."[22] In fiscal 1969 Univac announced the 1106, "a smaller, compatible version of the 1108 system."[23]

Univac 1108s were employed in a wide variety of contexts. A few examples from the late 1960s include the following: an 1108 scheduled trains for the French National Railway;[24] Fuji Bank Ltd., Tokyo, inaugurated a nationwide on-line banking system using an 1108;[25] the Sun Oil Company ordered an 1108 system for use in processing business and scientific problems;[26] and 1108s were used at the Marshall Space Flight Center and the White Sands Missile Range for various scientific real-time or administrative applications.[27] In 1970 Sperry Rand stated that its 1100 series computers were "acknowledged to be the most versatile processors available."[28]

Development of the 1108 was not without its problems, however; its operating system, EXEC-VIII, had "major problems in its initial stages."[29] These problems, similar to those encountered by other manufacturers with complex operating systems during the 1960s,[30] came relatively late for Sperry Rand "because it was not attempting to offer systems programs as complex and advanced as the other competitors were."[31] During the late 1960s Univac failed to deliver operating systems that completely met their advertised capabilities. Indeed, EXEC-VIII was delayed at least two or three years, not meeting its advertised capabilities until the early 1970s.[32]

The Product Line Task Force

The 1108, though successful, was not an answer to Univac's need for a compatible product line. It was announced at approximately the same time that Eckert, as head of Univac's Gemini Committee, was calling for unification of the dissimilar product lines. In 1965, in the wake of IBM's System/360 announcement, Frank Forster, Univac's president from July 1964 to early 1966,[33] set up the Product Line Task Force to review Univac products and to help him make decisions about their future.[34]

In February 1965, the task force reported that it believed Univac's manufacturing costs were higher than those of IBM, and that

> IBM's heavy investment in product research is beginning to bear fruit. Its developments in circuits, microprogramming techniques, memories, and mass storage suggest that for the first time in the short history of the industry, IBM has acquired a definite technological leadership; this, together with our cost situation, may leave us little to sell.[35]

In its next report, issued in March 1965, the task force observed that both Honeywell and RCA had committed themselves to the production of integrated computer families (the Honeywell 200 series and RCA's Spectra 70 line) in the "tailwind created by . . . IBM."[36] The report quoted the editor of *Datamation*:

> UNIVAC is the big question mark . . . every month until a new line is announced weakens their chances of success . . . and it's not clear they'll offer a complete line at all. Anything less could relegate them to the second division.[37]

Nonetheless, the task force was unsure whether Univac should try to match IBM's 360 or take some other action. Specifically, it expressed the concern

> that the RCA and Honeywell moves, although based on clever sales strategies, may not make such good sense financially. Both are based on the assumption that now that IBM has made its move, the pace of obsolescence will slow down, and longer writeoffs will be possible than in the past. It is our opinion that in about five years this assumption will prove to be catastrophic to anyone who bases his product line on it.[38]

Ultimately, Univac decided not to introduce a full-spectrum product line but to introduce only three machines, called models A, B, and C. In consonance with its concern about future technological developments rendering an entire product line obsolete, the task force called for accelerating development of the model at the low end of the line, the Model A, which was to be a 360-compatible processor targeted between the 360/20 and 360/30, to take advantage of the "large and barely exploited market for a low-priced scientific computer."[39] The task force observed, however, that:

> The announcement of Model A will have an effect on the whole product line, all the way up to the 1108A. Regardless of what is claimed, the fact that Model A contains the 360 repertoire will tell the world that our other products may be dead ends.[40]

The 9000 Series

The task force had been convened to consider Univac's product strategy nearly three years after IBM's SPREAD Committee Report; its reports appeared nearly a year after the announcement of System/360.[41] Univac finally announced its third-generation compatible computer family, the 9000 series (corresponding to the previously mentioned models A, B, and C) in the spring of 1966. Called a "line of small and medium-sized computer systems," Univac's initial offering included "the 9200, a low-cost, internally programmed punch-card system, and the 9300, a high-performance card and tape system."[42] The third machine of the line, the Model 9400, was announced in January 1968 and delivered in 1970 "from factories in the United States, West Germany and Japan."[43]

While the 9000 "aimed at compatibility" with IBM's 360,[44] it was not truly compatible. Eckert wrote:

[A] new line, compatible with IBM 360 coding . . . would have probably solved the problem. While the 9200, 9300 and 9400 are IBM like in their order code, they are not enough alike to do us any real good. We have had loads of people prove to us why we can't be IBM compatible and very little real effort to be IBM compatible, either in our software or our hardware efforts.[45]

The 9000 series was upward- but not downward-compatible among the three models. Thus, "if a person had programmed something for some of these smaller machines he could use it in one of the larger machines but not the other way around."[46] It also was not compatible with the 1100 series.[47]

Manufacturing and Marketing Policies

Univac both manufactured its own peripherals and purchased peripherals from others, remarketing them as part of its computer systems.[48] For a short period it marketed its peripheral devices to other manufacturers, who in turn remarketed them as parts of other systems.[49] Further, its own products were used as parts of systems in another way. The computers of the 9000 series, for example, were sometimes used as terminals to other manufacturers' systems.[50]

In addition to acquiring peripherals from other manufacturers, Univac contracted with software houses to have work done when it did not have sufficient in-house capability to meet its requirements and did not wish to expand internally to meet a peak load.[51] In particular, it purchased "software assistance from the Computer Sciences Corporation and also from University Computer Company."[52]

Univac both leased and sold its EDP equipment. McDonald wrote in 1967 that

Approximately 50 percent of the Division's products are sold outright with the remainder leased by customers on a one-year to five-year basis.[53]

Univac provided support services to its customers as well.[54] McDonald testified that Univac had to provide these services if it "were to compete successfully," since IBM did so.[55] However, Univac did not unbundle when IBM did in 1969, because

[W]e felt that there would be considerable anxiety in the marketplace . . . and we felt that it would be to our competitive advantage to maintain our previous pricing policy . . . and I think this was effective, at least for a period of time.[56]

McDonald testified that Univac's pricing policy between 1963 and 1971 was to set "a price that would generally be 10 percent, as a rule of thumb, below the price offered by IBM," not taking into account the performance of associated peripheral devices.[57] Univac attempted to set its products' price/performance between those of IBM's products, much as RCA had done with its Spectra series.[58] Considering that Univac's 9000 series was announced two years after System/360, its pricing approach was perfectly understandable.

IBM was not the only competitor about which Univac was concerned, however. While McDonald in 1967 identified "eight major hardware manufacturers" who were "[a]t the hard core of the industry" (IBM, Univac, CDC, RCA, GE, Honeywell, Burroughs, and NCR),[59] he recognized that

> By the 1960's, there were up to 50 major suppliers of automatic computing digital and analog computers and data processors. Over 700 organizations with some 30,000 persons were engaged in one part or another of the computer field.[60]

These included peripheral manufacturers, software suppliers, service centers, and leasing companies.[61]

In the mid-1960s Univac management became concerned about leasing companies. Forster wrote to McDonald in 1966, stating that he had

> some apprehension and also some prejudice in that I consider them to be parasitic. . . . If computers do not stay on rental, since they have no loyalty to any particular equipment their manner of disposal could be damaging.[62]

Univac's concern about the "manner of disposal" of leasing company equipment was that the leasing company would at some later time market it at very low prices, in effect "dumping it" on the market, knocking Univac's own equipment out of customer installations.[63]

Univac responded to this concern. In January 1969 management approved revisions in Univac's long-term lease plan that were designed to "decrease future vulnerability" to third-party leasing companies and that included the adoption of step-down payment plans for long-term leases and price-cutting of five-year lease rates for Univac's "most profitable systems."[64]

Univac's Success in the Late 1960s

Despite the fact that Univac did not offer a single compatible family with the breadth and compatibility of the IBM 360, it experienced substantial growth in its EDP business during the 1960s. At the end of 1965, prior to volume shipments of the 1108 or the announcement of the 9000 series, Univac's U.S. EDP revenues were $203 million; at the end of 1970 they were $478 million.[65]

By fiscal 1969 the Univac Division had become "the largest contributor to [Sperry's] revenues and earnings."[66] Withington wrote:

> The Univac Division became the largest single contributor to the profits of the corporation (it seems only a short time ago that Univac was castigated as the largest single drain on them!).[67]

Univac's growth was not limited to the United States. From at least the 1960s on, Univac offered a single worldwide product line.[68] In 1967 the firm's International Division conducted operations through 32 subsidiaries and distributors in Canada, Central and South America, Europe, and the Far East.[69] For 1970 Univac reported that its "international business [was] growing at an even higher rate than the domestic operations."[70]

Univac made great strides in the last half of the 1960s despite its slow start in undertaking a compatible family of products and its reluctance to accept disk technology. Writing in 1967, McDonald recognized what the problem had been and what would be required to solve it:

> Planning will be a requisite to survival on the basis upon which profitable business development can be structured. . . . The combined magnitude of both opportunity and risk superimposed upon the rapidly changing pace of the industry will rule out success based upon "seat of the pants" decision-making. The old technique of fumble and correct errors is out. There will not be time in the future to recover from serious mistakes without suffering severe penalties. We, therefore, must measure daily events against a flexible, preconceived plan of action in order to react in a timely fashion, competitively. Hard planning will be a part of daily activity. It will not be a luxury in the future.
>
> This is the precise area of one of UNIVAC's greatest past weaknesses. It is an area which has received concentrated attention since 1964 and will continue to receive emphasis in the future.[71]

Univac was finally back on its way to becoming a successful computer company. As we have have seen, it entered the 1970s acquiring RCA's computer business and profitably using it.

HONEYWELL

The history of Honeywell during 1964-70 turned on the success of the Honeywell 200 — a product that gave birth to a compatible family of computer systems that, in turn, sparked expansion of Honeywell's peripheral line and service capabilities. Despite some difficulties along the way, Honeywell ended the 1960s with a large and successful array of EDP products and services, with rising revenues and profits derived from them.

The 200 Series

In December 1963, Honeywell announced its 200 computer system. Richard Bloch, who before going to GE was vice-president for product planning at Honeywell, led the Honeywell team that designed the 200,[72] which was intended to make conversion from the IBM 1400 series as easy as possible.[73] An effort was made to replicate closely the file structure, media, and formatting of the 1400, and the LIBERATOR conversion aid was developed.[74] The LIBERATOR enabled 1401 programs to be converted to 200 series programs by means of assembly language and object code translators.[75] Because the conversion required only a very small amount of manual intervention, it resulted in a high degree of efficiency.[76]

Honeywell felt this strategy would give it an "accelerated move into the [general-purpose business data-processing] field, which we needed."[77] In 1963 Honeywell's EDP revenues were only 4 percent of its total revenues, and it had yet to make a profit in that area.[78]

The LIBERATOR successfully accomplished the conversion for which it was designed.[79] Further, the 200, which was also compatible with "most widely used small computers,"[80] offered users both an easy conversion method and price/performance superior to its preexisting competitors, including the 1401.[81] Both of these characteristics led the Honeywell 200 to enormous success.[82] Withington wrote in October 1964 that Honeywell had obtained many hundreds of orders for the 200, and that no computer manufacturer was gaining ground as fast as Honeywell.[83] McCollister of RCA testified that Honeywell expanded its sales force during the early 1960s, so that by 1965 it had 50 to 75 percent more people than did RCA, although the two companies had started the 1960s equal.[84] Sales were made to all kinds of customers.[85]

We have already seen in Chapter 5 the pressure that the Honeywell 200 put on IBM, tempting it to depart from the System/360 program to offer an SLT-based 1401 and making it urgent to announce the 360/30 — which was two or three times more powerful than the 1401 at less than one and a half times the price.[86] The 360/30, aside from its other desirable features, also offered better price/performance than did the Honeywell 200.[87] Nevertheless, despite the System/360 announcement in April 1964, Honeywell continued its successful course. In December 1964, T. V. Learson wrote to Thomas J. Watson, Jr., that "the Honeywell 200 story" had led to 300 losses to date for tape-oriented systems, with 1,000 such situations in the doubtful category, 40 percent of which he estimated as losses.[88]

Honeywell spent the remainder of the decade enlarging on and solidifying the 200's success. In a 1969 speech Honeywell's chairman, James H. Binger, outlined his strategy:

> In the beginning we made a conscious decision and adopted a strategy to compete in a broad segment of the computer marketplace, and to make significant penetration through a wide array of products and services. Our highly successful Series 200 computer line is the prime example of this strategy.[89]

In June 1964, after IBM's announcement of System/360, Honeywell announced the 2200, and followed it in February 1965 with three other compatible new members of the 200 series, giving it a "family of computer systems": the 120, the 1200, the 2200, and the 4200. Honeywell stated that "[t] he family concept of these new systems gives our customers the assurance that they can meet problems of growth by expanding through an extended range of central processors, continuing to use the peripheral equipment already in their EDP system."[90] The 200 series was also, through hardware design and programming adaptations, "accessible to [Honeywell's] 400 and 800 [users] who can shift to the higher levels of the newer series with a minimum of adjustment, and with the protection of a substantial part of their prior programming and file investment."[91]

Clarence W. Spangle, vice-president and general manager of Honeywell's EDP Division in 1965-69 and president of Honeywell Information Systems when he testified in 1975, stated that the 200 line was priced so that the three-year lease prices would be "roughly equal to those of IBM for equivalent price/performance on a system basis," with the one-year price "slightly above that of IBM" and the five-year price "5 to 10 percent below the one-year price of IBM."[92] According to Bloch, Honeywell gauged its pricing "against the nearest competitive IBM line or the IBM equipment which we were hoping to supersede, to a lesser extent some of the other competition," because "if we were to increase our penetration of the market we would obviously have to take away some of the captive business that was presently in IBM's hands."[93]

As IBM improved the capabilities of its 360 line, Honeywell further increased those of the 200 family through peripheral and software announcements. A number of new products, both hardware and software, were announced for the Series 200 line at the end of 1966, covering mass storage, data communications, and expanded multiprogramming, including four magnetic disk devices (which Honeywell purchased from CDC) for "random access information storage and retrieval" and a number of terminal devices.[94] In 1967 "more than a hundred hardware and software products and product modifications were added to the Series 200 EDP line and the control computer line."[95]

Honeywell's 200 series was sufficiently popular to be marketed by leasing companies. Leasco dealt in Honeywell equipment before 1967,[96] and Finalco was leasing Honeywell 200s and 1200s, a fact that made at least one Honeywell regional sales manager "a little nervous over what could happen if those systems come off lease."[97] Transamerica also leased Honeywell equipment in the late 1960s.[98]

Problems and Solutions

Other Systems

Honeywell was not without problems over this period, however. One of these was the 8200 computer system, which was planned to be the most powerful system in the 200 series and was announced in 1965.[99] The 8200 was intended to bring together the Honeywell 200 and 800 lines, the latter of which was installed at that time at about 100 different sites.[100] "At the time of the announcement the development of the machine had not begun. And as the development was undertaken, it turned out to be much more difficult to do those things than had been anticipated." Honeywell spent large amounts of money, more than it had planned, to develop the equipment and the software to supply with the equipment.[101]

Honeywell was not able to achieve the objective of having that system be an upgrade path for the 200 line, so, according to Spangle, "its market became limited really to those 800 customers who wanted to continue largely in the batch processing mode and wanted higher throughput."[102] As a result of all this, Honeywell was able to ship only about 40 of these machines, which Spangle testified was not enough to make the whole investment and development worthwhile. The particular problem that caused the 8200 to fall short of its objective was the need for two operating systems in one computer system — Honeywell could not get it to work.[103]

Honeywell tried to aid its customers with 800 systems installed in another way — by the provision of a larger system compatible only with the 800. Thus it announced the 1800 in 1962. The 1800, however, "sold in only very small amounts." Withington attributed this to the fact that the IBM 360 and GE 600 series, available at the same time, "were regarded as superior to the Honeywell 1800 by users and Honeywell users who outgrew their Honeywell 800 apparently more frequently left Honeywell for a competitor than accepted the 1800 instead." This was because the 360 and GE 600 "offered early versions of operating systems whose primary initial virtue was to permit multiple programming . . . plus automatic control of peripheral equipment in ways which would simplify the users' programming requirements."[104]

Peripherals

In the early 1960s, Honeywell still believed that magnetic card devices would be competitively superior to magnetic disk drives. It had under development such devices, which had been announced to customers. The slow speed and unreliability of the card devices, however, caused difficulties and hurt Honeywell in its marketing of systems.[105] Finally the effort was dropped, termed in IBM reports "a dismal failure."[106]

Honeywell made its decision to abandon the magnetic-card, mass-storage devices following IBM's announcement of the 2311 disk drive for the System/360. Withington testified that this was "a major change for Honeywell, because at the time there was no expenditure whatever for disk drive development, all of the mass storage development efforts being put into the magnetic card devices, so Honeywell had to start a new effort from scratch and also search the industry for OEM [original equipment manufacturer] sources for suitable disk drives."[107] By 1967 CDC was shipping its 9492 disk file to Honeywell, which subsequently became its principal customer for CDC 9433 and 9434 disk drives, taking in excess of 4,700 units.[108] Honeywell started to manufacture its own disk packs in 1967, but continued to purchase the drives.[109]

Honeywell began efforts to produce all of the peripheral devices contained in its EDP systems.[110] Prior to 1965 it purchased IBM card readers and card punches and offered them with its own computer systems, including the 200. Honeywell decided, however, to develop its own manufacturing capability in punch-card equipment, a decision that was accelerated by the announcement in late 1964 that IBM would no longer lease such equipment to Honeywell and other manufacturers planning to re-lease them to customers, but would only sell.[111] During 1965 Honeywell started deliveries of its own card reader and, later, its own card punches.[112]

During 1965 Honeywell introduced new models of printers and tape transports, and started deliveries of a variety of communications terminals as well.[113] It continued to acquire software or software development from outside companies, however.[114] In contrast with IBM's full-scale entry into the manufacture of its own components in 1961, Honeywell divested itself of its component operations in 1965, stating it "felt that we should concentrate our attention on electronic end products rather than components of this type. We intend to rely on the numerous well qualified suppliers of semiconductor devices for our substantial requirements."[115] It reversed that decision in 1969 with the announcement of a new integrated circuit development center.[116]

Marketing Practices

Bloch testified that during his tenure at Honeywell (1955-67) 80 to 90 percent of the firm's computer systems were leased. This was dictated "pretty much" by the customer.[117] Starting in 1965, Honeywell offered three- and five-year lease plans for systems and peripherals.[118] In 1967 nearly 70 percent of "commercial" Series 200 contracts signed were for five-year periods.[119]

To finance its leases, Honeywell in 1966 developed a sale and leaseback method. It would arrange to sell lenders an amount of installed equipment and then lease it back from them. The lenders gave Honeywell cash for the equipment, and Honeywell repaid in installments the amount of the cash advance plus a financing charge. According to Spangle, this "improved our profit and loss statement" and produced "more cash with which to operate."[120]

The sale and leaseback method continued until 1967, when a wholly owned subsidiary called Honeywell Finance was set up. That subsidiary "was able to accomplish much of the benefits of the sales and leaseback transaction in so far as creating or attracting cash and capital . . . although it did not have the effect of accelerating the profit from the lease part of it as the sale and leaseback transaction did." It did, however, preserve the residual value of the equipment for Honeywell.[121] Honeywell Finance borrowed money from banks and investors through the issuance of commercial paper and of long-term and medium-term bonds, on the security of the receivables from Honeywell's rental contracts.

The loan proceeds were passed through to Honeywell.[122] Honeywell's initial investment in this subsidiary was $15 million, half in a subordinated loan and half in common stock. A $60 million line of bank credit was established, of which $23,350,000 was being utilized at the end of 1967.[123]

During the middle and late 1960s, Honeywell bundled educational courses for customers, programming support, operating systems, and application software, supplying them without separate charge.[124] Bloch testified that this was due to "the dictates of the marketplace . . . the traditional way in which these services and equipments were being offered from the time that the field had begun."[125] When IBM announced its unbundling decision in 1969, Honeywell conducted a study to decide what action to take. The study recommended that Honeywell not follow IBM. Spangle testified that unbundling would have involved administrative difficulties and possible contractual problems. Moreover, Honeywell

> hoped to gain some temporary market advantage . . . because we thought there would be quite a bit of resistance to this change by the customers and prospects, and that because of that we might be able to get some customers that we otherwise would not have been able to get.[126]

Instead of unbundling, Honeywell increased its prices slightly, since it believed that IBM's change would be regarded as a price increase.[127] Honeywell then began to advertise its "package pricing" as its "same old bundle of joy . . . once in a while you move ahead just by standing still."[128]

Product and Service Acquisitions and Expansion

Prior to 1966 Honeywell had developed a series of small, high-speed, general-purpose digital computers to enhance its capability to provide control systems integrated with instrumentation of its own manufacture, a related business in which it had been involved for many years.[129] In 1966 Honeywell acquired the Computer Control Company, which at that time was a leading manufacturer of such small, high-performance hardware, and established it as Honeywell's Computer Control Division.[130] The Computer Control Company products included the DDP-116, DDP-416, and DDP-516 computer systems and a line of memories. These computer systems were used by customers in communications switching, engineering, and scientific applications. They were also offered to other computer firms that built systems for typesetting, plotting, and freight-yard distribution applications.[131]

Honeywell applied the "advanced digital techniques" gathered from the acquisition of Computer Control to its own products in the industrial process-control area, as well as to other areas of data processing.[132] For example, the DDP-516 was offered for time-sharing, communications, and medical applications.[133] It was made available for use aboard ships, aircraft, and vans. The modified DDP-516s had all the capabilities of the standard commercial version — software, price, delivery, flexibility, and proven design — while meeting the operational requirements of military, marine, and other users.[134] Ruggedized DDP-516s were used by the U.S. Coast Guard to gather data for weather forecasting.[135] A Honeywell press release stated that "using a general purpose machine rather than specially designed systems formerly employed will let the Coast Guard apply computers to many of its activities at sea."[136] American Airlines used 516s to control IBM 1977 terminals within its passenger services system.[137] The 116 was sold to Bunker Ramo for the "control and filing of up-to-the-minute freight booking information" on airline passenger planes. It was also used as part of a railroad car classification system by Westinghouse Air Brake Company, and in process-control applications by the Brown and Williamson Tobacco Corporation.[138]

In 1969 Honeywell introduced its first expansion of the old DDP line: the Honeywell 316, which it called a "minicomputer" and a "general purpose digital computer."[139] The 316 had a full line of peripherals and was offered for real-time control, data acquisition and communications applications, and as a front end for commercial computers made by others.[140]

Honeywell later incorporated these smaller computers into its larger computer systems and offered them for business data-processing. It also sold these smaller computers to its Control Systems Division for incorporation into systems that were then resold, and to outside buyers for use in specialized systems.[141]

In the late 1960s Honeywell expanded its EDP services offerings. It organized the Information Services Division. Sixteen data centers using a Honeywell 1648 for time-sharing were opened around the country. The Honeywell 1648, composed of several Series 16 computers, was introduced by the Computer Control Division.[142] According to Binger, it competed with the IBM 360/25 and 360/30, the Digital Equipment Corporation's PDP 10 and TSS/8 (based on the PDP 8), and the Hewlett-Packard 2000 A and B.[143]

Early in 1968 Honeywell combined its EDP Division and Computer Control Division into the Computer and Communications Group, to "bring into one organization those related activities that are essential to the computer and computer-oriented business." The new group was given the mission to involve Honeywell in the "total information systems market."[144] That group became Honeywell's contribution to Honeywell Information Systems in the 1970 merger with, and eventual acquisition of, GE's computer operations.[145]

Between 1963 and 1969 Honeywell's domestic EDP revenues increased from $27 million to $210.8 million, a more than sevenfold increase.[146]

In sum, Honeywell's EDP operations grew steadily throughout the 1960s, and that growth showed no signs of slackening at the end of the decade. By the end of 1969 Honeywell reported that its Computer and Communications Group continued to be the fastest-growing area of its business; indeed, its computer and communications business was growing faster than the industry, and the rate of profitability increase was exceeding the growth rate.[147] Domestic computer operations had been profitable for four years and overseas operations for two,[148] and Honeywell was investing, putting over half of all its research, development, and engineering dollars into the computer area.[149] In a speech given in 1969, Binger stated that the only possible factor limiting Honeywell's growth was the shortage of qualified people:

> . . . [W]e are not technology limited, we are not capital limited, we are not basically market limited. We may at some point be people limited to some extent.[150]

BURROUGHS

A slow starter in computers, by 1964 Burroughs still had not transformed itself into much of a computer company, having developed and marketed relatively few EDP products. Beginning in 1964, it shook up its operations, reduced expenses, and, while remaining profitable, increased its investments in research and development. The results were a proliferation of new products, substantial growth, and increased profitability over the decade.

Burroughs in 1964: Problems and Changes

Burroughs' situation in 1964 did not look promising for future growth in the computer industry. Its president, R. W. Macdonald, wrote in 1975:

> [I]n 1964, some analysts who observed the developing computer industry, had serious doubts about the ability of Burroughs to survive in the new environment as a computer company. Even some members of our own Board of Directors were concerned, and a highly respected financial journal predicted flatly that Burroughs either would have to merge into another company or fail.[151]

Those serious doubts were based on two factors: Burroughs' mediocre record in computers and the perceived strength of its competition.

> We faced giants such as RCA, with 1964 revenues of over $2 billion; Honeywell, with over $600 million; Sperry Rand, with its Univac Division, with $1.3 billion. IBM in those days had revenues of over $3 billion, but IBM was not the largest company we faced in terms of total revenues. General Electric, with serious intentions and a major program in computers, already was an industrial giant with revenues in excess of $5 billion.[152]

In contrast, Burroughs' total annual worldwide revenues were less than $400 million.[153] Its financial record since 1961 had been poor; its revenues had "remained on a plateau" and its earnings were "unsatisfactory."[154]

With regard to technical achievements, Macdonald wrote that by 1964, IBM was "well on their way to development of a truly impressive research and development capability," and "General Electric had been exploring the uses of the electron for years in both electrical and electronic applications." In contrast:

> Although [Burroughs] had been engaged in electronic research and had achieved initial success with a few very advanced new products, the products on which our revenue and profits depended remained primarily mechanical.[155]

Starting in 1964 and continuing through the 1960s, Burroughs set out to achieve its objective of "profitable growth" and "moderate growth commensurate with maintaining profitability" in computers.[156] As a first step, in 1964 Burroughs' president, Ray Eppert, formed the Profit Improvement Committee. The committee was to consider reorganization "with respect to all aspects of marketing, manufacturing and engineering operations, and the establishment of clear product development objectives." Its "primary charge was the swift improvement of the company's profitability."[157]

The changes instituted by this committee (of which Macdonald was a member) and further changes instituted by Macdonald, who in 1964 was given "broad administrative responsibilities" and in 1966 became chief operating officer, were intended to accomplish two things: first, reduced expenses, and second, improved development of computer products.[158]

Reduction of Expenses

The Profit Improvement Committee found that Burroughs' " 'problems' lay in the efficiency of its operations," and not in "spending levels associated with research and development." The committee instituted several changes to increase efficiency (those changes were in contrast with the policies implemented at RCA in the late 1960s, discussed in Chapter 8).

First, the productivity of the sales force was increased. To do this, the committee reduced salaries and commissions for salesmen, restructured the sales organization, and moved unproductive salesmen out of the division.[159] Burroughs found that

> The combined effect of these organizational changes gave us the equivalent of adding 500 highly productive salesmen — with no increase in budget costs.[160]

Second, the committee found that manufacturing costs "had been increasing as a percentage of revenue every year for ten years." It undertook to cut those costs by reducing the number of managers at its plants, specializing the plants by products, introducing a series of financial controls, designating each marketing district a "profit center," modernizing existing facilities, and building 17 new plants. With these changes, by 1966 manufacturing costs were reduced by more than 5 percent of revenue, and continued downward in ensuing years.[161]

The combined effect of these major changes, along with reductions in marketing and G&A expenses and other economies resulting from stricter overall control, produced an increase in net earnings of over 200 percent in two years, from $10 million in 1964, to $31 million in 1966.[162]

Increased Product Development

The Profit Improvement Committee decided that Burroughs' lack of profitability did not result from too much spending for research and development.[163] In fact, the reduction of expenses just discussed allowed increased expenditures in research and development, and Macdonald pushed to take advantage of this opportunity.[164]

Burroughs pressed ahead with its computer developments in two ways. First, it expanded its "product program to become more of a full range company."[165] Second, it offered greater capability and increased the diversity of its computer products. The addition of new products, in turn, made more money available for research and development.[166] By 1969 Burroughs' annual spending in research and development had doubled to $35 million.[167]

The changes that Burroughs began in the mid-1960s, particularly its increased research and development and improved manufacturing capabilities, required new investment. Macdonald described those investments between 1965 and 1972 thus:

> Since 1965, Burroughs had spent some $250 million in R&D. These funds came entirely from our own resources and were used for the development of our commercial and trademark product line.
>
> Over the same period, we have also invested just over one billion dollars to expand the manufacturing and marketing facilities to sell the products resulting from this R&D expenditure. Approximately $750 million of this represented a marketing investment. It went for facilities, inventory, receivables and lease funding. The remaining $250 million was for manufacturing facilities, men, machinery and equipment. I should also point out that this billion dollars was in addition to the $500 million that we had already invested by the end of 1965. Of the billion dollars invested over the last seven years, $250 million was generated through retained earnings and the remaining $750 million was raised in the financial markets through loans and equity issues.[168]

Computer Developments 1964-69

Burroughs moved both to extend the breadth of its product line and to increase the capabilities offered by its computer products. By the end of 1969 it had succeeded in adding many new products.

The 500 Systems Family

An important factor in Burroughs' success during the 1960s was the success of its 500 systems family. Nine systems in or related to that family were eventually announced: the B 500 (which was closely related to the smaller B 200 and B 300), B 2500, B 3500, B 4500, B 5500, B 6500, B 7500, B 8300, and B 8500. Because of problems that Burroughs, in common with other manufacturers, experienced with its larger machines, the B 7500, B 8300, and B 8500 were either not delivered or not operational at customer locations, and the B 6500 was delivered late. The B 4500 was never delivered.[169] Still, by 1969 Burroughs was able to report that "this family of balanced general purpose commercial data processors have [*sic*] helped the Corporation establish an excellent position in the EDP market."[170] However, the 500 systems "family" was not machine-language-compatible, as was the IBM 360, but was compatible only through the use of higher-level languages.[171]

Four months after IBM announced its System/360, Burroughs in August 1964 announced the B 5500, described as a "modular data processing system of advanced design for both commercial and scientific applications in the medium to large scale categories."[172] Burroughs reported that the B 5500 had "up to three times more productivity than its predecessor, the B 5000."[173] B 5500s were used for commercial and scientific applications, as well as in the space program.[174] By 1965 Burroughs reported that its orders for the B 5500 had exceeded its forecasts, and "included many diverse applications in national and state governments, advertising, manufacturing, ship building and research."[175]

Burroughs had two groups that marketed computers: Business Machines and Defense, Space and Special Systems. The relationship between the two groups was close, and involved marketing and designing the same or similar products.[176] Products designed and marketed commercially often were later modified or further developed and marketed for military use, and vice versa. For example, the B 5000, the foundation for the subsequent 500 product line, grew out of military work (the Burroughs D 825).[177] And when the Defense, Space and Special Systems Group was awarded a contract to produce a mobile communications system for the U.S. Army, it modified four B 3500 computer systems that had been developed by the Business Machines Group.[178]

During 1965 the Defense, Space and Special Systems Group announced the B 8500. It was marketed for "high volume, time-sharing, on-line business, scientific and government applications," and provided for "management information processing, including the full complement of business data processing, reporting and message handling as well as centralized or decentralized scientific and engineering computations." According to Burroughs, the B 8500 was a "logical extension" of the concepts of "modularity, multiprocessing and automatic scheduling programs used with the B 5500 and D 800 series systems." A good deal of the architecture came from the military D 825. The B 8500 made use of monolithic integrated circuits.[179]

By 1967 Burroughs reported that

Broadening customer interest in the giant self-regulating B 8500 system confirms the importance Burroughs has given the development and production of this supercomputer. It has the unique ability to multiprocess a number of batches of accounting routines, solve engineering and scientific problems, and deal with transactions as they occur, all at the same time. The interest of potential users in the B 8500 has greatly increased for on-line, real-time business and scientific applications.[180]

Burroughs experienced problems developing the B 8500, however, and none was ever delivered.[181]

It was not until 1966 that Burroughs began to turn its 500 systems into a family of computer systems somewhat comparable in breadth with IBM's System/360. In that year Burroughs introduced three new "members of the 500 systems," the B 6500, the B 2500, and the B 3500.[182]

The B 6500 central processors employed monolithic integrated circuitry throughout; had core or thin-film main memories; were "equipped for true multiprocessing, parallel processing, and real-time and time-sharing operations"; and had a "comprehensive, automatic operating system for program control, completely coordinated with the hardware elements."[183] The system was not delivered until 1969.[184] Even then its "full development" was delayed by problems in its system software, which were corrected in 1971.[185]

The "medium-priced" B 2500 and B 3500 were released for sale in April 1966.[186] Demonstrations of these systems "were made on a broad range of business applications programmed in COBOL, including remote processing and multiprocessing under the automatic control of the Master Control Program."[187] With these two systems Burroughs, for the first time, offered price/performance (roughly measured) comparable with that of System/360.[188] By 1967 it had received "an impressive number of orders" for the B 2500 and B 3500 from users in "such diverse fields as finance, manufacturing, government, retailing, insurance and publishing."[189]

In 1967 Burroughs announced the B 7500. Burroughs reported that this release "stimulated interest in other EDP products and strengthened the Company's position in this highly competitive field."[190] The B 7500 was never delivered, however.[191]

There were additional problems at the high end. In its 1968 Annual Report, Burroughs reported that it had installed the B 3800, "part of the B 8500 development program," to provide "a central passenger reservation system for a major world airline." That installation used "three central processors functioning under the automatic control of a single software operating system"; there were more than 2,700 input and display terminals throughout the United States with keyboard input and cathode ray tubes "to display data transmitted to and received from the computer."[192] Like Univac, however, Burroughs experienced difficulties with its airline passenger reservation system. The B 8300s at the airline (TWA) were never operational, because they "could not accommodate the projected workload" and Burroughs "had not demonstrated adequate availability or reliability of the system."[193] The effort was terminated, and in late 1970 TWA sued Burroughs for nondelivery of the B 8300.[194] In 1971 TWA installed one IBM 360/75 and two IBM 360/65s to perform the reservations function.[195]

By 1969 Burroughs reported that the production of its "'500 Systems' reached an all-time high during the year."[196] The firm described some of the reasons for the success of the 500 systems:

> With the Burroughs 500 Systems, the corporation gained an advantage by developing the software and hardware in parallel. Engineers in these two areas combined their efforts as the systems were developed, closing the time lag between installation and complete usefulness of the system to the customer. This advantage also insures the user maximum performance of the complete system.[197]

> Our systems software provides self-regulated operation which assures Burroughs customers of maximum work output through the techniques of multiprogramming in which a number of different programs are handled at one time. In the larger systems, simultaneous parallel processing of programs is achieved by use of multiple central processors. Another important advantage to users of our medium and large systems is a modular architecture which enables them to add processors and increase main memory and input/output capacity in increments as needs expand. Upward compatibility — from one "500" Systems computer to the next largest in size — is assured through the use of higher level programming languages.[198]

These characteristics were much the same as those IBM had earlier employed successfully in its System/360.

Smaller Computers

Burroughs marketed its smaller computers in three lines: the B 200 successors, the E series, and the L/TC line.

Burroughs had introduced the B 200 in 1961.[199] In early 1965 it introduced the compatible B 300 data-processing system and, also in 1965, the compatible smaller B 340 bank data-processing system.[200] By 1966 Burroughs reported that the B 200 and B 300 computers had been

> [l] eased or purchased by customers in many fields including transportation, data processing services, photo supplies, utilities, insurance, publishing, brewing, school systems, manufacturing, baking, textile milling, property management, retailing, wholesaling, distributing, government and public service, research and finance.[201]

During 1968 Burroughs introduced its B 500 computer, which had an automatic operating system and used COBOL. Although promoted by Burroughs as a "member of the '500' Systems EDP family," the 500 was compatible in assembly language with the B 100, B 200, and B 300 systems but was compatible with the larger 500 systems only through the use of COBOL.[202]

During 1964 Burroughs brought out its E 2100 computer.[203] Between 1964 and 1970 it added to the E series with the E 3000, E 5000, E 6000, and E 8000.[204] The machines of the E series were small, solid-state computers with electronic logic and data storage.[205] COBOL was available on the larger E series computers, the E 6000 and E 8000.[206]

In 1968 Burroughs took a major step forward with the announcement of its TC 500 terminal computer, expanding the line in 1969 with the TC 700 and TC 310 terminal computers.[207] The TC 500 was characterized by John Jones of Southern Railway as the first "intelligent terminal" — that is, the "first programmable terminal . . . that had in it a processor, a general purpose processor with memory and input and output, that could be programmed to perform in some way as the user desired as opposed to being hard wired." The TC 500

> [h]ad a keyboard for an operator to input data and a printer on which data could be printed, a character printer, and a processor inside of it which could be programmed to give that device any particular characteristics in its operation, as well as do other processing of the data as it [*sic*] was entered or before it was printed.[208]

Also resulting from the same engineering as the TC computers was the L 2000 computer. Introduced in 1969, the L 2000 was a computer designed for billing, with the property that "the addition of a data communications unit converts it to a terminal computer able to communicate with a central computer system."[209]

Macdonald described the L/TC series as follows:

> These internally programmed machines are programmed in COBOL and can operate under operator control or under program control.
>
> . . . .
>
> These small systems are, in terms of what they can perform, small full-scale computers.[210]

Peripherals

During 1964-69, Burroughs improved upon its existing peripheral equipment. It introduced several models of improved card readers, printers, sorter-readers, tape transports, multitape listers, and tape drives.[211]

By 1964 Burroughs had developed and was marketing a disk file with one head per track.[212] This head-per-track file had a slightly faster access time and a slightly higher cost per unit of storage than the movable-head devices.[213] During the mid-1960s Burroughs found that its disk drive was "a significant factor in the growth of the Company's business in EDP systems."[214]

When IBM introduced its 1311 disk drive with a removable disk pack in 1962, Burroughs did not offer a disk drive with a similar removable pack, nor did it offer such a disk drive after IBM introduced the 2311 and 2314 disk drives. Where Burroughs' customers wanted the advantages of a removable disk pack, Burroughs sought to convince them to keep their files on magnetic tape and to load and unload the files onto the Burroughs fixed-pack drives.[215] Finally, in the late 1960s Burroughs arranged to acquire disk drives with removable disk packs from Century Data, and in 1970 it began marketing those disk drives as part of its computer systems.[216]

Burroughs at the End of the 1960s

By the end of the decade the changes Burroughs had instituted in 1964 had begun to achieve its objective of "profitable growth."[217] The firm had reduced costs and increased efficiency in its manufacturing and marketing operations and had increased its expenditures in research and development.[218] Aided by those changes, Burroughs had expanded its product line in terms of both range and the capabilities offered. From a few midsize computers in 1964, Burroughs went to delivering several complete lines of computer systems ranging from small (E series, L/TC series) to very large (B 6500) by 1969. Its peripheral offerings also had expanded. Moreover, Burroughs was continuing its technological development of intelligent terminals, an area that became very important in the 1970s.[219]

Burroughs' management understood the close interrelationship of its extensive product line. In a 1969 presentation to the New York Society of Security Analysts, Ray Macdonald stated, concerning the relationship among various computer products:

> In 1967, I said that when I had the next opportunity of addressing this group we might refer to electronic accounting machines, electronic accounting systems, terminal units and electronic computers as one continuous market from small machine to giant computer. This blending of several markets into a single broad market has now become more evident.[220]

Burroughs' financial results reflected the growth of its computer products. From 1964 to 1969 its total corporate revenues did not quite double, increasing from $392 million to $759 million. During the same period its domestic EDP revenues increased from $61 million to $260 million, and its corporate profits jumped 500 percent.[221]

Writing in 1975, Macdonald looked back on the results of the changes that Burroughs had instituted in 1964:

> Our revenue has doubled every five years, and today, at $1.5 billion, is four times its level of ten years ago.
> Our net earnings have increased by 14 times during the 10-year period, and this is the best record of growth in the mainframe computer industry.
> Our manpower worldwide has increased from about 34,000 to more than 51,500. We are operating 54 plants in ten countries and two more plants are under construction.[222]

NATIONAL CASH REGISTER

Historically, National Cash Register (NCR) had concentrated on marketing its "traditional products" — cash registers, accounting machines, and adding machines — to customers engaged in retailing and banking.[223] By the beginning of 1964, while continuing to concentrate on customers in those areas, NCR had introduced and was marketing two models of its second-generation 315 computer system that had been announced in the early 1960s.[224] At the same time it was actively expanding "the functions of its traditional products."[225] In 1964 NCR's domestic EDP revenues ($46.3 million) accounted for only about 13 percent of its total domestic revenues.[226]

NCR's desire gradually to develop computers to support its traditional business was expressed by its president, Robert S. Oelman, in a November 1964 speech. He stated that the company had "recently" undergone "the most significant change in [its] long history . . . the advent of electronic data processing." However, this change did not mean the demise of NCR's "traditional products" for two reasons. First, the traditional products were "being integrated" into EDP systems; the traditional products served as an "input medium" for data and were thus in "the mainstream of the data processing revolution." Second, NCR could use "new technologies to add important machine features and to improve overall performance" of its traditional products.[227] Thus, NCR, rather than recognizing (as IBM had in the 1950s) that computers were going to make its "traditional business" obsolete and committing itself to the new technology, chose to split its resources between computers and its traditional cash register and accounting machine products.[228]

Outside observers also reported on NCR's desire to proceed gradually in computers. Withington described NCR as following a plan during the 1960s to proceed "methodically" in computers by using them "to complement its existing product and marketing positions." NCR did this because

> The risks and investments involved in introducing highly innovative products to rapidly achieve a major share of computer shipments do not appeal to NCR, and . . . as long as the company's overall position, growth, and profit objectives are supported the company's computer market share is not a primary objective.[229]

As a result of this strategy, NCR introduced only a few improvements to its second-generation equipment from 1964 to 1968. During this period it failed to come close to the price/performance (roughly measured) of IBM's System/360.[230] During the summer of 1964, NCR announced a follow-on member of the 315 family, the 315 Rod Memory Computer (RMC), which used thin-film memory technology.[231] Multiprogramming for the 315 RMC was announced during 1966.[232] During 1965 NCR announced the Series 500 computer, a general-purpose computer that attempted to combine "magnetic ledger bookkeeping with various combinations of punched card, punched paper tape or optical equipment."[233]

NCR did not readily abandon its existing products. Despite the fact that the CRAM file had been superseded by the disk drive, in 1966 NCR announced a more powerful version of that product rather than replace it entirely with disk drives.[234] In computer systems NCR continued to improve its second-generation 315 computer family, introducing increased modularity.[235]

It was not until March 5, 1968, almost four years after IBM's announcement of System/360, that NCR introduced its third-generation computers, the Century series. The first models announced were the Century 100 and 200, and NCR stated that it intended soon to announce a Century 400, which would be capable of performing time-sharing.[236]

NCR offered the Century 100 and 200 systems on one-, three-, or five-year rental terms, in addition to sale.[237] (By April 30, 1969, over half the orders were for a five-year term.)[238] Each system was marketed with a minimum amount of main memory, a card reader or paper tape reader, printer, and disk drive.[239] Other available peripherals included CRAM, a MICR sorter-reader, an optical journal reader, punched-card units, and visual display units.[240]

NCR promoted the Century series as its "most important new line of products,"[241] asserting that it incorporated many advances over its previous machines, including the following:

1. The Century series continued the use of thin-film main memory introduced on the 315 RMC. NCR called this an "important 'first,'" making the performance of the thin-film memory available at a lower cost.[242] Within about a year, however, NCR replaced the thin-film memory with core memory.[243]

2. The Century series used integrated circuits "throughout all Century computers and peripherals."[244]

3. The Century series provided for "complete upward compatibility," so that "as a user's needs increase, more powerful processors can replace original units as required."[245]

4. The Century series had more advanced peripherals — including, for the first time, disk drives: "The philosophy" of the Century series "is that the disc concept is an integral part of all members of the family." The series also included a new high-speed printer and, yet again, an improved CRAM unit.[246]

5. The Century series had the capability to use both COBOL and FORTRAN programs. NCR reported:
    Basic computer operating software as well as standard application programs have been prepared concurrently with equipment development. This has insured full program compatibility, plus a proper balance between "hardware" and "software" capabilities.[247]

6. The Century series provided for standardization in design, including standard cabinet frames and panels, power supplies, and cable connections. It also provided for standard interfaces so that "the many peripheral units

available with Century processors can 'interface' simply, and in a wide variety of configurations."[248]

Of course, while these features represented improvements over NCR's prior products, all of them, with the exception of the soon-to-be-discontinued thin-film memory, had been included in IBM's System/360 four years earlier. Perhaps because of NCR's late response to System/360, NCR (as J. J. Hangen, its senior vice-president of corporate affairs, testified) "as a general rule . . . attempt[ed] to price [its] products slightly less than the comparable IBM system" — that is, "5 to 10 percent less."[249]

In its Annual Report for 1968, NCR announced its marketing plans for the Century series:

> Over the years NCR has established itself as a leading supplier of business systems to thousands of manufacturing concerns, construction companies, whole-salers [sic], schools, hospitals, utilities, hotels and motels, business service firms, and local, state and federal government offices.
>
> The advent of the Century Series computer family has multiplied the company's opportunities in these fields. As users of NCR accounting machines grow and their data processing requirements increase, a Century 100 computer system can meet these greater needs just as the Century 200 can serve the larger organization. At the same time however, with thousands of new small businesses being established each year, the market for accounting machines has continued to grow.
>
> The largest single market for computer systems is in manufacturing. One out of every four Century Series computers currently on order, for example, is scheduled for use in this area.[250]

By April 1969 the majority of orders received for the Century were from "non-banking, non-retail industries."[251]

The Century series was "largely responsible" for the fact that in 1968 NCR's domestic orders for computers increased 98 percent over the prior year. Indeed, "for the first time domestic orders for computer equipment exceeded those for either cash registers or accounting machines."[252] To meet the demand, NCR expanded the Electronics Division plant facilities by 50 percent and planned a further increase in 1969.[253] Ninety percent of the Century series systems marketed were leased, and the start-up costs involved in creating and financing the lease base — an investment in the future — pushed earnings down in 1968.[254]

NCR understood the importance of support services — customer training, maintenance, systems design — in marketing computer products. It stated in its 1964 Annual Report that:

> The user of an NCR business system buys considerably more than the machine units which make up that system. In every case, an NCR systems specialist and in many instances teams of specialists design

the most efficient system possible to meet the customer's current and future needs, then thoroughly train the user's staff in its use. After the system is operational, further counseling and assistance including dependable maintenance are provided.[255]

The introduction of third-generation systems increased these needs. In its 1969 Annual Report, NCR stated:

Marketing requirements of the business equipment industry have changed significantly in recent years. In recognition of this, the company has taken various steps to provide the greater degree of support which customers need and expect.[256]

After IBM's "unbundling" announcement of June 1969, NCR announced (in October) that its "basic" package of software and support would remain bundled, but that it would separately price software and support services above its "basic" level.[257] Hardware prices were not changed.[258] On January 1, 1970, however, NCR partially reversed its unbundling decision and announced that it would separately price only on a "selective basis."[259]

As well as expanding its computer systems offerings, NCR enlarged its computer data center business, which had begun in 1960. By 1968 there were 69 centers worldwide. The data centers were "NCR's most successful effort in the data processing business" in the 1960s, according to Withington, and proved to be a "powerful stimulus to the sale and rental of data capturing" devices.[260] Many data center customers used NCR cash registers, accounting machines, or adding machines to produce "punched paper tape or machine readable 'optical' figures as a by-product of normal operations." The customers then sent the output media to NCR's data center for processing.[261]

NCR's use of its traditional products as input devices for its data center computers was an example of its attempt to integrate its traditional products with its computer systems. In 1963 NCR reported that those products could be used with computers in several ways:

Many different types of cash registers, accounting machines, adding machines and other peripheral units are available as basic input devices for [computer] systems. Some of these machines communicate with computers by means of punched tape or punched cards. Others record transactions or other data in slightly stylized print which can be read by optical or magnetic scanning machines. Still others can be cabled directly "on-line" to NCR electronic data processing systems.[262]

NCR did very little, however, in terms of developing and marketing on-line systems during the 1960s. During May 1969, H. M. Keller, NCR's manager of terminal communications products, wrote that in terminal and communication products NCR did "not have a great choice to offer our prospects," and listed only one on-line device, the 42-500, a bank teller's console.[263] Keller noted, however, that a change had recently occurred in NCR's commitment to on-line devices:

> Before we knew that our Company committed itself to creating and offering terminal devices for many, many purposes, we may have had reasons for not encouraging sales of on-line systems. Now that we know that NCR is committed, each of us must help to penetrate the on-line field.[264]

In support of that commitment, NCR was investing "tremendous sums of money in developing" terminal and communications devices.[265] In its Annual Report it predicted:

> More and more people will be brought into direct communications with computers through a variety of data terminals and data display devices. In fact, it is anticipated that by 1975 users of data processing systems will be investing as much or more in data terminals and related communications equipment as in the central computer itself. This will create major new opportunities for the business equipment industry and particularly for companies such as NCR which has extensive experience in data entry devices.[266]

And:

> A decade ago, almost all business machines were sold as free-standing equipment. Today, many of these products as well as entirely new types of equipment are linked together as "total" systems to meet individual customer needs. Such systems often include arrays of compatible computer equipment including communications networks.[267]

Those predictions turned out to be accurate. During the 1970s NCR found that "the capabilities and price/performance of its terminals [were] an important factor in convincing users to take NCR computer systems."[268]

By 1970 it was plain that NCR had proceeded "methodically" in the computer business, avoiding risks but also avoiding the great success that comes with successful risk-taking. Its domestic EDP revenues for 1969 were $179,298,000, over five times its U.S. EDP revenues in 1963.[269] Even with that growth, its domestic EDP revenues accounted for only 26 percent of total domestic revenues, as against 13 percent in 1963.[270] Between 1964 and 1970, NCR's most significant development was the introduction of two models (the Century 100 and 200) of a system whose principal features had been available on IBM's System/360, delivered three years earlier. With this gradual development, however, NCR reduced the chances that it would be a failure like GE and RCA and found itself in a position to turn the corner in the 1970s.

CONTROL DATA CORPORATION

The period from 1963 to 1969 was one of rapid expansion for Control Data Corporation (CDC). It added to its two principal product lines, the 3000 and 6000 series. It expanded the applications capabilities of its computers to include not only a scientific emphasis but also business-oriented software. For the first time it developed, manufactured, and marketed a broad line of peripheral equipment, including OEM sales to other companies and IBM plug-compatible equipment. It expanded its overseas operations. It made a large number of acquisitions, including, most important, that of Commercial Credit Corporation, a large financial services company. Finally, it greatly expanded its data center business. CDC's total EDP revenues grew from $85 million in 1963 to $570 million in 1969.[271] Its U.S. EDP revenues grew from $88 million in 1964 to $458 million in 1969.[272] Its assets increased from $71 million in 1963 to $761 million in 1969.[273] To finance that expansion, at least in part, CDC raised over $767 million between 1963 and 1969 through equity and long-term debt financings.[274]

CDC's 6000 and 3000 Series Offerings (1963-69)

The 6000 Series

CDC's most important product in the 1960s was the 6600 computer, announced in July 1962 in connection with a contract let by the Atomic Energy Commission's Lawrence Livermore Laboratory and first delivered in September 1964 (seven months later than the date contracted for).[275] CDC Chairman and Chief Executive Officer William Norris described the 6600 as a "very great risk" because "it was a trip into the unknown," and testified that CDC was "betting the future of the company" on it.[276] But, like IBM with System/360, CDC received considerable returns on its "bet." Despite early problems with the 6600, CDC ultimately was successful with it and with the other 6000 series computers.[277]

On December 15, 1964, some eight months after IBM's System/360 announcement, CDC formally announced the "6000 Series," then consisting of the compatible 6400, the 6600, and the never delivered 6800.[278] In the announcement press release, Norris described the 6000 series as "the industry's most extensive product line of super-scale computers . . . provid[ing] business, industry, science and government users the most comprehensive range of software and system compatibility ever announced in the computer industry."[279] Purchase prices for typical 6000 series systems were announced as ranging "from less than $1 million to several million," with rental prices from $25,000 to $150,000 or more per month.[280] (CDC later announced two more models of the 6000 series: the 6500, in March 1967, and the 6700, in May 1969.[281] Norris described the 6500 as "actually two 6400's connected together," and the 6700 as "somewhat more powerful," being "basically two 6600s."[282])

By the end of 1964, CDC had received "possibly five or six" orders for the 6600, although top officials at IBM had believed as early as the autumn of 1963 that as many as ten accounts were then planning to order CDC 6600s.[283] Deliveries of the 6600 were delayed, however, by unanticipated technological problems in 1964, 1965, and 1966.[284] Although those problems had been solved by the end of 1966, the time and effort required were greater than expected, and CDC "incurred increased penalties for late delivery and retrofit costs."[285]

CDC also found it difficult to establish a price for the 6600. In April 1964 it submitted 6600 proposals to the Bettis Atomic Power Laboratory (BAPL) and the Knolls Atomic Power Laboratory (KAPL) in competition with IBM, Burroughs, Philco, and Sperry Rand.[286] IBM proposed 360/90s, with the interim installation of Model 70s until the 90s were ready for delivery. The bidding process was highly competitive. Initially, BAPL and KAPL selected CDC and Burroughs, respectively. Later, however, both BAPL and KAPL changed their selections to IBM.[287]

Six months later, CDC was told by the government that it was interested in reopening the BAPL and KAPL negotiations if CDC was prepared "to sharpen [its] pencils."[288] According to Norris, BAPL and KAPL then misled CDC "in a deliberate manner" as to the terms of the IBM offering, telling CDC "that IBM had offered a computer at four times the power of the 6600 at a lower price," as well as misrepresenting the date at which IBM could deliver its equipment.[289] CDC made an "unsolicited proposal" to BAPL and KAPL in late February 1965, "at a price substantially lower than that previously proposed by CDC and substantially lower than the price proposed by IBM."[290]

CDC had earlier reduced the price of the 6600 because of "substantial reductions in prices of component parts (transistors, diodes, etc.) which . . . occurred in [1963 and 1964]."[291] CDC "proposed a combination deal which would involve replacing the 6600 within some period of time . . . with the computer that would be much more powerful than the 6600, . . . the 6800, and at the time the 6800 was delivered, that we [CDC] would take back in trade the 6600."[292]

CDC — "unfortunately" according to Norris — ultimately won the BAPL and KAPL contracts.[293] It was unable to meet the delivery dates, however, and as a result was required to pay substantial penalties that further reduced the effective price. The final settlement was "substantially disadvantageous to Control Data."[294] For a time, difficulties with the 6600 adversely affected CDC. According to Norris:

> We were losing money as a company in 1966/1967 primarily because of problems with the 6600 computer. Frankly, there was a great deal of conflict in top managment in 1966 over whether we should press forward or retrench — closing down data centers was high on the list of retrenchment possibilities. The decision was made to press on, however there were some deserters in top management as a result — they were afraid that the ship was sinking.[295]

Norris testified that CDC "had to rush into the 6600" because it had been "literally clobbered by IBM competition" with CDC's earlier 1604 computer system, and that with the 6600, CDC again faced the "enormous impact of competition from IBM."[296] Ultimately, however, the 6600 — and the 6000 series in general — proved to be "particularly" successful for CDC.[297] Indeed, CDC received more than $286 million in revenue and more than $185 million in gross profits from the 6600 computer systems during 1964-72. The firm's gross profits on the 6600 exceeded its gross profit objective.[298] CDC finally manufactured 94 6600/6700 computers (compared with some 17 360/90s manufactured by IBM, including four for use within IBM), and a total of 215 CDC 6000 series computers.[299]

In the late 1960s, as a successor to the 6600 and a replacement for the never delivered 6800, CDC developed the 7600 computer, which it officially announced in December 1968 and first delivered the following month — more than 21 months after the first committed delivery date for a 6800 and seven months later than the delivery date called for in the first contract using the machine designation "7600."[300] Norris characterized the 7600 as "several times more powerful than the 6600 and it addresses the same market."[301]

CDC Vice-President J. W. Lacey, speaking to a 1969 CDC graduate orientation class, described CDC's success as follows:

> [W] e have a world-wide leading position in large computers today. That position is widely recognized. Since 1964, with the delivery of the first 6600 Computer, followed recently by the 7600 Computer, Control Data has dominated this market. Second, there is a rapidly increasing trend towards very large computers used in data processing networks in which many users share the enormous power of machines like the 6600, and away from medium sized and small sized stand-alone computers. . . .[302]

Lacey added, "We believe that our position today and the direction we are giving our business puts us in an outstanding posture to share in the explosive future growth of our industry."[303]

The 3000 Series

Despite this, CDC was also expanding its line of smaller computers, its 3000 series. In September 1963 it announced its 3200 computer; in January 1964, the 3400.[304] Norris testified that the 3200 competed with "IBM, Univac, Burroughs, NCR to an extent, and possibly SDS."[305]

The following year saw the continued expansion of CDC's 3000 series. The 3300 was announced in November 1965 and delivered in that same month.[306] Norris described the 3300 as CDC's "entry into timesharing. And, again, I think it had some added features for business data processing. And it was a considerably lower-priced machine than, say, the 6600. It was what you term [sic] then a medium-size computer."[307] According to Norris, it competed with "IBM, Univac, Burroughs, SDS and NCR."[308]

The 3500 was announced in November 1965 but was not delivered until 1969.[309] Norris testified that it was "essentially the same computer" as the 3300 except for the use of integrated circuits and "somewhat larger memory options."[310]

In 1967 CDC announced its 3150 computer, the smallest of the 3000 series, stating that it "provides a complete business and scientific information handling capability with a minimum of hardware and software. The 3150 provides maximum throughput at low initial cost to the user and the capability for him to expand upward as his information handling needs grow."[311]

The 3000 series was a substantial success for CDC without, in large part, the start-up problems that beset the 6000 series. Indeed, as early as 1966 CDC was able to describe its 3200 — which had been introduced little more than two years earlier — as "highly successful."[312] And in 1968 CDC reported to its stockholders that "orders for our 3000 product line continue to increase — both in the number of systems ordered and in average dollar value."[313] The 3000 series was successfully marketed for applications in manufacturing, general business data processing, education, medicine, data services, and the brokerage business.[314]

CDC's Expansion into Commercial Data Processing

As the 1960s began, CDC perceived itself as offering large, "scientific" computers — "a supplier of large-scale digital computers to scientific and engineering applications."[315] Very quickly, however, CDC learned that the distinction between scientific and commercial data processing — if there ever was one — had blurred almost to the vanishing point, and by the end of the 1960s, the firm estimated that fully 40 percent of its business came from "pure business data processing."[316]

At the time of its announcement in 1962, CDC thought that the 6600 "would be unique to a great extent . . . it being so much more powerful and so well-suited to scientific work, it would just be outstanding in the eyes of those laboratories that have these very large scientific problems."[317] CDC Vice-President Gordon Brown described the entire 6000 series as announced as

> very definitely a scientific line of computers, and therefore, the analyses that we did showed that the strength of the 6000 product line prevailed . . . over IBM and Univac in most typical environments; and, on the other hand, proved to be deficient when it was employed in an environment requiring a lot of input/output of data, or commercial type requirement [because] the architecture of the 6000 series was designed with the scientific user in mind. It had a large, fast, central processor with a number of auxiliary processors to handle the input/ output functions. And it had a large, very fast disk storage capability associated with it.[318]

By October 1965, however, the CDC Executive Council "responsible for advising [the] Chief Executive Officer concerning major business questions" had recognized that there were no longer separate markets for scientific and business data processing.[319] Thus, between 1964 and 1968, according to Brown, "gradually additional capabilities were added to the 6000 computer system, and these included COBOL compilers . . . sort and merge packages and the ability to handle permanent files as opposed to using the input/output devices as auxiliary storage or temporary storage of data files."[320] By 1968 CDC had sold 6000 series systems in Mexico "which were devoted primarily to business data processing, using that COBOL compiler and the COBOL application programs." And in other situations, customers with business applications as well as scientific applications ordered a 6600 system to do both.[321]

The primary impetus for the broadened use of the 6000 series came from customers who wished to have a single machine capable of performing both commercial and scientific applications – one of the primary reasons that led IBM to develop, with System/360, the capability to do both applications equally well.[322] Norris testified:

> We found that there were large companies who, while the majority of the work that they wished to do was of an engineering and scientific nature, still they had a certain amount of business data processing and that they preferred to have only one computer as opposed to having two computers, one for scientific and the other for business.
>
> So, we set about to broaden out the software which was available with the 6600 so that we could meet the requirements of those customers where the bulk of the work was still scientific but still the 6600 would do the business data processing well enough so that the customer only had to have the one computer.[323]

While CDC also introduced the 3000 initially as "basically scientific," it realized from the outset that the 3000 series "had a little bit more versatility as a business data processing machine than the 6600."[324] Over time, CDC added hardware features and software packages to enhance the suitability of the 3000 series for business applications.[325] By 1966, according to Brown, "the 3000 product line . . . was evolving to a . . . better balanced product line between both the scientific and the commercial users. The initial base of customers had largely been scientific users, and many of them were starting to expand their applications for commercial usage."[326]

CDC's Expanding Peripheral Business

In its early years CDC did not manufacture its own peripheral equipment.[327] By the early 1960s, however, it recognized that the sale of peripheral equipment was potentially a highly profitable opportunity, and began to manufacture peripheral equipment not only for attachment to its own processors but also as an OEM (original equipment manufacturer) supplier for other EDP companies. In so doing, it laid the foundation for its later very successful entry into the IBM plug-compatible peripherals business.

In 1964, in CDC's news release announcing the 6000 series, Norris stated:

> [N]umerous peripheral devices . . .are under development and will be announced over the next two years to complete the implementation of products required for total management information systems. These peripheral devices include:
>
> Disk Files – not only low-cost units but very sophisticated, high capacity, low access time, extremely high transfer rate, mass memories. Mass core memory. Remote terminals and processors for on-line man/machine interaction. Optical character recognition readers. Line of visual displays. Line printers, card punches and readers.[328]

In 1965 CDC acquired Data Display, Inc., a manufacturer of "electronic display peripheral equipment."[329] It also announced its 852 disk drive, which was "in many ways like the IBM 1311." The 852 was marketed "in a very modest way" on an OEM basis to GE and Honeywell in Europe.[330]

The following year CDC announced its 9433/34 disk drive – an IBM 2311-type device, although it was not media-compatible with the 2311 drive – on an OEM basis, with first shipments occurring in 1967. CDC's principal OEM customers for the 9433/34 were Honeywell, GE, and RCA, as well as ICL in Great Britain and Siemens in Germany. CDC eventually sold some 16,000 9433/34 drives in the late 1960s on an OEM basis, at prices less than half that of the IBM 2311.[331] The development and marketing of such IBM-type devices foreshadowed CDC's later decision to produce IBM plug-compatible peripherals.[332]

In 1966-67 CDC also began to market peripherals originally designed for its 6000 series on an OEM basis, such as the 6638 disk file, which was sold in small numbers to Honeywell, ICL, and GE as the 9490.[333] In 1967 it introduced a new line printer, new tape transports, a card read-punch, a magnetic-drum storage unit, and several new versions of electronic display terminals.[334]

During 1968 CDC added to its peripherals product line "a 5 billion bit disk file, a 1200 line per minute printer, and a new generation of tape transports."[335] The following year it introduced six new peripheral products: a disk storage unit, two printers, a card reader, a display terminal, and a drum device.[336] CDC also announced an IBM 2314-type device for use with its 3000 series, 6000 series, and CYBER 70 product lines.[337]

CDC was of course not alone in developing peripherals. In 1968 it informed its stockholders that "independent suppliers and the in-house developments of major computer manufacturers do and can be expected to continue to intensify competition."[338]

By the end of the 1960s, CDC "had made major investments in technology in most of the principal peripheral areas. This started with the development of subsystems for use in [CDC's] own computers and carried through most of the Sixties . . . into the development of a fairly large base of OEM business."[339]

Data Centers

CDC also greatly expanded the data center (service bureau) portion of its business in 1963-69. In 1964 it operated six data centers.[340] These centers used CDC 3600 and 1604-A computer systems, forming a network — later known as CYBERNET — "tied together by Bell System Data-phones" and "providing complete data processing services to commercial and government users on a contract basis."[341] Typical of the many applications processed at the centers were "Operations Research applications," "traffic surveying and planning," "Hospital data processing," and "school scheduling and grade reporting."[342]

In the next few years CDC increased the number of centers and developed its network.[343] In the fiscal year ending June 30, 1968, it acquired C-E-I-R, a company that offered computer programming and other professional data-processing services, and Pacific Technical Analysts, Inc., claimed to be "the largest and most capable programming and service center company serving the Western Pacific area."[344] By the end of fiscal 1969, CDC was operating over 40 data centers worldwide with more than 13,000 miles of communication lines, and offering "an extensive inventory" of application programs.[345] It described its CYBERNET network as follows:

> Through the highly advanced CYBERNET service, customers have convenient access to the cost/performance advantages offered by both the CDC 3300 and 6600 computers without having to make large capital outlays.[346]

All this expansion required investment. As a result, "except for brief periods in the mid-60's, data centers in the aggregate operated at a loss until 1972 because [CDC] kept pouring money into expansion." Norris, in a draft of a speech in 1973, cited this as an example of CDC's "willingness to take risks."[347]

CDC's Acquisitions (1963-69)

The story of CDC's expansion in the 1960s cannot be fully understood without considering its acquisitions during that period. Between 1963 and 1969 CDC acquired some 43 companies, at a total cost of over $897 million.[348] All of those companies — with the exception of Cedar Engineering, Kerotest, and Commercial Credit Corporation — were supplying an EDP product or service at the time of acquisition.[349]

CDC also expanded internally, particularly through increased vertical integration. For example, it decided in 1966 to have its research division manufacture integrated circuits for use in the prototype of the 3500 computer rather than buy circuits from Texas Instruments.[350] Also in 1966, CDC reduced costs by bringing the manufacture of card module assemblies, memory cores, memory planes, memory stack assemblies, and logic chassis assemblies in-house.[351] Its numerous acquisitions, most of which were paid for with CDC stock,[352] enabled it to broaden its product and service offerings quite rapidly without the substantial development time that internal expansion would have required. Norris stated in a draft of a 1973 speech:

> Our high P/E [price/earnings] ratio stock, or Chinese money, as we often termed it, was used to acquire companies with complementary technology, products, services and markets. In other words, we were not trying to broaden our base as in a conglomerate, but rather to buy new computer products and services and markets to spread develop-ment costs and gain economies of scale as rapidly as possible.[353]

Norris agreed that this was "an alternative to investing money in research and development" and was "very successful for Control Data for that purpose."[354]

In fiscal 1964 CDC acquired companies with capabilities in: digital com-puters for use in power, chemical, petroleum, and oil industries; card punch and reader systems and other peripheral devices; optical character recognition equip-ment; data collection systems; data-processing services; printers; and analog-to-digital conversion equipment.[355] In the following year it bought companies with capabilities in electronic display devices and programming consulting services, as well as a business data-processing center and two companies whose products, involving radar, for example, incorporated the use of digital com-puters.[356] In fiscal 1966 CDC acquired the commercial computer operation of General Precision's Librascope Group; an electronic systems engineering company; a Hong Kong firm doing assembly of electronic components, particu-larly ferrite cores; and an Italian firm operating data centers in Italy.[357] The purchases in fiscal 1968 of C-E-I-R and Pacific Technical Analysts, Inc., have already been mentioned.[358]

CDC's single most important acquisition occurred in August 1968. In that month it acquired Commercial Credit, "a diversified financial institution . . . with nationwide and Canadian operations in financing, lending, leasing, factor-ing, and insuring."[359] Commercial Credit was acquired for 4,825,720 shares of CDC stock, with a total market value of $745,573,740 — by far the most expensive purchase made in the 1960s by Control Data.[360] The principal reason for the acquisition was to gain a financial services subsidiary in order to enable CDC better "to finance computer leasing."[361]

Initially CDC marketed its computer systems on a purchase-only basis. However, by 1961 or 1962 it had realized that many EDP customers demanded leases and, accordingly, it began to offer its systems for lease as well as pur-chase.[362] Over time CDC offered one-year, three-year, five-year, and longer leases, first offering three-year leases in 1966 and noncancelable five-year leases in 1967, both at a discount from its short-term lease price.[363]

CDC's changeover to leasing as well as purchase required additional sources of capital.[364] Thus, in 1966 it entered into an arrangement with Leasco whereby

Leasco would purchase CDC systems and then lease them to customers on a long-term basis.[365] CDC canceled that agreement the following year, however, "in light of current and prospective financing plans of the Company."[366] According to Norris, it was not until CDC acquired Commercial Credit Corporation in 1968 that CDC ultimately "solved the problem of financing leases."[367]

SCIENTIFIC DATA SYSTEMS

Scientific Data Systems (SDS) was formed in 1961 with an initial capitalization of approximately $1 million, raised from a San Francisco venture capital company and the firm's original founders.[368] It was the idea of Max Palevsky, who had first been concerned with computers in 1952 as a research analyst for Bendix and then organized Packard Bell's computer subsidiary in 1956.[369] In 1961 Palevsky left Packard Bell because

> that company had come on hard times. The ideas I had about how to proceed in the computer industry required much stronger backing from the parent company which they could not provide. . . . I also felt that the computer industry is a very unique kind of industry, and it was very difficult working under a management that really knew nothing about the industry itself, so that it made sense to be independent, and, of course, there were opportunities to make a great deal of money.[370]

Palevsky furnished approximately $60,000 to $80,000 of SDS's initial capitalization: half in cash and half as a note.[371] For his investment he received "something in excess of 15%" of SDS's equity.[372]

SDS initially conducted all its activities in a 5,000-square-foot facility with approximately 17 people, of whom 12 were professionals.[373] Its first product was the SDS 910 computer system, delivered in mid-1962, less than a year after its organization.[374] It then grew at an extraordinary rate while also achieving substantial profitability — in fact, SDS "produced continually increasing profits virtually from inception."[375] Its average annual compound growth rate from 1962 to 1968 was 115 percent. Even after the first two years it continued to grow at a rate of approximately 50 percent per year.[376] Its revenues, which by 1964 had reached $20.5 million, rose to $100.7 million by 1968. SDS was acquired by Xerox in 1969 (and then became XDS), in exchange for Xerox stock valued at approximately $980 million. Of this amount Palevsky received some $100 million worth of stock. He had also received several million dollars from previous sales of SDS stock.[377]

The SDS Entry Strategy

SDS implemented a consciously determined strategy to capitalize on what it saw as a market opportunity. Palevsky testified that at its formation in 1961, SDS had "two markets" in mind for its products, "one market being what I would characterize as the real time computer market, and the other, the small to medium scientific computer market."[378] It began to market computers consisting of high-performance hardware offered for real-time applications to customers that did not need a lot of software and support services from the manufacturer.[379]

Palevsky testified:

It was part of the market that essentially no one had attended to. At that time the other companies were really concentrating primarily on computers as devices into which one fed documents that contained data, cards, tapes, etc., and out of which one got printed answers.

Our computers were intended for a market which fed real time data, that is, data that came from centers in a steam generating plant or a missile launching site or some astronomical instrument and produced signals that, say, worked the valves on a steam generating plant or indicated to other pieces of equipment within the launch site the status of various functions within a space vehicle so that it didn't work as a computer works in an air-conditioned computing center, but rather as part of the whole complex of operational equipment.[380]

SDS did not initially attempt to market its product to "business data processing customers" because it "didn't have the kind of people who understood the business market and the need of the business market and we had not developed the software, the applications engineering, the general support that the customer needed."[381]

This strategy was highly successful. Palevsky testified that SDS was able to sell its products at "a very large gross profit":

We were able to do that at the beginning because we provided hardware, that range of hardware and other services that was relatively unique and consequently the customer was willing to pay a relatively large sum for it.[382]

Digital Equipment Corporation (DEC) was the only other firm Palevsky remembered producing products similar to those of SDS in the early 1960s.[383] Subsequently, and rapidly, SDS expanded its product line and its marketing approach.

The SDS 910

SDS's first computer was the SDS 910, which Palevsky described at the trial as a "special purpose general purpose computer" — by which he meant "a computer that had all the characteristics of what was generally known as a general purpose computer, with the added capability of operating . . . within a systems environment, that is, it was a computer that was easy to integrate with diverse types of special purpose equipment."[384] The "main frame" sold for $80,000 to $90,000; "[t]hen, depending on the peripherals, it got more expensive." Palevsky described the peripherals as being, "at the beginning, rather primitive equipment": paper tape punches, paper tape readers and card equipment. Also, at the beginning the SDS 910 was marketed with "very primitive software, really just an operating system."[385]

The Expansion of the SDS 900 Series

SDS did not actually manufacture its 900 series computers. Rather, it purchased the various parts (they were "readily available to anyone who wished to purchase them") and put them together in a system of its design at its facility, a practice SDS pursued for several years.[386] SDS purchased the following:

— Certain basic components for its central processing units and memory (that is, transistors, resistors, and capacitors) from the "[s]tandard avenues of supply — [f]rom the manufacturers of those components."[387]

— Core memories, "at the beginning from Fabri-Tek," which was "one of a number of companies that supplied core memories"; SDS acquired the memories in the form of core stacks, then assembled them in boxes.[388] SDS subsequently acquired core memories from Ampex, Magnetic Memories, "and probably one or two others"; when "we got to a certain size we generally had three sources of supply so that we were always assured that one of them would be there."[389]

— Tape drives and tape control units from Ampex, Computer Products, and Potter Instruments; eventually SDS made its own tape drives and controllers.[390]

— Printers and a few printer control units from NCR and Data Products and, in the case of "some specialized ones," from "small companies"; at the time of its acquisition by Xerox in 1969, SDS was buying printer mechanisms from NCR.[391]

— Disk drives and disk drive controllers from Control Data (and "perhaps some of them from California Computer Products").[392]

— Card punches from Univac; card readers were initially acquired from a third party, but SDS subsequently built them itself.[393]

— A few cathode ray tube terminals from Control Data; however, SDS built most of these itself.[394]

— "[S]tandard [Teletype] keyboard devices from Western Electric."[395]

SDS both wrote software for its computer systems and used outside software services. Software services were provided by Programmatics and another firm, and "a number of smaller firms for very specialized things." SDS also had "a number of users groups and a number of our users' programs became standard programs that were then widely distributed" by SDS. Additional software was obtained from a European company (a predecessor of CII) that was licensed by SDS "to build our computers in France."[396] SDS itself furnished maintenance service.[397]

SDS began the expansion of its line in 1963, announcing the SDS 920, 930, and 9300 systems, compatible with the 910 and designed with a "building block" philosophy.[398] The SDS 920 had certain instructions that were not included in the earlier 910 and "a slightly more sophisticated input-output system." It was marketed to essentially the same customers as the 910.[399]

The SDS 930 was "larger and faster and, again, somewhat more complex structurally." It was partially marketed to the same group of customers as the 910 and the 920, but also "to a greater extent to the general scientific community."[400] For example, at the Kennedy Space Center an SDS 930 performed off-line simulation of launch vehicle events for training, supplied input data to Mission Control in Houston, and handled a "fuel loading" system.[401] Palevsky testified that when it was first introduced, the SDS 930 competed with the IBM 1620 "[a]nd then when the 360 was introduced, the 360/30s, 40s and 44s."[402] Other competitors with the 930 were Computer Control Company (later bought by Honeywell) and DEC.[403] The SDS 929, "a modification of the 930 to . . . provide a faster low-priced machine," was introduced in 1964.[404]

Palevsky described the SDS 9300 as "conceived much more as a data processing system, as a computer that would sit in a central computing facility and essentially provide printed answers, as opposed to being interconnected on a real time basis with other sources of data." It was marketed "to the scientific community," but performed a still broader mix of applications than did the 930. One customer was DuPont, which had previously integrated SDS computers "into systems for controlling chemical processes." It acquired this new computer not only for a "specific process they wanted to control but rather for a general computing purpose, so that the customer may have been the same, but the part of the company would be different."[405] Similarly, Digicon, Inc., used a 9300 to process seismic data collected from oil fields as well as its accounting records.[406]

Palevsky testified that with the 9300, SDS "had now entered the more traditional and more highly developed market for computers and no longer had the edge of the innovations" it had made in "real time computers" on which to rely.[407] Indeed, "as the technology in the computer industry evolved, there were no longer those pockets, there were no longer those market areas that had relatively little competition."[408] Palevsky testified that SDS's "main competitors" in marketing the 9300 were IBM and Control Data (and later, DEC).[409]

SDS had supported a "growing program of research and development," and had committed "substantial capital to advanced product planning." One of the results was its announcement in 1964 of what it claimed was "the first computer to use monolithic integrated circuits, the SDS 92." As a result of the use of integrated circuits, SDS's manufacturing costs were "decreased while the reliability of SDS computers is improved at least three times over present models."[410] This was part of a more general development. Withington, writing in 1964, concluded that:

> The most significant development in components has been the approximately 50% reduction in the manufacturing cost of high-speed circuits over the past three years. This quite rapid development has enabled new small companies (e.g., Scientific Data Systems, Digital Equipment Corporation) to enter the computer market with low-priced computers of high performance. . . . This reduction in manufacturing cost has been at least partly responsible for the recent price reductions on older computers and the lower prices of new ones. The user has benefited, and the market has been enhanced.[411]

By the end of 1964 SDS told its stockholders that with the introduction of the "small, high-speed SDS 92 and the medium scale SDS 925, the company now offers a family of six compatible, general purpose computers — the SDS 92, 910, 920, 925, 930 and 9300 — providing the flexibility required for both industrial and scientific systems."[412] The number of SDS employees had increased from 438 in 1963 to 1,357 at the end of 1964, and the company was expanding abroad.[413]

Expansion and SDS's program of research and development required capital, as did the fact that SDS was leasing more of the 9300s than it had prior computers.[414] In 1964, "due to [its] rapid growth," SDS made its first public offering of common stock, selling 382,375 shares and raising almost $5 million.[415]

By 1965 SDS had announced the development of its own magnetic tape units, rapid-access disk files, and a line of digital logic modules.[416] In that year it increased the memory capacity of the 930 and integrated rapid-access data-storage units and communications equipment. A 930 system costing $250,000 was thereby transformed into a 940 system costing $1 million and designed for simultaneous access by multiple users at remote locations.[417] SDS called the 940 a "timesharing computer." It was used by several commercial time-sharing service bureaus as well as by a data center established by SDS to sell time to remote users in the Los Angeles area.[418]

SDS was finding it profitable to attempt to attract customers less sophisticated than those with which it had begun. In mid-1965 it "announced a new business programming package for all its computers to supplement the extensive library of programs presently available to scientific users." The package, known as MANAGE, was "expressly designed to facilitate corporate decision making by management personnel outside of the data processing department."[419] Similarly, SDS adopted some of the marketing practices of others in the industry. In 1965-66 it offered the federal government a 14 percent discount on equipment purchased "[f]or qualified Government schools and training institutions when primary application of the data processing system is for educational and training purposes."[420] It also offered to provide the government with "programming aids, including programs[,] routines, sub-routines, translation compilers and related items without extra charge."[421] By 1966 SDS was marketing its computers on a variety of lease terms as well as selling them.[422]

SDS continued to grow dramatically during 1965. It doubled its number of installations in one year. New business received during the fourth quarter of 1965 was greater than in any previous quarter in the company's history. To finance this continued expansion, SDS sold 47,500 shares of $100 par cumulative preferred stock to a group of insurance companies, raising $4,750,000 in the second quarter of 1965. And in February 1966 it sold $10 million in convertible subordinated debentures to a group of institutional investors.[423]

The Sigma Series

By 1965, the year after IBM's System/360 announcement, SDS had begun the development of its Sigma series of computers — its third-generation line. In fact, in that year the Sigma family "occupied the attention of virtually every department in the company."[424] The first of the series, the Sigma 7, was announced in March 1966 and the second, the Sigma 2, the following August. The remainder of the family was announced starting in 1967.[425] By 1971 the Sigma family included the 2, 3, 5, 6, 7, 8, and 9.[426] According to SDS that family delivered "more computations per dollar than any other commercially available machine." SDS praised its versatility: "The impact of Sigma, however, lies in its broad application for business, industry and science as well as its ability to perform an almost unlimited number of different applications at virtually the same time."[427]

The Sigma series was a response to the IBM 360 line. A Sigma 7 press release, dated March 15, 1966, stated that Sigma "represents the first family of computers with an entirely new design since the IBM 360 announcement" and that "Sigma 7 features a total capability for both business and scientific data processing."[428] SDS attempted to set its prices 10 to 15 percent lower than IBM's prices on the products that IBM had announced two years earlier. It also tried to have "an advantage over a company like Univac."[429]

Palevsky testified that, compared with the 9300, the Sigma computers "were more complex structurally. They were much faster, and some of the computers in that line were compatible so that we had on a very small scale something like the 360, that is, we had a number of computers of various sizes that were program compatible."[430] As IBM had done with the 360, SDS "designed standard interface units." It also "developed special programs which simplify the design, engineering, and final assembly of various building blocks or components into total systems."[431]

For the Sigma series SDS acquired Potter tapes, Control Data disk drives, NCR printers, Teletype console typewriters, and Uptime card equipment.[432] However, because peripheral equipment was viewed as a "critical element" in third-generation computer systems, SDS sharply increased its internal development and production of peripherals. SDS stated its reasons for undertaking peripheral equipment development programs internally rather than acquiring independent manufacturers or continuing to purchase from suppliers as follows:

> First, SDS can realize a significant improvement in profit margins on equipment which the company produces internally.
>
> Second, peripherals designed to complement the capabilities of Sigma computers provide an additional competitive advantage for SDS systems.
>
> Third, high reliability must be designed into the equipment and quality control assured during production, thus minimizing the cost for servicing faulty peripherals.
>
> Fourth, and most important, the technology is advancing too rapidly to permit SDS to rely primarily on suppliers. The new series of Rapid Access Data files [disk drives] is an example. Developed with a considerable investment, SDS RADs are among the most advanced secondary storage devices in the industry. The availability of the various RAD models provides SDS with a significant advantage in marketing Sigma computer systems.[433]

SDS provided "advanced software, including operating systems for real time, batch, and time-sharing operations, FORTRAN IV and COBOL compilers, assemblers," and various applications software, including a library with "[m]ore than 1000 utility and mathematical programs" for the Sigma family.[434] SDS obtained between 20 and 50 percent of this software — specifically, assembly languages, compilers, a data management system package, a linear programming package, and a communications package — from software houses such as Digitek, Programmatics, Bonner & Moore, Informatics, Computer Usage Corporation, Computer Sciences Corporation, Dataware, CII, and Scientific Resources.[435]

At first, according to Palevsky, the Sigma series was offered "to essentially the same market as before."[436] Gradually SDS "started to market it for applications that were mixed scientific and general data processing," and began to expand into applications for general business and industry, including marketing to business data-processing customers.[437] By this time "changes in the technology" had begun to "blur" the distinctions between business and scientific data processing.[438] More and more customers started using a single computer for both types of computation; if one were to ask "say in '65 how many installations used a single computer for both purposes and say by '68 how had that grown . . . I would guess that that had grown ten-fold."[439] Both because of that change and because of a perception that the area on which SDS was focusing was becoming too confining, SDS was "forced" to enter the market for business data-processing customers.[440]

Thus, at the time of the Sigma 7 announcement in March 1966, SDS issued a press release stating:

> Until now, explained SDS president Max Palevsky, computers were generally built either for business data processing or for solving problems

of a scientific nature or for real time control systems. "But because of its advanced internal architecture," Mr. Palevsky stated, "Sigma 7 is the only medium priced computer that can deliver outstanding performance in any of these applications."[441]

SDS advertised its Sigma 7 computer system as "unfair to IBM . . . Sigma 7 does everything a 360/50 does. At a fraction of the cost. Sigma 7 is a little cheaper than the 360/50 and a good deal faster. The combination gives Sigma a 25 to 65 percent edge in cost/performance."[442] According to Harvey Cohen, director of marketing operations at SDS in 1967-68, looking only at the CPU, input-output processors, and main memory, the Sigma 7 could in fact do everything that the IBM 360/50 could do, although this was not true when the array of peripherals and software available on the 360/50 was taken into account.[443] The Sigma 7 was indeed used for business processing applications.[444]

Similarly, the Sigma 5 was "designed for operating real-time programs simultaneously with general purpose scientific and business problems."[445] According to an XDS sales guide, a report based upon what was happening in the field, the IBM 360/40, 360/44, 360/50, 360/65, and 1800 were competitors of the Sigma 5 as late as 1972.[446] According to Cohen, IBM's 360/44, 50, 65, 67, and 75, as well as the 1130 and 1800, were the IBM systems SDS "most commonly competed with during this time."[447]

In the early 1970s the "prime competition" for the Sigma 5 consisted of the IBM 370 models 135, 145, and 155; the DECsystem 10; the SEL (Systems Engineering Laboratories) 86/88; and the Univac 418-III.[448] For the Sigma 6 and 9 the "prime competitors" were the IBM 370 models 135, 145, 155; the DECsystem 10; the PDP 10, models 1040, 1050, 1055 (dual processor); and the Univac 1106.[449] For the Sigma 8 the "prime competition" consisted of the IBM 370 models 145 and 155; the SEL 86/88; the DECsystem 10; the Univac 1106/1108; and the CDC 6200/6400.[450]

As this suggests, competition for the Sigma series included products from many suppliers besides IBM. Cohen listed 21 companies (plus leasing companies) as competitors of SDS/XDS "in the computer systems market" during the period 1966-72 — IBM, Honeywell, Univac, GE, CDC, Burroughs, DEC, SEL, Modular Computer Corporation, Fischer & Porter, Varian, Hewlett-Packard, Data General, Radiation, Inc., Harris, Collins, Comten, Interdata, Electronic Associates ("on occasion"), EMR, and RCA ("occasionally") — and said there were "very likely" others.[451] He went on to list the "effective competitors" (companies that won 20-25 percent of the competitions in which they were engaged) of SDS in specific application areas, as follows:[452] (1) in time-sharing, IBM, Honeywell (after the acquisition of GE's computer business), Univac, GE, and DEC; (2) in real time, IBM, Honeywell, Univac, CDC, DEC, and SEL; (3) in seismic, IBM and Univac; (4) in scientific batch, IBM, Univac, GE, Honeywell (after its acquisition of GE's computer business), CDC, and DEC; (5) in communications, GE, Univac, IBM, and Comten; and (6) in multiuse/multimode, IBM, Honeywell (after the GE acquisition), Univac, CDC, and DEC.[453] In particular, IBM was an "effective competitor" of SDS in every application area, and the systems that competed with those of SDS spanned the IBM product line: the 1130, 1620, 1800, 360/44, 360/50, 360/65, 360/67, 370/145, 370/155, and 370/158.[454]

That view was not one-sided. IBM was well aware of SDS during the mid- and late 1960s.[455] On December 22, 1964, T. V. Learson reported to Thomas J. Watson, Jr., about the serious competition SDS posed to IBM's 360/40 and 360/50.[456] That concern intensified over the next several years and, as we have seen, SDS competition was one of the pressures leading to IBM's development of the 360/44. SDS was considered one of nine "major computer manufacturers" reported on in internal reports.[457]

The Xerox Merger

The Sigma family brought still more growth for SDS. During 1966, which was described by SDS as "a crucial transitional year," SDS offered two issues of convertible subordinated debentures totaling $22.5 million and retired short-term bank loans.[458] From the fourth quarter of 1966 to the fourth quarter of 1967, the year that SDS saw as a "critical" period "during which the character of . . . future expansion" was "largely determined," SDS doubled its production of EDP equipment. It stated that in 1967, it "successfully completed its first product line transition, began a major facilities expansion, and initiated new product development and cost control programs to sustain orderly growth."[459]

By 1969 SDS had achieved that orderly growth and had reached what would be, for SDS as an independent entity, the pinnacle of its success. It told its stock-holders that it "ranks among the world's ten largest computer manufacturers," with assets of $113 million and more than 4,000 employees, and described itself as "one of the world's largest suppliers of commercial time-sharing systems."[460]

In 1969 SDS was acquired by the Xerox Corporation. Xerox's revenues for the year 1968 (excluding Rank Xerox, Ltd., its British affiliate that marketed its products abroad) were $896 million and its net income was $116 million (including the income from Rank Xerox).[461] SDS was acquired for approximately $980 million worth of Xerox stock.[462] (The history of SDS (then XDS) after the merger is discussed in Chapter 14.)

DIGITAL EQUIPMENT CORPORATION

Digital Equipment Corporation (DEC) was founded in 1957 by Kenneth Olsen and Harlan Anderson, both of whom had previously been associated with MIT's Lincoln Laboratory, where they had worked on Whirlwind and SAGE.[463] DEC set up production on one floor of a converted woolen mill in Maynard, Massachusetts, with three employees.[464] Its initial capitalization was $70,000, all of which was invested by the American Research and Development Corporation, a Boston-based venture capital firm.[465] Its first products were laboratory logic modules — "printed circuit boards containing components which are used to do logical functions in an electronic sense: add, etc." — that were used to build and test other manufacturers' computers.[466]

DEC acquired more and more space in its woolen mill, and its original three employees were joined by many others. By 1966 DEC occupied 338,000 square feet in its original location, employed 1,100 people, had 24 sales offices in 6 countries, and had about 800 computer installations.[467] By 1970 it had manufacturing plants in England, Puerto Rico, and Canada, as well as several in Massachusetts; employed 5,800 people; and had computer installations in 11 countries.[468]

The financing of this expansion required capital. In 1963, $300,000 was borrowed from American Research and Development. However, by the end of its 1964 fiscal year, DEC had accumulated over $3 million in retained earnings.[469] Retained earnings rose to $4.3 million in 1965, $15 million in 1968, $24 million in 1969, and $38.8 million in 1970.[470] DEC made its first public stock offering in August 1966, raising $4.8 million.[471] From 1968 to 1970 it had three additional public offerings, raising a total of $63.5 million.[472] A review of DEC's Annual Reports reveals that this outstanding record enabled DEC to meet its financing needs with no reliance on long-term bank loans. Vice-President Winston R. Hindle, Jr., testified, "Digital's expansion has not ever been limited by the ability to raise capital."[473]

It is interesting to note in this connection that DEC generally chose not to tie up its capital in financing leases for its customers, feeling that it had "better ways to invest" its money. When its customers wanted to lease, DEC would put them in touch with leasing agents who would "use their [own] capital and not Digital's capital." When DEC did offer leases directly to its customers, it generally sold them to financial institutions immediately thereafter.[474]

DEC's success was due in part to its commitment to product development. Hindle testified that "Digital has through the years spent between 8 and 11 percent of revenues annually on research and product development. . . . We have felt that product development was a vital part of our success. The rapid advances of technology in the computer field have meant that we must keep abreast of these advances and incorporate them and understand them in our product lines as rapidly as we could."[475] That commitment paid off and, as Withington testified, DEC "always maintained a position of technological leadership or at least currency with any significant competitor and always provided an adequate breadth of product line, maintenance and support."[476]

Like SDS, DEC began by producing computer systems with small, high-performance hardware, offered with relatively little support to sophisticated customers capable of providing the software and services for the application of those products to their needs.[477] Over time, DEC's products grew in capacity and capability, and DEC expanded its customer support, its marketing, and its software and service offerings. That process continued, and by 1980 DEC offered one of the broadest product lines in the industry and marketed it to the whole spectrum of EDP customers.

DEC's first computer, the PDP 1, was delivered in 1960, and was followed by the PDP 4 and 5 in 1962 and 1963, respectively. From 1964 through 1970,

DEC also introduced the PDP 6 (1964), PDP 7 (1964), PDP 8 (1964), PDP 8S (1966), LINC 8 (1966), PDP 9 (1966), PDP 10 (1967), PDP 8I (1968), PDP 8L (1968), PDP 12 (1969), PDP 14 (1969), PDP 15 (1969), and PDP 11 (1970). All of these were classified by Hindle as "general purpose computers," except the PDP 14, whose program was preset.[478] As we shall see, each of DEC's successive announcements expanded the breadth and capabilities of its product line, contributing to the firm's phenomenal success.

PDP 1, 4, 5, and 7

DEC's first computer was the PDP 1, delivered in 1960 and withdrawn in 1963 or 1964.[479] Its original purchase price was in the neighborhood of $125,000-$243,000.[480] The machine was designated "PDP" (Programmed Data Processor), a nomenclature that DEC used throughout the 1960s for its products, because "EDP people could not believe that in 1960 computers that could do the job could be built for less than $1 million."[481]

The PDP 1 was "an outgrowth of the technology that was incorporated into the line of logic modules, although there was a completely separate design from the logic modules in our product line prior to that."[482] Its uses included early research on time-sharing, input-output as a remote station in a larger time-sharing system, and "scientific and engineering" applications at the Atomic Energy Commission's Livermore Laboratory, where it was selected over an IBM 1401 in 1962.[483]

DEC introduced the PDP 4 system in 1962, and the PDP 5 in 1963.[484] The PDP 5 was offered with keyboard-printer, paper tape reader and punch, and a software package including FORTRAN.[485] According to Hindle, "although the term 'minicomputer' wasn't used during the time of the PDP-5" (and indeed "is not a precise term"), DEC would have considered the PDP 5 a "minicomputer" (by which he meant that "the smallest available configuration could be configured for less than $50,000").[486] According to the 1964 DEC Annual Report, the PDP 5 was used in "numerous applications in physics, biomedicine, industrial process control, and systems applications."[487]

In the early 1960s DEC's research and development effort produced the "flip chip" modules that, like IBM's SLT, combined printed circuits with discrete components and made possible the introduction in 1964 of the smaller, faster, and cheaper PDP 7 and 8 to replace the PDP 4 and 5.[488] An IBM Win and Loss Report for August 1964 reported competition between the DEC PDP 4 and the IBM 1401 and between the PDP 7 and the 360/30.[489] The Atomic Energy Commission selected a PDP 7, installed in January 1967, over a 360/30, as well as over systems bid by CDC, SDS, Univac, and Honeywell.[490]

PDP 6

The PDP 6 was first delivered by DEC in 1964.[491] DEC's Annual Report for 1964 described the PDP 6 as "an expandable system which can start as a very basic configuration and grow through the addition of processor, memory and input-output options into a major computation facility equivalent to the largest commercial systems currently offered."[492] At the time the PDP 6 was the largest of DEC's computer systems, ranging in price from $350,000 to $750,000. It was used in "large data processing assignments" at Brookhaven National Laboratory, the Rutgers University Physics Department, the universities of Aachen and Bonn, Germany, the University of Western Australia, Lawrence Radiation Laboratory, United Aircraft Corporation, Applied Logic Corporation, Yale, MIT's Laboratory for Nuclear Science, the University of Rochester, Stanford University, and the University of California at Berkeley. DEC described it as "equivalent to the very large computers used by scientific laboratories."[493]

The PDP 6 was "designed for time-shared use," and DEC proposed a multi-processor version of it to MIT's Project MAC. DEC was "in among the finishers" for this award, which included CDC, offering a 6600; IBM, offering a 360/50; GE, the winner of the contract with a modified 635; and RCA, with a 3301. A $1 million PDP 6 was chosen by Project MAC as a peripheral processor for the time-sharing system.[494]

At Lawrence Livermore Laboratory, two PDP 6s were acquired in 1965-66 and used as control computers in the OCTOPUS network. Because Lawrence Livermore required a faster memory than DEC could supply, it solicited bids for add-on memory, receiving bids from five companies in addition to DEC, and awarding contracts to Lockheed and Ampex.[495] That acquisition was an indication of things to come: there was later, primarily in the 1970s, substantial development of DEC plug-compatible equipment, in part reflecting the great popularity of DEC computer systems.[496]

PDP 8

The PDP 6 procurements were prestigious, but DEC's financial growth was more affected by the PDP 8 series of computer systems. The PDP 8 was introduced in 1964 as a replacement for the PDP 5. Through the use of integrated circuits, it was four times faster than the PDP 5 at two-thirds the price.[497] Using the price/performance improvements made possible by "FLIP-CHIP circuit modules and automated production techniques," the PDP 8 opened new market opportunities for DEC (such as typesetting) and expanded its base of scientific-oriented users.[498] The PDP 8 was offered with "disk storage units, terminals, tape units, line printers, cathode-ray tube display units."[499]

Alan Perlis testified that the PDP 8 "generalized very nicely to other machines and it itself gave birth to a whole line of offspring"; and the "parent" "received a remarkably immediate acceptance."[500] As a result of the greater-than-expected demand, DEC expanded its manufacturing facilities in 1965. By mid-1966 over 400 PDP 8s had been installed.[501]

The various other members of the PDP 8 family in existence at the time of Hindle's testimony in November 1975 were introduced from 1966 (the

PDP 8S) through 1974 or 1975 (the PDP 8A), with the later members of the family still being delivered.[502] After the first PDP 8, each new member of the family was introduced at a lower price than the one before because of "changes in manufacturing technology, semiconductor prices, and peripheral prices as purchased from our vendors."[503] The systems of the PDP 8 family were soft-ware-compatible, with DEC providing three "general purpose operating systems" for them.[504] It was "generally true," although "not . . . one hundred percent true," that the same peripherals could be used on all systems in the family.[505]

First deliveries of the PDP 8 went to Stanford Research Institute, Harvard Medical School, MIT, and the University of Wisconsin. The PDP 8 was also offered to newspaper and book publishers for automatic typesetting and to laboratory, industrial, and educational users.[506]

In addition, approximately 30 to 50 percent of the PDP 8 family was sold to original equipment manufacturers (OEMs), systems vendors, or manufacturers that incorporated the PDP 8s into their systems or products. Some PDP 8s were sold as processors alone, some as processors plus memory, and some as total systems.[507] When a PDP 8 was sold OEM as a processor only, the purchaser would acquire "from another manufacturer the appropriate devices necessary to perform input or output functions," with either the customer or DEC providing "interfacing services" for the input and output devices.[508] Beginning in 1964, these OEM purchasers marketed PDP 8 systems for business data processing, including "invoicing, accounts payable, inventory control, order processing," and other applications.[509] Different users used the quite versatile PDP 8 to perform different applications, and in some cases the same user might have the same PDP 8 computer system doing, for example, both business data processing and industrial control applications.[510]

DEC itself, prior to 1972, was largely unsuccessful in marketing the PDP 8 directly for business data-processing applications because it had not worked "on the packaging to make the product suitable and attractive to the business data processing customers."[511] Then, in 1972, DEC introduced the Datasystem 300, an adaptation of the PDP 8 specifically designed for business data processing. The "primary difference" between the PDP 8 and the Datasystem 300 was that the latter was packaged in a different type of console and used a business-oriented language called DIBOL.[512]

Prior to 1975 the PDP 8 competed with IBM's 360 and 370 computer systems when used as part of larger DEC computer systems such as the PDP 10, and singly against the IBM System/3, System/32, and 1130.[513] The PDP 8 also had the ability to perform terminal or input-output applications as part of a computer system with an IBM or some other manufacturer's CPU.[514]

By any standards the PDP 8 was a successful and significant product. At the time of Hindle's testimony in late 1975, between 30,000 and 40,000 PDP 8s had been sold, and the PDP 8 was being marketed "to a wider variety of customers," including "communications customers" and "business data processing customers."[515]

PDP 10

In 1967 DEC introduced the PDP 10, the first of a family of computer systems later marketed as the DECsystem 10.[516] The new offering superseded the PDP 6, whose features it incorporated, and the earlier machine was withdrawn.[517] The PDP 10 was "introduced to serve . . . laboratory users, industrial users, education users, a class of users we call the data service industry. . . . This is a class of computer users who purchase — or lease or rent — computer equipment and then offer various kinds of services to clients."[518] When introduced, the PDP 10 could be purchased "for prices in the vicinity of $450,000, all the way up to configurations which would be a million and a half dollars."[519] It was not actively marketed on an OEM basis, but generally was sold directly to end users.[520]

In 1969 DEC described the PDP 10 as

serving business, industry, and science in a multitude of installations throughout the world. They keep track of bubble chamber events in physics laboratories, analyze blood chromosomes, work in banks, teach in high schools and universities, and perform a myriad of other tasks. New applications are constantly appearing and current applications steadily grow. Customers find new approaches, add new equipment, develop more software. Systems designed solely for real-time tasks often expand to include program development or business data processing. The applications described here demonstrate the PDP-10's inherent flexibility.[521]

The PDP 10 (which Hindle did not consider a "minicomputer") competed on a "one for one basis" with the IBM 360, 370, and System/3 computer systems.[522] In establishing its price DEC looked at the IBM System/360, specifically models 30, 40, and 50, as well as systems offered by Honeywell, GE, and Scientific Data Systems.[523]

The DECsystem 10 was announced in 1971 as a family of systems "spanning virtually the entire large-scale range," and was based upon the PDP 10 processors.[524] It offered improvements in peripherals, in particular a better-quality printer and a disk drive with a removable disk pack.[525] Both the PDP 10 and the DECsystem 10 were highly successful. By 1974 over 400 such systems had been installed.[526]

PDP 15

The PDP 15, introduced in 1969, was originally "marketed to laboratory users, industrial users, education users," but with the addition of another programming language (MUMPS) — a "business-oriented language" — it was also marketed for business data-processing applications starting in the early 1970s.[527] "Representative applications" performed by the PDP 15 were "nonbusiness computation applications, business data processing applications, real time data collection and instructional computing applications as well as industrial control applications."[528] Hindle testified that the PDP 15 competed "on a one for one basis" with the IBM 1130, 1800, System 7, 360, and 370 computer systems.[529] By late 1975 between 800 and 1,200 PDP 15s had been installed.[530]

PDP 11

As with the PDP 8, the PDP 11, introduced in 1970, was the designation for a whole family of computer systems.[531] At the time of introduction DEC expected to market it "to the entire group of users . . . described for the PDP 8, which would include laboratory users, education users, industrial users, engineering users, [and] communications users." As with the PDP 8, between 30 and 50 percent of the PDP 11s were sold to OEM purchasers who wrote applications programs and offered the PDP 11 for business data-processing applications.[532] But DEC preferred to market the PDP 11 as a system rather than offering just the processor.[533] In 1972 the DEC Datasystem 500 series was introduced for marketing to business data-processing customers. DEC took the PDP 11, added software capabilities, including BASIC, and put it in a "separate type of package" that looked different to the user. "But other than that, there were no significant differences."[534]

Hindle testified that the PDP 11/15 and 11/20, smaller members of the PDP 11 family, competed on a one-for-one basis with the IBM 1130, System 3, and System 7 computers, and also with the 360 and 370 in configurations that included the PDP 10.[535] Like the PDP 8, the smaller PDP 11 computer systems might "be used to perform terminal or input/output applications" as part of computer systems whose main CPU was manufactured by IBM or by manufacturers other than IBM or DEC.[536] Larger members of the PDP 11 family, such as the 11/45 and 11/70 (announced in 1971 and 1975, respectively), competed on a one-for-one basis with IBM 360 and 370 systems, as well as with System 3, System 7, and 1130.[537] These were not small machines. DEC did not consider the PDP 11/70 to be a "minicomputer," and even some PDP 11/45s were configured in systems with prices as high as $250,000.[538] In pricing the products in the Datasystem 500 series, DEC looked at the prices of the IBM System 3, System 7, System 32, 360, and 370 systems.[539]

Peripherals and Software

The rapid proliferation of DEC's product line during the 1960s extended to peripheral and software offerings. Although as late as 1969 Memorex was marketing disk file products to DEC on an OEM basis, with 1969 sales of approximately $5 million, by 1970 DEC had "introduced many new peripherals including those of our own internal design and manufacture, such as disks, paper tape, DECtape, display systems, and real time interface equipment."[540] DEC had also worked on software, introducing new software features "[w]ith each mainframe that is a new version of a previous machine."[541] It had provided DIBOL, a business-oriented language, for the PDP 8, and added COBOL to the PDP 10.[542]

In 1967 DEC developed application packages called Computerpacks, which until 1969 were marketed with the DEC hardware at no separate charge.[543] The Computerpack was actually a complete turnkey system for users desiring systems that required a minimum of programming and computer experience. DEC merely added an application package to a PDP 8 and marketed the result as a Computerpack. For example, the Quickpoint-8 was offered for numerical-control tape preparation; the Communic-8 was offered for data communication applications; the Time-Shared-8 was offered for general-purpose time-sharing applications; and the Lab-8 was offered for nuclear magnetic resonance spectroscopy applications.[544]

Competition

DEC's approach to the market was different from that of IBM. In the 1960s it offered fast, inexpensive hardware with less versatile and generalized software and service than that offered by IBM. DEC marketed most of its machines announced in the 1960s to "experienced" and "moderately experienced" users.[545] Perlis described the PDP systems as they were perceived in the university environment: "[I] t was generally felt that . . . PDP systems . . . for delivering the same amount of work, were cheaper than the IBM systems." He estimated that the PDP 10 was about 20 percent cheaper than a 360/50 because the latter machine required an "attendant staff of operators, people to handle the variety of software that is used . . . and so forth," whereas PDP 10s were operated "without any staff whatsoever in attendance on the machine during its period of operation, which runs 24 hours a day, seven days a week."[546] In this respect the bundle of services associated with the IBM 360 line provided an opportunity for DEC to obtain a price advantage with those users who did not want or need those services. DEC offered hardware and software more specifically tailored than the generalized System/360 to enable users to perform one or a few applications in a decentralized way rather than on a central IBM computer.

The competition between DEC and IBM was not only on a "one-for-one" basis. As Hindle explained, "it would be possible that in a given computer application a customer could choose one powerful machine to do the job or could choose several less powerful machines and decentralize the job. In that type of situation we would have one machine competing with several machines from a different manufacturer." Such competition would arise, for example, because "considering the total system cost of both software and hardware, a distributed network of smaller computers can often be a cost-effective alternative to the single, centralized computer." Alternatively, as Hindle said, "it is possible to have several smaller computer systems which are not interconnected electronically" competing with a single larger computer system.[547]

The IBM Commercial Analysis Department described this competition in the Quarterly Product Line Assessment for the first quarter of 1970: "Mini-computers affect IBM's business potential by implementing one application out of several possible applications in a prospect's business." And, according to the report, the application selected for the minicomputer was frequently the application having the greatest economic justification. The off-loading of that application could eliminate the opportunity for IBM to supply the customer with a "larger and more comprehensive computer installation." The report also commented on the success of minicomputers:

> Mini-computers have established a substantial base and continue to widen their base each year. Digital Equipment Corporation is now ranked #3 in total CPU's representing about 5,600 units (8%) out of the 70,000 total domestic CPU's reported for year end 1969 by Diebold.[548]

Competition from DEC was felt by IBM and others in the 1960s, and was to become even greater.[549] From its beginning and throughout the 1960s, DEC achieved extremely rapid growth by taking advantage of new technology and its own research and development to manufacture an ever-expanding product line. Its total assets grew from $5.7 million in mid-1964 (when financial information first became publicly available) to $114.8 million in mid-1970.[550] DEC's profits after taxes went from $889,000 in 1964 to $14.4 million in 1970.[551] Its worldwide EDP revenues rose from $4.3 million in 1961 to $12.6 million in 1964, to $142.6 million in 1970, a compound growth rate of 44 percent per year.[552] By virtue of the $70,000 investment in 1957, American Research and Development had acquired 78 percent of DEC's common stock.[553] In 1968 it sold 215,000 shares of DEC stock for a gain of more than $26 million, and in 1972 it distributed the remainder of its DEC stock, valued at $382 million, to its shareholders.[554]

DEC entered the 1970s a large and profitable company with a successful and popular product line. It had some 500 computers installed with the federal government, almost 10 percent of the total, making it the third-ranked supplier in terms of numbers of computers (behind IBM and Univac).[555] But, despite the impressiveness of these indicators of success, they were but small indications of the DEC that was to emerge in the next decade.

AMERICAN TELEPHONE AND TELEGRAPH

Despite the continuing restrictions of its 1956 consent decree, American Telephone and Telegraph (AT&T) expanded its offerings of computer-related products and services during 1964-69. Its U.S. EDP revenues, as a result, grew from $125.6 million in 1964 to $477.75 million by 1969.[556]

As it had done in the 1950s, AT&T competed in the computer industry in at least two ways during the 1960s. The first involved Western Electric's manufacture and marketing to the Bell System operating companies of stored-program-controlled electronic switching systems and automatic intercept systems. The Bell System's enormous size and the fact that the Bell operating companies were free to, and did in fact, buy EDP products and services from non-Bell-affiliated companies, made them a very important source of business to computer vendors who vie with Western Electric for the business of the Bell System. During the 1960s equipment developed and manufactured by AT&T competed for the business of the Bell System with the equipment of other EDP vendors, including IBM.[557]

The second form of competition consisted of AT&T's offering of EDP products and services to non-Bell customers. While this business was also a large one, AT&T was restricted in the extent to which it could compete in this area by its 1956 consent decree.[558] Those restrictions did not apply, however, to sales to the U.S. government, including the military, and AT&T was active in such sales.[559]

For 1964-69 AT&T's revenues from the sale of EDP products and services to the U.S. government were as follows:

1964 — $37,856,000

1965 — $40,216,000

1966 — $51,373,000

1967 — $50,964,000

1968 — $51,949,000

1969 — $65,746,000[560]

Competition for Bell System EDP Business

By at least mid-1963 IBM executives understood that their firm was facing direct and substantial completion from AT&T and that its new computer systems would more and more be competing with AT&T's. IBM Senior Vice-President T. V. Learson wrote to IBM Chairman Thomas J. Watson, Jr., and President A. L. Williams in August 1963, less than a year before the announcement of System/360:

> 1. IBM, as well as most of our well-known competitors, are competing directly with AT&T in both the terminal and the message switching equipment area today.

> 2. The next generation of machines will handle indistinguishably data and voice.

> 3. The product serving the market area above will also include our new processors [System/360].

4. The present central plant of AT&T will be replaced by this same equipment.

5. We plan to expand our sales effort into the plants of the independent telephone companies, both here and abroad.

6. Since the equipment we will supply to our customers will be identical to what AT&T will require for their plant, they may well represent a possible new market.[561]

Learson's observations were borne out in 1965, when AT&T's first electronic switching system (No. 1 ESS), developed by Bell Labs and manufactured by Western Electric, went into service.[562] AT&T in 1964 described the No. 1 ESS in the following terms:

The central processor controls the operation of the No. 1 electronic switching system by executing sequences of program instructions. . . .

. . . .

[A stored program system, as used in ESS,] consists of memories for storing both instructions and data, and a logic unit which monitors and controls peripheral equipment by performing a set of operations dictated by a sequence of program instructions. . . .

. . . .

. . . Therefore the central control can be described as an input-output processor superimposed on a general-purpose data processor.[563]

That sounds like the description of a computer, and indeed it is.[564] Tapes and disks, as well as memories and logic, were involved.[565] By 1970 AT&T engineers described the Stored Program Control No. 1A processor (a follow-on to the No. 1 ESS processor) as "a general purpose stored program electronic processing system."[566]

In the first part of the 1960s IBM was actively marketing its computer systems for telephone applications, including switching. Beginning in 1963, for example, Southwestern Bell and IBM began to study the design of a computer-controlled automatic intercept system (a system providing assistance to callers who have dialed a number no longer in service).[567] The resulting computer system, installed in 1965, contained two IBM 1447 processors, four IBM 1311 disk drives, an IBM 1442 card reader, two IBM 7770 audio response units, and an IBM 2910 automatic intercept switch, as well as some nonstandard hardware.[568] Western Electric later developed and marketed such equipment itself, using a control complex that was described as "a data processing system operating through the use of stored programs to process intercepted calls."[569] Other vendors offered such systems as well.[570]

IBM offered its computer systems for other network switching applications as the Bell System moved to electronic computers for its central office exchanges.[571] Indeed, IBM proposed the use of a System/360 instead of No. 1 ESS to AT&T.[572] As IBM Vice-President John F. Akers testified, one of the "major ways" IBM has competed with AT&T

> is in the electronic switching systems that the American Telephone & Telegraph Company employs to switch messages and to switch lines and to do customer billing and accounting information.
> IBM over the years has competed with those systems. We have bid System 360 products, we have bid Series 1 products, we have bid System 7 products, and perhaps others.[573]

In 1965 IBM engaged in contract negotiations with Canadian Bell "for over ten 360 systems for use in network switching."[574] IBM's sales strategy, according to IBM employee G. W. Woerner, Jr., was "to convince the Bell System that the telephone companies should solve their problems with general purpose computers procured directly from IBM."[575] (Similarly, in 1966 IBM entered into negotiations with General Telephone & Electronics and Automatic Electric "on the feasibility of IBM building the computer processor portion of a message switching system."[576])

A principal reason for this activity was the convergence of the technologies involved. In September 1963 an IBM memorandum compared the data-processing capabilities of No. 1 ESS and System/360. It concluded that *the two systems architectures are similar and most ESS1 instructions have equivalents in System 360.*[577] Two months later an IBM task force to consider communications policy reported:[578]

> Technologically there will be no distinction between an electronic switching center and a computing center. Both will be able to perform the same functions. . . .
>
> . . . .
>
> Communications should be recognized as part of our business. . . . In our judgment by 1970 fifty per cent of our business will involve communications-oriented products.[579]

A further report of the Communications Task Force in 1966 stated:

> All IBM products have the technical characteristics necessary for a communications system. System/360 — in both its equipment and programming support — is specifically designed with an advanced capability in data communications.
>
> . . . .
>
> ESS is a form of computer, a stored program transistorized digital system. . . .
> *The professional level of the [common] carriers' research and engineering* is fully competitive with IBM's.
>
> . . . .
>
> . . . [T] here is no question that the resources and entrenched communications position of AT&T make it potentially a formidable competitor indeed.
>
> . . . .

. . . Although AT&T is a major customer for IBM data processing systems, its manufacturing subsidiary, Western Electric, has the ability to gear up to volume computer production.[580]

Western Electric did "gear up." Its revenues from the sales of its stored-program central data processors and related equipment and software (such as No. 1 ESS) to the Bell System operating companies for 1964-69 were as follows:

1964 – $ 20,419,000

1965 – $ 37,013,000

1966 – $ 62,458,000

1967 – $ 61,789,000

1968 – $108,546,000

1969 – $227,285,000[581]

AT&T itself well understood what was happening. In 1968 its chairman, H. I. Romnes, stated:

[O]ne way and another we have been involved with computers a long time. . . .

I believe we understand the potentials of computers and the importance of communications in achieving them. I likewise believe we can contribute a great deal toward the realization of great aims.

It is sometimes said, . . . , that the nationwide dial system is like a giant computer. Is this merely – or mainly – a figure of speech?

No, not at all. It is a fact. . . .

. . . .

Today, as direct dialing has extended over the whole nation, our data processing equipment has become much more complex. . . .

Now, with the development of transistor technology, we have started to use electronic processors to handle calls, rather than those that employ electromagnetic relays and switches. These processors of ours . . . have a vastly increased memory capacity and operate at electronic speed. . . .

These new systems of ours, I might add, are big and complex. Their executive programs range from 70,000 to 200,000 or more words, and thus are in the range of the largest time-sharing general-purpose computer operations.[582]

That view was not a minority opinion. In 1971 the Federal Communications Commission found:

There is virtually unanimous agreement by all who have commented in response to our Inquiry, as well as by all those who have contributed to the rapidly expanding professional literature in the field, that the data processing industry has become a major force in the American economy. . . . There is similar agreement that there is a close and intimate relationship between data processing and communications services and that this interdependence will continue to increase. . . . We stated in our Notice of Inquiry, and no respondent has challenged the finding, that common carriers "as part of the natural evolution of the developing communications art" were rapidly becoming equipped to enter into the data processing field, if not by design, by the fact that computers utilized for the provision of conventional communication services could be programmed additionally to perform data processing services.[583]

Other Competition from AT&T

In addition to competition with outside EDP vendors for sales within the Bell System, AT&T also competed in other areas in the 1960s. For example, it continued to offer its modems (devices for intercomputer communication) for sale generally.[584] Its 200, 300, 400, and 800 series modems, as well as the AT&T 10A Data Line Concentrator, were manufactured and marketed for use as part of a communications processor.[585] As such, they competed with IBM's modems and those of other vendors marketed for the same purpose. More generally — as AT&T's brochures put it — by "reduc[ing] the need for separate data processing equipment at other locations" and "mak[ing] possible centralized data processing operations," AT&T's modems provided customers with an alternative to other forms of data-processing equipment.[586] AT&T's revenues from the sale of modems for 1964-69 were as follows:

$$1964 - \$\ 5,893,000$$
$$1965 - \$13,699,000$$
$$1966 - \$21,470,000$$
$$1967 - \$25,297,000$$
$$1968 - \$37,791,000$$
$$1969 - \$48,825,000[587]$$

Perhaps the most familiar example of AT&T's presence, however, was provided by its terminal products, most of which are manufactured and sold by Western Electric's subsidiary, Teletype Corporation. As IBM and the Justice Department stipulated in 1975:

American Telephone and Telegraph Company manufactures and markets in the United States electronic digital computer terminals which perform input and output functions for electronic digital computers. Some or all of American Telephone and Telegraph's electronic digital computer terminals are used by end users as a part of "general purpose electronic digital computer systems."[588]

Not surprisingly, competition from AT&T terminals was felt within IBM, where AT&T was considered the "major" competitor in terminals.[589]

Teletype Corporation's EDP revenues for 1964-69 were as follows:

1964 — $ 61,422,000

1965 — $ 83,554,000

1966 — $ 87,188,000

1967 — $ 67,290,000

1968 — $ 76,101,000

1969 — $110,722,000[590]

10

THE GROWTH OF
OTHER FORMS OF
COMPETITION

THE EMERGENCE OF IBM PLUG-COMPATIBLE MANUFACTURERS

As discussed previously, the introduction of System/360 presented IBM's competitors with a business opportunity.[1] By marketing plug-compatible devices to end users of System/360, they could take advantage of the same benefits that accrued to IBM from the modularity and standardized interface features of System/360, and especially from the product line's compatibility.[2] Because the same peripheral equipment could be used with any model of the System/360 family, the number of models of a given type of peripheral device could be minimized, resulting in at least three benefits to IBM — and to a manufacturer of IBM plug-compatible products: (1) the reduction of development expenses, especially those associated with developing the various models; (2) the reduction of unit manufacturing costs as a consequence of higher production volume for each type of unit; and (3) the reduction of administrative overhead by virtue of simplifying the management of the lease base.[3] In addition, competitors could copy IBM's design and, in particular, use its systems software, thus having lower development costs than IBM.

IBM management recognized this competitive risk as early as 1961 in the SPREAD Committee Report.[4] A System/360 Compatibility Committee was formed for the purpose of examining "possible competitive developments compatible to System/360" and recommending possible responses to that competition.[5] The committee concluded that competing systems manufacturers would investigate the possibility of developing processors compatible with System/360 and that input-output (I/O) manufacturers, both independents and divisions of systems manufacturers, could achieve a position to market plug-compatible peripheral devices at prices approximately 20 percent below those of IBM.[6] The committee also foresaw "concerted activity from competitors in marketing I/O devices on System/360 in the Federal Government."[7]

But even IBM's Compatibility Committee very much underestimated the surge in plug-compatible manufacturers' (PCM) business that would take place. The extraordinary success of System/360 attracted a number of companies — especially those original equipment manufacturers (OEMs) that were producing peripherals for other systems manufacturers — into the business of replacing IBM System/360 peripherals with comparable plug-compatible equipment.[8] These plug-compatible devices (first attaching to the IBM control unit and later involving PCM control units and complete peripheral subsystems) were transparent to the IBM operating system and hence involved minimal effort to attach.[9] Ironically, the success of the System/360 had spawned even more competition for IBM.[10]

From OEM to PCM

In the 1950s and 1960s companies offering computer systems, such as Burroughs, DEC, GE, Honeywell, RCA, SDS, and Sperry Rand, often did not manufacture their own components and peripherals, but purchased that equipment from companies producing computer components and peripherals on an OEM basis.[11] Burroughs, for example, purchased printers and tape drives from Potter.[12] CDC, GE, NCR, and Sperry Rand all bought tape drives from Ampex.[13] GE purchased disk drives from Bryant, Telex, and CDC.[14] As we have seen, SDS was able to enter the systems business in the early 1960s by assembling components and peripheral equipment manufactured by OEMs. SDS obtained core memories from Fabri-Tek, Ampex, and Magnetic Memories; printers from Data Products and NCR; tape drives and tape control units from Computer Products and Ampex; disk drives and disk control units from CDC and CalComp; card readers and card punch equipment from Univac; cathode ray tube terminals from CDC; and keyboard devices from Western Electric.[15] RCA acquired equipment from OEMs in order to improve the functional capability of its system; RCA computer systems incorporated IBM card I/O equipment, Anelex printers, and Bryant disks.[16]

Companies such as Ampex, Collins Radio, and Potter entered the OEM field from the technical, electronics, or communications business, and new companies were formed by EDP industry employees who sought to take advantage of these opportunities.[17] These OEMs sold their products to attach to the computers of several different companies.[18] OEMs also benefited from the emergence of computer leasing companies (discussed below), which were organized to purchase CPUs, memories, and peripherals for lease to end users at rates below those of the major computer system suppliers. With the vast expansion of leasing companies in the late 1960s, manufacturers making the transition from OEM sales to the production of IBM plug-compatible equipment found it convenient to enter into OEM-like agreements with leasing companies. This enabled them to have their products marketed to end users without having to provide their own marketing force. Leasing companies profited by being able to take advantage of the peripheral manufacturers' lower prices.[19]

The OEM business had its "vagaries and unpredictabilities" because OEMs depended upon the business decisions of the systems manufacturers.[20] As the 1960s progressed, peripherals became an area of increasing profitability and consequence to systems performance. In 1960 peripherals had represented only about 20 cents of every hardware dollar spent on a computer system.[21] But by the late 1960s peripherals had grown to constitute more than half of the systems price, and the expectation was that they would continue to increase as a portion of the computer user's budget.[22] Accordingly, systems manufacturers turned to in-house development and production of peripherals in response to the growing business opportunity in that area.[23] By July 1970, Burroughs, GE, NCR, RCA, and Sperry Rand, which had previously purchased tape products on an OEM basis, were producing their own tape products; CDC, GE, and Honeywell, which had previously purchased OEM disks, were producing their own disk products.[24] Subsequently newer companies, such as DEC and SDS, also began to produce some of their own peripheral devices.[25]

At about this time CDC became an active OEM supplier. In 1968-75 CDC marketed card equipment, disks and drums, memories, printer equipment, tape equipment, and terminal equipment to as many as 150 companies on an OEM basis.[26] In particular, CDC was active in the late 1960s in marketing, on an OEM basis, its non-IBM plug-compatible disk drives.[27] It began shipping 2311-type non-IBM-compatible drives in 1967, announcing a 2314-type non-IBM-compatible disk drive with a hydraulic actuator. The following year its customers included SDS, ICL, Saab, and CII.[28] Competing with CalComp for OEM contracts with Burroughs, CDC then developed voice coil actuator versions of its 2314-type non-IBM plug-compatible disk drives.[29] These were announced and delivered in 1970 to Siemens, ICL, CII, XDS, and Telex, among others.[30] CDC also announced in 1969, for delivery in 1970, a 2314-type non-IBM plug-compatible disk drive for use in its own systems.[31]

As the systems manufacturers built their own peripherals capability, a number of OEMs began selling plug-compatible peripheral equipment directly to end users of IBM System/360 equipment in 1967 and 1968.[32] Successful PCM installation required overcoming customer reluctance to have a multivendor computer system. But that reluctance started disappearing in the late 1960s as computer users matured.[33]

A significant event marking the acceptance of multivendor installations occurred in June 1969, when the comptroller general formally reported to Congress the results of a study conducted by the General Accounting Office on the acquisition of components and peripheral equipment for federal government computer installations. The report found that a number of private organizations had installed plug-compatible equipment and achieved substantial savings; it recommended that federal agencies take immediate action to require replacement of leased computer components and peripherals with cheaper plug-compatible units.[34] The Veterans Administration acted upon this study, examining plug-compatible replacements for its IBM 2311 disk drives and recommending leasing Marshall, Linnell, and MAI 2311-type compatible drives.[35] The result of this examination by the Veterans Administration, and then other federal agencies, was the institution of government-wide peripheral equipment replacement programs, involving the procurement not only of disks but also of tapes, memory, communications equipment, terminals, printers, and drums at cost savings to the government.[36]

As a result of this increasing acceptance, PCMs were quite successful.[37] By 1970 they were shipping IBM-compatible tape drives, disk drives, terminals, communications controllers, and add-on memories. Some companies offered more than one type of plug-compatible peripheral, beginning with one product and then branching out.[38]

Moreover, the business of these PCMs did not stop with IBM; they also marketed their IBM plug-compatible peripherals, with minor modification, on an OEM basis to non-IBM systems manufacturers.[39] For example, Information Storage Systems (ISS) sold its 2314-type IBM plug-compatible disk drive not only to Telex for marketing to users of IBM computers but also to Hewlett-Packard.[40] Memorex marketed its 630 (2311-type) and 660 (2314-type) disk drives not only directly to users for attachment to IBM computers but also to a number of different systems manufacturers, including RCA, Burroughs, Univac, Honeywell, DEC, Datacraft, SEL, Hewlett-Packard, NCR, Siemens, Phillips, and ICL.[41] Ampex sold its tape drives and add-on memories, which were used for attachment to IBM systems, to 75 or 100 different manufacturers.[42] And CalComp marketed its Century Data disk drives to BASF, Burroughs, Univac, Nixdorf, and some 25 other OEM customers.[43]

PCM Entrants

We now consider the history of some of the early plug-compatible manufacturers during the 1960s.

Telex

From its organization in the 1930s until 1959, Telex was a family-owned business devoted to making hearing aids and a limited line of acoustic products.[44] In 1959 Telex experienced a "significant change in the ownership of the Company," and the new owners began "to implement a comprehensive growth program."[45] In the next few years the firm became "a broadly-based electronics manufacturer" of "instruments, controls, components and special products for the electronics industry," as well as "phonographs and radio phonographs for the retail market."[46] In 1962 Telex acquired Midwestern Instruments, a supplier of telemetric and specialized electromechanical devices for the space program, and instruments and magnetic tape devices for industry.[47] Following the acquisition, Telex sold magnetic tape drives "to small, special purpose computer-type companies, making equipment for special, narrow purposes."[48]

In the mid-1960s the large number of IBM tape drives in service attracted Telex's interest in the IBM plug-compatible tape business. In January 1966, Stephen J. Jatras, Telex's president, wrote to Roger M. Wheeler, Telex's chairman and chief executive officer:

> The fact that there are 53,000 IBM Digital Tape Transports in the field has represented a tempting target for ourselves and others who

build equipment of this kind. The greatest problem in penetrating this market has been that of convincing potential customers that they would be supplied with service equal to that they are accustomed to from IBM. In addition to convincing the customer of this, there was also the problem of actually carrying out such a [service effort].

We have recently found a method for satisfying the service requirements for this kind of equipment. Several of the large leasing companies such as Data Processing Associates (formerly Doheny Leasing Company) and Management Associates, Inc. have recently sprung up and made a major penetration into the IBM replacement market. Both of these companies have established service branches primarily staffed with ex-IBM personnel.[49]

Jatras also estimated that the engineering costs for the design of "a modification list for the standard M4000 Digital Tape Transport [which Telex was then marketing] so that [Telex could] offer an IBM compatible machine" was "approximately $42,000."[50]

Telex entered the business of manufacturing IBM plug-compatible tape drives after receiving a contract from DuPont. Jatras described this turn of events in his testimony:

[O]ne of the men who worked for Midwestern Instruments had earlier made a proposal that we undertake the idea of trying to convert or redesign one of our digital tape drives, such that it would interface with an IBM CPU, and we studied that for a while and appropriated some money to do some preliminary work and to actually begin the development program of the interface electronics.

We . . . had, up until that time, been a manufacturer for OEM markets primarily, and the prices that prevailed in the IBM plug-to-plug market . . . looked quite attractive to us, and we saw a good profit opportunity.

Subsequently, the DuPont Company, on some independent means, decided they wanted to replace their IBM 729s, and by that time we were probably halfway done with our engineering program, and when we responded to the request for a quotation, apparently we were the only ones that could, in a convincing way, meet their delivery requirements, and we won that order.

After we won that order and put some equipment in the field with them and put another installation in, we became convinced that we understood how to make the machines work in that environment, and we then eventually reached the decision to go into the market in the broader sense.[51]

Telex began deliveries of its 729-type drives in 1967, and its tape drive sales increased rapidly.[52] Tasting success in its computer-related business, it expanded its product line to include disks and printers as well as tapes.[53] On April 21, 1969, Telex entered into an agreement with Information Storage Systems (ISS), to market and service ISS-built 2311-type and 2314-type disk drives.[54] In early 1970 Telex reached an agreement with CDC for the marketing of "a complete printer subsystem, utilizing a train type mechanism manufactured by CDC" and a controller manufactured by Telex.[55]

Telex's rapidly expanding EDP business was reflected in its domestic EDP revenues, which increased from $870,000 in 1966 to $23,006,000 in 1969, and almost tripled to $65,628,000 in 1970.[56]

Ampex

In 1955 Ampex produced its first tape drive for use with a computer, manufacturing magnetic tape drives for sale on an OEM basis.[57] Its biggest customer was GE, but it also sold to NCR, CDC, Burroughs, Collins, Sperry Rand, and several European manufacturers.[58]

In 1960 Ampex stated its "plans to continue development and introduction of memory devices tailored to the advanced requirements of manufacturers of computers and other data-processing equipment."[59] In the next few years Ampex offered several new tape systems as well as core memory.[60] In 1964-74 Ampex sold its tape drives to 75-100 different manufacturers of computer systems, including not only IBM but also Burroughs, General Automation, RCA, Honeywell, DEC, GE, Hewlett-Packard, NCR, Sperry, and Varian Data Machines. The tape drives sold to all of these companies were substantially the same product.[61]

Ampex was one of the first companies to enter the IBM plug-compatible replacement business.[62] Like Telex, it entered the business after being asked to bid on replacing DuPont's IBM 729 tape drives. Although Telex received the contract, the event brought a change in Ampex's marketing emphasis, and in 1968 it began marketing a replacement for IBM 729 and 2401 tape drives directly to end users.[63]

Ampex was the first company to offer add-on memory to end users of IBM systems. In its 1969 Annual Report, Ampex stated:

> While most Ampex core products are sold to manufacturers, the first end-user installations of Ampex core memories were made during the year at major data processing centers. Two Ampex Model RM extended core memories, each capable of storing nearly 10 million bits, were installed for use with two IBM 360/50 computers at the Kaiser Foundation Research Institute in Oakland, California.[64]

According to M. K. Haynes, IBM's director of storage technology:

> The Ampex LCS [Large Core Storage] was originally designed and built for IBM attachment to the Model 91. After we had terminated the contract, Ampex continued the development to make it into a product which they had marketed and installed. The present Ampex situation is that they have installed three LCS units, all on 360/Model 50's.[65]

Subsequently, Ampex also sold a core memory that was used with computer systems made by GE, Litton, RCA, DEC, Univac, and CDC, as well as IBM. In the five or ten years prior to 1974, Ampex sold its core memory products to as many as 100 different companies for incorporation in their computer systems. The core memory module sold by Ampex to all of these purchasers was "for all practical purposes identical." The only difference in terms of cost was the interface, but that was "relatively nominal compared to the cost of the core memory."[66]

Like other PCMs Ampex prospered in the late 1960s. Ampex's net sales and operating revenues increased from $170 million in 1966 to $298 million in 1969 and $314 million in 1970.[67] Its domestic EDP revenues increased from $13.8 million in 1960 to $30.6 million in 1969 and $35.7 million in 1970.[68]

Memorex

Memorex was incorporated in February 1961 by four former employees of Ampex, each of whom invested $3,125, for a total investment of $12,500.[69] Additional capital of $1.25 million was raised from "a group of some two dozen institutions and individuals," including the Allstate Insurance Company and the Bank of America.[70] The company was formed to go into the business of manufacturing magnetic recording tape for computer and commercial broadcasting applications.[71]

In the summer of 1962 Memorex began operations, marketing computer tape to IBM systems users, as well as instrumentation tapes.[72] In the next few years the firm established itself as one of the three principal manufacturers of precision magnetic tape.[73] From 1964 to 1967 Memorex marketed its computer tape to Burroughs, Honeywell, CDC, Univac, NCR, DEC, and ICT.[74]

In 1967 Memorex began developing disk packs for IBM and other systems manufacturers' disk drives.[75] Laurence Spitters, who had been Memorex's president, chairman, and chief executive officer, testified about the attraction for Memorex to enter into the disk pack business:

> Beginning in 1964, the market for disk packs developed with the shipment into the computer marketplace of 2311 type removable disks, and subsequently, I believe in 1967, with the shipment of 2314 type equipments, which called for a higher quality disk pack, a higher valued disk pack, these products were used by a large number of the several thousand customers to whom Memorex was daily calling upon selling its computer tape.
>
> These products involved, to some extent, some of the magnetic coating formulation technologies that Memorex had for some years employed in its tape business.
>
> So, consequently, with this congruence of marketplace and its opportunities and technologies to some extent, it seemed most advisable for the company to enter the disk pack business.[76]

Memorex began marketing its disk packs in September 1967.[77] Through its entrepreneurial subsidiary, Disk Pack Corporation, it sold disk packs both on an OEM basis and to users of IBM, CDC, and Honeywell computer systems.[78]

The "entrepreneurial subsidiary" was a device used by Memorex in the late 1960s to enter the disk pack, the disk drive, and the output microfilm printer businesses.[79] The parent firm retained a majority ownership interest in an entrepreneurial subsidiary and provided financial support, marketing assistance, management expertise, and manufacturing capabilities. The remaining minority ownership was retained by "technically skilled individuals" who developed a certain product under contract and who were given an incentive in the form of potential capital gain. If the enterprise was successful, Memorex had the right to acquire the minority ownership interest in exchange for shares of Memorex common stock according to a predetermined ratio based upon the degree of success.[80]

As is described later, the use of "entrepreneurial subsidiaries," as well as other accounting techniques, while enriching Memorex's founders and original shareholders, eventually led to substantial criticism of the firm in the financial community. The use of entrepreneurial subsidiaries was part of the speculative financial strategy of Memorex under Laurence Spitters, who made speeches about the strategy to members of the financial community. That strategy most notably included the use of debt leverage to minimize the issuance of equity, in an attempt to achieve capital gains for Memorex shareholders, especially for original shareholders such as Spitters himself. The use of high leverage, which received criticism from "conservative investors and from bankers," later caused Memorex to have difficulties in paying its debt service and in obtaining capital.[81]

A natural direction of growth was from disk packs to disk drives.[82] In 1966 another entrepreneurial subsidiary of Memorex, Peripherals Systems Corporation, was formed to develop a key-to-disk entry-recording system.[83] Although that device was not developed, the Peripherals Systems Corporation did successfully develop Memorex's first disk file.[84]

The Memorex 630 was an IBM plug-compatible 2311-type disk drive that attached to the IBM 2841 control unit.[85] It was sold "primarily" on an OEM basis and to leasing companies, especially Management Associates, Inc. (MAI), which marketed it to IBM System/360 users; initial deliveries were made to MAI in 1968.[86] At that time Memorex had "no marketing and no service organization," and it required MAI's support.[87] Similarly, Potter IBM plug-compatible tape drives had first been offered to end users and serviced by MAI; and, as we have seen, the availability of such service had been an attraction to Telex.[88] Memorex also marketed the 630 to Digital Equipment Corporation, which attached the file to its own computer systems. The 630 files marketed to MAI had an interface different from those marketed to DEC.[89] Memorex 630 drives with different interfaces were also marketed to other systems manufacturers.[90]

In 1969 Memorex adopted a plan to organize the company into two parts: (1) the magnetic media business and (2) the equipment group, which would consist largely of two subsidiaries, Peripherals Systems Corporation and Image Products Corporation.[91] In May 1969 the equipment group had only the 630 disk file on the market but was developing a computer output microfilm system. It planned to expand its disk file product line.[92]

D. James Guzy (Memorex's executive vice-president and chief operating officer when he left the company in 1973)[93] testified that Memorex's strategy for its equipment group was to begin by expanding its disk file line, selling to OEMs. This would "produce some cash to finance the forward development of the corporation." The second part of the program was to take these same products directly into the end-user marketplace. The objective was to develop an end-user sales and service organization. The combination of the volume of product being manufactured for OEMs and the additional volume sold to end users "would give us overall lower costs," which would allow the third phase of the program, the development of Memorex's own systems.[94] Such lower costs through higher volume of course relied on the fact that Memorex had a single product line or at least common facilities for production of OEM and plug-compatible products.[95]

OEM sales were to come first because they were easiest. Spitters testified:

> To market to MAI required a skeletal sales organization, principally consisting of Mr. Guzy and one or two assistants. There was no service capability required, and of course, Memorex had none. And it was principally relating to the absence of an end user marketing force and service force that we undertook selling to a very small group of OEM customers; and, secondly, OEM customers were cash customers, and that was important to the cash requirements of the company.[96]

The first two phases of this strategy depended on producing IBM-like disk drives, and Memorex hired a large number of disk drive engineers who had worked at IBM, writing to its customers to inform them of this fact.[97] Between 1968 and 1971 Memorex hired approximately 600 former IBM employees and attempted to recruit nearly 600 current IBM employees. Among those hired was a cadre of engineers with experience in disk drive design.[98]

Memorex followed its 630 disk file with its 660 disk drive, which was "styled and intended to be an IBM 2314 type disk drive."[99] The 660 was announced in 1968, with volume production beginning in the second quarter of 1969.[100] Memorex initially marketed the 660 to a number of OEM customers.[101] For example, it shipped about 1,200 660 disk drives to RCA, the drive attaching through an RCA controller.[102] It obtained an agreement from Univac for similar shipments, the drive attaching through the Univac controller, but Univac terminated the agreement because of the poor performance of the disk drives.[103]

Memorex subsequently marketed the 661 control unit for the 660 disk drive. The 661 was plug-compatible with IBM's System/360 and could replace the IBM 2314 control unit at 15 percent below IBM's price.[104] The control unit was announced December 17, 1969, one day after Memorex had signed an agreement with a group of former IBM employees to develop such a product for Memorex.[105]

Phase two of Memorex's strategy — marketing directly to end users — began shortly after the equipment group was formed in May 1969.[106] In its 1970 Annual Report, Memorex stated:

> Concurrent with growth was the Company's transition from a reliance upon OEM customers (original equipment manufacturers) to an equipment products business based upon marketing to computer users. In 1969 and early 1970, an insignificant volume of products had been marketed to users. In the second half of 1970, approximately 90% of production was shipped to computer users.[107]

During 1969 and 1970 Memorex's disk sales grew substantially. The firm stated in its 1969 Annual Report that its sales of disk drive products had been $15 million in 1969, the first full year of production. However, "throughout most of the year, sales were production limited and production was restricted by facilities. Manufacturing space tripled during the year, but it was not until October that the major expansion occurred which accommodated a sharp increase in production."[108] Memorex's employees increased from 1,916 at the end of 1968 to 3,409 at the end of 1969, and to 6,101 at the end of 1970.[109] By October 1969, Memorex had commenced phase three, the development of its computer systems.[110]

The 1960s were years of great growth for Memorex. Spitters stated in 1968 that the company's sales volume had grown from zero to more than $60 million in seven years.[111] Its domestic EDP revenues increased from $390,000 in 1962 to $41.5 million in 1970.[112]

Spitters explained that this expansion was financed by utilizing both the public securities market and bank credit. Starting with $1.25 million of external capital, Memorex increased that capital in 1962 by $608,000. In late 1962 and early 1963 sales and leaseback arrangements brought Memorex more than $650,000. Memorex also borrowed from the Bank of America: by 1966 the amount was $6 million. Memorex had a public offering of $12 million in 1966, and with those proceeds it repaid its bank debt. But by 1969 Memorex had again borrowed approximately $40 to $50 million from the Bank of America.[113]

In March 1969, Spitters stated:

> Our original investors who provided the 1961 and 1962 funding have enjoyed a capital appreciation of their investment of more than 80 times.
>
> And our original public stockholders, who purchased Memorex shares of the first public offering in March 1965, have received a 10-times appreciation of their investment.[114]

Information Storage Systems

Information Storage Systems (ISS) was formed by 12 IBM employees who had resigned in December 1967 from the IBM San Jose facility, which had responsibility for disk drive development and manufacture.[115] These 12 people had worked in key disk development positions, and some of them had been part of the crucial Merlin (3330) program discussed in Chapter 11.[116]

In April 1969, ISS granted Telex the "marketing rights to end user customers for disc pack drives manufactured by [ISS]...."[117] Before ISS had shipped any product on its own, Telex also assumed responsibility for servicing the ISS drives. This initially meant that Telex had rights to the 701, a plug-compatible replacement for the 2311.[118] Other disk products were added to the ISS line later in 1969. In September ISS announced its 714 disk, which was a plug-compatible replacement for the IBM 2314. In November ISS announced the 728 control unit, allowing the "728/714 system [to be] plug-for-plug compatible with the 2314 on an IBM selector channel."[119] Telex also marketed these products to end users.[120]

ISS began its product shipments in August 1969, and its sales for that year were $648,000. By 1970 its revenues were $24,247,000.[121]

CalComp/Century Data Systems

California Computer Products (CalComp) was incorporated in September 1958, and the company's primary business for the next decade was computer plotter systems, associated electronic equipment, and related software. By 1972 CalComp laid claim to being the pioneer in, as well as the world's leading supplier of, digital plotter hardware and software.[122] IBM marketed a CalComp-manufactured plotter as the IBM 1627.[123] Century Data Systems was formed in 1968 by several former SDS engineers to enter the plug-compatible disk drive field.[124] In October 1968, CalComp made an initial investment in Century Data Systems, becoming the major investor.[125] This investment was increased "from 49% to 66%" in March 1970, and to 94 percent in October 1971.[126]

Century Data shipped its first plug-compatible disk drive (a 2311 type) in June 1969.[127] It later became the "first company to produce and ship a 2314 equivalent."[128] CalComp purchased these disk drives from Century Data for resale to end users.[129] Century Data also marketed the disk drives to leasing companies such as Randolph and to other computer companies such as Nixdorf (through BASF), and later Burroughs and Univac on an OEM basis.[130]

CalComp's gross revenues increased from $16.8 million in 1968 to $20.4 million in 1969, and in 1970 Century Data's revenues for the fiscal year ending June 30 were $4 million.[131] CalComp's U.S. EDP revenues rose from $11.2 million in 1967 and $13.3 million in 1968 to $22.6 million in 1970.[132]

PCM Price Competition and Success

As one would (and IBM did) expect, where largely imitative products are introduced some time after the originals, PCMs were able to, and did, offer their products at prices below those of IBM. PCMs were able to offer lower prices because they placed their products in existing IBM installations, thereby avoiding the substantial costs that IBM had incurred and continued to bear, not only in product research and development but also in software support, systems development, and marketing.[133] IBM would configure the system and do whatever else was necessary to make the installation. After the installation had been made, the PCM would offer its replacement device at a lower price.[134]

The PCM price advantage was at least 10 to 15 percent.[135] In many cases, however, the price discounts over IBM equipment were even more substantial. For example, in November 1968, Frank Cary wrote to Thomas J. Watson, Jr., about the Telex and Potter price advantage in tape drives:

> Midwestern Instruments (a division of Telex) and MAI (Management Assistance, Inc.), the sales organization for Potter Instrument tape drives, are actively marketing direct replacement of IBM's 2400 Series drives. The OEM's predominate [*sic*] thrust has been replacing leased drives on purchased CPU's and their current purchase prices range from 25% to 50% less than IBM's 2400 Series.[136]

There were similar reports inside and outside IBM.[137]

In addition to their lower list prices, PCMs did not charge for additional use of equipment beyond 176 hours per month (as IBM did). Free overtime use was most attractive to the high-usage customers, who were running their systems on a two- or three-shift basis.[138] PCMs also offered other financial incentives that further reduced their prices. These discounting practices included long-term leases with lower monthly charges; free trial periods of 30 days or more; special discounts off list price; volume discounts; free transportation from the plant to the customer's site; and "rent forgiving practices." These practices in some cases increased PCM discounts by as much as two or three times the figure indicated by their list prices.[139]

In July 1970, H. G. Figueroa, vice-president of marketing development in IBM's Data Processing Division, wrote:

> We lose due to *price* and secondarily as a result of lack of function. . . .
> [T]he *OEM* discount averaged 27% below IBM's cost in loss situations.[140]

As a result of the lower prices, by 1968 there was "a sudden and very rapid growth" in the quantity of equipment shipped by PCMs who were "displacing, or replacing the installed IBM equipment." This phenomenon started in the tape drive area and spread to disk drives. The growth of these companies "in terms of the number of pieces of IBM equipment which were being displaced was very rapid."[141] By the end of 1969, IBM was receiving plug-compatible competition in add-on memories, as well as in disks, tapes, printers, and terminals.[142]

The success of the PCMs in displacing IBM equipment was a significant concern within IBM in the late 1960s. At a July 15, 1968 meeting of the IBM Management Committee (then IBM's second highest committee), a presentation on plug-compatible peripherals was made by the Data Processing Group (DPG) staff at the request of IBM's president, T. V. Learson.[143] The presentation reported on the substantial competition in the areas of compatible disk drives, tape drives, control units, printers, and card I/O, as well as an anticipated growth in PCM shipments. Among the reasons given for the tremendous success of PCM competition were the "explosive growth" in tapes and disks, the availability of technology, the mobility of people, the availability of service and sales support with the advent of leasing and service companies, the availability of capital to new companies seeking to exploit a more mature technology, and the questioning of the one-vendor concept, especially by the government.[144] The Management Committee agreed with the DPG staff that IBM "should maintain [its] position in the I/O area through technical superiority."[145]

The August 1968 Quarterly Product Line Assessment (QPLA), prepared by the Commercial Analysis Department of the Data Processing Division (DPD), also reflected the increasing competition that IBM was facing in the peripherals area:

> IBM has produced superior I/O equipment. Now it is freely copied, or improved upon, and presented to our customers as "plug-for-plug" compatible. And it is! We have reached a point where every piece of I/O gear *must* be able to hold its own, in terms of price/performance, in a highly competitive market.[146]

At the October 17, 1968, Management Committee meeting a more optimistic note was struck with respect to tapes. While PCMs were considered to be established in the business, it was believed that IBM's new tape products would be an effective competitive response, since

> Increased investment in tape drive engineering in 1967 and 1968 had produced products which are technically superior to competitive offerings.[147]

In November 1968 Frank Cary, then IBM vice-president and general manager of the Data Processing Group, emphasized the need to compete with "superior technology and function, and not price alone." In reporting to Thomas J. Watson, Jr., as quoted above, that Midwestern Instruments and MAI were "actively marketing direct replacement of IBM's 2400 series drives," he stated that "the strategy of new technology announcements [was] the most effective way" to respond to the PCM competition in tapes.[148]

Nevertheless, PCM competition in tapes grew stronger. Indeed, PCMs were expanding their facilities in an effort to keep up with the demand for their products.[149] In May 1969, R. A. Whitcomb, the DPD product marketing manager for input-output products, informed DPD President F. G. Rodgers that IBM had already lost over 1 million points (dollars of monthly rental value) to competitors' tape drives; that 2.5 million more points were "doubtful"; that competition was "installing all they can produce"; and that IBM's estimate of its losses through 1971 was going to be exceeded by 50 percent. Whitcomb's recommendations included reducing delivery times and cutting prices on IBM's most advanced tape drives.[150] At the July 8, 1969 Management Committee meeting, PCM competition in tape drives was reported to be growing at 13 percent per month.[151]

Also in July 1969 Rodgers, in response to a request from IBM President Learson, told Learson that the "plug-to-plug tape and disk market [was] growing at a rate in excess of 70%." Rodgers reported that the PCM activity would continue for at least four reasons: (1) systems manufacturer activity in the IBM plug-compatible peripherals business had increased; (2) leasing companies had committed approximately $170 million to PCM peripheral manufacturers for the purchase of disk and tape drives that the leasing companies would market; (3) the federal government was encouraging multiple vendor systems; and (4) contract terms and conditions would become more varied, with pricing tailored for quantities, cluster installations, and long-term leases. Rodgers added that IBM's strategy in response to this PCM activity was to cut prices and enhance performance on existing drives.[152]

IBM employees recognized the substantial threat PCMs presented to IBM's systems business. The competitive evaluation done for the forthcoming Merlin disk file in January 1970 included an analysis of disks offered both by systems manufacturers and by PCMs, and took into account the PCM-leasing company marketing arrangements.[153] A February 1970 talk on competition in the tape area by W. J. Hollenkamp (a talk he was later to characterize as "optimistic" and "mild in describing the threat that we face from competition") concluded that "the problem we face in IBM today" is that "it takes all the running you can do to keep in the same place. If you want to get somewhere else, you must run at least twice as fast as that."[154] Looking back, Whitcomb, who left IBM for Itel in September 1971, testified that if IBM had taken no price or product action, there would have been "[a]n increase in an accelerating rate of the plug compatible manufacturers versus the IBM inventory," and it would have been only a short time before the PCMs would have replaced a very large portion, if not most or all, of the tapes and disks attached to IBM central processing units.[155]

The PCM competitive threat accelerated in 1970 with the issuance on February 2, 1970, of the Bureau of the Budget's (BOB) Bulletin no. 70-9. The bureau directed federal agencies "to review and make certain determinations on whether leased peripheral equipment components in computer systems supplied by the system manufacturer should be replaced with less costly equipment available from independent peripheral manufacturers or other sources."[156] To facilitate this review, the General Services Administration (GSA) was to send a listing to each agency of all installed leased components scheduled to be retained. Each agency was required, upon receipt of the listing, to review it and determine whether "substitution action should be taken." If action should not be taken, the agency was to indicate the reason and return the annotated listing to the GSA "no later than April 15, 1970."[157]

On learning of the BOB Bulletin, V. R. MacDonald, DPD vice-president and manager of the GEM Region (which was responsble for marketing to the federal government), estimated that there were 8.27 million points of IBM tape drives and disk drives that were subject to replacement by PCMs.[158] That concern was well-founded. A substantial amount of IBM's peripheral equipment was replaced in government agencies. By February 1970 the Defense Department alone had identified 480 IBM tape units and 99 IBM disk drives to be replaced.[159] H. S. Trimmer, Jr., of GSA later advised Congressman Jack Brooks, chairman of the Subcommittee on Government Activities, that "of approximately 3300 such components in the Government inventory as of June 30, 1970, over 1800 have been replaced."[160]

The BOB Bulletin prompted H. E. Cooley, vice-president of development of IBM's Systems Development Division (SDD), to write to B. O. Evans, then SDD president:

> I consider this, along with other Government action . . . to be extremely serious.
> I am seriously considering appointing myself as a one man task force to try to come up with some new ideas on the problem.[161]

Evans conveyed the message to higher management.[162] He testified about the appointment of the Cooley Task Force:

> [E]arly in 1970, the peripheral marketplace was in a lot of trouble. System manufacturers, the plug compatibles, the leasing companies, were hitting us hard. We didn't know it at the time, but the beginning of the economic adjustment was on us and our lack of success in the marketplace was startling.
> Mr. Cooley came to see me in February or March of 1970 and, at that time, he suggested that the problem was getting so serious and the pressure was going to be on us for solutions even more than they had, and Cooley suggested that he go over and work full-time alone on the problem of what more we might do.
> I felt the problem was indeed serious and thought it was of such consequence that perhaps we ought to have a broader group than that, and it ended that we brought in, under Mr. Cooley's stewardship, a number of top professionals from the business. We brought in the Director of the Boulder Laboratory, the man most responsible for magnetic tape development; we brought in the Director of the San Jose Laboratory, the man most responsible for disk file development; we brought in an executive from the Data Processing Division in the United States from an area that was being hit hardest at that time by the competition; we brought in a representative from World Trade; and this group went to work then for some time looking at whether we

could accelerate our technologies that were emerging, or if there was anything that we could do with technologies at hand to find a better way.[163]

The next month (March 1970) the IBM Management Committee designated peripherals as a "key corporate strategic issue."[164] (Such a designation was "their way of telling the operating unit that that's an issue. . . . they want to review more frequently than at operating plan review time."[165] IBM used that designation procedure from 1969 to June 1971, when it was stopped because key corporate strategic issues "became so numerous that they . . . really weren't very meaningful any longer. . . ."[166]) The Management Committee was interested in establishing "a long range, well-defined and understood peripheral strategy," and included specific products in the scope of the intended review: "magnetic tape drives, direct access storage products, impact printers, card readers and punches, associated control units, and main and large capacity memory products."[167] The scope of the review was expanded a few days later "to include multiplexors (local and remote) and competitive compatible displays," because the purpose of examining peripherals as a key corporate strategic issue was "to examine [IBM's] policies and [IBM's] strategies vis à vis [sic] competition and not individual products," and because it was felt "that by confining it to local systems I/O gear we may be ignoring some key policy and strategic issues dealing with the communications problem."[168] Ralph Pfeiffer, the IBM director of marketing, was assigned the lead corporate staff responsibility for the review, in which role he was to supply a statement of "Corporate concerns" to the Cooley Task Force.[169]

At the March 11, 1970 meeting the Management Committee concluded that the business opportunity for PCMs remained attractive, and gave this assessment of their competitive position:

> Continuing financial backing is likely. Larger volumes and broader product lines should aid OEM's in reducing manufacturing costs as well as reducing marketing expense and enhancing maintenance coverage. Users will use cost savings as a prime reason for procurement. The entrepreneurial opportunity will continue to be attractive to quality personnel. Therefore, accelerated competitive penetration is possible. . . .[170]

The Management Committee requested that the work being coordinated by Cooley proceed "as rapidly as possible," since by May of that year it would be necessary to price the not yet announced System/370.[171] And in its report to the Management Review Committee (then IBM's highest committee), the Management Committee stated that the peripherals area was IBM's "number one challenge."[172]

The initial finding of the Cooley Task Force was that "there was nothing terribly significant that could be done through existing technologies."[173] Cooley, along with Evans, conveyed this finding to G. B. Beitzel, vice-president of IBM's DP Group, with the recommendation that IBM was "going to have to find price/performance through some policy pricing."[174] Beitzel did not believe that was "a proper recommendation from his development forces" and, according to Evans, "threw us out . . . and sent us back to the drawing board, so to speak, to see if we could find anything more."[175] Cooley came back in the late summer of 1970 with several recommendations. His conclusion then was that the best way to compete was through technological excellence.[176] Evans testified about Cooley's recommendations:

> [W]e would have to intensify the assignment of resources, have to assign more resources to the development of disk[s] and tapes and their successor equipment.[177]

Throughout 1970 PCM competition rapidly "accelerat[ed] in volume and scope," posing "a serious threat to IBM's potential for growth."[178] The April 1970 QPLA reported that IBM faced serious competition in both tapes and disks: "IBM's most serious problem" was "the replacement of installed 2400 series units by compatible drives."[179] The August QPLA called PCM replacement of IBM 2311 disk drives a "major competitive problem," and proceeded to sound a warning about several types of competitors marketing disk products like IBM's 2311 and 2314 that were challenging the superiority of IBM's disk products:

> Memorex builds 2310, 2311 and 2314-type files, marketing direct to end users. Their marketing agreement with MAI for the 2311-type file is still in effect.
>
> G.E. is providing Greyhound with 1000 disk drives for 2311 replacement.
>
> Potter offers 2311 and 2314-type files and storage control units to end users. ISS markets their 2311 and 2314-type files in conjunction with Telex. Friden manufactures and markets a 2311-type file in conjunction with Talcott.
>
> Marshall Laboratories markets a drive interchangeable with the 2311, but with two R/W [read/write] heads per arm. They also announced a 2314-type file.
>
> Century Data Systems builds 2311 and 2314-type files, and markets them through CalComp. Century Data has licensed BASF to manufacture and market these units in Europe, and they are particularly active in West Germany.
>
> In addition to the above, CDC, ICL, and Fujitsu are manufacturing 2311-like drives for their own use, and also are selling them OEM to other computer manufacturers.
>
> Hitachi manufactures and markets 2311 and 2314-type files for their own use, and are selling them OEM to other computer manufacturers. They do not presently have a U.S. outlet but are actively seeking one.
>
> Univac announced their 2314-type device (Univac 8414 Disc Subsystem) for use on the Univac 9000 and 1100 Series computers. Honeywell has delivered the H274 (2314-type device) for attachment

to the H200 and larger Honeywell systems. NCR announced a 2314-type device (NCR 657 Disk Drive) for the Century 200 system.

. . . .

A recent trend in the competitive market reveals potential exposure in the disk drive area for IBM 1130 and 1800 systems. Intercomp, BCD Computing Corporation, IOMEC, Caelus, Memorex, and Community Computing Corporation have announced files in competition with the IBM 2310, 2311, and 1810 disk drives on the 1130 and 1800 systems. . . .[180]

IBM was having trouble keeping track of the activity of the PCMs and forecasting their future success. Forecasts of installed PCM 2314 spindles were done on April 10, October 3, and October 31, 1970. The April 10 forecast saw 5,800 spindles of PCM 2314s installed by 1972. The October 3 forecast revised this figure to 8,700, and the October 31 forecast raised that figure again to 15,000. The April 10 forecast predicted that 12,500 spindles of PCM 2314s would be installed by 1974, but the October 31 forecast revised this figure to 17,300. Moreover, the DP Group forecast that if the PCMs introduced a double-density 2314, the number of PCM 2314 spindles would by 1974 increase to 21,400 – 60 percent of all 2314-type disk drives installed on IBM systems.[181]

The effects on IBM were not limited to its peripheral devices. As the Management Committee recognized in March 1970, pricing of System/370, IBM's new family of computers, and System/370 peripherals required taking PCM competition into account.[182]

In short, despite the spectacular success of System/360, IBM was facing increasingly intense competition as a result of the growth of PCM competition, the efforts of systems manufacturers in peripherals, and the continuing importance of OEM relationships. Productive resources were channeled into the increasingly profitable field of peripherals, both by systems manufacturers and by independents, resulting in more alternatives for users in configuring EDP systems. As the decade ended, IBM faced the choice of responding to this vigorous competition or losing more and more business.

LEASING COMPANIES

An Overview of Leasing Company Operations

Computer leasing companies acquire equipment from various sources. They purchase new computer equipment from manufacturers, thereby qualifying for an investment tax credit when and to the extent it is available. They also purchase through customers who have leased equipment already installed, using the credits toward purchase accumulated by those customers.[183] In some instances they obtain EDP equipment through used equipment brokers or through acquisition of companies that own such equipment.

Having purchased the equipment, leasing companies become new sources of supply for the same equipment, offering the user lower prices or terms and conditions, as well as financial alternatives in addition to those available directly from the manufacturer. Although leasing companies are customers of manufacturers when purchasing from them, they are competitors when they lease the equipment to users.

Leasing companies also compete across product generation cycles by reducing prices on older equipment (for example, System/360), thereby making it price/performance-competitive with newer equipment (for instance, System/370 or the 4300 series).[184] This competition is heightened by the fact that some leasing companies not only reduce prices on older IBM equipment but also enhance equipment performance through the addition of peripherals or software from vendors other than IBM. As discussed below, this competition from leasing-company-owned equipment constrains the pricing of IBM's products and affects IBM's terms and conditions.[185]

Moreover, leasing companies have had another important competitive effect. Beginning in the 1960s, they acted as systems integrators, combining hardware and software from more than one manufacturer into systems.[186] In so doing, they encouraged the wider acceptance of mixed systems. In addition, they provided a source for the sale of the products of the plug-compatible suppliers and, in effect, augmented the marketing forces of those suppliers, facilitating their entry and initial growth.[187]

The opportunity for profitable leasing company operation arises primarily from differences in suppliers' expectations about future prices. The rate at which prices for existing equipment will decline in the future is uncertain, for it depends on the pace of technological change and the rate of introduction of competing equipment. Because of this uncertainty a leasing company may perceive an opportunity to make a profit based upon its particular expectation about the future value of the computer equipment it is seeking to acquire. If a leasing company believes that the equipment can be leased at relatively high prices for a longer period than the current market prices for lease and purchase indicate, then it can act upon that belief and acquire the equipment at current purchase prices, hoping to make a profit by keeping it on lease long enough to more than recoup (in present value terms) the purchase price plus its associated costs. Of course, if the leasing company miscalculates, it will suffer losses.[188]

There are many factors that affect the profitability (or the projected profitability) of leasing companies:

> The financial results achieved by, and reported by, leasing companies depend on a host of factors including, but not limited to, the cost of EDP equipment purchased, the timing of purchase of EDP equipment, the rental charged and the terms and conditions of lease agreements, the availability of capital, the interest rates paid on funds borrowed to purchase EDP equipment, marketing and remarketing costs, maintenance and reconditioning costs, the amount of EDP equipment that comes off rent, the length of time required to re-lease EDP equipment, the availability and utility of the investment tax credit, the accuracy of the forecast of the period for which and the rate at which EDP equipment will produce revenue, the rate of price-performance improvement

offered by manufacturers and other leasing companies, the accounting principles utilized to record income and expense, the success or failure of ancillary activities and the skill of management.[189]

Some of these items deserve further comment.

The Investment Tax Credit

A purchaser acquiring computer equipment has, over the years, often been entitled to an investment tax credit (ITC) for some percentage of the investment in new equipment. This was a key factor in the operations of leasing companies.[190] Generally, leasing companies could take full advantage of the ITC because (unlike EDP manufacturers) they universally depreciated their equipment beyond the eight years necessary to qualify for the full ITC during the periods it was available in the 1970s. They could thus pass the ITC through to customers in one form or another, or make use of it themselves.[191] However, the availability of the ITC was controlled by law and changed significantly over time. In addition, the use of the ITC by leasing companies themselves depended upon the existence of sufficient taxable income to utilize the entire credit as an offset against tax liability.

Marketing Costs

The costs and efforts associated with the marketing and remarketing of EDP equipment are key factors in a leasing company's eventual profitability.[192] A manufacturer offering a computer system to a user must configure it to suit the user's application needs and must convince the user that his proposal is better than that of his competitors. Such proposals can be quite elaborate.[193] A leasing company, when it offers the identical equipment, generally incurs no such costs. It often can simply wait until after the customer has chosen his configuration and the marketing effort has been accomplished, then offer the equipment that has already been selected at a lower price.[194] This practice enabled leasing companies to operate with small marketing staffs and low marketing costs during the 1960s. For example, in 1968 SSI (which became Itel) signed lease contracts for equipment having an original cost of more than $100 million with a marketing staff of perhaps one person at the beginning of the year and between five and eight at the end.[195]

When a leasing company has to re-lease equipment to new customers, however, it may not be able to do so by simply walking in and offering a configuration that the user has already selected.[196] Even if it has in its inventory equipment identical to that sought by the prospect or being proposed by the competition, it has to bear the reconditioning, transportation, and installation costs. Moreover, a leasing company must bear the risk that when the equipment comes up for re-lease, it will have "odd" configurations or pieces of equipment left over after the new lessees have chosen the configurations they require. Furthermore, when a leasing company markets older equipment in competition with new equipment, it has to convince the customer that its proposal is superior to proposals for newer equipment. Such a proposal takes some effort and expense. The leasing company can no longer "piggyback" entirely on the manufacturer's efforts.

Capital Availability and Cost

Among the most important factors in the growth and profitability of leasing companies are the availability and the cost of capital. All leasing operations depend on their ability to raise capital with which to purchase equipment.[197] Thus, an increase in capital costs, in general, or interest rates, in particular, significantly affects the profitability of leasing operations.[198]

Capital can be raised by leasing companies as debt or as equity. The ability to raise capital either way depends in large part on how a leasing company's profitability appears to prospective investors or lenders.[199] The basic assumption underlying leasing companies' profitability, and indeed their ability to do business in the first place, is the belief that purchased equipment will continue to be leased at relatively high prices for a longer time than expected by the manufacturer.[200] That assumption was crucial to the leasing companies' apparent profitability in the 1960s, because the leasing companies purchasing 360 equipment in the middle and late 1960s depreciated that equipment at a considerably slower rate than did IBM (or other manufacturers generally).[201] Whereas manufacturers used a life of four to six years and accelerated depreciation, some leasing companies used straight-line depreciation over a minimum of eight years (a sufficient period to take full advantage of the ITC), but more typically ten years, and assumed a 10 percent residual value thereafter.[202] Such relatively slow depreciation tended to make reported profits appear high in the early years, as did the leasing companies' practices of "flowing through" ITC to the early years and deferral of certain expenses (such as marketing, interest, and start-up costs) beyond the initial lease term.[203] It was "child's play to show very substantial profits" using the accounting methods of the leasing companies.[204]

"The profits *inter alia* reported in accordance with the accounting policies they adopted made risk leasing companies attractive to the capital markets where they raised billions of dollars in the period 1966-1969."[205] They were thus able to raise money relatively easily and to buy more equipment.[206] Additional purchases, accounted for in the same manner, cumulated the effect and made leasing company profits appear to grow even more, making leasing companies even more attractive to investors. However, as described below, when the accounting practices and the reality of the depreciation assumptions were called into question, the bubble burst, and the situation changed from one of easy credit to one of tight credit almost overnight.

The History of Leasing Companies in the 1960s

After the 1956 consent decree required IBM to sell as well as lease, the opportunity existed for companies to purchase IBM equipment, then lease and sell it to users in competition with IBM. (Indeed, it was the potential for such additional competition to IBM that was apparently one of the Antitrust Division's goals in requiring IBM to accept the consent decree provision.) Leasing companies such as MAI soon began to offer leases on IBM equipment in competition with IBM, dealing initially in unit record equipment.[207] However, Greyhound claimed to be the first firm to execute a third-party lease for a computer system, having leased an IBM 7090 to "a major aerospace company" in 1961.[208] In 1966 Greyhound created the Greyhound Computer Corporation to take over its computer leasing operations.[209]

By 1965 a number of what were to become the largest computer leasing companies were already in existence. MAI and Bankers Leasing were founded in 1955; Leasco was established in 1961; Levin-Townsend was in operation by 1963; and Randolph was founded in 1965.[210] Nevertheless, EDP leasing started slowly, relative to its post-1965 expansion. Thomas Spain, who was in charge of IBM's relations with leasing companies in the late 1960s, estimated that from 1961 through 1965, annual leasing company purchases of IBM EDP equipment (principally second-generation equipment) were between $10 million and $24 million. By comparison:

> In the first nine months of 1966 . . . leasing company purchases of IBM EDP equipment had climbed to over $75 million, and over $60 million of these purchases were of the newer IBM 360 equipment. As of October 1, 1966, leasing companies owned over 33% of all purchased 360 central processing units.[211]

Randolph alone had purchased over $24 million of System/360 equipment – as much as all leasing companies together had invested in any prior year.[212]

Leasing company growth continued to be very rapid throughout the rest of the decade. In 1969 IBM estimated that cumulative leasing company purchases of IBM equipment totaled $2.5 billion, up from $200 million in 1965.[213] Annual revenues of leasing companies showed similar growth. Boothe's domestic EDP revenues went from $440,000 in 1967 to $44.3 million in 1969; Diebold's, from $258,000 in 1967 to $30.8 million in 1969; Greyhound's, from $1 million in 1962 to $50 million in 1969; Itel's, from $1.4 million in 1967 to $38.7 million in 1969; Leasco's, from $8.5 million in 1967 to $37.7 million in 1969; Levin-Townsend's, from $371,000 in 1964 to $34 million in 1969; MAI's, from $17 million in 1965 to $63 million in 1969; and Randolph's, from $1.5 million in 1965 to $41.7 million in 1969.[214]

The number of leasing companies also grew dramatically. By 1970 IBM listed over 250 leasing companies as competitors, compared with 92 in 1966.[215]

Leasing Company Growth

A number of factors combined to produce the explosive growth of leasing companies in the middle to late 1960s. Important among these was the nature of System/360 itself. Leasing company success is dependent on, among other things, the ability either to remarket equipment easily or to keep it on rent for a long time.[216] The widespread customer acceptance of System/360 indicated that there would be a large set of potential customers for equipment remarketed by leasing companies.[217] Further, leasing companies perceived that the compatibility of the 360 processors and peripherals, the standardization of 360 peripherals, the modularity and flexible configurability, and the all-applications nature of 360 greatly enhanced the remarketability of a 360 inventory.[218] Finally, IBM had made a huge investment in programming systems for System/360 consonant with its efforts to produce an architecture that would be long-lasting.[219] Leasing companies thus expected that 360 equipment was likely to remain usable for a very long time, even by customers using later IBM equipment.[220] Hence, while leasing companies also dealt in equipment of other manufacturers, they bought very large amounts of IBM 360 equipment.[221]

Another factor contributing to the growth of leasing companies dealing in IBM equipment was the fact that in the 1960s leasing companies were able to offer longer-term leases than IBM offered. During the 1960s IBM (which until January 1966 was constrained to leases of less than one year by the 1956 consent decree) offered its products only on a month-to-month basis or for purchase.[222] This created a "gap" that leasing companies sought to use to their advantage — an opportunity to offer IBM equipment on leases of several years' duration with reduced monthly charges.[223]

Partly as a result of leasing company competition, in the 1960s other systems suppliers began to offer longer-term leases with reduced rates, or equivalent plans.[224] IBM itself only began offering longer-term leases in 1971.

Other factors facilitated the growth of leasing companies in the late 1960s. The investment tax credit, which during this period provided for a credit against taxes of up to 7 percent of the purchase price of new equipment, was in full effect for all but a five-month period from the IBM 360 announcement until 1969. Additionally, in 1966 the General Services Administration enhanced the opportunity for leasing company deals with the federal government by permitting the purchase and leaseback of EDP equipment on commercial prices, terms, and conditions.[225] The door was opened even further when, on July 1, 1966, IBM modified its procedures "to allow the United States Government to assign to leasing companies the right to purchase at IBM's standard commercial terms, prices and conditions most EDP equipment already installed at facilities of and leased by the United States Government."[226]

Leasing company purchases of 360 equipment were high through the first ten months of 1966. In October 1966, however, the investment tax credit was suspended and the money market was tight.[227] As a result, leasing company purchases declined despite IBM's announcement of the "3X3" price change on September 29, 1966, by which purchase prices were lowered and lease prices raised by 3 percent.[228]

In March 1967 the investment tax credit was reinstated, the "credit crunch" began to ease, and leasing company acquisitions picked up.[229] The pace of leasing company purchases continued to rise rapidly, and in 1968 the heaviest concentration of 360 purchases occurred.[230] Leasing company stock prices also soared, and many new firms entered the business in 1967 and 1968.[231] Some of the largest leasing companies, such as Boothe and Itel, started during this period.

These were the "go-go years" of the stock market, and "computer" was a magic word.[232] It was "a time when it appeared that the financial community, those who were supposedly sophisticated . . . had lost their reason."[233] It was "a mania" in which virtually all EDP companies could sell stock and convertible and subordinated debentures, and leasing companies were part of the mania.[234] They were glamour companies, which meant "there [was] a presumptive contagion . . . from one company in a particular industry to others."[235]

Leasing companies, through a combination of depreciating their equipment relatively slowly and taking other liberties with their accounting, were showing impressive book profits.[236] This relationship was noted by, among others, the Morgan Guaranty Trust Company and Professor Abraham Briloff of City University of New York.[237] Leasing company stocks soared and traded at astronomical price-to-earnings ratios.[238] Their revenues increased dramatically as well. It was quite easy for leasing companies to raise capital during that period; indeed, they raised billions.

Leasing companies did not limit their capital-raising efforts to the issuance of securities. They were able to secure sizable lines of credit from banks as well. For example, Leasco had a credit line of $51.5 million in 1967 (up from $5 million in 1966). In 1968 Greyhound Computer Corp. had a credit line of nearly $100 million, Randolph had a credit line of $81 million, and Boothe Computer Corp. had a $93.5 million credit line.[239]

Some leasing companies also used IBM as a major source of credit by paying for equipment purchased on IBM's installment payment plan. In fact, they availed themselves of $313.5 million in installment credit from IBM between 1968 and 1970 alone.[240] A report on leasing companies prepared by IBM employees stated: "In a current prospectus, one company has indicated IBM installment credit as its primary debt source. Others use it essentially in the same manner but without formal announcement."[241]

The ease with which leasing companies were able to raise capital can be seen in both the size and the pace of their equipment purchases. Boothe, for instance, wrote its first lease in November 1967. Less than one year later, when it stopped purchasing 360 equipment, it had an inventory of over $140 million. Itel showed similar growth. It wrote its first lease in March 1968, and by the end of the year had leases on equipment valued at over $130 million, of which it owned $104 million. Both these companies moved in less than one year from inception to being regarded within IBM as among the ten largest leasing companies.[242]

The Emergence of New Challenges

By 1969, however, things began to change again for leasing companies. The investment tax credit was withdrawn, interest rates rose sharply, the stock market fell, and the financial press soured on the leasing companies. Regarded as glamour companies just several months earlier, leasing companies began to lose their glitter.[243]

Starting in 1969 and continuing through 1970, economic conditions were such that capital was not readily available. As noted in the 1969 Diebold Annual Report: "Record high interest rates during 1969 together with the scarcity of credit brought the computer leasing business in the U.S. to a virtual standstill."[244] Leasco reported that "despite the company's strong record, Leasco stopped writing new leasing business. . . . That decision was predicated on one especially salient fact: the continued high cost of money which would erode future profit margins."[245] DPF&G also cut back its purchases, due "principally to prevailing tight money conditions."[246]

General economic conditions seemed especially dismal for leasing companies because of a changing — much more skeptical — perception of them in the financial community. Articles began to appear in the financial press criticizing leasing companies' accounting practices.[247] In a December 2, 1968 *Barron's* article entitled "All a Fandangle," Briloff voiced his concern that leasing companies' practices and procedures had "one primary objective — to create an air of excitement regarding performance, to give an unreal appearance of accomplishments and to offer the promise of even greater attainments tomorrow."[248] Briloff severely criticized the leasing companies' depreciation practices, their use of the "flow through" method of allocating the investment tax credit, and their deferral of costs beyond the initial lease term. He called for a "halt to the game" because of the "bedazzlement and the delusion spreading to ensnare the multitudes."[249]

The changing perception of the leasing companies was reflected in the prices of their stocks, which declined very sharply.[250] Their access to credit also was affected.[251] By 1970 the stock market had collapsed, and a recession was in full swing, compounding the fiscal problems peculiar to the leasing companies.

Leasing companies were beginning to encounter other difficulties. As initial leases expired, equipment came off lease. Many leasing companies were for the first time faced with the task of remarketing their equipment. As already indicated, this was a much more substantial undertaking than the initial placement of the equipment, in which, by and large, the leasing companies relied upon the manufacturers to configure and sell the systems.[252] Hence, marketing staffs had to be enlarged.

Marketing was difficult. The number of leasing companies had grown substantially, which intensified the competition for favorable prospects.[253] Leasing companies also began to experience new competition from plug-compatible manufacturers marketing their own peripherals in competition with leasing-company-owned peripherals.[254] As a result of this heightened competition and the changing demands of users and prospects, features and peripheral products that were included in systems coming off rent did not always match the demands of the new users to whom the leasing companies were market-ing.[255] Perhaps most important of all, by 1969 System/360 equipment was five years old, and in the interim other manufacturers had introduced products with improved price/performance, and the announcement of a new line of IBM equipment (System/370) was on the horizon.[256]

The result of all this was a decline in lease rates together with an increase in marketing costs, all coinciding with the higher cost of money.[257] As one would expect, leasing company acquisitions of IBM equipment in 1969 were substantially lower than in 1968, and the decline of 360 purchase activity con-tinued in 1970.[258]

Diversification

By the end of the decade, many leasing companies had diversified their operations. They developed various marketing relationships with PCMs, assem-bling systems from different sources.[259] For example, MAI was marketing Memorex disk drives and Potter tape drives, and DPF&G was marketing Ampex tape drives.[260] Greyhound was marketing a disk storage unit made to its specifi-cations by GE, and DPF, by the end of 1970, was marketing IBM-compatible tape drives under its own name.[261]

These relationships were beneficial to both the leasing companies and the PCMs. By integrating the lower-cost plug-compatible peripherals into systems they owned, the leasing companies were able to increase the price/performance and, hence, the competitiveness of their systems. In return, leasing companies substantially reduced the capital required by the PCMs from whom they pur-chased by providing ready cash and reducing the marketing costs of those manufacturers.[262] As noted above, however, PCMs also offered their lower-priced peripheral products in competition with the peripheral products in the leasing companies' inventories.

Some Individual Companies

Leasing companies had many similarities, but each company had its particu-lar history and characteristics. A few of the important leasing companies of the 1960s will be discussed in more detail.

Greyhound

The Greyhound Corporation claimed to be the first third-party computer lessor by virtue of a lease written in 1961.[263] It acquired the Boothe Leasing Corporation (not to be confused with Boothe Computer Corporation discussed below) as a subsidiary in 1962.[264] Its U.S. EDP revenues were $1 million in 1962 and had increased to $13.4 million by 1965.[265] In that year Greyhound changed the name of its subsidiary from Boothe Leasing to Greyhound Leasing and Financial Corp. (GL&FC).[266] In 1966 Greyhound Computer Corporation (Greyhound) was organized as a subsidiary of GL&FC, and shares and convertible debentures were sold to the public.[267]

Greyhound reported that by the end of 1966, it had an EDP portfolio at cost (not including accumulated depreciation) consisting of $47.3 million of second-generation IBM equipment, $20.2 million of IBM 360 equipment, and $5.6 million of other equipment.[268] Its 360 portfolio increased to $75.6 million by the end of 1967, $154.8 million by the end of 1968, and $188.2 million at the end of 1969.[269] Greyhound "had completed by mid-year [of 1969] most of its purchases of computer equipment."[270]

Greyhound depreciated its second-generation IBM equipment on a straight-line basis over eight years or to December 31, 1973, whichever came first. It depreciated its 360 equipment over ten years, and the other computer equipment over three to eight years.[271]

During the period 1965-69 Greyhound's EDP revenues rose steadily. Its U.S. EDP revenues went from $13.4 million in 1965 to $17.3 million in 1966 to $49.9 million in 1969.[272] Not all of those revenues came simply from purchasing and leasing IBM equipment. Like many other leasing companies, Greyhound also marketed equipment of peripheral manufacturers, and it purchased and marketed the 3311 disk drive made for it by GE.[273] In addition, Greyhound offered data services. By 1967 it had begun to diversify into computer service centers and project management, forming a Data Services Division to operate service bureaus and provide consulting services to customers in computer planning, installation, and operation.[274] In 1969 it offered time-sharing services through Greyhound Timesharing Corporation, formed in September 1968.[275]

Computer leasing, however, was Greyhound Computer Corporation's major area of operations in the 1960s. It stated in 1967 that its leases ranged in general from those terminable on 30 days' notice to those with initial terms of up to eight years. It reported that most of the early leases of the company, by dollar volume, were for initial terms of one to three years.[276] However, in 1968 Greyhound reported that in the previous year it had "modified our rate structure to encourage longer term leases. The result: 'Many leases written in the last half of 1967 encompassed terms of two to five years.'"[277]

Boothe Computer Corporation

Boothe Computer Corporation (Boothe) was founded in 1967 by two former officers of Greyhound Computer Corporation.[278] Boothe wrote its first 360 lease in November of that year. Approximately eight months later internal IBM estimates ranked Boothe as the seventh largest computer leasing company in the United States.[279] In the last two months of 1967 alone, Boothe purchased nearly $12.8 million in EDP equipment.[280] Boothe was "the leading 1968 purchaser [of 360 equipment] with acquisitions amounting to $131 million."[281] Boothe announced in October 1968 that its "planned acquisition program" was virtually complete, and by year's end its EDP portfolio exceeded

$144 million.[282] Nevertheless, Boothe added to its already substantial 360 port-folio in 1970 through the acquisition in November of the $50 million System/360 portfolio of GAC Computer Leasing Corporation, on what it called "very favorable terms." By so doing, Boothe, which also operated in Europe, increased its "ownership in the United States and Canada of IBM 360 equipment to $220 million."[283]

Boothe's acquisitions were financed in part through the sale of common stock. In May 1968 its initial public offering of 150,000 shares of common stock reached the market at $18 per share, closing near $50 by the end of the first day.[284]

Boothe's revenues increased nearly as dramatically as its acquisitions. From 1967 to 1969 its U.S. EDP revenues went from $440,000 to $44 million.[285]

Boothe reported that it wrote leases of one to five years, generally providing "for early termination after 12 months upon payment of a termination fee."[286]

Boothe depreciated its 360 equipment on a ten-year, straight-line basis.[287] It decided fairly early to use the cash flow generated by its computer leasing business to invest in "other phases" of the EDP industry.[288] To accomplish this end, it formed its Brokerage Division in 1968, "to engage in the purchase and sale of computer systems and components from existing non-manufacturer users."[289] This was an obvious adjunct for a leasing company. In 1969 the company formed Boothe Resources International, which "specializes in the computer services and software field" and which marketed peripheral equip-ment manufactured by Viatron Computer Systems Corporation.[290]

In 1969 Boothe formed yet another subsidiary to engage in the marketing of EDP equipment, Dataware Marketing, Inc., which "engaged in marketing peripheral equipment internationally, and in the domestic brokerage of second-user computers and computer equipment." It immediately began to distribute the products of Courier Terminal Systems, Inc., "a manufacturer of CRT data entry and retrieval terminals and quality line printers."[291] Through another subsidiary, the Boothe Computer Investment Corporation, Boothe "placed equity investments in companies manufacturing peripheral gear or engaged in computer-related services. At year end, 1969, equity interest in 11 such companies had been acquired."[292] One of those companies was Courier Termi-nal Systems.[293]

Itel

Itel was incorporated in December 1967 as SSI Computer Corp. It wrote its first computer lease in March 1968 and by the end of that year had lease contracts covering computer equipment at original cost of $130 million, of which it owned approximately $104 million.[294] Gary Friedman, who was executive vice-president of the corporation in 1968, testified that all of this equipment was marketed by a sales force that went from perhaps one person at the beginning of the year to somewhere between five and eight at the end of it.[295] An IBM report on leasing companies listed Itel (SSI Computer) as having the ninth largest IBM computer portfolio at the end of its first full year of operation.[296] By the end of 1969, Itel owned approximately $195.5 million of computer equipment.[297]

Itel's U.S. EDP revenues rose sharply as well, going from $9.6 million in 1968 to $38.7 million in 1969 and to $46.9 million in 1970.[298]

Itel offered leases "normally written for initial terms of 24 to 60 months" to fill the "gap" between purchase and the short-term lease offered by IBM.[299] It "typically" either purchased equipment already on order or purchased installed equipment, using the customer's purchase option credits.[300] It leased to companies in a "wide range of industries," including "utilities, transportation, general manufacturing, aerospace, textiles, petroleum, chemicals, publishing, banking, insurance, auto manufacturing, finance, food processing and medical services."[301]

Itel also diversified its activities in order "to build a diversified company concentrating on data processing activities. . . ."[302] In 1969 it acquired the Statistics for Management Data Processing Corporation, a specialized service bureau.[303] It also "entered the peripheral equipment field through the formation of an affiliate, Diablo Systems, Inc.," which would "concentrate initially on the manufacture of mass memory devices and then intends to produce other related peripheral equipment."[304] In April 1970 it acquired Intercontinental Systems, Inc., a manufacturer of word processors, data terminals, and off-line systems.[305] Its most important acquisition, however, did not come until early 1971 with the purchase of Information Storage Systems, which it sold to Sperry Rand in July 1973.[306] Diablo Systems was sold to Xerox in 1972 at a substantial profit.[307]

The Effects of Leasing Companies on IBM

The dramatic growth of computer leasing companies in the 1960s had two kinds of effects on IBM. First, IBM's annual revenues increased immediately as purchases by leasing companies and others spurted in the late 1960s — a phenomenon that IBM had difficulty in projecting accurately.[308] Second, IBM faced accelerating competition from leasing companies, culminating in the impact of the large amounts of 360 equipment in leasing companies' portfolios on IBM's pricing of System/370.

Certain IBM employees early recognized the competitive impact of leasing companies (as did those of other manufacturers).[309] An analysis of leasing companies prepared within IBM in September 1966, for example, stated:

> With capable marketing personnel, substantial inventories, and attractive rental rates, leasing companies represent an increasing potential for replacing IBM installed rental equipment. We are aware of current proposals which would result in the replacement of IBM rental units.[310]

The report also recognized potential effects on future generations of IBM equipment.

Even though newly announced machines reputedly "obsolete" older equipment, there is always a price at which the "obsoleted" equipment has a better price-performance . . . than newer equipment. It appears that leasing companies will be in a position to offer this price-performance advantage for some years to come.[311]

The recognition of leasing companies as competitors dictated their treatment as such, and IBM salesmen were so directed.[312] By February 1968 an internal report on leasing company activities stated: "[C]ollectively leasing companies are potentially IBM's biggest domestic competitor. . . ."[313] In March 1969 it was estimated that, as of year-end 1968, leasing companies owned 16.1 percent of the total installed base of IBM equipment (up from 5 percent on December 31, 1965) — some 41.5 percent of all purchased IBM equipment, and an increase in both percentages was projected.[314]

Leasing company competition constrained IBM's pricing of System/370.[315] For example, a February 20, 1969 Quarterly Product Line Assessment prepared by the Commercial Analysis Department of IBM's Data Processing Division stated: "When NS0 and NS1 [to become System 370/135 and 145, respectively] are announced, IBM will be faced with competition from three sources: (1) other computer vendors, (2) owners of IBM computer systems, and (3) computer-oriented service companies." And, the report continued, "competition from owners of IBM computer systems will come primarily from leasing companies and from System/360 purchase customers who sell their used systems. Both of these sources could make lower-priced System/360s available to compete with NS0 and NS1 with competitive price/performance."[316]

In March 1969, Gil Jones, IBM senior vice-president, wrote in a report of the Management Committee to the IBM Management Review Committee: "Our old 360 purchase inventory will remain a major competitive product. There is an added unknown in the possible merger of OEM's, software houses and leasing companies." This report also stated that System/360 equipment offered at a price discount of only approximately 30 percent would be an effective competitive product against System/370 at the prices then planned for the new systems. Particular exposures identified were the projected 370 purchase prices and maintenance charges.[317] Thereafter the purchase prices on System/370 were reduced.[318] (As discussed in Chapter 11, renewed efforts were also made to reduce the projected maintenance expenses and charges; those efforts led to an extension of the warranty period and then to a substantial reduction in monthly maintenance charges.)

The competitive effects of leasing companies' 360 offerings on IBM's pricing of 370 continued beyond the initial 370 announcement date. In January 1971, Learson and Cary, then president and senior vice-president, respectively, considered a proposal for a general price increase by the Data Processing Group. They each visited four to five sales offices. Learson wrote:

What we found there was . . . strong activity by the leasing companies in reinstalling available equipment at reduced rentals for very short terms — 12 to 18 months. In truth, what is happening to the 360 line is that prices are being reduced instead of being increased. In some cases, they are selling their leased inventories at 50% off original price, with payments deferred 24 to 36 months. Coupled with this atmosphere is our own action in reducing prices on files and tapes and the OEM's reacting with a further price cut.[319]

Leasing company competition was not to disappear.

SERVICE BUREAUS

A service bureau "purchases or rents a computer from a computer manufacturer or systems manufacturer and then proceeds to perform problems for a customer, or to let a customer perform problems on the apparatus for himself. . . . The service bureau may assist the customer with his software problems, they may assist him with printed copies of the material and other things as part of their service."[320]

Entry and Growth

Service bureaus were a natural development in the computer industry. They began before 1960 but grew rapidly in number thereafter. It was easy to start a service bureau; all that was needed was a computer system and the ability to run it. For example, Digicon, Inc., had six founders in 1965, each of whom put up about $330.[321] By 1970 Digicon had $1.5 million in U.S. EDP revenues.[322]

Like Digicon, many service bureau companies grew fantastically in just a short time. Optimum Systems, Inc., had $300,000 in U.S. EDP revenues in 1967, its first half-year of operation, and $10.5 million in 1970;[323] TCC, Inc., started in 1968 and had $6.7 million in U.S. EDP revenues in 1970;[324] and there are many other examples.[325] The Association of Data Processing Service Organizations reported that the average service center firm's revenues increased 50 percent in 1965-66 alone, and that by 1966 there were 700 such firms with total revenues over $500 million.[326]

Some service bureaus primarily offered computer time; others offered programming and other services ancillary to the use of computer time, such as systems and software design, application packages (often proprietary to the service bureau), and other specialized services.[327]

Entrants sprang from a number of sources. New firms such as Digicon and ADP started from scratch and offered computer services as their principal business. Firms already in the EDP business saw an opportunity for profit and opened service bureaus. Those ventures often began as an attempt to gain customers for their other computer products and services.[328] Such firms included both leasing companies, such as Greyhound Computer and Itel, and systems manufacturers.[329] By the end of the decade, CDC, NCR, IBM, Honeywell, and GE had extensive service bureau operations.[330]

In addition, businesses that owned their computer systems but were not utilizing them fully for their own needs naturally found it attractive to offer unused time to others for a fee.[331] Banks and aerospace companies, in particular, began to sell computer services.[332] As time went on, brokers made it a business to find computer time for users and often then went into the service bureau business directly.[333] For example, the Bergen-Brunswig Corp., a drug company, began in the EDP business because it "had idle capacity on an IBM 1401 computer, and at first we started offering it to some of our customers who we sensed needed help in accounts receivables. It mushroomed after that and six months later we had to add a second computer to render those services."[334] By 1970 Bergen-Brunswig had U.S. EDP revenues of $2.5 million.[335]

The federal government also saw the benefits to be derived from selling excess computer time and, through the General Services Administration (GSA), set up a program that by 1966 facilitated the use by one government agency of the EDP services of another.[336] GSA also operated federal data processing centers, service bureau enterprises that offered processing, systems design, programming, and applications software to government agencies for a fee.[337] In addition, a full-service remote computing network was developed for GSA by Computer Sciences Corp.'s INFONET Division, "to provide Federal agencies with an economical and broadly based supply of certain types of computer services."[338]

Time-Sharing and the "Computer Utility"

The development of service bureaus was given a substantial impetus in the 1960s by the growth of time-sharing. Instead of physically transporting data between the customers' premises and the service bureau, time-sharing services allowed terminals to be placed at the users' installations to provide on-line access to a central computer.[339] F. Rigdon Currie of Xerox testified that "when the time sharing technique was developed . . . many entrepreneurs saw an opportunity to start a business and offer this service to users, and so many commercial time sharing service bureaus were established in the late sixties, and [SDS] provided computers to many of these companies."[340]

GE, in particular, emphasized time-sharing services, although it started off in the service bureau business offering batch services.[341] The GE time-sharing service was originally based on the GE 235 and "was primarily aimed at solution of small engineering or technical problems."[342] As the number of languages available for the 235 increased, the applications grew into "somewhat larger scientific and into the commercial sphere."[343] But the success of the GE time-sharing service bureaus rested on the larger 635, which was "aimed at solving bigger problems." As more languages became available, "there were more and more" business applications for the 635.[344] GE remained in the service bureau business after selling most of its computer operations to Honeywell in 1970.[345]

Other time-sharing service bureaus also started off performing scientific and engineering applications, but progressively shifted their emphasis to commercial applications. For example, whereas in the late 1960s 75 percent of Tymshare, Inc.'s income came from engineering/scientific applications, by mid-1971 more than half of the firm's income was from commercial applications.[346] The president of Time Share Corp. wrote in a 1968 article:

> Today the typical [time-sharing] user is no longer buying just raw computer power alone. He is beginning to buy both applications and computing power. And the applications are increasingly being found in the business area. Time-sharing is being recognized as a powerful aid to business decisions. The once-remote computer has been replaced by the familiar teletypewriter . . . at the manager's point of contact.[347]

As time-sharing developed in the middle and late 1960s there was growing talk of an "equipment utility" that would "directly connect terminals on the users' premises with networks of computers and data transmission links," eliminating the need for each user to possess its own computer.[348] In 1966 Western Union was advertising a complex "designed to provide information, communications and processing services in much the same way as other utilities supply gas and electricity."[349] The ARPANET network of the Advanced Research Projects Agency was seen as pointing the way in the late 1960s. Alan Perlis testified:

> [I]n effect, what the ARPA network showed was that we were about at the beginning of what we might call the Network Age of computing where computers will be tied together in a network like the telephone network, using satellites, etc.[350]

Only later did it become apparent that the increasing capability of small stand-alone systems would provide an alternative to that vision.[351]

Competition

In providing computer time, programming, and other computing services, service bureaus competed with manufacturers in furnishing users with alternatives to the acquisition, use, or expansion of their own hardware and software.[352] McDonnell Douglas Automation, among others, advertised to this effect, urging users to "expand your computing capacity without leasing or buying computers" and saying of the IBM 7094 that "You *could* buy one, you *could* lease one but it's cheaper and simpler to hire ours by the hour."[353] ADP advertised: "[Y]ou don't have to buy a computer to get [answers]. You can buy computing, instead."[354]

The small user, contemplating the acquisition of his first computer system, could forgo or delay that acquisition by having his work done at a service bureau.[355] Large users with heavily loaded equipment could off-load some of their work and thereby postpone or forgo the acquisition of additional EDP equipment.[356] Users also turned to service bureaus in place of their own equipment to acquire flexibility, to fill in gaps in their own data-processing equipment without acquiring new hardware, to take advantage of the additional services offered, and to automate new applications (often at lower cost because of less overhead expense than the alternative of installing hardware).[357] Thus, the service bureau's customers included both those with their own data-processing installations and those without.[358]

Examples of the choices made by customers include the following:

1.   Datamatic, Inc., submitted a proposal in 1967 to the Southwest Louisiana Electric Membership Corporation "to automate and process their accounting and engineering functions," and won over a proposal submitted by IBM involving IBM hardware.[359]

2.   DP&W provided Medical Associates of Chelmsford, Massachusetts, services "which eliminated the complete installation of IBM equipment" previously on lease from IBM.[360]

3.   The Aerojet Company of Sacramento had two 360/65s installed. When its four operating divisions were organized into three separate independent companies, two of those companies came to Information Systems Design (ISD), a service bureau, to do their processing, and one of the Model 65s was returned to IBM. When the remaining company's business declined a year or so later, it returned the other 65 to IBM and gave its business to ISD.[361]

The competition provided by service bureaus was well understood within IBM. As early as 1964, Frank Cary, at the time president of the Data Processing Division, received a report entitled "Remote Scientific Computing" that projected "an immediate, rapid development of interest in the service bureau form of business."[362] The Quarterly Product Line Assessment (QPLA) of November 1968, written by members of IBM's Commercial Analysis Department, examining competition for the 360/25 and 360/30, stated:

> Computer-oriented service company competition is getting stronger every day as new service bureaus and time-sharing companies spring up and existing ones expand. Both of these sources compete by reducing prospective customers' computer needs.[363]

The May 1969 QPLA reiterated that such companies "offer services which may substitute for additional computer function and/or capacity," and noted the "explosive growth of this segment of the data processing market."[364] Service bureau competition was analyzed in assessing the competitiveness of IBM's planned 370 line, and Cary testified that service bureau competition constrained IBM's prices.[365]

Other hardware manufacturers saw the same thing. For example, Currie of Xerox testified that Xerox Computer Services (XCS) salesmen, in accounts with small computer systems, had "been successful on a number of occasions in replacing the computer hardware." In other instances XCS competed with "the hardware vendors, the small computer system vendors in providing a solution to a customer" currently using another service bureau for accounting or doing its accounting work on accounting machines.[366] The services of XCS were offered as competitive alternatives to the use of a centralized data-processing system.[367] Although XCS services were offered only after 1970, the same phenomena were equally present in the 1960s, and Xerox's experience was widely shared.[368]

By the end of the 1960s service bureaus had become a major force. In 1970 the Federal Communications Commission estimated that there were more than 800 of them, with total annual sales exceeding $900 million. The commission estimated that more than 5,000 companies had sold excess computer time and capacity.[369]

Some Successful Service Bureaus

As all this indicates, there were many successful service bureaus in the 1960s. We illustrate their different activities by briefly considering three of them.

McDonnell Automation

In 1959 the McDonnell Corporation was a major aircraft manufacturer, with sales of $436 million.[370] It established the McDonnell Automation Center in 1960, to provide "complete electronic data processing services both for scientific work as well as in administrative fields such as inventory control, marketing analyses, production control and accounting." The company had 300 EDP employees and was about to acquire an IBM 7080 and 7090.[371] The center later advertised that its equipment "encompass[ed] virtually every size and type available. . . . This variety of machines enables the Center to process any size or type of program at the lowest possible hourly rates, because a customer is not bound to a single machine."[372] The center stated that it was the first commercial user to install an IBM 360/30, the first to install a CDC 6400, and the first to install an RCA Spectra 70/55.[373]

By 1970 McDonnell Automation had combined with McDonnell Douglas' West Coast computer operation to form McAuto.[374] It offered systems design, consulting, and programming services.[375] Its inventory of computer equipment was valued at over $125 million, its staff had grown to 3,000, and its clients included the Federal Reserve Board, General Motors, Atlantic Richfield, the Social Security Administration, and Illinois Bell Telephone Company. Revenues for 1970 exceeded $47 million.[376]

Automatic Data Processing

Automatic Data Processing (ADP) had begun in the late 1940s by performing payroll services for customers using manually operated bookkeeping and accounting machines, later converting to IBM punched card equipment. It installed its first computer, an IBM 1401, in November 1961, "to offer a substantially broader range of services for its many clients."[377] By 1964 ADP had placed orders for System/360 and called itself "the largest independent payroll processor in the nation, preparing payrolls for approximately 500 firms with 80,000 employees whose annual wages total almost a half-billion dollars."[378] ADP had decided that "major growth was in order." It assembled a marketing force, which undertook a "missionary and educational program" to sell ADP's services to the business community. This was supported by advertising and direct mail promotions. The result, according to ADP, was "unlike anything the data processing services industry had seen." Revenues increased twenty-twofold and earnings fifty-eightfold in six years.[379] Along the way ADP acquired a number of other companies; developed capabilities in "back office" processing applications for brokerage houses, accounts receivable processing, time-sharing, and portfolio applications; and expanded its geographic coverage.[380] By 1970 ADP was processing the payrolls of 7,000 firms, totaling $5 billion in wages.[381] ADP's U.S. EDP revenues rose from $187,000 in 1957 to about $2 million in 1963, $4.7 million in 1964, $20 million in 1968, and $37 million in 1970.[382]

Tymshare

Tymshare, Inc., began offering time-sharing services in 1966, and in the following year generated $1 million in U.S. EDP revenues.[383] One of the first time-sharing concerns not associated with a hardware manufacturer, Tymshare developed its own applications packages, programming systems, and such hardware as channels and interfaces.[384] In 1970 it acquired Dial-Data, another service bureau, to broaden and increase its customer base and to expand its technical research and development capability.[385] Prior to 1970 Tymshare "relied quite heavily on engineering and scientific computation." Beginning in 1969, it "began to develop applications packages and programming systems designed to open the use of our services to a much broader group of customers, primarily in the business, commercial, and financial activities." By 1970 Tymshare's "market profile" had "shifted to one that is approximately balanced between engineering and business use."[386]

By the end of the decade Tymshare had accomplished its "most significant" achievement, its TYMNET communications network. Nineteen cities were connected through 25,000 miles of telephone lines over which traffic was directed by a "combination of specialized hardware and software" developed by Tymshare. There were more than 20 terminals compatible with this service, including one designed to Tymshare's specifications. Compatible plotters were also available.[387] By 1970 Tymshare's domestic EDP revenues had risen to more than $10 million.[388]

SOFTWARE COMPANIES

In the late 1950s and early 1960s, a few independent software firms were founded that "for the most part . . . started doing Government contract work. To some extent, then, in addition, they also began undertaking work for some of the computer manufacturers as well."[389] Such firms included Computer Sciences Corporation, Planning Research Corporation, Computer Usage Corporation, Informatics, Applied Data Research, and System Development Corporation.[390] Lawrence Welke, president of International Computer Programs, Inc. (ICP), which published catalogs of available software packages, testified that by about 1965 there were 40 to 50 independent suppliers of software programming.[391] The leaders in this field "were still at that point working with government, in large part, they were still . . . doing work for the computer manufacturers themselves, and increasingly they were getting involved in the commercial marketplace, the private sector."[392] The work done for computer manufacturers was extensive. Welke estimated that between 30 and 50 percent of the systems software developed for third-generation computers was done by independent software suppliers.[393]

The work that software vendors were doing for computer manufacturers, together with advances in software technology, the proliferation of computers, and the shortage of qualified people, combined to stimulate the growth of independent software houses in the mid-1960s.[394] Welke testified that there

> was a general recognition . . . that there was more money to be made programming with an independent software firm than in a user shop or working for a computer manufacturer.
>
> A lot of firms were formed by people leaving the computer manufacturer's employment, and that wasn't just IBM, everybody was experiencing that loss. IBM had the most to lose because they had the most people to lose. But I guess word spread rather easily and quickly that it was possible to get a government contract and go into business with a very low entry fee for going into business as a contract programming firm.[395]

Almost no capital was needed to enter the business. "All you need is a coding pad and a sharp pencil."[396]

In the period after 1964, the entry and growth of independent software companies were stimulated by the introduction of System/360. Users needed help in planning for and converting to the more complex hardware and software. "And this, in turn, caused a demand that was reflected back onto the software firms." Also, during the period of the introduction of System/360 "people expanded the use of computers and put more and more applications on," which required more programming.[397] Users found that "with the increased complexity of solving the problem, if you are going to do your own program, your costs for the programming will increase . . . the comparative cost of buying the product becomes more attractive as the cost of the in-house programming, the cost of the in-house solution goes up."[398] In terms familiar to economists since the days of Adam Smith, as the market grew, it became efficient to have an increasing division of labor, and opportunities for specialists increased.

A number of independent software companies formed in the late 1950s or early 1960s had enjoyed rapid growth by the end of the decade. For example, in 1969 Computer Sciences Corporation, established in 1959, had U.S. EDP revenues of $67.2 million;[399] Informatics, Inc., formed in 1962, had U.S. EDP revenues of $19.8 million;[400] and Applied Data Research, formed in 1959, had corporate revenues of $6.2 million.[401]

In the late 1960s the growth of suppliers of software "exploded."[402] Martin Goetz, vice-president of Applied Data Research, wrote in late 1969 or early 1970 that starting from "about 20 major programming firms . . . and perhaps several hundred smaller organizations" in 1965, "the number of and size of individual concerns within the independent programming software field have doubled each year."[403] Welke estimated there were about 2,800 vendors of software in 1968, at the end of the period he described as "the flowering of the independent software industry."[404] He estimated that by 1969 contract programming accounted for revenues of $600 million, while software products accounted for another $20-25 million.[405]

Despite this growth, revenues of independent software vendors represented only a minor fraction of the aggregate expenditures for programming made by users, and this continued into the 1970s. Welke estimated that user expenditures for programming went from around $200 million in 1960 to $3-4 billion in 1965, to $8 billion in 1970, and to $12 billion in 1975.[406] Most of that expenditure was for software written by the users themselves; less than 10 percent was for software written by systems manufacturers.[407]

Once a program has been developed, the cost of distributing it to additional users is essentially zero. As computers developed, therefore, it became relatively inexpensive for users to help each other learn how to use the equipment more efficiently and to avoid needless duplication of programming effort.[408] Alan Perlis testified concerning SHARE, an IBM users' organization:

[C]ertainly during those days [the early to mid-1960s] the SHARE meeting was a scene where a large amount of information about the practical use of the IBM 704, 709 and 7090, was passed back and forth and it represented to the acquirers of those machines a real, positive benefit — increase in value of those machines.[409]

Such user groups assisted software sellers by providing constant feedback on desirable modifications and enhancements.[410]

The free exchange of software contributed to its growth. Writing in 1966 "to state the opposition of the Department of Justice to the issuance of patents on computer programming methods," Donald F. Turner, then assistant attorney general in charge of the Antitrust Division, described the situation eloquently:

The computer industry is one of the most dynamic in the American economy, in terms of absolute as well as relative growth, and further rapid expansion is anticipated. . . . Current investment in programming, or the "software" portion of the computer industry, is approximately equal to the equipment or "hardware" portion, and should surpass it in the very near future. Growth in the software portion of the computer industry has been facilitated by a remarkably free and easy exchange of ideas, concepts, and programs. One of the notable features of the programming industry, indeed, has been the widespread establishment, sponsorship, and universal acceptance of joint user groups to facilitate the exchange of programs and algorithms. As a result, for the past twenty years, almost all basic ideas in computer programming have been available openly to all computer users.

One of the major policy arguments advanced for extension of patent protection to computer programs is a supposed need to encourage individuals and companies to invest in programming development. But it is difficult to conceive how the field of programming could have grown faster, or that its past growth has been hampered in any meaningful fashion by a lack of investment funds. If anything, the current free interchange of programs has lead [sic] to an extraordinarily efficient use of scarce programming talent and has kept needless duplication of existing programs and techniques to a minimum. Furthermore, many small software companies have achieved financial and technical success by producing more efficient versions of widely used manufacturer-developed programs. These more efficient versions of operating programs benefit other software producers, computer manufacturers, computer users, and the general public. In the light of past experience, any step which could upset the vital interchange of programming material should be approached with the utmost caution.[411]

Programming supplied by software companies competed against the bundled software provided by hardware manufacturers.[412] For example, Autoflow, which was supplied by Applied Data Research, QUICKDRAW, which was marketed by NCA, and other independently supplied software competed with IBM's Flow Chart software.[413] Welke estimated that between 75 and 85 percent of the systems software products listed in the ICP quarterly catalog in 1969 were systems software usable on IBM computers, and said that "in most cases" IBM had a competitive offering.[414] Successful independent software efficiency-derived products offered higher performance or cost savings over manufacturer-supplied programming.[415]

Moreover, operating system enhancements and other software provided by independent software companies reduced the amount of computer equipment required by users.[416] Software solutions to performance problems substituted for the installation of additional or larger systems. For instance, the Bank of Virginia acquired a spooling system as an alternative to an additional System/360 Model 30 or migration to a Model 40.[417] The Computer Software Company's EDOS software (marketed as a product in 1972) could improve the performance of an IBM system, permitting the installed system to do 20 to 33 percent more work "for the same amount of money."[418] Abacus Programming improved the compiler at Hughes Aircraft, making additional core memory unnecessary.[419] Data Processing Consultants, Inc., a service bureau, used add-on memory plus GRASP, a spooling package marketed by Software Design, Inc., to increase capacity by approximately 20 percent, thereby avoiding the upgrading of its 360/30 to a 360/40 or the acquisition of an additional Model 30.[420] There are many other examples.[421]

We now consider the history of two of the active and successful software firms in the 1960s.

Computer Sciences Corporation

In 1973 Computer Sciences Corporation (CSC) described its early history as follows:

> The initial technical capability on which Computer Sciences Corporation was founded in April 1959 was Systems Software. CSC has designed, developed and implemented more programming systems than any independent company in this field. CSC's first contracts were with computer manufacturers and required the development of systems programming packages for their machines. The first project was the production of a FACT compiler for Honeywell, closely followed by the LARC scientific compiler for Univac, and then a major effort for Univac in which CSC developed the complete operating system, the executive system, and all of the processors and compilers for the 1107. The latter project represented a significant state-of-the-art advance at that time, an advance which immediately brought industry-wide recognition of CSC as a major force in the software industry. Major design and development projects for IBM and other manufacturers followed soon after. Since that time, programs have been developed for over 50 machines, and customers have included virtually all major computer manufacturers, large companies in other industries, and Federal, state, and local governmental agencies. Compilers designed and developed at CSC are rated among the fastest in the industry and are noted for their object code efficiency. Many CSC-developed computer languages, compilers, and software systems are standards for the Armed Forces.
>
> Through its history, CSC systems programming activities have expanded from simply completing a specified project to functioning as a system architect for a computer manufacturer or other user. In this role, CSC helps to determine the operational characteristics required of the software to realize and even amplify the rated maximum effectiveness of the computer equipments.[422]

CSC also developed software products in the 1960s, including an income tax preparation program for accountants, a ticket service program, and a series of package programs for users of the IBM System/360 performing "such standard functions as payroll, general ledger, accounts receivable, personnel management, commercial loan and systems activities."[423] As of 1970 CSC had "a product line of 12 packages in the field, all satisfactorily installed and operational with multiple clients, and all verifying the ability to design standard applications which can serve many different users."[424] CSC also developed its own communications network (INFONET) that provided time-sharing information services with the Univac 1108 as a nucleus, utilizing its own proprietary time-sharing operating system.[425]

CSC grew rapidly during the 1960s. Its U.S. EDP revenues were $5.7 million in 1964, $17.8 million in 1965, $67.2 million in 1969, and $82 million in 1970.[426]

Informatics, Inc.

Informatics was formed in 1962 and initially provided programming services to the federal government.[427] Between 1962 and 1969 it expanded its product offerings to include programming services to computer manufacturers and nongovernment end users, proprietary program products, and data center computer services. By 1969 Informatics had U.S. EDP revenues of $19.8 million.[428]

Informatics' major proprietary software product in the 1960s was Mark IV, which was first delivered in 1967. Mark IV was "a general purpose data base management system" initially developed to operate on IBM 360 computers.[429] It competed with IBM's unpriced "generalized retrieval system."[430]

Mark IV was very successful.[431] By September 1968 there were over 60 installations.[432] In 1969, only 13 months after the product was first marketed, Informatics reported that there were 171 installations that made a "significant contribution to [Informatics'] revenues and income."[433] By 1973 Informatics had implemented Mark IV for IBM 370 and Univac Series 70 equipment, and stated that "large and small users throughout the world are using Mark IV in a complete spectrum of applications. 600 Mark IV installations . . . at the present time make Mark IV one of the most successful software products ever developed."[434] In 1969 Informatics began its first data center operations in Los Angeles and San Francisco as "the first steps in a planned nationwide data center operation using the Mark IV system and eventually offering on-line and timesharing Mark IV service for business applications."[435]

11

IBM INTRODUCES
NEW PRODUCTS

Even in 1964 IBM management realized that however successful 360 would turn out to be, the competition would not stand still. Thomas J. Watson, Jr., wrote in November 1963:

> I believe that whenever we make a new machine announcement, we should set up a future date at which point we can reasonably assume that a competitor's article of greater capability will be announced. We should then target our own development program to produce a better machine on or before that date.[1]

Accordingly, planning commenced for future generations of equipment even before System/360 was delivered. On October 9, 1964, A. K. Watson, IBM senior vice-president, wrote to John W. Gibson and Emmanuel Piore, both IBM vice presidents and group executives:

> . . . I think it is extremely important that you put together a group of engineers from each of your divisions who will now be starting to design the next generation machine and do this on a continuing basis, taking advantage of possible improvements in monolithics technology, any new memory technology, printing, etc.[2]

It was recognized that the future competitiveness and price/performance advances of IBM's computer systems would depend on new peripheral devices as well as on processors and memory. IBM's System/360 Compatibility Committee reported in August 1964:

> The heretofore heavy emphasis on processor planning as the criterion for improved price/performance should be re-oriented towards I/O [input/output] developments. The across-the-board improvements in price/performance which will be required in the 1967-68 time period will probably be brought about more by improved I/O capability than by CPU and memory improvements.[3]

In particular, continued improvements in input-output equipment were expected to be needed "to keep System/360 a viable product line. . . ."[4] As we have seen, IBM did in fact announce greatly improved disk and tape drives in the two years following the announcement of System/360. Peripheral developments were also to contribute significantly to the next generation of computer systems.

Design planning for what would become System/370 started in 1965, and the engineering work began "in earnest in 1966."[5] Richard Case, who was director of architecture at IBM during the planning for the new systems, described the objectives for the development of System/370: IBM was to develop its own integrated logic circuits, monolithic systems technology (MST), and integrated memory circuits. It was "to extend the architecture of System/360 in order to make System/370 more valuable to users and, therefore, more attractive to them." System/370 was to be upward-compatible from System/360. Dynamic Address Translation, developed in the Model 67, and related systems software were to be added to support virtual memory, a feature that would make the memory available to the programmer appear essentially unlimited. Various other improvements, related to program control facilities, reliability, and availability, were also to be included. All of these features contributed to an overall goal: "It was our objective in designing System/370 to design . . . a new family of central processing units utilizing new circuitry and new technology to achieve new levels of price performance for the user."[6]

Such new levels of price/performance for central processing units were to be accompanied (as would be required if system performance were not to be limited by input-output performance) by improved price/performance in peripheral equipment.

> Similarly, we had an objective to make available new technology and new circuitry to achieve new levels of price/performance for the auxiliary storage devices, that is, for the direct access storage devices and for the magnetic tape devices.[7]

In addition, there were to be fixed-head file devices, block multiplexer channels, new terminals, a 3705 communications control unit, a mass storage system that Case described as an "ancestor" of the later 3850, and a new high-speed printer, the 3211.[8]

Fifteen months prior to announcement of the first System/370 models (then called "NS" for "new system"), the planning goals were discussed by the Management Committee:

> [George] Kennard [vice-president, development, SDD] summarized the intent of the meeting as being to review basic NS objectives and strategy, terminal-oriented and data base computing systems, NS plans, and marketing plans as they relate to the NS systems. The basic NS objectives are to allow customers and IBM to meet market requirements on an evolutionary basis. Kennard depicted the marketplace of 1970-75 as moving towards communications oriented, on-line usage. He enumerated the basic functions which would have to be improved, increased

or added to satisfy this demand. Improvements are required in CPU's and channels, availability, access methods and front-end tie-ins. Increased function is required in memory size, channels, and on-line data files. New functions are required in I/O devices, such as tape, terminals, displays, printers, and conversational compilers with associated control programs.[9]

The strategy for the new systems, however, was "evolution not revolution."[10] This applied to IBM itself as well as to its customers. Thus, IBM planned to stagger the announcements of its next generation of CPUs to avoid the excessive strains and demands that the simultaneous announcement of the entire 360 line had placed on the business. Since the concept of compatible families was now well established, this approach, unlike the situation at the announcement of System/360, would not subject the customer to unnecessary uncertainties. The new processors were to be announced "one or two at a time at approximately six month intervals," starting with the two largest models in the summer of 1969.[11]

The design and development of the new systems were to involve a complex interaction among the development and application of new technologies for memory, logic circuitry, disk drives, and tape drives, and the achievement of advances in operating systems architecture. Each of these developments played a crucial role in the ultimate announcements of System/370 and in the achievement of the basic goals for the next generation: the attainment of a substantial price/performance improvement over System/360, the extension of the System/360 architecture, the maintenance of upward compatibility from System/360, and the addition of improved capabilities and functions.

TAPE DRIVE DEVELOPMENTS: THE 2420 AND 3420

In the early 1960s IBM "in essence took development monies away from magnetic tapes . . . [and] other technology areas," and concentrated on System/360. "As the development bulge of System/360 began to pass," however, IBM reassigned development resources to "programs of technical excellence . . . that led to . . . the development of what became the 2420 and later the 3420 tape subsystem family."[12] Thus, in 1965-66, after its announcement of the 2401 and 2415 tape drives, IBM began a longer-range program to develop new and superior tape drives to supplant the ones just announced.

The 2420

Development of the 2420 (known in development as the D30R) was reviewed in late 1966:

We started early in 1965 to develop a truly superior tape drive that uses the latest technology to achieve improved reliability and faster thruput while staying compatible with the 2400 line. The technologies chosen provided increased tape speed, faster access time and linear rewind characteristics far superior to any known drive. These characteristics substantially improve the thruput of our Medium and Large Scale Systems/360.[13]

Among the features of that new tape drive technology were automatic threading, the use of a single capstan to enhance reliability, the use of SLT technology throughout, and the use of fewer components, leading to greater reliability and serviceability.[14] It was anticipated that the D30R drive with these advantages could be manufactured at the same or even less cost than the existing 2400 line.[15] It was also proposed in late 1966 that a new tape drive (later called the D30X), utilizing the D30R mechanism, be introduced to supersede the existing 2400 line for "small and medium system users," in order to give them the same advantages.[16]

The need for such improved tape drives was very apparent by the time they were announced. In December 1967 the Management Committee reported to the Management Review Committee that although the Data Processing Group analysis of "peripheral equipment exposures and related action programs" indicated that IBM's peripheral products were superior to competitors' alternatives in most areas, tape drives faced at least a potential threat.

> Frank Cary recognizes an immediate exposure, especially in the tape drive area, which stems mainly from an improving marketing and service capability, and the attention the trade is giving to these obviously better performing tape drives. Frank feels this exposure can be contained at the level of about 1,000 drives, since at the announcement of the D30R in January we will reestablish technical superiority and indicate to the market that our entire tape line will be renovated.
>
> . . . .
>
> In retrospect, it is recognized that our strategy in tapes, which stretched old technology too far, too long, created the threat we are now experiencing. Conversely, because of our technical superiority in the [disk] file area, we are able to react and keep ahead. The Group is committed to avoid this problem in the future.[17]

On April 15, 1968, C. B. Rogers, Jr. (vice-president, marketing, Data Processing Division), wrote to F. G. Rodgers (president, Data Processing Division): "The competitive tape unit market is moving fast and we anticipate even greater acceleration in the future," pointing out the agreement by which Potter and MAI would market Potter tape drives.[18]

The IBM 2420 Model 7 was announced on January 30, 1968, for use with the System/360 Models 50, 65, 75, and 85. Using a unique high-torque, low-inertia motor developed at IBM, it incorporated a single capstan drive, 2.0 millisecond access time, 200-inch-per-second tape speed, automatic threading, cartridge loading, and compatibility with all IBM 1600 bpi (bits per inch) phase-encoded tapes.[19]

Because of its high data rate, the 2420 Model 7 could not be used with systems smaller than the 360/50, but other aspects of its technological advances were desirable for the users of smaller IBM systems.[20] Thus plans were made to extend the D30R technology to slower-speed tape drives (D30X program) for use with the 360/30 and up.[21] That program was given a "kickoff" meeting on January 5, 1968.[22] By February it was reported that "Boulder is making real progress on the slower speed D30R-like drives."[23] Important goals of the program were improvements in reliability and serviceability as well as cost reduction.[24]

In July 1968 the Management Committee received a presentation on peripherals. It was told that "the 2401 Models, one through six, are the most vulnerable to the competitive compatible products in that they are roughly half the price of our products and are of a newer technology." The DPG strategy "to compete in the competitive compatible products area" was, among other things, to "[m]aintain technical superiority."[25] The Management Committee (MC) reported to the Management Review Committee:

> We have announced a tape drive which is technically equal in the high performance area, and have plans to announce technically competitive products in the other capacity ranges in October 1968 and June 1970. At those periods of time we will be equal in technical performance. We will be technically equal, but not equal in price/performance basis. DPG is actively working on strategies to combat this exposure but in the MC's opinion, we are at best, in a weak posture in this area today.
>
> Based on the extended capacity of the competitive manufacturers, we stand to lose a significant amount of highly profitable business unless a plan can be implemented to plug the dike. DPG has been asked to report back to the MC by September with a validated forecast of expected impact of competitors and their plans to respond to this threat.[26]

IBM had caught up and was pushing ahead in its technological development of tape drives. A presentation to the Management Committee in mid-October 1968 stated: "[W]hile we were behind in technological development in the tape drive area in 1965 and 1966, the increased investment in tape drive engineering in 1967 and 1968 had produced products which are technically superior to the competitive offerings."[27] In November 1968, Cary (then IBM senior vice-president and general manager, Data Processing Group) wrote to Board Chairman Watson concerning tape drives and discussing competition from Telex and MAI, which were "actively marketing direct replacement of IBM's 2400 Series drives." He stated:

> Our tape strategy is to compete with superior technology and function, and not price alone. . . .
>
> We believe the new 2420 single capstan technology . . . will narrow the price differential between us and the other manufacturers, increase customer satisfaction, and regain technical leadership for IBM. . . .

Our next move is the planned announcement of the second model of our new technology tape drive, the 2420 Model 5, which is scheduled within the next 30 days.[28]

The 2420 Model 5 was announced on December 2, 1968. According to the announcement, it was attachable to System/360 models from the 30 through the 91; offered a format compatible with the 2400 and the 2415 series Models 4, 5, and 6, as well as the 2420 Model 7; but had half the speed of the 2420 Model 7.[29] Although the component parts of the Model 5 differed greatly from the parts of the earlier Model 7, the Model 5 embodied most of the advantages of design that the Model 7 had introduced, including automatic threading and cartridge-loading capability.[30] The goal had been to "cost reduce [the Model 7] to make it a more manufacturable machine," and that was accomplished by changes in its organization and packaging.[31] The 2420 Model 5 was offered at a substantially lower price than the 2420 Model 7.

Outside IBM the 2420 Model 5 was perceived as an important development. A memorandum written by three engineers of the Telex Corporation stated:

The [IBM 2420] Mod 5 is a very well planned, designed, engineered and production-designed machine, taking advantage of high production type tooling. It has been cost reduced far better than any IBM drive I have ever seen.

. . . .

The IBM 2420 Model 5 is a completely different tape drive from the IBM 2420 Model 7. It is very apparent that the Mod 5 is the drive that they have spent the greatest amount of time and money on. It has been cost-reduced and highly styled.[32]

The 3420 (Aspen)

Around 1967 a new, more ambitious program emerged from the development effort that had produced the 2420 Models 7 and 5. That program, known within IBM first as PRIME, then as HATS, and then, in 1968, as Aspen, resulted in the 3420, announced in November 1970 as part of the System/370 announcements.[33]

In August 1967 a phase review of the project, then called HATS (High Availability Tape Subsystem), set forth as objectives the improvement of availability, price/performance, reliability, and serviceability with the use of half-inch compatible tape. Drives were planned for 3,200 and 1,600 bits per inch, and were to have 360 programming compatibility and to incorporate NS (System/370) architecture. They were to have a much higher data rate than any existing IBM drive, including the D30R (2420 Model 7). Announcement was planned for September 1969.[34]

By September 1968, however, with the name of the project changed to Aspen, announcement had moved farther away, being scheduled for June 1971.[35] That 1971 announcement was one piece of a multipart strategy. The strategy, which included the announcement of the 2420 Model 5 and the first customer shipment of the 2420 Model 7 in 1968, was to go on in 1970 with the announcement of a mass storage device and then to the announcement of the first Aspen drive in 1971.[36]

That timetable proved to be too slow. By October 1969 activity by leasing companies and peripheral manufacturers was increasing. It was reported within IBM that while the 2420 was "currently competitive," competition was "expected to equal or exceed the capabilities" thereof with rental or purchase prices lower than or comparable with IBM's. That competition included both systems companies that by 1969 had announced tape subsystems equal to or better than the 2400 line and leasing companies and peripheral manufacturers.[37]

In order to accelerate the development effort, the Aspen program was divided into two parts, Aspen Intermediate and Aspen Advanced, to be announcd in September 1970 and June 1973, respectively.[38] "The Aspen Intermediate Program is currently targeted to meet the OEM competitive pressures that are increasing in the field today. . . ." With the Aspen program concentrating only on Aspen Advanced, "it has become apparent that this product by itself would not stop erosion of our tape products inventory. . . . To meet the competition then, the Aspen 'Intermediate' Program has been introduced to supplement the Aspen 'advanced' high performance plan."[39] Aspen Intermediate was planned to have a density of 1,600 bits per inch; Aspen Advanced, a density of 6,400 bits per inch. Aspen Intermediate was to have tape speeds of 50, 100, or 200 inches per second; Aspen Advanced, tape speeds of 100 or 200 inches per second. As a result, Aspen Intermediate would have a data rate ranging from 80 to 320 kilobytes per second; and Aspen Advanced, from 640 to 1,280 kilobytes per second. Aspen Intermediate was seen as "protecting our tape investment" on 360/40s and 50s and early A48s (subsequently announced as the 370/155), while Aspen Advanced, to which Aspen Intermediate was "a more logical step," was seen as a way of ensuring long-term system price/performance.[40]

There were pressures within IBM to speed up delivery of Aspen Intermediate and the announcement of Aspen Advanced.[41] Indeed, Corporate Marketing expressed doubts that the entire strategy would be in time or would be sufficient. In early October 1969, R. A. Pfeiffer (IBM director of marketing) wrote to W. D. Winger (product manager, tape devices, Systems Development Division) concerning the Tape Devices Strategic Plan:

> Corporate Marketing disagrees with the subject strategy for the following reasons:
>
> 1. The strategy does not address critical requirements in the ½ inch tape marketplace identified by market requirements statements and increasing competitive penetration of IBM's tape drive base.
>
> . . . .
>
> 3. The strategy does not positively indicate that IBM will regain and maintain price/performance superiority over competitive manufacturers.

4. The risks of insufficient advanced technology efforts are identified in your strategy, but resolution is not addressed.[42]

In particular:

The growth of the OEM [PCM] installed/on-order position, coupled with their projected production capability, requires immediate IBM response to protect and grow our market.[43]

Further, with reference to price/performance comparisons:

Inclusion of OEM plug-compatible units shows IBM price/performance deficient in the critical Intermediate and Large Systems areas.
We do not see positive assurance that IBM will regain price/performance superiority from competitive manufacturers.[44]

Winger replied on October 30: "I believe this has been answered by the funding of Aspen Intermediate to permit announcement 9/70." Aspen Intermediate was to be announced for both System/360 and the new systems.[45] It was "price competitive with system manufacturers and OEM at their lowest quote prices," but the long-range strategy called for "additional functions and improved performance."[46] These efforts, however, presented

a problem of adequate resources to bring out a burst of products while at the same time building a technology base for future products and product enhancements. The alternatives are to add resources or to accept the risks or to cut out product programs. I have listed the choices in order of my preference. This is an SDD funding issue.[47]

Pfeiffer replied in mid-November, saying: "The first customer shipment date and delivery schedules for Aspen Intermediate drives should be improved. . . . The lack of advanced product technology efforts has not been resolved."[48] In particular, "in light of current OEM [PCM] strength, first customer shipment [of Aspen Intermediate] should be reduced to 9-12 months after announcement to maximize competitiveness of the new drives." Also, while it was understood that advanced technology efforts were "primarily a funding issue, [w]e are not satisfied that acceptance of the risks involved with insufficient new product technology development is a proper strategy."[49]

By the time it was shipped, IBM had spent more than $10 million on Aspen.[50] Aspen Intermediate was announced on November 5, 1970, as the 3420 tape drive, Models 3, 5, and 7, with first customer shipment scheduled for October 1971. As announced, the drives were attachable to all 360 models above the Model 20 and to all models of System/370.[51] The three models had tape speeds of 75, 125, and 200 inches per second and provided format compatibility with all IBM 240X and 2420 tape drives through the ability to accept both NRZI and phase-encoded tapes.[52]

Although IBM capitalized on the basic design of the 2420 in its development of Aspen, the end result was a significantly improved tape drive and control unit.[53] Some of the differences between the 2420 and its control unit (the 2803) and the 3420 and its control unit (the 3803) were the following:

1. A wider choice of recording formats, densities, and tape speeds, giving the user greater flexibility.[54]

2. An improvement in access time on the order of 20 percent.[55]

3. A 25 percent improvement in rewind time.[56]

4. Simplified maintenance and automatic, instead of manual, adjustments of pneumatics.[57]

5. A built-in programmable diagnostic capability of the 3803 controller that could detect and identify problems in the tape subsystem as they occurred.[58]

6. Use of monolithic circuitry with more logic capability on fewer cards and in a smaller space, with a resulting improvement of more than 25 percent in reliability over the 2420 family. As a result of the reduction in space requirements, the 3803 controller was only half the size of the 2803, and the switching circuitry (which in the 2420/2803 was contained in a stand-alone box) could be included under the covers of the 3803.[59]

7. A new method of attaching the tape drive to the tape control unit — a radial attachment with the control unit at the center and drives attached like the spokes of a wheel, rather than a "daisy chain" attachment, with a whole string of drives attached at one end to the control unit. Whereas in the "daisy chain" attachment the failure of one tape drive would mean the failure of the whole string, radial attachment meant that "if a tape unit malfunctions it could be worked on while the rest of the tapes were on line."[60] In addition, the radial attachment increased users' flexibility in the physical arrangement of the computer installation.[61]

8. A digital instead of an analog interface between the tape drive and controller, giving better noise rejection characteristics.[62]

The 3420, with its faster rewind and faster mounting and dismounting of tape reels, provided higher throughput than the 2420.[63] In addition, it had considerably lower manufacturing costs than the 2420 Model 7.[64] The advantages of the 3420 were widely acknowledged.[65]

DISK DRIVE DEVELOPMENTS: THE 3330 (MERLIN), 2319, AND 3340 (WINCHESTER)

With System/360 IBM had placed disk drives in a position of central importance. By the late 1960s disk drives had proved a major competitive success, and IBM again planned its new systems (System/370) around new, high-performance disk drives, including the Merlin and the Winchester.[66]

The 3330 (Merlin)

So important was the 3330 (Merlin) disk file perceived to be to the success of System/370, that the initial announcement of the 370 line was held up for almost a year because the Merlin was not ready at the planned announcement time of late 1969.[67] The delay in the announcement of Merlin was seen as serious, not only because it was needed to make 370 systems competitive but also because of the increasing pressure from plug-compatible disk drive competition. For example, in April 1969 T. V. Learson (then president) wrote to F. T. Cary (then senior vice-president) concerning a recent ISS disk announcement:

> You have read of the ISS 701. I am quite alarmed that it has been announced prior to and at superior specifications to our 2314A-3. They have moved to the new electromagnetic actuator which we are postponing until announcement of the Merlin file. Their average access time is one half the speed that we are planning on the 2314A-3 and is 25% faster than the Merlin file.
> I realize that we have more capacity planned, but there is nothing to stop them from adding capacity.[68]

ISS had been founded in 1967 by 12 former employees of IBM's San Jose disk drive facility, some of whom had worked on Merlin development. The actuator involved was the voice coil actuator (or high-speed electromagnetic actuator), which was considerably faster than the hydraulic actuator used on the 2314 and the development of which was responsible for some of the 3330 delays.[69] In fact, as Cary informed Learson, the Merlin as planned would give IBM a "significant edge" in "both technology and product performance" over "all the competition."[70]

By July 1969 a number of competitors had announced equipment comparable with IBM's 2314, which had first been delivered in 1967.[71] By January 1970 an evaluation of the "file facility environment," in connection with Merlin Phase III-level forecast assumptions, stated:

> From the announcement of the 2314 in 1965 until late 1968 IBM had significant competitive advantages in this product area, as no competitor could offer a direct access device with the price, capacity, performance, and interchangeability characteristics of the IBM 2314. The situation today, however, has changed radically as most system manufacturers now have announced devices which are virtually identical in specifications to the IBM 2314.[72]

Moreover, ISS and Memorex were expected to announce, in late 1970 or early 1971, "modular Merlin-type drives at 10% to 15% below the IBM equivalent price and no extra shift charges"; first shipment of those devices to customers was expected by late 1972. By 1973 Merlin-type announcements were expected from major systems manufacturers, with first shipment to customers anticipated late in 1974, by which time it was expected that "plug-compatible devices of the Merlin-Type will be in heavy production."[73]

Thus, even before the announcement of Merlin, competitive responses were expected:

> MERLIN competition will be from both plug-compatible and system vendors. The key point here is the timing of this competition. It is our opinion that the significance of the MERLIN release will force the data processing industry to react faster than the assumptions predict. This reaction will probably be in two areas — MERLIN equivalents and 2314 price cutting and/or enhancements. We expect the latter to be the key competitor to MERLIN initially and improved MERLIN equivalents in the '73 time frame. . . . Experience has shown that the competition is not limited to direct plug-compatible devices.[74]

The 3330 disk drive and associated 3830 control unit were announced with the initial processors of the 370 line on June 30, 1970, for use with System/370 and with the 360 Models 85 and 195.[75] The 3330 was a very substantial advance in IBM disk drives. It offered disk capacity up to 800 million bytes in a single facility. It had almost double the number of tracks and the density, and over three times the capacity of the 2314. Its data rate was 2.5 times that of the 2314; its average access time with the high-speed, electromagnetic actuator was half that of the 2314.[76] It was widely recognized as a significant innovation and advance.[77]

The 2319 and 3340 (Winchester)

While the 3330 was the most important disk drive development planned for System/370, it was not the only one.[78] The need for a broader line of disk drives was stressed by Erich Bloch (director of the Poughkeepsie laboratory, SDD) in March 1969 when he wrote to Al Shugart (product manager, Direct Access Storage Products [DASD] SDD), concerning disk file development:

> Our systems are competing across an increasing spectrum of performance and applications against improving competition. At the same time DASD devices are becoming more important to good system balance and performance. In this environment it is important that IBM market a full set of DASD products in order to fit the right combination of cost, capacity and performance to the application. . . . It is important that you understand and recognize this need so that you can plan for a broader and more flexible DASD product line than the very limited one we now have.[79]

It was evident that Merlin would not provide "the right combination of cost, capacity and performance" for the lower end of the 370 line – that is, for processors from the 370/145 down.[80]

In 1969 Kenneth Haughton, an IBM senior engineer, was attempting to develop a low-cost, low-end file by looking at "new technology" rather than at the heads and disks developed for Merlin or the 2314. After a number of iterations, "by mid-summer we had come up with a rather revolutionary new approach," which would involve the removability not only of the disk pack itself but also of an entire disk "module" in which both the heads and the pack would be contained. This development was to become Winchester, the 3340.[81]

Mid-1969 was very late, however. The announcement of the first processors of the System/370 line, the 370/155 and 165, had already been delayed from mid-1969 to mid-1970, because of the lateness of the Merlin program. It was evident that Winchester would not be ready for the planned announcements of the 145, 135, and 125 processors, which were expected to begin in the fall of 1970.[82] As a result the Data Processing Division wanted to announce attachment of the 2314 to those processors as an interim step.[83]

IBM faced a dilemma. On the one hand, it could not do without a relatively low-cost disk drive for the low-end processors. C. T. Carter, product marketing manager for intermediate systems, wrote to J. J. Keil, director of systems marketing, in April 1970 that the attachment of a 2314-type device was believed to be

> needed to enhance the NS [370] systems price in the 1970-1973 time frame. It is in this period that we must maximize our competitive posture in the Model 20/25/30 marketplace. The competition in this market will include not only today's NCR 100/200, MH [Minneapolis Honeywell] 115, and UN [Univac] 9200/9300 but new competitive announcements as well as discounted leasing companies 360's.[84]

On the other hand, plug-compatible manufacturers (PCMs) were already replacing IBM 2314s. To use the 2314 as the disk drive of choice until Winchester was ready meant continued exposure to replacement by PCM competition. Moreover, customers, having acquired these 2314s from IBM or 2314-type devices from PCMs, might be reluctant to move up to Winchester or Merlin – moves that would be necessary if they were to expand their usage of data processing to take advantage of the full capacity of the 370 line.[85]

The 2314s that had been marketed for System/360 were at this time "coming back almost by the trainload" because the competition was displacing them.[86] The attachment of the 2314 at its current prices to the new processors was, of course, out of the question. It would simply invite a flood of replacements by PCMs already supplying 2314-type disk drives.[87] Moreover, it would not fill the need for a low-cost disk device and would raise the 370 systems' prices to unacceptable levels. Therefore, a new, low-priced disk drive of the 2314 type was the chosen solution. The result was the 2319. Even though it was recognized that the low price of the attachment would put "[p]ressure on Winchester Price/Performance Improvements,"[88] Group Finance took the position, in the financial analysis of the 2319 in September 1970, that IBM should announce it at "the low-price assumption of the *$1000* price in that this price level assures *maximum revenue* and *profit* to IBM."[89]

The new, low price of the 2319 disk drive was achieved through a combination of factors. IBM employed a reuse program for the 2314 spindles that were being returned to it as a result of competitive displacements, incorporating those spindles into the 2319.[90] In addition, the 2319 was announced with "native attachment" to the CPU, meaning that an entire box — the control unit — had been eliminated by the incorporation of its functions into the disk drive and into an integrated file adapter in the CPU. The use of new, more compact monolithic systems technology (MST) (as opposed to SLT) facilitated the integration of that function in a cost-effective way.[91]

The native attachment represented a long-recognized approach to cost reduction: minimization of the number of boxes.[92] Analyses conducted within IBM indicated that such attachment was a feasible approach for the 2319, and that it would provide significant cost-saving benefits both to IBM and to users.[93] Native attachment for System/370 was first announced as the optional integrated file adapter (IFA) for attachment of the 2319 to the 370/145 in September 1970 and to the 370/135 in March 1971.[94] It constituted a product improvement as well as a cost savings.[95]

Winchester was eventually announced as the 3340 direct-access storage facility in March 1973.[96] It was a highly innovative and successful product and was widely copied by others.

NEW PROCESSOR PLANNING: SYSTEM/3 AND SYSTEM/370

Coincidentally with IBM's planning and development of improved peripherals, particularly tape drives and disk drives, its strategy for the development of a new generation of CPUs and memories was formed and implemented.

Monolithic Logic and Memory

During the development of SLT from 1961 to 1966, IBM laid the groundwork for the eventual use of monolithic semiconductor circuits. The same substrates and tooling used to manufacture SLT were applicable to the assembly of monolithic circuitry.[97]

IBM's work on development of monolithic semiconductor memories (of which the two principal types are bipolar and FET memories) began around 1964, "in an attempt to find a memory technology which could overcome the speed, cost and size limitations of magnetic core technology."

The potential advantages of monolithic semiconductor memories were based on projections that they would be denser, would require fewer external connections, less power and less cooling and would be fabricated using existing semiconductor processes and would avoid duplication by using the same technology and packaging as monolithic semiconductor logic circuitry.[98]

Another goal and potential benefit of the new technology was the integration of memories into the CPUs, with the resulting benefits of improved performance and reliability as well as cost savings.[99] (That goal could not be achieved with the initial 370 processors, the 370/155 and 165, because of IBM's inability to produce sufficient components in time.)[100]

Logic technology moved to monolithic systems technology (MST), first used in the 360/85 and the System/3 Model 10 computers, which were announced in January 1968 and July 1969, respectively.[101] The MST modules, cards, and boards used the same packaging techniques as those of SLT modules, cards, and boards, which provided cost saving.[102] Advantages over SLT were greater density, a higher level of integration, and a substantial increase in reliability (by a factor of ten over SLT).[103] Monolithic semiconductor circuitry was used for logic circuitry and buffer storage in the 370/155 and 165, announced in 1970.[104]

IBM's first use of monolithic semiconductor memory was in the storage protect memory of the 360/91 and 360/95, the first of which was delivered in October 1967.[105] The experience gained by 1968 through design and development of monolithic semiconductor memories led IBM's memory designers and developers to a recommendation accepted at the highest level of management. "On January 25, 1968, IBM's Management Review Committee decided to abandon any further magnetic core memory development and it was decided that from that point on, IBM would develop only monolithic memories."[106] Cary testified:

> We took a tremendous risk in doing this, because a lot of people continued to cost reduce and improve core memories. We stopped our development on them and we went full bore into the development of semiconductor memories.[107]

As in other areas, competiton was increasing and certainly was not going to stand still. By July 1969 J. A. Haddad, IBM vice-president, wrote to G. E. Jones, IBM senior vice-president, nominating memory as a key corporate strategic issue:

> The last year has seen a drastic increase in competition in memory, with every indication that we shall soon be facing major inroads to both installed and on-order memory as well as increasing price competition in all phases of the memory market. We must have a strategy to lead the competition (we no longer possess our previous lead position), rather than to be pushed around by it.

. . . .

. . . Memory is central to our products, processors, and profits. Memory profit is a major factor in processor profitability as well as the key new factor in performance. In large systems we are lagging in speed and price, and in very small systems we are non-competitive in both price and speed. Memory prices affect memory size, which affect programming requirements, I/O and storage requirements, and total systems thruput.[108]

As June 1970, the announcement date for the first 370 processors, approached, it was apparent that IBM would not be ready to produce monolithic memories in adequate quantity, and it was decided to announce the 155 and 165 with core memory. The smaller 145, which was announced a few months later, was to have bipolar monolithic memory derived from SLT; field effect transistor (FET) memory was preferred but could not be readied in time.[109]

It was recognized that the memories announced with the 155 and the 165 were "very old technology" and "were going to go very shortly noncompetitive in the sense of the availability of semiconductor memories."[110] Cary testified:

[W]e knew that they did not have long life and that if we didn't get competitive technology in the marketplace that we wouldn't be competitive either with the plug compatible type of manufacturer or with the other systems manufacturers. Every one was going this way just as hard as they could go.[111]

Despite the use of the old, slow core memory, the new processors were two to five times as fast as the earlier 360/50 and 65, because of the use of the new monolithic circuitry in processor logic and buffer storage.[112] Monolithic logic and memory circuitry, including FET memory, were to be utilized in subsequent products when available.[113]

System/3

In designing the 360, IBM produced a long-lasting architecture that was suitable for processors in the range initially announced on April 7, 1964. However, while compatibility was extended to larger processors, as in the 360/90 series, it was recognized as early as the SPREAD Report that extending compatibility to less powerful processors was a more doubtful matter.[114] IBM's attempt in this direction, the 360/20, resulted in a system only partly compatible with the rest of the line.[115] In 1969 IBM announced a small, low-cost system that departed from System/360 architecture: the System/3.[116] This was the first of several such low-end IBM systems.

IBM was able to introduce its low-cost system in July 1969, in part because "as of 1968 the development of monolithic semiconductor circuitry at IBM had reached a point where major performance and cost improvements could be achieved by using monolithic semiconductors instead of SLT circuits and logic circuitry." The System/3 Model 10 was one of the first two IBM computers to use monolithic system technology (MST).[117]

The System/3 announcement was not merely the announcement of a new processor. It also involved "new families of disk files and printers, a keyboard and console typewriters, and unique programming capabilities."[118] The initial announcement (the Model 10) offered both a card-oriented and a disk-oriented system.[119] The card involved was a new 96-column one. This card was "about 1/3 the size" of earlier cards but could contain 30 percent more information. This meant "less space and storage requirements, easier handling, reduced mechanical [sic] loads, smaller sized machines for processing the cards and, therefore, a lower cost system. Hence, the 96-column card made it possible for System/3 to become the economical, high performance system that it is."[120]

The System/3 "was a new, low entry computer system . . . that was aimed at bringing total computer capability to the small user at the thousand dollar a month rental price, approximately, having full capability of I/O function and programming support."[121] Some forecasts within IBM indicated discontinuance of 40 percent of the accounts using leased unit record equipment. "Without System/3, it was estimated that 50% of these discontinuances would go to competition (Univac 9200, Honeywell 110, GE 105/115, NCR C-100). System/3 will allow the company to save approximately one-half of these losses."[122] System/3 was not intended merely for small users, however. IBM's 1969 Annual Report stated:

> Although it was designed primarily for small business, it is also expected to find application in large firms that wish to decentralize their data processing capabilities.[123]

To manufacture and develop System/3 enhancements and other products not using the System/360 architecture, IBM formed the General Systems Division within the Data Processing Group in early November 1969.[124] A marketing and service capability was provided in the General Systems Division five years later.[125]

Customer reaction to System/3 was "enthusiastic."[126] By the end of 1970, its first year of deliveries, more than 1,600 had been installed in the United States.[127]

Virtual Memory

As we have already seen, pressured by leading-edge users, IBM had developed Dynamic Address Translation (DAT) as a hardware device in the 360/Model 67, combining it with systems software to enhance the system's time-sharing capabilities. That effort had proven difficult and expensive, and despite earlier plans to include those features, by 1969 the plans were proceeding, with DAT (or relocate) not to be included in the initial 370 line.[128] B. O. Evans, on returning from the Federal Systems Division to become president of the Systems Development Division in 1969, was "quite surprised" to discover that omission. He considered it "fundamentally wrong."[129]

Evans' surprise was natural. He had been sent to the Federal Systems Division as "a little punishment" because the "very demanding IBM management" viewed it as a "fundamental mistake" that Dynamic Address Translation had not been included in System/360 architecture.[130] He testified:

> I felt so intensely about Dynamic Address Translation and the advantages of virtual memory that within the first hour that I was in my new job I hand-picked several professionals from across the development team to go to work full-time immediately and get me a plan for virtual memory on System/370.[131]

Virtual memory would give the appearance to the user of having a very large memory at his disposal and would facilitate multiprogramming and communications-oriented applications. System/360 had been built in part on the belief that communications-oriented processing would grow in importance, but awareness of the growing importance of time-sharing and communications-oriented processing now became a reason for concern about the absence of the relocate feature and virtual memory in the plans for the 370.[132] The Management Committee reported to the Management Review Committee in March 1969 that IBM's position in this area was felt to be weak, with IBM "behind in both hardware and software."[133]

The need for virtual memory was being felt by others in IBM. In June 1969, C. B. Rogers, Jr. (vice-president of marketing and development, Data Processing Division [DPD]), wrote to C. E. Branscomb (president of SDD), stating DPD's view that "progress has been unsatisfactory" toward the production of "a viable NS announcement plan." He stated:

> Market requirements are not being met with SDD's current announcement and support plan. The CPU's provide improved price/performance for doing today's processing, but do not offer significant new function for continued growth.
>
>   . . . .
>
> Implementation of the virtual memory concept — with functional compatibility throughout the NS line, combined with multiprocessing — can extend NS's price/performance range dramatically. We view virtual memory implementation as necessary and fundamental to meeting market requirements in the early 1970's.[134]

The anticipated solution was a phased introduction of the relocate hardware, with the initial machines designed to utilize it when it was available. Specifically as to time sharing, an interim plan involved increased funding under the DOS and OS operating systems and re-emphasis of the TSS time-sharing operating system. New software implementing that plan was announced in

December 1969.[135] The long range plan consisted of two parts, the first being the new NS (370) operating system and a new DOS operating system both "designed to enhance time sharing."

> The second, and equally important part of the strategy, is the relocation hardware necessary to really do this job. This is scheduled for announcement in 1973 with installations in 1974.[136]

That plan was adequate in concept, if attainable, but it raised two timing questions: Could the initial 370 announcements be made in 1970 with provision for relocate and virtual memory? When could relocate be ready? The plan's response to the second question was mid-1973 or 1974. That was too late according to C. B. Rogers, Jr.:

> Not having relocation support until 6/73 or 1/74 is totally wrong. It's too far out. The logic that we can't support it until then is unsatisfactory. We think TSS could be modified to accommodate the '67 scheme on NS.[137]

The market, moving toward remote computing, would not wait for the IBM development effort. The need for relocate was a matter of increasing concern through the fall of 1969.[138]

By late 1969 it was too late to get relocate into the first System/370 announcements, scheduled for mid-1970.[139] Evans considered delaying those announcements or shipments until the design of Dynamic Address Translation was finished and the monolithic memory technology was available.

> But the situation was . . . that System 360 had been out in the field for about six years and competition had become [more severe] since 360's announcement, with ever-improving components and systems, and so, competitively speaking, the System 360 was out of gas, and when we looked at the users' requirements, as we saw them in late 1969, . . . delaying System 370 another two years or more to get dynamic address translation, et cetera, into the machines, didn't seem reasonable.
>
> So we made a thoughtful decision to proceed with the 155 and the 165 and the so-called vanilla version of the System 370 phasing in dynamic address translation and semi-conductor memory technology as quick [sic] as we could.[140]

The 370/155 and 165 were announced in June 1970, on a schedule that had already been delayed because of the unavailability of the Merlin disk drive.[141] Relocate and virtual storage were not included in the initial System/370 announcements; the first announcement of virtual storage for System/370 was made in August 1972, when IBM announced the 370 Models 158 and 168, containing Dynamic Address Translation. IBM also announced at that time that DAT could be purchased to implement virtual storage on the 370/155 and 165, and was available on the 370/145 (announced in September 1970) and 370/135 (announced in March 1971) without additional charge.[142] By mid-1972 the principal goals of System/370 had been attained.[143]

System/370 Pricing

The Commercial Analysis Department of the Data Processing Division, in its Quarterly Product Line Assessment of February 1969, reported:

> When NS0 [370/135] and NS1 [370/145] are announced, IBM will be faced with competition from three sources: (1) other computer vendors, (2) owners of IBM computer systems, and (3) computer-oriented service companies.
>
> It is expected that Burroughs, NCR, and Sperry Rand will be our strongest competition in respect to marketable products when NS is introduced. . . .
>
> Honeywell is expected to announce a new series in 1970. Thus, they could once again be a formidable competitor. . . .
>
> . . . .
>
> In World Trade, American or American-associated companies should be the prime competitors. However, ICL will continue strong; Philips may have gotten a foothold with their P1000 series; and Siemens may have introduced a new series. In addition competition may come from Japanese companies such as Fujitsu offering their products outside of Japan.
>
> Competition from owners of IBM computer systems will come primarily from leasing companies and from System/360 purchase customers who sell their used systems. Both of these sources could make lower-priced System/360's available to compete with NS0 and NS1 with competitive price/performance.
>
> Computer-oriented service company competition will come from time-sharing companies and service bureaus. Both offer services which may substitute for additional computer function and/or capacity.[144]

The report went on to compare the price/performance (on a monthly lease price basis) of IBM's new systems configurations with the lease prices then expected for the "best of competition," concluding that "NS0 and NS1 are rated superior to competition. . . ."[145] Similar conclusions were expressed with respect to the price/performance of the NS2 (370/155) and the NS3 (370/165), assuming the availability of the Merlin disk drive.[146]

As of March 1969 it appeared that the price/performance of the NS systems would represent an average improvement of 1.8 times over System/360.[147] That meant, however, that System/360s owned by leasing companies and users would "remain a major competitive product." In addition, "[t]here is an added unknown in the possible merger of OEM's [PCMs], software houses and leasing companies," with the possible marketing of 360 CPUs enhanced in price/performance by plug-compatible peripherals and independent software.[148] As of

March 1969 it appeared to IBM management that with the planned prices for the NS CPUs, "a leasing company can compete on an equal basis with NS by discounting the 360 30%."[149] As expressed by Cary, a principal concern was that high purchase prices and high maintenance charges would cost IBM sales of System/370 CPUs, with many of the losses being to leasing companies and other owners offering discounted System/360 CPUs for sale or lease.[150]

That concern continued through early 1970.[151] As announced in June 1970, the purchase prices on the 370/155 and 165, as well as on the 3360 processor storage, were lowered substantially from their values in the earlier planning assumptions.[152]

The substantial differential between 360 and 370 maintenance prices also contributed to the competitive exposure. The planned maintenance charge for the NS2 (370/155) was $4,930, although cost reduction actions were expected to reduce it to $2,620.[153] The differential was due in part to the fact that maintenance prices for the 360 were felt to be too low, "probably by half," in relation to the cost of the "increased inventory of maintenance parts, brought about in part by integrated circuitry" for the new machines, and to the time necessary for field engineers to gain experience with the new software and hardware.[154]

As had been forecast, by the time of announcement, substantial improvement had been made in reducing costs, and thus prices, of NS maintenance.[155] Thus, at the time of announcement, the monthly maintenance charges on the 155 were about $2,200 — less than half those contemplated in the planning assumptions.[156] Moreover, IBM decreased the effective maintenance price of System/370 still further by increasing the warranty time on purchased CPUs, channels, and memories to one year from the three-month warranties on System/360.[157] In 1972, as warranties began to expire on the purchased System/370 units, IBM announced further reductions in maintenance charges on those machines amounting to, for example, about 15 percent on the 155 processor. This made monthly maintenance charges on the 155 about $1,750.[158] Adjusted for inflation, the decrease was even greater.

CONCLUSION

Notwithstanding the enormous success of the System/360 as announced in 1964, and IBM's continued technological improvements thereafter, by 1969 the firm confronted serious competitive challenges to its position of technological leadership and price/performance superiority. The state of technological development and implementation for the new products being planned in the face of those challenges caused consternation among IBM top management. Pressures were exerted throughout the organization by the insistence that the new products had to be better, and announced and delivered sooner. The organization responded, but IBM was unable to announce on schedule the range of product capabilities that management felt necessary to sustain the firm's superiority. Consequently, IBM entered the 1970s engaged in a struggle to achieve the ambitious goals it had established, in response to competition, for its next generation of systems.

THE 1960s, CONCLUSION:
THE GROWTH OF
THE EDP INDUSTRY

THE EXPLOSION OF DEMAND

One fact about the EDP industry is so clear and unequivocal that its significance can be easily overlooked. That fact is the extraordinary growth in the use of computers over the first 20 years of the EDP industry's existence — a phenomenon that continued unabated over the next decade and made the industry the fastest- or one of the fastest-growing industries in the world, as many observers have remarked.[1] The growth in the use of computers is shown in estimates of the numbers of computers installed and also in estimates of the value of EDP equipment shipped by the manufacturers. For example, the comptroller general of the United States, in a report to Congress in June 1969, estimated that the computer industry had grown from "a few experimental computers" in the late 1940s, to "400 computers installed in the United States" in 1955, to "approximate[ly]" 6,000 in 1960, to "installations" in excess of 67,000 in 1968. He stated: "The computer hardware market is believed to have reached a value of about $7.2 billion during 1968 and is expected to grow at a 15 to 20 percent annual rate over the next 5 years."[2]

The 1972 Census of Manufactures reported that the value of shipments by all producers of "electronic computing equipment" grew from $4,048.8 million in 1967 to $6,108.0 million in 1972.[3] *U.S.* v. *IBM*'s Census II (a joint deposition program of suppliers of EDP products and services over the period 1952-72) shows that of the 618 companies reporting U.S. EDP revenue in 1972, only 9 had such revenue in 1952, 75 in 1960, and 188 in 1964. The total U.S. EDP revenues reported by those companies grew from $39.5 million in 1952 to $1.3 billion in 1960, to $3.2 billion in 1964, to $12.8 billion in 1972. These revenues grew at a compound growth rate of 33.5 percent over that period.[4]

The rate of growth in the demand for computers was continually underestimated by most participants in and observers of the industry — and, in retrospect, called "startling," "unique," and "tremendous."[5]

Increase in the Number of Users of Computers

Frederic Withington of Arthur D. Little wrote in 1964, after the announcement of System/360:

> The single most important factor in the historic growth of the computer market has been the increasing number of computer users. This increase has been made possible by constant reduction of the minimum cost of computers and greater understanding of how computers might be used.[6]

But, he went on to project, "new users will become increasingly hard to find in the United States." He reasoned that "there are approximately 25,000 companies with net worth of over one million dollars. In general, it is fair to assume that any company smaller than that is not likely to acquire a computer: in fact, many firms with a net worth of five million dollars do not use a computer."[7]

By the very next year, however, Withington had changed his mind. He stated:

> The number of organizations using computers continues to increase rapidly, primarily because computer systems with complete capabilities are becoming available at steadily lower costs. Thus they come within the reach of organizations that could not previously afford such computer systems: for example, the IBM 360/20 and 1440, the Honeywell 120, and the Univac 1004. More than 2,000 such machines were installed during 1965, representing shipments of considerable dollar value to the manufacturers.[8]

By 1967 it had become apparent to Withington how wrong he had been in 1964:

> [T]he experience of recent years has shown that, as the costs of small computer systems decline, great numbers of new users enter the market. We expect this trend will continue, and by the end of 1971 there should be many thousands of new computer users who do not now have machines.[9]

> The situation is becoming more dynamic rather than less so, and the only safe prediction at this point is that pace of change, and the growth of the industry as a whole, will remain extremely rapid.[10]

Withington's observation that the number of users continued to expand was repeated in 1968 and 1969.[11] The importance of the phenomenon was clearly recognized within the industry.[12] As we have seen, when IBM announced its 360/20 in 1964 and the System/3 in 1969, an important goal was to attract new users of computers and to compete with other manufacturers' efforts to do so — a goal that continued to motivate IBM product announcements in the 1970s.

Expansion by Existing Computer Users

Another substantial contribution to the growth of the industry came from the almost insatiable demand of existing users of computers for additional computing power. Donald Hart, of General Motors Research (GMR), stated that through 1970 the "demand for computing power supplied by GMR . . . doubled every year and a half since we installed the 701 in 1954." He continued, "We fully expect this growth to continue over the next 20 years."[13]

An important example of the trend in computer use in general was the increasing use of computers by the U.S. government, the world's largest user of computers.[14] That growth reflected expansion by existing users as well as the introduction of new agencies to the use of computers. According to reports by the comptroller general and by the General Services Administration, the number of computers installed in the federal government went from 5 in 1952 to 531 in 1960, to 1,862 in 1964, to 5,277 in 1970, and kept on growing.[15] Moreover, merely counting the number of computers very much understates the growth in computer capability and use as computational power per computer (or per dollar) also increased very rapidly.[16]

The Explosion of New Applications of Computers

The initial development of computer applications consisted of applying computers to jobs that had previously been performed by other means. Thereafter, computers were increasingly applied to jobs that could not previously have been performed without computers.

For example, when Consolidated Vultee (later Convair), the aircraft company, first acquired an IBM 701 in the early 1950s, the work that was undertaken "was in part a transfer of work from unit record equipment, but it was very largely, and . . . within a matter of months predominantly, work of the type that could not have been done in the same form or perhaps at all on unit record equipment."[17] Computers could "perform problems which punched card equipment simply could not perform." General Motors and North American Aviation "were processing data which involved a totality of applications such as order entry, checking the validity of orders, placing requirements on the factory, scheduling production, controlling inventory, and controlling manufacturing, all in a single, integrated operation and with no human intervention." Oak Ridge Laboratories "was using computers to simulate a diffusion plant, the purpose of which was to enrich uranium." And various "property, casualty and life insurance companies were using computers to maintain and update on a daily or weekly basis files which, in the case of large companies, continued millions and even tens of millions of policies."[18] The General Accounting Office, in a report to Congress in 1960, stated that the "[p]rogress achieved in the development and application of . . . automatic information processing systems have [*sic*] borne out earlier predictions" that computers will cause "a second industrial revolution."[19]

By the early 1960s, however, although more and more ways in which computers could be applied were being conceived, only the first steps toward realizing such applications had been taken. Withington stated in 1964:

> In the past decade, most computers were sold to do simple jobs — payrolls and scientific applications. Most computers today are still doing simple tasks. The exotic computer applications that abound in the literature are the exception, not the rule.
>
> We believe that the next wave of computer applications is just beginning. If the first generation of computer applications consisted mainly of record keeping and scientific computations, the second generation will consist of automatic decision rules (for inventory control, credit, etc.) and design automation. Third-generation applications will involve real-time systems. . . . No one has begun to define the limits of computer technology.[20]

In the 1960s real-time systems were increasing in importance as users actively developed real-time applications.[21] Scientific Data Systems, perceiving this trend early, capitalized on it by building on the uses of computers for real-time applications, such as process control, to achieve an impressive success. Others saw real-time applications in terms of interaction between man and computer. In June 1964, John Weil, in a presentation to GE's executive office, stated:

> The single most important trend in the information processing market today is that we are moving away from batch processing, where information is collected for a far-flung organization by fundamentally manual methods and then processed in a batch through a computer system. . . .
>
> The information processing business of tomorrow . . . will have transaction data entered into the system through communications lines, processed against massive central files on a random-nonscheduled basis and returned via communication lines to the user, frequently all in a matter of seconds. Prototypes of this kind can be found in the airline reservations systems, in military command and control systems and in process computer installations.
>
> . . . .
>
> The direct access system . . . will play a large part in the growth of the computer business in the next few years. We predict by 1974 80% of the domestic shipment volume of information processing systems will be serving the direct access market and almost one-half of this will be remote terminals. The classic batch system, which dominates today's market, will continue to exist but will play a diminishing role in the equipment market.[22]

The Department of Justice told the Federal Communications Commission (FCC) in 1968:

> The following categorization of existing applications is sufficient to underscore the commercial and practical importance of the entire

remote access computer industry:

> (a) Conversational time-sharing systems (always real-time) — these involve the simultaneous sharing of a central computer among a group of users located at remote terminals and connected to the central computer by communications circuits.
>
> (b) Inquiry systems (usually real-time) — in such systems, typified by stock quotation services, a large number of terminals are connected to a single data processing center by means of communication lines; the system enables remote users to query a frequently updated central store of information.
>
> (c) Remote batch processing systems — these systems permit the central processing of tasks that originated at and are transmitted from distant locations.
>
> . . . .
>
> (f) Information distribution systems — these systems, capable of operating on either real-time or batch basis, often operate like inquiry and document-production systems without the need for specific, repeated customer inquiry.
>
> (g) As information relevant to the needs of a particular subscriber is received by a central computer of such a system, the information is automatically and selectively transmitted to the subscriber via communications lines.
>
> (h) The distribution of railroad freight traffic information to railroad traffic agents, shippers, and consignees is an example of such a system.[23]

As a consequence of such developments:

> The number and variety of remote access data processing systems, both real-time and batch processing time, is already very large and rapidly growing.[24]

People were exploring and discovering new ways to use computers. As the Justice Department told the FCC:

> The growth of computational capability has been accompanied by a rapid growth in the diversity of computer applications.
>
> [One source listed over] 1,200 computer applications in such diverse fields as business, government, manufacturing, education, law, medicine, sports, science, engineering, national defense, social welfare, music, and language.[25]

In June 1966, President Lyndon B. Johnson urged the federal government to participate. He directed the head of every federal agency "to explore and apply all possible means" to "use the electronic computer to do a better job," and to "manage computer activity at the lowest possible cost." He went on to list the ways in which the "electronic computer is having a greater impact on what the Government does and how it does it than any other product of modern technology," including applications in the space program, medical research, tax administration, Social Security and Medicare, defense logistics, atomic energy, and highway design.

> In short, computers are enabling us to achieve progress and benefits which a decade ago were beyond our grasp.
> The technology is available. Its potential for good has been amply demonstrated, but it remains to be tapped in fuller measure.
> I am determined that we take advantage of this technology by using it imaginatively to accomplish worthwhile purposes.
> I therefore want every agency head to give thorough study to new ways in which the electronic computer might be used. . . .[26]

Improved Price/Performance and Ease of Use

The increase in the ways in which computers were used and the large influx of new users were made possible by sharp price/performance improvements, increases in computer capabilities, and, in particular, by increasing ease of use. Alan Perlis of Yale testified that as the "price/performance of the hardware side of the computer" improved, "our appetites as users of the computers" increased.

> [C]omputers are so much more capable of doing things than we know how to tell them to do at any stage, that they represent a reservoir for our wishes, as it were, and everything seems to indicate that we are just going to continue to load these computers with more and more software in order to perform the tasks that we have in mind. . . .[27]

Withington wrote in 1965 that "the improved economics . . . make it possible to use computers for previously unprofitable work. As users discover this, total usage grows."[28] In 1968:

> As the costs of complete computer systems decline, thousands of new users appear and marginal applications of existing users become justified.[29]

The computer was becoming more familiar and easier for human beings to use. A good deal of this was due to the improvement in software. Higher-level languages had made it possible to program in terms more readily accessible to human beings than the ones and zeros that characterized machine languages. Advanced operating systems made it possible to program without the annoyance of having to keep track of memory addresses or do hexadecimal arithmetic. This increased the productivity of scarce programming talent, and, as we have seen, software houses developed that specialized in providing such programs to users.[30]

The increase in interactive computing was interrelated with the increasing ease of use of computers. Hart, of General Motors, wrote in 1971:

> There are two phenomena which we have noticed with the advent of interactive computing: (1) the threshold [*sic*] of complexity — of the difficulty associated with using a computer — has been lowered significantly. As a result, the number of new users has increased rapidly during the past five years. Probably more than half of the 2000 or so users of our Honeywell (GE) time-sharing system were previously non-computer users — and would not have become users of a batch system.
>
> The other phenomenon has to do with human productivity. Whereas the average engineer may be able to get five times as much work done per unit time, the outstanding creative man may get 10-20 times as much done. With a batch system, this man was frustrated by turnaround time — whereas with an interactive system, he can proceed full speed without the computer getting in his way.
>
> If it sounds like I am promoting interactive computing, it's because I am. I believe it represents a revolutionary new way of using computers to solve problems, and we are only beginning to understand what it means.[31]

Computer price/performance was also improving very rapidly in quantifiable ways. Some examples for IBM products make the point. The IBM 650 processor, announced in 1953, was able to process 700 instructions per second; the 1401 processor, announced in 1959, was able to process 5,000 instructions per second; the 360/Model 30 processor, announced in 1964, was able to process 30,000 instructions per second, a fortyfold increase in speed over about ten years.[32] Maximum main memory increased from 10,000 bytes on the 650 to 65,536 bytes on the 360/30, or by 6.5 times.[33] The rental price of the 360/30 at announcement, however, was about equal to the rental price of the 650 at announcement.[34]

Similar improvements were achieved in peripheral devices. For example, IBM's 350 magnetic disk drive, announced in 1956, had a data rate of 8,800 characters per second, an access time of 600 milliseconds, and a capacity of 4.4 million characters per spindle.[35] The 2314 disk drive, announced in 1965, had a data rate of 312,000 characters per second (over 35 times faster), an access time of 75 milliseconds (80 times faster), and a capacity of 25.87 million characters per spindle (5 times greater).[36] The storage capacity per dollar of rental increased from 7,692 characters to 38,255 characters.[37] IBM magnetic tape drives from the 729-III, announced in 1957, to the 2420 Model 7, announced in 1968, achieved a threefold increase in recording density and a sixfold increase in data rate per dollar of rental.[38]

These advances and those made by the other manufacturers translated directly into the economics of computer acquisition and use.[39] Perlis estimated in 1975 that the price per operation had decreased "a thousand to one" during the period 1948-68 and projected the same decrease for the period 1968-88.[40] Hart, writing in 1971, stated that "the changes which occurred in the 14 years between the 701 in 1954 and the 360/65 in 1968 can only be described as revolutionary." The cost per problem had improved by a factor of 100. "For $20,000 you can now purchase a whole minicomputer which could run rings around the 701." This, of course, made possible more efficient use of increasingly expensive scientific personnel. "It is interesting to note, during the past 20 years . . . while computing cost has gone down by a factor of 1,000, costs of engineers and scientists has [*sic*] tripled." These improvements "have largely come about from revolutionary changes in computer hardware technology"; however, "there has also been a revolution in software technology which has helped to make more efficient use of computer hardware — this is the operating system (currently typified by IBM's OS/360)."[41]

These improvements in ease of use, price/performance, and capabilities attracted new users, enabled existing users to expand their data processing, and contributed to the explosion of the uses of computers. To take advantage of such improvements, existing users upgraded and converted their old equipment. Withington testified that "during the entire eight-year period, 1955 to 1963, something in the range of 30 to 40 percent of users having acquired one computer system changed to a computer of another manufacturer."[42] Further, perhaps 40 to 50 percent of users acquiring an initial system from one manufacturer subsequently converted to a noncompatible computer system of the same manufacturer."[43]

Such changes generally cost users time and money. Personnel had to be retrained and programs had to be converted, processes facilitated by the use of higher-level languages and conversion aids.[44] Customers made such changes because the conversion costs were less than the resulting benefits. Hart informed his colleagues at GM:

> While [a user who disliked having to convert] was groaning, his roommate was cheering because he could now solve his problem faster, cheaper — or at all! And many new users were attracted by new capabilities. . . . The overall benefits (to the computing community) from each change have overshadowed the conversion costs required.[45]

THE ROLE OF THE FEDERAL GOVERNMENT

Particularly in the 1950s and early 1960s, the federal government played an important role in promoting the advance of computer technology. The government viewed the development and application of ever more advanced computers as critical to the nation's security and accordingly encouraged and financed leading-edge work throughout the industry. The National Security Agency was particularly active in this regard — an activity that continued throughout the 1960s.[46]

Many military-related applications required capability for performing in "real-time," and it was in military applications that such capability was first achieved, SAGE being one of the earliest examples.[47] Further, in the late 1950s and early 1960s the government supported work to build the most advanced and most powerful computers then possible (including NORC, LARC, and STRETCH) for, among other things, weapons systems development and testing and the design of nuclear weapons. Defense needs also spurred later efforts to build smaller but more powerful computers for use in aircraft, satellites, missiles, and other small spaces.[48]

The establishment of the National Aeronautics and Space Administration and the manned space flight program in 1958, followed by President Kennedy's 1961 commitment to the goal of landing a person on the moon before the end of the decade, provided still further impetus for the development of both large-scale, advanced computers and powerful, small computers. It is amazing to think that in 1961 "the computing capability did not exist" even to make the decision whether to abort an orbital flight, let alone make a lunar landing possible.[49]

The needs and the assistance of the federal government provided opportunities for companies starting out in the EDP field. William Norris, the founder of Control Data Corporation, stated in 1961:

> The huge government expenditure for research and development is the equalizer between large and small companies. Approximately 70% of all basic research done in the United States is financed by the government. This means that most of the new additions to scientific knowledge are just as available to the little company as to the large company.[50]

Of course, companies participating in military development contracts benefited directly, particularly as computer developments originally undertaken for military purposes carried over into other uses.[51] This was particularly so with the development of real-time applications.[52]

In addition to its role in supporting and funding special research and development efforts, the federal government was important as the largest user of computer equipment in the world.[53] It "increased its inventory of computer systems from 531 in June 1960 to 5,277 in June 1970, when it owned ADP [automatic data processing] equipment which cost $1.9 billion and rented equipment which would cost $1.2 billion to purchase."[54]

By the middle of the decade, governmental acquisition of computers had become sufficiently important to warrant special attention in the form of legislation — the Brooks Bill. Prior to 1965 the government's EDP equipment was acquired in essentially the same manner as other property, with each agency responsible for its own equipment requirements. Such acquisition decisions were made largely on a decentralized basis, with a view only to the individual agency's needs. This decentralized decision making failed to take into account the availability of computer equipment elsewhere in the government or the possibility that the equipment chosen by a particular agency might be used by another. As the government expanded its acquisition of EDP equipment, the potential benefits from the coordination of acquisitions decisions increased. In 1965 the Brooks Bill was enacted, amending the Federal Property and Administrative Services Act of 1949 to include general-purpose computers (essentially stored-program computers) and related services under the General Services Administration's (GSA's) procurement authority.[55]

As summarized in a report to Congress by the comptroller general in 1971, the new law

> [g]ave GSA the operational responsibility for coordinating a Government-wide ADP management program. . . . GSA was given exclusive authority to acquire all general-purpose ADP equipment for use by other agencies.
> . . . GSA was to administer an ADP Fund for the acquisition of agencies' equipment requirements. The agencies were to obtain annual appropriations from the Congress to reimburse the ADP Fund.
> The law also provided for the establishment of a management information system of inventory and fiscal data. . . . [for] efforts to achieve optimum utilization of ADP resources and to ensure that the Government evaluates all acquisition alternatives so that equipment is acquired in the most economical manner practicable.[56]

Among other things, GSA was to consider the "possibility that additional procurement sources could be cultivated to serve as competitive alternatives to the exclusive procurement of equipment directly from manufacturers and the "possibility of procuring equipment and software . . . as separate items."[57] The Bureau of the Budget (later renamed the Office of Management and Budget – OMB) and GSA encouraged the use of plug-compatible peripherals and the acquisition of EDP equipment from third-party leasing companies.[58]

The resulting effort was implemented by the General Accounting Office (GAO), the OMB, the National Bureau of Standards, and the GSA. The OMB put out instructions designed to ensure that the agencies satisfied their EDP needs in the most economical manner. The GAO assured that the implementing instructions issued by OMB and GSA were adhered to. The Bureau of Standards provided technical advice. The operation of these agencies in combination was analogous to the organization of a commercial establishment with top management, those responsible for daily operations, and technical advisers.[59]

Three of the programs arising from the Brooks Bill deserve additional description. They are the GSA Reutilization Program, the ADP Fund, and the ADP Sharing Program.

The GSA Reutilization Program

The federal government began taking advantage of its size as a user by actively seeking to efficiently reutilize EDP products that it owned. As with leasing companies and used equipment brokers outside the government, such efforts led to older, purchased equipment competing for business with the new offerings of EDP manufacturers.

Federal agencies were expected to determine whether their needs could be met either by utilizing excess EDP equipment or by sharing installed equipment before seeking new acquisitions.[60] Such determinations were actively assisted. In particular the Defense ADPE (automatic data-processing equipment) Reutilization Office acted "as a marketing type agency with respect to the disposal of excess computer equipment within the Department of Defense, and through GSA to other Federal agencies and programs."[61]

Reutilization of EDP equipment by the government was boosted, in part, by the increase in the amount of EDP equipment purchased, rather than leased, by the government beginning around 1963, when the GAO urged more extensive purchasing of EDP equipment. The percent of government-installed computer equipment that was purchased rose from 17.0 percent in 1962 to 21.3 percent in 1963, to 59.8 percent in 1969.[62] Reutilization was also facilitated by the general-purpose nature of the equipment, which by definition could be utilized in many different applications.

The reutilization program involved hundreds of millions of dollars. The acquisition cost of government ADP equipment transferred or reutilized during fiscal years 1965-70 totaled almost $563 million.[63] The GSA reported that between 1966 and 1970 the government realized cost reductions through reutilization of government-owned excess EDP equipment totaling over $330 million.[64] These savings, of course, came about because the reutilized equipment competed successfully with new equipment that the government would otherwise have acquired.[65]

Excess equipment that could not be reutilized efficiently within the federal government was disposed of elsewhere. Surplus government-owned equipment (including such unusual items as the guidance computer of the Minuteman I missile) was donated to approved recipients, such as state and local governments or educational institutions, or sold on the open market.[66]

The ADP Fund

The Brooks Bill authorized the establishment of a fund, the ADP Fund, to be managed by the GSA. GSA was authorized to "acquire excess government owned equipment and rent the equipment to agencies through the ADP Fund at rates which would ensure the continued solvency of the fund but which would be lower than the rates charged by suppliers."[67] The fund was "activated" in fiscal 1968 with an initial capitalization of $10 million in appropriations and an additional appropriation of $20 million in January 1971.[68]

The ADP Fund functioned as a leasing company for government agencies.[69] Because it was established without fiscal-year limitation, the fund could be used by certain federal agencies to enter into long-term leases (at reduced rentals) for EDP equipment in situations where their own budgetary or statutory constraints would prevent them from entering into a lease with a term beyond one year.[70]

The ADP Sharing Program

The reutilization program and the ADP Fund increased the extent to which federal agencies actively considered old equipment in competition with new computers they might otherwise have acquired. Such competition was further enhanced by the possible use of excess computer time in lieu of hardware acquisition. Where the GSA acted as an internal government computer broker/dealer and the ADP Fund as an internal government leasing company, the sharing of computer time created internal government service bureaus. As with service bureaus outside the government, this took two forms: the use of excess time on computers otherwise utilized by primary users, and the creation of data-processing centers with computers dedicated to the provision of time and services to a variety of users.[71] Such service bureaus provided users with further alternatives to hardware and software procurement.[72]

As with the other EDP-using activities of the government, the sharing of excess time was systematized under GSA following the Brooks Bill. There were substantial savings in avoiding the acquisition of additional EDP equipment or services. For fiscal 1966-70 such savings were estimated to total $250.8 million.[73]

Separate service bureau operations were also set up. GSA operated twelve federal data processing centers (financed through the ADP Fund) that offered the following services to government agencies and contractors: computer processing, systems design and programming, data conversion, and applications software.[74] In addition to these larger centers, a number of joint use centers were created "in which more than one agency with a data processing requirement joins together to do their work either by time-sharing or splitting shifts."[75]

MODULAR ACQUISITION AND INCREASING COMPETITION

As computer technology and applications changed, so did the ways in which users acquired and changed their computer systems. In the 1950s and early 1960s, customers installing their first systems typically acquired a complete system from a single supplier.[76] Because of the limited number of options and limited configuration possiblities of those systems, users who wanted to upgrade or significantly expand their computing capability typically acquired complete new systems.[77] During that time period, however, competitive necessity was ringing in a new order, and manufacturers were being forced to make their systems more and more modular. Withington described the process thus:

> As users' demands for . . . breadth of hardware functionality grew, the manufacturers attempting to compete were forced to maintain continuous developments of different modular types of equipment that could be configured together into models offered to the user. . . . This occurred in the late 1950s . . . perhaps 1958 through 1962.[78]

Customers were interested, for example, in having the option of moving to a larger central processing unit without reprogramming and without replacing all the other parts of their system:

> Through this process [of replacing and adding individual boxes without a single conversion] it would have evolved to a point where the computer system, both in terms of the individual machine model as entirely replaced, and the modes of use as changed, and the systems programs being replaced in a modular fashion along the way as well, has become entirely different. Thus, the beginning and the end point of the process are totally distinct, and yet at no one point in time would there have been a moment at which one could say: at this point the entire system changed from one to another.[79]

Whether or not a system offered that flexibility was one factor that users took into account in making procurement decisions.[80]

As we have seen, IBM responded first and most forcefully to this competitive impetus and reaped the greatest benefits from doing so. But as IBM and other systems suppliers accommodated users by making their product lines more modular, they also created opportunities for new competitors to begin marketing boxes directly against the individual boxes in those new computer systems, which now could be reconfigured at will.[81] Moreover, entry of such box suppliers was facilitated by their ability to tap the software support of the systems suppliers and copy the designs of their products. Thus, as James O'Neill of American Airlines testified:

> [In] the latter part of the Sixties and into the early part of the Seventies, and I will say from about 1966 through about 1973-74, manufacturers, . . . manufacturers other than IBM, started to develop and sell compatible tape drives, disk drives, printers that would operate with little conversion, although some conversion was involved, . . . on the IBM processors.
>
> That doesn't mean to say that the Honeywells and the Burroughs and the NCRs and the CDCs were not there, because they were also putting in their systems. But what happened was more choices became available.
>
> Ampex was selling memory, for instance; Calcomp [sic] was selling disk drives; Potter was selling tape drives.
>
> There were a number of alternatives that one could evaluate, which meant that they did not have to buy all their equipment from one manufacturer. . . .
>
> What that means is that we can get our data processing done at a lower cost.[82]

O'Neill continued:

> We [American Airlines] tend to buy boxes [rather than systems].
>
> . . . .

We can put together the pieces and pick and choose the best boxes at the lowest cost from the various manufacturers that are offering those boxes.[83]

Nor did the box competitors limit their focus to IBM. According to V. O. Wright, who was chairman of RCA's Peripheral Task Force in 1970, RCA performed a market survey and was both "surprised" at the amount of non-RCA equipment attached to its systems and "quite shocked" at the number of users who expressed an intention to attach non-RCA peripherals to RCA systems in the future.[84]

This was clearly a continuation of that trend . . . where many users who used to be really dependent upon one manufacturer for all of the boxes comprising a system, had learned that it was possible for them to achieve certain benefits by procuring and mixing boxes from different manufacturers in the same system. It was a continuation of that trend.[85]

The increasing trend toward modular replacement permeated the area of systems software as well. That trend, coupled with users' unslakable thirst for applications programming, triggered an explosion in the number of software suppliers during the latter half of the 1960s. In the meantime, leasing companies and service bureaus were also burgeoning, providing a host of new alternatives for users and increasing competitive pressures on hardware manufacturers.

For all of System/360's spectacular success, IBM could not match the growth of all these competitors. The expansion of EDP companies during the 1960s was astounding in both number and size. From 1961 through 1970 the number of companies reporting U.S. EDP revenues in Census II increased from 98 to 582.[86] Moreover, from 1961 through 1970 the U.S. EDP revenues of those companies, excluding IBM, grew from $796,386,000 to $6,820,225,000, an amazing compound growth rate of 27.1 percent per year. During those same years IBM's U.S. EDP revenues grew at an impressive, but considerably lower compound growth rate of 17.6 percent per year.[87] As a result, IBM's share of total U.S. EDP revenues fell: from 1961 to 1970 its share of the reported U.S. EDP revenues dropped dramatically from 51 percent to 34 percent.[88]

For IBM and other EDP companies, the influx of competitors during the 1960s required constant vigilance and a readiness to respond quickly with new and better products. Any other course would have amounted to going out of business. As GE's APL (advanced product line) "Master Plan" stated:

One of the key aspects of technology in the computer field is its high rate of obsolescence. Never in the history of technology has the pressure of competition and the lure of highly rewarding markets created such a dynamic evolution.[89]

PART III
THE 1970s

IBM IN
THE FIRST HALF OF
THE 1970s

The computer industry followed numerous multiple and interacting lines of technological development during the 1970s. While the emergence of IBM's System/370 at the beginning was perhaps the most important event at the time, many other significant technological developments and breakthroughs in machines, systems, software, applications, and organization appeared cumulatively throughout the decade. These included monolithic semiconductors and very large-scale integration, advanced communications technologies and time-sharing systems, minicomputer and super-mini systems, microprocessors, intelligent terminals, distributed data processing and networking, mass storage devices and very high-speed printers, plug-compatible processors, and data management service packages. This torrent of new developments is narrated primarily in terms of interrelated technological developments and new-product announcements, at the risk of unduly minimizing the broad consequences as perceived by commercial, governmental, and scientific users and others affected by them.

The story cannot be told exclusively in terms of IBM or only as it was seen by IBM. It is not easy to describe the complex events of the 1970s, which involved rival technological developments, actions, reactions, challenges, responses, quantum leaps, and occasional failures by IBM, its established system-supplier rivals, makers of particular elements of systems, new suppliers of products, and suppliers of services. The present chapter concentrates on IBM in the first half of the 1970s, beginning with the introduction of System/370 and proceeding to detail developments introduced by IBM in the next few years. Chapter 14 traces the development of the established systems suppliers in two phases: their reactions to the introduction of System/370 and their own contemporaneous product initiatives, and their later product and service evolution up to the end of the decade. Chapter 15 follows the evolution of the plug-compatible manufacturers (PCMs) that remained competitively active through most of the 1970s, and also surveys leasing companies. Chapter 16 details the development of new entrants of various types, and their contributions to and impacts on electronic data processing during the 1970s. Finally, Chapter

17 returns to IBM in the second half of the decade, and shows not only its reactions to the innovations of competitors detailed in earlier chapters but also some new product and service initiatives of its own. This organization is designed to illuminate both the lines of development and their interaction in the rivalry of the marketplace.

INTRODUCTION OF SYSTEM/370

IBM's System/360, introduced in the mid-1960s and enhanced and augmented by new products and programming during the second half of that decade, had been by any measure one of the most successful product lines in the history of American industry. As detailed above, deliveries of that line of equipment — in volumes unprecedented in the computer industry — transformed IBM into one of the largest and most successful companies in the world.

But by the end of the 1960s, IBM's position and growth in the industry were feeling the effects of obsolescence and of competitive pressures: pricing actions and product line enhancements and improvements from systems manufacturers; rapid introductions of "plug-compatible" peripheral equipment — particularly tape drives, disk drives, and memories — by Memorex, Telex, Ampex, and other companies; and the activities of leasing companies that had acquired large volumes of IBM-manufactured equipment from customers or directly from IBM, and were marketing that equipment on a variety of terms and conditions against the equipment IBM's sales force was marketing. Hence, despite the overwhelming market acceptance of its System/360 line, IBM's U.S. EDP revenues had peaked in 1968 and remained essentially flat through 1972. Over the same period, as measured by Census II, the U.S. EDP revenues of IBM's competitors almost doubled.[1]

Two other factors added to the competitive pressures on IBM at the beginning of the 1970s. First, by January 1970 IBM was implementing its "unbundling" announcement of June 1969, in which it announced the separate pricing of certain support services. Some of IBM's largest competitors, such as Sperry Univac and Honeywell, did not unbundle at that time because they saw competitive opportunities in remaining bundled.[2] Second, beginning in late 1969, the country slid into a serious recession. For a time the growth in demand for EDP products and services slowed; users became extremely cost-conscious. IBM was no exception. Both its lease rentals and its outright sales of computer products declined in 1970.[3]

On the other hand, users' increased concern with cost resulting from the recession aided some suppliers — those able to offer virtually identical products at lower prices than the System/360 components.[4]

The leveling of demand and the increased user concern with cutting EDP costs added to the pressure for price reductions and heightened the direct price competition among all suppliers of computer equipment and services, including IBM. That pressure became particularly visible when the federal government, the largest customer for computer products and services, increased its pressure for price competition among EDP suppliers. The Brooks Bill, passed by Congress in 1965, had given the General Services Administration authority over the federal government's procurements of general-purpose computer equipment and had given the Bureau of the Budget fiscal control over those procurements. Beginning in early 1970, the Bureau of the Budget required all federal agencies to consider peripheral equipment offered by independent peripheral manufacturers as well as peripheral equipment from systems manufacturers when cost savings could be achieved. In addition, in early 1971 the General Services Administration solicited proposals from over 300 suppliers for multiyear leases, with price discounts, for computer equipment.[5]

Setting the Stage

IBM had begun the planning for its new systems (NS) in the mid-1960s, even while the early System/360s were being shipped. Its management was planning for a staggered announcement of NS processors beginning in the second half of 1969. Those dates slipped, in large part because IBM's Merlin disk storage system — then in development — encountered technical difficulties and was not ready for announcement. Merlin was to be a major technological advance over the 2314, significantly faster and more reliable, and offering at least twice the storage density. Because IBM management considered Merlin to be critical to the competitive success of NS as a whole, the announcement of NS was delayed until Merlin was available.[6]

By June 1970 NS equipment — Merlin included — was ready and IBM began to announce the System/370 product line, starting with the largest processors, Models 165 and 155 (followed by the 145 and 135 in September 1970 and March 1971), and the Merlin disk file and its control unit, the IBM 3330 and 3838.

The System/370 line made the entire System/360 line obsolescent, and led to massive returns of leased System/360 equipment to IBM, which sharpened the effects of the recession on the firm.[7]

Model 155 and 165 Processors

The 155 and 165 CPUs and their high-performance channels were announced on June 30, 1970. Both processors were System/360-compatible, and hence were capable of being used with existing System/360 peripheral equipment and software.

The advantages of the 155 and 165 processors were largely in speed and memory capacity, which in turn permitted greater data handling and programming capabilities. The 155 processor used the "buffer" memory techniques first introduced by IBM with the 360/85 in 1968. It offered greatly improved internal speed: as much as four times that of the 360/50. The 155 also could accommodate up to 2 million bytes of main memory, compared with about 256 kilobytes on the 360/50 — a nearly eightfold increase in maximum memory capacity. The 370/155 Model H, with a main memory of 256 kilobytes, was priced only about 50 percent more than the 360/50 Model H, also with 256 kilobytes of main memory. Thus the user was offered an improvement in terms of internal processing speed per dollar of over 150 percent. Even comparing the higher-priced 370/155 Model J (with one megabyte of memory) with the 360/50 Model E (with 256 kilobytes), the improvement in internal processing speed per dollar was almost 90 percent.[8]

The 370/165 processor offered internal processing speed up to five times faster than that of the 360/65. The 370/165 Model J, with one megabyte of main memory, was priced only slightly higher than the 360/65 Model J, also with one megabyte of memory. That offered the user an improvement in internal processing speed per dollar of over 350 percent. The higher-priced 370/165 Model K, with two megabytes of memory, offered an improvement over the 360/65 Model J in internal processing speed per dollar of 280 percent. The main memory capacity of the 165 extended up to 3 million bytes, as compared with 1 million bytes on the Model 65, a threefold improvement in the maximum memory capacity. Also, the price of the main memory dropped by two-thirds.[9]

The 155 and 165 were not "virtual memory" processors; IBM's virtual memory systems control programming was not ready for announcement in 1970. However, the 155 and 165, with some additional hardware, as well as the later 370/145 and 370/135 processors as originally shipped, were equipped to accept virtual memory control when the software became ready. (The virtual memory announcements of August 1972 are described below.)

IBM 3330/3830 Disk Subsystem

IBM's forecast assumptions for the 3330/3830 disk subsystem indicated that by 1970 many of its system, plug-compatible, and leasing company competitors were offering disk devices that were highly competitive with the existing 2311 and 2314 products.[10]

The 3330/3830 disk drive and control unit, as announced, represented a major technological and price/performance improvement over those existing disk subsystems. The 3330's data transfer rate was two and a half times that of the 2314, and the storage capacity per disk spindle was more than three times greater.

The 3330's combination of a voice coil actuator and a new track-following "servo" system was a major innovation. Also, for the first time in the industry the disk drive control unit was programmable and contained sufficient processing and storage capability to permit the subsystem itself to execute extensive error detection and correction, and to take over various control functions otherwise performed by the CPU and/or its channels. In addition, the 3830 control unit included IBM's innovation of a writable control store consisting of a disk cartridge housed within the unit to load and store control and diagnostic programs.[11]

IBM 3211 Printer

Together with the 370/155 and 370/165 processors and the 3330, IBM announced a new high-speed printer, the 3211. This printer used improved versions of the "train" printing technologies of the popular 1403 printers.[12] The 3211 was capable of printing 2,000 lines per minute, compared with about 1,100 lines per minute for the 1403-N1 provided with System/360.[13]

IBM System/370 Model 145 Processor, the IFA, and the 2319 Disk

In September 1970 IBM announced the System/370 Model 145 processor, the first processor in the computer industry to be offered with main memory made exclusively with the new monolithic semiconductor technology. The internal performance of the 370/145 was up to five times that of the 360/40, although the 370/145 Model H was priced only about 26 percent higher than the 360/40 Model H, both with 256 kilobytes of memory. Thus, the 370/145H offered an improvement in internal processing speed per dollar of almost 300 percent over the 360/40H. In addition, the 145 offered up to 500,000 bytes of main memory, while the Model 40 had a maximum capacity of 250,000 bytes of main memory.[14]

The use of monolithic semiconductor memory in the 370/145 represented a significant technological step, and was a direct result of IBM's earlier decision to shift memory development away from magnetic core technology and into semiconductor technologies.

The 145 could be used with the 3330/3830 disk subsystem. But, with the 145 processor, IBM also announced a low-priced optional integrated file adapter (IFA). The IFA consisted of disk control electronics that were integrated into the cabinet of the 145 processor and could control a maximum of eight 2314/ 2319 disk spindles (totaling 233 million bytes of storage); with that limit the IFA eliminated the need for separate, more costly disk control units. The IFA was priced at less than half the rental price of the control unit used with IBM's 2314 disk drives. With the IFA, as noted above (Chapter 11), IBM also announced the 2319 drive, which was essentially a repackaged, price-reduced, three-disk spindle version of the successful 2314 disk drive family.[15] The combination of the lower-priced 2319 and the IFA gave IBM a competitive disk offering for smaller 145-based systems, and at the same time made its disk products more competitive with those of the plug-compatible manufacturers.[16]

IBM was able to offer the 2319 drives at a lower rental for the three-spindle configuration than the 2314 at least in part because it expected to reuse returned 2314 drives, which it modified with the addition of new control electronics.[17]

IBM 3420 Tape Subsystem

In November 1970 IBM introduced the Aspen tape subsystem, which consisted of the IBM 3420 Models 3, 5, and 7 tape drives and the 3803 control unit. This new subsystem could be used with 360 as well as 370 systems. IBM's announcement of this product came at a time when it was facing stiff competition in tape products from plug-compatible equipment manufacturers and from systems vendors. During 1969 and 1970 over 20 companies announced a total of 30 to 40 tape systems, promising better price/performance than IBM's current tape product line.[18]

The new 3420/3803 subsystem gave IBM a lower-priced tape offering and embodied significant innovations in reliability and performance. As already said, the Aspen project had been under way within IBM for about four years, under different code names. One of the original goals of that program was a quadrupling of the recording densities on the magnetic tape. That goal was not achieved until 1973.[19]

IBM 2319B and Disk Price Reductions

In December 1970 IBM announced the 2319 B disk drive. The original 2319, announced for use on the 370/145, was renamed the 2319A. The 2319B was not, strictly speaking, a System/370 announcement. The 2319B drives were offered for attachment to System/360, although they were capable of being upgraded to 2319A drives in the field, and as such could be used with System/370 systems equipped with IFAs, if users chose to install the newer IBM equipment. Like the original 2319, the 2319B reused 2314 disk spindles. With the 2319B IBM offered its System/360 users the same price-reduced disk drives — reduced compared with prices of 2314 drives — that it was offering to its System/370 users with the 2319A: a monthly rental price of roughly $1,000 for three disk spindles.[20]

Also in December 1970 IBM further reduced prices for its disk storage products by eliminating "additional use" charges for IBM 2314, 2319, and 3330 disk drives.[21] Those charges had been made for additional hours of use above the number included in the basic rental contract for the equipment.

System/370 Model 135 Processor

In March 1971 IBM announced what was then the smallest member of the System/370 family: the Model 135 processor, which was compatible with System/360 programming and was capable of using System/360 and 370 peripheral equipment, including the 3330 and the 2319/IFA.

This processor was two to four and a half times faster than the System/360 Model 30. The 370/135 Model FE, with 96 kilobytes of main memory, for example, was priced less than 50 percent above the 360/30 Model F, with 62 kilobytes of memory. Thus, the 370/135FE offered the user an improvement in internal processing speed per dollar of almost 220 percent over the 360/30F. Even the 370/135 Model DH, with almost four times the main memory of the 360/30F, offered an improvement in internal processing speed per dollar of over 100 percent. The 370/135's memory, like that on the 145 processor, was monolithic semiconductor rather than the older core memory technology. Moreover, the 370/135 offered up to roughly four times the memory capacity available on the Model 30.[22]

IBM 3270 Terminal Subsystem

In May 1971 IBM announced a new family of terminal subsystems, the IBM 3270, which included terminal displays and printers, and controllers for the subsystem. The 3270 was IBM's first major CRT (cathode-ray tube) or display terminal announcement since 1965, when the 2260 terminals were announced. In the intervening years display terminals had become an increasingly attractive alternative method for computer output and input: unlike computer-roombound printers, consoles, and card readers, display terminal equipment could be located closer to where data were created, and could be used to enter and display or print data in a form directly readable by the ultimate user, rather than requiring that user to go to a computer room and deliver card decks or pick up computer printouts. A number of manufacturers had begun offering display terminal equipment for use in computer systems during the 1960s and early 1970s.

The 3270 display system could be used as part of System/360 or System/370 computer systems and could handle a variety of on-line information-processing applications, including data base inquiry, data entry, transaction processing, and on-line programming — either attached locally or via remote communications links.

The 3270 systems, however, were still essentially "dumb" terminals, in the sense that little, if any, processing and storage were performed in this peripheral equipment, rather than in the system's main processing and storage equipment. Hence, this terminal announcement may be looked upon as a continuation of a "centralized" approach to data processing in which, in systems using the 3270, storage, control, and processing remained largely in the other equipment. As we shall see, in the late 1960s and early 1970s other suppliers in the computer industry, particularly Burroughs, Data 100, and Four Phase, were already introducing equipment capable of substantial "distributed" processing and storage.

IBM's Fixed-Term Plan

Also in May 1971 IBM announced an optional lease plan for several of its System/370 and System/360 peripheral products. The Fixed-Term Plan (FTP) eliminated any remaining extra shift usage charges, and provided an 8 or 16 percent discount from IBM's monthly rental rates for customers who chose the plan's one- or two-year leases.

Through the 1950s and 1960s IBM had offered its computer equipment under either purchase contracts or rental agreements generally cancelable by customers on 30 days' notice. During the 1960s, however, some of IBM's competitors had begun offering longer-term lease plans ranging from one to seven or more years, and discounts to computer customers who agreed to commit themselves for longer periods. Those competitors included systems manufacturers, plug-compatible peripheral manufacturers, and leasing companies. And, as noted, in the spring of 1971 the GSA formally requested proposals for firm multiyear leases for computer equipment, at discounted prices. Thus, IBM's largest customer was soliciting specific terms and conditions not then available from IBM but offered by most, if not all, of its competitors. By early 1971 IBM's other customers were becoming quite vocal about their desires for long-term leases.[23]

Another significant impetus for introducing a fixed-term lease plan with discounts was IBM's continuing losses to plug-compatible peripheral manufacturers and leasing companies, both of which were marketing PCM equipment with those kinds of leases. By early 1971 PCMs were replacing IBM 2314-type disk drives at the rate of over 1,000 spindles per month. At that rate IBM's intallations of 2314-type disk drives would have reached zero by mid-1973.[24]

By May 1971 IBM forecasters projected that, in the absence of an IBM fixed-term lease with rental rate reductions, PCMs would have replaced essentially all of its 2314 and 2319 disk products and all but 12 percent of its new 3330 disk drives by 1975. In that month IBM announced FTP for its disks and tapes and their control units, as well as for printers, data cells, and magnetic drums and their controllers.[25]

When IBM's top management decided to introduce the company's first term lease plan on these products in 1971, it expected that term leases of some kind would ultimately be offered with all the company's data-processing products. And, in fact, IBM later offered such lease plans for virtually every computer product it markets.[26]

On the same day FTP was announced, May 27, 1971, IBM announced purchase price decreases of approximately 15 percent, effective June 1, for most disk, tape, and printer products, and their associated control units. Among those products were the 3330/3380 disk subsystem; 3211 printer; 2314, 2319A, and 2319B disks; and the 3420/3820 tape subsystem.[27] Other manufacturers quickly followed suit.

SYSTEM/370 DEVELOPMENTS, 1972-74, AND NOTES ON SOME COMPETITIVE REACTIONS

While IBM was making the first volume shipments of the System/370 products announced in the first 18 months of the 1970s, it continued to develop newer equipment and programming for the System/370 line.

3705 Communications Controller

In March 1972 IBM announced the 3705 programmable communications controller, which was made available under the Extended-Term Plan (ETP), as well as under the regular purchase and rental contracts. (Announced in March 1972, the ETP was a two-year rental plan that applied to certain peripheral products and provided for about a 15 percent discount from the monthly rates.) The 3705 replaced IBM's earlier 270X line of communications controllers, originally announced in the mid-1960s. Those earlier controllers were not programmable and, hence, did not offer the flexibility of the 3705, which could act as preprocessor to large host systems.[28] By 1972 other firms, such as Comten, Honeywell, Data General, and Modcomp, were offering programmable communications controllers (or front-end processors) superior to the IBM 270X multiplexors, usually at lower prices.[29]

The 3705 could emulate the 270X line or operate in native mode under IBM's new Network Control Program (NCP). In either mode the 3705 was more cost-effective than the 270X line, and it could handle a greater number of and more varied communications lines. And when operating under NCP, it relieved the CPU of many teleprocessing tasks, supported a wide range of terminals and functions (including the processing and translation of data as it passed from the network to the host processor), and increased the overall flexibility of the system.[30]

In February 1973 IBM announced the 3704, a programmable communications controller that was smaller than, though compatible with, the 3705.

158/168 Processors: FET Memory

The 158 and 168 processors, announced in August 1972, were designed with advanced semiconductor memory, called field effect transistor (FET) memory. Because FET semiconductor devices generally required fewer process steps to fabricate, and offered higher circuit densities than the bipolar semiconductor memory used on the 135 and 145, they were less expensive to manufacture than bipolar devices, though bipolar circuits could operate at higher speeds. Moreover, with those products IBM was able to achieve in its larger processors the economies of a single integrated package for logic and memory circuitry.

Significant advantages in price and performance were achieved with the 158 and 168. The internal speed of the 158 was 20 to 40 percent faster than that of the 155. With main memory of one megabyte, the 158 cost only 15 to 20 percent more than the 155, giving the customer an effective improvement in internal processing speed per dollar of up to 20 percent, without taking into account such additional features and capabilities as virtual storage. The 168 offered as much as 30 percent faster internal performance than the 165. They had a maximum main memory of three megabytes for the 165 and four megabytes for the 168, but about the same purchase and monthly rental prices, so that the customer was offered an improvement in internal processing speed per dollar of up to 30 percent.[31]

A major advantage of FET memory, as installed on the 158 and 168 processors, was its compactness. The 155 and 165 processors' main core memory had to be housed in separate boxes, each holding up to 500,000 bytes of memory storage capactiy. Since the maximum memory size of the 155 was 2 million bytes and the maximum size of the 165 was 3 million bytes, up to four of these separate memory boxes could be required with the 155 and up to six with the 165. By comparison, the memory circuits for the 158 and 168, at announcement, were one-fortieth as large, five times more reliable, used one-seventh as much power, and cost half as much to manufacture as the core memories used in the 155 and 165 processors. In addition, by 1973, when the 158 and 168 processors were first being shipped to customers, IBM had doubled the density of each memory chip. Thus, as shipped, the 158 and 168 FET memory was only one-eightieth as large as the core memory of the 155 and 165.[32]

The faster FET memory, at lower cost to the user, contributed to an unprecedented demand for add-on main memory capacity on IBM's computer systems. Whereas the average amount of add-on memory marketed to users of the System/360 Model 65 was half a megabyte, the average add-on for the 370/168 was estimated in 1975 at five and a half megabytes.[33]

Virtual Memory Operating Systems

All new System/370 processors could use the new virtual memory capability. (The predecessors of System/370 Models 158 and 168, the Model 155 and 165 processors announced in June 1970, had included the option of Dynamic Address Translation [DAT] hardware, which permitted those processors to function as virtual memory machines.) Virtual memory, or virtual storage, as it is sometimes called, is a combination of hardware and software that provides EDP users with an apparent main memory capacity substantially greater than the actual main memory capacity of their systems. The system automatically handles the "overhead" of memory allocation. Virtual memory made a System/370 processor appear to the user to have 16 million bytes of memory when, in fact, it could have as little as 130,000 actual bytes of memory.[34]

Virtual storage in various forms had been introduced during the 1960s by Burroughs, GE, CDC, RCA, and others – including IBM; but these early virtual memory offerings encountered difficulties of various kinds. IBM's virtual memory announcement built upon its experience derived from the System 360 Model 67/TSS program of the 1960s. In that program IBM also encountered unexpected difficulties, and even considered abandoning it entirely in late 1966. In the end, its decision to continue the Model 67 program and to push development of "relocate" hardware and programming technologies contributed to the success of the virtual storage announced in 1972.

The New Attachment Strategy

IBM's August 1972 announcement also included a new disk control unit, the 3830 Model II, and an optional integrated storage control (ISC) feature for the 145, 158, and 168 processors that permitted attachment of 3330 disk drives. IBM also announced an integrated file adapter (IFA) to handle 3330 disk drives on Model 135 processors.[35]

In these disk control hardware announcements, IBM retained the interface between controller and processor that had been used on System/360. Hence IBM designers — or, for that matter, designers of competitors' plug-compatible disk subsystems — could continue to design products (such as controllers) to attach to that channel interface. An advantage to IBM of the "new attachment strategy," however, lay in its creation of a single disk-drive-to-control-function interface for new disk products and processors, whether those processors were used with integrated controllers or with separate control units. In the past most IBM disk drive products had different and unique interfaces, and thus rquired different control units. The new attachment strategy created a single interface that permitted the use of a single disk control unit, the 3830 Model II, for the 370 disk drives. Suppliers of plug-compatible disk drives had to redesign the interface if those drives were to connect to the new IBM controllers. The new single interface was also used in the integrated controllers for IBM 370 processors. Hence, IBM's 3330 and the later 3340, 3344, 3350, and 3370 disk drives and the IBM 3850 mass storage subsystem all utilized the new interface.[36]

IBM System/370 Models 125 and 115

In October 1972 IBM announced the System/370 Model 125 and, in March 1973, the System/370 Model 115. These smaller members of the 370 family offered virtual memory and monolithic memory technology. The 125 provided approximately two to four and a half times the internal speed of a System/360 Model 25, and one and one-third to three times the speed of the Model 22. The 115 offered approximately one and a half to three times the internal speed of a System/360 Model 25, and up to one and a half times the speed of a System/360 Model 22. The 115 and 125 were compatible with the larger 370 processors (unlike the earlier System/360 Model 20, which was not compatible with the larger System/360 processors). At the same time IBM announced its 3330 Model 2, a one-spindle version of the 3330, and a new 3340 disk drive for the Model 115.[37]

The plans for the 115 and 125 processors had originally included a selector channel that would have permitted attachment of all of the high-speed peripherals that were attachable to selector channels on the older System/360 processors. However, IBM ultimately worked out a plan for "native" attachment of its disk and tape drives, thereby reducing development expense. At the same time it reduced the operating speed of the byte multiplexor or slow-speed attachment channel on the 115 and 125. Both of these decisions required redesign of existing peripheral devices before they could be used with these CPUs.[38]

Term Lease Plan

In March 1973 IBM announced the Term Lease Plan (TLP), an optional four-year, fixed-term lease for virtual memory System/370 processors. It eliminated additional use charges on the processors and memory, and offered users 48 months of price protection, plus the right to accrue rentals of up to 50 percent toward the purchase price of the processor.[39] TLP was IBM's first longer-term lease on processors, although such terms and conditions were already common among its system and leasing company competitors. In June 1976 IBM modified TLP to offer roughly a 9 percent price reduction of the monthly rental charge under the plan.

1973 Disk and Tape Subsystem Announcements

In 1973 IBM made three major product announcements in computer storage: the 3420 Models 4, 6, and 8 tape drives (internally called Birch), the 3340 disk drive (internally known as Winchester), and the 3330 Model 11 disk drive (Iceberg).

Birch

The 3420 Models 4, 6, and 8 tape drives, announced in March 1973, represented nearly a fourfold increase in storage density over any tape drive in the computer industry.[40]

Winchester

Also in March 1973 IBM announced the 3340, or Winchester, disk drive. It was a high-performance, intermediate-capacity disk storage device that introduced the 3348 data module, which combined in one removable sealed unit both the disk surfaces and the read/write heads. In disk drives with removable disk packs, there was danger of errors when different packs were used on different drives; costly mechanisms and tolerances had to be built into the equipment to prevent such errors from occurring. The use of the data module gave the disk drive greater reliability at lower cost, because the same disk heads would always read and write data on the same disk surfaces. It also reduced the danger of contamination of the disk surface. In addition, the 3340 featured a new low-mass read/write head assembly that eliminated the need for much of the hardware that had previously been used to keep heavier heads from coming into contact with and destroying disk surfaces.[41]

Iceberg

In July 1973 IBM announced a double-capacity version of its 3330 disk drive, the 3330 Model 11, with 200 million bytes of storage per spindle, compared with 100 million on the original 3330. The density of the tracks was almost doubled from 192 per inch on the 3330 to 370 per inch on the 3330 Model 11. IBM was able to increase the recording densities because of its development of a new disk coating process called "zapping" that allowed the head to fly lower on the disk surface.[42]

In 1970-73, as noted subsequently, there were numerous competitive disk subsystem developments. Vendors including Ampex, CalComp, CDC, Marshall, Memorex, and Telex announced double-density versions of the 2314. Firms announcing equivalents of the 3330 Merlin included Memorex, Century Data Systems, Potter, Telex, CDC, Ampex, Itel, and STC. STC, Memorex, and Cal-Comp delivered 3330-compatible products within eight months of IBM's first 3330 Model 11 shipment, and Itel (through ISS) went into full production and shipment within one year.

IBM 3600 Terminal Subsystems

During the second half of 1973 IBM announced a series of terminal sub-systems, the IBM 3600, 3650, and 3660. These subsystems were designed to perform input and output as well as a range of additional storage and processing functions commonly needed in specific industries: banks and other financial institutions, retail stores, supermarkets, and insurance companies. Each operated as part of IBM 370 computer systems.

These terminal subsystems were IBM's first major industry-oriented ter-minals since the announcement of the 3670 brokerage communications system in September 1971. The subsystems operated to bring the power of a System/ 370 processor directly to the point where a customer's data were created, whether the source was a bank deposit or a supermarket purchase. Through their use information could be captured, translated into machine-readable form, and processed or stored for subsequent additional processing. The supermarket terminal, for example, was able to read data (prices) directly off grocery items marked with the Universal Product Code, compute totals, print out a sales slip, and forward information to the terminal controllers for storage and pro-cessing in those controllers or for entry into larger processors located else-where.[43]

Other companies introduced industry-oriented terminal subsystems, with substantial remote processing capability, at the same time as or before IBM announced its 3600 line. For example, in 1970 NCR introduced its 280 Retail System, which included an intelligent terminal, input-output equipment, data storage and communications hardware, and software permitting the subsystem to operate as part of NCR computer systems. The following year it introduced its 270 Financial System, which performed on-line bank teller transactions, linked directly to central processors. By 1973 National Semiconductor was offering its Datachecker, a point-of-sale terminal system for the retail industry. It provided electronic registers and scales for each checkout stand plus a micro-computer and disk storage.[44]

System/3 Model 15

In July 1973 IBM announced the System/3 Model 15, a more powerful model of the System/3 computers.[45] The Model 15 offered a variety of software capabilities, including RPG, COBOL, FORTRAN, and a Communication Control Program for handling communications applications. It also offered greater on-line disk capacity. By 1973 IBM had added control programming to its System/3 line to permit the various models not only to be used as stand-alone systems but also to be linked to other processors in a larger 370 system.

IBM 3850 Mass Storage Subsystem

In October 1974 IBM announced the 3850 mass storage subsystem for use with System/370 processors above the Model 135. The 3850 was a "mass" storage device because it was capable of storing, under the control of a single control unit, 472 billion bytes of data that could, in turn, be accessed by as many as four different System/370 processors at any one time. That volume of data, on-line and available to processors through a single control unit, was a quantum jump in the amount of on-line data available. By comparison, the IBM 2314 direct access storage facility, an advanced disk drive system when it was announced in 1965, held about 200 million bytes of data. The IBM 3330 Model 11 disk subsystem, which appeared in 1973, was capable of storing about 6.4 billion bytes of data under a single control unit.[46] And the IBM 3420 Model 4, 6, and 8 tape subsystem, also announced in 1973, was capable of storing about 1.3 billion bytes of data under a single control unit that could handle eight tape drives.

The 3850 mass storage subsystem used an IBM 3330 disk storage device in combination with an innovative "honeycomb" of new magnetic tape media. Electromechanical devices accessed the information and read it onto the disks for processing. The information was "staged" — that is, taken from the magnetic strips within the 3850's cartridges to a disk subsystem and then from the disks to the CPU. In this way vast amounts of information could be stored and retrieved under the control of the computer within seconds, without the need for anyone to select, mount, and unmount reels of tape. The advantage of the 3850 was that it combined some of the benefits of disk storage with some of the benefits of tape storage: rapid access, automatic control, very large capacity, and a low unit cost.[47]

Within a year after IBM's announcement of the 3850, CDC announced its 38500, equivalent to the 3850 and capable of storing up to 16 billion bytes. CDC marketed the 38500 to users of IBM System/370 computer systems, to other systems manufacturers, and for use with its own computer systems. The CDC machine was different from the IBM machine in that it did not use the rotating head, diagonal stripe recording mechanism and did not automatically stage the information from tape to disk.[48]

Other competitors also offered "mass storage" devices in competition with IBM's 3850 or other tape and disk subsystem products. For example, in October 1973 Storage Technology Corporation (STC) announced its 8000 series Super Disks, with a capacity of 800 million bytes of information per module. STC marketed the Super Disk in combination with its high-performance tape subsystem as an alternative to IBM 3850 and other mass storage devices.[49]

In 1974 CalComp began marketing an "automated tape library" after acquiring the Xytex Corporation, the company that developed the device. The "automated tape library" permitted the automatic mounting and dismounting of magnetic tape reels on as many as 32 tape drives under the control of a host computer. The library could store up to 7,000 reels of tape. Much later, in June 1979, the trade press reported that a joint venture of Japanese firms had introduced a mass storage system designed to replace the IBM 3850. As reported, that system consisted of a mass storage device, a disk control device, and a disk drive.[50]

Antitrust Developments

A private antitrust suit was filed by CDC against IBM in 1968.[51] The CDC suit was settled out of court in 1973.[52] As part of the settlement CDC obtained the Service Bureau Corporation (SBC) from IBM for SBC's net worth as of December 31, 1972 (approximately $16 million), and IBM withdrew from the "data services" business in the United States for a period of six years.[53]

Meanwhile, a rash of other private antitrust cases were filed, principally the following:

Greyhound v. *IBM*, 1969[54]

Telex v. *IBM*, 1972[55]

CalComp v. *IBM*, 1973[56]

Hudson v. *IBM*, 1973[57]

Marshall v. *IBM*, 1973[58]

Memorex v. *IBM*, 1973[59]

Transamerica v. *IBM*, 1973[60]

Forro v. *IBM*, 1974[61]

Memory Tech v. *IBM*, 1974[62]

Sanders v. *IBM*, 1975[63]

Some of these plaintiffs (Greyhound, Hudson, and Transamerica) were leasing companies; other (Memorex, CalComp, Telex) were manufacturers of plug-compatible equipment. Most cited several of IBM's practices, policies, and decisions mentioned earlier in this chapter as factors contributing to alleged competitive injury — notably the New Attachment Strategy, the IFA, the disk drives 2319A and B, the elimination of the selector channel on the 115 and 125 CPUs, the Fixed-Term Plan, and changing ratios between purchase and lease prices on IBM equipment.

These private suits were variously decided or settled throughout the 1970s. Nine additional minor ones not listed above were also settled or dismissed. To avoid fragmenting the discussion, we shall summarize these developments in Chapter 17.

The trial in the government case, *U.S.* v. *IBM*, which had been filed in January 1969,[64] began in May 1975. The outcome of that case was mentioned in Chapter 1.

ACTIONS AND REACTIONS OF OTHER COMPUTER SYSTEMS MANUFACTURERS IN THE 1970s

FIRST PHASE, 1970-73

A number of established computer systems manufacturers introduced new computer lines of their own and also reduced prices or enhanced the performance of their existing lines in the early 1970s, partly in response to IBM's initial announcements of its System/370.

Burroughs

In October 1970, four months after IBM's System/370 Model 155 and 165 announcements and less than a month after the 370/145 announcement, Burroughs formally announced a new family of computers, the 700 System, including the B 5700, B 6700, and B 7700 series — all of which had monolithic integrated circuitry. As part of the initial 700 System announcement, Burroughs also introduced new disk subsystems, including an IBM 3330-type, to be manufactured by Century Data Systems.[1]

A year later Burroughs added the B 4700 to its 700 family, and in June 1972 it announced the lower-cost, lower-performance B 1700. B 1700 systems were marketed as replacement products for, among others, IBM System/360 Model 20 and System/3 computer systems. IBM's new low-end System/370 processor, the 370/115, was not announced until March 1973.[2]

In the fall of 1970, at approximately the same time as its original 700 System announcement, Burroughs brought out new processors in its Series L minicomputer line, originally introduced in early 1969. It described the Series L line in 1970 as "advanced, self-contained systems designed to handle the multitude of medium-sized data processing tasks which face most businesses." The series was, according to Burroughs' chairman, a "COBOL machine," and represented product offerings from Burroughs ". . . to respond to the needs of users, either an individual user that is a relatively small company, or small operation, or the small operation of a large organization."[3] The announcement of one of the new Series L machines, the L 5000, included 48 standard application programs for such areas as manufacturing, contracting, finance, hospitals, and government.

During 1971 and 1972 Burroughs announced larger, more advanced members of the Series L line: the L 7000 and L 8000 series, which offered up to 40 times the processing speed of the earlier Series L computers.[4]

In a "common development program" with the Series L, Burroughs continued to develop its intelligent terminal products, the Series TC "terminal computers," first introduced in 1967. In 1970 Burroughs described these products as ". . . one of the most successful product families Burroughs has ever introduced. They are designed to operate as remote data communications terminals functioning on-line to a central computer system, or as self-contained, off-line systems."[5] Those terminal products contained a significant amount of processing and storage capability. In 1970 two new models of the Series TC line were introduced, increasing the range of applications that could be handled by the TC family of terminal computers. John L. Jones of Southern Railway made the following observations on the significance of the Burroughs TC line:

> I wanted to point out for the Court that this equipment was installed in 1970, and that, to my knowledge at least particularly on Southern Railway Company, was one of the first times that processing began to migrate, I will say, out of the main processor into the peripheral devices. For example, because of the programmable nature of the Burroughs TC 500, there were certain formats and edits which had been made and checked previously in the main processor, which we now took and moved and put in the Burroughs TC 500 itself.
>
> That made eminent good sense, because now, as the operator was keying to that device, if an error was made of a type of the changes that we had made, the device itself, the processor in the TC 500 itself, would stop the operator and indicate the nature of the error immediately, but long before in the prior system the data would have had to go through the central processor, be checked, and then sent back again.
>
> So I wanted to point out this was the start of the concept of the distributed process in Southern Railway Company. . . .[6]

After a recession-induced slowdown in 1971, Burroughs' worldwide corporate revenues increased in 1972 to just over $1 billion, for the first time in the corporation's history. Electronic data-processing (EDP) systems and products, including business minicomputers, showed the fastest growth. The company's U.S. EDP revenues in 1972 were over $471 million. New orders for EDP systems and products, including business minicomputers, increased another 27 percent in 1973.[7]

Control Data

CDC had been one of the spectacular success stories of the 1950s and 1960s. In 1970 it was making initial shipments of several of its newer processors, including the CDC 6700 and 6200. In the early 1970s CDC announced more new products.

In September 1970 CDC announced the development of the Star 100, which it claimed could handle 100 million instructions per second; however, this machine did not meet performance or schedule expectations and, after delivery of only three systems, was discontinued in 1974.[8]

In March 1971 CDC announced a new family of computers, the Cyber 70 series. The Cyber 70 offered price/performance improvements over CDC's existing products, including the 6200, 6400, 6600, and 7600 computer systems, and was designed for a broad range of industrial, financial, and institutional applications.[9]

As already noted, by 1970 CDC had become quite active in producing peripheral equipment for other manufacturers (the OEM business). In 1972 it was probably the largest OEM supplier of peripheral products, selling to as many as 150 other computer system manufacturers and systems integrators.[10] Beginning in 1970, CDC added to those activities the marketing of IBM plug-compatible peripheral devices (the PCM business.) Its first major offering was the 23141 disk subsystem, designed as a plug-compatible replacement for IBM's 2314; it was marketed directly to IBM end users. In early 1971 CDC entered into an agreement with Telex to manufacture 3330-type disk drives, which Telex would market with its control units to IBM end users. CDC also began marketing an IBM-compatible add-on memory manufactured by Fabri-Tek.

Following IBM's FTP announcement in May 1971, CDC announced a variety of new lease options to users both of CDC's own EDP equipment and of its IBM plug-compatible equipment lines. It countered the IBM two-year lease with a three-year lease plan offering a 15 percent reduction.[12]

In 1971 CDC announced a "double density" 2314-type disk subsystem. It marketed this product both on a plug-compatible basis, as the 23122, to users of IBM computer systems and on an OEM basis, as the 9742, to such customers as Siemens, ICL, CII, XDS, and Telex. It was highly successful in both types of use.[13]

CDC encountered some problems with other new IBM plug-compatible products. Although there was good market acceptance for the 23141 subsystem, profitability was low because Control Data was late to market. Also, CDC's initial 3330-type drives were unacceptable to Telex, and their OEM deal was canceled. CDC experienced similar problems with the memories supplied to Fabri-Tek for attachment to 360/50 and 360/65.[14]

In 1972-73, however, CDC made a corporate decision to expand its product lines of IBM plug-compatible peripherals. Hence, in 1973 it announced new IBM plug-compatible semiconductor memory equipment, this time manufactured principally by AMS.[15]

From a financial viewpoint, CDC's computer business ended years of outstanding growth with a recorded $46 million loss in the recession year 1970, said to be due to poor computer business operation, including some year-end adjustments and write-offs of unsuccessful ventures. But by 1972 its business had returned to a profitable course.[16]

Digital Equipment

By 1970 DEC had grown into a company with over $130 million in revenues and was manufacturing several lines of computer systems.

In January it introduced a new family of computers, the PDP 11. Two models were announced: the 11/15 and 11/20. Within six months DEC had received over 500 orders, and by August 1971 had installed more than 1,200 PDP 11 systems worldwide. It enhanced the line in late 1970, and throughout 1971 and later, adding processors (including the 11/10, 11/40, and 11/45), peripherals, and software, then cutting prices in 1972. Also in 1972 DEC announced a version of the PDP 11, the Datasystem 500, with a separate type of packaging for business data processing.[17]

The PDP 11 family, including, in those years, the PDP 11/45, could be configured into systems that were offered in competition with products ranging from the IBM 1130, System/3, and System/7 systems to the lower end of the 360 and 370 series. The range of "representative applications" for the PDP 11 family included business data processing, real-time data collection and instructional computing, industrial control, commercial typesetting, and data communications. The larger PDP 11 systems, such as the 11/40 and 11/45, were marketed in competition with IBM's System/360 and 370 systems, both as one-for-one competitive alternatives and in configurations including DEC's larger PDP 10 equipment, which had been announced in the 1960s. In those larger systems the PDP 11 might function as an intelligent terminal, giving users remote from the central computer installation substantial local processing capability.[18]

In the early 1970s DEC continued to enhance its successful PDP 8 line, first introduced in 1964. Those enhancements included the announcement of the Datasystem 300, for business data processing. Hence, in the opening years of the 1970s the PDP 8 line was being marketed to a wider variety of customers, including "communications customers, business data processing customers, newspaper typesetting customers."[19] The PDP 8 computers were offered in competition with a variety of IBM equipment, including the System/3 and 360 and 370 systems.

In September 1971 DEC announced a series of large-scale systems called the DECsystem 10. It announced five DECsystem 10 processors with configurations ranging in purchase price from roughly $390,000 to $2 million. The systems were, according to an IBM analysis sent to corporate headquarters, direct competitors of the IBM System/370 Model 135 through Model 165.[20] The DECsystem 10 was based on DEC's PDP 10 processor. The COBOL programming language and certain additional peripheral equipment and software, enhancing the system's batch processing capabilities, were added to the PDP 10 to make it more successful in the business data-processing marketplace. DEC adopted the "DECsystem 10" nomenclature in order to give the machines a new marketing emphasis.[21]

In 1970 DEC's worldwide revenues were roughly $135 million; by 1972 they were $187.5 million. Its domestic EDP revenues in that year were about $140 million.[22]

Honeywell

During 1970 Honeywell announced and completed its acquisition of a large part of GE's worldwide computer manufacturing and marketing organizations. For the full year 1970 Honeywell Information System (HIS), the company's major computer subsidiary, had revenues of $859 million, which represented a 13 percent increase over the combined data-processing revenues of GE and Honeywell in the preceding year.[23] In its 1970 Annual Report Honeywell emphasized that successful merger of GE's computer business had added growth that otherwise would have required at least five years.[24]

In February 1971 HIS announced the 6000 series, a family of systems with six different processors that offered improved performance over the older GE 600 line and improved peripherals, including newer disk subsystems of the IBM 3330 and 2319 type, tape subsystems, communications controllers, and display terminals. The 6000 series utilized GE's existing operating system software (GECOS), developed originally for the GE 600 family. Orders for the 6000 series quickly exceeded Honeywell's expectations, according to the company's Annual Report, and significant new customers were won in the U.S. government for the series, with over 45 systems shipped or ordered in 1972-73. During 1972 the main memory capacity of these systems was quadrupled.[25]

In January 1972 Honeywell introduced a second major new product line, the 2000 series, to replace its older H200 series, which had been so successful in the 1960s. The 2020 and 2030 were directly responsive to the new products of Burroughs and IBM, such as the B 1700 virtual memory and the 370/125.[26]

The 2000 series was a family of systems that offered advanced performance capabilities in data communications and data base management. Included in its announcement was the introduction of a new, programmable communications processor, the DATANET 2000. (IBM's programmable communications controller, the IBM 3705, was announced in March 1972.) According to Honeywell:

> An advantage of the Series 2000 is an advanced data communications controller, the DATANET 2000. It manages the transmitting and processing of the data in the 2000 System arriving from many locations at frequent intervals. More than 12 percent of Series 2000 orders worldwide include this important new subsystem, illustrating the growing significance of data communications to medium-scale computer users. The heart of the DATANET 2000 is a minicomputer developed and produced at our Framingham, Massachusetts facilities.[27]

Honeywell reported in 1973 that its shipments of the 2000 series equipment as a whole were at record levels, including large orders from Ford Motor Company, the U.S. Internal Revenue Service, and the Italian Justice Department.[28]

NCR

NCR's corporate earnings fell precipitously between 1969 and 1972, from a $30 million profit to a net loss of nearly $60 million. According to its management, this decline was due to several factors, including the slowdown in the U.S. economy, retraining expenses, an unusually large $11 million write-off of inventories for LIFO valuation, and a 16-week strike by the United Auto Workers in 1971.[29]

In 1973 NCR reversed its poor earnings record: its corporate revenues increased by 17 percent, from about $1.5 billion to $1.8 billion; its earnings rose from a loss of nearly $60 million to profits of about $74 million, the highest in the company's history. And by that year NCR had all but completed its transition from mechanical to electronic products, and its computer business moved into the black.[30]

During the early 1970s two significant developments affected NCR's data-processing business. First, in May 1972 William S. Anderson became NCR's president, and in July 1973 he was named chief executive officer. He had formerly headed NCR Japan. When he assumed control, Anderson recognized that NCR was in trouble. He stated that his first task was to arrest the steep decline in profits that had begun in 1970 and ". . . to move the company successfully through the transition from mechanical to electronic products."[31] In the first two years of his tenure, Anderson directed extensive reorganization of NCR's manufacturing, research, development, marketing, and administrative operations. He also made a number of management changes and reduced the size of the work force.

Second, during these years NCR made no major "systems" announcements of the type undertaken by IBM, Burroughs, DEC, Honeywell, and others. It had been late in announcing its third-generation family, the Century series, and did not begin shipments until 1968. In 1970 and 1971 NCR did not try to replace that line, but instead announced two additions, Models 50 and 300.[32]

The company also expanded its network of data services. From a nucleus of three domestic data centers in 1960, NCR had by 1970 established a worldwide network of 80 such facilities. During the early 1970s these centers steadily increased their volume of data-processing applications. The data centers performed a variety of types of work, including merchandising, inventory control, banking, and payroll applications.[33]

The other new computer products that NCR announced at the outset of the 1970s were industry-oriented terminal subsystems and their associated on-line control software.

In 1970 the company introduced the NCR 280 Retail System, another example of an intelligent terminal system, capable of performing stand-alone processing and similar in concept to Burrough's TC equipment. The NCR 280, as announced, included input-output equipment (even electronic wands), data storage equipment, and communications equipment, together with the necessary software to permit the subsystem to operate as part of larger NCR computer systems. By 1971 the 280 system was highly successful.[34]

In 1971 NCR introduced its 270 Financial System, a series of teller-terminal subsystems that could be linked directly "on-line" to NCR central processing units. The 270 was, according to NCR's management, the most advanced system developed for the handling of customer transactions in savings institutions and commercial banks.[35]

Also in 1971 NCR announced the 399 series, which was said to combine the advantages of a general-purpose, operator-oriented accounting machine with the speed and computational abilities of a computer. The following year it introduced an enhanced version of the 270 Financial System, the 275, which was a free-standing financial terminal for commercial banks. The 275 could be used either as an independent unit or as part of a single computer system if the using bank moved to an on-line configuration of its computer system.[36]

NCR's growing experience and capability in the on-line approach to data processing, involving remote storage, processing, communications, and supporting control programs, was the kind of capability that later turned out to be highly relevant to the development of distributed processing systems. Moreover, terminal subsystems were one of the most rapidly growing products in the data-processing industry in the 1970s. NCR's management observed in 1973: "Just as the computer provided the most dramatic advances in information processing during the 1960s, so the data terminal is emerging as the key development of the 1970s."[37]

Sperry Rand

In November 1970 Univac announced a new, large-scale, general-purpose processor, the 1110, with advanced software, ". . . for today's full range of applications, whether local or remote, batch, time-sharing or real-time, business or scientific."[38] This system built on the success of the company's 1108. However, Sperry apparently perceived itself as trailing behind IBM in processor design. In a 1971 memorandum, J. Presper Eckert, one of the pioneers in computing, wrote to Robert E. McDonald of Sperry Rand:

> The engineering problem that Univac faces is that every program to build a large computer and much else, has been a sort of "crash" program. In the case of the 1110 and 1195, the crash has not been due to any lack of time or facilities or manpower, but just due to awful planning and poor technical foresight. The 1195 is now being planned as a "cache memory" machine which, except for some interesting and valuable improvements in the cache design and an adaptation of the cache design to Univac 1100 series and 490 series techniques, is simply following *IBM's lead almost exactly*. Now what doesn't make sense is this. IBM gave out at talks, and in papers, sufficient information to enable us to go the cache memory route if we liked in 1968. The plans for the 1110 were not very advanced at that time. In addition to the information in IBM's own publications, Dr. Spandorfer and I attended meetings at which Gibson of IBM explained the cache memory and

we of course, relayed this additional information to Univac. No serious work however, apparently took place on a cache memory until about six months ago. In other words, we knew about the cache memory three years ago but only looked into the matter seriously, six months ago. Now on the 1195 we find ourself not only copying IBM but we have wasted two and a half years of lead time in the copying we are doing.[39]

In 1971 IBM employees and the trade press reported that Sperry had taken several actions to reduce the prices of its current UNIVAC 9200 and 9300 computer systems, including new long-term leases at discounted rates (in April) and packaged configurations (August and October).[40]

In November 1971 Univac introduced the 9700 computer in its 9000 line. In the same month Sperry and RCA reached an agreement in principle for Sperry to acquire RCA's computer business. The agreement, which became final in December, called for an initial payment by Sperry of $70 million, and a future percentage of revenue payments that would total $60 million. Sperry's management expected the acquisition of the RCA business to enhance Univac's competitive position in the computer industry. RCA then had more than 1,000 computer installations and in excess of 500 customers. In 1972 Univac shipped more than $130 million in new equipment to former RCA customers.[41]

As of December 1974 the RCA equipment had yielded Sperry a revenue stream (sales, rentals, and maintenance) of approximately $370 million. In May 1976 approximately 76 percent of the RCA equipment acquired by Sperry Rand was still on rent.[42]

In 1973 Sperry Rand made another important acquisition: Information Storage Systems (ISS), a major manufacturer of computer disk subsystems. Its acquisition provided Univac with significant in-house peripheral capability. At the time of the acquisition ISS was also a major supplier of IBM plug-compatible disk products to such firms as Telex, Itel, and Storage Technology Corporation. As part of Univac it continued to supply plug-compatible replacements for IBM disk products and also became the developer and manufacturer of disk subsystems for use in Univac systems. Univac's appraisal of the proposed acquisition emphasized the fact that without ISS, Univac was lagging behind its competition in disk storage capability by two years. That appraisal also forecast a further profit of $50 million resulting from the sale of additional computer systems. ISS products were expected to enhance the marketability of entire computer systems as well as the disk subsystems themselves.[43]

THE ESTABLISHED SYSTEMS MANUFACTURERS IN THE MID- AND LATE 1970s

Burroughs

Revenues of Burroughs' Business Machines Group, whose activities include domestic marketing of EDP products and services, grew from $483 million in 1972 to $1.2 billion in 1979.[44]

In 1973 Burroughs introduced the B 700 series of "small scale computers," which fit between its B 1700 series of small-scale computer systems and its Series L business minicomputers.

In 1976 it further expanded its small computer line with the introduction of B 80 — "... a fully featured general purpose system whose price range begins at minicomputer levels."[45]

Still further announcements were made in 1979: the B 1900 and B 90 series, part of Burroughs' newly announced 900 family and, like the earlier B 1700 systems, capable of being used either as stand-alone computers or as part of distributed data-processing systems in an on-line network.[46]

Between 1975 and 1980 Burroughs also introduced new "medium and large-scale" computer systems. In 1975 it brought out the initial members of its 800 family — the B 2800, B 3800, and B 4800. According to Burroughs these new systems offered one and a half to four times the power of B 2700, B 3700, or B 4700 systems. In 1976 and early 1977 Burroughs completed the introduction of the 800 family with the announcement of the B 6800 and B 7800, which offered two and two and a half times the performance of the B 6700 and B 7700 systems, respectively.[47]

In mid-1977 Burroughs brought out two new models of the B 3800, reportedly designed to compete with IBM's 370/138.[48] One model, expandable to 1 million bytes of main memory, featured new chip technology; the other, capability to be configured into dual-processor systems.

In 1978 Burroughs announced new models in the B 2800, B 3800, and B 4800 series that featured engineering enhancements to central processors, increases in basic memory capacities, and new software capabilities. It also announced new system and communications processors that enhanced the performance of its medium-scale computers when serving as network "host" systems.[49]

The following year Burroughs introduced an entire new "family" of computers, the 900, initially consisting of the B 90, B 1900, B 2900, B 3900, and B 6900 series. The B 3900 was capable of supporting from 2 million to 5 million bytes of main memory, and reportedly offered approximately the same performance as the IBM 4341 processor, announced in January of that year.[50]

Control Data

The revenues from Control Data's computer business (including systems, peripheral equipment, and EDP services) increased from $948.2 million in 1973 to nearly $2.3 billion in 1979, a compound annual growth rate of over 15.9 percent.[51]

In the 1970s CDC's peripheral products business was the fastest-growing part of its EDP operations. Its revenues from the marketing of peripheral products nearly tripled between 1975 and 1979, from approximately $317 million to about $909 million.[52] CDC marketed peripheral products as part of its own computer systems, directly to users of computers manufactured by others, and on an OEM basis to other computer equipment manufacturers. Much of CDC's end-user peripherals business in the 1970s involved marketing compatible replacements for IBM peripherals. In 1977 CDC reported that it had installed IBM-compatible products at more than 1,300 IBM user installations. Its OEM peripherals business grew from 215 customers in 1973 to 720 in 1977.[53]

CDC's peripheral products have included disk drives and controllers, tape drives and controllers, printers, card readers and punches, terminals, data entry systems, mass storage devices, optical character recognition devices, and add-on memory. CDC had acquired a number of these products from joint ventures formed in 1972 and 1975. In 1972 CDC and NCR, later joined by ICL, formed Computer Peripherals, Inc. (CPI), to manufacture card, tape, and printer equipment. In 1975 CDC and Honeywell formed Magnetic Peripherals, Inc. (MPI), to develop and manufacture rotating mass-memory products. At the time of its formation MPI was 70 percent owned by CDC and 30 percent owned by Honeywell.[54]

CDC's peripheral products that were plug-compatible with IBM systems included add-on memory for IBM System/370 Model 135 through Model 168 and 303X, manufactured by AMS and Memory Technology Corporation; IBM plug-compatible 2314-type disks; IBM plug-compatible 3330-type disks, including single- and double-density versions; a disk subsystem, the 33801, that could be used in either 3330-type or 3350-type systems (a double-density version of the 33801, the 33802, was announced in 1978); a plug-compatible replacement for IBM's 1403N1 printer; and a line of plug-compatible peripherals, introduced in 1978, including disks, printers, terminals, and storage module drives, for IBM's Series/1 computers.[55]

In 1973, as a result of the settlement of its lawsuit with IBM, CDC acquired the Service Bureau Corporation (SBC) from IBM. (CDC had already been supplying data-processing services to customers through its CYBERNET computer network.) The acquisition of SBC expanded CDC's service offerings.

In its 1977 Annual Report CDC summarized the evolution of the data services business from the offering of computer time to a complete service:

> The data services business started by providing raw machine time to organizations having peak loads that they could not handle on their own equipment and to those having no equipment at all. In the intervening years, the business has moved increasingly toward providing a complete service rather than just computer time. Today, Control Data offers a wide range of application services that meet the specific requirements of selected industries or technical/scientific disciplines.
>
> . . . .
>
> A partial list of areas of specialization includes: petroleum exploration, nuclear reactor design and radiation safety monitoring, structural design and engineering, financial analysis, basic accounting and budgeting systems, sales statistics, planning models, credit union membership accounting and electric utility services.[56]

In the years after 1973 CDC introduced several new lines of computers. In mid-1975 it began to deliver the initial members of its CYBER 170 family of computers, to perform scientific, engineering, and business data processing in time-sharing, batch, remote batch, and transaction modes.[57]

In 1975 CDC introduced the CYBER 18 series of "small computers," primarily for customers in petroleum, manufacturing, distribution, and education.[58]

In March 1977 it introduced two new models in the CYBER 170 series, the CYBER 171 and the CYBER 176. Both of these used a distributed network processing architecture. Later that year it announced the OMEGA 480-I and 480-II systems, the company's first IBM plug-compatible processors. CDC claimed that OMEGA offered 10 to 100 percent performance improvements over comparable IBM systems at a 5 to 30 percent decrease in price.[59] The OMEGA processors marketed by CDC were manufactured by IPL, a small Massachusetts corporation partly owned by Cambridge Memories.

In January 1978 CDC announced three lower-priced models of its CYBER 175 series and a lower-priced version of the CYBER 176. In April 1979, it introduced four computers, the CYBER 170 Series 700, which replaced five of the six models in the earlier CYBER 170 line.

In June 1979 CDC announced three new IBM plug-compatible OMEGA processors, all manufactured by IPL. It claimed that the new OMEGAs were one and a third times faster than the specifications for the IBM 4341.[60]

Digital Equipment

From 1972 through 1979 DEC continued its spectacular growth. Revenues increased from $188 million in fiscal 1972 to $1.8 billion in fiscal 1979, a compound annual growth rate of 38 percent.

In June 1972, shortly after IBM's 3705 communications controller announcement, DEC offered the PDP 11D23, a communications processor version of its successful PDP 11 line, which could attach directly to an IBM System/360 or System/370 channel and perform functions similar to those of the IBM 3705. In August 1973, a few months after IBM's System/370 Model 115 announcement, DEC expanded its Datasystem 500 series with several new processors based on the PDP 11/40 or 11/45 CPU. In January 1973, less than six months after IBM's announcement of virtual memory on its System/370 systems, DEC announced virtual memory system hardware and software for its DECsystem 10 line. The DECsystem 10 was soon performing diverse applications for time-sharing organizations, universities, and commercial and industrial firms. The DECsystem 10 replaced DEC's earlier PDP 10 systems.[61]

By 1973 DEC's PDP 11/45, introduced in 1971, reached volume production. The PDP 11 computers were then being used in scientific and engineering applications, business data processing, real-time data collection and instructional computing, industrial control, commercial typesetting, and data communications. The PDP 11/45 offered performance capabilities comparable with those of processors in IBM's System/370 line. A 1974 IBM analysis estimated that the 11/40 and 11/45, then the largest members of DEC's PDP 11 series, had ". . . functional capability varying from that of an IBM System/3 to an IBM System/370 Model 135, depending on the application for which it is being used."[62]

In 1974-75 DEC announced additional members of its DECsystem 10 family — Models 1080, 1088, and 1090. The 1080 and 1090 systems cost roughly between $600,000 and $1.5 million, and were capable of performing time-sharing, transaction processing, batch processing, remote batch, and real-time user requirements. The 1088 was expected to compete with System/370 Models 158 and 168.[63]

In 1975 DEC introduced the PDP 11/70, at that time the high-end computer of its PDP 11 series. At the same time it introduced a new operating system for the 11/70 called IAS, which provided support for 16 interactive terminals and simultaneous use of several programming languages.[64]

The following year, shortly after IBM's System/370 Model 148 and 138 announcements, DEC introduced the first members of a new computer family: the DECsystem 20. The DEC 2040 and 2050 were designed for commercial, scientific, and educational applications. The new system could support as many as 128 simultaneous users in an interactive, time-sharing environment. In early 1978 DEC announced two additional members of the DECsystem 20 line — the 2020 and 2060. The DECsystem 2020 was a full, general-purpose mainframe computer system, with concurrent interactive time-sharing, multistream batch, and transaction-oriented processing. As announced, it supported up to two megabytes of main memory and 1.4 billion bytes of on-line disk storage; the 2060, as announced, had a main memory capacity of 5 million bytes and was supported by up to 56 disks. In 1979 DEC expanded the main memory capacity of the DECsystem 2040 and 2060 to 12 megabytes — six times the maximum memory capacity of the IBM 370/148, and twice that of the 370/158.[65]

In October 1977, within weeks of IBM's 3031 and 3032 processor announcement, DEC announced the VAX-11/780 as an upward-compatible expansion of the PDP-11 family. The VAX-11/780 was introduced with a main memory capacity of 2 million bytes, and offered the FORTRAN, COBOL, and BASIC programming languages. In September 1978 DEC announced that it was increasing the main memory capacity of the VAX computer to eight megabytes.[66]

By this time other manufacturers were supplying plug-compatible equipment for DEC systems. Its hardware included a full line of peripheral devices, and it offered a wide range of software operating systems.[67]

Honeywell

Honeywell Information Systems' revenue grew from $856 million in 1975 to $1.5 billion in 1979.[68]

One important aspect of Honeywell's business activities in the second half of the 1970s was a series of acquisitions and joint ventures. During this period the firm took over the domestic installed base of Xerox (see below) and agreed to service it; entered into a joint venture with CDC for the manufacture of peripheral equipment; completed the purchase of GE's ownership interest in Honeywell Information Systems; and effected the merger of CII and Honeywell-Bull in France. It also acquired Incoterm, manufacturer of intelligent terminals; Synertak, a manufacturer of semiconductor (MOX/LSI) devices and microprocessors; and Spectronics, a manufacturer of optical switches and fiber optics. It launched a joint venture with GE in Europe and Australia, combining part of Honeywell's time-sharing operations with those of GE.[69]

Honeywell devoted much attention during the 1970s to developing distributed processing. In 1974 it introduced the Series 60 computers, designed to support distributed processing. In early 1976 Honeywell announced the initial models of its Level 6 family of "minicomputers," which could operate in both stand-alone mode and distributed-processing systems. (Level 6 computers also were widely used in control systems produced by other Honeywell divisions, such as Industrial Systems and Controls.) Honeywell also established a broad line of intelligent terminals.[70]

From 1978 to 1980 Honeywell introduced several members of its Distributed Processing series (DPS) computers. These announcements, as well as the introduction of other computers, were specifically aimed at IBM's computers ranging from the System/3 to the 3000 series. In 1978 Honeywell introduced its Level/66 DPS, which was roughly equivalent to the IBM 3031, 3032, and 3033 in performance.[71] It also "reconfigured" its Level 64 "medium-scale computers" and substituted a single expandable model for the line's five submodels, in order to provide IBM System/3 users with an "upward migration path."[72] These moves were directed at the "low end" of IBM's System/370, Models 115 through 138.

In 1979 Honeywell introduced various additional models of its Level 66 and Level 64 systems that, according to the firm, were price/performance-competitive with IBM's 4341 and 4331 processors.[73]

NCR

NCR's "computer systems" revenues increased from $385 million in 1974 to $838 million in 1979, and revenues from retail, financial, and general-purpose terminals and systems increased from $295 million to $959 million over the same period. NCR achieved this growth largely through internally generated funds.[74]

By the end of 1975 — and in the face of ever-increasing competitive activity — NCR's Century series, announced in 1968, had effectively reached the end of its product life. In 1976 NCR introduced the first models of a new computer line, the Criterion 8000 series, which it characterized as ". . . an advanced general-purpose computer which provides solution-oriented data processing for industrial, financial, retail, commercial, educational and governmental organizations."[75]

In 1977 NCR expanded its 8000 computer series from 3 models to 15. The following year it announced the Criterion 8600, which was reported to have a capacity of up to 16 million bytes of main memory and 15 percent greater performance than the IBM 3033 processor, which had been announced in March 1977.[76]

NCR announced the NCR 499 small-computer series, replacing the successful NCR 399, in 1976. Its 499 product plan analysis preceding this announcement had some perceptive comments on the current atmosphere in the market:

> The major characteristic of today's competitive marketplace is the increasing velocity of change. A few major producers of Accounting Systems such as NCR, Burroughs, IBM, and Litton once produced most of the offerings to the marketplace. This is no longer true. Data Pro reports that 40 vendors offer over 150 small business systems models. An increasing number of new vendors are offering small data processing systems to the entry level commercial market. Just a few years ago the Singers, Basic/Fours, Quantels, and the Datapoints were unheard of. Major producers of scientific minicomputers and calculators, such as DEC, Olivetti and Wang have recently introduced small business processing oriented versions. Major overseas producers such as Nixdorf and Phillips have penetrated the U.S. market.
>
> This multiplication of competitors has produced two major results in the marketplace. First, the acceleration of technology and its introduction into the marketplace is producing shorter market lives for most small business systems. Secondly, this multiplication has promoted decreasing price stability as the various vendors react to these new introductions in the marketplace. A good example of these forces at work is the change in the marketplace since IBM introduced the System 32. Burroughs reconfigured and repriced their B700 series, DEC introduced their 310 Diskette Based Business System, and Quantel announced new Models 850 and 900 (6M Bytes Disk Systems) at purchase prices under $25,000.[77]

In 1979 NCR acquired Comten, a successful manufacturer of IBM-compatible, programmable communications controllers. It was probably the leading manufacturer of IBM and PCM front-end processors.[78]

NCR was now in second place in total EDP revenues (sales and rentals) and was a full-line integrated supplier of hardware, software, and services of all types.

Sperry Rand

Sperry's computer operations grew throughout the 1970s. Its Univac Division revenues, $635 million in fiscal 1970, had grown to $2.319 billion by fiscal 1980.[79]

In 1973 a major portion of Univac's product line was its 1100 series of computers, which, with enhancements, continued to win business well into the decade. In November 1976 Univac introduced the 1100/10. It was described as a "medium-scale" computer that offered capabilities available in large-scale systems such as the 1100/20 and 1100/40 (2-4 million bytes of main memory).[80]

During fiscal 1977 Univac announced the 1100/80, which was reported to have a main memory capacity of 16 million bytes and on-line disk capacity of about 6 billion bytes. It was the most powerful member of the 1100 line.[81]

In June 1979 Univac announced the 1100/60, reported to be its response to IBM's 4341 processor, which had been announced in January 1979. It combined LSI (large-scale integration) circuitry with a unique framework of multiple microprocessors.[82]

Another major portion of Univac' product line in the 1970s was its 90 series, the first members of which, the 90/60 and the 90/70 — follow-on products to the RCA Spectra series — were announced in 1973. These were later improved in price/performance to enable them to compete closely with the IBM 370/138 and 148.[83]

In January 1975 Univac started deliveries of the 90/30 small-to-medium-class computer. The following year the company reported that nearly 60 percent of its more than 1,000 orders for the 90/30 were from new customers, who had formerly used competitors' products or who had not previously had a computer doing the work assigned to the 90/30.[84]

At the same time that it was adding products to its 1100 and 90 computer lines, Univac was pursuing its "distributed communications architecture" through the introduction, in 1976, of its Universal Terminal Systems (UTS) line. The UTS also could be used with equipment of other manufacturers including IBM, through emulating IBM software protocols.[85]

As noted earlier, in the early 1970s Sperry acquired ISS and RCA's computer business. The ISS acquisition provided it with substantial in-house disk capability, and ISS continued to develop and manufacture disks both for Univac systems and as plug-compatible replacements for disks on IBM systems. The RCA customer base subsequently bought or rented significant quantities of Univac equipment.[86]

During fiscal 1976 Sperry acquired the disk manufacturing facility of Caelus Memories, Inc. The following year it bought Varian Data Systems, a manufacturer of computer systems. In 1978 Sperry introduced an extension to Varian's existing computer line, the V77 series. The new product, called the V77-800, was a general-purpose microprogrammable "minicomputer" with scientific, commercial, and data communications applications. It supported up to 2 million bytes of memory, languages such as COBOL, FORTRAN, and RPG II, and the TOTAL data base management system. Sperry's V77 series also supported its PRONTO transaction processing system, which permitted the user to install a V77 computer between an IBM 3270 remote terminal subsystem and an IBM 370 computer. This configuration allowed local applications to run off-loaded from the host 370.[87]

XEROX AND THE FATE OF SDS/XDS

In the late 1960s Xerox saw a need to acquire digital technology capability for use in its advanced information-handling systems. With the primary purpose of obtaining that technology for those systems, it had acquired Scientific Data Systems (SDS), which offered a range of computer systems to perform a variety of applications, including commercial, scientific, and time-sharing work, in 1969.[88]

At the outset Xerox was very optimistic about the prospects for SDS (which was renamed Xerox Data Systems, or XDS). However, almost from the beginning Xerox experienced serious difficulties with its XDS operations. While revenues increased to $124 million in 1969, they declined sharply to $82 million in 1970, and dropped again to $65 million in 1971. Xerox explained to its shareholders that these losses were caused by the recession in 1970 and the decline in government business during this period.[89] It also began to suffer from obsolescence of XDS products. At the time of the SDS acquisition, the company's primary product line was the Sigma series, Models 3, 5, and 7. The Sigma 7 was announced in 1966, the Sigma 5 in 1967, and the Sigma 3 in 1969. The Sigma 5 and 7 reached the peak of their competitive effectiveness in approximately mid-1969, and Sigma 3 by the end of 1970; they declined thereafter at an accelerating rate.[90]

Replacements for the Sigma 5 and 7, which would have been competitively desirable in 1970-72, were not announced until February 1974 and not delivered until the latter part of 1974 or early 1975. By that time IBM and other manufacturers were already replacing their 1960s product line for the second time in the 1970s.[91]

In 1972-73 XDS also began to encounter severe manufacturing problems, complicated by the fact that the computer manufacturing facilities in El Segundo, California, were given responsibility for certain noncomputer products and by the apparent tendency of management to give first priority to duplicator/copier products.[92] It had decided to stop purchasing disk drives from CDC and to use those of its own manufacture, but then was unable to deliver them in anything like the volume needed, thus disrupting and delaying shipments of systems to customers. Donald E. McKee, XDS vice-president for computer marketing, wrote in 1973:

> The disk drive problem has virtually eliminated our ability to make firm commitments on delivery to our customers, aggravated over fifty customers with units on order, made us liable for liquidated damages in some situations and cost us orders for new equipment. Morale in the field is terrible because of delivery schedules and made worse because commitments are missed with no notification from Manufacturing.[93]

In 1972 Xerox reorganized its computer operations on a functional basis and incorporated them into other parts of the company. There was now no president of the computer operation as such, and each of its departments was merged with the equivalent function in the Xerox Corporation. The heads of the functional departments reported to someone who had no computer experience. At the end of 1973 the computer functions were again reorganized — back into a separate entity called the Data Systems Division. The head of the Data Systems Division, however, never recovered all of the functions that the head of the computer operations had had prior to the 1972 reorganization. The former data-processing vice-president of XDS believed that the 1972 reorganization delayed the development of products to replace the Sigma series by at least six months, and probably a year.[94]

In July 1975 Xerox announced its withdrawal from the manufacture and sale of mainframe computers — which, in fact, were in direct competition with the growing number of minicomputer systems as well as other large systems.[95] But it by no means left the EDP industry. Indeed, that 1975 announcement applied to only about half of Xerox's computer business.[96] In fact, its data-processing revenues in 1979 were estimated by the *Datamation* annual survey at $475 million — considerably larger than in 1974.[97]

Xerox continued to operate its Xerox Computer Services, which provided shared accounting and management services for small and medium-size companies, as well as for utilities and municipalities, based on a nationwide communications network.[98] It also remained a supplier of hardware, both to its own service division and to OEM suppliers of systems. Beginning in 1972, Xerox acquired a number of companies that manufactured EDP equipment, including Diablo Systems, Inc., a manufacturer of disk units, printers, and terminals; and in late 1975, a few months after the discontinuance of the XDS operations, it bought Daconics, a maker of shared-logic word-processing systems utilizing minicomputers, and Versatec, a manufacturer of electrostatic printers and plotters. In December 1977 Xerox acquired Shugart Associates, a manufacturer of flexible disk drives for minicomputers, terminals, and word-processing systems. It purchased Century Data Systems (CDS), a manufacturer of rigid disk drives and controllers, from California Computer Products in 1979.[99]

In the late 1970s Xerox moved aggressively into automated office and interoffice operations, which included word processing, data management, and information reproduction and distribution, combining the technologies of computers and data processing, communications, and xerography. In 1977 it introduced two word-processing systems, the 850 and Visual Type III. Each featured display work stations and substantial processing and text editing capability.

Xerox also introduced the 9700 electronic printing system, which employed xerography and other technologies to print 18,000 lines per minute either directly from a computer or from magnetic tape. In 1979 it was reported that Xerox had begun to offer 6,250 bits-per-inch (bpi) and 1,600 bpi tape drives and controllers, manufactured by Storage Technology, for the 9700. According to Xerox, ". . . 9700 combines computers, which can store any number of different kinds of formats, with the advanced technologies of lasers and xerography."[100]

In 1978-79 Xerox announced the 860 information processing system, which combined text editing, computation, and the processing of business office records; it filed an application with the Federal Communications Commission to provide, through the Xerox Telecommunications Network, communications services for document distribution, teleconferencing, and data transmission; and it completed the acquisition of WUI, Inc., which operated a worldwide network of telecommunications facilities, including submarine cables and satellites. It also announced Ethernet, which through cables links work stations, printers, and electronic files within a building. Ethernet networks could be linked to one another and to outside communications facilities.[101]

PLUG-COMPATIBLE PERIPHERAL EQUIPMENT MANUFACTURERS AND LEASING COMPANIES IN THE 1970s

PCMs FROM S/360 TO S/370

The firms that had been engaged primarily in the manufacture of plug-compatible memory and peripheral equipment for IBM System/360 computer systems before 1970 hastened to respond to IBM's introduction of System/370 in 1970 and 1971.

Telex: Difficulties and Recovery

Telex, one of IBM's earliest plug-compatible peripheral equipment competitors, reacted quickly to IBM's 360 and 370 announcements in 1970-71.

One day after IBM announced its 3420 tape subsystem in November 1970, Telex told its salesmen that it would have comparable products ready for delivery very shortly after IBM deliveries. In December 1970 Telex formally announced its 6420/6803 tape subsystem, a plug-compatible version of the IBM 3420/3803. Telex had hired Howard Gruver away from IBM. Gruver had been IBM's product engineer with responsibility for development of the 3803 tape drive control unit, announced with the 3420 in November.[1]

Telex began deliveries of the 6420/6803 subsystem in November 1971, and in 1972 reported that it was one of the firm's most successful product introductions. Shipments of the 6420/6803 subsystem through 1972 exceeded Telex's announcement forecast: over 2,000 6420 tape drives were shipped by December 1972, compared with the 1,575 that had been forecast in November 1970; nearly 700 Model 6803 controllers were shipped by December 1972, compared with the 520 originally forecast.[2]

Telex also responded to IBM's Fixed-Term Plan announcement of May 1971 with additional downward adjustments in its own lease rates, effective July 1, 1971. The new rate reductions were incorporated in formulas that related to length of lease term and other variables. In general they preserved historical rental differentials between Telex and comparable IBM units.[3]

In 1969 Telex began marketing IBM plug-compatible 2314-type subsystems manufactured by ISS. In the fall of 1970, following IBM's 3330/3830 disk announcement in June, Telex hired or recruited several IBM engineers for its disk development program.[4]

While that recruiting activity was under way, Telex also tried to negotiate an OEM agreement with ISS to obtain 3330-type IBM-compatible products; that effort was unsuccessful. Telex then turned to CDC, with which it reached agreement in early 1971 to obtain 3330-type disk drives to be marketed by Telex with its own 3830-type controllers. However, as late as February 1972, approximately six months after IBM had begun shipments of its 3330/3830 subsystem, CDC's disk drive development failures made it apparent to Telex that the project was unlikely to succeed. During this same time Telex also encountered difficulties in producing the control unit for the CDC drives, and terminated its in-house program after learning it could purchase the controllers more cheaply than it could manufacture them. Telex ultimately acquired 3330-type products from ISS but was able to ship less than 200 units by the end of 1972.[5]

For its fiscal year ending March 31, 1969, to that ending March 31, 1970, Telex had reported dramatic rises in revenue and in net income. Beginning in fiscal 1971, however, that picture changed significantly.[6] After moderate declines in 1971 and 1972, Telex revenues dropped further in fiscal 1973, and it reported a net loss of $13.3 million.[7]

Several factors contributed to this business reversal. In May-August 1971 Telex had a production line strike that created serious problems for its field service personnel, affecting field service costs and morale, and customer satisfaction.[8] In 1970-73 Telex had manufacturing and performance problems with its older 5420 tape systems, a PCM version of IBM's 2420, as well as with its newer 6420. By mid-1972 Telex field executives viewed the entire 6420 program as "a major disaster," and considered the quality of parts to be "pitiful."[9]

While Telex was experiencing these manufacturing and reliability problems, a new company, Storage Technology Corporation (STC), was announcing and delivering newer plug-compatible products and offering new terms and conditions. In the weeks prior to April 1972, STC displaced more than 100 Telex tape drives, primarily because of Telex's inability to deliver its 6420/6803s.

By April 1972 Telex salesmen had been told to decline any orders for delivery of the 6420s until September 1972. Later in 1972 STC bid against Telex, and won, on a five-year lease of 218 tape drives and 24 controllers to the Ford Motor Company, at prices 10 to 12 percent below Telex's prices. It was not until December 1972 that Telex was able to equal STC's production of tape units.[10]

During Telex's fiscal year 1974 the company increased its revenues to above the 1971 levels but still reported a loss. The next year, however, the company returned to a profitable position, with revenues of $106.1 million. By 1979 revenues were $148.2 million.[11]

During the remainder of the decade, Telex further expanded its product line. Much of that expansion resulted from a series of acquisitions. In December

1976 Telex acquired the terminal product division of United Technologies Corporation. By 1979 this division's products included REACT (remote access communications terminals), ". . . a programmable terminal which dramatically enhances the communication network and thus reduces total operating costs of users with their own message switching networks."[12] In January 1977 Telex acquired Gulliver Technology, which resulted in the introduction in 1978 of a 6,250-bits-per-inch (bpi) tape drive for use by minicomputer manufacturers. The following year Telex introduced an end user version of this same tape drive that, like its OEM counterpart, featured data storage density for "minicomputers" equivalent to the top of IBM's tape drive line, the 3420-4, 6, and 8 (Birch).[13]

In 1978 Telex acquired General Computer Systems (GCS). GCS's major product was a system (2100) that linked terminals employing keyboards and video display tubes to a central processing unit that also supported magnetic disk drives or tape drives, card readers, communications lines, line printers, and other devices.[14]

Storage Technology Corporation

STC was founded in August 1969 by Jesse Aweida and three others who left IBM's tape subsystem development program in Boulder, Colorado, to set up the new company. The start-up investment for STC was about $250,000, supplied by the founders and J. H. Whitney and Company, a venture capital concern.[15]

The company's first product was a line of IBM 24XX plug-compatible tape drives, announced and exhibited in May 1970, nine months after the company was formed. The first deliveries of those products were made in September 1970. Later that same year — within one month of IBM's 3420 tape subsystem announcement — STC announced an IBM 3420-equivalent system. During the 1970s STC became the industry's leading independent tape subsystem supplier (one not producing complete systems).

STC grew phenomenally in the early 1970s and beyond. From $3.6 million in 1971 its revenues had climbed to over $75 million by 1974 — about three times what had been projected by STC's investment bankers in 1969[16] — and grew to $479 million by 1979.

This growth was fueled by an aggressive product and marketing program. In 1971 STC signed an agreement with Decimus Corporation, a subsidiary of the Bank of America, for Decimus to purchase up to $21 million worth of STC equipment over three years, to be leased to end users. In 1972 the company announced a new IBM-compatible tape drive, the 3480, reportedly featuring greater speed and transfer rate than any of IBM's 3420-series tape products. In September of that year STC branched into disk products and began shipments of 3330-compatible disk subsystems that it acquired from ISS. It also began to market IBM plug-compatible semiconductor memory, acquired from Intel. STC's first memory products were semiconductor replacements for IBM's core memory on the 370/155 and 165 processors.[17]

In January 1973 STC formed a subsidiary, Disk Storage Systems (DSC), to develop and manufacture disk subsystems, and in October of that year it announced its first disk product developed in-house, the 8000 series super disk. First deliveries were made in early 1975. The 8000 series offered storage capacity of up to 800 million bytes per module — four times that available with IBM's 3330 disk drive, announced in June 1970, and twice that of IBM's 3330-11, announced in July 1973. According to STC, in certain configurations the 8000 series offered savings of as much as 50 percent over IBM's 3330/3830 subsystems of equal storage capacity. In March — the same month that IBM announced its 3420-4, 6, and 8 (Birch) tape drives — STC announced plug-compatible products of equivalent storage density and speeds.[18]

In 1973 and 1974 STC expanded its product line still further by marketing tape drives and controllers for use with computers manufactured by companies other than IBM. In January 1973 STC entered into an OEM agreement with CII, a French computer manufacturer, for STC tape subsystems. In September STC introduced 3400 series subsystems for attachment to Univac processors. And in October 1974 STC signed agreements with DEC, CII, and Siemens to supply their requirements for high-performance tape subsystems.

In 1976 STC announced its model 8350, a plug-compatible version of IBM's 3350 Madrid disk (described below). Two years later it doubled the capacity of the 8350, with a 1.2 billion byte capacity for each two-spindle subsystem. It also introduced the 4305 solid state disk, which used charge-coupled devices for data storage.[19]

By the late 1970s STC was marketing its data storage subsystems to end users of IBM processors and, on an OEM basis, to a large number of systems manufacturers: Burroughs, Univac, DEC, Siemens, CII, Honeywell-Bull, and 38 others. It also continued in the latter 1970s to offer add-on memory for the IBM System/370 line.[20]

STC simultaneously moved into new product and technology areas. By 1976 it had introduced peripherals for minicomputers with the announcement of the Model 1900 tape drive with a 6,250 bpi capacity. In 1978 STC announced its 2700, an intelligent disk drive for attachment to minicomputers. The 2700 contained a built-in microcomputer that could absorb overhead functions from the CPU and a built-in controller permitting most manufacturers to adapt it for attachment to their processors at low cost.[21]

STC had established the STC Communications Corporation to take advantage of the growing complementarities between data processing and telecommunications. In 1978 STC introduced telephone digital voice multiplexors and concentrators, using microprocessors, for telephone companies, government agencies, and corporate communications networks. The firm acquired Microtechnology Corporation in 1979 to assist it in developing its own large-scale integration (LSI) devices.[22]

Memorex

Following IBM's announcement of its 3330/3830 disk subsystem in June 1970, Memorex moved to develop a competitive offering. In October 1971 it announced its 3670 disk subsystem, which was a plug-compatible replacement for the 3330/3830.

In late 1970, through the spring of 1971, and beyond, Memorex announced price reductions first on its 2314 and then on its 3330-type subsystems in response to price reductions and changes in lease terms by IBM and other disk subsystem suppliers.[23]

In those years Memorex experienced a continuing strong demand for its disk products. In each of the years 1973 through 1976, its 3660 family of disk products was profitable, as was the 3670 line.[24]

Memorex as a whole, however, experienced severe difficulties in the early 1970s. In 1970 its total corporate revenues were about $79 million, with net income of approximately $3.2 million. The majority of these revenues came from computer tape media sales, not from EDP equipment. By 1971-73 Memorex recorded substantial losses. By the latter year it also had senior debt, principally to the Bank of America, totaling more than $180 million, but had had to shelve at least two proposed equity offerings.[25]

Contributing to these financial woes was a series of product failures and revenue and profit shortfalls. In 1970-73 a principal part of Memorex's business, the media business — disk packs, video tapes, and computer tapes — suffered from lowered demand and severe price competition. As a result Memorex's media revenue for the entire 1970-75 period fell nearly $450 million short of expectations. In 1970 Memorex began shipping computer output microfilm (COM) equipment, for use in computer systems (without a market research study), but by 1973 the COM business had achieved less than 10 percent of its 1970 projections.[26]

Through 1973 Memorex missed its sales volume projections in its new computer terminal business by over $44 million. The program lost money; Memorex's chairman at the time advised his successor to cancel the program.[27]

In 1972 and 1973 Memorex encountered manufacturing and quality problems with its new IBM plug-compatible disk products. For example, in December 1972 and early 1973, Manufacturing was so seriously behind its original commitments for the 3670 that the company's management feared a loss of credibility and of customers; problems persisted until at least November 1973.[28]

In 1972 Memorex introduced two computer systems, the Memorex Model 40 and Model 50. At that time the firm did not have adequate financing for systems. After delivery the largest single customer for the systems canceled because of the product's poor performance. Memorex's systems program was canceled in July 1973.[29]

A combination of management upheavals and adverse publicity over its unorthodox accounting practices also contributed to Memorex's difficulties during the early 1970s, and hindered its acquisition of additional capital. Public skepticism had been expressed about Memorex's accounting practice of deferring expenses for lease acquisitions and for research and development, even in the early part of 1970. Matters became worse in November 1970 when, following a *Wall Street Journal* article criticizing its accounting, the New York Stock Exchange suspended trading in Memorex stock and an SEC investigation began. The SEC subsequently sued the company and two of its executives for securities fraud. The government's suit was settled in 1971, but private suits continued and more controversies arose over the firm's accounting practices until, in 1973, Memorex changed these practices and wrote off over $37 million of accumulated expenses.[30]

During these ongoing controversies and various product program shortfalls and cancellations, Memorex's top management underwent major upheavals. Most of the principal officials left between early 1971 and early 1974.[31]

Beginning in 1974, Memorex attempted to recover from the problems and poor financial performance it had experienced in the first years of the 1970s. By 1979 its worldwide EDP revenues were over $600 million, and its total revenue over $700 million — up from $177 million in 1973.[32]

In this period Memorex offered new disk, tape, memory, and communications products, including the 3673 disk controller, which permitted its disk drives to attach to IBM's integrated storage controller; the 6000 series add-on memory, which Memorex described as a cost-effective expansion of internal memory capacity of IBM's System/360 and 370 processors; the 1380 programmable communications controller, a plug-compatible replacement for IBM 3705 controllers; and the 1377 display terminal, a plug-compatible replacement for IBM terminals used with 360 and 370 processors.[33]

Memorex continued to expand its product line in subsequent years. In 1976 it announced the 3640, an IBM 3340-type disk drive manufactured by Nippon Peripherals, Ltd., and marketed by Memorex. In the same year Memorex introduced the 3650 disk drive, which was announced as incorporating the latest Winchester technology and offering full functional compatibility with the IBM 3350, which had been announced in 1975.[34]

Also in 1976 Memorex announced a new memory system, the 6268, and a new tape system that used the latest 6,250 bpi technology — the same storage density available on IBM's highest-performance tape drives.[35]

In 1978 Memorex announced its 3770 disk cache, which consisted of a microprocessor and semiconductor memory device. The 3770 was intended for use with the Memorex 3670 and 3675 disk drives, to permit faster access time and increased system throughput. That same year Memorex opened a new flexible ("floppy") disk drive manufacturing plant and expanded other production facilities. In 1979 it introduced the 3652 disk subsystem, a double-density 3350-type disk drive featuring 635 million bytes of storage, and a low-capacity drive with an 11.7-million byte capacity, for use with word-processing and minicomputer equipment.[36]

In addition to product developments, Memorex acquired Business Systems Technology, a supplier of storage and communications products, and in 1978 entered into a joint venture with a Japanese industrial concern, Teijin, to produce Memorex flexible media in Japan. That same year it acquired Telex Europe, which increased Memorex's customer base in Europe. However, these innovations in product, service, and organization had uneven success, and in 1980 Memorex incurred its first annual loss since 1974.[37]

Advanced Memory Systems

Advanced Memory Systems (AMS) was incorporated in October 1968 to design, manufacture, and market semiconductor memory equipment for computer systems. It began operations at a time when memory technology was moving from core to semiconductors.[38]

In the fall of 1970 AMS announced its semiconductor storage unit (SSU), which was marketed as a "completely compatible" add-on memory product for IBM System/360 and System/370 processors. This product featured 1,024 bit-per-chip metal oxide silicon (MOS) technology. At that time IBM offered only older core memory technology for its System/360 processors and for the 370/155 and 165 processors, announced in June 1970. In 1971 AMS announced the development of a memory chip featuring twice the density of its original MOS product. This 2,048 bit-per-chip design was marketed beginning in mid-1972.[39]

AMS's IBM plug-compatible semiconductor memory equipment won customer acceptance quickly. By 1971 its add-on memories had been installed by a variety of IBM systems users, including the Mennen Company, Hyster, Beckman Instruments, Hughes Aircraft, Time, Inc., Getty Oil, Stanford Research Institute, and American Savings & Loan. In 1973 AMS's OEM business was expanded through an agreement with CDC that gave the latter nonexclusive, worldwide rights to market AMS's System/370-compatible memory product line. AMS also entered into marketing arrangements with Itel in 1970 and Memorex in 1974, and during the early 1970s marketed its memory products on an OEM basis to a number of processor and peripheral manufacturers, including CDC, Data General, Univac, Amdahl, Raytheon, STC, Honeywell, Fujitsu, Nixdorf, Siemens, Hitachi, and Wang. Also in 1973 AMS introduced an MOS main memory system for the IBM 370/145, which the company claimed offered better price/performance than IBM's bipolar semiconductor memory on that machine, and announced a 4,096-bit MOS device.[40]

In the period 1972-74 AMS ran into cost and production problems. Though its revenues grew to over $30 million in 1973 and 1974, it reported losses of $196,000 and $2.1 million for those years. In 1974 and 1975 the company returned to a profitable position.[41]

Fiscal 1976 (ending September 26) was the best year in the history of the company, with revenues over $40 million and profits nearing $4 million.

In November 1976 AMS merged with Intersil, Inc., a manufacturer of integrated circuits and microprocessors. In 1979 Intersil introduced the UMS-3 universal memory system, thereby becoming the first add-on memory supplier to offer a complete line of 16K memory products for use on the IBM 370/138,

148, 158, and 168, and the 3031, 3032, and 3033 computers. The UMS-3 product line consisted of one basic design that required only the change of a few interface cards from one model to the next. Intersil posted over $140 million in revenues in 1979.[42]

LEASING COMPANIES

Computer leasing companies had emerged as major competitors in the EDP industry in the late 1960s. Leasing companies generally had concentrated on purchases of IBM System/360 computer equipment, which they leased to customers on a variety of terms and conditions, at rates typically lower than those charged by IBM under its monthly rental plan.

In 1969 IBM estimated that leasing companies had purchased $2.5 billion worth of its equipment — $1.1 billion of System/360 CPUs and memory alone.[43]

In response both to IBM's introduction of the System/370 in 1970 and 1971 and to other competitors' product and price announcements, leasing companies in the early 1970s took a number of steps to make their System/360 equipment more competitive. They cut prices and offered more attractive terms and conditions for the System/360 equipment they were marketing. With these lower prices the price/performance of that equipment made it an attractive alternative to the newer System/370 equipment. System/370 models 135 and 145 were soon in close competition with discounted leased System/360 Models 50 and 65.[44]

Leasing companies also increased the price/performance of their System/360 equipment by modifications of existing hardware and software. For example, the Computer Company developed an "extended disk operating system" (EDOS). This software operating system was compatible with IBM System/360 hardware and, according to its suppliers, enhanced performance of that hardware beyond that available under IBM's disk operating system (DOS). EDOS was marketed with System/360 equipment by 10 or 11 leasing companies, including DPF, Greyhound, CLC, Itel, and Boothe, against IBM 370 equipment. The availability of EDOS caused several users to "migrate backwards" from 370s to 360s. Itel offered software that enabled customers with certain 360 equipment to use the DOS/VS operating system, which was offered by IBM on some 370 equipment.[45]

Leasing companies continued to market plug-compatible equipment with their IBM-manufactured processors — again as a means of enhancing the price/performance of their 360 systems. For example, leasing companies offered modified 3330-type disk subsystems, with somewhat reduced data rates, for use with their larger System/360 processors. The 3330 itself was not generally offered by IBM for attachment to 360 processors below the Model 85. In addition, a number of leasing companies offered "packaged" systems. Itel, for example, offered 360/50s, which they claimed performed better than IBM's 370/135, for $50,000 a year less. This system included add-on monolithic memory, 3330-compatible disks, 3420-compatible tapes, and a fast 3215 console.

Itel also offered a DAP Box, a combination of plug-compatible memory, tapes, and disk, and software that it claimed could make a 360/40 as powerful as a 370/125, a 360/50 more powerful than a 370/135, and a 360/65 more powerful than a 370/145.[46]

These actions by leasing companies allowed their 360 equipment to remain competitive with IBM's 370 equipment well into the 1970s. IBM's 370 equipment was sometimes being replaced by leasing company 360s; low rentals on leasing company 360s caused users to cancel orders for IBM's 370 equipment; and leasing company 360s were frequently chosen over IBM proposals of 370 equipment.[47]

Despite competitive successes with their 360 equipment, however, some long-term problems were beginning to build up for the leasing companies. We have already described the accounting policies used by many leasing companies in the late 1960's. Depreciation policies were at the core of the problem. Leasing companies based their pricing on assumed equipment lives that were substantially longer than those used by IBM and other leading manufacturers of computer equipment. They also followed straight-line depreciation policies that made no provision for the fact that the revenues derived from leasing EDP equipment would naturally be highest when the equipment was newest, and lower as the equipment became older.[48] Instead, leasing companies depreciated their equipment in equal amounts each year throughout their lengthy depreciation periods, and in effect assumed their revenue stream would be constant, despite the obvious rapid technological change in the computer industry.

In fact, the price structures of the leasing companies were overtaken by events: their estimates of obsolescence proved too optimistic. When IBM brought out the first models of its System/370 in the early 1970s, and other manufacturers did likewise, System/360 became something less than a state-of-the-art system. It could not match the improved price/performance of System/370 without substantial price reductions — which leasing companies' depreciation rates had not anticipated.

Problems of leasing companies were exacerbated if they had bought their System/360 equipment relatively late in the product life of that system. At the time of IBM's initial 370 announcement, the average age of the System/360 inventory held by leasing companies was between one and a half and two years, with seven to seven and a half years remaining on the ten-year book value life that most of them were using for depreciation purposes. IBM's internal estimates indicate that over 85 percent of leasing company purchases of 360 CPUs and memory were made after January 1968.[49] As the obtainable rentals of their 360 systems declined, leasing companies had to write off many millions of dollars in lost capital values.[50]

Though some leasing companies (such as Boothe, Greyhound, and DPF) chose not to make early investments in System/370 equipment, a number of older leasing companies, such as Itel, Leasco, and Randolph Computer Corp., began to lease 370 equipment soon after it was first delivered. As the 1970s progressed, leasing companies as a group acquired IBM 370 equipment for leasing in volumes that considerably exceeded the earlier totals for their acquisition of System/360 equipment, even adjusted for price changes.[51] Later they launched programs to purchase and lease IBM 303X computers, announced in 1977.[52] Leasing companies with System/370 inventories again began to discount them in competition with the 303X equipment; thus did history repeat itself, in part.

New leasing companies, with no prior history of System/360 leasing, entered the market in the 1970s with System/370 and (later) 303X equipment. Among them were Alanthus, Decimus Corporation (a subsidiary of Bank of America), Ford Motor Credit Company, and General Electric Credit Corporation. Several of these adopted leasing policies that avoided the mistakes of some of the earlier System/360 leasing companies: they used shorter depreciation periods and avoided linear cost allocations. Some leasing companies also carried equipment produced by other manufacturers.[53]

During the 1970s many leasing companies, such as Boothe and Greyhound, were also active as dealers and brokers of used equipment, including 360 and 370 products as well as non-IBM equipment. Conversely, some companies that began largely as brokers and dealers of used equipment expanded into a variety of leasing activities. (Perhaps the best known is Comdisco, founded in 1969.)[54]

16

ENTRY AND EXPANSION OF OTHER COMPETITORS FROM 1970 TO 1980

The 1970s witnessed the entry of numerous computer systems and equipment suppliers, as well as expansion of some of the smaller systems suppliers that had entered the business late in the 1960s. These competitors included suppliers of minicomputers, which were sometimes arrayed with peripherals into complete systems; producers of CPUs that were plug-compatible with IBM's systems and those of a few other large manufacturers; semiconductor firms that expanded into EDP equipment; communications firms that developed data-processing equipment and services; makers of microprocessors; software houses and service bureaus; and several large firms that entered the U.S. market, such as Exxon (by acquiring some existing suppliers), and foreign manufacturers, notably from Japan.

Firms that were already in the U.S. market, including those mentioned in preceding chapters, also developed their versions of minicomputers and minisystems, and distributed-processing microprocessors and intelligent terminals that embodied processors and often were hard to distinguish from mini- and microcomputers.[1]

MINICOMPUTERS AND MINISYSTEMS SUPPLIERS

By the mid-1970s so-called minicomputers or minisystems, often used as parts of distributed-processing systems, had grown in sophistication and power, and were already in widespread use as alternatives to larger computer systems and processors from the established systems manufacturers. The following were among the most prominent of the firms that entered the industry as minicomputer suppliers or expanded from other products into minicomputer CPUs and minisystems.

Data General

Data General was formed in April 1968 by some former DEC employees. The company announced its first product, the Nova computer system, in the fall of that year and began shipments in February 1969. Its first offices were located in a storefront in Hudson, Massachusetts. Data General's original capitalization was less than $1 million. In 1970 its domestic EDP revenues were $6.8 million. By that year the company's second full year of operation, it had become profitable. In 1972 Data General's U.S. EDP revenues climbed to approximately $25.8 million; by fiscal 1979 its worldwide revenues had reached $507 million.[2]

The Nova computer system was a 16-bit word, small-scale, general-purpose digital computer. Its basic price was $7,950, including 4,096 words of core memory as a teletype interface. The Nova processor was designed to operate with as many as 60-odd peripheral devices. It was an immediate success. By the end of 1970 Data General had delivered over 700 Nova computers.[3]

In 1970 Data General brought out more powerful processors and a multiprocessor communications adaptor (MCA), which enabled a user to combine up to 15 Novas and/or Supernovas into a single multiple-computer system. It also developed a hardware/software interface to IBM System/360 and System/370 processors that permitted the Nova line of computers to be treated as standard IBM peripherals by the 360 or 370 system. Its Supernova SC processor was built with monolithic, as opposed to core, main memory.[4]

In 1974 Data General expanded its computer line further with the introduction of the Eclipse series, which was enhanced and expanded throughout the 1970s.

By the mid-1970s Data General's computer systems were being used for a variety of data-processing tasks, including process control, computation and data processing, time-sharing networks, front-end processors in larger computer systems, intelligent terminals in distributed-processing systems, user-oriented interactive data processing, real-time tracking, scheduling, and data base management.[5]

In January 1978 Data General introduced the Eclipse M/600 computer system, with a purchase price of $500,000 or more. The M/600 supported up to 2 million bytes of main memory and up to 6 billion bytes of on-line disk storage. It used the AOS operating system, which permitted users to perform time-sharing, batch, and real-time data-processing operations simultaneously. The M/600 also supported a variety of programming languages, such as PL/1, FORTRAN, and COBOL, and Data General's data base management system. The Eclipse computers used Data General's XODIAC networking system, which allowed users to manage large numbers of interconnected computers and to access large commercial data-processing networks.[6] Meanwhile, Data General had introduced its new Commercial System (CS) line of small computers, primarily for business applications, which have often been used in distributed-processing networks.

Hewlett-Packard

Hewlett-Packard shipped its first computers, designed to complement the company's measuring instruments, in 1967. It soon began to introduce a variety of other computer products.

Hewlett-Packard has achieved a high rate of growth in its EDP business. In 1972 its domestic EDP revenues accounted for about 15 percent of total corporate revenues — $68 million out of a total of nearly $480 million; in 1979 they were over $1 billion, almost 50 percent of total corporate revenues.[7]

Early in 1972 Hewlett-Packard announced the HP 3000 computer system line, which was, according to the company's management, a general-purpose line. The equipment and operating system software were designed to handle simultaneously ". . . time-sharing, real-time, multi-programmed batch, and on-line terminal operations — each in more than one computer language."[8]

In the early stages of HP 3000 shipments Hewlett-Packard encountered difficulties with its performance. But between 1976 and 1979 it enhanced its 3000 series with the introduction of the 3000 series II in 1976, the 3000 series III and the Series 33 in 1978, and the 3000 series 30 in 1979. The newer 3000 series computers offered main memory capacity up to 2 million bytes, as well as communications and networking capability permitting interaction of remotely located Hewlett-Packard processors and terminals. In addition the 3000 series was provided with operating system software that could simultaneously handle traditional batch processing and interactive processing for up to 63 terminals, and support languages such as COBOL, FORTRAN, and BASIC as well as Hewlett-Packard's IMAGE data base management system.[9]

In addition to its processors and terminals, Hewlett-Packard offered a full range of peripheral products, largely manufactured in-house, for use with its HP 3000 series. These included disk memories, magnetic tape units, high-speed plotters, and card readers.[10]

Hewlett-Packard described customer uses of the HP 3000-II as including customer order, production, and warehousing applications for a textile manufacturer; customer account and advertising accounting for a cable TV and radio company; accounting, personnel, and management work for a retail store chain; and accounting, management, and engineering applications for a municipal water utility.[11] To give another example, in 1977 Hewlett-Packard equipment was among the alternatives bid in response to Union Carbide's major request for proposals for production scheduling applications. Comserv, one of six bidders, proposed HP 3000 equipment in a distributed-data-processing configuration. IBM bid System/3, System/34, and System/370 equipment; Univac, the winner, bid a "clustered" network of 90/30 computer systems equipment.[12]

Prime Computer, Inc.

Prime Computer, Inc., was formed in 1971. Its first computer was the Prime 200, introduced in 1972. In 1979 Prime's revenues were about $153 million. As of March 1980 it reported that more than 3,500 of its computer systems were in use around the world.[13]

Prime's investment growth curve during 1974-79 was striking. In 1974 it had total assets of $7.5 million. By 1979 that had increased to $142.7 million.

The funds for this expansion came from retained earnings and a variety of external financing arrangements.[14]

By 1977 the top of Prime's line of systems, the Prime 400 and Prime 500, provided up to 8 million bytes of main memory and up to 2.4 billion bytes of on-line disk capacity. That disk capacity was available on drives offering up to 300 million bytes of storage each. Prime also offered a broad line of other peripheral products, including floppy diskettes; matrix, chain, and brand printers; card readers and punches; magnetic tape drives; plotters; and paper tape readers and punches.[15] The 400 and 500 were capable of supporting up to 63 concurrent users and offered programming in languages including FORTRAN, COBOL, BASIC, and RPG II. In addition, they supported a CODASYL-compliant data base management system. The Prime 500 was adept at both interactive business data processing and computational time sharing.[16]

In addition, Prime offered communications and networking capabilities through PRIMENET, which was a geographically dispersed network allowing Prime computers to communicate with other Prime computers, with computers from other vendors, and with terminals attached to packet switching networks.[17]

In January 1979, the same month as IBM's 4300 series announcement (see Chapter 17), Prime announced four new computers for large-scale processing that were compatible with one another — the Prime 450, 550, 650, and 750. The largest, the 750, was offered with up to eight megabytes of main memory and a variety of programming tools, such as COBOL, FORTRAN, PL/1, and Prime's data base management system. Prime advertised these as alternatives to IBM's 4331 and 4341 processors.[18]

Perkin-Elmer

Perkin-Elmer is a diversified manufacturer of analytical instruments, optical equipment, and avionic instruments as well as small- and medium-scale computers and peripherals. In 1974 it acquired Interdata, a manufacturer of minicomputers, which had been founded in 1966. In 1976 Perkin-Elmer further expanded its EDP product line through the acquisition of Wangco, a peripheral equipment manufacturer selling tape and disk drives primarily to OEMs. During 1974-79 its EDP business grew from $42 million to $168 million.[19]

Underlying that growth was Perkin-Elmer's expansion and enhancement of Interdata's computer product line. In 1975 the firm introduced the 8/32 Megamini computer and began delivery of the 7/32 computer. Perkin-Elmer described the 7/32's performance as roughly equivalent to the IBM System 370/135.[20] Of the 8/32 the company stated:

> The 8/32, with 1 million bytes of directly addressable memory, is positioned at the point where the traditional minicomputer market intersects the large scale mainframe computer market. It combines the

advantage of large scale mainframe architecture and performance with minicomputer packaging and pricing and is ideally suited to a broad range of applications. The 8/32's first customers are using it for flight simulation, seismic data processing, commercial data processing and distributive data processing.[21]

By 1977 Perkin-Elmer reported that it offered its customers a broad array of complementary computers, peripheral products, and terminals.[22]

In February 1979, soon after IBM's 4331/4341 processor announcement, Perkin-Elmer announced the first of two new computer systems, the 3220, followed by the 3240. The 3240 was reported as supporting up to 16 million bytes of main memory — the same capacity available at the top of IBM's line, the 3033 — and up to 115 billion bytes of on-line disk storage; both were offered for a diverse range of scientific, control, business, and real-time applications.[23]

Harris Corporation

Until the early 1970s the principal business of Harris was the manufacture of typesetting and other printing equipment. In 1969 it began deliveries of the Fototronic-CRT typesetter, a computerized cathode ray tube unit. There soon followed additional systems to perform typesetting and other applications related to the printing business. In 1971 Harris acquired a minority interest in Datacraft Corporation, a manufacturer of computer systems in the range of the PDP 11 and IBM System/360 Model 50, and of core memory for its own processors and for IBM System/360 processors. The following year Harris acquired CSI, a subsidiary of UCC, which later became the Wyly Corporation. CSI manufactured programmable communications controllers compatible with IBM processors, as well as a line of terminals, printers, and card readers.[24]

In 1976-79 Harris introduced a series of new computer products, including computer systems, front-end processors, and terminal equipment.

In 1979 Harris enhanced its 1600 distributed-data-processing product line by introducing a faster processor with double the memory capacity of the previous 1600, which permitted ". . . simultaneous execution of all five distributed data processing functions — remote batch, local batch, data entry, local interactive and remote interactive processing."[25]

The previous year Harris had introduced the "high-performance" Series 500, consisting of the 550 and 570 systems, a family of powerful, disk-oriented virtual-memory computer systems for educational, scientific, and industrial end users. It could perform concurrent interactive time-sharing, multistream batch, remote job entry, and real-time processing.[26] Harris followed up in 1979 with the Series 800, which could support up to 128 interactive terminals simultaneously. The 850 processor was marketed with main memory expandable to over 3 million bytes.[27]

Wang Laboratories

Wang Laboratories was founded in 1951. It first marketed EDP products in 1964, and by 1972 its U.S. EDP revenues were reported to be about $30 million. By fiscal 1979 its data-processing revenues were $280 million.[28]

Wang produced computers and peripheral devices for data-processing systems for use in business, technical, and scientific applications and for word-processing systems. Its major line of computer systems for information processing has been the 2200, first introduced in 1973. In October 1977 Wang introduced the 2200VS, which had multiple-terminal, multiple-language, and improved programming capabilities. It could support up to 23 work stations and 2.3 billion bytes of on-line disk storage. The 2200VS was offered with 512,000 bytes of main memory.[29]

In June 1979 Wang introduced an additional member of the 2200VS family — the VS-100, which supported up to 128 work stations and expanded disk storage capacity to 4.6 billion bytes. The VS-100, which sold for up to $800,000, had multiprocessing capabilities using several languages, and supported a variety of telecommunications options and data base management software. In September of that year Wang's management stated that the company's major competitors, at least at the "higher end" of its business systems, included ". . . larger IBM System 3 configurations, the low end of the IBM 370 line, the IBM E Series 4331 and 4341 and the IBM 8100, Digital Equipment Corp. (PDP 11/34-11/70 series), Data General's CS 20/40/60 series and Eclipse series, and Hewlett-Packard's 3000."[30]

Tandem Computers

Tandem Computers, Inc., was formed in 1974, and shipped its first computer system in May 1976. Its revenues grew from $581,000 in fiscal 1976 to $55,974,000 in fiscal 1979.[31]

Tandem's computer systems consisted of multiple processors that operated as a single system. Its systems were expandable from a basic two-processor system to a system utilizing 16 processors. Its use of multiprocessors permitted nonstop operation because, in the event of one processor's failure, another processor automatically took control of the work being performed. In 1979 Tandem described the scope and capabilities of its NonStop system thus:

> The Tandem NonStop System is the first general purpose, commercial computer system designed specifically to fulfill the critical needs of on-line transaction processing. The innovative, fault-tolerant Tandem architecture virtually eliminates the risk of system failures and protects the customers' data bases from damages caused by electronic malfunctions. The system is also the only one on the market that can be

expanded modularly — without any programming changes and even while the system is running — from a two-processor, mid-sized system up to a 16-processor, large-scale system, creating a continuous range of models priced from approximately $150,000 to over $3,000,000.[32]

Each Tandem processor in the 1979 configuration supported up to two megabytes of main memory, large disk capacity (for example, a ten-processor Tandem system could support 9.6 billion bytes of on-line disk storage), a variety of programming languages, including COBOL and FORTRAN, and a data base management system. (Tandem obtained its peripheral equipment from OEM suppliers.) Tandem also offered the EXPAND network operating system, which permitted users to build a distributed-data-processing network of up to 225 geographically dispersed Tandem systems. Under EXPAND the network could grow to be as large as 4,080 processors, each capable of accessing a geographically distributed data base as if it were in the local system. It was practically immune to failure of particular processors or communication lines.[33]

Datapoint

In 1969 Datapoint introduced its first product, a solid-state terminal used as a teletypewriter replacement in computer systems. Thereafter Datapoint manufactured a variety of processors, intelligent terminals, communications equipment, and software, emphasizing throughout the distributed-data-processing capabilities of its products.

In 1977 Datapoint announced the 6600 advanced business processor for stand-alone processing, time-sharing with up to 24 terminals, and network applications, and the attached resource computer, which was a distributed-processing system with multiple time-sharing capabilities.[34]

The following year Datapoint introduced the attached support processor, a front-end processor for IBM 360 and 370 computer systems.[35]

In fiscal 1979 Datapoint's revenues were $242 million, a nearly sevenfold increase over its fiscal 1974 revenues of $34 million.[36]

PLUG-COMPATIBLE PROCESSOR MANUFACTURERS

Beginning in 1975, with the first shipment of a plug-compatible CPU by the Amdahl Corporation, a new type of competitor in the computer industry emerged. Thereafter, additional manufacturers began to make and market computer processors that used IBM's software and could, in effect, be plugged into IBM or IBM-compatible peripheral equipment to replace an IBM-manufactured processor, much as plug-compatible storage or input-output equipment was marketed to replace compatible IBM peripheral equipment.

Amdahl Corporation

Amdahl Corporation was founded in 1970 to develop, manufacture, and market large-scale computer systems for general-purpose applications. The principal founder of the company was Gene Amdahl, who had been one of IBM's chief processor designers for the System/360 and who left IBM to start his new company.

As of 1975 the two principal stockholders in Amdahl were the Japanese computer manufacturer Fujitsu, with a 41 percent interest, and Heizer Corporation, a U.S. venture capital company, with a 31 percent interest. Fujitsu manufactured major subassemblies for Amdahl computers.[37]

In mid-1975, after a five-year gestation, Amdahl introduced the 470 V/6 processor, the first IBM plug-compatible CPU. It was designed as a one-for-one replacement for the IBM 370/168 processor, at that time IBM's largest, most powerful computer. Amdahl processors could use existing IBM-designed systems control programming. Computer systems with an Amdahl processor and plug-compatible peripheral equipment could conceivably be constructed with no IBM-manufactured hardware included in them, and no connection with IBM except the IBM-created system control programming.[38]

Amdahl's IBM plug-compatible processors were an immediate success. By 1978 the firm achieved revenues of $321 million and had introduced several new processors, all IBM plug-compatible: the 470 V/6 II processor, comparable with the 3032; the 407 V/7, comparable with the IBM 3033; the 470 V/5, comparable with the IBM 3031 and 370/168-3; the 470 V/5-II; and the 470 V/8, its most powerful processor, comparable with IBM's 3033.[39]

In addition to its expanded hardware offerings, in 1978 Amdahl began to market software enhancements for its product line, including operating system performance enhancements called the MVS/SE Assist and the VM/Performance Enhancement.[40]

Others

Following the introduction of Amdahl's 470 V/6, other companies brought out IBM-compatible CPUs.

National Advanced Systems manufactured and marketed IBM-compatible processors (at first marketed by Itel) that offered performance equivalent to IBM's 4300 series and 3031/3032 processors. It also marketed a processor in the 3033 range, manufactured in Japan by Hitachi.[41]

Nixdorf announced in May 1980 its plans to offer a 4331-compatible system in the United States.[42]

In May 1977 Control Data Corporation (CDC) announced six models of two IBM-compatible computer systems, developed and manufactured by IPL Systems, Inc. Called the Omega 480-I and Omega 480-II, they were, according to CDC, in the 370/135 through 148 performance range. CDC also stated at the time of their announcement that Omega systems could be ". . . configured with Control Data plug-compatible peripherals that include disk, tape and printer subsystems, and the CDC 38500 Mass Storage System."[43] In March 1979 CDC announced the Omega 480 Model 3, manufactured by IPL, said to be in the performance range of IBM's 3031.[44]

Magnuson Systems Corporation, founded in 1977, announced the first models of its M80 line of CPUs, compatible with the IBM 370/138 and 148 in May 1978. In March 1979 it announced three new IBM-compatible CPUS, and reduced prices for its original processors and memory. The new processors reportedly exceeded the performance of IBM's 4331 and 4341 processors.[45]

Two Pi Co., Inc., a subsidiary of Philips of Holland, manufactured IBM plug-compatible CPUs in the performance range of IBM's 370/138 and 4300 series processors. In April 1978 Two Pi announced its first plug-compatible processor, the V32, which could support up to 4 million bytes of main memory. Two Pi in May 1980 announced that it had added integrated controllers to the channels of its V32 processor, which enabled it to attach a variety of non-IBM-compatible peripherals. Two Pi marketed the V32 on an OEM basis to other companies.[46]

Nanodata Computer Corporation, formed in 1971, developed the QM-1 Emulator, which could emulate IBM, DEC, and Data General computers, as well as computers of 23 other companies. In June 1980 Nanodata introduced the IBM-compatible QMX 6300 series, which consisted of three models in the 4331 and 4341 performance range and could be configured with up to 4 million bytes of main memory.[47]

In March 1980 Formation, Inc., introduced the 4000 Information System; expandable to 4 million bytes of main memory, it was said to consist of multiple microprocessing units, microcoded to emulate IBM 370 channels and controllers. Formation stated that the 4000 system could utilize IBM software, was compatible with the 370 program library, and could accommodate the DOX/VS, OS/VSI, and VM 370 operating systems.[48]

Paradyne Corporation during the 1970s expanded its product offerings to include communications and network controllers of the IBM 3705 type, and incorporated IBM-compatible microcoded minicomputers in its PIXNET data network system.[49]

SEMICONDUCTOR MANUFACTURERS

During the 1970s advances in semiconductor technology played a major role in lowering the price and increasing the performance and reliability of computer equipment. Semiconductor components were and are manufactured by a large number of companies, including computer equipment manufacturers like IBM and many others. A number of semiconductor component companies have expanded into the manufacture of computer equipment.

Texas Instruments

Texas Instruments (TI) was one of the early developers of transistors for commercial purposes. Since that time it has marketed a broad range of computer equipment, including, in recent years, the DS 990 Commercial Computer System and the TI Series 700 Distributed Processing Systems. The 990 computer system supported over 2 million bytes of main memory, a data base management system, and programming languages such as COBOL, FORTRAN, and BASIC. As part of its Series 700, TI offered a family of intelligent terminals, disk storage, printers, and bubble memory devices.[50]

Intel Corporation

Intel, founded in 1968, became a leading supplier of large-scale integrated circuits. Intel capitalized on its capabilities in the fabrication of semiconductor memory and large-scale integrated circuits to expand beyond the production of semiconductor memory circuits to microprocessors and to complete memory systems, including IBM and DEC plug-compatible memory systems.

By the end of the decade Intel's microprocessors were employed in Wang word processors, Hazeltine terminals, and Aydin video graphics terminals. Intel enhanced the capabilities of its microprocessors by developing and marketing sophisticated software, a variety of programming languages, and peripheral chips to enable its microprocessors to control floppy disk drives, CRT displays, and a variety of communications protocols. Intel offered a number of languages for its microprocessors, including FORTRAN 77, BASIC, PL/M (which was said to be similar in concept to IBM's PL/1), and PASCAL.[51]

In addition to its microprocessor products Intel, beginning in 1971, offered a line of add-on memories for the IBM 370 series. In 1975 it began to market its IBM-compatible memories directly to end users and through leasing companies. Intel also manufactured memory for Digital Equipment computers. For the PDP 11 line it offered products to expand memory to 4 million bytes; the company also offered memory for DEC's LSI-11 family.[52]

Over the past several years Intel has also moved into new, high-technology computer storage devices: charge-coupled devices, bubble memory, semiconductor disk storage subsystems, and data base processors. For example, in 1979 Intel announced the FAST-3805 semiconductor disk storage subsystem, which used semiconductor technology with far faster access times than other disk technologies. Intel described the FAST-3805 as a random-access, memory-based device that emulated the IBM 3830/3350 and 2835/2305 disk subsystems, and stated that it could triple disk traffic without requiring additional channel or controller capacity.[53]

Early in 1979 Intel acquired MRI Systems Corp., which developed and marketed the System 2000 data base management system for IBM, IBM-compatible, CDC, and Univac computers. About a year later Intel introduced its FAST-3805 data base assist processor. This processor used Intel's FAST-3805 to increase the speed of certain System 2000 functions.[54]

National Semiconductor Corporation

National Semiconductor Corporation was formed in 1967, and quickly became one of the leading manufacturers in the semiconductor industry. In 1973 National began a seven-year evolution from components supplier to manufacturer of semiconductor-based computer systems.[55]

As the first step in that evolution, in 1973 National Semiconductor began to market point-of-sale terminal equipment comparable with the equipment of other manufacturers, such as NCR and IBM. By 1974 it had developed a laser scanning system for use with point-of-sale systems.

National then began to manufacture IBM-compatible memory systems that were marketed by Itel and others to end users of IBM processors. It also started to produce processors plug-compatible with the IBM 370/148 and 158. This equipment, known as the AS-4 and AS-5 processors, was at first also marketed by Itel. In 1978 National began marketing its memory products directly to end users.[56]

In 1979 National Semiconductor acquired Itel's computer sales, service, and support operations. The renamed organization, National Advanced Systems, was to market a complete line of medium-to-large-scale IBM-compatible computer products, including current and future systems from National and other computer and peripheral manufacturers. National Advanced Systems later announced the AS/3000 series, equivalent to the IBM 4341 processor and the 370/158-3; the AS/5000 series, equivalent to the IBM 3031 processor; and the AS/7000 series, equivalent to the upper end of the IBM 303X series. The three models of the AS/7000 series were manufactured in Japan by Hitachi, which had been marketing these larger IBM-compatible processors through Itel.[57]

COMMUNICATIONS FIRMS

When all computer equipment that was part of a general-purpose computer system was located in a single room, data communications — across distances — played no significant role in computer systems. But even in the 1950s customers, at least advanced customers, were seeking methods of configuring computer systems that were not bounded by a computer room, systems in which input and output, and even processing and storage, could be performed at remote locations. The military's SAGE system of the 1950s and the IBM/American Airlines SABRE airlines reservation system were examples of these early efforts. By the 1970s such systems had become commonplace, and users routinely configured their computer systems with substantial and growing proportions of geographically dispersed equipment of all kinds.

Firms originally in the communications business have moved into the computer industry.

AT&T

AT&T is, of course, one of the world's largest corporations and a leader in communications technologies. It had been a major participant in the computer industry and a competitor of IBM for many years and was in fact manufacturing EDP systems for its affiliated companies and others by 1965 at the latest. The scope of its efforts increased in the 1970s as communications and data-processing technology rapidly converged. AT&T began to introduce a number of new EDP products and services.

The Dataspeed 40 Terminals

Western Electric Corporation's Teletype subsidiary was already a prime competitor of IBM in computer terminal equipment when, in 1975, AT&T announced new models of its Dataspeed 40 (later called 40/4) terminal as a direct replacement for the IBM 3270 terminal. IBM faced substantial competition from the Dataspeed 40/4 in marketing to the Bell System operating companies. For example, in January 1978 New York Telephone selected 7,000 Dataspeed 40/4s, 20 Comten 3650 communications processors, and 16 CDC CYBER 1000 communication switching systems for AT&T's Bell Administrative Network Communications System. This equipment displaced 7,000 installed IBM 3277 terminals.[58]

Dimension Private Branch Exchange (PBX). Early in 1975 AT&T introduced the first of a family of PBXs known as the Dimension PBX. This system used solid-state technology and a miniaturized computer. By 1980 *Electronic News* reported that the Dimension 2000 provided automatic wake-up service, room status, inventory reports, and itemized telephone call billing for hotels. These applications could be, and often were, performed by System/3 and other IBM products, including 370 systems.[59]

Transaction Network Service (TNS). In 1976 AT&T introduced TNS, which was developed to handle large volumes of business transactions that call for short inquiries and responses. It included terminals and message-switching software. Among its applications were credit authorization and check verification; electronic funds transfer systems; reservation systems; and inventory control and quotation services — applications commonly performed by other computer systems.[60]

Advanced Communications Service (ACS). In July 1978 AT&T filed a petition asking the FCC to tariff AT&T's proposed Advanced Communications Service. Through ACS, AT&T would provide, with the use of its own computer hardware and software, unified network control of customers' processors and remote terminals or storage devices. Both communications and data-processing functions would be performed by ACS, which was planned to offer program and data storage and a variety of other computer services on a shared basis.[61] These were functions commonly performed by other distributed-data-processing systems.

Software. AT&T also licensed computer software. An advertisement that appeared in *Datamation* for February 1978 stated:

[A]s one of the world's largest computer users, the Bell System has developed a lot of software for its own use. For data management, statistical analysis, practically anything done with computer. A limited amount of this software has been made available for licensing . . . [including] : The UNIX system . . . a multi-programmed, time-sharing operating system for the DEC PDP 11/40-45-70 minicomputers. It has features seldom found even in larger systems, including over 100 subsystems and utilities.[62]

Other software products marketed by AT&T included a computer management system and a text-editing system.

ESS and Other Switching Systems. In the early 1970s AT&T continued its changeover to its electronic switching system (ESS) stored-program computer, which it had begun in the mid-1960s. IBM was bidding System/360, Series/1, and System/7 products, among others, against ESS at Bell operating companies. IBM marketed the System/7 in competition with the Bell Labs TDR System for traffic data collection applications at Bell telephone companies. IBM also promoted the System/7 and Series/1 for computerized directory assistance systems, and duplexed Series/1 processors to perform computerized electronic billing system applications in competition with Bell System products, such as LAMAC, ETS — which used ESS processors — and BDT, which performed the same applications.[63]

Northern Telecom, Ltd.

Northern Telecom, a Canadian company, is the principal supplier of telecommunications equipment in Canada and the second largest in North America. In 1979 roughly 40 percent of its revenues came from operations in the United States.[64]

The management of Northern Telecom recognized the progressive merging of data-processing and communications capabilities and technologies. In 1975 Northern Telecom introduced a digital switching system, and in 1976 it announced its Digital World line of telecommunications systems based on digital technology. Digital World systems included computers. According to Northern Telecom:

The basic technique used in digital telecommunications systems is identical to that used in most computers: information is transformed into numerical codes and represented by electrical pulses. Each system is programmed to identify, sort and compare electrical pulses and to make decisions as to what to do with them. This decision-making process constitutes the intelligence of an electronic system. It is essential to digital telecommunications equipment, such as Northern Telecom's Digital Multiplex System (DMS) family of products, and to computers.[65]

In 1978 Northern Telecom completed three significant acquisitions in the United States: Danray, Data 100, and Sycor. In addition, as of 1979 it owned a 21.9 percent interest in Intersil, a manufacturer of integrated circuits and IBM-compatible memory systems. Also in 1978 Northern Telecom created Northern Telecom Systems Corporation (NTSC) to manage its electronic office equipment business; Data 100 and Sycor were placed under NTSC management. For 1979 Northern Telecom reported NTSC's revenues as $349.8 million, 18.4 percent of total corporate sales.[66]

Danray manufactured the auxiliary data exchange, which permitted users to connect computers, terminals, word-processing machines, and other information-generating equipment to their internal telephone systems.[67]

Data 100 was formed in 1968. When acquired by Northern Telecom, it offered a family of multifunction terminals and processors that could be used for remote job entry, data entry, remote or local file management, stand-alone processing, or any combination thereof.[68]

Sycor was formed in 1967 and began shipment of its first products, terminals, in 1969. By 1977 it had expanded its offerings to include an array of products for distributed data processing. Sycor's products were described by Northern Telecom thus:

> Northern Telecom's Sycor intelligent terminal systems enter information and process data at sites remote from a central computer. One of Northern Telecom's most sophisticated terminal systems, the Sycor 445 distributed data processing system, is equipped with a central processing unit and up to eight individual work stations. These work stations concurrently and independently perform a variety of different tasks such as data entry, data communications and data processing. An innovative software package introduced in 1977, called SYCOR-LINK, enables the Sycor 445 and other Sycor distributed data processing systems to communicate with each other and to share printing devices and information stored on magnetic disks.[69]

FCC Computer Inquiry II

Perhaps the most significant development of the 1970s affecting the role of AT&T and other large communications firms in the EDP industry, at least up to the decision in January 1982 that ended the U.S. government's antitrust case, was the FCC's decision in May 1980, in Computer Inquiry II (Docket no. 20828). In that decision the FCC adopted a policy of regulating only basic transmission services, defined as "limited to the . . . offering of transmission capacity for the movement of information."[70] The FCC expressly determined that it was not in the public interest for it to regulate "enhanced services," which it defined as

> . . . any offering over the telecommunications network which is more than a basic transmission service. In an enhanced service, for example,

computer processing applications are used to act on the context, code, protocol, and other aspects of the subscriber's information.[71]

Similarly, the FCC ruled that it would no longer regulate any customer premises equipment (CPE). It declined to distinguish, in determining tariffs, among CPE used for different functions. In its ruling the FCC stated:

> We have concluded that CPE should not be classified as to its communications or data processing characteristics and that no classification scheme should be adopted. Implicit in this is the fact that no demarcation can be drawn for differentiating CPE for tariff purposes.[72]

Further, AT&T, in the FCC's view, was free to compete on a unregulated basis in all areas of the EDP industry.[73]

By that time several firms, including Xerox, Fujitsu, Exxon, and IBM itself, were developing total integrated systems of data and word processing and communications for the market.[74]

SOFTWARE SUPPLIERS, SERVICE BUREAUS, AND TIME-SHARING COMPANIES

Software Companies

As noted earlier, software companies, which began to emerge in the 1950s, entered the industry in large numbers in the 1960s. They provided software and technical assistance to both hardware manufacturers and users, and they offered software as alternatives to similar goods produced by hardware manufacturers and, in many cases, as alternatives to hardware marketed by those manufacturers. In 1975 there were approximately 1,000 independent firms offering slightly more than 3,000 software products, as well as contract programming services, and having total revenues of approximately $1.3 billion.[75]

Some examples of software suppliers and their products follow.

The Computer Software Company (TCSC) offered a product called EDOS, which was claimed to enhance IBM's disk operating system for 360 and 370. Early in the marketing of EDOS, which was announced in 1972, TCSC encouraged leasing companies ". . . to utilize EDOS as a means of enhancing or extending their system 360 portfolio."[76]

Informatics marketed SHRINK, a file compression system that could reduce a user's requirements for large disk and tape files. Other companies, such as Computer Action, Inc., Applied Data Research, and Electronic Data Preparation Corp., also marketed data compression and data management products that reduced disk storage requirements.[77]

Cincom Systems, Inc., was formed in October 1968. Its major product in the 1970s was the TOTAL data base management system, which offered a variety of data base functions. TOTAL was written initially to operate on IBM computers and ultimately on IBM's System/360, System/370, System/3, and System/34 computers. It was designed to reduce core requirements and increase effective disk storage capacity and performance.[78] It was also compatible with and portable to other machines. In addition to IBM computers, TOTAL could run on those manufactured by DEC, Perkin-Elmer, Prime, Honeywell, Univac, CDC, NCR, Varian, International Computers, Ltd., Harris, and Modcomp.[79]

A November 1979 survey of data base management (DBM) systems described the data base software offerings of 18 software companies that operated on a broad spectrum of computer systems, including minicomputers manufactured by DEC, Systems Engineering Laboratories, BTI Systems, Inc., Data General, Modcomp, Perkin-Elmer, Basic Four, and Wang. In addition, some manufacturers themselves offered DBMs, including Data General, DEC, Hewlett-Packard, Honeywell, Prime, Tandem, and Texas Instruments.[80] Data services companies also developed DBMs that they offered with their data services. These included NOMAD, marketed by National CSS; MANAGE, marketed by Computer Sciences; and MAGNUM, marketed by Tymshare.[81] More recently companies began offering DBM software for implementation on microcomputers. For example, Micro Data Base Systems, Inc., reportedly offered its MDBS data base management system for both the Zilog Z80 and the Intel 8080 microcomputers.[82]

System Development Corporation (SDC) was organized as a not-for-profit corporation in 1956 to support the U.S. Air Force with system training and computer program development, installation, and maintenance for the SAGE Continental Air Defense System. This was the first giant real-time information system, and it soon unlocked the door to a dynamic new technology with multiple applications. In 1969 SDC decided to convert to a for-profit corporation; thereafter it expanded into a variety of contract, programming, and data services while continuing its development of command and control communications systems.

By 1980 SDC offered turnkey systems, utilizing its own software and hardware it purchased from manufacturers, including the TEXT II newspaper automation system, which employed a network of minicomputers and SDC software to provide a complete system capability for automated entry, editing, and composition of news and advertising copy as well as automated billing, accounts receivable, cash posting, and management reports.[83] It also marketed an on-line retail banking system, consisting of a minicomputer and SDC software linked to terminals for teller inquiry, instant signature verification, on-line account information, and automatic teller machines.[84]

SDC also provided a variety of service offerings, both through its own computer facilities and by developing or managing users' systems. Through its support service offerings it operated its customers' computing facilities and provided other technical and operations support. SDC developed information systems for many users, including municipalities and hospitals, and provided facilities management services for a variety of users. SDC's transaction services enabled many customers to access its special information management systems, paying for service on a "per transaction" basis. SDC offered a variety of services through its own computer facilities: a claims administration system that provided computerized processing of medical and dental claims for corporations and insurance companies; several automated services for banking applications, including investment and dividend reinvestment, account records maintenance, and processing of time deposits and mortgage loans; and search services, which provided on-line bibliographic information retrieval from SDC's information banks in science, technology, engineering, patents, and commerce.[85]

SDC built upon its experience in fabricating hardware subassemblies to move toward the manufacture of hardware products, an unusual development for a software company.[86]

Computer Sciences Corporation (CSC) continued its growth through the 1970s in contract services and data services. Contract services were performed to a client's contractual specifications. They ranged from the development of custom-designed systems to the management of a client's complete computer requirements, and included Medicaid management and informatiion systems and order-entry and inventory control systems. Data services consisted of proprietary services, such as INFONET, that were marketed to numerous clients (including, prominently, the federal government), transaction services for a specific industry or market, and other data base-oriented or applications-oriented computer services.[87] CSC's annual revenues reached $452 million in 1980.[88]

In 1978 CSC announced a data base manager (called MANAGE); it also offered, through INFONET, data base management capabilities utilizing MRI's System 2000 and TRW's generalized information management system.[89] By 1980 CSC had inaugurated its distributed network services, which combined CSC-provided DEC PDP-11/23 and PDP-11/44 processors, configured to CSC specifications, and CSC software with INFONET's communications and computer facilities. A subset of CSC's MANAGE data base management system had been adapted to operate on these DEC computers.[90]

Service Bureau/Time-Sharing Companies

As noted earlier, in the 1970s a number of computer equipment manufacturers, including CDC and Xerox, purveyed a variety of sophisticated data-processing services. There were, in addition, many service bureau and time-sharing companies that offered computing services to users as alternatives to the installation of in-house computer equipment — either entire systems or additions of equipment to already installed systems. We cite only a few examples.

Automatic Data Processing, Inc. (ADP), was 21 years old in 1970. In 1972 it began to offer order-entry, billing, and inventory services via terminals in the client's offices that were to be connected to ADP's computer complex through a nationwide network of dedicated telephone lines. Other services available were accounts receivable, sales analysis, profit analysis, payroll, accounts payable, general ledger, financial statement preparation, and a host of analytical management reports.[91] By 1977 ADP offered an extensive line of data base applications in finance, securities analysis, economics, foreign exchange rates, demographics, and chemistry.[92]

In the 1970s ADP also began to market hardware products manufactured by others in ADP-engineered systems. For example, in 1975 it first reported that it had developed a minicomputer system, which it programmed to deliver service similar to that provided by ADP's central installation, for on-line clients with large processing volumes at their locations. The first applications for the minicomputer service were inventory control and accounting.[93] In 1978 the company introduced ADP/Onsite, a service using an on-site computer that could perform local processing and could access the ADP computer network, and that provided several data bases, four standard languages, customer programming assistance, and day-to-day service support.[94]

By 1979 ADP served more than 75,000 users and provided computing services to virtually every segment of industry, finance, and government. Its revenues that year were $371 million.[95]

General Electric (GE) began the 1970s with a highly successful time-sharing/service bureau business. At the time GE merged its computer business into Honeywell, GE's Ventures Task Force recommended that the company retain its services business, which it did. By the late 1970s GE's computer service network reached over 600 cities in 24 countries. Its 1979 data-processing revenues were estimated to be about $350 million.[96]

GE also marketed a line of computer printers and communications controllers, the TermiNet family, which, according to GE, were capable of emulating Univac and IBM remote print stations.[97] In the late 1970s GE began offering the Marklink III computer system, for distributed data processing. The Marklink III minicomputer processor was manufactured by Texas Instruments and could operate at a customer's location as part of GE's time-sharing computer network.[98]

A GE subsidiary, General Electric Credit Corporation, was engaged in leasing computer equipment and, by 1978, had over $600 million of such equipment on lease.[99] GE also advertised that the company offered computer maintenance services on a worldwide basis ". . . to OEM's and computer manufacturers who need a ready-made service organization."[100]

McDonnell Douglas Automation Company (McAuto) was formed in 1970 from the consolidation of in-house computer service organizations throughout the McDonnell Douglas Corporation and the former McDonnell Automation Company, which had been operating as a service bureau since 1960. In 1970 McAuto's revenues were about $47 million. For 1979 the company was ranked twenty-fifth in data-processing revenues in *Datamation's* "Top 100" company list, and its revenues from data services were $150 million.[101]

During the 1970s McAuto expanded the scope of its announced offerings to include the following:

– A Service called CO-OP (Customer On-Line Order Processing System). By renting this CO-OP "system" and acquiring only terminal equipment, which would be located on its premises, a customer could process orders, handle inquiries, print acknowledgments, and screen parts sent out against its inventory.

— The LAND package, which performed subdivision platting for condominium and shopping center projects.

— The Automated Shareholder Records System (ASRS), a software program used by corporations to keep track of shareholder data

— An inventory control system

— A facility planning service and an educational management service.

By 1979 McDonnell Douglas, McAuto's parent, announced that it had formed a subsidiary, the McDonnell Douglas Finance Corporation, to engage in the leasing of "major equipment," including computer systems.[102] Also in 1979 McDonnell Douglas acquired Microdata Corporation, which had about $94 million in revenues that year. Microdata manufactured several lines of computer systems, including the Reality family. In 1979 Microdata expanded the Reality line: three models were said to compare in performance with the IBM System/34 and System/38, Univac BC/7, and MCR 8200 series; the fourth and largest model reportedly supported up to 512,000 bytes of main memory, 514 million bytes of on-line disk storage, and the Reality data base manager.[103]

EXXON'S DIVERSE ENTRY PROGRAM

During the 1970s Exxon — the nation's largest industrial firm, with 1979 revenues of $84 billion — entered the computer industry by acquiring control of several firms, mostly suppliers of hardware. It appeared, for a time at least, that Exxon was determined to become one of the leading suppliers of EDP products and services. For 1979 it reported that the combined revenues of these computer companies had reached $194 million.[104]

Zilog, Inc.

Zilog started business on May 15, 1975, and soon thereafter received financing from Exxon. Its product line ranged from chips to microcomputer systems.

Zilog's microcomputer systems in 1978 constituted a line of general-purpose electronic digital computer systems ranging in price from $6,000 to $18,000.[105] The software that Zilog made available for its MCZ series of systems included an operating system and programming languages such as BASIC, FORTRAN IV, 1974 ANSI, standard COBOL, Level 1, and a variety of utility packages. Zilog advertised that the disk capacity of the MCZ 1/90, for instance, could be expanded to 40 million bytes.[106]

By 1978 Zilog had announced the Z8000 chip, which had a 16-bit word length, was faster than the Z80 by a factor of five to ten, and showed significant advances over the Z80 in its ability to support parallel processing, networking, and file maintenance. As was the case with the Z80, the Z8000 had an operating system and supported various languages such as BASIC, COBOL, and FORTRAN.[107]

Zilog microcomputers were used for business, engineering, and scientific applications, as intelligent terminals, and as front-end processors in other computer systems. Zilog components (boards and chips) also were used in a wide variety of peripheral products.[108]

Periphonics Corp.

Periphonics, a wholly owned affiliate of Exxon, in 1980 offered a variety of communications and terminal products. It marketed the T-COMM communications system, which had a programmable telecommunications processor designed to support a variety of terminal devices, including those offered by IBM, Burroughs, and NCR. Periphonics advertised that T-COMM could effect communication between terminals and an IBM processor without the use of IBM telecommunications access methods, network control programming, or the one megabyte of memory or extra CPU cycles needed to support that software.[109] In addition, it marketed add-on memory for DEC PDP-11 computers that could extend the main memory of a PDP-11 to 2 million bytes.[110]

Ramtek Corp.

Ramtek, in which Exxon owned a minority interest, manufactured graphics and other intelligent terminals. The Ramtek 9000 series terminals, for example, were programmable, microprocessor-controlled, graphics terminals with a main memory expandable to 16,000 bytes. Ramtek also offered stand-alone graphics terminals that included a Zilog Z80 microprocessor that functioned as a terminal controller, and the 8000 series of programmable intelligent terminals, which included models that emulated certain Univac Uniscope terminals.[111]

Vydec, Inc.

Vydec was a division of Exxon Enterprises, the new business development arm of Exxon. It manufactured and marketed word-processing systems. In 1979 Vydec announced new word-processing systems built around Zilog Z80 microprocessors. The largest system included six Z80s and supported up to 64,000 bytes of main memory. In addition the system offered two Shugart minidiskette drives, printers, and a communications processor that permitted Vydec word processors to communicate with similarly equipped Vydec and other processing equipment as well as Telex and TWX networks.[112]

In 1980 Vydec announced its 1800 word processor, which, among other things, offered a records processing package allowing users to maintain a data base of records, and a math package that handled certain calculations. It also announced a shared-resource office system. This system consisted of a micro-processor-based system controller or CPU, various Vydec work stations, and Exxon's QYX intelligent typewriter, which could be equipped with memory and diskette storage and could communicate with other QYX machines, with Vydec word processors, and with computers.[113] The controller could support up to 75 million characters of disk storage and could address up to 1 million bytes of directly addressable memory.[114]

Others

By 1980 Exxon also owned Qwip, which manufactured facsimile transmission equipment; Optical Information Systems, Inc., which manufactured semiconductor laser products for computers; and Dialog Systems, Inc., an affiliate of Exxon Enterprises. Dialog reportedly had developed speech recognition equipment for voice input and voice response for computer data entry, information retrieval, and telephone network applications. According to Dialog, its products were intended to permit users ". . . to transmit data directly to and retrieve data directly from a computer by speaking over any telephone."[115]

FOREIGN COMPETITORS

Most American computer manufacturers plan, develop, manufacture, and market their product lines on a worldwide basis. In this worldwide business IBM and other American companies have faced increasingly aggressive competition from foreign rivals, both inside and outside the United States.

Japanese Manufacturers

The Japanese have made the EDP industry a national priority of the highest order.[116] It is supported not only by the Japanese successes around the world in other electronic industries — radios, televisions, home videotape recorders — but also by the expressed policy of the Japanese government.[117]

Under government guidance the major Japanese companies by the latter part of the 1970s were paired into three groups — Fujitsu/Hitachi, Nippon Electric/Toshiba, and Mitsubishi/Oki — for purposes of research and development. The Japanese government gave them assistance through special depreciation allowances, the sharing of developmental costs, special tax concessions, and export subsidies in some cases.[118]

The Japanese clearly intended to acquire a significant share of American computer markets, perhaps similar to their share of the U.S. automobile market (18-20 percent.)[119] By the late 1970s they certainly had the technical capability and products to meet that goal. Japanese computer companies manufactured and marketed a full menu of computer products, from LSI semiconductor components to peripheral equipment of all kinds, to some of the largest computers in the world.

The sophistication of the Japanese industry was especially evident in its response to IBM's Model 4300. Within six months of that announcement, NEC, Mitsubishi, Fujitsu, and Hitachi had all announced competing products. In addition, the Japanese were already exporting significant amounts of computer and computer-related products to the United States.

One class of products in which the Japanese exhibited growing strength was semiconductor components. By 1980 they had captured an estimated 42 percent of the American memory market.[120] Japanese semiconductor technology often equaled or surpassed that of IBM. For example, they had developed the use of E-beam technology to produce memory and logic circuits — a process that increased yields, reliability, and density.[121]

In October 1979 Fujitsu committed $10 million for the construction of a memory and logic assembly facility in California, and Hitachi was completing an assembly plant for semiconductor memories in Texas. In Japan the government helped companies fund research and development efforts — for instance a research program in Josephson (supercooled superconducting) technology by Fujitsu.[122] The Japanese semiconductor manufacturers were part of a program sponsored by the Japanese government, called the VLSI (very large-scale integration) effort to develop products, circuits, and tools for the manufacture of these components. The program was also developing and doing research in computer products. These Japanese programs involved an outlay of approximately $500 million — comparable with the expenditures of IBM in its Stanford Program, which was also an effort to develop very large-scale integrated circuitry.[123]

Japanese computer products were already being marketed in the United States by the late 1970s. For example:

— National Advanced Systems marketed Hitachi computer systems. In addition, Hitachi marketed bubble memory to CDC and printers to Centronics.

— Fujitsu owned about 41 percent of Amdahl and provided Amdahl with CPU subassemblies. Moreover, Fujitsu entered into a joint venture with TRW to market Fujitsu computers. In addition, Fujitsu marketed high-speed tape drives to Memorex and Winchester-type disk drives to OEMs. It also supplied 64K memory chips to NCR, and logic to CDC for the STAR computer.

— Nippon Peripherals, Ltd., a joint venture of Fujitsu and Hitachi, marketed its advanced tape and disk subsystem through Memorex.

— Nippon Electric Company marketed small computers through a U.S. subsidiary, NEC Information Systems. Honeywell used systems control programming developed by NEC for some of its Series 60 computers, as well as certain printers, logic, and memory manufactured by NEC.

— Melcom Business Systems, Inc., a U.S. subsidiary of Mitsubishi, marketed the Melcom 80 small computer. Mitsubishi also marketed peripherals on an OEM basis.

— Toshiba sold its TOSBAC small computers through Toshiba America. It also supplied consoles to Honeywell.

— Sharp, NPL, and Oki offered a variety of EDP products, including microprocessors, printers, card readers, and IBM plug-compatible disk drives.[124]

European Manufacturers

European computer manufacturers also were introducing new products and increasing their sales in the United States in the late 1970s. Three were of particular note: Siemens AG, ICL, Ltd., and Nixdorf Computer.

Siemens AG in 1975 was the sixth largest company in the world in the field of electrical engineering. In EDP equipment it manufactured semiconductors and memory components, microprocessors, and small to very large computers and peripherals.

Siemens-USA's business included a variety of semiconductor products, communications equipment, and computer products. In 1979 Siemens-USA began to market 16K memory chips along with its specialty semiconductor components, teleprinters, and computer-controlled switching systems.[125] In the same year Siemens-USA acquired the "mini-floppy" disk product line from Perkin-Elmer, which it proceeded to market on an OEM basis. In 1979 it was reported that Siemens had agreed to sell its laser printers, similar to IBM's 3800 printer, to Univac on an OEM basis.[126]

Siemens-USA also manufactured an OEM disk line in the United States that ranged in capacity up to 500 megabytes. In 1979 it entered into an agreement with Rockwell International for product exchange and the distribution of magnetic bubble memories and their associated subsystems.[127]

ICL, Ltd., was formed in England in 1968 from a number of smaller computer companies. It grew steadily. ICL's worldwide sales in 1978 exceeded $956 million. It manufactured and marketed a range of computer products, from small to very large systems.[128]

In 1975 ICL acquired a one-third interest in Computer Peripherals, Inc., which at the time was jointly owned by CDC and NCR. In the next year ICL acquired Singer's foreign computer base and its marketing force, as well as certain of the U.S. manufacturing facilities of Cogar, a Singer subsidiary, which manufactured intelligent terminals.[129] In 1977 ICL began to offer the ICL 220 series as a Singer System Ten upgrade.

In 1980 ICL introduced the Model 320, to be manufactured in the United States, which could be used as a stand-alone system or as part of a distributed network.[130] The company also announced that it would begin to market its array processor and large configurations of ICL's 2900 systems, as well as its recently introduced ME 29 computer systems, in the United States. ME 29 could support 1 million bytes of main memory and up to 16 billion bytes of on-line disk storage.[131] ICL continued to market the 1500 "expandable mini-computer" in the United States and the 9500 point-of-sale series of terminals.[132]

Nixdorf Computer was founded in the 1950s, but achieved its most rapid growth in the 1970s; its worldwide revenues were $723 million in 1979.[133] Nixdorf began marketing computer equipment in the United States in 1969 and has expanded its U.S. activities since that time. In 1977 it acquired Entrex Corporation and integrated it into Nixdorf Computer Corporation. Nixdorf's U.S. revenues increased from $42 million in 1977 to over $100 million in 1979, by which time it had sales and maintenance offices in 110 cities in the United States.[134] Nixdorf's product line in the United States included a variety of systems and equipment. The products were primarily designed for distributed-processing configurations.

In May 1980 Nixdorf announced that it would market an IBM 4331-compatible computer in the United States and elsewhere. At the same time it announced its acquisition of the Computer Software Company, which designed and marketed IBM-compatible systems control programming.[135]

17

IBM FROM 1975 TO 1980, AND SOME COMPETITIVE INTERACTIONS

THE EDP MARKET ENVIRONMENT

At the end of 1974 IBM was confronted with a complex situation. The company, although still growing, was not growing as rapidly as the EDP industry as a whole. By the beginning of 1973, based on data collected in Census II, IBM's share of EDP revenues in the United States had fallen to about 33 percent, from about 49 percent in 1963.[1] Looking at the domestic data-processing revenues of only the top 50 firms in the industry, based on *Datamation*'s estimates, IBM's domestic data-processing revenues in 1976 represented about 44 percent of that total, and declined to 34 percent by 1979.[2]

Other suppliers in the industry were announcing and delivering many new and improved computer products and services. IBM's competition had expanded beyond the systems competitors of the 1960s — such as Univac, Honeywell, CDC, DEC, NCR, and Burroughs — to include newer systems manufacturers, at first called minicomputer makers, which in the mid-1970s — whatever their label — had become substantial manufacturers of competitive computer systems. These companies included Hewlett-Packard (which had actually become a major systems supplier), Data General, Perkin-Elmer, Wang, Datapoint, and newer companies such as Prime and Tandem.

Plug-compatible peripheral equipment manufacturers had appeared for virtually every box of peripheral equipment IBM was marketing, including disk subsystems, tape subsystems, printers, communications controllers, memory systems, and terminals of all kinds, products that by the 1970s amounted to 70 percent or more of the value of computer systems. Plug-compatible processor manufacturers had entered the market, led by Amdahl and quickly joined by National Semiconductor, Fujitsu, Hitachi, Magnuson, and others — all of them marketing box-for-box replacements for what traditionally had been the "heart" of IBM's computer systems line. Leasing companies offered an alternative channel of acquisition for 360 and 370 processors and a variety of plug-compatible equipment. Service bureau and time-sharing suppliers had been increasing the sophistication and variety of their service and software offerings and had themselves begun to supply their customers with advanced computer hardware, largely manufactured by others.

The IBM System/370 equipment, which had been announced in the first three years of the 1970s to replace System/360, was facing stiffer competition from the newer products and services being announced by competitors.

IBM's management circulated a revealing summary outline of the competitive environment affecting the company in late 1975.[3] Below are pages 2 and 3 of the document, prepared by the Commercial Analysis Department for V. J. Goldberg, assistant group executive of the Data Processing Marketing Group (DX 9404, November 1975):

1975 MARKETPLACE ENVIRONMENT

MANAGEMENT INFORMATION SYSTEMS

- Growth of DB/DC [Data Base/Distributed Computing]
- Requirement for larger systems and larger storage
- Demand for easier installation and adaptability to end user needs
- Emergence of device independent networking[1]

DISTRIBUTED COMPUTING

- Availability of low cost, remote intelligence
- Increase in small minisystems/terminals at remote sites
- Growth in autotransaction[2]
- Distributed Data base and intelligence[3]
- Stand-alone departmental computers

OFFLOADING – CYCLE STEALING FROM HOST

- Communication front-end processors/regional concentrators
- Intelligent terminals[4]
- Data entry[4]
- Minisystem stand-alone applications

MAJOR TRENDS

- Shift toward purchase
- Alternative solutions: Minisystem stand-alone applications
  Distributed processing
- Emphasis on non-traditional systems approaches

1975 MAJOR COMPETITIVE OFFERINGS

- Minisystems
- Wide variety of data entry/terminal products[5]
- Multi-vendor networking[6]
- Software compatible processors[7]
- Enhanced time-sharing products and services[8]
- Competitive independent peripherals
- Continued third party activity
- Traditional competitors shift to distributed processing

IBM CONFIDENTIAL

FOOTNOTES

1. Device independent networks will allow diverse terminals and processors, manufactured by different vendors, to communicate with one another using standardized network protocols.

2. Autotransaction is a term used to describe data processing tasks generated by event driven terminal devices which are used for one or a limited number of applications. Some examples are POS, Teller Terminals, Airline Reservation Systems, Brokerage Terminals.

3. Distributed Data Base is an extension to Distributed Computing where the remote computer has its own data base. The addition of 3330-like files to minisystems makes this a practical alternative for positioning "local" data.

4. Offloading by intelligent terminals and data entry devices can take two forms. In one case the device can process data that would normally be processed by the host and transmit summary data only. In the second case the remote device does all processing and little or no data is transmitted to the host.

5. The distinction between terminal and data entry products is disappearing as both acquire intelligence through embedded minisystems. However, there is expected to be a profusion of device types, many limited to specific applications.

6. It is anticipated that many of the networks will be developed to encompass a variety of hardware from different manufacturers. Moreover, the networks will be used to communicate among terminals and processors produced by different vendors.

7. The Japanese, both through Amdahl, and with their own M and V Series, represent the greatest threat. However, should this approach be successful we can expect some of our domestic competitors to market IBM compatible systems.

8. Enhanced timesharing encompasses not only competitive offerings for in-house timesharing (e.g. DECsystem 10 and minisystems) but also enhancements to competitive data servicer offerings (e.g. CDC Cybernet).

An important trend that appears throughout this outline is the competitive impact on IBM of minisystems, remote intelligence, intelligent terminals, and off-loading — cycle stealing from host. These were viewed as "alternative solutions" to the traditional IBM approach and competitive with IBM's intermediate and large systems.

Earlier in 1973 Ralph Pfeiffer, Jr., then president of IBM's Data Processing Division, wrote to his superior, Dean McKay, IBM vice-president and group executive of the DP Marketing Group, expressing his growing concern regarding the impact of minicomputers.[4] The attachment to his memorandum read in part:

The minicomputer has emerged from its traditional role as the small OEM processor and has developed into a full-function, low-price entry, general-purpose computing system, spanning a variety of application areas, such as:

— Stand-alone processors (business and scientific systems)

— Telecommunications (including multiplexors, line concentrators, RJE terminals)

— Time sharing systems

— Sensor-based systems

— Peripheral processors/controllers

The economy of scale favoring large scale computers is disappearing.[5]

The memorandum further noted: "The distributive and/or decentralized computing strategy underlying minicomputers is in direct contrast with IBM's centralized systems approach."[6] In 1973 and 1974, to be sure, IBM offered a variety of products for use in on-line systems, which included remote — distributed — equipment. Its terminal products such as the 3270 are examples. IBM also offered System/3 and System/7 equipment that could be used to perform remote processing on-line as part of larger 370 systems and, of course, the 370 processors were also used in this way. But one of IBM's marketing approaches at this time focused on the belief that users desired centralized control of programming and centralized location of processing and storage.

IBM came to realize not only that comeptitors' minicomputers were affecting its smaller systems sales but, more fundamentally, that the availability of smaller, sophisticated computers was expanding the equipment and systems choices for general-purpose computer systems and, hence, was affecting its entire computer product line. The traditional notion of a "central" processor of the 1950s and 1960s was only one of many alternative configurations for getting the data-processing jobs done.

NEW PRODUCTS

In the years after 1974 IBM introduced new items in every part of its computer product line, including new processors, memory, disk and tape storage subsystems, terminal subsystems, printing devices, mass storage devices, and a variety of program products.

System/32 and System/34

In January 1975 IBM announced the System/32, a very low-cost, general-purpose computer system. As announced, a System/32 could be rented for as little as $809 per month.[7] Its processor was capable of supporting up to 32,000 bytes of main memory. The System/32 memory was made of the FET semiconductor memory IBM used in its larger processors. Storage was available through nonremovable disk drives with a capacity of up to 9.1 megabytes and through removable diskette drives, each of which could store up to approximately 250,000 bytes. Both line and serial printing equipment was offered with the System/32. Input could be handled via diskettes, the keyboard of the operator console, or cards.[8] In addition, IBM announced new systems control programming, called System/32 Operation Control Language, as well as a number of separately priced standard applications programming products.[9]

The low cost and ease of use, including programming packages, of the System/32 made the equipment immediately attractive to smaller businesses. These systems were also marketed to individual locations within much larger enterprises, to perform processing at such locations as opposed to performing it at the enterprises' central complexes of computer equipment.[10] The System/32 was quickly enhanced. Between June and September 1975 IBM offered additional applications packages for a variety of distribution industries, such as appliances, plumbing/heating, paint/chemical, and tobacco. In January 1976 IBM announced enhanced disk storage for the System/32 by offering five new models, each providing 13.7 million bytes of nonremovable disk storage – a disk capacity increase of more than 50 percent. In June 1976 it announced nine new, low-cost models of System/32 featuring reduced disk capacity and/or slower printing speed. These new models were fully upgradable in the field and compatible with other System/32 models.[11]

In June and July 1975, about six months after the appearance of System/32, IBM announced software control programming that permitted the System/32 to function on-line as a remote job entry "work station" in a larger computer system that included an IBM 370 processor.[12] With this capability System/32 equipment could be used as part of distributed-data-processing system configurations, with diverse types of processing, storage, input-output, and control products, situated in multiple locations – all functioning as a single computer system.

In April 1977 IBM announced the System/34, a compatible follow-on to the System/32. Like the System/32 it was physically compact, easy to install and operate, and supported by various industry application programs. In addition, the System/34 had the capacity for multiprogramming, as well as the capability of communicating with other systems or devices at other locations.[13] The System/34 featured a disk capacity of 27.1 million bytes, as announced, nearly twice as much as the enhanced System/32, and also offered twice the memory available for the System/32: 64,000 bytes, compared with about 32,000 bytes.[14]

By 1978 System/32 and 34 equipment was being marketed by IBM and installed by customers for many distributed-data-processing system configurations, including airlines, drug wholesalers, hotel reservation systems, and banks.[15]

IBM 3800 Printing Subsystem

In April 1975, a few months after the initial System/32 announcement, IBM moved to improve the printer peripheral for its System/370 processors larger than the 135. That month it announced the 3800 printing subsystem. In the 3800 a laser beam replaced the traditional mechanical parts used to form the characters in IBM's "chain" and "train" mechanical impact printers, the IBM 1403 and 3211 series.[16] Using these newer, nonmechanical technologies, IBM was able to offer printing rates of up to 13,360 lines per minute — over six times the speed of IBM's fastest printer at that time, the 3211, announced with System/370 in 1970 and capable of printing about 2,000 lines per minute.

When introduced, the 3800 was the fastest on-line computer printer available. Moreover, it was designed to include sufficient processing and storage capability within the printing subsystem to permit users to control and vary printing type styles, print sizes, and forms.

In the year immediately following the 3800 announcement, IBM announced an increase in its maximum printing speed to 20,040 lines per minute. With this increase IBM was able to offer printing over 130 times faster than the IBM 716 printer used on the IBM 701 computer (150 lines per minute) at only about four times the purchase price — that is, $310,000 for the 3800, compared with $78,050 for the IBM 716 in 1957, leaving aside changes in the value of the dollar.[17] A report that would have taken 10 hours for an IBM computer to produce 20 years earlier could be printed by the 3800 in less than five minutes.

The 3800 was not the only nonimpact printer to appear on the market. For example, Honeywell had announced its PPS (page printing system) in 1974. The PPS was an electrostatic printer capable of printing up to 18,000 lines per minute. However, it could not operate "on-line," required certain tape input, and had to be used with Honeywell-supplied electrographic paper.[18]

In 1973 Xerox had announced its 1200 printer, which could print 4,000 lines per minute via a nonlaser electrophotographic process. In mid-1977, two years after the announcement of the 3800, Xerox announced its Model 9700 printer, capable of printing 18,000 lines per minute by means of a nonimpact electrophotographic-laser technology — a substantial speed improvement over the Xerox 1200.[19] The 9700 could be attached to various processors, including the IBM 370/158 and 168.

At about the time of the Xerox 9700 announcement, Siemens AG introduced its ND-2 nonimpact printer, which offered printing speeds up to 21,000 lines per minute. This printer was marketed in competition with the IBM 3800 overseas and in the United States.[20]

IBM 3350/3344 Disk Systems

In July 1975 IBM made two major announcements in its disk storage subsystems. Two years earlier its Iceberg and Winchester disk announcements had put IBM ahead of most, if not all, of its disk competitors. The 3330 Model 11

(Iceberg) doubled the storage capacity of IBM's 3330 disk drive, announced in 1970, and the 3340 (Winchester) introduced new, highly innovative head/disk assembly packaging in a lower-capacity, lower-priced disk subsystem. In September 1974 and May 1975 IBM announced attachment features that would permit use of the 3340 disk drives with IBM's System/3 and System/7 product lines, which enhanced the storage capabilities of those systems.[21]

During the two years following the original announcements, however, important competitive disk announcements were made. (Some have already been mentioned above.) For example, in July 1973 CalComp announced a disk storage system that was marketed as media-compatible with the IBM 3330 Model 11. In October, Memorex announced a disk drive said to be plug- and media-compatible with the IBM 3330 Model 11.[22] In the same month STC announced the first of its super disks, a box that had four stacks of disk packs and one centralized actuator, capable of storing under one cover in one box 800 megabytes of information. The super disk thus offered in one cabinet twice the storage available in one 3330 Model 11 two-spindle box.[23]

In January 1974 Memorex announced the new 3673 controller, making its 3330-type disk systems directly attachable to the IBM System/370 Models 125 and 135 integrated controls. That October Memorex expanded the function of the 3673 to include attachment to the ISC of the System/370 Models 145, 158, and 168. In February, Univac introduced an IBM 3330-equivalent disk drive manufactured by ISS, designed for use with Univac's 90/60 and 90/70 systems. In March 1974 CDC announced a double-density 3330-type disk drive for attachment to IBM System/370 and larger models of System/360. CDC reportedly included a high-capacity, double-density disk subsystem in its CYBER 170 system, announced in April 1974.[24]

In the summer of 1975 came some IBM countermoves. On July 1 it reduced the purchase prices on its Model 2319, Model 3330, 3330 Model 11, and Model 3340 disk drives by 10 percent.[25] Two weeks later IBM announced two new disk storage products, the 3350 and the 3344 (Madrid) disk drives. These drives were attachable to System/370 processors through IBM's existing control units and integrated controllers.[26]

The 3350 offered significant improvements in price/performance over IBM's earlier disk products, including the 3330 Model 11. It provided 635 megabytes of storage per two-spindle box, allowing more than 2.5 billion bytes of storage per string of disk drives, compared with a capacity of 400 million bytes per two-spindle box and 1.6 billion bytes per string on the 3330 Model 11. Data could be transferred from the 3350 to a CPU at the rate of almost 1.2 million bytes per second, approximately 50 percent faster than the 3330 and 3330 Model 11. One dollar of monthly rental bought 470,000 bytes of storage on the 3350, compared with 207,000 bytes on the 3330 Model 11 and 145,600 bytes on the 3330.[27] The 3350 represented a 1,500-fold increase in areal density, measured in bits per square inch, over the first IBM disk drive, introduced 19 years earlier. This rapid advancement in recording density was coupled with a 136-fold increase in data rate and a 24-fold decrease in average access time.[28]

The 3344, which was compatible with the 3340 Winchester, attached to a standard 3340 in a string combination. Available for use on System/370 Models 135 and above, it featured a capacity of approximately 280 megabytes per spindle, with a maximum configuration of more than 1.8 billion bytes per 3340/ 3344 string, compared with approximately 70 megabytes per spindle and 560 million bytes per string for the 3340 (with 3348 Model 70 data modules).[29]

With the 3350 IBM came full cycle, returning to the fixed disk file design that had existed prior to IBM's introduction of the industry's first removable disk pack, announced in 1962 with the IBM 1311 disk subsystem. The removability feature had been highly attractive to computer users because it enabled them to store disk packs and transfer them from one drive to another, the way magnetic tapes were stored and moved. But removable and interchangeable disks entailed substantial engineering and manufacturing problems, since rigorous manufacturing tolerances were required, particularly at the high recording densities being achieved on disk packs by the mid-1970s.[30]

The 3340 Winchester data module approach had reduced these problems by keeping the disks and read-write heads together in one sealed pack. The "fixed file" design, used in the 3350 and 3344, integrated the head-disk assemblies that then were not designed for customer handling. With the 3350 disk drive IBM offered sufficient storage capacity on a single disk drive to make removability unnecessary for most users. In many cases users of earlier designs were not taking the disks off in any event; hence a mixture of fixed and removable disks seemed an appropriate option to offer.[31]

By the spring of 1977 IBM analysts in the DPD Commercial Analysis Department found that the major system manufacturers were offering a price differential about 5 percent less than IBM's for 3330-type drives and were announcing 3350-type drives; the PCM disk competitors were offering price differentials of up to 50 percent on new leases of 3330-type drives and were beginning early installations of their 3340 and 3350 types.[32]

In April 1977 IBM again reduced the purchase prices of its 3330 Model 11, this time by about 15 percent.[33]

IBM 5100 Computer System

In September 1975 IBM announced the 5100, a portable "desk top" computer system weighing 50 pounds. It featured FET memory expandable from 16,000 to 64,000 bytes — equivalent to the maximum memory capacity available on the System/360 Model 30; however, the 5100 system's purchase price was only five times what it cost to rent a similar configuration of a Model 30 processor for one month. It also included APL and BASIC programming languages, a 1,024-character CRT screen for output, an optional 80-character-per-second printer, and an optional auxiliary tape unit. At announcement the 5100 had a purchase price of under $9,000, for a minimum configuration, up to approximately $27,000, when configured with full 64K memory, printer, tape unit, and I-O adapter.[34]

IBM introduced the 5110 in January 1978, and the 5120 in February 1980. Each of these newer systems retained the "desk top" design of the 5100, despite the increased capabilities each offered over the 5100. The 5110 offered a new diskette storage device with a maximum capacity of 4.8 million bytes.[35] IBM supported the 5100/5110/5120 series of computers with a variety of applications programs, including project control, business planning, business report and application development, construction payroll, labor costing, linear programming, international airfreight rating, general ledger, fixed-asset accounting and control, general accounting, inventory reporting, administrative control, and dealer parts inventory.[36] The 5110 was equipped to operate as a complete stand-alone system that could communicate with a host when required.

System/370 Processors

In February 1976 IBM announced the 3062 Lexington attached processor for the 370 Model 168. This new processor would provide a 168 processor with 1.5 to 1.8 times the power of a single 168-3 processor, for only a 50 percent increase in price. Similarly, the new 158 AP processor, announced in October 1976, would provide a 158 processor with 1.5 to 1.8 times the power of a single 158-3 processor, for less than a 25 percent increase in price.[37] The 138 processor, a "growth system" for 370 Model 125 and 135 users, offered up to 36 percent increased internal processing speed over the 135; and the 148 processor offered up to 43 percent increased internal processing speed over the 370 Model 145. The 138 and 148 processors used IBM's most advanced circuitry, including Riesling and SNIPE memory circuits, which offered the advantage of greater circuit density than other technologies and lower price.[38] In the same month IBM also introduced "accelerated processors" for the 135 and 145 — the Models 135-3 and 145-3. These new models constituted field upgrades that allowed existing 135 and 145 users to achieve performance similar to the new 138 and 148 models, without changing processors.[39]

In addition, as noted previously, at that time IBM began to offer approximately a 9 percent price reduction for customers who took any of its virtual-memory System/370 processors under the optional Term Lease Plan.

In March 1977 IBM announced roughly a 35 percent price cut on the purchase, rental, and lease prices for memory on all of the following 370 processors: 168, 158, 148, 138, 125, and 115, and 3704 and 3705-II communications controllers.[40]

IBM Series/1 Computer System

The Series/1, at announcement in November 1976, consisted of a variety of processing, storage and input-output equipment, including two processors that could support up to 128,000 bytes of memory, monolithic semiconductor main memory, and fixed disks with 9.3 megabyte capacities, as well as "diskette" disk subsystems, each with one-half megabyte of storage capacity.[41]

At announcement the Series/1 equipment was offered for purchase only, with little applications or systems control programming. It was at first designed for the self-sufficient customer who had the capability to do much of his own application programming. IBM explained the Series/1 as ". . . an alternative to the fully supported, application-oriented, product that IBM has traditionally offered. It is a 'tools-oriented' offering which allows the user to customize his system to fit his application needs."[42]

IBM quickly announced improvements and enhancements to the Series/1 equipment and software. In April 1977, for example, it announced new operating system software, called the Realtime Programming System, to support both real-time and batch program processing. By March 1979 the Series/1 "menu" of equipment included 11 processors, up to 1 billion bytes of on-line disk storage, 6 tape drive models, an IBM System/370 channel attachment device, communications control programming that permitted Series/1 equipment to operate on-line as part of larger IBM systems, higher-level language compilers including COBOL, PL/1, and FORTRAN, three systems-control programming systems, and a series of separately priced programming packages for such applications as energy management, data management, networking, intelligent data entry, interactive processing, and remote job entry.[43] The Series/1 was being used or marketed for such applications as auto dealer services, security and vehicle testing, warehouse document preparation, international banking/foreign exchange operations, customer order service and invoicing, production monitoring and process control, telephone directory assistance, and research laboratory automation.[44]

The 303X Processors

In March 1977 IBM announced its 3033 processor. The 3033 was a compatible member of the System/370 family of computers and was, like other 370 processors, capable of using existing IBM peripheral equipment and programming. The price/performance improvement represented by this processor was impressive. According to IBM's announcement literature, the 3033 processor with four megabytes of memory offered nearly twice the processing power of a four-megabyte 370/168-3 processor, IBM's previous largest model, at only a 12 percent increase in purchase price. And, according to IBM, a 3033 with eight megabytes of memory offered nearly twice the processing power of an eight-megabyte 168-3 processor, at only a 13 percent increase in purchase price.[45]

Along with the 3033 processor IBM introduced the System/370 Extended Facility, supported by a new enhancement to its operating system software, the MVS/System Extensions program, which speeded up processing considerably.[46]

In October 1977 IBM introduced the 3031 and 3032 processors. Both were 370-compatible and both offered major price/performance gains for users. The 3031 processor, according to IBM's announcement, offered up to two to two and a half times the internal processing speed of an IBM 148 processor at less than a 4 percent increase in purchase price. The 3032 processor offered internal processing speed of up to two and a half to three times greater than the 158-3 processor for only a 2 percent increase in purchase price.[47]

In March 1978 IBM introduced the 3033 multiprocessor complex, which was capable of performance rates 1.6 to 1.8 times greater than a 3033. The multiprocessor could accommodate a maximum of 16 megabytes of main memory and 32 channels. That September IBM announced the 3031 attached processor complex, 1.6 to 1.8 times faster than a single 3031, for at most a 45 percent increase in price.[48]

THE 4300 PROCESSORS AND OTHER ANNOUNCEMENTS
AT THE END OF THE 1970s

In October 1978 IBM announced two new computer systems, the System/ 38 and the 8100. Both were based on IBM's new 64K semiconductor chip, manufactured through its newly developed FET process, SAMOS (silicon and aluminum metal oxide semiconductor). This chip was the densest ever announced up to that time. Its single-device memory cells were so tiny that 200 of them could be covered by an amoeba.[49]

System/38

The System/38 was an intermediate-size system. At announcement it offered 50 percent more memory than the System/370 Model 138. In December 1979 the System/38's maximum memory capacity was increased from 1.5 million bytes to 2 million bytes — the same capacity available on the System/ 370 Model 148.[50]

The System/38 was announced with new operating system software, called Control Program Facility, which offered, among other capabilities, data base management and communications — including the ability to use the System/38 as a terminal to System/370. It was the first computer system to have a full-function data base facility designed as a part of the basic machine.[51]

The 8100 and Other Announcements

The 8100 was designed for distributed data processing. It included, at announcement in October 1978, two processors (8130 and 8140) that could support up to 512K bytes of main storage, more storage than had been available on the System/360 Models 30, 40, or 50; removable diskette storage of up to one megabyte; new CRT input-output equipment as well as software and hardware to permit attachment of existing IBM I-O equipment; and data base management software and system control programming to allow the integration of networks of 8100s and System/370s. New system control or operating system software was also announced with the 8100.[52]

Also in October, IBM cut rental, lease, and purchase prices on its 3350 and 3344 disk systems.[53]

In November 1978 IBM announced enhancements to the 3850 mass storage system, consisting of features that permitted the system to use the advanced 3350 disk drives as data staging devices in place of 3330 Model 11s.[54]

In December IBM announced additional memory increments for the 3033 processors, raising the maximum memory available on that processor to 16 megabytes, twice the maximum memory on the IBM 370 Model 168 and approximately two and a half times that of the 158. It also again cut rentals and lease prices up to 20 percent, and purchase prices roughly 30 percent, for FET memory increments on most System/370 and 303X processors, and on the 3704 and 3705-II communications controllers.[55]

In January 1979 IBM announced the "attached processor" for the 3033 processor, called the 3042, which improved the 3033 instruction execution rate generally in the range of 60-80 percent for a 37 percent additional cost.[56]

The 4300 Processors

In January 1979 IBM announced two more new System/370-compatible processors, the 4331 and 4341. Both were built on IBM's advanced 64K chip technology. The price/performance improvements represented by these processors were recognized as dramatic, even against the background of IBM's price/performance jumps of the preceding two years or so. The 4341 had approximately the same internal performance as the 370/158 for about the price of a 370/138 (less than one-quarter the price of the 158), and nearly the same internal performance as the 3031 for about half the price.[57]

The 4300 computers also represented significant price/performance improvements in terms of memory. The memory on each 4300 processor had a purchase price of $15,000 per megabyte, less than one-fifteenth the cost of memory on the 158 and 168, approximately half the cost of memory on the System/38, and over 15 percent less than the cost of the memory on the 8100.[58]

The 4300 series processors also offered reductions in power consumption and cooling and space requirements, and improved reliability and serviceability.[59]

The 3370 Disk Drive

As part of the 4300 announcement, IBM announced several new peripheral products, including the 3370 disk drive. It presented major improvements in technical performance and in price over IBM's 3350 drive, introduced in 1975. For example:

It offered 571.3 megabytes of storage per disk spindle, compared with a maximum storage capacity on the 3350 of 317.5 megabytes per spindle.

Recording density was more than twice that of the IBM 3350.

The announced average access time of the 3370 was 20 percent faster than that of the 3350, and the rate at which data could be transferred from the disk device to a CPU was more than 50 percent higher on the newer drive.[60]

The 3370 achieved these performance advances in part through new read/ write heads and high-density, large-scale-integration circuitry combined with fixed media. The 3370's read/write head was an advanced "thin film." IBM's use of this film technology dates back to work done in the 1970s on thin-film main memory for certain System/360 processors. In the course of that work, IBM researchers developed an advanced electroplating technique that was adaptable to the construction of disk heads, and thus was able to make a smaller, cheaper head, which in turn facilitated the recording and reading of smaller magnetic bits of data, packed more closely on the disk surface. At announcement the 3370 was offered for attachment to the IBM 4341 processor, via a new 3880 control unit, and to the IBM 4331 processor, via a DASD Adapter physically integrated within the 4331 CPU.[61]

In June 1980 IBM announced two more new disk drives, the 3380 and 3375, with fixed head and disk assembly and still greater capacities. The 3380, the higher-capacity drive of the two, provided 1.25 billion bytes per disk spindle — over a twelvefold increase compared with the 3330 announced ten years earlier. In addition, the 3380's data rate exceeded by 60 percent that of the 3370, announced only a year and a half earlier.[62]

Prices per unit of storage continued their steep decline. For the 3330 disk drive, one dollar of monthly rental bought about 145,000 bytes of disk storage; for the 3350, announced in 1975, a dollar bought 470,000 bytes; for the 3370, announced in 1979, a user obtained 810,300 bytes of storage per rental dollar; and for the 3380, 1,191,500 bytes.[63]

Responses by IBM's Competitors

Competing suppliers attempted to respond to IBM's late 1978 and early 1979 announcements even before the products could be shipped. There were many competitive pricing and product reactions. (Some have been mentioned already in connection with preceding discussions of specific firms.)

In November 1978 NCR announced two new computers, the I-8270 and I-8410, that extended the 8200 line. They utilized the 16K-bit chip instead of the 4K-bit chips used in the earlier models, and offered, in the larger model, up to one megabyte of memory and up to 648 megabytes of disk storage.[64]

STC announced what it claimed to be a major breakthrough of disk drive technology: the doubling of the track density on its IBM-compatible, 3350-type disk drive. Two months earlier CDC had announced an IBM 3350-compatible disk drive, the Model 33502, with double the capacity of the IBM 3350: 635 megabytes per spindle and 1,270 megabytes per cabinet.[65]

In December 1978 Nippon Electric Company (NEC) announced the NEAC MS10 at the low end of its MS computer line, reportedly designed to compete directly with the Series/1, and the N4700 system, reportedly designed to compete with IBM's 8100 and other systems. The MS10 was announced with a maximum memory of 64K words and was intended for distributed processing, communications, and industrial process control applications. The N4700 system was announced with two models, the larger having a memory of one megabyte.[66]

Prime introduced four new computers in January 1979. The 750, the largest, could support eight megabytes of main memory, a variety of programming tools, such as COBOL, FORTRAN, and PL/1, and Prime's data base management system.[67]

Burroughs announced a dual-processor version of its B 1800 computers and two "repackaged" models, reportedly priced to respond to the IBM System/38 and effectively replacing the existing B 1800 line.[68] In February 1979 Burroughs introduced the B 900 series with the announcement of the B 2930 and B 3950 computer systems. The two processors were compatible with Burroughs' earlier B 800 series systems, and could be linked to form loosely coupled multiprocessor complexes with up to four CPUs. They were specifically aimed to compete with the IBM 4331 and 4341.[69]

Itel announced a new IBM plug-compatible processor, the AS/3 Model 5, which it claimed provided up to 22 percent better internal performance than the 4341. The AS/3 Model 5, an extension of Itel's Advanced System (AS) series of IBM-compatible processors, was manufactured by National Semiconductor. The AS/3 Model 5 could support a maximum of 8 million bytes of memory, compared with the 4341's maximum capacity of 4 million bytes.[70]

NCR introduced four new processor models in the Criterion line that could be run in either uniprocessor or multiprocessor configurations. The top two systems were said to offer performance equal to the 4341, while the lower two bracketed the 4331 in performance.[71]

Siemens announced a new model of its 7.000 series, the 7.706, with a minimum configuration of 384K bytes of main memory and two 60-megabyte disk drives, reportedly as its answer to IBM's System/38 and 4331.[72]

CDC announced a new IBM plug-compatible processor in March 1979 in its Omega line, developed by IPL and reported to range in cost from $360,000 for a CPU with 2 million bytes of memory to $560,000 for an 8 million-byte system. CDC claimed that ". . . the Model 3 is 1.3 times faster than the published specifications for the IBM 4341."[73]

Kardios Systems announced a new version of Perkin-Elmer's 3220 Supermini, which Kardios was acquiring on an OEM basis from Perkin-Elmer. Kardios described the new processor, the Duo 70-E, as offering full IBM 370 compatibility and as matching the throughput of the 4341. Kardios reportedly created the system through changes in the 3220's firmware, which permitted the processor to run IBM programming code and to accept IBM peripherals under Perkin-Elmer's operating system.[74]

Magnuson introduced three new IBM plug-compatible processors, the M80/32, M80/42, and M80/43; upgraded its earlier M80/3 and M80/4; and reduced the prices of those earlier models. Magnuson claimed the new processors bracketed the 4341 in performance and had faster machine cycle times than the 4341, and that the top of the line, the M80/43, offered 30 percent better performance than the IBM 4341 and a maximum memory capacity of 16 million bytes, four times the maximum capacity of the 4341.[75]

Data General reduced prices for its Eclipse computers by more than 50 percent and also announced expanded memory capacity for most of the Eclipse systems. It reduced memory prices on those systems to $28,000 per megabyte.[76]

Mitsubishi announced a pair of new processors: the 700S, which, the firm stated, offered four times the power of IBM's 4331; and the 700 III, which it claimed was twice as powerful as the 4341. Mitsubishi also stated that the computers featured interactive and distributed processing capabilities.[77]

Honeywell introduced four new processors in its DPS series. The new systems were designed to work within the Honeywell Distributed Systems Environment as host or cohost processors, and they offered software compatibility with the firm's Level 6 minicomputers. The memory for the Honeywell processors was priced at $23,680 per megabyte, compared with IBM's price of $15,000.[78]

In April 1979 CDC introduced four computers, the CYBER 170 Series 700, which replaced five of the six models in its earlier CYBER 170 line. In addition it reduced prices of incremental memory on its processors by 20 to 53 percent.[79]

DEC reduced prices by up to 30 percent on the memory for its DECsystem 20 line, following the price/performance improvements of the 4300 series. It also increased the maximum memory capacity to six megabytes for the 2060 and 2040 processors, compared with a maximum of four megabytes for the 4341.[80]

Fujitsu introduced four new processors in its M series of 370-type computers: the FACOM M-130F, M-140F, M-150F, and M-160F. It rated the 130F about equal in performance to the 4331 but 20 percent cheaper, and the 140F equal in price to the 4331 but 60 percent more powerful. The 150F was graded slightly below the performance of the IBM 4341 but featured a 25 percent price advantage, and the 160F was approximately the same price as, but 10 percent more powerful than, the 4341.[81]

During May and June 1979 Two-Pi introduced an IBM plug-compatible processor, the 3200-V, said to offer approximately twice the performance of the 4331,[82] and Univac announced the 1100/60 system in four single-processor and two multiprocessor configurations that were said to range from slightly below the performance of the 4341 to about the performance of the IBM 3032.[83] Wang introduced the VS/100, which it claimed provided eight times the performance of the prior Wang virtual-storage computers and supported up to two megabytes of main memory and 4.6 billion bytes of on-line storage. The trade press stated that the Wang VS/100 was directed primarily at the IBM 4300 series but that the company claimed capabilities extending into the IBM 3032 range.[84]

DEC cut its memory prices by as much as 60 percent for the VAX-11/780, PDP-11/70, and PDP-11/34A, and announced additional price reductions for its

DECsystem 20 line. Industry observers attributed these price cuts to ". . . the pressures established by IBM in the past six months with its 8100 and 4300 processors, which use 64K bit chip technology, priced at $15,000 per megabyte."[85]

In July Hewlett-Packard reduced the prices of its largest systems by 12 to 18 percent, in part by reducing the price of memory. In September it announced a new, low-price version of its 3000 series, the HP 3000 Series 30, and a new intelligent network processor that was to use ". . . silicon-on-sapphire microprocessors and 32K bytes of on-board RAM to take over communications management tasks from the CPU."[86]

Nixdorf introduced a new series of systems offering higher performance and lower prices than its previous line and reportedly aimed directly at IBM's 8100 systems. It was claimed that the new series bracketed the 8100 in terms of price/performance.[87]

ANTITRUST DEVELOPMENTS

Almost all of the private antitrust suits against IBM were disposed of by 1980.

One of the first such suits, *Greyhound* v. *IBM*, was dismissed by the District Court in 1972,[88] but Greyhound appealed the decision. The Appeals Court ordered a new trial,[89] which was set to begin in 1981; shortly before its scheduled opening, however, IBM, recognizing that further substantial resources would be required to resolve the matter in court, settled with Greyhound for a payment of $17.7 million without admitting any wrongdoing.[90] (This was actually the latest of the private cases to be settled, though Hudson was still in limbo in 1982.)

Meanwhile, in the Telex case the District Court found that IBM had exercised monopoly power in a "market" for plug-compatible peripheral equipment and had injured Telex in so doing, and assessed triple damages.[91] However, the Court of Appeals reversed the District Court and remanded the case for entry of a judgment in favor of IBM.[92] Telex requested a Supreme Court hearing but settled with IBM before it began.[93]

The CalComp case went to trial in 1976; the District Court judge dismissed it without even hearing a defense early in 1977.[94] The Forro case went to court in August 1977; the trial judge dismissed the antitrust claim one month later, after the jury was unable to reach a verdict.[95] The Memorex trial, which took place in 1978, ended in a directed verdict for IBM, again after the jury was unable to reach a decision.[96] The Transamerica trial in 1979 likewise resulted in a hung jury, and the judge decided that case in IBM's favor.[97] Appeals by Forro and Memorex were rejected by the Court of Appeals;[98] Transamerica's appeal was still pending in 1982.

Several of the smaller private suits were settled out of court: Marshall, Memory Tech, and Sanders.[99]

Thus, by the end of the decade (January 1981 in the case of Greyhound) IBM had either won or settled all of the private cases except the pending cases noted above. (The Telex loss in the District Court had been reversed.) No monopolization of any market by IBM had been finally established in any private case, and it had paid no court-ordered damages to anyone. The government ultimately abandoned its antitrust case in January, 1982.

AT THE THRESHOLD OF THE 1980s

Stepping back from the multitudinous product and service innovations of the 1970s, we can see the dominant trends over the three decades of the EDP industry before 1980.

One was the exponential increase in the number of suppliers of various kinds, and the even larger increases in the number and diversity of product and service alternatives made available to users. Another intertwined trend was the very rapid rate of technological change driving the industry, which had enormously reduced the cost of computation and expanded its capabilities and scope beyond recognition.

No slackening of these trends was visible as the industry entered the 1980s. The microprocessor was taking its place in the market and had begun to invade what had been the territory of much larger computers; microcomputers with the capacity of the largest computers of the mid-1950s now cost little more than high-performance typewriters. Office automation, word processing, new approaches to storage and memory, new EDP service and data management concepts, and continued innovations in software and data communications were making their initial impacts on the market and creating new opportunities for entry and growth of suppliers of all sizes. Finally, some of the largest corporations in the world, most notably the successor to AT&T, were developing new programs of competitive equipment and service to enlarge and transform the EDP market throughout the 1980s.

APPENDIX:
LISTS OF WITNESSES

PLAINTIFF'S DIRECT CASE

Witness	Identification at Time of Testimony
Allen, David D.	Vice-president, Management Information Systems, CBS; formerly with IBM
Andreini, Richard C.	Vice-president, System Marketing, Intersil (formerly known as AMS)
Andrus, William E., Jr.	Program manager, Engineering and Information Processing Standards, National Bureau of Standards; formerly with IBM
Armstrong, Robert W.	Vice-president, Marketing, Amdahl; formerly with IBM
Ashbridge, G. Harry	Vice-president, Business and Market Opportunities, Telex
Aweida, Jesse I.	President and chairman of the board, STC
Beard, Arthur D.	President, Formation; formerly with RCA
Beitzel, George B.	General manager, DP Group, IBM
Binger, James H.	Chairman of the Executive Committee and member of the board of directors, Honeywell
Bloch, Richard D.	Private consultant with Genesis Group, an investment and venture capital concern; formerly with GE and Honeywell
Brooks, Frederick P., Jr.	Professor of computer sciences, University of North Carolina; formerly with IBM

Witness	Identification at Time of Testimony
Brown, Gordon R.	Senior vice-president, Marketing and Planning, Peripheral Products Company, a subsidiary of CDC
Brueck, Robert L.	President and member of the board of directors, MRI Systems
Bullen, Richard H.	Consultant; formerly with IBM
Butters, Stephen J.	Institutional funding manager, Putnam Management
Clapp, William M.	Loan officer, Western Region, Corporate Banking Division, Crocker National Bank
Cohen, Harvey	President and chief executive officer, International Communications Sciences; formerly with SDS/XDS
Conrad, Anthony L.	President and chief executive officer, RCA
Cooley, Henry E.	Director, development staff, Systems Product Division, IBM
Currie, F. Rigdon	Director, Special Businesses, Xerox
DeSio, Robert W.	Director, High Performance Systems, DP Division, IBM
Eckert, J. Presper	Vice-president, Univac Division, Sperry Rand; cofounder, Eckert-Mauchly Computer Co., later acquired by Sperry Rand
Enfield, Jerry A.	President, the Computer Software Company
Fassig, Gerard J.	Program administrator, IBM
Faw, Hillary A.	Retired assistant treasurer and director, Business Practices, IBM (assisting IBM's legal staff)
Feigenbaum, Edward	Professor, Computer Science Department, Stanford University
Femmer, Max E.	Corporate resident manager, Mountain States, IBM
Fernbach, Sidney	Head of Computation Department, Lawrence Livermore Laboratory
Figueroa, Howard G.	Vice-president, Management Services, DP Division, IBM
Folger, Jay D.	Senior account marketing manager, DP Division, IBM

Witness	Identification at Time of Testimony
Forese, James J.	Assistant general manager, Finance, IBM Europe
Friedman, Gary B.	Vice-chairman and executive vice-president, Itel
Gardner, Thomas E.	Member, Memorex litigation staff
Gartner, Gideon I.	Oppenheimer & Co.; formerly with IBM
Gibson, John W.	President, Components Division, IBM
Goetz, Martin A.	Senior vice-president and director, Software Products Division, Applied Data Research
Guzy, D. James	Vice-president, CDC; formerly with Memorex
Hangen, John J.	Senior vice-president, Corporate Affairs, NCR
Hewitt, James M.	Vice-president, Product Marketing, IBM
Hindle, Winston R., Jr.	Vice-president and group manager, Digital Equipment
Hochfeld, Burton M.	Security analyst, F. Eberstadt and Company; formerly with IBM
Horton, Thomas R.	Director, University Relations, IBM
Howe, Robert H.	Director, Marketing, Corporate Headquarters, IBM
Hume, Warren C.	Senior vice-president, IBM
Humphrey, Watts S.	Director, Endicott Laboratory, IBM
Imershein, Richard E.	Manager, Commercial Analysis Programs, IBM
Ingersoll, John L.	Manager, Investor Relations, GE
Jackson, Robert S.	Real estate evaluator, World Trade, IBM
Jakes, Andrew M.	Vice-president, Continental Illinois Bank
James, Jack	President, Telex Computer Products
Jatras, Stephen J.	President, Telex
Jones, Gilbert E.	Chairman of the board, World Trade, IBM
Jones, Reginald H.	Chairman of the board and chief executive officer, GE
King, Jack H.	Manager, Applications Services Department, Xerox
Kuykendall, Eugene L.	Manager, Market Analysis, IBM
Lacey, John W.	Senior vice-president, Corporate Plans and Development, CDC

Witness	Identification at Time of Testimony
La Veau, Phillip J.	Manager, Commercial Analysis, DP Division, IBM
Learson, T. Vincent	Retired chairman of the board, IBM
Lee, Warren	Senior investment officer, Bank of America
Macdonald, Ray W.	Chairman of the board and chief executive officer, Burroughs
Mather, Winton E.	Marketing manager, Oakland Public Sector, IBM
Maurer, Joseph P.	Manager, Corporate Pricing, IBM
McAdams, Alan K.	Associate professor, managerial economics, Cornell University School of Business
McCollister, Edwin S.	Director, Market Development, International Group, Burroughs; formerly RCA vice-president
McDonald, Robert E.	President and chief operating officer, Sperry Rand
McDermott, James P.	Director, Business Evaluation, Corporate Headquarters, IBM
McManus, Frank L.	Manager, Market Research, Corporate Headquarters, IBM
Metropolis, Nicholas C.	Life scientist, Theoretical Division, Los Alamos Scientific Laboratory
Morse, Philip M.	Professor emeritus, Massachusetts Institute of Technology, and member of the board of directors, CDC
Navas, John	Member, Memorex litigation staff
Norris, William C.	Chairman of the board and chief executive officer, Control Data (CDC)
Oelman, Robert S.	Chairman of the Executive Committee of the board of directors, NCR
Opel, John R.	Senior vice-president, IBM (currently IBM's chairman)
Page, Otis S.	Assistant to vice-president, Marketing, Memorex; formerly with IBM
Palevsky, Max	Partner, Bart/Palevsky Productions, a motion picture production company; founder of Scientific Data Systems, later acquired by Xerox

Witness	Identification at Time of Testimony
Peirce, E. Read	General auditor, Burroughs
Perlis, Alan J.	Professor of computer science, Yale University; formerly with Carnegie-Mellon University
Pfeiffer, Ralph A.	Corporate vice-president and president, DP Division, IBM
Pier, Howard J.	Assistant, Management Systems, DP Division, IBM
Preston, Lee E.	Professor of economics, University of Maryland; formerly professor of economics, SUNY Buffalo
Rathe, Gustave H., Jr.	Corporate resident manager, South Central States, IBM
Rice, Alvin C.	Executive vice-president, Bank of America, and executive officer of its World Banking Division
Rizzo, Paul J.	Vice-president, Finance and Planning, IBM
Robinson, Louis	Director, Standards and Systems Development Division, IBM
Rodgers, Francis G.	Vice-president, Marketing, IBM
Rooney, Joseph W.	Executive vice-president, Data Services Group, Itel; formerly with IBM and RCA
Saalfeld, Richard L.	Personnel director, European, Middle Eastern, and African Division, Bank of America
Scherer, Frederick M.	Director, Bureau of Economics, Federal Trade Commission
Schmidt, Robert D.	Executive vice-president, CDC
Scott, Orland M.	Corporate vice-president and president, Field Engineering Division, IBM
Shoemaker, Delbert L.	Chief, Standards Branch, Automated Data and Telecommunications Services, General Services Administration
Smith, Paul C.	Manager, Financial Operations, RCA Computer Systems
Spangle, Clarence W.	Executive vice-president, Honeywell, and president, Honeywell Information Systems (HIS)
Spitters, Lawrence L.	Former chairman of the board, president, and chief executive officer, Memorex

Witness	Identification at Time of Testimony
Strickland, Edward E.	Vice-president and senior staff officer, Corporate Growth, CDC
Sturges, David M.	Assistant to vice-president of finance, World Trade, IBM
Teti, Louis J.	Manager, Market Requirements and Special Systems, General Systems Division, IBM
Vaughan, James R.	General manager, Engineering Services Marketing, CDC
Vilandre, Paul C.	Headquarters Operations, Itel; formerly with IBM
Watson, Thomas J., Jr.	Retired chairman of the board, IBM
Weil, John W.	Vice-president and chief technical officer, Honeywell
Weiss, Leonard W.	Professor of economics, University of Wisconsin
Welke, Lawrence A.	President, International Computer Programs
Whitcomb, Richard A.	Director, Product Planning, Itel; formerly with IBM
Withington, Frederic G.	Senior member of professional staff, Arthur D. Little
Wright, V. Orville	President and chief operating officer, MCI Communications; formerly with IBM, RCA, Xerox, and Amdahl
Wyngarden, H. Dale	District manager, DP Division, IBM
Zeman, Morton I.	Corporate director, Marketing, IBM

PLAINTIFF'S REBUTTAL

Witness	Identification at Time of Testimony
Kost, John C.	Director of administration, Data Processing Division, IBM
McAdams, Alan K.	See "Plaintiff's Direct Case"
McGovern, Patrick J.	President and chief executive officer, IDC
McKie, James W.	See "IBM's Direct Case"
McPherson, Kenneth A.	Senior market research consultant, IDC
Preston, Lee E.	See "Plaintiff's Direct Case"
Weiss, Leonard W.	See "Plaintiff's Direct Case"
Withington, Frederic G.	See "Plaintiff's Direct Case"

PLAINTIFF'S SUR-SURREBUTTAL

McAdams, Alan K.	See "Plaintiff's Direct Case"

IBM'S DIRECT CASE

Witness	Identification at Time of Testimony
Ahearn, George R.	Manager, Systems Attachment, Los Gatos, IBM
Aikman, Walter M.	Vice-president, Paine Webber
Akers, John F.	Vice-president and group executive, DP Marketing Group, IBM (currently IBM's president)
Anderson, William S.	President, NCR
Bangle, David	Manager, Memory Systems, Telex
Barbour, Robert T.	Vice-president and regional manager, CIT
Baumol, William J.	Professor of economics, Princeton University and New York University
Benscoter, Don L.	Chairman of the board and chief executive officer, NRG
Bloch, Erich	Manager, East Fishkill Facility, and vice-president, Data Systems Division, IBM
Borch, Fred J.	Retired chairman of the board and chief executive officer, GE
Briloff, Abraham J.	Emanuel Saxe distinguished professor of business and professor, Accounting Department, Bernard M. Baruch College, City University of New York
Brown, H. Dean	Manager, Market Analysis, Zilog (a subsidiary of Exxon Enterprises)
Buffett, Warren E.	Chairman, Berkshire-Hathaway; member of the board of directors of *The Washington Post* and various other companies
Calvin, Donald L.	Manager, Production Engineering, Telex
Cary, Frank T.	Chairman of the board, IBM
Case, Richard P.	Group director, Advanced Systems, IBM
Cochlan, Paul T.	Director, Service, Sycor
Crago, Robert P.	Manager, Advanced Programs, Federal Systems Division, IBM; former manager of SAGE Program, IBM
Custard, Raymond L.	Vice-president, Divisional Management Systems, Westinghouse

Witness	Identification at Time of Testimony
Dallenbach, Robert B.	Director, Sales, Telex
Daniel, Richard H.	Senior vice-president and department administrator, Security Pacific National Bank
Davidson, Sidney	Arthur Young professor of accounting and director of business research, Graduate School of Business, University of Chicago; lecturer in law, University of Chicago Law School
Day, Rion G.	Manager, Communications Development, Telex
Deacon, Amos R. P., Jr.	President, MDB Systems
DuBois, Russell C.	President and chief executive officer, Varadyne Industries; formerly with Data Pathing
Dubrowski, Raymond J.	Partner, Price Waterhouse & Co.
Dunlop, Robert B.	Vice-president, Manufacturing, Corporate Staff, IBM
Dunwell, Stephen W.	Retired engineer and manager of STRETCH Program, IBM
DuVernay, David E.	Manager, Transportation Leasing and Financing Business, GE Credit
Egan, Richard J.	Senior vice-president, Manufacturing, Cambridge Memories
Evans, Bob O.	Vice-president, Engineering Programming and Technology, IBM; former president, Systems Development Division, Federal Systems Division, and Systems Communication Division, IBM
Evans, Thomas L., Jr.	Senior associate programmer, Raleigh, IBM
Findley, Gerald I.	Advisory programmer, San Jose, IBM
Fisher, Franklin M.	Professor of economics, Massachusetts Institute of Technology
Forrest, Henry S.	Senior vice-president, Government Relations, CDC
Friend, Phillip A.	Consultant, Quantum Science
Gomory, Ralph E.	Director, Research, IBM
Gruver, Howard L.	Vice-president, Engineering Peripheral Equipment, Telex

Witness	Identification at Time of Testimony
Hague, Merl T.	Manager, Advanced Requirements, World Trade, IBM
Hambrecht, William R.	Partner, Hambrecht & Quist
Hansen, Robert H.	Advertising specialist, CDC
Harris, Thomas I.	President, Optical Research Associates
Hart, Donald E.	Head, Computer Science Department, General Motors Research Laboratories
Haughton, Kenneth E.	Manager, Advanced [Disk] File Development, IBM
Heavener, James R.	Manager, Profit Planning and Control, Telex
Heinzmann, Frank M., Jr.	Vice-president, Computer Sciences, Eastern Airlines
Herzfeld, Valerius E.	Vice-president, Business Planning and Development, Sperry Rand
Hill, David H.	Manager, Information Systems, General Motors
Holzer, Nathaniel L.	President and chairman of the board, Datawest
Hughes, Ernest S., Jr.	Retired manager, Technical Operations, Boca Raton, IBM
Hurd, Cuthbert C.	President, Cuthbert Hurd Associates; formerly with IBM
Ice, Winston E.	Manager, Product Assurance, Telex
Jacoby, Neil H.	Professor of economics, Graduate School of Management, U.C.L.A.
Jones, Desmond	Director, Program Development, Telex
Jones, John L.	Vice-president, Management Information Services, Southern Railway
Justice, Robert E.	Manager, Printer Systems, Telex
Kaysen, Carl	Professor, School of Humanities and Social Science, Massachusetts Institute of Technology
Kevill, John F.	President, Disk Systems; formerly with Telex
Knaplund, Paul W.	Vice-president, Corporate Headquarters, IBM; former group executive, Development Group, IBM

Witness	Identification at Time of Testimony
Liptak, Thomas M.	President, General Technology Division, IBM
Mancke, Richard B.	Associate professor of international economic relations, Fletcher School of Law and Diplomacy, Tufts University
Mascho, John G.	Former controller, Telex
Mauchly, John W.	Cofounder, Eckert-Mauchly Computer Co., later acquired by Sperry Rand
McCarter, G. Berry	Director, Systems Development, DP Product Group Headquarters, IBM; former head of Product Test, IBM
McColough, C. Peter	Chairman of the board and chief executive officer, Xerox
McDowell, William W.	Retired resident vice-president, Endicott, IBM
McGrew, J. Douglass	Director of operations, Computing and Telecommunications services, Union Carbide
McKee, Donald E.	Member, corporate marketing staff, Xerox
McKenna, Bernard J.	Manager and senior loan officer, Capital Equipment Financing and Leasing Department, Ford Motor Credit
McKie, James W.	Professor of economics, University of Texas at Austin
McNamara, Thomas J.	Director, Data Systems, Honeywell
Meyer, Raymond F.	Senior consultant, Network Consulting Group, Professional Services Division, CDC
Miller, Arjay	Dean, Stanford Graduate School of Business
Morison, T. Lincoln, Jr.	Vice-president, First National Bank of Boston
Morris, John R.	General manager, Product and Service Strategy Forecasting, CDC
Mueller, George E.	President and chairman of the board, System Development Corp.
Nelson, James R.	Professor of economics, Amherst College
Nevitt, Peter K.	President, First Chicago Leasing
Northrop, C. Arthur	Controller, IBM

Witness	Identification at Time of Testimony
O'Neill, James J.	Vice-president, Data Processing and Communication Services, American Airlines
Peltzman, Samuel	Visiting research professor, business economics, University of Chicago
Perkins, Gordon P.	President and chairman of the board, Monolithic Systems
Peterman, Neil R.	Independent consultant and engineer
Pfeiffer, Jane C.	Chairman of the board, National Broadcasting Company, and member of the board of directors, RCA; former vice-president, IBM
Phillips, Almarin	Professor of economics and law, University of Pennsylvania
Pickle, Robert J.	Director, Finance and Administration, Telex
Ponton, Mark	Vice-president, Marketing, N.Y. Banking Group, First National City Bank
Powers, Jonathan G.	Director, Financial Analysis, DP Group, IBM
Prieto, Anthony	Engineer, Telex
Quist, George	Partner, Hambrecht & Quist
Rademacher, Hollis W.	Senior vice-president, Continental Illinois Bank
Repp, Dennis A.	Assistant treasurer, Allstate Insurance
Ritter, James J.	President, Technology Equities
Robelen, Russell J.	Consultant
Rosovsky, Henry	Professor of economics and dean of the Faculty of Arts and Sciences, Harvard University
Sampson, Ralph	President, Computer Information Systems
Sapienza, Samuel R.	Dean, Wharton School, University of Pennsylvania
Sells, Raymond T.	Development engineer, Telex
Spain, Thomas A.	Corporate director, Industry Relations, IBM
Stigler, George	Professor of economics, University of Chicago
Sullivan, Neal A.	Manager, Management Systems and DP, Rockwell Industries
Talvola, Michael A.	President, Systems Enhancement Associates

Witness	*Identification at Time of Testimony*
Terry, William E.	Vice-president and general manager, Data Products Group, Hewlett-Packard
Wade, Forrest L.	Engineer, San Jose, IBM
Walker, Brooks J.	Chairman of the board, U.S. Leasing International
Walkowicz, Thaddeus T.	Employee, National Aviation and the Rockefeller family
Welch, James F.	Senior vice-president, Chemical Bank
Williamson, James V.	Manager, Manufacturing Operations, Telex
Wilmer, Richard K.	Senior engineer, San Jose, IBM
Winger, Wayne D.	Manager, Storage Products Planning, Boulder Laboratory, IBM
Witschey, Walter R. T.	President, the Computer Company
Woodward, Harper	Managing partner, Venrock Associates
Yang, Harold S.	President, Enhancement Technology; formerly with IBM

IBM'S SURREBUTTAL

Fisher, Franklin M.	See "IBM's Direct Case"

GOVERNMENT AGENCY WITNESSES

As a part of its direct case, IBM offered 97 depositions of employees of government agencies. A tabular list of the deponents, their titles, and their agencies follows.

Deponent	Title	Affiliation
Abbadessa, J. P.	Assistant general manager and controller	Atomic Energy Commission
Allen, C. L.	Manager of computer operations, Computer Science Division, Union Carbide Corporation/ Nuclear Division	Atomic Energy Commission
Andrews, T. B., Jr.	Associate chief, analysis and Computation Division	NASA Langley Research Center
Aufenkamp, Dr. D. D.	Head, Computer Applications and Research Section, Computer Research Division	National Science Foundation
Beutel, A. E.	Head, Computer Sciences Department	Naval Electronics Laboratory Center
Black, J. E.	Chief, Electronics Branch, Data Collection Division	Army White Sands Missile Range
Blakelock, Col. J. H.	Director, Computer Center, Aeronautical Systems Division	Air Force Systems Command
Blaso, A. M.	Acting director, Logistics Data Management Division, Office of Standards and Quality Control	General Services Administration
Blue, A. G.	Assistant to the director, Information Processing Techniques Office	Department of Defense, Advanced Research Projects Agency
Bowers, D. A.	Head, Technical Liaison and Support Division	Navy ADPE Selection Office
Brachman, R. J.	Chief, Fire Direction and Diagnostic Systems Division	Army Frankford Arsenal

Deponent	Title	Affiliation
Brennan, F. W.	Deputy director, operations Support Division	General Services Administration
Bright, L. G.	Director, Research Support	NASA Ames Research. Center
Brodsky, R. S.	Assistant director, Reactor Safety and Computation, Division of Naval Reactors	Atomic Energy Commission
Brown, R. P.	General engineer	Ballistics Missile Defense Program Office
Bruns, Dr. R. H.	Division chief, Computer Systems Division	NASA Kennedy Space Center
Budd, P. J.	Chief, Management Directorate	Veterans Administration
Carter, Dr. H. P.	Manager, Computer Sciences Division, Union Carbide Corporation/ Nuclear Division	Atomic Energy Commission
Cook, R. S.	Director, Management Information Systems Division	General Services Administration
Crone, D. A.	Deputy Director, ADP Procurement Division	General Services Administration
Daunt, J. J.	Chief, Uniform Crime Reporting Section	Federal Bureau of Investigation
Davis, Dr. R. M.	Director, Institute for Computer Sciences and Technology	National Bureau of Standards
Deakins, G. E.	Head, Test Data Division	Navy Pacific Missile Range
Dines, T. R.	Chief, Computation Division	NASA Ames Research Center
Doane, R.	Deputy Commander, Command and Management Systems, Electronic Systems Division	Air Force Systems Command
Donegan, J. J.	Chief, Operations Support Computing Division	NASA Goddard Space Flight Center

Deponent	Title	Affiliation
Doty, A. B., Jr.	Chief, Simulator and Human Factors Division	Wright-Patterson Air Force Base
Douglas, R. F.	Chief, Data Processing and Control Branch, Directorate of Range Operations	Air Force Eastern Test Range
Dumke, Lt. Commander D. R.	Contracts Division officer, Supply Department	Naval Air Station, Point Mugu
Farrar, B. L.	Chief, ADP Operations	Defense Communication Agency
Fife, Dr. D. W.	Supervisory computer systems analyst and chief, Computer Science Section, Institute for Computer Sciences and Technology	National Bureau of Standards
Francis, W. W.	Director, Information Systems Office	Department of State
Frazier, H.	Executive assistant to the director, Geophysical Fluid Dynamics Laboratory	National Oceanic and Atmospheric Administration
Friedman, G.	Assistant bureau director, Methods and ADP Systems	Social Security Administration
Fullerton, Col. G. R.	Commander	Army Computer Systems Support and Evaluation Command
Gold, E.	Director, ADP Procurement Division	General Services Administration
Green, D. T. J.	Head, Amphibious and Mine Warfare Analysis Division	Naval Weapons Laboratory
Hanna, W. E., Jr.	Director, Bureau of Data Processing	Social Security Administration
Higgins, Col. W. W.	Deputy comptroller, Data Automation	Office of the Assistant Secretary of Defense

Deponent	Title	Affiliation
Hiniker, G. N.	Chief, Leaseback Branch, Automated Data Management Services	General Services Administration
Hintze, Dr. G.	Director, Flight Simulation Laboratory	Army White Sands Missile Range
Holden, T. A.	Chief, Excess Equipment Utilization Branch	General Services Administration
Jeffery, S.	Chief, Systems and Software Division, Institute for Computer Science and Technology	National Bureau of Standards
Johnson, R. W.	Chief, Data Systems Division	U.S. Coast Guard
Koschmeder, L. A.	Mission operations manager, Orbiting Astronomical Operations	NASA Goddard Space Flight Center
Kraft, C. C., Jr.	Director, Johnson Space Center	National Aeronautics and Space Administration
Lawrence, W. R.	Chief of operations, Surplus Property Utilization Program	Department of Health, Education and Welfare
Lealman, R. E., Jr.	Chief, Electrical Guidance and Control Systems Division, Launch Vehicle Operations	NASA Kennedy Space Center
Levine, R. H.	Associate director, Defense Communications Engineering Center	Communications Agency, Department of Defense
Luce, Capt. T. R.	Project officer, Directorate of Computer Technology	Air Force Space and Missile Systems Organization
Mahoney, E. J.	Deputy director, Division of Financial and General Management Studies	General Accounting Office
Markey, B. A.	Director, Centralized Mail List Services, Region 8	General Services Administration

Deponent	Title	Affiliation
Masson, V. W., Jr.	Assistant head, Computation Department	Lawrence Livermore Laboratory
Mayer, J. M.	Chief, Computer Engineering Branch, Navigation and Guidance Division, Avionics Directorate, Aeronautical Systems Division	Air Force Systems Command
McCue, Capt. H. F.	Chief, Automatic Data Processing Systems Center	Defense Intelligence Agency
Medlock, J. R.	Deputy chief, Checkout Automation and Programming Office	NASA Kennedy Space Center
Melmed, A. S.	Head, Special Projects Section, Office of Computing Activity	National Science Foundation
Menardi, P. J.	Director, Administration, Region 8	General Services Administration
Morin, M. K.	Project manager, STAR Project Office	NASA Langley Research Center
Moss, Maj. G. G.	Chief, Requirements and Applications Division, and director, Teleprocessing	Air Force Communications Service
Mount, B. H., Jr.	Manager, Mathematics Section	AEC Bettis Atomic Power Laboratory
Normile, J. J.	Head, Special Projects Division	Navy Automatic Data Processing Equipment Selection Office
Onks, D. H.	Director, ADP Plans and Review, Directorate of Data Automation	Office of the Assistant Secretary of Defense, Comptroller
Owen, R. L.	Chief, Networks Engineering Division	NASA Goddard Space Flight Center
Parten, R. P.	Chief, Spacecraft Software Division, Data Systems and Analysis Directorate	NASA Johnson Space Center

Deponent	Title	Affiliation
Pasta, Dr. J. R.	Director, Division of Computer Research	National Science Foundation
Purcell, J. J.	Project manager, Orbiting Astronomical Observatory	National Aeronautics and Space Administration
Pyke, T. N., Jr.	Acting chief, Computer Networking Section, Computer Systems Engineering Division, Institute for Computer Sciences and Technology	National Bureau of Standards
Ramsay, W. B.	Chief, Computer Services Division Institute for Computer Sciences and Technology	National Bureau of Standards
Ream, N. J.	Special assistant to the secretary of the navy	Navy ADPE Selection Office
Reeves, R. L.	Director, Slidell Computer Complex	NASA Marshall Space Flight Center
Renninger, C. R.	Staff assistant to director, Institute for Computer Sciences and Technology	National Bureau of Standards
Robbins, Maj. Gen. J. B.	Director and commander, Directorate of Data Automation	Air Force Data Automation Agency
Roberts, Dr. L. G.	Director, Information Processing Techniques Office	Department of Defense Advanced Research Projects Agency
Rose, Dr. M. E.	Chief, Mathematics and Analysis Branch	Atomic Energy Commission
Row, M. F.	Chief, Data Processing Section, Computer Processing Division	Federal Bureau of Investigation
Ruth, Lt. Col. J. C.	Director, Digital Avionics Information Systems Program of the Avionics Laboratory	Air Force Systems Command

Deponent	Title	Affiliation
Ruths, C. F.	Deputy commander	Army Computer Systems Support and Evaluation Command
Siegel, N. B.	Attorney	NASA
Slaughter, Dr. J. B.	Head, Information Systems Technology Department	Naval Electronics Laboratory Center
Smagorinsky, Dr. J.	Director, Geophysical Fluid Dynamics Laboratory	National Oceanic and Atmospheric Administration
Springer, M. L.	Director, Management Information and Data Systems Division, Office of Planning and Management	Environmental Protection Agency
Stokes, J. C., Jr.	Chief, Ground Data Systems Division	NASA Johnson Space Center
Strong, H. D.	Manager, Automatic Data Processing Requirements Office	NASA Jet Propulsion Laboratory
Swearingen, C. N.	Chief, Computers Division, Astrionics Laboratory	NASA Marshall Space Flight Center
Tallman, J. J.	Chief, Computer Branch, Electronics Engineering Division	Air Force Communications Service
Thomas, E. F.	Chief, Airborne Instrumentation Engineering and Test Division, Weather Instrumentation System Program Office	Air Force Electronic Systems Division
Thombs, H. W.	Head, Programming Systems Branch	Naval Weapons Laboratory
Tindall, H. W., Jr.	Director, Data Systems and Analysis Directorate	NASA Johnson Space Center
Turney, W. O.	Chief, Contracts Office	Army Ballistic Missile Defense Command

Deponent	Title	Affiliation
Videan, E. N.	Director, Data Systems	NASA Flight Research Center
Walker, J. H., Jr.	Assistant head, Technical Applications, acting head, Computer Programming Division, Warfare Analysis Department	Naval Weapons Laboratory
Webster, K. R.	Chief, ADP Management Branch, Office of Tracking and Data Acquisition	National Aeronautics and Space Administration
Wojtalik, F. S.	Chief, Guidance and Control Division, Astrionics Laboratory	NASA Marshall Space Flight Center
Woodling, C. H.	Chief, Flight Simulation Division, Data Systems and Analysis Directorate	NASA Johnson Space Center
Wynn, S. G.	Director, Office of Surplus Property Utilization	Department of Health, Education and Welfare
Zimmerman, M. B.	Technical adviser to the assistant vice-chief of staff for automation	Army Management Systems Directorate

NOTES

NOTE FORMAT

Virtually all citations are from the record of U.S. against IBM. "DX" denotes exhibits introduced into the record by IBM; "PX" denotes exhibits introduced by the Antitrust Division; "JX" denotes exhibits introduced by agreement of both parties, and "Tr." denotes sworn testimony appearing in the transcript. Transcript references are prefaced with the last name of the person testifying to the cited point. When a DX or PX exhibit references deposition testimony, the last name of the deponent is cited and followed by the abbreviation "dep." References to documents originally produced as part of Telex vs. IBM are identified by "(Telex)."

CHAPTER 1

1. DX 7532.
2. Eckert, Tr. 729, 770-71; Plaintiff's Admissions, set II, para. 800.2.
3. Eckert, Tr. 758; Fernbach, Tr. 439.
4. Plaintiff's Admissions, set II, para. 800.13.
5. Eckert, Tr. 778; Metropolis, Tr. 1141-44; DX 5423.
6. Hughes, Tr. 33881, 33886-87.
7. Eckert, Tr. 780-81; PX 5657.
8. Hurd, Tr. 86327-28; DX 44, p. 5.
9. DX 13526: Forrest dep., p. 66.
10. Hurd, Tr. 86327-28, 88206; DX 5423; DX 13526.
11. Perlis, Tr. 1853.
12. Eckert, Tr. 773, 782; R. Bloch, Tr. 7566-70; Hurd, Tr. 87662; DX 280.
13. Eckert, Tr. 805-08; Norris, Tr. 5599; Oelman, Tr. 6120-21; Hangen, Tr. 6262; McCollister, Tr. 10995-96; Withington, Tr. 55983; Hurd, Tr. 88028; DX 280, p. 1; DX 12694.
14. Crago, Tr. 85961-62, 86008-09; Hurd, Tr. 86324-26, 88089-90, 88156, 88213-15.
15. DX 75841: Mauchly dep., p. 37.
16. Eckert, Tr. 715-19, 783, 960-61; Norris, Tr. 5599-5601.
17. Eckert, Tr. 715, 772; PX 1, p. 2.
18. Eckert, Tr. 772.

19. Eckert, Tr. 772-74, 781-82; PX 1, p. 2.
20. Eckert, Tr. 782-84, 790, 867; DX 280, p. 2.
21. Fernbach, Tr. 460; Perlis, Tr. 1854, 1875; Withington, Tr. 55980; J. Jones, Tr. 78716; DX 69, p. 5.
22. J. Jones, Tr. 78741; PX 1, p. 2; PX 127, p. 70; DX 280, p. 2.
23. Perlis, Tr. 1855, 1874-75; PX 299.
24. Eckert, Tr. 867.
25. J. Jones, Tr. 78704; DX 7584: Mauchly dep., pp. 24-25.
26. DX 7584: Mauchly dep., p. 38.
27. Ibid., p. 32.
28. J. Jones, Tr. 78810; DX 7584: Mauchly dep., pp. 31-32.
29. DX 7597, p. 4.
30. DX 7584: Mauchly dep., pp. 32, 205-07; DX 9070: Ream dep., p. 33; Eckert, Tr. 783-84.
31. J. Jones, Tr. 78719-20, 79342.
32. Norris, Tr. 5598-99; DX 280, p. 1.
33. DX 280, pp. 1-2.
34. Eckert, Tr. 807-08; Norris, Tr. 5599; DX 280, p. 2.
35. DX 13526: Forrest dep., pp. 55-56.
36. DX 13526: Forrest dep., pp. 75-77; DX 280, p. 2.
37. DX 13526: Forrest dep., p. 78;

see DX 280, p. 2.

38. DX 280, p. 2; DX 438, p. 2.

39. DX 13526: Forrest dep., pp. 45-46; DX 280, p. 3.

40. DX 280, p. 2.

41. DX 13526: Forrest dep., pp. 46-48; Plaintiff's Admissions, set II, para. 146, 1-3.

42. DX 13526: Forrest dep., pp. 46-48, 53-55, 84; DX 280, p. 2.

43. DX 13526: Forrest dep., pp. 84-85.

44. Ibid.

45. DX 280, pp. 2-3; Withington, Tr. 57481.

46. Eckert, Tr. 809; DX 280, pp. 2-3.

47. Eckert, Tr. 808; DX 280, p. 3.

48. Eckert, Tr. 808.

49. DX 280, p. 3.

50. Also see J. Jones, Tr. 79344; Bloch, Tr. 7570, 7736.

51. Hurd, Tr. 86423-24.

52. DX 13526: Forrest dep., pp. 44, 100-01.

53. DX 7596, p. 1; DX 7597, p. 3.

54. Norris, Tr. 5722; DX 305, p. 1.

55. Hurd, Tr. 86324; DX 8888, p. 5.

56. Eckert, Tr. 760; Metropolis, Tr. 1135, 1204; Hurd, Tr. 86335.

57. Hughes, Tr. 33889-99, 33912-93, 71948-50; Hurd, Tr. 86335.

58. Hughes, Tr. 33874-76; Hurd, Tr. 86327, 86334-35.

59. Hurd, Tr. 86338; PX 3330A, p. 17; PX 6054, pp. 23-24.

60. Hurd, Tr. 86339.

61. Ibid.

62. Hurd, Tr. 86333-38; DX 7594: McDowell dep., pp. 193-94.

63. DX 7594: McDowell dep., pp. 187-88.

64. Dunwell, Tr. 85521.

65. Dunwell, Tr. 85522; see Hughes, Tr. 33874-75.

66. Hurd, Tr. 86328-32; see Dunlop, Tr. 93607-08; DX 7594: McDowell dep., pp. 190-92.

67. DX 7594: McDowell dep., p. 189.

68. Hurd, Tr. 86334.

69. Ibid., pp. 86336, 86008-09.

70. DX 7594: McDowell dep., p. 191.

71. Dunwell, Tr. 85523.

72. Hurd, Tr. 86326.

73. Dunwell, Tr. 85522-23.

74. Hurd, Tr. 86343.

75. Hurd, Tr. 86334, 86341-46; DX 7594: McDowell dep., pp. 200-02.

76. Hurd, Tr. 86345-46.

77. Hurd, Tr. 86345-46, 86360, 87679.

78. Hurd, Tr. 86440.

79. Hart, Tr. 80203-04; Hurd, Tr. 86352, 86904, 87679.

80. Case, Tr. 72248; see Crago, Tr. 86175; Hurd, Tr. 86357; Hart, Tr. 80204; DX 8952.

81. Hurd, Tr. 86411; see J. Jones, Tr. 78717.

82. Hurd, Tr. 86407.

83. Case, Tr. 72337, 72655, 72660; Hurd, Tr. 86355-56, 85633-36; Fernbach, Tr. 442.

84. Plaintiff's Admissions, set II, paras. 559-60.

85. Hurd, Tr. 86352-54.

86. DX 9070: Ream dep., p. 33; Withington, Tr. 56885, 56893-94.

87. Hurd, Tr. 86362.

88. Ibid.

89. Ibid.

90. Hurd, Tr. 86362-64; see Hughes, Tr. 33902-04.

91. Hurd, Tr. 86363-64.

92. Hurd, Tr. 86363.

93. Ibid.

94. Hurd, Tr. 86363-64.

95. DX 1402, p. 2.

96. Hughes, Tr. 33905; McCollister, Tr. 11016-17; PX 1900, p. 6.

97. Hurd, Tr. 86438; see McCollister, Tr. 11278.

98. Withington, Tr. 56901-02; Hughes, Tr. 33902, 33906-07, 34058-60, 71892-93.

99. J. Jones, Tr. 78763-64.

100. Hurd, Tr. 86431-34; H. Brown, Tr. 82963-69.

101. Hughes, Tr. 33905-07; Hurd, Tr. 86436-37.

102. Hurd, Tr. 86366-67, 86436-38; Perlis, Tr. 1334-35; Welke, Tr. 17065, 17294-98.

103. Hurd, Tr. 86368.

104. Hurd, Tr. 87692.

105. Hurd, Tr. 86459-60, 87649-50.

106. DX 7604.

107. Ibid.; see PX 1, p. 2.

108. Eckert, Tr. 905.

109. Hart, Tr. 80164.

110. Hart, Tr. 80163.

111. Hart, Tr. 80166.

112. Hart, Tr. 80166-67.

113. Bloch, Tr. 7753.

114. Welke, Tr. 17378-79; see also R. Bloch, Tr. 7751-54; Welke, Tr. 17327-30,

17377-81; Goetz, Tr. 18537-38.

115. Hurd, Tr. 86415; see R. Bloch, Tr. 7675-76; McCollister, Tr. 11088-89; Rooney, Tr. 12126-27; Welke, Tr. 17345-46; Withington, Tr. 55737, 55886-89.

116. Hurd, Tr. 86415; see Rooney, Tr. 12124-28; Beard, Tr. 8546-47; Welke, Tr. 19619; J. Jones, Tr. 79037-40.

117. Norris, Tr. 6049-50; R. Bloch, Tr. 7675-76, Welke, Tr. 19619.

118. Norris, Tr. 6049-50; R. Bloch, Tr. 7675-76; J. Jones, Tr. 79036-37; JX3, p. 2.

119. Withington, Tr. 56637-40, 56459-60; JX3, p. 2; DX 7528, p. 17.

120. Brown, Tr. 83138-39.

121. J. Jones, Tr. 78818.

122. Ibid.; see Norris, Tr. 6049; Rooney, Tr. 12498-99.

123. R. Bloch, Tr. 7603-05, 7751-54; Beard, Tr. 10090, 10094; Withington, Tr. 56782-86, 56789.

124. McCollister, Tr. 11042.

125. Hurd, Tr. 86361.

126. DX 7596, p. 1; DX 7597, pp. 1-2.

127. R. Bloch, Tr. 7577, 7751-55.

128. R. Bloch, Tr. 7753.

129. R. Bloch, Tr. 7751-52.

130. DX 7596, p. 2.

131. DX 1096, p. 1.

132. Welke, Tr. 17111.

133. Spangle, Tr. 5092.

134. R. Bloch, Tr. 7577, 7603-04, 7751-55; J. Jones, Tr. 78796-97.

135. Welke, Tr. 19225-26.

136. Welke, Tr. 19228.

137. Withington, Tr. 56782-83.

138. Withington, Tr. 56783.

139. DX 7597, p. 11.

140. DX 3979, p. 16.

CHAPTER 2

1. Crago, Tr. 85956, 85962.

2. Crago, Tr. 85956, 85960; Hurd, Tr. 86371-72.

3. Morse, Tr. 30963; Crago, Tr. 85961, 86010, 86023.

4. Crago, Tr. 85962; see J. Jones, Tr. 78745-46.

5. Crago, Tr. 85962; Hurd, Tr. 86463-64.

6. Crago, Tr. 85962-63.

7. Crago, Tr. 85962, 85965; Hurd, Tr. 86370.

8. Hurd, Tr. 86465.

9. Hurd, Tr. 86466.

10. Crago, Tr. 85960-61, 85963-64; Hurd, Tr. 86371.

11. Crago, Tr. 85956-57, 85959-60.

12. Crago, Tr. 85956-58.

13. Hurd, Tr. 86372.

14. Hurd, Tr. 86372-73; see Crago, Tr. 85970-72, 86059-60.

15. DX 8948, pp. 2-15; see Crago, Tr. 85980-81, 85985-87.

16. DX 8948, p. 15.

17. Crago, Tr. 85966.

18. E. Bloch, Tr. 91466-67; 91526; see Fernbach, Tr. 451.

19. Crago, Tr. 85967-68; Hurd, Tr. 86374.

20. Crago, Tr. 85970-71.

21. Crago, Tr. 85975; Weil, Tr. 7044.

22. Hurd, Tr. 86377.

23. DX 2609A, pp. 34-50.

24. Hurd, Tr. 86378; DX 8955, p. 1.; DX 8956.

25. Hurd, Tr. 86377, 86529-32; E. Bloch, Tr. 92850.

26. DX 8955, p. 3.

27. Beard, Tr. 8657-58, 8700-01; Morse, Tr. 30963; PX 6088, p. 5; Hurd, Tr. 88216; E. Bloch, Tr. 91529.

28. Perlis, Tr. 1876; see PX 299.

29. Perlis, Tr. 1997-98; see Case, Tr. 72345-47.

30. Withington, Tr. 56894; Case, Tr. 72375-76, 78191-92.

31. Hart, Tr. 80213.

32. Ibid.; see Perlis, Tr. 1848.

33. Hart, Tr. 80213-14.

34. Hart, Tr. 80134.

35. Weil, Tr. 7220; Case, Tr. 73152.

36. Goetz, Tr. 17651; Enfield, Tr. 19948-49; Perlis, Tr. 1349, 1352; Spangle, Tr. 5124; Case, Tr. 73016, 73019.

37. Fernbach, Tr. 519-20; Case, Tr. 73021-23; Perlis, Tr. 1857, 1973; Gomory, Tr. 98322-23; Palevsky, Tr. 3259, 3262.

38. Hart, Tr. 80215-16.

39. Hart, Tr. 80189.

40. Perlis, Tr. 1857; see Perlis, Tr. 1999-2000.

41. Case, Tr. 73023; see Hart, Tr. 80216.

42. Perlis, Tr. 1857.

43. Case, Tr. 72973-76; 72985-86.

44. Perlis, Tr. 1973, 2000; McCollister, Tr. 11309; Case, Tr. 72974.

45. Case, Tr. 72971-72.

46. Withington, Tr. 56512-16.
47. DX 3717, p. 1; DX 3727, pp. 4-5; J. Jones, Tr. 78856-57, 78864-65.
48. Consent Decree, part IV, para. (a).
49. Ibid., part V, paras. (a), (b).
50. Ibid., part VI, para. (a).
51. Ibid., part VI, para.(b).
52. Ibid., part VI, para. (c).
53. Ibid., part VII, para. (a).
54. Ibid., part VII, para. (c).
55. Ibid., part XI, para. (a).
56. Friedman, Tr. 50384-85.
57. Hurd, Tr. 86379.
58. Ibid.
59. PX 6072.
60. Ibid., p. 1; McCollister, Tr. 9592; Spitters, Tr. 54313; Withington, Tr. 56494; Haughton, Tr. 94861.
61. McCollister, Tr. 9591; Spitters, Tr. 54313.
62. Hurd, Tr. 86558-61, 86568-69.
63. Haughton, Tr. 94807-08, 94859-60, 94862, 94892-94.
64. DX 25.
65. Hurd, Tr. 86381.
66. Withington, Tr. 56240-41.
67. Beard, Tr. 8996-97; McCollister, Tr. 9591; Withington, Tr. 56246-47, 56253-54.
68. PX 4714, p. 1.
69. Ibid., p. 2; Case, Tr. 72526-27.
70. Perlis, Tr. 1844, 1998-99; Case, Tr. 72381, 72704; Hurd, Tr. 86408.
71. Case, Tr. 72381.
72. PX 4714, p. 4; Perlis, Tr. 1844, 1846-49.
73. Hurd, Tr. 86382; PX 4714, p. 1.
74. PX 4714, pp. 1-2.
75. Withington, Tr. 56465; see E. Bloch, Tr. 91677-80.
76. DX 280, p. 3; DX 7584: Mauchly dep., pp. 37-38.
77. DX 305, p. 1.
78. DX 280, pp. 3-4.
79. Norris, Tr. 5721-22.
80. Norris, Tr. 5722-23, 5846-47; DX 284, pp. 4-5; DX 305, p. 1.
81. DX 13526: Forrest dep., pp. 90-91.
82. Ibid., p. 91.
83. Ibid., pp. 98-99.
84. Ibid., pp. 100-01.
85. Ibid., pp. 101, 103-04.
86. Ibid., p. 104.
87. DX 7597, p. 4.
88. Ibid., pp. 2, 6.
89. DX 7584: Mauchly dep., p. 34.
90. DX 7597, pp. 2-3.
91. Ibid., p. 3.
92. DX 7584: Mauchly dep., pp. 27-28.
93. Ibid., pp. 90-101; for the advertisement see DX 12610.
94. Ibid., pp. 101-03.
95. Ibid., pp. 97-99.
96. J. Jones, Tr. 79344.
97. DX 7596, p. 1.
98. Ibid., pp. 2-3.
99. DX 7597, p. 7.
100. Ibid., pp. 17-19.
101. DX 7598, pp. 1-2; J. Jones, Tr. 79342.
102. J. Jones, Tr. 79344.
103. DX 7584: Mauchly dep., p. 55.
104. Ibid.
105. Ibid., p. 62.
106. Withington, Tr. 56478-79.
107. Ibid., pp. 56488-89.
108. DX 7584: Mauchly dep., p. 65.
109. DX 7597, p. 10.
110. Norris, Tr. 6010.
111. DX 280, p. 4.
112. DX 13526: Forrest dep., p. 115.
113. Ibid., pp. 115-16.
114. DX 7595, pp. 1, 3; see DX 7584: Mauchly dep., p. 71.
115. DX 7596, p. 2.
116. DX 280, pp. 3-4; DX 8; DX 7584, Mauchly dep., pp. 18-23.
117. DX 7584: Mauchly dep., p. 21.
118. DX 272, p. 2; see Norris, Tr. 5707-09.
119. DX 280, p. 3.
120. DX 10, p. 1.
121. DX 105, a *Business Week* article dated November 22, 1969; see also McDonald, Tr. 3813; J. Jones, Tr. 79339-44.

CHAPTER 3

1. Dunwell, Tr. 85528-29, 85555; Brooks, Tr. 22717; Fernbach, Tr. 509-10; Eckert, Tr. 974.
2. Dunwell, Tr. 85530-31; Hurd, Tr. 86386-87.
3. Case, Tr. 74591; Dunwell, Tr. 85530-31; Hurd, Tr. 86386-87.
4. Dunwell, Tr. 85536-37.
5. Hurd, Tr. 86388-90.
6. Dunwell, Tr. 85536.
7. Dunwell, Tr. 85527; see also Fernbach, Tr. 470-71; E. Bloch, Tr. 91482,

91678-80.

8. Hurd, Tr. 86387; Dunwell, Tr. 85527-28.

9. Hurd, Tr. 86630.

10. Hurd, Tr. 86631-32.

11. Dunwell, Tr. 85555-56; Hurd, Tr. 86390, 86642-51.

12. Dunwell, Tr. 85555-56; DX 4767, pp. 31, 33; PX 5942.

13. Dunwell, Tr. 85550.

14. Fernbach, Tr. 510-11.

15. Withington, Tr. 56464-65.

16. DX 5423: Smagorinsky dep., p. 94.

17. Fernbach, Tr. 515-16.

18. Case, Tr. 73606-08; Dunwell, Tr. 85539-49, 85894; Hurd, Tr. 86592-96; E. Bloch, Tr. 91485-89; DX 3171.

19. E. Bloch, Tr. 91485-89; see also Case, Tr. 72268-69; Hurd, Tr. 86394, 86594-98.

20. Case, Tr. 73606-08.

21. Norris, Tr. 5608, 5611, 5916.

22. DX 13683, p. 13; see also Fernbach, Tr. 471.

23. PX 343, p. 1.

24. DX 372, p. 2; see Weil, Tr. 7172-73.

25. DX 13674, pp. 10-11.

26. DX 7566, pp. 10-11.

27. Withington, Tr. 55918, 56500; see also Case, Tr. 72258, 72261.

28. DX 571-A; DX 572-A.

29. Dunwell, Tr. 85536; Hurd, Tr. 86394-95.

30. Dunwell, Tr. 85536; Hurd, Tr. 86395.

31. Hart, Tr. 81935; Dunwell, Tr. 85536; DX 572-A.

32. Welke, Tr. 17314; Case, Tr. 73278-79; O'Neill, Tr. 76005-08; DX 4109.

33. O'Neill, Tr. 76005-06; see also Crago, Tr. 86152.

34. O'Neill, Tr. 76005-08, 76231, 76776.

35. Hurd, Tr. 86537-40; Crago, Tr. 86152-53.

36. DX 571-A; Dunwell, Tr. 85894; Withington, Tr. 56500.

37. DX 4769, p. 1.

38. Norris, Tr. 5923-24; Case, Tr. 73276, 73282.

39. J. Jones, Tr. 78804-05, 78982, 79625; Case, Tr. 73277.

40. Weil, Tr. 7026; see Hart, Tr. 80208; Withington, Tr. 56904.

41. DX 573; Hurd, Tr. 86383; DX 925, p. 13; DX 4589, p. 7; DX 4590, p. 17.

42. James, Tr. 35017-18; see also Beard, Tr. 8708-09.

43. Withington, Tr. 56171; Plaintiff's Admissions, set II, para. 928.3.

44. Withington, Tr. 56173-74.

45. Plaintiff's Admissions, set II, para. 931.1.

46. Withington, Tr. 56251.

47. Withington, Tr. 56253; see also Hurd, Tr. 86384-85.

48. Case, Tr. 72929; O'Neill, Tr. 76227.

49. Fernbach, Tr. 547-48.

50. J. Jones, Tr. 78953-54.

51. PX 114, pp. 4, 25, 27.

52. Eckert, Tr. 838.

53. Spangle, Tr. 5021-23; R. Bloch, Tr. 7605-06; McCollister, Tr. 11237; Withington, Tr. 55866-67.

54. Weil, Tr. 7031-32.

55. Haughton, Tr. 94824, 94829; DX 3554-D.

56. Haughton, Tr. 94853-54, 94875.

57. Haughton, Tr. 94877; 94875-76.

58. Case, Tr. 72737-38; Haughton, Tr. 94826-28, 94856.

59. Haughton, Tr. 94833-42, 94864-75, 94943; DX 421, p. 9.

60. Case, Tr. 72740.

61. DX 571-A, p. 1; Welke, Tr. 17305, 19298; Andreini, Tr. 47728-33.

62. Withington, Tr. 56173-75.

63. Withington, Tr. 57678-79.

64. McDonald, Tr. 3787-91.

65. McDonald, Tr. 3788-91.

66. McDonald, Tr. 3787.

67. Eckert, Tr. 1008-13; McDonald, Tr. 3785-88; PX 4829, p. 20.

68. PX 4829, p. 20.

69. Fernbach, Tr. 508-09; Eckert, Tr. 825-27.

70. Fernbach, Tr. 508-11.

71. Eckert, Tr. 974.

72. Plaintiff's Admissions, set IV, para. 82.0 (d).

73. Eckert, Tr. 827.

74. DX 8, p. 2.

75. Eckert, Tr. 1101.

76. Withington, Tr. 56454-55, 56477.

77. Fernbach, Tr. 516-17.

78. Fernbach, Tr. 518.

79. Eckert, Tr. 836-37.

80. Eckert, Tr. 817-18; DX 14221-A, p. 6.

81. Withington, Tr. 56479-81; DX 14221-A, p. 6.

82. Withington, Tr. 56481.

83. Hughes, Tr. 33902-03; DX 1402;

Hurd, Tr. 86436-37.
84. Withington, Tr. 56481-82.
85. DX 8, p. 5.
86. Ibid., p. 2.
87. PX 4829, p. 20.
88. PX 6119, pp. 35, 37; DX 14221-A, p. 9.
89. DX 7608, p. 1.
90. DX 10, p. 1; Eckert, Tr. 1018-19.
91. DX 8, p. 2.
92. DX 8, pp. 2-3.
93. Ibid., p. 4.
94. Ibid., p. 5.
95. Withington, Tr. 56486-88; DX 8, p. 5.
96. DX 8, p. 6.
97. Ibid., p. 4.
98. Ibid., p. 6.
99. Ibid., p. 4.
100. DX 15, pp. 2-3.
101. DX 69, p. 5.
102. Eckert, Tr. 1021; DX 10, p. 1.
103. DX 13912, p. 21.
104. Eckert, Tr. 1019-23.
105. DX 69, p. 6.
106. Eckert, Tr. 863-65.
107. DX 14222, pp. 19-20; see Eckert, Tr. 1024-25.
108. DX 14222, p. 20.
109. DX 13912, p. 20.
110. DX 6119, p. 16; DX 13912, p. 21; DX 69, p. 11.
111. Eckert, Tr. 1013-17.
112. DX 10, p. 1.

CHAPTER 4

1. DX 14208, p. 24.
2. DX 14208, pp. 17-18, 34.
3. DX 10448, p. 14; see also DX 6888, pp. 3, 4, 120-22; DX 10447, p. 6.
4. Eckert, Tr. 767-69.
5. DX 10447, p. 6.
6. DX 10448, p. 19.
7. DX 10447, p. 3.
8. DX 7604, p. 1.
9. Fernbach, Tr. 469; DX 6888, pp. 3, 123-24.
10. DX 5333, p. 6.
11. DX 14209, pp. 20, 22.
12. *U.S.* v. *Western Electric Co.* (1956) Trade Regulation Reporter, para. 68, 246 (D. N. J. 1956).
13. DX 6893, pp. 2-3.
14. DX 10448, p. 18.
15. DX 6886, p. 2.
16. DX 14210, p. 7.
17. DX 8224, p. 133.
18. DX 5945: Dunnaville dep., pp. 10-12.
19. R. Bloch, Tr. 7570, 7575; Hurd, Tr. 86326; DX 13684-A, p. 8.
20. R. Bloch, Tr. 7570.
21. DX 13684-A, p. 27.
22. R. Bloch, Tr. 7567-70, 7572-73.
23. R. Bloch, Tr. 7570, 7736.
24. Crago, Tr. 85962; Hurd, Tr. 86463-64.
25. R. Bloch, Tr. 7570, 7739.
26. R. Bloch, Tr. 7573, 7575.
27. R. Bloch, Tr. 7571-72; Binger, Tr. 4502-03; PX 318, p. 33.
28. DX 13670, pp. 5, 7-11.
29. Binger, Tr. 4502; R. Bloch, Tr. 7573, 7739-42.
30. R. Bloch, Tr. 7748-49; see R. Bloch, Tr. 7746.
31. DX 130, p. 12; see R. Bloch, Tr. 7571-72.
32. DX 13670, pp. 5, 16; DX 13685, pp. 4, 18.
33. Binger, Tr. 4502-04, 4512-13, 4549-50; DX 13671, p. 16.
34. Binger, Tr. 4504-05.
35. DX 13855, p. 7.
36. DX 9070: Ream dep., p. 37.
37. Ibid., p. 36.
38. Ibid.
39. DX 13672, pp. 8-9; see Binger, Tr. 4550.
40. DX 13673, pp. 27-28, 43.
41. Binger, Tr. 4550; DX 13674, pp. 10-11; DX 13675, pp. 35-36.
42. DX 13675, p. 37; Spangle, Tr. 5092-93; Withington, Tr. 56512-16.
43. DX 13676, p. 29.
44. DX 13676, p. 31.
45. DX 198, p. 25.
46. DX 198, p. 26; see DX 167.
47. DX 8631, pp. 31, 37; DX 14484, p. R1.
48. DX 198, p. 4.
49. PX 343, p. 3.
50. PX 344-A, p. 1; Beard, Tr. 8652.
51. Beard, Tr. 8651.
52. DX 658, p. 17.
53. Crago, Tr. 85962; Hurd, Tr. 86463.
54. DX 658, pp. 19-23; Eckert, Tr. 768.
55. DX 658, p. 13.
56. DX 659, p. 16.

57. PX 344-A, pp. 1-2; PX 343, p. 3; DX 661, p. 21; Hurd, Tr. 88213.

58. DX 661, p. 21.

59. Ibid.; see Beard, Tr. 8449-50.

60. McCollister, Tr. 9254-55; Beard, Tr. 8710-11; Withington, Tr. 56507-08.

61. McCollister, Tr. 9255; PX 343, p. 1; PX 114, p. 18; Beard, Tr. 8711.

62. McCollister, Tr. 9542-43.

63. PX 114, p. 5.

64. McCollister, Tr. 9541-42.

65. McCollister, Tr. 9593-94; Withington, Tr. 55958, 56487.

66. Beard, Tr. 8450-51, 8676, 8684-86, 8983-84.

67. PX 114, p. 5.

68. McCollister, Tr. 9255.

69. Beard, Tr. 8717.

70. DX 562, p. 2; see PX 344-A, p. 1; Beard, Tr. 8454, 8958.

71. McCollister, Tr. 9543-44, 9622; Beard, Tr. 8458.

72. J. Jones, Tr. 79347-48.

73. McCollister, Tr. 9544.

74. Beard, Tr. 8457-58; McCollister, Tr. 9545.

75. McCollister, Tr. 9624.

76. McCollister, Tr. 9623.

77. Beard, Tr. 8724, 8983.

78. McCollister, Tr. 9362-63.

79. Beard, Tr. 8955; McCollister, Tr. 9622.

80. Beard, Tr. 8998-99.

81. Beard, Tr. 9009-10.

82. Withington, Tr. 56508-09.

83. Beard, Tr. 10323.

84. McCollister, Tr. 9245-46.

85. Beard, Tr. 9003-04; see Beard, Tr. 8451.

86. Beard, Tr. 9004.

87. McCollister, Tr. 9552-53.

88. DX 14192; Weil, Tr. 7174-75; R. Bloch, Tr. 7744-45.

89. DX 4993, p. 4; see Weil, Tr. 7012.

90. Weil, Tr. 7012-13, 7155-56; see PX 318, p. 34; PX 320, p. 4.

91. PX 318, p. 34.

92. Weil, Tr. 7157-59.

93. Weil, Tr. 7158-59.

94. Weil, Tr. 7157-58, 7004.

95. PX 353, p. 43.

96. Weil, Tr. 7006; see Weil, Tr. 7173; DX 387, p. 12.

97. DX 401, p. 1.

98. Weil, Tr. 7166-67.

99. Weil, Tr. 7006-07, 7016, 7167-70; PX 320, p. 4.

100. Weil, Tr. 7171.

101. Weil, Tr. 7171-72.

102. R. Bloch, Tr. 8033; PX 353, p. 43.

103. PX 353, p. 43.

104. Weil, Tr. 7159-60.

105. R. Jones, Tr. 8752, 8874.

106. R. Jones, Tr. 8875.

107. R. Jones, Tr. 8869, 8875-76.

108. PX 320, p. 18.

109. R. Bloch, Tr. 7623-24; see R. Bloch, Tr. 7616.

110. PX 320, p. 4.

111. Weil, Tr. 7174-76.

112. Weil, Tr. 7009-10.

113. Weil, Tr. 7010.

114. McCollister, Tr. 10995-99; DX 12674; DX 14329, p. 3.

115. McCollister, Tr. 10995-96.

116. McCollister, Tr. 11001, 11006-07; DX 698, p. 6; DX 700, p. 9.

117. DX 698, pp. 4-7; McCollister, Tr. 11000-01.

118. McCollister, Tr. 9164-65.

119. DX 698, pp. 3-4.

120. McCollister, Tr. 9165-66.

121. Withington, Tr. 55506.

122. DX 700, pp. 3-4.

123. DX 10257, p. 5.

124. Ibid.

125. Withington, Tr. 56470.

126. DX 700, p. 6.

127. DX 10282, p. 2; see DX 10283, p. 1.

128. DX 10283, p. 1.

129. DX 427, p. 4.

130. DX 427, p. 2.

131. Ibid.

132. DX 10254, p. 15.

133. DX 10720, p. 2; see DX 10255, p. 8.

134. DX 10256, p. 8.

135. Ibid.

136. Withington, Tr. 56499; DX 5652: Bruns dep., pp. 5-6.

137. DX 10281, pp. 22-23.

138. Withington, Tr. 56498-99.

139. DX 10713, p. 11.

140. Withington, Tr. 56499.

141. DX 10256, p. 4.

142. DX 10282, pp. 5-6.

143. DX 10713, p. 9; DX 10257, p. 5.

144. DX 10714, p. 8.

145. Ibid.

146. DX 10281, p. 28; see DX 10713, p. 9.

147. DX 10283, p. 2; DX 10257, p. 4.

148. Withington, Tr. 55918.
149. Withington, Tr. 55918-19.
150. DX 10283, pp. 6-7.
151. Ibid.
152. DX 427, pp. 4-5.
153. DX 427, p. 4.
154. DX 372, p. 1.
155. Oelman, Tr. 6120; DX 337, p. 24.
156. DX 9097, Oelman, p. 9.
157. DX 360, p. 10; see Oelman, Tr. 6120-21.
158. DX 360, p. 12; see DX 481, p. 20; Oelman, Tr. 6121.
159. DX 372, p. 1; DX 9097, Oelman, p. 10; Withington, Tr. 55983; DX 12655.
160. Oelman, Tr. 6121, 6123, see DX 9097, Oelman, p. 10.
161. Oelman, Tr. 6121-22.
162. Oelman, Tr. 6122-23.
163. DX 337, p. 24; see Oelman, Tr. 6121, 6124.
164. Hangen, Tr. 6292-93.
165. Ibid.; DX 9097, Oelman, p. 14.
166. DX 8224, p. 3; DX 400, p. 1.
167. DX 387, p. 12; DX 400, p. 14; DX 482, p. 14.
168. DX 9097: Oelman dep., p. 15.
169. Oelman, Tr. 6127; Hangen, Tr. 6293-94.
170. DX 401, p. 1; DX 400, p. 15.
171. Oelman, Tr. 6158; DX 401, p. 1; DX 330, p. 2; DX 331, pp. 4-5.
172. Withington, Tr. 56510-11.
173. Oelman, Tr. 6163.
174. DX 403, p. 11.
175. Oelman, Tr. 6130; DX 382, pp. 3, 12.
176. DX 382, pp. 3, 10; DX 746, p. 1; Hangen, Tr. 10762, 10764; DX 9097, Oelman, p. 16.
177. Hangen, Tr. 6311.
178. Withington, Tr. 56469-70; 56511.
179. DX 350-B; see Hangen, Tr. 6314; DX 342, p. 7.
180. Hangen, Tr. 6319.
181. Ibid.
182. DX 8224, p. 3.
183. DX 14196, pp. 1-2.
184. DX 7512, p. 190.
185. DX 7512, p. 20; see p. 190.
186. DX 7512, pp. 25, 190-96.
187. Fernbach, Tr. 513; Weil, Tr. 7072; DX 7512, pp. 191-92.
188. PX 3624, p. 2; Goetz, Tr. 17454-55, 17792-93.
189. Fernbach, Tr. 512-13; DX 5642:

Hintze dep., pp. 7-8.
190. DX 7581.
191. DX 8387, pp. 1, 6.
192. Miller, Tr. 85191-92, 85186.
193. Norris, Tr. 5604-07, 5713; DX 271, p. 7.
194. Norris, Tr. 5606.
195. Norris, Tr. 5607-08, 5713-15, 5738, 5742-43; DX 271, p. 7; DX 280, pp. 4, 6.
196. Norris, Tr. 5611.
197. DX 271, p. 7.
198. Norris, Tr. 5608; DX 271, p. 7.
199. Norris, Tr. 5608-09; PX 6066, p. 1.
200. Schmidt, Tr. 27236, 27521; PX 355, pp. 33-34.
201. Norris, Tr. 5611, 5733-37.
202. Norris, Tr. 5611-15, 5923-25.
203. PX 355, p. 33; Norris, Tr. 5614-15, 5979.
204. DX 331, pp. 4-5.
205. DX 13666, p. 7.
206. PX 355, p. 33.
207. Norris, Tr. 5611.
208. DX 284, p. 3.
209. Ibid.
210. DX 284, pp. 3-4.
211. Ibid.; DX 13666, p. 7.
212. DX 284, p. 7.
213. Ibid.
214. DX 296; PX 355, p. 3; DX 280, p. 6; DX 284, p. 7; Norris, Tr. 5794.
215. DX 13666, p. 8.
216. DX 331, p. 5; see Norris, Tr. 5789; DX 355, p. 3; DX 296.
217. DX 331, p. 1.
218. DX 331, p. 9.
219. DX 331, p. 5.
220. Norris, Tr. 5934, 5938; DX 308; DX 309; DX 310; DX 13526.
221. JX 10, p. 2; PX 355, pp. 34-35.
222. Norris, Tr. 5853-54.
223. PX 355, p. 34; Norris, Tr. 5615-16.
224. Norris, Tr. 5615.
225. Norris, Tr. 5793; PX 355, pp. 3, 5.
226. DX 13538, pp. 3, 15-21; DX 12664; Perlis, Tr. 1331; Crago, Tr. 85964; DX 6086, p. 13.
227. PX 355, pp. 3-4; DX 296.
228. Norris, Tr. 6010.
229. DX 284, pp. 4-5.
230. DX 302.
231. Dunwell, Tr. 85522-23.
232. R. Bloch, Tr. 7742-43.
233. R. Bloch, Tr. 7743.
234. Rooney, Tr. 12385.

235. Withington, Tr. 55974; see McCollister, Tr. 9553.
236. DX 7594: McDowell dep., p. 187.
237. DX 7594: McDowell dep., p. 188.
238. Rodgers, Tr. 16842; Spain, Tr. 88790; Akers, Tr. 97352; Cary, Tr. 101618.
239. Perlis, Tr. 1887; O'Neill, Tr. 76224-28; Hurd, Tr. 86726; Beard, Tr. 9048, 10272.
240. Binger, Tr. 4512-13; Norris, Tr. 5608-09; Beard, Tr. 8999-9000; Withington, Tr. 56510.
241. Hurd, Tr. 86345, 86360; E. Bloch, Tr. 91530; Dunlop, Tr. 94377-81.
242. Cary, Tr. 101716-17.
243. DX 3979: Johnson dep., p. 16.
244. Liptak, Tr. 84619-21, 84644-46; Miller, Tr. 85046, 85105-06; McCarter, Tr. 88433-35; Spain, Tr. 89645-47; Cary, Tr. 101328-29, 101503-04, 101608-13, 101718-19.
245. Knaplund, Tr. 90468-69.
246. Macdonald, Tr. 6904.

CHAPTER 5

1. DX 4740: Evans, Tr. (Telex) 3925.
2. DX 4740: Evans, Tr. (Telex) 3925-26.
3. Knaplund, Tr. 90464-65; DX 13890, pp. 16, 18; see also DX 1404A, p. 10 (App. A to JX 38).
4. DX 4740: Evans, Tr. (Telex) 3919; DX 13890, p. 16; see also DX 1404A, p. 10 (App. A to JX 38).
5. DX 1404A, pp. 81-82, 85, 86, 89 (App. A to JX 38).
6. DX 1404A, p. 75 (App. A to JX 38); DX 2609B, p. 94.
7. DX 8886, p. 43.
8. Hughes, Tr. 33915.
9. Brooks, Tr. 22771; Evans, Tr. 101047.
10. Brooks, Tr. 22665-66.
11. Evans, Tr. 101045-46, 101269.
12. Evans, Tr. 101048-51; see also DX 4773, p. 3.
13. Evans, Tr. 101049; see also DX 4773, p. 1; DX 14059.
14. JX 38, p. 2; see DX 1404A, p. 7 (App. A to JX 38).
15. DX 1404A, p. 3. (App. A to JX 38); DX 8081 (Tr. 101035).
16. Brooks, Tr. 22806-07; Tr. 71984-85; JX 38, p. 5; DX 1404A, p. 3 (App. A to JX 38); DX 4779.
17. JX 38, pp. 2-3; the report is DX 1404A (App. A to JX 38).
18. Case, Tr. 73571.
19. DX 1404A, pp. 73-91 (App. A to JX 38).
20. Evans, Tr. 101271-73; see also Knaplund, Tr. 90473.
21. DX 1404A, p. 75 (App. A to JX 38).
22. DX 1404A, p. 57 (App. A to JX 38).
23. Evans, Tr. 101126; see also Friedman, Tr. 50378; Case, Tr. 73561-62.
24. Evans, Tr. 101129.
25. DX 4795.
26. DX 4806.
27. Rooney, Tr. 12123-24; Welke, Tr. 17079-80, 17304-05; see also Northrop, Tr. 82711; PX 3638.
28. DX 3726 (Tr. 78990); see also DX 4740: Evans, Tr. (Telex) 4034-35; DX 4755.
29. DX 573, p. 6; JX 38, p. 33.
30. DX 573, p. 3; JX 38, p. 32.
31. DX 4740: Evans, Tr. (Telex) 4034-35; DX 4755.
32. DX 572A, p. 6; JX 38, p. 394.
33. DX 572A, p. 5; JX 38, p. 394.
34. Case, Tr. 74220.
35. A statistical analysis comparing the price/performance of System/360 with the systems of competitors in terms of processor and memory characteristics is given in Franklin M. Fisher, John J. McGowan, and Joen E. Greenwood, *Folded, Spindled, and Mutilated: Economic Analysis and U.S. v. IBM* (Cambridge, Mass.: MIT Press, 1983), Ch. 5. Such processor-memory comparisons are referred to below as "price/performance, roughly measured."
36. PX 1099A; see also Knaplund, Tr. 90503; DX 1525.
37. Knaplund, Tr. 90504-05; see also PX 1099A, p. 1; PX 6204, p. 1.
38. Withington, Tr. 56590-92; PX 4829, p. 16.
39. PX 320, pp. 13-14.
40. PX 243, pp. 5-6.
41. DX 4773, p. 3.
42. Case, Tr. 73244; Evans, Tr. 101048.
43. JX 38, p. 5; DX 1404A, p. 7 (App. A to JX 38).
44. Case, Tr. 72303.
45. JX 38, p. 5.
46. E. Bloch, Tr. 91468-69, 91492, 91686; see also DX 9117, p. 2.
47. E. Bloch, Tr. 91492-93.

48. E. Bloch, Tr. 91690-92; see also PX 1900, p. 7.

49. E. Bloch, Tr. 91686-87; see also DX 9117, p. 3.

50. E. Bloch, Tr. 91492.

51. Case, Tr. 72265; E. Bloch, Tr. 91486-87.

52. E. Bloch, Tr. 91493; see DX 9117, pp. 4-5, 8.

53. E. Bloch, Tr. 91492.

54. E. Bloch, Tr. 91694-95.

55. E. Bloch, Tr. 91492-94; see also Gibson, Tr. 22625-27; DX 4782.

56. E. Bloch, Tr. 91492-94.

57. E. Bloch, Tr. 91699-701.

58. Case, Tr. 72301-03; E. Bloch, Tr. 91705; see also PX 3587 (Tr. 25334).

59. E. Bloch, Tr. 91496-97; see also McCarter, Tr. 88380; Evans, Tr. 101132.

60. Evans, Tr. 101132.

61. E. Bloch, Tr. 91705.

62. E. Bloch, Tr. 91497-98; see also Case, Tr. 72298-301.

63. Case, Tr. 72301; E. Bloch, Tr. 91497.

64. E. Bloch, Tr. 91708.

65. Evans, Tr. 101131.

66. E. Bloch, Tr. 91695-96.

67. E. Bloch, Tr. 91704-05; see also Withington, Tr. 56591.

68. E. Bloch, Tr. 91698; Dunlop, Tr. 93991.

69. See E. Bloch, Tr. 91494, 91500, 91703; Case, Tr. 72300-14 for details of the carry-over of SLT development into monolithics.

70. E. Bloch, Tr. 91499.

71. E. Bloch, Tr. 91562.

72. Case, Tr. 71998-99, 72008-12, 73235-38, 73514, 77966-67, 77977, 77982; DX 3538.

73. Case, Tr. 73515.

74. PX 1900, p. 9.

75. Case, Tr. 73245-48; see also E. Bloch, Tr. 91563.

76. Case, Tr. 73250.

77. E. Bloch, Tr. 91929; see also Case, Tr. 73251-52.

78. E. Bloch, Tr. 91928-29.

79. Case, Tr. 73253, 73267.

80. DX 1404A, p. 12 (App. A to JX 38).

81. DX 4740: Evans, Tr. (Telex) 3925-28.

82. DX 1404A, p. 13 (App. A to JX 38).

83. Case, Tr. 73329.

84. Case, Tr. 73274-83.

85. DX 4740: Evans, Tr. (Telex) 3927-28.

86. Evans, Tr. 100152.

87. DX 1404A, p. 44 (App. A to JX 38).

88. Case, Tr. 73268-69, 73321.

89. Evans, Tr. 101129.

90. Evans, Tr. 101052, 101129; see also Case, Tr. 73538-39.

91. Case, Tr. 73538-39.

92. Brooks, Tr. 22843-44; Case, Tr. 74574.

93. Evans, Tr. 101187-88, 101275-76; Hughes, Tr. 33970-71.

94. Evans, Tr. 101144.

95. PX 320, p. 13.

96. Weil, Tr. 7189; see also Beard, Tr. 10342; Friedman, Tr. 50378; O'Neill, Tr. 76194-96.

97. Weil, Tr. 7190.

98. Evans, Tr. 101132-33. A sample list of the diverse applications for which System/360 has been used is given in DX 14971, pp. A1-A21.

99. Case, Tr. 73327-28; see also Weil, Tr. 7059-60.

100. Case, Tr. 73328-29, 73387-89.

101. Case, Tr. 73368-69; see also Brooks, Tr. 22681-82.

102. DX 1404A, p. 8 (App. A to JX 38).

103. DX 1404A, pp. 16, 25 (App. A to JX 38).

104. Evans, Tr. 101141.

105. Welke, Tr. 19193; Case, Tr. 73406-10; Evans, Tr. 101140-41; PX 4829, pp. 17-18.

106. DX 1404A, pp. 35-40 (App. A to JX 38).

107. See McCollister, Tr. 11068; Brooks, Tr. 22692; Friedman, Tr. 50377; Case, Tr. 73427-28; J. Jones, Tr. 80007-08; Knaplund, Tr. 90507-08; PX 1215, p. 1.

108. Rooney, Tr. 12550-51; see also Spangle, Tr. 5026; Beard, Tr. 10325.

109. DX 1404A, p. 8 (App. A to JX 38).

110. DX 1404A, pp. 36-41 (App. A to JX 38); see also PX 1215, p. 2.

111. Case, Tr. 73387-88.

112. DX 1404A, p. 40 (App. A to JX 38).

113. Case, Tr. 73520; see also Evans, Tr. 101057-58; DX 1404A, p. 17 (App. A to JX 38).

114. Case, Tr. 73520.

115. Case, Tr. 73223; JX 38, p. 5.

116. Case, Tr. 73521.

117. Case, Tr. 73225; see also Evans, Tr. 101142-43.

118. Brooks, Tr. 22806-07.

119. Case, Tr. 73347.

120. Evans, Tr. 101133; see also H. Brown, Tr. 82972; PX 4505, p. 1; PX 4531, p. 1; DX 860, p. A; DX 9405, pp. 552, 1013.
121. Withington, Tr. 56592-93.
122. DX 1404A, p. 12 (App. A to JX 38). Emphasis in original.
123. Ibid.
124. DX 1404A, p. 39 (App. A to JX 38).
125. Weil, Tr. 7029-32.
126. DX 561, p. 13.
127. R. Bloch, Tr. 7578, 7588-89, 7605-06, 7886-89; Goetz, Tr. 17652-54, 18822-23; Enfield, Tr. 20052-54; DX 6661, p. 6.
128. Hughes, Tr. 34047-48.
129. DX 2872.
130. Brooks, Tr. 22656-57, 22666-67, 22673-74; Case, Tr. 77966-67; DX 2900.
131. JX 38, pp. 30, 289, 292, 334, 526; DX 14305.
132. Case, Tr. 74557-62.
133. Withington, Tr. 56606.
134. Withington, Tr. 56371-72; see also DX 2900.
135. PX 449, p. 9.
136. Beard, Tr. 9057-58, 9956-57, 10029-30, 10318-19; see also R. Bloch, Tr. 7608-09, 7614-15, 7881-82; McCollister, Tr. 11287-89; Rooney, Tr. 11853, 12395-96; Goetz, Tr. 17655, 18778.
137. Beard, Tr. 9058-59, 9953-60, 10324-25; McCollister, Tr. 11069; Goetz, Tr. 18935-36; Enfield, Tr. 20020-21.
138. Weil, Tr. 7060-61.
139. J. Jones, Tr. 79042-43; see also Hart, Tr. 81936.
140. See Withington, Tr. 57677-83; Hart, Tr. 80222-24.
141. Hart, Tr. 81938-39.
142. DX 3753 (Hart, Tr. 80193).
143. Hart, Tr. 80222-24.
144. DX 5440, pp. 2-3, 5.
145. DX 5440, p. 9.
146. PX 449, p. 9.
147. McCollister, Tr. 11287-88.
148. PX 2161, p. 3.
149. Perlis, Tr. 1848-49; Welke, Tr. 17113; Goetz, Tr. 17476-77; Enfield, Tr. 20737-38; Case, Tr. 73443.
150. DX 1404A, pp. 7, 8, 9, 54 (App. A to JX 38).
151. Case, Tr. 73438-41.
152. Perlis, Tr. 1887.
153. PX 1092, p. 4; PX 1900, p. 8.
154. Perlis, Tr. 1887; Welke, Tr. 17313; Rooney, Tr. 12576.

155. Case, Tr. 73526.
156. Case, Tr. 73527-30.
157. Perlis, Tr. 1887.
158. Ibid.; see also Palevsky, Tr. 3180; Rooney, Tr. 12576; Currie, Tr. 15186; Welke, Tr. 17308-12.
159. Withington, Tr. 58596-600; Enfield, Tr. 20947-52, 21120; Brooks, Tr. 22759, 22853-54, 22862-63; McCarter, Tr. 88388; JX 38, para. 9, p. 6; PX 6217; DX 1410.
160. Enfield, Tr. 20088-89, 20299-300, 20741-42, 20943-48.
161. Case, Tr. 73416.
162. DX 1172, p. 1.
163. JX 38, para. 6, p. 4.
164. Evans, Tr. 101134; JX 38, pp. 14-25; PX 4829, pp. 16-18; see also Withington, Tr. 56770.
165. Withington, Tr. 56475-76, 58534; Case, Tr. 72787-88, 74205-06; JX 38, pp. 346-47; PX 2990, p. R3; PX 6671, pp. 15, 26; DX 13949.
166. Evans, Tr. 101134; see also PX 4829, p. 18; Withington, Tr. 56770-71.
167. Gibson, Tr. 2948-49; see also JX 38, p. 28; PX 3638, p. 1; PX 4829, p. 18.
168. PX 320, p. 13.
169. Evans, Tr. 101136.
170. Evans, Tr. 101135.
171. Norris, Tr. 6019-20; Currie, Tr. 15495-96; Rooney, Tr. 12048-49; Withington, Tr. 56239, 56246-47; DX 13949.
172. Evans, Tr. 101137; DX 3617; see also Enfield, Tr. 20266; JX 38, p. 207; DX 573, pp. 4, 6.
173. Evans, Tr. 101137; see also Case, Tr. 72881.
174. Beard, Tr. 10322-23.
175. Currie, Tr. 15459.
176. Currie, Tr. 15006-08.
177. G. Brown, Tr. 51528-29.
178. G. Brown, Tr. 51541-46.
179. DX 94B.
180. DX 2782A; DX 7984.
181. Case, Tr. 72741-42; JX 38, p. 86; PX 4252, p. 1; DX 3554D; see also Enfield, Tr. 20264-65; Haughton, Tr. 94998.
182. Case, Tr. 72742-43; JX 38, pp. 86, 439; DX 3554D; see also Haughton, Tr. 94998.
183. Beard, Tr. 9048-49; McCollister, Tr. 9597; Withington, Tr. 56240-41, 58800.
184. Knaplund, Tr. 90506.
185. Case, Tr. 73527.
186. Evans, Tr. 101139.

187. Case, Tr. 73451-53.

188. McCollister, Tr. 9591; Rooney, Tr. 12142; Case, Tr. 73468-70.

189. Case, Tr. 72743.

190. Case, Tr. 73452-53.

191. Withington, Tr. 56240-41.

192. McCollister, Tr. 9370, 9591-92; Rooney, Tr. 12122; Knaplund, Tr. 90506-07; Evans, Tr. 101138.

193. Withington, Tr. 56246-49.

194. Rooney, Tr. 12193.

195. PX 1967, pp. 1, 3; see Page, Tr. 33122.

196. Case, Tr. 73468-70.

197. JX 34, pp. 1-2.

198. Guzy, Tr. 32858-64; Gardner, Tr. 38585, 39143.

199. Gardner, Tr. 39143; DX 1418, p. 151; see also Spitters, Tr. 55259-61; DX 2572.

200. Guzy, Tr. 32316, 32776, 32899.

201. Guzy, Tr. 33168; DX 1302, pp. 1-3; DX 1308, p. 1.

202. Whitcomb, Tr. 34555-56; DX 4756B, p. 96; DX 4739: Wilmer, Tr. (Telex) 4266; DX 4741: Yang, Tr. (Telex) 6116.

203. PX 4732A, p. 12; DX 4242, p. 8; DX 4250, p. 7; DX 4756A, pp. 36, 72.

204. DX 86A, p. 2; DX 4113: Terry, Tr. (Telex) 3310-12.

205. Page, Tr. 33072-73; Ashbridge, Tr. 34812-13.

206. DX 86A, pp. 1, 4, 5; DX 87, p. 12.

207. Eckert, Tr. 988-89; McDonald, Tr. 45060-63.

208. DX 10735, pp. 10-11.

209. PX 5324, p. 46; DX 4756A, p. 8.

210. PX 3707A, p. 38; DX 10735, p. 10.

211. PX 3146A, p. 1; PX 5581, p. 10; PX 5582, p. 7; DX 1886, p. 7; DX 12194.

212. G. Brown, Tr. 51056-57, 51080-81, 51095-96.

213. McCollister, Tr. 9370.

214. Beard, Tr. 8575.

215. Ashbridge, Tr. 34812-13; G. Brown, Tr. 51536-37; Spain, Tr. 90227.

216. G. Brown, Tr. 51536.

217. Spain, Tr. 88753, 88755.

218. DX 7858, p. 2.

219. Hughes, Tr. 34102-03; Case, Tr. 73446, 73474-75, 73523; DX 1404A, pp. 19-20 (App. A to JX 38).

220. Case, Tr. 74079-83; Haughton, Tr. 95010-32.

221. Hughes, Tr. 71939.

222. Case. Tr. 73447.

223. Case, Tr. 73446-48.

224. Hughes, Tr. 71939-40; Case, Tr. 73448.

225. Hughes, Tr. 71939-40; see also Case, Tr. 73533.

226. Case, Tr. 73416.

227. Case, Tr. 73448; see also Hughes, Tr. 34109.

228. Withington, Tr. 58268-69, 58271-75.

229. Case, Tr. 73427-28; see also Navas, Tr. 41394-95; Withington, Tr. 56193.

230. Case, Tr. 73531-32.

231. See DX 1656; DX 1657; DX 1658; DX 1659.

232. Case, Tr. 73474-75; Navas, Tr. 41395-96.

233. Case, Tr. 73523; Cary, Tr. 101333-37, 101339, 101374, 101629-31; see also Wright, Tr. 13236-38; Enfield, Tr. 20765-68; G. Brown, Tr. 51812; Powers, Tr. 95376-89, 95412-13, 95475-82; PX 3312A, p. R14; PX 3594A, pp. 4, 26, 36, 40; PX 3681A, p. R1; PX 4880, p. 3.

234. Shoemaker, Tr. 30867; Case, Tr. 74125-50; Peterman, Tr. 99441-43; DX 7590: Perkins dep., pp. 21, 24; DX 7591: Hilyer dep., p. 15. IBM's OEMI (original equipment manufacturers information) Manual for System/360 was first made available in 1965 (Case, Tr. 74145).

235. Knaplund, Tr. 90497-98; DX 1404A, p. 40 (App. A to JX 38); see also PX 3908A.

236. Withington, Tr. 56174.

237. Knaplund, Tr. 90495-500; Akers, Tr. 96665, 96675-76; Cary, Tr. 101386-87.

238. Knaplund, Tr. 90496-98.

239. Cary, Tr. 101359; see also Brooks, Tr. 22868; Case, Tr. 73561; Evans, Tr. 101126.

240. Knaplund, Tr. 90515; Evans, Tr. 101126; PX 1092, p. 1; DX 1172, pp. 1-2.

241. PX 1900, p. 4.

242. McCarter, Tr. 88377; DX 1404A, p. 8 (App. A to JX 38).

243. Hughes, Tr. 33921-22, 71942-43; Dunlop, Tr. 93647-51.

244. Knaplund, Tr. 90470-71.

245. DX 1404A, pp. 7, 49 (App. A to JX 38).

246. Case, Tr. 74469, 74487-88, 74492-99.

247. Dunlop, Tr. 93651-52.

248. Dunlop, Tr. 93641, 93646.

249. Dunlop, Tr. 93642-43, 93645.

250. Knaplund, Tr. 90471.
251. Brooks, Tr. 22706.
252. Brooks, Tr. 22669.
253. PX 6671, p. 6.
254. PX 6671, pp. 5-6.
255. Knaplund, Tr. 90546; E. Bloch, Tr. 91562.
256. PX 1900, p. 9.
257. E. Bloch, Tr. 91562-64, 91891-93.
258. Case, Tr. 73561; Evans, Tr. 101128.
259. Case, Tr. 73562.
260. Friedman, Tr. 50378; Case, Tr. 73561-62; Evans, Tr. 101126.
261. Evans, Tr. 101128.
262. Case, Tr. 73606.
263. See, for instance, Case, Tr. 73589-92; PX 1074; PX 1090.
264. Evans, Tr. 101277; see also DX 4806.
265. PX 1099A.
266. Knaplund, Tr. 90511-13.
267. McCollister, Tr. 9298-300; Palevsky, Tr. 3145-46; Spangle, Tr. 5531; Oelman, Tr. 6160.
268. Withington, Tr. 56524, 56539.
269. DX 1406.
270. Hughes, Tr. 33962-66, 33972-73, 34062.
271. J. Jones, Tr. 78991-97.
272. Hindle, Tr. 7447.
273. R. Jones, Tr. 8867.
274. R. Bloch, Tr. 7761-62.
275. For example, Hindle (DEC), Tr. 7448; Hangen (NCR), Tr. 10423-24, 10431; Currie (XDS), Tr. 15175-76; Brooks, Tr. 22705, 22795-96; Withington, Tr. 56560, 56565; DX 426, pp. 7-8.
276. See Withington, Tr. 56459-60.
277. DX 4806.
278. PX 1077, pp. 1-2.
279. PX 1099A, pp. R2-R3.
280. PX 2952.
281. PX 3624, p. 4.
282. Weil, Tr. 7026-30, 7033-38, 7060-62, 7181; DX 488; DX 490.
283. Weil, Tr. 7031-34.
284. Norris, Tr. 5937-38; JX 10, para. 4.
285. PX 1045.
286. PX 1026A.
287. PX 1025.
288. PX 2807.
289. PX 3619.
290. PX 3620.
291. DX 13958.
292. PX 320, p. 15.
293. See Case, Tr. 73561, 73589; Evans,

Tr. 101128.
294. DX 13526: Forrest dep., pp. 748-50.
295. PX 320, pp. 4-15.
296. McCollister, Tr. 11367; PX 1079; DX 167.
297. McCollister, Tr. 11237; Knaplund, Tr. 90475; Evans, Tr. 101188; DX 167.
298. R. Bloch, Tr. 7605-06; McCollister, Tr. 11237; Goetz, Tr. 17652; DX 167; DX 488.
299. PX 1079.
300. Evans, Tr. 101186; PX 3912.
301. Evans, Tr. 101196.
302. Knaplund, Tr. 90475; JX 38, para. 16; PX 1079; PX 1095; DX 2983.
303. See, for instance, Case, Tr. 73512, 73590; Evans, Tr. 101127.
304. PX 1074, pp. 2-3.
305. Hughes, Tr. 33952-53; McCarter, Tr. 88394; JX 38, para. 7; DX 4800.
306. Hughes, Tr. 33953-54; Evans, Tr. 101188, 101195.
307. PX 3913.
308. PX 1090.
309. DX 2983.
310. Evans, Tr. 101195-96.
311. Evans, Tr. 101275-76; PX 6668 (DX 14514).
312. Evans, Tr. 101277.
313. Hughes, Tr. 33953-54.
314. Evans, Tr. 101190, 101198-99.
315. Knaplund, Tr. 90477; see also Hughes, Tr. 33933-34, 33947-49; PX 1107, p. 7; DX 1405.
316. Brooks, Tr. 22695-96.
317. Brooks, Tr. 22785.
318. Hughes, Tr. 33952-55; JX 38, para. 7, p. 5; DX 4800.
319. McCarter, Tr. 88383; JX 38, para. 19.
320. Brooks, Tr. 22699.
321. McCarter, Tr. 88382-83.
322. DX 1172, p. 2.
323. McCarter, Tr. 88390-93; Evans, Tr. 101065-66, 101082; DX 1172, pp. 2, 5; see also DX 4815.
324. See Spangle, Tr. 4997-99; Weil, Tr. 7232-35; McCollister, Tr. 9635-41.
325. DX 1172; DX 2983; DX 4815.
326. DX 4815; see also Evans, Tr. 101072-75.
327. DX 1172; see also Brooks, Tr. 22782-84; Knaplund, Tr. 90486-88.
328. Knaplund, Tr. 90486-88.
329. See JX 38, para. 24.
330. Weil, Tr. 7064; see McCollister, Tr.

9635, 9641, 9646; Hangen, Tr. 10761-62; Knaplund, Tr. 90483-84; PX 355, pp. 33-36; PX 2226A, pp. 13, 19, 27; PX 2432, pp. 19, 22, 28; DX 573; DX 4769; DX 4774; DX 8962.

331. Weil, Tr. 7064-65; Withington, Tr. 58738-46; J. Jones, Tr. 79034-36; Akers, Tr. 96537-40; DX 3726.

332. DX 1172, p. 1; see also DX 3726; DX 4815.

333. Withington, Tr. 58738-46; J. Jones, Tr. 79034-36; Knaplund, Tr. 90483-88; Akers, Tr. 96537-41; DX 1172, pp. 1-2; DX 3726; DX 4815.

334. Knaplund, Tr. 90474-77.

335. Gibson, Tr. 22648; Brooks, Tr. 22799-800; Hughes, Tr. 34003; Knaplund, Tr. 90483, 90493; E. Bloch, Tr. 93311; JX 38, paras. 18, 22; DX 1165; DX 9161.

336. McCarter, Tr. 22568-70, 88362-93; 88434-55; Brooks, Tr. 22786-88, 22850-53; Evans, Tr. 101065-66, 101083-95, 101174-78; PX 2126, pp. 2-5, 35-37; PX 4005; DX 1165; DX 1172, pp. 2, 5; DX 1409; DX 4815; DX 8083.

337. McCarter, Tr. 88404.

338. McCarter, Tr. 88371-72, 88602-05; Evans, Tr. 101093-94; DX 4768; DX 7680; DX 9005.

339. JX 38, para. 24.

340. Brooks, Tr. 22853.

341. JX 38, para. 25; DX 4740: Evans, Tr. (Telex) 3933-34; Welke, Tr. 19410, 19631; see also Enfield, Tr. 20947-48; PX 4834, p. 23.

342. McCarter, Tr. 88390-93; Evans, Tr. 101119; DX 5609.

343. Fernbach, Tr. 517-18; Perlis, Tr. 1320, 2001-03; Spangle, Tr. 4997-99, 5008; Weil, Tr. 7215-21, 7232-35; McCollister, Tr. 9694-98, 9707-08, 9710-11; Rooney, Tr. 12132-34, 12335-36, 12349-50, 12358; Wright, Tr. 13373-76; Conrad, Tr. 14088-89, 14133; Currie, Tr. 15303, 15352-54, 15704; Welke, Tr. 19281-82; Brooks, Tr. 22762-63; Withington, Tr. 55914, 56599-600, 56729-31; McCarter, Tr. 88390-92; Evans, Tr. 101119; DX 872, p. A.

344. McCarter, Tr. 88544-45.

345. Enfield, Tr. 20294-97; see also Perlis, Tr. 1347-48.

346. Perlis, Tr. 1887-88; Palevsky, Tr. 3180; Rooney, Tr. 12576; Currie, Tr. 15186; Welke, Tr. 17308-13; McCarter, Tr. 88389;

PX 1900, pp. 3-4, 8; PX 4833, p. 16; PX 4834, p. 23.

347. See Knaplund, Tr. 90515; DX 4740: Evans, Tr. (Telex) 3932-33.

348. Gibson, Tr. 22636-37; Case, Tr. 73258; Knaplund, Tr. 90547; Evans, Tr. 101123; Cary, Tr. 101780-81; JX 38, para. 28; PX 1900, pp. 7, 10; DX 9331.

349. JX 38, para. 28.

350. PX 1900, p. 10.

351. Gibson, Tr. 22635-37; Knaplund, Tr. 90545-46; E. Bloch, Tr. 91895-96; DX 7691, p. 4; DX 9333.

352. Knaplund, Tr. 90547; E. Bloch, Tr. 91899-906; Dunlop, Tr. 94774-75; DX 9331; DX 9332; DX 9333; DX 9334.

353. DX 9331; see also E. Bloch, Tr. 91899-900, 91905-06; Dunlop, Tr. 94774-75; DX 9332; DX 9333.

354. Knaplund, Tr. 90547-48; E. Bloch, Tr. 91905-08; Dunlop, Tr. 93670; PX 5771, p. 28; DX 9038.

355. E. Bloch, Tr. 91908.

356. DX 9038.

357. Dunlop, Tr. 93670.

358. PX 5771, p. 3; DX 13680, pp. 3-4; see also Knaplund, Tr. 90549-50; Dunlop, Tr. 93670; DX 4740: Evans, Tr. (Telex) 3934.

359. Knaplund, Tr. 90549-50; DX 4740: Evans, Tr. (Telex) 3934.

360. Knaplund, Tr. 90548-51; DX 1154; DX 1155; see also E. Bloch, Tr. 91915; DX 9333.

361. Knaplund, Tr. 90551-52; E. Bloch, Tr. 91915-18.

362. Knaplund, Tr. 90551-52; E. Bloch, Tr. 91917-19.

363. Knaplund, Tr. 90551-52; DX 9038.

364. Knaplund, Tr. 90943-46; E. Bloch, Tr. 91917.

365. Knaplund, Tr. 90552-53.

366. JX 38, para. 27, p. 10.

367. See Knaplund, Tr. 90849-54; JX 38, para. 25.

368. DX 8886, p. 107.

369. Cary, Tr. 101359-60; PX 1900, pp. 4, 8; DX 4740: Evans, Tr. (Telex) 3932-34; DX 8886, pp. 107-08, 111; DX 13677, p. 5; DX 13678, pp. 6-7.

370. Cary, Tr. 101359.

371. PX 468, p. 31; DX 13677, p. 7; see also DX 4740: Evans, Tr. (Telex) 3932-34.

372. Case, Tr. 73590; Evans, Tr. 101127-28; DX 1172.

373. Cary, Tr. 101525-26; DX 8886, p.

111; DX 13677, p. 5; DX 13678, p. 7.

374. PX 5771, p. 36.

375. DX 13677, pp. 6-7; DX 13678, pp. 7, 39; DX 13889, p. 20.

376. Cary, Tr. 101525-26; PX 4481A, p. 1; PX 6153, p. 2.

377. Cary, Tr. 101781.

378. DX 13677, p. 5.

379. PX 5767, p. 3.

380. Cary, Tr. 101360, 101781; DX 4740: Evans, Tr. (Telex) 3934-35.

381. PX 1900, pp. 8-9.

CHAPTER 6

1. PX 320, pp. 12-13.
2. DX 1525.
3. PX 2956, p. 1; DX 1525; see also PX 4829, p. 19.
4. PX 2956, p. 1.
5. PX 4829, p. 19.
6. Beard, Tr. 8459.
7. Beard, Tr. 9113-14.
8. McCollister, Tr. 9630.
9. Beard, Tr. 8459.
10. DX 960.
11. PX 320, p. 14; see also Weil, Tr. 7060.
12. PX 320, p. 16.
13. DX 1525.
14. PX 2996, p. 3.
15. DX 13445.
16. Franklin M. Fisher, John J. McGowan, and Joen E. Greenwood, *Folded, Spindled and Mutilated: Economic Analysis and U.S. v. IBM* (Cambridge, Mass.: MIT Press, 1983), Ch. 5.
17. PX 320, p. 16.; cf. Fisher, McGowan, and Greenwood, loc. cit.
18. Weil, Tr. 7060-61.
19. Weil, Tr. 7062.
20. PX 320, p. 16.
21. DX 1525.
22. PX 4829, p. 21.
23. Norris, Tr. 5626, 5965-67; DX 319, p. 1.
24. PX 355, p. 35.
25. DX 14, p. 1.
26. DX 1525.
27. DX 14, p. 1.
28. PX 4829, p. 20.
29. PX 4830, p. 22.
30. DX 16, p. 2.
31. McDonald, Tr. 3821; DX 70, p. 9.
32. Eckert, Tr. 908.

33. PX 2082, p. 95.
34. PX 4829, p. 22.
35. PX 4832, p. 21.
36. Ibid.; DX 10262, p. 8.
37. DX 13849, p. 27.
38. DX 44, p. 5.
39. Palevsky, Tr. 3223-24.
40. DX 52, p. 1.
41. DX 14295, p. 44.
42. DX 13824, p. 2.
43. DX 1525.
44. DX 13823.
45. DX 13640, p. 1.
46. PX 1265, pp. 2, 4.
47. DX 14134.
48. DX 13824, p. 2.
49. DX 13825.
50. PX 3630, p. 2.
51. PX 1214.
52. PX 1256 (DX 14504).
53. JX 38, pp. 329-30; JX 10, App. A, paras. 3, 5, pp. 2-3; DX 13827.
54. DX 14322.
55. Evans, Tr. 10111-12.
56. PX 1389, pp. 1-2.
57. JX 38, p. 393.
58. PX 1288, p. 2; PX 1637, p. 2; DX 14135.
59. PX 3908A, p. 4.
60. PX 3908A, p. 22.
61. PX 6671, pp. 15, 26-27.
62. PX 1251 (DX 14503), pp. 1, 4.
63. PX 1271, pp. 3, 6, 8, 12, 14; PX 1288, pp. 1-2.
64. PX 1272 (DX 960), p. 2.
65. PX 1288, pp. 1-2; see DX 13955, p. 4.
66. JX 38, pp. 377, 484.
67. PX 4256; DX 13950, p. 2.
68. Case, Tr. 72742-43; see also PX 3226A, p. 4.
69. PX 3226A, pp. 4-5.
70. Case, Tr. 72742; PX 1967 (Tr. 35690); see also McCollister, Tr. 9597.
71. Beard, Tr. 9049.
72. Case, Tr. 72743.
73. PX 1967 (Tr. 35690).
74. PX 1967 (Tr. 35692).
75. DX 1404A, pp. 35-36, 69 (App. A to JX 38).
76. Hughes, Tr. 71942-43; Knaplund, Tr. 90478.
77. Knaplund, Tr. 90489.
78. DX 13829, p. 1.
79. DX 13829, pp. 1-2.
80. DX 14477.

81. PX 4830, p. 20.

82. Case, Tr. 73575; JX 38, p. 297.

83. Hughes, Tr. 71992; Case, Tr. 74085.

84. PX 3773, p. 2.

85. DX 4841, pp. 5-6; see also Wright, Tr. 13348-49.

86. DX 2609B, p. 182.

87. PX 4830, pp. 20-21.

88. The NSA projects are discussed at. length in the classified NSA stipulation (DX 3420A), paras. 79-86, 333-69.

89. DX 4775.

90. Brooks, Tr. 22844.

91. Brooks, Tr. 22713-14; Knaplund, Tr. 90477-78, 90517; DX 1404A, p. 16 (App. A to JX 38).

92. JX 10, para. 5.

93. Knaplund, Tr. 90571-72; PX 1034; PX 1036; PX 1041.

94. Wright, Tr. 12903-94; JX 10, paras. 4, 7, 9, 13; PX 1061.

95. JX 10, para. 15; see Knaplund, Tr. 90920-21; Plaintiff's Admissions, set IV, paras. 37.0, 53.0-53.6, 82.0; PX 1061; DX 7518: Mount dep., pp. 63-64.

96. Robinson, Tr. 23049.

97. Knaplund, Tr. 90518-19; see Wright, Tr. 12893-94, 12897.

98. Knaplund, Tr. 90519-20.

99. PX 1040; see also Norris, Tr. 5617; Wright, Tr. 12893-94; Brooks, Tr. 22718-19; Knaplund, Tr. 90920.

100. Dunwell, Tr. 85840; Wright, Tr. 12899-900; PX 1041; PX 1082; PX 1160.

101. Dunwell, Tr. 85549-50; Crago, Tr. 85979-80.

102. Eckert, Tr. 836-37; Lacey, Tr. 6657; DX 13526: Forrest dep., pp. 106-07.

103. Gibson, Tr. 22593; Case, Tr. 73606-08; Dunwell, Tr. 85338-49, 85791-94, 85880-82; Hurd, Tr. 86592-93, 86595-98; E. Bloch, Tr. 91485-89; JX 10, para. 3; DX 3171; DX 5423: Smagorinsky dep., p. 94; DX 8923; DX 13526: Forrest dep., pp. 106-07.

104. PX 1469.

105. DX 7692, p. 3; see also Gibson, Tr. 22644; McCarter, Tr. 88408; DX 1141.

106. Norris, Tr. 5934, 5938; DX 308; DX 309; DX 310; DX 13526: Forrest dep., pp. 191-97, 205-06, 225-30, 232-42, 245, 504-08, 570-74, 580-81.

107. PX 1045.

108. Knaplund, Tr. 90519-20; JX 10, para. 7.

109. PX 1049; see also PX 1051.

110. JX 10, para. 7; see also Knaplund, Tr. 90520; PX 1021; PX 1036; PX 1041.

111. JX 10, para. 8; PX 1021; PX 1041; PX 1082; PX 1204.

112. Knaplund, Tr. 90520-21; see also DX 9080.

113. Knaplund, Tr. 90521; JX 10, para. 1.

114. See the classified NSA stipulation (DX 3420A), paras. 387-415, esp. 403, 411-15.

115. Knaplund, Tr. 90523-24.

116. McCarter, Tr. 88409; JX 10, paras. 17, 21; PX 1177.

117. McCarter, Tr. 88413; DX 3162; DX 3167; DX 3224; DX 3266.

118. E. Bloch, Tr. 91940-43; JX 10, paras. 30, 33.

119. Gibson, Tr. 22640-41; E. Bloch, Tr. 91940.

120. Case, Tr. 73594-95.

121. Case, Tr. 73593; Gomory, Tr. 98273-75; JX 10, para. 32; PX 3050; DX 3164.

122. JX 10, para. 35.

123. JX 10, para. 36.

124. DX 1189, pp. 3-4; see also Norris, Tr. 5849-51; DX 438, p. 7.

125. Knaplund, Tr. 90539.

126. PX 1288, p. 2.

127. See PX 1439A; PX 3566; PX 3615; PX 3630.

128. Knaplund, Tr. 90539.

129. PX 1439A.

130. PX 1589A, p. 1; see also Knaplund, Tr. 90539.

131. Knaplund, Tr. 90540; PX 1439A; PX 1538; PX 1589A, p. 1; DX 9036.

132. Knaplund, Tr. 90540.

133. PX 1541, p. 6; see also PX 1589A. The inability could be eliminated at some sacrifice in throughput (Knaplund, Tr. 90541; PX 1589A, p. 1; PX 3563A).

134. PX 1541, pp. 4, 6.

135. Knaplund, Tr. 90542; DX 1155; DX 11515, p. 2.

136. PX 2163A, p. 4; PX 2419, pp. 6-8.

137. PX 1979; PX 2099; PX 3555.

138. PX 2125, p. 48.

139. PX 2567, p. 93; see PX 2871A.

140. Perlis, Tr. 1862-63; JX 1, p. 115.

141. PX 299; see also Perlis, Tr. 1881; Brooks, Tr. 22739-40; Morse, Tr. 30986. The other developments included SAGE and SABRE (Wright, Tr. 13664-65; Crago, Tr. 85975-76); the "dynamic address

translation unit" (Brooks, Tr. 22866; Wright, Tr. 13332); and other efforts (Perlis, Tr. 2042-43; Wright, Tr. 13325-28; Knaplund, Tr. 90533; DX 4823).

142. Brooks, Tr. 22859-60; DX 1404A, pp. 12, 18, 19, 24, 26, 33 (App. A to JX 38).

143. Brooks, Tr. 22859-60; Knaplund, Tr. 90532-33.

144. PX 1194A, p. 3; see also Weil, Tr. 7287-88; Wright, Tr. 13331-32; Knaplund, Tr. 90532-33.

145. Wright, Tr. 13332; Brooks, Tr. 22743, 22866; Knaplund, Tr. 90532-33.

146. Weil, Tr. 7108.

147. PX 2961, pp. 1, 3. Emphasis omitted.

148. Weil, Tr. 7111-12.

149. Knaplund, Tr. 90533.

150. Weil, Tr. 7116-17.

151. PX 3502, p. 1.

152. PX 3502, pp. 3-7.

153. PX 1194A, p. 1.

154. PX 1194A, p. 3.

155. PX 1194A, p. 4.

156. PX 1194A, pp. 2-3.

157. PX 1194A, p. 1.

158. PX 2811, p. 1.

159. PX 2811, pp. 2-3. Emphasis in original.

160. PX 2811, pp. 4-5, 7. Emphasis in original.

161. PX 2964A, pp. 4-6.

162. PX 2964A, pp. R28-29.

163. Perlis, Tr. 1968-69, 2043-44, 2054-55; Weil, Tr. 7116; PX 4830, p. 14.

164. Hart, Tr. 80278-79.

165. Wright, Tr. 13287-92.

166. DX 894. Emphasis in original.

167. Wright, Tr. 12799.

168. Wright, Tr. 12802-07.

169. Wright, Tr. 12807, 12843-45; PX 2964A, pp. R28-29.

170. Wright, Tr. 12813.

171. DX 895.

172. PX 1238A, p. 4.

173. PX 1191; PX 1246A.

174. Cary, Tr. 101808-09.

175. Wright, Tr. 12793-95, 12814-15; Knaplund, Tr. 90535; PX 1318.

176. Wright, Tr. 12842-43.

177. Wright, Tr. 12825-26.

178. Wright, Tr. 12829-33.

179. Wright, Tr. 12842.

180. Perlis, Tr. 1963-69.

181. Perlis, Tr. 2054.

182. Wright, Tr. 12842-43.

183. Wright, Tr. 12905-08; see also Hart, Tr. 80293.

184. Wright, Tr. 12843, 13316-24; DX 901.

185. Wright, Tr. 12843-45.

186. PX 6209.

187. Brooks, Tr. 22760; Wright, Tr. 13357; PX 2029, p. 1; DX 898.

188. PX 1427.

189. Wright, Tr. 13334-35.

190. Wright, Tr. 13336-37.

191. Wright, Tr. 12881-84, 13359.

192. DX 898, p. 2.

193. Perlis, Tr. 1981-82; Knaplund, Tr. 90538; see also DX 13348. Product Test issued a "formal" nonconcurrence with the announcement, although it believed the program was "in good shape." The nonconcurrence was resolved by management (Wright, Tr. 13352-54, 13667-68; Knaplund, Tr. 90536-37; McCarter, Tr. 88416-17). The difficulties that the 67 eventually experienced were unrelated to Product Test's reasons for not supporting it. (McCarter, Tr. 88418).

194. PX 1826, p. 2.

195. PX 3471.

196. Wright, Tr. 12876-78, 13363-66; see also DX 897.

197. Wright, Tr. 12879; see also Wright, Tr. 13364-65; Hart, Tr. 80294.

198. Weil, Tr. 7227-28.

199. Weil, Tr. 7232-35.

200. Weil, Tr. 7234.

201. Weil, Tr. 7234-35.

202. Weil, Tr. 7232-33; Wright, Tr. 13375-76, 13673-74.

203. Weil, Tr. 7232.

204. Weil, Tr. 7232-33.

205. Wright, Tr. 13375-76.

206. Weil, Tr. 7236.

207. PX 1955 (DX 13866).

208. DX 3282A.

209. Wright, Tr. 12842, 13375; DX 905; see also Hart, Tr. 80296-300, 81961-63; Cary, Tr. 101809; cf Perlis, Tr. 2118-19.

210. DX 2609B, p. 182; see Cary, Tr. 101809.

211. DX 4740: Evans, Tr. (Telex) 3950.

212. PX 2487A, p. R2; DX 4740: Evans, Tr. (Telex) 3937-41.

213. DX 4740: Evans, Tr. (Telex) 3943-54.

214. Cary, Tr. 101809-10.

215. Case, Tr. 73612-13, 73578-79, 73403; Cary, Tr. 101809-10; see also PX 2487A, p. R2; DX 8066.

CHAPTER 7

1. DX 5424: Pasta, dep., pp. 11-13; DX 5504, p. 43.
2. DX 5504, p. 15.
3. Ibid. The Rosser Report is DX 5504.
4. DX 5504, p. 66.
5. DX 5504, pp. 18, 21.
6. Morse, Tr. 30965.
7. DX 5462, p. 20.
8. Macdonald, Tr. 6986; JX 28, para. 11; DX 347, p. 2; DX 5504, p. 20.
9. DX 7514, p. 8.
10. DX 5504, p. 44.
11. DX 5504, pp. 28-30.
12. DX 7514, p. 6.
13. See, for instance, Hangen, Tr. 10448-49; Rooney, Tr. 11880.
14. See, for instance, Perlis, Tr. 2033; Wright, Tr. 12910; Morse, Tr. 30985; Andreini, Tr. 47880-82.
15. Morse, Tr. 30965; Hurd, Tr. 86421; DX 7514, p. 33.
16. Norris, Tr. 5647-48, 5988; Morse, Tr. 30980.
17. DX 5504, p. 57.
18. DX 5500, p. 3.
19. DX 5476, p. 18; see also Hurd, Tr. 86715.
20. DX 7514, p. 8; DX 12150, pp. 17-18.
21. Hurd, Tr. 86712-13; DX 12150, pp. 11, 23.
22. Hurd, Tr. 86420; DX 12150, p. 32.
23. Perlis, Tr. 2009; JX 28, para. 12.
24. JX 28, para. 13.
25. DX 7514, p. 30.
26. JX 28, paras. 15-17.
27. JX 28, para. 19.
28. See, for instance, DX 12435: Armstrong dep., pp. 80-81.
29. See, for instance, Macdonald, Tr. 7534; Wright, Tr. 12958; PX 2963, pp. 7, 9.
30. Norris, Tr. 5647-48, 5989-91, 5993-95; DX 278, pp. 1, 6.
31. DX 983, p. 10; DX 11011, p. 10; DX 13846, p. 6; DX 13847, p. 7.
32. See, for instance, PX 1468 (University of Pennsylvania); PX 1558 (University of Colorado); PX 1824 (University of California, Berkeley).
33. PX 1088.
34. Wright, Tr. 12912-13; PX 1652, p. 1; PX 1661, p. 1; PX 1679, pp. 1-2; PX 3871: Armstrong dep., pp. 145-46.

35. PX 1706, p. 2; PX 1745, p. 2; PX 1746, p. 2.
36. JX 28, paras. 26, 29.
37. R. Bloch, Tr. 7603-04.
38. See Norris, Tr. 6058-59; R. Bloch, Tr. 7751-54; McCollister, Tr. 11041-43; Welke, Tr. 17343-46, 17380-81.
39. Goetz, Tr. 17500-01; see also Spangle, Tr. 5092; Norris, Tr. 6066; R. Bloch, Tr. 7604; McCollister, Tr. 11042-43.
40. Enfield, Tr. 19908; Akers, Tr. 96554-56.
41. Welke, Tr. 17009.
42. Welke, Tr. 17007-10, 17069-70, 17372-73.
43. Welke, Tr. 17010; Akers, Tr. 96555-56.
44. McCollister, Tr. 9648-49.
45. McCollister, Tr. 11370-72; DX 402, p. 10; DX 426, p. 12; DX 427, p. 4.
46. Akers, Tr. 96555-57; see Welke, Tr. 17017; Enfield, Tr. 19878-79, 19886-88; DX 4793.
47. Welke, Tr. 19225-26.
48. Enfield, Tr. 19862; see also Welke, Tr. 17373-75; DX 4793.
49. Enfield, Tr. 20249-50.
50. Pfeiffer, Tr. 16019-20.
51. R. Bloch, Tr. 7751-54; Welke, Tr. 19230.
52. Beard, Tr. 9944-46.
53. Beard, Tr. 8497.
54. McCollister, Tr. 9647-53; DX 69, pp. 3, 5; see also DX 98, p. 12.
55. Welke, Tr. 19617-18; Withington, Tr. 56591-93; PX 4833, p. 9; DX 1172, pp. 1-2; DX 4815.
56. PX 4833, p. 9.
57. DX 981, pp. 4-5.
58. DX 982, p. 3; DX 983, pp. 16-17.
59. McCollister, Tr. 9649-53, 11403-06.
60. DX 65, p. 2; DX 69, pp. 3, 5; DX 98, p. 12; DX 366, p. 3; DX 368, p. 3; DX 370, pp. 5, 19.
61. PX 3390.
62. PX 3351; PX 3352.
63. PX 3351, p. 4.
64. Ibid.; PX 3352.
65. PX 3351, pp. 1-2.
66. PX 3351, p. 3; PX 3390, pp. 1-2.
67. PX 2804A, pp. 1, 2; PX 2805A, p. 1; PX 4053, p. 1.
68. PX 1748, p. 11.
69. JX 57, p. 2.
70. Watson, Tr. 16602; see also Welke,

Tr. 17172-73.

71. Welke, Tr. 17361-62; see also DX 1096, pp. 1-2.

72. See Welke, Tr. 17093-95, 19180-82.

73. Watson, Tr. 16601; PX 3351, p. 3.

74. Welke, Tr. 19211-13; PX 1651, p. 6; DX 1031.

75. For instance, PX 3351, p. 3.

76. Watson, Tr. 16602.

77. Welke, Tr. 17172-73.

78. Welke, Tr. 19226.

79. McDonald, Tr. 2896-97.

80. Spangle, Tr. 5086-87;McCollister Tr., 11206-09; Withington, Tr. 56786-87.

81. DX 346, p. 1. Emphasis in original.

82. Hangen, Tr. 10721-24; DX 346.

83. DX 386, p. 2. Emphasis in original.

84. Norris, Tr. 5647; Goetz, Tr. 17530.

85. PX 3351, p. 4; see also PX 2454, p. 1; PX 3352, p. 5.

86. Withington, Tr. 55919-20; see also Perlis, Tr. 1344, 1348, 1986; Enfield, Tr. 20740-41, 21074; DX 491, p. 5.

87. PX 4834, p. 11; see also Macdonald, Tr. 6977-78.

CHAPTER 8

1. R. Jones, Tr. 8754; DX 556, p. 2; DX 13667, p. 1.

2. PX 5771, p. 3; DX 3364, p. 5.

3. See PX 5771, pp. 32, 36; DX 3364, pp. 47, 48, 53, 54; DX 3811; DX 13677, pp. 33, 37;DX 13678,pp. 33,37;DX 13679, pp. 33, 37; DX 13680, pp. 45, 46, 53, 54.

4. Weil, Tr. 7260; PX 326 (DX 13668), pp. B, 3; PX 327, pp. 2, 36; PX 328, pp. 2, 23; DX 556, pp. 2, 18; DX 7320; DX 8224, p. 6; DX 8631, pp. 31, 37; DX 13667, pp. B, 14; DX 13669, pp. 3, 4; DX 14484, p. R1.

5. PX 325, p. 10.

6. R. Bloch, Tr. 7615-17.

7. Weil, Tr. 7007-08, 7072, 7173.

8. PX 4829, p. 19.

9. R. Bloch, Tr. 7788-89;PX 353, p. 43.

10. Weil, Tr. 7005-06.

11. DX 488; DX 490.

12. PX 353, p. 44.

13. Weil, Tr. 7031-35.

14. Weil, Tr. 7018, 7038.

15. Weil, Tr. 7188-89.

16. Weil, Tr. 7263-64; DX 489. Emphasis in original.

17. See Chapter 6 in this volume; Franklin

M. Fisher, John J. McGowan, and Joen E. Greenwood, *Folded, Spindled and Mutilated: Economic Analysis and U.S. v. IBM* (Cambridge, Mass.: MIT Press, 1983), Ch. 5; PX 2966, pp. R-1, R-2,3; DX 1525; DX 13445.

18. PX 353, pp. 43-44.

19. Weil, Tr. 7197-98; DX 491, p. 1.

20. Weil, Tr. 7198.

21. PX 4829, p. 18.

22. PX 320, p. 16.

23. Weil, Tr. 7192.

24. PX 4829, p. 18.

25. PX 4829, p. 19.

26. Weil, Tr. 7206.

27. Weil, Tr. 7026-27.

28. Weil, Tr. 7029.

29. Weil, Tr. 7030.

30. Weil, Tr. 7031, 7034-35.

31. Weil, Tr. 7060-61.

32. Weil, Tr. 7062.

33. Weil, Tr. 7207.

34. Weil, Tr. 7212.

35. Weil, Tr. 7269.

36. Weil, Tr. 7207, 7209-11, 7215.

37. Weil, Tr. 7212.

38. Weil, Tr. 7019.

39. Weil, Tr. 7192.

40. Weil, Tr. 7190-91.

41. Weil, Tr. 7192; DX 491, p. 1; DX 492B, p. 3.

42. Weil, Tr. 7270-72; see PX 328, p. 21.

43. PX 4829, pp. 18-19.

44. PX 4829, p. 18.

45. Weil, Tr. 7178-79, 7192-93.

46. Weil, Tr. 7200; DX 556, p. 5.

47. DX 491, p. 1; see also Weil, Tr. 7199-203.

48. Weil, Tr. 7215-16.

49. Weil, Tr. 7216-17.

50. Weil, Tr. 7217-18.

51. Weil, Tr. 7217-19; see Perlis, Tr. 2001-04; McCollister, Tr. 9694-97, 9706-08; Rooney, Tr. 12132-36, 12349-50, 12358; Conrad, Tr. 14088-89, 14133; Withington, Tr. 56727-30.

52. Weil, Tr. 7220-22.

53. Weil, Tr. 7224-25; see also Withington, Tr. 55735-36, 56727-28, 56754, 57671-72.

54. PX 327, p. 9.

55. Ingersoll, Tr. 8339.

56. Weil, Tr. 7106-07.

57. Weil, Tr. 7106-08, 7225-26, 7231.

58. Perlis, Tr. 1881; Weil, Tr. 7226-27;

Brooks, Tr. 22739-40.

59. Weil, Tr. 7108.

60. Weil, Tr. 7111-12.

61. PX 2961, pp. 1, 3.

62. Weil, Tr. 7115.

63. Weil, Tr. 7116, 7251-52, 7254-55; see Perlis, Tr. 2117-18; PX 320, pp. 9-10.

64. Weil, Tr. 7122-23.

65. Weil, Tr. 7225-26, 7231.

66. Weil, Tr. 7227-28.

67. Weil, Tr. 7233.

68. PX 326 (DX 13668), p. 15; see also Hart, Tr. 80284-87.

69. Weil, Tr. 7234.

70. Weil, Tr. 7234-35.

71. Weil, Tr. 7236-37.

72. Weil, Tr. 7236.

73. Wright, Tr. 13375-76.

74. Weil, Tr. 7232.

75. Weil, Tr. 7233.

76. Perlis, Tr. 2001-04; McCollister, Tr. 9694-97, 9706-08; Rooney, Tr. 12132-36, 12349-50, 12358; Conrad, Tr. 10488-89, 14133; Currie, Tr. 15704-06; Withington, Tr. 56727-30.

77. Weil, Tr. 7238-39.

78. Weil, Tr. 7239; see also PX 326 (DX 13668), pp. 3, 15; PX 328, p. 18.

79. Weil, Tr. 7239-40.

80. DX 13668, pp. 15, 33.

81. Weil, Tr. 7240.

82. PX 327, pp. 9, 33.

83. Weil, Tr. 7223-24, 7240-42; PX 327, pp. 9, 33.

84. Weil, Tr. 7242.

85. Weil, Tr. 7243.

86. R. Bloch, Tr. 7615-16, 7755.

87. Weil, Tr. 7242-46; R. Bloch, Tr. 7756.

88. R. Bloch, Tr. 7592, 7611, 7757; PX 327, p. 28.

89. R. Bloch, Tr. 7757-59.

90. R. Bloch, Tr. 7759.

91. R. Bloch, Tr. 7759-60.

92. PX 328, p. 18. The lines included the 50 series, produced in France; the 100 series, produced in Italy; and the 200, 400, and 600 series, designed in the United States.

93. In July 1963 the Computer Department was headed by Harrison Van Aken, who reported to the general manager of the Industrial Electronics Division (Weil, Tr. 7085; PX 320, pp. 1, 2, 19; DX 485; DX 491). In 1964 Dr. Louis T. Rader was hired to be in charge of GE's worldwide computer activities. He was named vice-president and general manager of the Industrial Electronics Division and reported to Hershner Cross, vice-president and group executive of the Industrial Group (J. Jones, Tr. 79357-58; DX 13667, p. 31). In 1965 GE realigned its organization and formed an Industrial and Information Group headed by Cross. Within that group was the Information Systems Division, headed by Rader (DX 13668, pp. 15, 33). In 1966 still another new division was formed, called the Industrial Process Control Division, and Rader was transferred from the Information Systems Division to the new division to become its general manager. Cross remained group executive of the Industrial and Information Group and at the same time served as acting general manager of the Information Systems Division (Weil, Tr. 7223-24; PX 327, pp. 9, 33). Early in 1967, J. Stanford Smith, formerly vice-president of marketing and public relations services, became the general manager of the Information Systems Division (DX 13668, p. 33; PX 327, p. 33). In January 1968, GE again changed its organization, going from 5 groups to 10 groups and from 29 divisions to 46 divisions. Hershner Cross's Industrial and Information Group was split into two groups. Cross remained vice-president and group executive, heading up the Industrial Group, which included the Industrial Process Control Division, led by Rader. Smith was promoted to vice-president and group executive in charge of the Information Systems Group, and John Haanstra, who had recently come from IBM, became general manager of the Advanced Development and Resources Planning Division within that group (R. Bloch, Tr. 7755-56; DX 13669, pp. 27-29). Later in 1968 Haanstra became general manager of the Information Systems Equipment Division (PX 328, p. 28), and Richard M. Bloch replaced Haanstra as general manager of the Advanced Development and Resources Planning Division (later the Advanced Systems Division) (R. Bloch, Tr. 7623-25; PX 328, p. 28; DX 556, p. 30). In early 1969, Hilliard W. Paige, who was vice-president and group executive of the Aerospace Group, replaced Smith as head of the Information Systems Group (PX 328, p. 27; DX 556, p. 29). Later that year J. F. Burlingame succeeded Haanstra, who was killed in a plane crash, and became vice-president of

the Information Systems Equipment Division (DX 556, p. 30).

94. Weil, Tr. 7247-49.
95. Weil, Tr. 7259.
96. Withington, Tr. 56731.
97. PX 353, p. 45.
98. J. Jones, Tr. 79354-55.
99. R. Bloch, Tr. 7646-47.
100. PX 328, p. 7.
101. Weil, Tr. 7153-54; DX 485.
102. R. Jones, Tr. 8794-95.
103. Weil, Tr. 7247-48.
104. Weil, Tr. 7174-76.
105. R. Bloch, Tr. 7623-24, 7616.
106. R. Jones, Tr. 8751, 8752, 8869-70.
107. R. Jones, Tr. 8875.
108. R. Jones, Tr. 8874.
109. PX 328, p. 18.
110. PX 328, pp. 3-4.
111. PX 328, pp. 18, 21.
112. PX 328, p. 18.
113. DX 556, p. 13.
114. Ingersoll, Tr. 8329-30; DX 554, p. 9.
115. DX 148, p. 1; DX 13977.
116. R. Jones, Tr. 8876.
117. PX 4834, p. 29.
118. R. Bloch, Tr. 7787-88; PX 328, p. 18.
119. R. Bloch, Tr. 7762-68; see Weil, Tr. 7252-54.
120. R. Bloch, Tr. 7761-62; see R. Jones, Tr. 8866-67; PX 353, p. 23.
121. PX 331A, p. 18.
122. PX 353, pp. 43-44. Footnote omitted.
123. R. Bloch, Tr. 7757.
124. Weil, Tr. 7243; R. Bloch, Tr. 7798; Ingersoll, Tr. 8104.
125. R. Bloch, Tr. 7648-49, 7799.
126. R. Bloch, Tr. 7647-48.
127. R. Bloch, Tr. 7803.
128. R. Bloch, Tr. 7792-93.
129. R. Bloch, Tr. 7873; see also PX 353, p. 119.
130. PX 353, pp. 53-54, 57.
131. R. Bloch, Tr. 7881-84, 7889-90; PX 353, pp. 53, 62-63, 67, 118, 119, 164-65, 171, 175, 178, 179.
132. R. Bloch, Tr. 7663-64, 7866.
133. R. Bloch, Tr. 7867-68.
134. R. Bloch, Tr. 7868-72, 7880; PX 353, p. 64.
135. R. Bloch, Tr. 7654-59.
136. R. Bloch, Tr. 7695-96; PX 362, p. 4.
137. R. Bloch, Tr. 7699.
138. Ingersoll, Tr. 8378-82; PX 362, p. 10.

139. R. Bloch, Tr. 7703, 7935-36; see also PX 362, p. 10.
140. R. Bloch, Tr. 7908-10, 7929; PX 362, p. 5.
141. R. Jones, Tr. 8756-57.
142. PX 331A, p. 5.
143. PX 331A, p. 6.
144. PX 331A, p. 5; see also DX 550; DX 551.
145. Ingersoll, Tr. 8266-67; see also PX 331A, p. 5; DX 556, p. 3.
146. PX 331A, pp. 5-6.
147. At the time of their task force assignment, Jones was vice-president of finance, McKitterick was vice-president of corporate planning, and Estes was vice-president, secretary, and general counsel (Ingersoll, Tr. 8267-69).
148. R. Jones, Tr. 8778-79.
149. R. Jones, Tr. 8767-68.
150. R. Jones, Tr. 8758-59.
151. R. Jones, Tr. 8801.
152. PX 331A, p. 9.
153. PX 331A, p. 49.
154. PX 371A, p. 39.
155. PX 371A, p. 40.
156. PX 371A, p. 20.
157. PX 371A, p. 34.
158. R. Jones, Tr. 8886-87.
159. Ingersoll, Tr. 8431.
160. PX 331A, p. 7. Emphasis in original.
161. PX 331A, p. 28.
162. R. Jones, Tr. 8769.
163. Weil, Tr. 7244-45.
164. Ingersoll, Tr. 8370; see also R. Jones, Tr. 8768; PX 363, p. 15.
165. Ingersoll, Tr. 8128-29; PX 363, p. 15.
166. Ingersoll, Tr. 8127.
167. R. Jones, Tr. 8866-67; see PX 353, p. 23.
168. Ingersoll, Tr. 8271-72.
169. PX 371A, p. 73.
170. PX 371A, p. 76.
171. PX 371A, pp. 75-76; see also pp. 7, 10; R. Jones, Tr. 8831-32, 8843; PX 331A, p. 7.
172. PX 371A, p. 76.
173. Ingersoll, Tr. 8288-91.
174. R. Jones, Tr. 8838-41.
175. DX 555, p. 3.
176. See Ingersoll, Tr. 8242, 8252-53; DX 7259: Borch dep., pp. 13-14.
177. PX 380; see Ingersoll, Tr. 8353-56; R. Jones, Tr. 8756.
178. Ingersoll, Tr. 8359-60, 8365-66.

179. Ingersoll, Tr. 8377-78.
180. DX 554, p. 9; see Ingersoll, Tr. 8329-30.
181. PX 362, p. 10; see Ingersoll, Tr. 8378-79.
182. PX 331A, p. 32; see Ingersoll, Tr. 8376-77.
183. DX 555, pp. 22-24; see Ingersoll, Tr. 8393-96; DX 14073, p. 32.
184. Ingersoll, Tr. 8388-89; DX 555, pp. 26, 31; DX 14064, p. 164.
185. Ingersoll, Tr. 8393-96.
186. DX 14073, p. 32.
187. DX 14130, p. 164; DX 14131, p. 172; DX 14132, p. 172; DX 14133, p. 173.
188. DX 13980, p. 40; DX 13981, p. 40.
189. DX 13887, p. 40; DX 13981, p. 40.
190. McCollister, Tr. 9622.
191. DX 580, p. 1.
192. McCollister, Tr. 9161-62, 9247, 9622.
193. McCollister, Tr. 9622-23.
194. DX 580, p. 1; see also Beard, Tr. 8994-95.
195. Beard, Tr. 8458-60, 10276, 10307.
196. Beard, Tr. 8447-51, 10276.
197. Beard, Tr. 9004, 10307; see also McCollister, Tr. 9622-23.
198. McCollister, Tr. 9657.
199. Beard, Tr. 9046.
200. Beard, Tr. 9046-47.
201. Withington, Tr. 56511.
202. McCollister, Tr. 9658.
203. Beard, Tr. 8458-59; PX 4830, p. 25.
204. PX 4830, p. 25.
205. Beard, Tr. 8458-59, 9986-87, 10235.
206. McCollister, Tr. 9624.
207. Beard, Tr. 8483-85; McCollister, Tr. 9635-36; DX 669, p. 11.
208. PX 338, p. 22; DX 670, p. 16; DX 674, pp. 8-9.
209. McCollister, Tr. 9635-36.
210. Beard, Tr. 8460.
211. Beard, Tr. 8461-63; McCollister, Tr. 9269-70; Rooney, Tr. 12117.
212. Beard, Tr. 8526-28.
213. Beard, Tr. 10073; Rooney, Tr. 12126-27.
214. Beard, Tr. 8493-94; 10095, 10103; Rooney, Tr. 11826, 12414-15, 12420-21; Wright, Tr. 13083. See Fisher, McGowan, and Greenwood, loc. cit.
215. Beard, Tr. 10103; Wright, Tr. 13083-84.
216. Beard, Tr. 10103-05.
217. Rooney, Tr. 12421.
218. Beard, Tr. 10092-93, 10097-99, 10106-07, 10113, 10121-22; Rooney, Tr. 12129-31.
219. Beard, Tr. 10097-99, 10106-07.
220. Fisher, McGowan, and Greenwood, loc. cit.
221. Beard, Tr. 8519-20; see also Rooney, Tr. 11857.
222. Beard, Tr. 8526.
223. Beard, Tr. 8524-26.
224. McCollister, Tr. 9630-32.
225. McCollister, Tr. 9273.
226. McCollister, Tr. 9644-45.
227. Rooney, Tr. 11802-03; see also Beard, Tr. 8460.
228. DX 617, p. 2; see Beard, Tr. 9099-100.
229. Beard, Tr. 9100-01.
230. Beard, Tr. 9101-02.
231. DX 619, pp. B, 1, 39. Emphasis in original.
232. Rooney, Tr. 12190-91.
233. Rooney, Tr. 11687-88.
234. DX 621; see also Rooney, Tr. 12145-48, 12186, 12202-03.
235. Rooney, Tr. 12197-201.
236. Rooney, Tr. 12175-76.
237. Rooney, Tr. 12204-05; DX 620.
238. DX 620; see Rooney, Tr. 12205-06.
239. McCollister, Tr. 9647-50, 9653.
240. McCollister, Tr. 9649-50.
241. McCollister, Tr. 9640.
242. Beard, Tr. 8460; McCollister, Tr. 9719, 9740-41.
243. McCollister, Tr. 9642; Beard, Tr. 10110.
244. McCollister, Tr. 9719; see also PX 127, p. 77.
245. McCollister, Tr. 9730-31.
246. Beard, Tr. 9071-73.
247. McCollister, Tr. 9729.
248. McCollister, Tr. 9740-41.
249. McCollister, Tr. 9724-25.
250. McCollister, Tr. 11355.
251. McCollister, Tr. 9646.
252. McCollister, Tr. 9640-42, 9665.
253. Rooney, Tr. 12139.
254. Beard, Tr. 10111-12.
255. Beard, Tr. 10112.
256. DX 620, pp. 1, 3-4.
257. Beard, Tr. 10109-10.
258. Beard, Tr. 10109, 10233.
259. Beard, Tr. 10111-12; see McCollister, Tr. 11216.
260. Rooney, Tr. 12137-39.
261. DX 674, p. 8.

262. McCollister, Tr. 9673-74; DX 672, p. 21.
263. McCollister, Tr. 9679.
264. McCollister, Tr. 9680.
265. DX 674, p. 8.
266. McCollister, Tr. 9694.
267. McCollister, Tr. 9695.
268. McCollister, Tr. 9697.
269. McCollister, Tr. 9710-11.
270. McCollister, Tr. 9694.
271. Rooney, Tr. 12134.
272. McCollister, Tr. 9674, 9717-18.
273. Rooney, Tr. 12135-37.
274. McCollister, Tr. 9659-60.
275. Beard, Tr. 9935.
276. Beard, Tr. 9913.
277. Beard, Tr. 8575.
278. Beard, Tr. 9924-28; DX 4556, p. 2; DX 12543.
279. Beard, Tr. 8574-75.
280. Beard, Tr. 10246, 10254-55.
281. Beard, Tr. 9915, 9922.
282. Rooney, Tr. 12123, 12192-94.
283. Rooney, Tr. 12192-94.
284. DX 11101. p. 1.
285. McCollister, Tr. 9604.
286. PX 338, p. 49.
287. DX 840, p. 1.
288. McCollister, Tr. 9246-48.
289. DX 669, p. 2.
290. DX 670, p. 7.
291. DX 671, pp. 4, 15.
292. PX 338, p. 5; DX 671, p. 4.
293. PX 338, p. 5.
294. DX 674, pp. 8, 9.
295. DX 8224, p. 2.
296. PX 338, p. 49; DX 674, p. 36.
297. McCollister, Tr. 11156-57; PX 338, p. 49; PX 339, p. 49.
298. PX 341, p. 38.
299. PX 400; DX 677, p. 13.
300. PX 339, p. 11.
301. Rooney, Tr. 12022-24; Conrad, Tr. 14002-05; DX 671, p. 5; DX 674, p. 21; DX 677, pp. 14-19.
302. Conrad, Tr. 14027-28; PX 339, p. 49.
303. Rooney, Tr. 12025.
304. McCollister, Tr. 22590.
305. Rooney, Tr. 11687-88.
306. Wright, Tr. 12785.
307. McCollister, Tr. 11590.
308. McCollister, Tr. 11156-57; Withington, Tr. 56702-03.
309. McCollister, Tr. 11156-58.
310. PX 340, p. 3.
311. McCollister, Tr. 11158; see Withington, Tr. 56707-09.
312. McCollister, Tr. 9809.
313. Rooney, Tr. 12225-26.
314. Wright, Tr. 13173.
315. Withington, Tr. 57079.
316. Rooney, Tr. 11814; DX 2666.
317. Withington, Tr. 56715-16.
318. Withington, Tr. 56716-20; DX 2666, pp. 5, 15-16.
319. Rooney, Tr. 11820-21.
320. McCollister, Tr. 9837-38.
321. McCollister, Tr. 9816-17.
322. Rooney, Tr. 12234-36.
323. Rooney, Tr. 11814.
324. Rooney, Tr. 12242-43.
325. Wright, Tr. 13175-76.
326. PX 340, p. 17.
327. DX 675, p. 16.
328. McCollister, Tr. 9819-20.
329. McCollister, Tr. 9816-17, 9819-20.
330. McCollister, Tr. 9837-38.
331. Rooney, Tr. 11811-12.
332. McCollister, Tr. 9819-20; Wright, Tr. 13577-78; Withington, Tr. 56454-55.
333. Withington, Tr. 56710-11.
334. McCollister, Tr. 9838-39; Withington, Tr. 56720.
335. McCollister, Tr. 9837-39; see Withington, Tr. 56711; PX 4836, p. 23.
336. McCollister, Tr. 11491-94.
337. McCollister, Tr. 9818; see Wright, Tr. 13577-78.
338. McCollister, Tr. 11491-94.
339. McCollister, Tr. 9838-39.
340. Rooney, Tr. 12275-77; Wright, Tr. 13581-83; DX 873, p. 24.
341. McCollister, Tr. 9820-21.
342. Wright, Tr. 13589-96.
343. McCollister, Tr. 9820-21.
344. McCollister, Tr. 9819-20.
345. Rooney, Tr. 12247-48, 12249-50, 12252-53.
346. DX 11101, p. 2.
347. DX 11099, p. 5.
348. See DX 937.
349. DX 862.
350. Rooney, Tr. 12335.
351. DX 872, pp. A, B, C.
352. Rooney, Tr. 12349-50.
353. Rooney, Tr. 12352-53.
354. McCollister, Tr. 9814-15.
355. PX 208, p. 1.
365. PX 340, p. 3.
357. DX 11108, p. 1.

358. DX 952, pp. 7-8, 12.
359. DX 952, pp. 1, 2.
360. DX 955, p. A.
361. McCollister, Tr. 9814-15.
362. Conrad, Tr. 14125.
363. DX 952, pp. 7-8.
364. McCollister, Tr. 10964-65; see also Tr. 9814-16.
365. DX 952, p. 21.
366. Wright, Tr. 13559-60.
367. Wright, Tr. 13560-61.
368. Wright, Tr. 13563-66.
369. DX 11108, p. 1.
370. DX 873, p. 33.
371. PX 349, pp. 6-7.
372. Ibid.; DX 955, p. 2; DX 11106, p. 1.
373. PX 349, pp. 6-7.
374. PX 349, p. 7.
375. Wright, Tr. 13589-91.
376. Conrad, Tr. 14057-58.
377. Wright, Tr. 13590.
378. DX 956, pp. 5-6; see Conrad, Tr. 14058-65, 14069-70.
379. Rooney, Tr. 12264.
380. Rooney, Tr. 12682.
381. DX 873, p. 24.
382. Rooney, Tr. 11910-11, 11913-14, 11922-23, 12583-90, 12649-50; PX 349, pp. 6-7.
383. Rooney, Tr. 11923, 12048-60.
384. A "Computer Industry Survey" prepared by RCA in February 1970 listed 102 companies (other than IBM) offering "computers," "peripherals and components," and "software and services" (DX 11107, pp. 4-6).
385. Wright, Tr. 13555-57; see also DX 852, pp. 14, 17, 19-20.
386. DX 11099, p. 4; see also Beard, Tr. 9021.
387. McCollister, Tr. 9804-07, 11088.
388. DX 11099, p. 5; see McCollister, Tr. 9290-92.
389. PX 192, pp. 2-4; see Conrad, Tr. 13939-40.
390. Conrad, Tr. 13942; PX 201; PX 349.
391. Conrad, Tr. 13942-44.
392. Conrad, Tr. 13942-43, 13948, 14145.
393. Rooney, Tr. 12369; Wright, Tr. 13172, 13570-71.
394. Rooney, Tr. 12368-71; Wright, Tr. 13572.
395. Conrad, Tr. 14072; PX 208, pp. 4-5, 8.

396. Rooney, Tr. 12370-74; Wright, Tr. 13572-73.
397. PX 208, p. 5.
398. PX 208, p. 6.
399. Conrad, Tr. 14047-48; see also Tr. 13944-47.
400. Rooney, Tr. 12094.
401. Withington, Tr. 56711, 56720-21.
402. PX 208, p. 6.
403. PX 208, p. 7.
404. Ibid.
405. PX 208, p. 8.
406. Conrad, Tr. 13953-54, 13968-70; PX 402.
407. PX 405A, p. 8.
408. Conrad, Tr. 14130.
409. PX 410.
410. Smith, Tr. 14247-48.
411. Conrad, Tr. 14008-12, 14022-27, 14102-06; DX 13854, p. 15; DX 13860, p. 8; DX 13902, pp. 2, 36-37.
412. Conrad, Tr. 14048-49, 14157-58.
413. McDonald, Tr. 3873-74; DX 63, p. 1; DX 71, p. 9.
414. DX 63, p. 1.
415. DX 68, pp. 11-12.
416. McDonald, Tr. 4045-46.
417. DX 8224, p. 2.

CHAPTER 9

1. Eckert, Tr. 1008-13; McDonald, Tr. 3785-88.
2. PX 4829, p. 20.
3. DX 10; Eckert, Tr. 1014-17.
4. See PX 4829, p. 20; DX 8, pp. 1-2; DX 10; DX 14, p. 1.
5. Withington, Tr. 56455, 56485-87.
6. Guzy, Tr. 33170-71; Withington, Tr. 56243-44; PX 2267B, p. 27; PX 5584, p. 16; DX 1302, p. 1.
7. DX 69, p. 3.
8. McDonald, Tr. 3813; DX 8224, p. 624.
9. DX 13983, p. 6.
10. McDonald, Tr. 2769, 2776-78, 2890-91.
11. PX 4830, p. 22; DX 13913, p. 16.
12. DX 13913, p. 12.
13. DX 69, pp. 12-14; see DX 2992, pp. 592-93, 1123; DX 5123, p. 3; DX 5410: Fullerton dep., pp. 36-37.
14. DX 9088; Plaintiff's Admissions, set II, paras. 768.0-.4; see also paras. 702.0,

702.15, 748.2-.4.
15. DX 13913, p. 13.
16. DX 61, p. 9.
17. O'Neill, Tr. 76015-17, 76231-32.
18. O'Neill, Tr. 76231.
19. DX 14, p. 1; DX 13983, p. 14.
20. PX 4829, p. 20.
21. PX 4830, p. 22; PX 4832, p. 18.
22. PX 4833, p. 17.
23. DX 3271, p. 5.
24. DX 13914, p. 5.
25. DX 3271, p. 7.
26. DX 13914, p. 16.
27. Plaintiff's Admissions, set II, paras. 746.4, 748.0-.7; Plaintiff's Admissions, set IV, paras. 386.0, 390.0, 392.0, 394.1, 401.0.
28. DX 13915, p. 5.
29. J. Jones, Tr. 79631; PX 4834, p. 25.
30. See Perlis, Tr. 2002-03; Weil, Tr. 7217-19; McCollister, Tr. 9694-97; Rooney, Tr. 12132-36, 12349-50; Conrad, Tr. 14088-89; Withington, Tr. 56727-31.
31. Withington, Tr. 56736.
32. Perlis, Tr. 2003; Withington, Tr. 56737; DX 5654, pp. 114-15, 231-32.
33. DX 61, pp. 2-3; DX 13983, p. 6.
34. McDonald, Tr. 3804-05; see also DX 13.
35. DX 15, p. 2.
36. DX 16, p. 2.
37. *Datamation*, February 1965, p. 88, quoted in DX 16, p. 2.
38. DX 16, p. 2.
39. DX 16, pp. 2-3.
40. DX 16, p. 5.
41. DX 16, p. 1.
42. DX 70, p. 9.
43. DX 3271, p. 7; DX 13914, p. 6.
44. Eckert, Tr. 908.
45. DX 10, p. 1; see also McDonald, Tr. 3803-04.
46. Eckert, Tr. 906-07.
47. Eckert, Tr. 908.
48. Guzy, Tr. 33170-71; Ashbridge, Tr. 34851; PX 5584, p. 16; DX 1302, p. 1; PX 2267, p. 27.
49. McDonald, Tr. 4053-55.
50. McDonald, Tr. 3969; Withington, Tr. 56981; DX 13939, p. 176.
51. Eckert, Tr. 915-16.
52. McDonald, Tr. 4024.
53. PX 1, p. 3.
54. McDonald, Tr. 2893-96.
55. McDonald, Tr. 2895-96.

56. McDonald, Tr. 2896.
57. McDonald, Tr. 2883-84, 4190-91.
58. McDonald, Tr. 4182-83.
59. PX 1, pp. 6, 12; see also McDonald, Tr. 2804-06.
60. PX 1, p. 1.
61. PX 1, p. 12.
62. DX 78.
63. McDonald, Tr. 4017; DX 76.
64. McDonald, Tr. 3988; DX 76, p. 5.
65. DX 8224, p. 625; see McDonald, Tr. 3867-68; DX 71, p. 7.
66. DX 3271, p. 2.
67. PX 4834, p. 24.
68. Withington, Tr. 57602-03.
69. PX 1, pp. 4-6; see also McDonald, Tr. 3839-42.
70. DX 13915, p. 7.
71. PX 1, p. 7.
72. R. Bloch, Tr. 7575-76, 7886.
73. Binger, Tr. 4823; R. Bloch, Tr. 7886; DX 198, pp. 25-26.
74. Spangle, Tr. 5025; R. Bloch, Tr. 7605-06.
75. R. Bloch, Tr. 7606; Goetz, Tr. 17652-53.
76. Spangle, Tr. 5021-22; Goetz, Tr. 17652; see also R. Bloch, Tr. 7888-89.
77. R. Bloch, Tr. 7585-86.
78. DX 132, p. 11; DX 198, pp. 4-5; DX 8224, p. 387; DX 8631, pp. 31, 37; DX 14484, p. R1.
79. Binger, Tr. 4823; R. Bloch, Tr. 7888-89; see also Goetz, Tr. 18780-81.
80. DX 167; DX 198, p. 26.
81. McCollister, Tr. 11237, 11365-66; Evans, Tr. 101187-88; PX 6204, p. 4; DX 167.
82. R. Bloch, Tr. 7602-03, 7888; McCollister, Tr. 11235-36; Withington, Tr. 55863-67; J. Jones, Tr. 78989-95.
83. PX 4829, pp. 20-21.
84. McCollister, Tr. 10962-63.
85. G. Brown, Tr. 50985; DX 13849, p. 27.
86. Hughes, Tr. 33924; JX 38, p. 33; DX 573, p. 6.
87. Franklin M. Fisher, John J. McGowan, and Joen E. Greenwood, *Folded, Spindled and Mutilated: Economic Analysis and U.S. v. IBM* (Cambridge, Mass.: MIT Press, 1983), Ch. 5.
88. PX 1288, p. 2.
89. DX 132, p. 12.
90. DX 13849, p. 27.

91. DX 199, p. 32.
92. Spangle, Tr. 4882, 4887-89, 5056.
93. R. Bloch, Tr. 7596-97.
94. DX 199, p. 31.
95. DX 200, p. 31.
96. Spain, Tr. 88749.
97. Spangle, Tr. 5191-92; DX 161A.
98. Spangle, Tr. 5190.
99. DX 13849, p. 27.
100. Spangle, Tr. 4997.
101. Ibid.
102. Spangle, Tr. 4997-98.
103. Spangle, Tr. 4998.
104. Withington, Tr. 56491-93.
105. Withington, Tr. 56494-95.
106. PX 3481, pp. 75-76.
107. Withington, Tr. 58562-63.
108. G. Brown, Tr. 51033-34, 51056-57.
109. G. Brown, Tr. 51056-57; DX 200, p. 31.
110. DX 13849, p. 28.
111. Binger, Tr. 4512-13, 4549-50; Spangle, Tr. 5102-07.
112. DX 13849, p. 28.
113. Ibid.
114. Spangle, Tr. 5092-94.
115. DX 13849, p. 6.
116. DX 123, p. 41.
117. R. Bloch, Tr. 7673, 7675-76.
118. Spangle, Tr. 4953; G. Brown, Tr. 52613; Withington, Tr. 56624.
119. DX 200, p. 32; DX 13849, p. 5.
120. Spangle, Tr. 5076-77.
121. Spangle, Tr. 5082.
122. Spangle, Tr. 5082-84.
123. DX 200, p. 9.
124. Spangle, Tr. 5084-86.
125. R. Bloch, Tr. 7604.
126. Spangle, Tr. 5086-89.
127. Spangle, Tr. 5089.
128. DX 13713.
129. DX 13849, p. 20.
130. DX 199, p. 3; DX 4917.
131. DX 199, p. 32.
132. See, e.g., DX 200, p. 24.
133. DX 7561, pp. 5, 9, 10.
134. DX 7727.
135. DX 7561, p. 10; DX 9087.
136. DX 9087.
137. O'Neill, Tr. 76000.
138. DX 5789.
139. DX 123, pp. 1-2.
140. DX 7583.
141. Binger, Tr. 4540-42, 4689-91; Spangle, Tr. 4916-18, 4930.

142. DX 123, p. 33.
143. Binger, Tr. 4593-94.
144. DX 201, p. 31.
145. Binger, Tr. 4531.
146. DX 8224, p. 387; DX 14484, p. 1; DX 8631, pp. 31, 37.
147. DX 123, pp. 7, 28, 33; DX 132, p. 11.
148. DX 132, p. 11; see also DX 123, p. 7.
149. DX 123, p. 33.
150. DX 132, p. 17; see Binger, Tr. 4818-20.
151. DX 427, p. 2.
152. DX 427, p. 3.
153. DX 10260, p. 22.
154. DX 427, p. 3.
155. Ibid.
156. Withington, Tr. 56732; DX 10262, p. 6.
157. DX 427, p. 5.
158. Macdonald, Tr. 6883-91; DX 427, pp. 7-8; DX 10260, p. 4.
159. DX 427, pp. 6-7.
160. DX 427, p. 7.
161. DX 427, pp. 7-8.
162. DX 427, p. 8.
163. DX 427, p. 6.
164. Macdonald, Tr. 6886; DX 427, p. 8.
165. Macdonald, Tr. 6888-89.
166. Macdonald, Tr. 6889-90.
167. DX 10285, p. 3.
168. DX 426, pp. 19-20.
169. PX 5048D (DX 14506): Pierce dep., p. 62.
170. DX 10264, p. 5.
171. PX 5525A, p. 218; DX 10264, pp. 6, 8.
172. DX 10260, p. 12; DX 13920.
173. DX 10260, p. 12.
174. Ibid.
175. DX 10261, p. 9.
176. DX 10260, p. 19; DX 10261, p. 17; DX 10263, p. 17.
177. Withington, Tr. 55976-77, 58527-28.
178. DX 10716, p. 8; DX 13665, p. 19.
179. Macdonald, Tr. 7556-57; DX 10261, p. 17.
180. DX 10263, p. 9.
181. Perlis, Tr. 2001-02; PX 5048D (DX 14506): Pierce dep., p. 62.
182. DX 10262, p. 8.
183. Ibid.
184. DX 10264, p. 8.

185. DX 3269, p. 3.
186. DX 10262, pp. 3, 8.
187. DX 10262, p. 3.
188. Fisher, McGowan, and Greenwood, Ch. 5.
189. DX 10263, p. 9.
190. DX 10263, p. 11.
191. PX 5048D (DX 14506): Pierce dep., p. 62.
192. DX 13665, pp. 3, 5.
193. O'Neill, Tr. 76014-15.
194. O'Neill, Tr. 76015; see DX 10265, p. 42.
195. O'Neill, Tr. 76013-14.
196. DX 10264, pp. 6-8.
197. DX 10262, p. 10.
198. DX 10264, pp. 6-8.
199. PX 5525A, p. 53.
200. DX 10260, p. 12; DX 10263, p. 11.
201. DX 10262, p. 12.
202. DX 13665, p. 5.
203. DX 10260, p. 8.
204. DX 10263, p. 11; DX 10264, p. 18.
205. DX 10260, p. 9; DX 10264, p. 18.
206. DX 10264, p. 18.
207. DX 13665, pp. 1, 7; DX 10264, p. 14.
208. J. Jones, Tr. 79044-45; see also DX 13665, p. 7.
209. DX 10264, p. 18.
210. DX 10285, p. 6.
211. DX 10261, p. 11; DX 10264, p. 10.
212. Withington, Tr. 56244; DX 10260, p. 10.
213. Withington, Tr. 56244-45.
214. DX 13665, p. 5; see also PX 4834, p. 31.
215. Withington, Tr. 58802.
216. PX 4445, pp. 7-8; DX 10716, p. 12.
217. DX 427, p. 8.
218. Macdonald, Tr. 6889; DX 427, pp. 6-8; DX 10264, pp. 4, 6.
219. See DX 10264, pp. 2, 14.
220. DX 10285, p. 5.
221. DX 8224, p. 1; DX 10260, p. 5; DX 10264, p. 5.
222. DX 427, pp. 2-3.
223. DX 344, p. 1; DX 372, p. 1.
224. DX 344, p. 14; DX 382, pp. 3, 10.
225. DX 344, p. 1.
226. DX 361, p. 22; DX 8224, p. 3.
227. DX 342, pp. 2-6.
228. See, e.g., DX 361, p. 1; DX 370, p. 16.
229. PX 4834, p. 34; see also PX 2050, p. 4.
230. See Fisher, McGowan, and Greenwood, Ch. 5.
231. Hangen, Tr. 6314; DX 361, p. 14; DX 401, p. 2.
232. DX 370, p. 16.
233. Hangen, Tr. 10402; DX 361, p. 13.
234. DX 370, p. 16; see Withington, Tr. 56469-70. The CRAM file was discussed in Chapter 4.
235. DX 368, p. 6.
236. DX 348, p. 1.
237. DX 348, pp. 1-2.
238. DX 372, p. 4.
239. DX 348, p. 1.
240. DX 421, p. 17; DX 469, p. 14.
241. DX 366, p. A.
242. DX 366, p. 5.
243. Hangen, Tr. 6329-30.
244. DX 366, p. 6.
245. DX 366, p. 8.
246. DX 366, pp. 6-7.
247. DX 366, p. 10.
248. DX 366, p. 7.
249. Hangen, Tr. 6239, 6350-51; see Fisher, McGowan, and Greenwood, Ch. 5.
250. DX 340A, p. 8.
251. DX 372, p. 4.
252. DX 340A, p. 2.
253. Ibid.
254. Hangen, Tr. 6358-59; DX 340A, pp. 2-3.
255. DX 361, p. 8; see also DX 370, p. 5.
256. DX 367, p. 4.
257. DX 346, p. 1.
258. Hangen, Tr. 6365.
259. DX 386, p. 2.
260. PX 4832, p. 22; DX 340A, p. 3.
261. DX 340A, p. 10.
262. DX 344, p. 3.
263. DX 719, p. 1; see Oelman, Tr. 6164.
264. DX 719, p. 1.
265. Ibid.
266. DX 367, pp. 9-10; see also DX 719, p. 1.
267. DX 367, p. 19.
268. Oelman, Tr. 6183.
269. DX 8224, p. 3.
270. DX 367, p. 6.
271. DX 298.
272. DX 8224, p. 5.
273. DX 302.
274. DX 300.
275. JX 10, para. 4.
276. Norris, Tr. 5616.
277. See Norris, Tr. 5849-51.

278. Norris, Tr. 5967; JX 10, para. 34; DX 319.
279. DX 319, p. 1.
280. DX 319, p. 3.
281. PX 355, pp. 36-37; see Norris, Tr. 5626.
282. Norris, Tr. 5626.
283. Norris, Tr. 5624; JX 10, para. 3.
284. See Norris, Tr. 5853-54; JX 10, para. 34.
285. DX 13839, p. 2.
286. Norris, Tr. 5620; JX 10, para. 12; DX 4960, p. 5.
287. JX 10, para. 12.
288. Norris, Tr. 5620.
289. Norris, Tr. 5970-73; PX 367, p. 5.
290. JX 10, para. 12; DX 324.
291. Schmidt, Tr. 27416; DX 13838, p. 4.
292. Norris, Tr. 5621.
293. Norris, Tr. 5963, 5976; JX 10, para. 12.
294. Norris, Tr. 5976-78.
295. DX 284, p. 6; see also Norris, Tr. 5678-79.
296. Norris, Tr. 5625.
297. See Norris, Tr. 5849-51.
298. DX 1185, pp. 3-5.
299. JX 10, paras. 35, 36; see also Schmidt, Tr. 27469-76.
300. Norris, Tr. 5628; JX 10, para. 34; PX 355, p. 39.
301. Norris, Tr. 5628.
302. DX 438, p. 7.
303. DX 438, p. 13; see also Lacey, Tr. 6676-77.
304. Norris, Tr. 5627; PX 355, p. 34.
305. Norris, Tr. 5627.
306. PX 355, p. 35.
307. Norris, Tr. 5627-28.
308. Ibid.
309. PX 355, pp. 35-36.
310. Norris, Tr. 5628.
311. DX 13840, p. 8.
312. DX 13839, p. 5.
313. DX 13842, p. 2.
314. DX 13843, p. 4.
315. Norris, Tr. 5624.
316. Schmidt, Tr. 27476-78.
317. Norris, Tr. 5617-18.
318. G. Brown, Tr. 50996.
319. Lacey, Tr. 6556; DX 276; see Norris, Tr. 6002-06, 6081-82.
320. G. Brown, Tr. 53064-65; see also Schmidt, Tr. 27457; DX 13841, p. 4.
321. Schmidt, Tr. 27457-58.
322. Norris, Tr. 5618; see JX 38, pp. 27-29.
323. Norris, Tr. 5618.
324. Norris, Tr. 5627.
325. G. Brown, Tr. 50990-91.
326. G. Brown, Tr. 50990, 50997; see also DX 13838, pp. 7, 9; DX 13840, p. 8.
327. Norris, Tr. 5609; see PX 6066, p. 1.
328. DX 319, p. 3.
329. PX 355, p. 5; DX 296.
330. G. Brown, Tr. 51015-17.
331. G. Brown, Tr. 51056-58.
332. See G. Brown, Tr. 51063-67.
333. G. Brown, Tr. 51032-34.
334. DX 13840, p. 8.
335. DX 13841, p. 8.
336. DX 13843, p. 6.
337. G. Brown, Tr. 51068-69.
338. DX 13841, p. 8.
339. G. Brown, Tr. 51212; DX 438, p. 12.
340. DX 13838, p. 8.
341. DX 284, p. 4; DX 13838, p. 8.
342. DX 13838, p. 8.
343. DX 284, p. 4.
344. DX 13841, p. 2.
345. DX 13841, p. 7; DX 13843, p. 6.
346. DX 13843, p. 6.
347. DX 284, p. 4.
348. Norris, Tr. 5788-89; PX 355, pp. 3-9; DX 296.
349. Norris, Tr. 5794-95.
350. DX 432.
351. DX 13839, p. 9.
352. Norris, Tr. 5789.
353. DX 284, p. 7; see also Norris, Tr. 6092-93.
354. Norris, Tr. 5804-07.
355. DX 13838, p. 5.
356. PX 355, pp. 5-6.
357. DX 13839, p. 3.
358. See Norris, Tr. 5796-97; Lacey, Tr. 6632-33.
359. PX 355, p. 8; DX 13842, p. 16.
360. PX 355, pp. 3-9.
361. Norris, Tr. 5643; see Lacey, Tr. 6586-88.
362. Norris, Tr. 5641-42.
363. Norris, Tr. 5644; DX 295.
364. Norris, Tr. 5642-43.
365. DX 13839, p. 2.
366. DX 13840, p. 12.
367. Norris, Tr. 5643-44.
368. Palevsky, Tr. 3128, 3193.
369. Palevsky, Tr. 3121.

370. Palevsky, Tr. 3127-28.
371. Palevsky, Tr. 3127, 3193.
372. Palevsky, Tr. 3193-94.
373. Palevsky, Tr. 3196, 3198; DX 45, p. 4.
374. PX 5774, p. 13.
375. PX 5774, p. 6.
376. DX 46, summarizing data contained in DX 44 and DX 45.
377. Palevsky, Tr. 3195-96.
378. Palevsky, Tr. 3133.
379. Palevsky, Tr. 3137; PX 2103 (Tr. 23290).
380. Palevsky, Tr. 3135; see also DX 982, p. 4.
381. Palevsky, Tr. 3137.
382. Palevsky, Tr. 3155.
383. Palevsky, Tr. 3136.
384. Palevsky, Tr. 3132, 3134.
385. Palevsky, Tr. 3134.
386. Palevsky, Tr. 3198-204.
387. Palevsky, Tr. 3198-200.
388. Palevsky, Tr. 3199.
389. Palevsky, Tr. 3200-01.
390. Palevsky, Tr. 3201-02.
391. Palevsky, Tr. 3202; Plaintiff's Admissions, set I, 9, paras. 191.0-.2.
392. Palevsky, Tr. 3203.
393. Ibid.
394. Ibid.
395. Palevsky, Tr. 3204.
396. Palevsky, Tr. 3205-06.
397. Palevsky, Tr. 3134-35.
398. DX 44, p. 7.
399. Palevsky, Tr. 3162.
400. Ibid.
401. DX 5652, pp. 116, 123, 164; see also DX 5836: Reeves dep., pp. 55-56.
402. Palevsky, Tr. 3185.
403. Palevsky, Tr. 3165.
404. Palevsky, Tr. 3214; DX 44, p. 3.
405. Palevsky, Tr. 3163.
406. DX 4085: Poe dep., pp. 18-19, 21.
407. Palevsky, Tr. 3164.
408. Palevsky, Tr. 3155-56.
409. Palevsky, Tr. 3165.
410. DX 44, p. 5.
411. PX 4829, p. 31.
412. DX 44, p. 7.
413. DX 44, pp. 3, 17.
414. Palevsky, Tr. 3164.
415. DX 44, pp. 3, 21.
416. DX 981, p. 3.
417. Ibid.; DX 982, p. 12.
418. DX 45, p. 7; DX 982, p. 12; DX 983, p. 3.
419. DX 981, p. 4.
420. DX 47, p. 16.
421. DX 47, p. 3.
422. Palevsky, Tr. 3207.
423. DX 981, p. 3.
424. DX 981, p. 9.
425. Palevsky, Tr. 3226.
426. PX 5774, p. 13; DX 13400, p. 22; DX 13401, p. 19.
427. DX 981, p. 6.
428. DX 52, p. 1.
429. Currie, Tr. 15175-76; see also Palevsky, Tr. 3149-50, 3176, 3269-72; Fisher, McGowan, and Greenwood, Ch. 5.
430. Palevsky, Tr. 3165-66.
431. DX 982, p. 12.
432. Currie, Tr. 15507.
433. DX 982, p. 10; see also Palevsky, Tr. 3277-78.
434. DX 49, pp. 2, 8.
435. Currie, Tr. 15388-89.
436. Palevsky, Tr. 3166.
437. Ibid.; Cohen, Tr. 14684-86.
438. Palevsky, Tr. 3137.
439. Palevsky, Tr. 3254-55.
440. Palevsky, Tr. 3137.
441. DX 53, p. 1.
442. DX 54.
443. Cohen, Tr. 14427-28, 14622-24; see also Palevsky, Tr. 3243-45.
444. Cohen, Tr. 14610-11, 14631.
445. DX 982, p. 8.
446. DX 50, p. 102/001-29; see Palevsky, Tr. 3185, 3228-29, 3232-33.
447. Cohen, Tr. 14555-56; PX 433.
448. Palevsky, Tr. 3231-32; DX 50, p. 102/001-29.
449. Palevsky, Tr. 3247; DX 51, p. 103/001-13.
450. Palevsky, Tr. 3238; DX 50, p. 102/001-30.
451. Cohen, Tr. 14600-09; see also Palevsky, Tr. 3166, 3233; DX 50, p. 102/001-30.
452. Cohen, Tr. 14723-24.
453. Cohen, Tr. 14729-30.
454. Cohen, Tr. 14555-60; PX 433.
455. See Wright, Tr. 12993.
456. PX 1288, p. 2.
457. See, e.g., PX 3451; see also Wright, Tr. 12993.
458. DX 982, p. 3.
459. DX 983, p. 3.
460. DX 45, pp. 4, 6.
461. DX 13857, p. 3.

462. Palevsky, Tr. 3195.
463. Hindle, Tr. 7318; DX 13833, p. 5.
464. DX 13858, p. 1.
465. Hindle, Tr. 7476.
466. Hindle, Tr. 7318-19; DX 13858, p. 1.
467. DX 517, p. 1; DX 13847, p. 19.
468. DX 511, p. 3; DX 517, p. 2.
469. DX 13845, pp. 10-11.
470. DX 511, p. 15; DX 13846, p. 12; DX 13979, p. 7.
471. PX 5026 (DX 13848), p. 15; DX 13847, p. 3.
472. PX 4562, p. 17; DX 511, p. 17; DX 512, p. 11; DX 13979, p. 8.
473. Hindle, Tr. 7313-18, 7337, 7476; DX 12323, p. 47.
474. Hindle, Tr. 7369-70.
475. Hindle, Tr. 7383-84.
476. Withington, Tr. 56016.
477. Palevsky, Tr. 3133-36.
478. Hindle, Tr. 7321-24, 7327, 7388; PX 377A.
479. Hindle, Tr. 7318-19, 7321; DX 507, p. 10.
480. DX 13858, p. 2; Plaintiff's Admissions, set II, paras. 240.2, 371.3(d).
481. DX 13858, p. 2.
482. Hindle, Tr. 7319.
483. Feigenbaum, Tr. 29531-33, 29535-36; DX 2992, pp. 18, 1113; DX 7622, p. 3; DX 13858, p. 3.
484. Hindle, Tr. 7321.
485. DX 13928.
486. Hindle, Tr. 7325, 7453.
487. DX 13845, p. 8.
488. DX 13845, pp. 2-3; see the passage by Withington quoted on p. 267 (PX 4829, p. 31).
489. PX 3630, p. 6.
490. DX 2992, p. 49.
491. Hindle, Tr. 7321.
492. DX 13845, p. 6.
493. DX 13845, p. 3; DX 13846, p. 8; DX 13847, p. 7.
494. PX 2961, pp. 1, 3; DX 13845, p. 3.
495. DX 4572.
496. See, e.g., Hindle, Tr. 7422-23, 7444-45.
497. Hindle, Tr. 7321; DX 13845, p. 3; DX 13846, p. 3.
498. DX 13846, p. 3; DX 13847, p. 8.
499. Hindle, Tr. 7334.
500. Perlis, Tr. 1877; DX 13847, p. 8.
501. DX 13846, p. 3; DX 13847, p. 8.
502. Hindle, Tr. 7322.
503. Hindle, Tr. 7347-48.
504. Hindle, Tr. 7346-47, 7421.
505. Hindle, Tr. 7421-22.
506. Hindle, Tr. 7331; DX 13846, p. 6.
507. Hindle, Tr. 7330-31.
508. Ibid.
509. Hindle, Tr. 7332, 7389.
510. Hindle, Tr. 7389-91.
511. Hindle, Tr. 7489-90.
512. Hindle, Tr. 7333-34.
513. Hindle, Tr. 7338-39, 7341, 7442; PX 377A; see also Akers, Tr. 96713.
514. Hindle, Tr. 7394.
515. Hindle, Tr. 7329, 7331-32.
516. Hindle, Tr. 7324.
517. Hindle, Tr. 7321; PX 5026 (DX 13848, p. 3).
518. Hindle, Tr. 7359.
519. Ibid.
520. Hindle, Tr. 7358.
521. DX 519B, p. 7.
522. Hindle, Tr. 7325-27, 7358-59, 7442; PX 377A; see also DX 2992, pp. 73, 86, 118, 858.
523. Hindle, Tr. 7361-62.
524. DX 511, p. 1; DX 522, p. 3.
525. Hindle, Tr. 7362-63.
526. Hindle, Tr. 7380; DX 525, p. 10.
527. Hindle, Tr. 7323, 7377.
528. Hindle, Tr. 7441; PX 377A.
529. Ibid.
530. Hindle, Tr. 7380.
531. Hindle, Tr. 7323.
532. Hindle, Tr. 7349-51.
533. Hindle, Tr. 7349.
534. Hindle, Tr. 7351-52, 7355-57.
535. Hindle, Tr. 7441; PX 377A.
536. Hindle, Tr. 7394.
537. Hindle, Tr. 7414-15; PX 377A.
538. Hindle, Tr. 7323, 7325-27, 7456.
539. Hindle, Tr. 7354.
540. Spitters, Tr. 42067-68, 42072; DX 517, p. 2; see also DX 511, p. 10.
541. DX 517, p. 2.
542. DX 517, pp. 3, 5.
543. Hindle, Tr. 7426.
544. DX 6868, pp. 7-10; DX 10776, pp. 8-13.
545. PX 377A.
546. Perlis, Tr. 1976-78.
547. Hindle, Tr. 7415-17.
548. PX 2567, p. 186.
549. Palevsky, Tr. 3228-29; Binger, Tr. 4593-94; Spangle, Tr. 4933-34; Rooney, Tr. 11733; Wright, Tr. 12993; Akers,

Tr. 96713-14.

550. DX 511, p. 14; DX 13845, p. 10.
551. DX 511, p. 1; DX 13845, p. 10.
552. DX 526.
553. DX 13833, pp. 5-6, 21.
554. DX 514, p. 6; DX 13835, p. 4.
555. DX 924, p. 6.
556. DX 8224, p. 133.
557. See DX 5945: Dunnaville dep., pp. 4-8.
558. See *United States* v. *Western Electric Co.*, Trade Reg. Rep. (CCH), para. 68, 246 (D. N.J. 1956).
559. DX 5057, pp. 3-7; DX 5061.
560. DX 5945: Dunnaville dep., pp. 12-13.
561. DX 12408.
562. DX 14210, p. 7.
563. DX 6886, pp. 1, 3; see also DX 6880, pp. 1-2.
564. DX 12419, pp. 6-7; see also DX 6883, p. 1; DX 10447, pp. 4-5; DX 13831, pp. 14, 16; DX 13832, pp. 14-15.
565. DX 12412.
566. DX 6883, p. 1.
567. Ibid.; DX 12411, p. 4.
568. DX 12411, pp. 5-7.
569. DX 6881, esp. p. 2.
570. DX 12422.
571. See DX 5612; DX 12410.
572. DX 9016A, pp. 448-50; see also Akers, Tr. 97036-37; DX 5612; DX 12410; DX 12416; DX 12420.
573. Akers, Tr. 97036-37; see also Akers, Tr. 96704-05.
574. DX 12413, p. 13.
575. DX 12420.
576. DX 12421, p. 2; see also DX 12418.
577. DX 12414, p. 2. Emphasis in original.
578. DX 12419, p. A.
579. DX 12415, pp. 1-2.
580. DX 12419, pp. 2, 6-9. Emphasis in original.
581. DX 5945: Dunnaville dep., pp. 7-9.
582. DX 10447, pp. 3-5; see also DX 13831, pp. 14, 16.
583. In the Matter of Regulatory and Policy Problems Presented by the Interdependence of Computer and Communication Services and Facilities, 28 F.C.C. 2d 268-69 (1971) ("Computer Inquiry I"); see also Plaintiff's Admissions, set II, paras. 312.2, 312.13-.14.
584. See DX 6890; DX 6893.
585. DX 2891, pp. 2-4.
586. DX 6893, p. 3; see Knaplund, Tr. 90897-98.

587. DX 5945: Dunnaville dep., pp. 9-10.
588. DX 4906, pp. 6-7; see also DX 2930, pp. 2-4.
589. Knaplund, Tr. 90897-98; PX 2125, p. 121; PX 2238, pp. 149-50, 201; DX 9083, p. 24; DX 12408; DX 12419, pp. 5-6.
590. DX 5945: Dunnaville dep., as amended by letter from Dunnaville to Deutsch, February 27, 1975, included as part of DX 5945.

CHAPTER 10

1. See PX 3908A, p. 5.
2. Case, Tr. 73473-75; PX 3908A, p. 5; see also PX 2262.
3. Navas, Tr. 41394-96; Hughes, Tr. 71939-40.
4. Knaplund, Tr. 90497-98; DX 1404A, p. 40 (App. A to JX 38).
5. PX 3908A, pp. 4, 21-24.
6. PX 3908A, p. 4; see Knaplund, Tr. 90497-98.
7. PX 3908A, p. 4.
8. PX 4847, p. 1.
9. Gardner, Tr. 36880; Wright, Tr. 13236-38; Welke, Tr. 19191-92; Enfield, Tr. 20765-68; Ashbridge, Tr. 34900-02; G. Brown, Tr. 51064-65; PX 4472, p. 7; PX 5593, pp. 7-8; DX 4242, p. 8; DX 4249, p. 5; DX 12446; DX 13851, p. 9; DX 13900, pp. 5-6.
10. See DX 2583; DX 2585, DX 2587; DX 2589.
11. Palevsky, Tr. 3198-205; Binger, Tr. 4549-50; Macdonald, Tr. 6898-99; Beard, Tr. 8999-9000, 9935-36, 10197-99; McCollister, Tr. 9598-607; Spitters, Tr. 42067-68; Withington, Tr. 56243-44, 58365-66; PX 2267B, p. 27; DX 1482B, p. 80.
12. Macdonald, Tr. 6898; Peterman, Tr. 99944; DX 13899, p. 8.
13. Ashbridge, Tr. 34793-96, 34850-53.
14. Ashbridge, Tr. 34792-94; G. Brown, Tr. 51017, 51057, 51542; DX 14475, p. 9.
15. Palevsky, Tr. 3198-204.
16. McCollister, Tr. 9598-606; Beard, Tr. 9935-36, 10197-99.
17. Guzy, Tr. 33168-69; Navas, Tr. 41240-42; Aweida, Tr. 49071-73; PX 4847, p. 1; DX 4741: Yang, Tr. (Telex) 6116.
18. Guzy, Tr. 33584; Ashbridge, Tr. 34792-95, 34850-54; G. Brown, Tr. 51056-65, 51427-31, 51433-35; DX 1302; DX

1482, p. 1; DX 4122; DX 12544.

19. Enfield, Tr. 20827-29; Spitters, Tr. 42071; Friedman, Tr. 50458-60; PX 4834, p. 43; PX 4847, p. 2.

20. Spitters, Tr. 54352-58; DX 1270, p. 5.

21. PX 4201, p. 3; DX 1553A, p. 13.

22. Binger, Tr. 4596-98; Spangle, Tr. 5338-39; Norris, Tr. 6018-19; McCollister, Tr. 9587-91; PX 2530, p. 3; see also PX 2267B, p. 9.

23. Palevsky, Tr. 3277-78; Binger, Tr. 4550-51; PX 4201, pp. 3-5.

24. PX 3135B, pp. 1, 8-9.

25. See the discussions of DEC and SDS in Chapter 9.

26. Norris, Tr. 6021-30; G. Brown, Tr. 51002; DX 297; see also DX 4228, p. 3.

27. G. Brown, Tr. 51032-34, 51056-87.

28. G. Brown, Tr. 51056-59, 51078-79, 51087.

29. G. Brown, Tr. 51082.

30. G. Brown, Tr. 51080-81.

31. G. Brown, Tr. 51068.

32. Guzy, Tr. 32400-04, 33168-69; Ashbridge, Tr. 34852-54; DX 2851; DX 6740. See detailed discussion below.

33. Brueck, Tr. 22251; PX 401, p. 4; DX 7568, pp. 45-51.

34. DX 7568, pp. 3-4. 33-34.

35. DX 7582.

36. DX 6257: Gold dep., pp. 111-15, 128-31; DX 9071: Crone dep., pp. 114, 118-19, 123-25.

37. Withington, Tr. 56033-34.

38. PX 4847. pp. 1-2.

39. Guzy, Tr. 33168-74; Navas, Tr. 41235-41; Spitters, Tr. 42066-69; G. Brown, Tr. 51057-59; DX 1302; DX 1482, p. 1; DX 4113: Terry, Tr. (Telex) 3310-12.

40. DX 4113: Terry, Tr. (Telex) 3310-12.

41. Guzy, Tr. 33168-74; DX 1302; DX 1482.

42. DX 4004: Flanigan dep., pp. 62-65.

43. Navas, Tr. 41235-37; PX 5584, p. 16; DX 1886, p. 7.

44. DX 10658, p. 9.

45. DX 14474, p. 2.

46. DX 10657, p. 15; DX 10658, pp. 8-9.

47. DX 10658, pp. 2-3.

48. Jatras, Tr. 35209.

49. DX 1721.

50. Ibid.

51. Jatras, Tr. 35209-10; see also Ashbridge, Tr. 34799.

52. DX 4249, p. 5; DX 10654, p. 6; DX 13856, p. 3.

53. DX 4242, p. 2; DX 4250, p. 6.

54. DX 13856, p. 3.

55. DX 4250, pp. 4, 7.

56. DX 8224, p. 554.

57. PX 4847, p. 1; DX 13884, p. 22.

58. Ashbridge, Tr. 34794; PX 3237A, p. 7; DX 13883, p. 9.

59. DX 13880, p. 5; see also DX 13881, pp. 1-2.

60. Ashbridge, Tr. 34794; DX 4004: Flanigan dep., pp. 65-66; DX 13882, p. 8.

61. DX 4004: Flanigan dep., pp. 62-63.

62. PX 4847, p. 1.

63. Ashbridge, Tr. 34797-800; PX 3237A, pp. 7-8; DX 4756, p. 36; DX 13836, p. 9.

64. DX 13884, p. 22.

65. PX 3656A, p. 3.

66. DX 4004: Flanigan dep., pp. 65-68.

67. DX 2978, pp. 16-17.

68. DX 8224, p. 526.

69. Spitters, Tr. 42040-53.

70. Spitters, Tr. 42052-53.

71. Guzy, Tr. 32330-31; Spitters, Tr. 42040-43.

72. Spitters, Tr. 42066; DX 1264, pp. 8-10.

73. PX 4336, p. 5.

74. Guzy, Tr. 32356-57.

75. Guzy, Tr. 32373, 32377-78; PX 4336, p. 5; DX 1265, p. 17.

76. Spitters, Tr. 42090; see also DX 1265, p. 17.

77. DX 1266, p. 4.

78. Guzy, Tr. 32373.

79. DX 1267, p. 7; DX 1268, p. 7.

80. DX 1267, p. 5; DX 1268, p. 7; DX 1547, pp. 9-11; see also Spitters, Tr. 42094-102.

81. Spitters, Tr. 43106, 54187-206, 54207-08; DX 1547; DX 1548.

82. DX 1268, p. 17; DX 1482B, p. 1.

83. Guzy, Tr. 32364-66.

84. Guzy, Tr. 32368-69.

85. Gardner, Tr. 36880; DX 1267, p. 17.

86. Guzy, Tr. 32370; DX 1267, p. 17.

87. Spitters, Tr. 42071; DX 1482, p. 1.

88. J. Jones, Tr. 79037-38.

89. Guzy, Tr. 32383-84.

90. Guzy, Tr. 33168-73, 33587-603; DX 1302.

91. Guzy, Tr. 32380-82.

92. Guzy, Tr. 32382-83.

93. Guzy, Tr. 32316.

94. Guzy, Tr. 32385-86.
95. Navas, Tr. 41395-96.
96. Spitters, Tr. 42071; see also DX 1267, p. 6.
97. Guzy, Tr. 32862-64, 32899-908, 33255-58; DX 1296, p. 2.
98. Guzy, Tr. 32863-64, 32899-907, 33257-58; JX 34; DX 1418, p. 30.
99. Guzy, Tr. 32776.
100. DX 1267, p. 17; DX 1268, p. 17.
101. Guzy, Tr. 33168-73, 33590-602; DX 1302.
102. Guzy, Tr. 33177-79; DX 1302, p. 1.
103. Guzy, Tr. 33179-82; DX 1302, p. 1.
104. DX 1268, pp. 17, 19; DX 4756A, p. R-84; DX 4756, pp. 16-17; see also Case, Tr. 74117-18.
105. Guzy, Tr. 33255-74; JX 34; DX 1297; DX 1298; DX 1299.
106. Guzy, Tr. 32513-15.
107. DX 1269, p. 7.
108. DX 1268, p. 17.
109. DX 1269, pp. 28-29.
110. Guzy, Tr. 32423.
111. DX 1547, p. 12.
112. DX 8224, p. 547.
113. Spitters, Tr. 42101-07.
114. DX 1548, p. 13.
115. DX 4741: Yang, Tr. (Telex) 6116.
116. Whitcomb, Tr. 34566; DX 4756B, p. 96; DX 4739: Wilmer, Tr. (Telex) 4266.
117. DX 4756A, p. 36; see also PX 4732A, p. 12.
118. DX 4250, p. 7; DX 4756A, p. 36.
119. DX 4756A, pp. 50, 71-72.
120. DX 4242, p. 8; DX 4250, p. 7; DX 4741: Yang, Tr. (Telex) 6117-20.
121. PX 4732A, pp. 11, 14.
122. PX 4445, p. 7; PX 5583, p. 8; see also PX 5581, p. 10; DX 10736, pp. 3, 6; DX 13844, pp. 3, 6-13; DX 13885, p. 1.
123. Northrop, Tr. 82500.
124. PX 3655, p. 9; PX 4298, p. 1.
125. PX 5582, p. 7.
126. PX 5581, p. 32; PX 5582, pp. 5, 7; PX 5583, pp. 5, 26.
127. PX 5324, p. 46.
128. DX 4756A, p. 8; DX 10735, p. 10.
129. PX 5581, p. 10; DX 10735, p. 8.
130. PX 3146A, p. 1; PX 5581, p. 10; PX 5582, p. 7; DX 1886, p. 7; DX 12194; see also Guzy, Tr. 33201-02.
131. PX 4201, p. 13; DX 10735, pp. 26-27.
132. DX 8224, p. 531.

133. Spitters, Tr. 55286-87; Haughton, Tr. 95169-70; Cary, Tr. 101336-48; PX 2308, p. 220; DX 1542, p. 4; DX 1673; DX 1848; DX 1926, p. 10; DX 4226, p. 20.
134. Whitcomb, Tr. 34454-55.
135. Whitcomb, Tr. 34459-60; Navas, Tr. 39678-81; PX 4472, pp. 15-16; see also Aweida, Tr. 42974-87; Lacey, Tr. 6574; Haughton, Tr. 95169-70.
136. PX 2343.
137. Andreini, Tr. 47542-45; JX 38, pp. 938-39; PX 2392, p. 2; PX 2441A, p. 1; PX 3086; DX 1682, p. 11; DX 4555; DX 4756A, p. 3; DX 4756B, p. 102.
138. Whitcomb, Tr. 34460-62; PX 3847A, p. 19.
139. Whitcomb, Tr. 34460-62; Ashbridge, Tr. 34911; Spitters, Tr. 54432-33; Withington, Tr. 56630-32; Powers, Tr. 95386-87; PX 4201, p. 6; DX 1743; DX 4243.
140. PX 2615A, p. 1. Emphasis in original. See also Whitcomb, Tr. 34458-61.
141. Whitcomb, Tr. 34454-55; see also Withington, Tr. 56427-31; PX 4875, p. 1; DX 6257: Gold dep., pp. 143-45.
142. McCollister, Tr. 9327; Cooley, Tr. 31841-42; Andreini, Tr. 46986; PX 2552B, p. 3; PX 2558B, p. 2.
143. PX 2267B, pp. 1, 4.
144. PX 2267B, p. 13.
145. PX 2267B, p. 14.
146. PX 2308, p. 220. Emphasis in original. See PX 2306, p. 2.
147. PX 3096A, p. 3.
148. PX 2343.
149. DX 1268, p. 4; DX 4249, p. 2; DX 4250, p. 6; DX 13884, p. 22; DX 13900, pp. 3, 8.
150. PX 2430A, pp. 2, 4; see also PX 3654, pp. 5-6.
151. PX 3201A, p. 1.
152. PX 3117.
153. DX 7858.
154. PX 2530, pp. 1, 21-22.
155. Whitcomb, Tr. 34183-86, 34456-57; DX 5, p. 166.
156. PX 3829, p. 2; see also PX 3960.
157. DX 5212, pp. 2-4; see also PX 3829.
158. PX 3829, pp. 4-5; PX 3960.
159. PX 3127A, p. 10.
160. DX 4323, p. 1.
161. PX 3829, p. 1.
162. DX 1260.
163. DX 4740: Evans, Tr. (Telex) 4005-06; see also PX 3829; DX 1260.

164. PX 2546A.
165. Cary, Tr. 101388.
166. Cary, Tr. 101390.
167. PX 2546A.
168. PX 2550A, p. 1.
169. PX 2546A; PX 2548A.
170. PX 2552B, p. 3.
171. PX 2552B, pp. 3-4.
172. PX 2558B, p. 2.
173. DX 4740: Evans, Tr. (Telex) 4007.
174. Ibid.
175. DX 4740: Evans, Tr. (Telex) 4007-08.
176. PX 3135B, pp. 1, 47, 49, 59-62; see also Whitcomb, Tr. 34488.
177. DX 4740: Evans, Tr. (Telex) 4008; see also PX 3925, p. 8; PX 3991, p. 3.
178. PX 3854A, p. 1.
179. PX 2567, pp. 212-13.
180. PX 2627, p. 179. Emphasis in the original.
181. PX 3965.
182. See Fassig, Tr. 31997-98; Whitcomb, Tr. 34288-89; DX 7858; see also Withington, Tr. 56412, 56520-21; PX 2360, p. 112.
183. Friedman, Tr. 50558-59; Spain, Tr. 88735; DX 14136, pp. 1-3.
184. JX 3, para. 23.
185. See, e.g., Withington, Tr. 57023-29, 58630-31.
186. JX 3, paras. 13-14.
187. JX 3, paras. 15-16.
188. JX 3, paras. 9-10.
189. JX 3, para. 18.
190. DX 10640, p. 5; see also Friedman, Tr. 50752-53; Spain, Tr. 89619-21.
191. Friedman, Tr. 50752-55; DX 14190, p. 2.
192. DX 10640, p. 3; DX 14326, p. 5.
193. See, e.g., the various proposals made to Union Carbide for its major computer procurement (DX 3703; DX 3705; DX 3710).
194. Spain, Tr. 88735, 88752-53.
195. Friedman, Tr. 50382; DX 2223, p. 3.
196. Spain, Tr. 88752-53.
197. See, e.g., DX 10208, p. 150; DX 10495, p. 5; DX 14190, p. 1.
198. See, e.g., JX 3, para. 18; DX 10208, p. 150.
199. Spain, Tr. 88730; JX 3, paras. 20, 21.
200. See Spain, Tr. 88734.
201. Davidson, Tr. 98761-68.
202. Spain, Tr. 88733-34; Davidson, Tr. 98761-63; JX 3, para. 19; PX 4436, p. 2;
PX 4834, p. 43; DX 122, p. 14; DX 2231, p. 28; DX 6966, p. 22; DX 10495, p. 16; DX 14197, p. 11; DX 14476A, p. F-10.
203. Davidson, Tr. 98761-68; Buffett, Tr. 100377-80; PX 4437, pp. 1-2.
204. Briloff, Tr. 80724-25.
205. JX 3, para. 20.
206. JX 3, para. 21.
207. DX 14084, pp. 4-5; DX 13850, p. 5.
208. DX 10347, p. 1.
209. DX 14195, p. 9.
210. DX 4043: Coonan dep., pp. 6-7; DX 10208, p. 4; DX 14084, p. 9; DX 14089, p. 2; DX 14446, p. 3.
211. Spain, Tr. 88729; see also PX 4260, pp. 3, 23, 24.
212. See Spain, Tr. 88729; PX 4260, pp. 12, 21-23.
213. PX 4504, pp. 3, 7.
214. DX 8224, pp. 73, 150, 152, 157, 162, 530, 539, 543. Some of these revenues include EDP revenues of acquired EDP leasing companies.
215. PX 2414, pp. 62-78; PX 4315A, pp. 129-34; DX 9416B.
216. DX 10640, p. 3; DX 14326, p. 5.
217. PX 4834, p. 43; see also Spain, Tr. 88729-30.
218. Friedman, Tr. 50376-79.
219. Ibid.; Case, Tr. 73239-40, 73345-57; DX 3635A; DX 14201, p. 1.
220. Friedman, Tr. 50376-79.
221. Spain, Tr. 88749; JX 3, para. 13; PX 4436, p. 2.
222. JX 4, para. 41.
223. Friedman, Tr. 50372-73; PX 4832, p. 10; DX 2223, p. 16; DX 10208, p. 4; DX 14075, p. 9; DX 14188, p. 8; DX 14189, p. 17.
224. Spangle, Tr. 4953; Norris, Tr. 5991; Hangen, Tr. 6371-72; McCollister, Tr. 9802-05; G. Brown, Tr. 52609-10, 52613-14; Withington, Tr. 56624; PX 4832, p. 10; DX 75; DX 76, p. 2; DX 278.
225. PX 4315A, p. 18; see also DX 14486.
226. JX 3, para. 28(a).
227. DX 14085, p. 6; DX 14191, pp. 21, 22, 24.
228. PX 4322, p. 11.
229. PX 3056, p. 3.
230. DX 9416A; see PX 2414, p. 5.
231. Briloff, Tr. 80725-26; PX 4495, p. 5; PX 4499, p. 4.
232. Welke, Tr. 17401-03; Briloff, Tr. 80696-706; Buffett, Tr. 100358-63.

233. Briloff, Tr., 80705.
234. Welke, Tr. 17403-04.
235. Briloff, Tr. 80705, 80720-28; Buffett, Tr. 100359-62.
236. Spain, Tr. 88730-34; Davidson, Tr. 98763; JX 3, para. 20; PX 2181A, p. R1; PX 3056, p. 13.
237. PX 2181A, p. R1; DX 2263.
238. Briloff, Tr. 80725-26; PX 4322, p. 9.
239. DX 10208, p. 28; DX 14076, p. 24; DX 14090, p. 4; DX 14326, p. 5.
240. JX 3, para. 25.
241. PX 2414, p. 20.
242. PX 2414, p. 56.
243. PX 4371, p. 6; DX 2263.
244. DX 14190, p. 1.
245. DX 10208, p. 150, see also p. 143.
246. DX 10495, p. 5.
247. See, e.g., PX 4371, pp. 4, 7; DX 2263.
248. DX 2263, p. 1.
249. DX 2263, p. 10.
250. Briloff, Tr. 81081-82.
251. PX 4371, p. 4.
252. Spain, Tr. 88752-53.
253. Spain, Tr. 88754; PX 2181A, p. R14; PX 3105, pp. 5-6.
254. Spain, Tr. 88754; DX 1494, as discussed in Navas, Tr. 40120-21, 41265-66; see also DX 14327, p. 2.
255. See DX 14211, p. 6.
256. See, e.g., DX 14340, p. 4; DX 14485, p. 37.
257. Spain, Tr. 88754; DX 14190, p. 1; DX 14340, p. 6.
258. DX 9416A.
259. See JX 3, para. 14.
260. Spitters, Tr. 42067-68; PX 4436, pp. 6, 9; PX 4834, p. 43.
261. DX 4756A, p. 39; DX 10495, pp. 2-3. The GE disk drives marketed by Greyhound had reliability problems (see DX 14331, p. 41).
262. JX 3, paras. 15-16.
263. DX 10347, p. 1.
264. DX 14193, p. 5.
265. DX 8224, p. 539.
266. DX 14194, p. 7.
267. DX 14195, p. 9.
268. DX 14195, p. 10.
269. DX 14075, p. 24; DX 14076, p. 24; DX 14341, p. 41.
270. DX 14341, p. 18.
271. DX 14074, p. 21.
272. DX 8224, p. 539.
273. DX 4756A, p. 39.
274. DX 14075, p. 6.
275. DX 14076, pp. 9-10.
276. DX 14195, p. 9.
277. DX 14075, p. 9.
278. DX 14188, p. 2; DX 14195, p. 2.
279. PX 3082, p. 34.
280. DX 14188, p. 2.
281. PX 2414, p. 5.
282. DX 14326, p. 2.
283. DX 14189, p. 5; DX 14326, p. 3.
284. See DX 14101.
285. DX 8224, p. 530.
286. DX 14095, p. 13; see also J. Jones, Tr. 79039-40.
287. DX 14340, p. 14.
288. DX 14340, p. 4.
289. DX 14326, p. 2.
290. DX 14340, pp. 6-7.
291. DX 14340, p. 7.
292. Ibid.
293. DX 14071, p. 5; DX 14096, p. 6.
294. DX 2223, p. 3.
295. Friedman, Tr. 50382.
296. PX 2414, p. 56.
297. DX 2226, p. 16.
298. DX 8224, p. 543.
299. Friedman, Tr. 50373; DX 2223, p. 16.
300. Friedman, Tr. 50558-59.
301. DX 2223, p. 9.
302. Ibid.; see also DX 2226, p. 7.
303. DX 2226, pp. 8-9.
304. DX 2226, p. 10.
305. DX 2229, p. 18.
306. Friedman, Tr. 50438-39; DX 2232, p. 35; DX 14260; DX 14280.
307. Friedman, Tr. 50400; DX 2231, p. 29.
308. Spain, Tr. 88737-38.
309. McDonald, Tr. 3995-96; McCollister, Tr. 9802-05; James, Tr. 35048; G. Brown, Tr. 52609-10; DX 75; DX 76; DX 78, p.1.
310. PX 4315A, p. R-4, see also p. R-16.
311. PX 4315A, p. R-16.
312. See Akers, Tr. 96868-69, 97112-13; PX 2512A, p. 17.
313. PX 3455A, p. R-37.
314. PX 2414, pp. 53, 55.
315. Compare Withington, Tr. 57023-29, 58630-31.
316. PX 2388, p. 117.
317. DX 14201, pp. 1-2; see also DX 14479, p. 1.
318. See PX 4505.
319. DX 8063.

320. Eckert, Tr. 917; see also Weil, Tr. 7159; O'Neill, Tr. 76020.
321. DX 4085: Poe dep., p. 11.
322. DX 8224, p. 356; see also DX 4076: DiPietro dep., p. 10 (DP&W, Inc., began with $75,000); DX 5930: Davenport dep., p. 12 (Davenport Data Processors began with $5,500).
323. DX 6015: Roach dep., pp. 12-13; DX 8224, p. 504.
324. DX 3975: Moranz dep., pp. 5-6; DX 8224, p. 504.
325. DX 5816: Vallario dep., p. 9; DX 8224, p. 621 (Bergen-Brunswig Corp. entered the EDP business in 1964, $2.5 million in U.S. EDP revenues in 1970); DX 5933: Biegel dep., p. 3; DX 8224, p. 50 (Bradford Computer and Systems started in 1968, $9.8 million in U.S. EDP revenues in 1970); DX 5988: Leslie dep., p. 3; DX 8224, p. 95 (Insco Systems started in 1968, $15.4 million in U.S. EDP revenues in 1970); DX 6190: Stapp dep., p. 10; DX 8224, p. 521 (Middle South Services started in 1963, $5.1 million in U.S. EDP revenues in 1970); DX 8122: Larribeau dep., p. 10; DX 8224, p. 577 (Information Systems Design started in 1966, $1.6 million in U.S. EDP revenues in 1970); DX 8224, p. 557; DX 13916, p. 6 (Tymshare started in 1966, $10.2 million in U.S. EDP revenues in 1970).
326. Plaintiff's Admissions, set II, paras. 325.0, 325.9, 325.10, 325.11; Withington estimated the number of firms at 1,400 (PX 4832, p. 6).
327. See, e.g., DX 6914, p. 4; DX 7425, pp. 4, 12; DX 10324, pp. 52, 55, 57, 86, 119; DX 10667, pp. 3, 10; DX 13917, pp. 2, 7.
328. See, e.g., Lacey, Tr. 6611, 6687; DX 340A, pp. 3, 10; DX 367, pp. 21-22; DX 13912, p. 20.
329. Friedman, Tr. 50355, 50361; DX 2226, p. 8; DX 10346; DX 14193, p. 5. See the discussion of individual systems manufacturers in Chapters 8 and 9.
330. Lacey, Tr. 6634-35; PX 328, p. 21; PX 4832, p. 21; DX 123, pp. 28, 33; DX 284, pp. 1, 4; DX 340A, pp. 3, 10; DX 367, p. 21; DX 13843, p. 6.
331. See, e.g., Plaintiff's Admissions, set II, paras. 321.8, 341.5, 345.2.
332. See, e.g., DX 5637: Allen dep., pp. 24-25 (Fulton National Bank); DX 5819: Hammaker dep., p. 4 (Connecticut Bank

and Trust Co.); DX 6150: Pettit dep., p. 4 (Grumman Corp.); DX 6151: Lynch dep., p. 4 (Harris Trust and Savings Bank); DX 6180: Hager dep., pp. 4-6 (Marine Midland Bank subsidiaries); DX 13943 (Westinghouse).
333. See, e.g., DX 13924.
334. DX 5816: Vallario dep., p. 10.
335. DX 8224, p. 621.
336. Plaintiff's Admissions, set II, paras. 368.0-.2; see, e.g., 369.11, 369.15, 369.21.
337. Plaintiff's Admissions, set II, paras. 364.0-.2, 364.4.
338. Plaintiff's Admissions, set II, paras. 367.2-.4.
339. See Norris, Tr. 5828-29.
340. Currie, Tr. 15346.
341. Weil, Tr. 7133-34.
342. Weil, Tr. 7134-45.
343. Weil, Tr. 7135-36.
344. Weil, Tr. 7137-38.
345. R. Jones, Tr. 8799-8800.
346. DX 2765; see also DX 13917, p. 1.
347. PX 2404A, p. 25; see also Currie, Tr. 15346-47.
348. Weil, Tr. 7203-04; PX 4832, p. 27; DX 5324, pp. 1-5.
349. DX 13942, p. 26; see also DX 6872; Plaintiff's Admissions, set II, paras. 304.21-.23.
350. Perlis, Tr. 1869; see also Plaintiff's Admissions, set I, paras. 39.0, 41.0, 45.0, 48.0; DX 7528: Mahoney dep., pp. 81-83.
351. Weil, Tr. 7257-58.
352. Currie, Tr. 15439; Withington Tr. 56986-89, 56993, 57001-02; DX 4076: DiPietro dep., pp. 6-7; DX 5652: Bruns dep., pp. 156-57; DX 5821: Brownell dep., p. 16; DX 5937: Alkema dep., p. 9; DX 5816: Vallario dep., p. 16; DX 6026: Gehring dep., pp. 12-14; DX 6088: Zweifel dep., pp. 19-20; DX 6128: St. Amant dep., pp. 11-12; DX 6243: Mortensen dep., p. 6; DX 8122: Larribeau dep., pp. 11-12; DX 8175: Finelli dep., pp. 17-19; see also DX 84, pp. 2-3.
353. DX 10324, pp. 59-60. Emphasis in original.
354. DX 11202; see also DX 6872, p. 1 (Keydata — "all the benefits of a large computer with none of the problems"); DX 11759 (Martin Marietta Data Systems — on-site remote job entry computing service "as a replacement for an existing facility . . . e.g. manufacturer replaces 370/135").

355. Currie, Tr. 15605-06.
356. Norris, Tr. 5819; Currie, Tr. 15350-51; J. Jones, Tr. 79982-84; DX 4085: Poe dep., pp. 19-20; DX 6088: Zweifel dep., pp. 16-17.
357. See Norris, Tr. 6078-79; PX 4832, pp. 11, 32; DX 5821: Brownell dep., pp. 16-17; DX 6026: Gehring dep., pp. 14-15; DX 7532: Parten dep., pp. 188-91.
358. DX 4085: Poe dep., p. 19; DX 6016: Gehring dep., pp. 12-14; DX 6080: Dale dep., pp. 10-11; DX 6088: Zweifel dep., p. 18; DX 7393, pp. 110, 117.
359. DX 6128: St. Amant dep., pp. 4, 11.
360. DX 4076: DiPietro dep., pp. 3, 6-7.
361. DX 8122: Larribeau dep., pp. 5, 12-13.
362. Cary, Tr. 101325; PX 2964A, pp. R29-R30.
363. PX 2360, p. 139.
364. PX 2437, pp. 108, 294.
365. Cary, Tr. 101642; PX 2388, p. 117.
366. Currie, Tr. 15603-06.
367. Currie, Tr. 15477-90, 15611-12.
368. See, e.g., Norris, Tr. 5698, 5997 (CDC); R. Jones, Tr. 8848 (GE); Macdonald, Tr 6900 (Burroughs); Rooney, Tr. 12039-40, 12482 (RCA).
369. The FCC's estimate was in its tentative decision in Computer Inquiry I (Docket no. 16979); Plaintiff's Admissions, set II, paras. 306.7-.9; see also PX 4835, pp. 36-38.
370. DX 11074, p. 2.
371. DX 11074, p. 14.
372. DX 10324, p. 155.
373. DX 10324, pp. 82, 234.
374. DX 11075, p. 12.
375. DX 10324, pp. 52, 55, 57, 86.
376. DX 11075, p. 12.
377. DX 13875, p. 3.
378. DX 13876, pp. 3-4.
379. DX 14212, pp. 6-7.
380. DX 10320, p. 18; DX 13877, pp. 5, 12; DX 13878, pp. 4, 5, 8; DX 13879, p. 3; DX 14212, p. 9.
381. DX 13879, p. 3.
382. DX 8224, p. 135.
383. DX 8224, p. 557; DX 13916, p. 6.
384. DX 13917, pp. 1, 7.
385. DX 13917, p. 1.
386. Ibid.; see also DX 2765.
387. DX 13917, pp. 3, 8.
388. DX 8224, p. 557.
389. Welke, Tr. 17383; see also Tr. 17072; DX 1049, pp. 5-6.
390. Welke, Tr. 17014, 17071-72, 17382.
391. Welke, Tr. 17003-05, 17040-41, 17051-53, 17384.
392. Welke, Tr. 17082-83; DX 1049, pp. 5-6.
393. Welke, Tr. 17388-91; see also Spangle, Tr. 5092-94; Macdonald, Tr. 6901-02; Currie, Tr. 15385-89; Goetz, Tr. 17489-90.
394. Welke, Tr. 17383-84; DX 1049; see also Withington, Tr. 56790.
395. Welke, Tr. 17083.
396. Welke, Tr. 17083, 17404-05; DX 1049, p. 3.
397. Welke, Tr. 17078-81, 17385-87, 19195; DX 1049, p. 5.
398. Welke, Tr. 19195-97.
399. DX 7425, p. 5; DX 8224, p. 532.
400. DX 8224, p. 542; DX 8796, p. 7.
401. Goetz, Tr. 17441, 18580.
402. Welke, Tr. 17392.
403. Goetz, Tr. 18773-74; DX 1096, p. 2; see also Withington, Tr. 56791.
404. Welke, Tr. 17392-96.
405. Welke, Tr. 17167-68, 17180-81.
406. Welke, Tr. 17318-20.
407. Welke, Tr. 17326, 19206-07; Withington, Tr. 56772.
408. Perlis, Tr. 1996-97; McCollister, Tr. 11063-65; Case, Tr. 73151-53; see Palevsky, Tr. 3206; Spangle, Tr. 4907-09.
409. Perlis, Tr. 1921-22.
410. Welke, Tr. 17248.
411. DX 9110, pp. 1-2.
412. DX 1049, p. 8.
413. Goetz, Tr. 17506-07, 18662-66; Welke, Tr. 19217-19; DX 1064.
414. Welke, Tr. 19216-17.
415. Welke, Tr. 17156-58, 19217, 19267-70, 19349-50, 19354; J. Jones, Tr. 79417-19; PX 4833, p. 28; DX 3950, pp. 17-18.
416. Welke, Tr. 19267.
417. Enfield, Tr. 19910-11.
418. Enfield, Tr. 20134-36.
419. DX 4028: Oppenheim dep., pp. 8-10, 14-15.
420. DX 6123: Smith dep., pp. 2, 8-10.
421. DX 3970: Benton dep., pp. 6, 8-9; DX 6145, p. 13; DX 6169: Lissner dep., pp. 11-12; DX 6244: Clay dep., pp. 17-18.
422. DX 7425, p. 5; see also DX 7426, pp. 8-9.
423. DX 7426, pp. 13-15.
424. DX 7426, p. 15.
425. DX 5194, pp. 2-5; DX 7426, p. 15.

426. DX 8224, p. 532; see also DX 7426, p. 21.
427. Welke, Tr. 17071-72; DX 2985: Thomas dep., p. 7.
428. DX 8224, p. 542; DX 13891, pp. 4-5, 11.
429. Withington, Tr. 57662-63; DX 7116, p. 3; DX 13982, p. 6; DX 14082, p. 2.
430. Welke, Tr. 17156-58, 19218.
431. Welke, Tr. 17163, 19217.
432. DX 10611.
433. DX 13891, p. 4.
434. DX 7116, p. 2.
435. DX 13891, p. 5.

CHAPTER 11

1. PX 1077, p. 2.
2. DX 14394.
3. PX 3908A, p. 22; see also PX 6671, p. 27.
4. PX 3908A, p. 22.
5. DX 4740: Evans, Tr. (Telex) 3937.
6. Case, Tr. 73609-13, 73732.
7. Case, Tr. 73732-34.
8. Case, Tr. 73695-99, 73734-35, 73737-48; DX 1437.
9. PX 2399, p. 1.
10. PX 5621, p. 17.
11. Cary, Tr. 101359-61.
12. Evans, Tr. 101294-96.
13. DX 7751, p. 3.
14. DX 7751, pp. 3-6.
15. DX 7752, p. 3.
16. DX 7752, p. 1.
17. PX 2152A, pp. 1-2.
18. PX 3958, p. 1.
19. JX 38, p. 840; DX 7751, p. 5; DX 12689, p. 9.
20. See DX 5155: Gruver dep., pp. 42-43; see also DX 7838, p. 3.
21. DX 7710, pp. 5-6.
22. DX 7710, pp. 1, 4.
23. DX 7669.
24. Ibid.; DX 7698.
25. PX 2267B, p. 1.
26. PX 3086.
27. PX 3096A, p. 3; see also PX 3104, p. 2.
28. PX 2343.
29. JX 38, p. 932.
30. Ibid.; DX 7710, p. 2.
31. See Aweida, Tr. 49091-94; DX 5155: Gruver dep., pp. 38-40.

32. DX 1769, pp. 1-2.
33. Cooley, Tr. 31942; Aweida, Tr. 49617-22; DX 2158; DX 4740: Evans, Tr. (Telex) 4122-24; JX 38, p. 981.
34. DX 3116, pp. 1, 2, 3, 6, 13, 28.
35. DX 3087, pp. 1, 2, 5, 7, 9.
36. See PX 2343.
37. PX 4033, pp. 28, 33; see also PX 5360.
38. PX 4033, p. 20.
39. PX 5360, pp. 1-2.
40. PX 5360, pp. 2-3.
41. PX 5564; see also PX 5360; DX 14388.
42. PX 4212, p. 1.
43. PX 4212, p. 2.
44. PX 4212, p. 3.
45. PX 5563, p. 1.
46. PX 5563, p. 2.
47. Ibid.
48. PX 5564, p. 1.
49. PX 5564, p. 2.
50. DX 7619: Winger, Tr. (Telex) 5695.
51. JX 38, pp. 981, 983.
52. JX 38, pp. 981-83, 985.
53. PX 4033, p. 48.
54. JX 38, pp. 840, 932, 982, 985; DX 7619: Winger, Tr. (Telex) 5709-10.
55. DX 2137, p. 1; DX 7619: Winger, Tr. (Telex) 5714-15.
56. DX 2137, p. 1; DX 7619: Winger, Tr. (Telex) 5716.
57. Cooley, Tr. 31941; DX 4253, pp. 6, 9.
58. PX 3784B, p. 36; PX 3962, p. 8; DX 2137, p. 6; DX 4253, pp. 17-22; DX 5155: Gruver dep., pp. 62-64, 73, 96-97; DX 7619: Winger, Tr. (Telex) 5706-08, 5713.
59. Case, Tr. 73736; JX 38, pp. 981, 985; DX 4253, p. 7; DX 4740: Evans, Tr. (Telex) 4129-31; DX 5155: Gruver dep., pp. 59-60, 65-67, 89, 94; DX 7619: Winger, Tr. (Telex) 5698.
60. DX 4740: Evans, Tr. (Telex) 4130; see also PX 3962, p. 8; DX 2137, p. 5.
61. Case, Tr. 73735-36.
62. Cooley, Tr. 31940-41; DX 2137, pp. 4-5; DX 5155: Gruver dep., pp. 91-92.
63. DX 4740: Evans, Tr. (Telex) 4135-37.
64. DX 4740: Evans, Tr. (Telex) 4139-43.
65. DX 3119, pp. 1-4; DX 4201, pp. 1-6; DX 4421, pp. 1-2.
66. Case, Tr. 73734; see also DX 13442, pp. 2-3.

67. Cary, Tr. 101360-63; see also Case, Tr. 73732-34; PX 2399, p. 4; PX 2468A, p. 2; PX 2474B, p. 1; PX 2502B, p. 3.
68. DX 12115.
69. Haughton, Tr. 94857; PX 2474B, p. 1; DX 1437, p. 3.
70. DX 12116.
71. PX 2474B, p. 1.
72. DX 7858, p. 2.
73. DX 7858, pp. 4-5.
74. DX 4237, pp. 2-3.
75. DX 1437, p. 1; see also PX 4505.
76. PX 6414A, p. 6; DX 1437, pp. 1, 3.
77. Rooney, Tr. 12048-49; Wright, Tr. 13131-33; Currie, Tr. 15495-501; Withington, Tr. 56250-51.
78. See Case, Tr. 73733-34.
79. DX 13442, pp. 2-3.
80. Haughton, Tr. 94913-14; PX 3696A, p. 5.
81. Haughton, Tr. 94912-21; PX 3696A, pp. 1, 5, 8; PX 4538, p. 1.
82. DX 4740: Evans, Tr. (Telex) 4010–11; PX 4143; PX 4149.
83. PX 4143; see also DX 1456.
84. PX 4138, p. 2.
85. See, e.g., PX 5343.
86. DX 4740: Evans, Tr. (Telex) 4011.
87. See, e.g., PX 4214.
88. DX 9374, p. 6.
89. DX 9374, pp. 5, 7; emphasis in original. See also Powers, Tr. 95336-40.
90. Whitcomb, Tr. 34505-07; DX 4740: Evans, Tr. (Telex) 4012, 4023-25; see also Dunlop, Tr. 93812-13.
91. Haughton, Tr. 95021-22; DX 4740: Evans, Tr. (Telex) 4023-25, 4076-77.
92. Hurd, Tr. 86622-23; DX 1656; DX 1657; DX 1658; DX 7630: Herzfeld dep., pp. 21-22.
93. PX 4132, p. 1; DX 7619: Winger, Tr. (Telex) 5686-87; see also DX 1662.
94. PX 4527, pp. 1, 3; PX 4528, pp. 1, 3.
95. See DX 4740: Evans, Tr. (Telex) 4023-25, 4084; DX 4742: Kevill dep., pp. 523-26.
96. Case, Tr. 73734; PX 4538.
97. E. Bloch, Tr. 91500-01.
98. E. Bloch, Tr. 91537-38; see also E. Bloch, Tr. 91563; PX 4401; PX 6312, p. 3.
99. E. Bloch, Tr. 91548-51, 93324-26.
100. E. Bloch, Tr. 93325-26.
101. E. Bloch, Tr. 91501.
102. E. Bloch, Tr. 91502; see DX 3564.
103. E. Bloch, Tr. 91502.

104. PX 4505, pp. 2, 4.
105. E. Bloch, Tr. 91539-40.
106. E. Bloch, Tr. 91541; Cary, Tr. 101428-29; PX 2177A, pp. 3-4; DX 8056.
107. Cary, Tr. 101428.
108. PX 4565.
109. E. Bloch, Tr. 91542, 92294, 92910-12; Cary, Tr. 101412-13; DX 4740: Evans, Tr. (Telex) 3937-42, 3959-63; PX 3130A, pp. 2-3; PX 4324; PX 4400, pp. 2, 4.
110. Cary, Tr. 101403-04.
111. Cary, Tr. 101429.
112. DX 4505, pp. 2, 4.
113. E. Bloch, Tr. 91501, 91543-45, 91550-51; Cary, Tr. 101430; PX 3256C; DX 9157A.
114. JX 38, para. 2, pp. 2-3; DX 1404A (App. A to JX 38).
115. JX 38, p. 297; see also Case, Tr. 73370-71.
116. DX 8073.
117. E. Bloch, Tr. 91501.
118. PX 2459, p. 7.
119. DX 8073.
120. PX 2459, p. 9.
121. James, Tr. 35037.
122. PX 2459, p. 16.
123. DX 3364, p. 8.
124. DX 8072.
125. Akers, Tr. 97401-03.
126. DX 3364, p. 8; see Withington, Tr. 58435.
127. DX 2609B, p. 185.
128. PX 2500, pp. 1, 2; PX 6672, p. 2; DX 4740: Evans, Tr. (Telex) 4184.
129. DX 4740: Evans, Tr. (Telex) 3938, 4184-85; see Evans, Tr. 101299-301.
130. DX 4740: Evans, Tr. (Telex) 3950-51.
131. DX 4740: Evans, Tr. (Telex) 3941.
132. DX 4740: Evans, Tr. (Telex) 3942-52; see Evans, Tr. 101300-01.
133. DX 14201, pp. 5-7; see also PX 2399, pp. 1-2.
134. PX 4270, p. 1; see also PX 4272.
135. DX 1091, p. 1; DX 14335.
136. PX 2412, p. 3; DX 14201, p. 6; see PX 2399, pp. 1-2.
137. PX 4270, p. 4.
138. PX 2487A, p. 2; PX 4033, p. 13; PX 4233.
139. PX 2502B, p. 3.
140. DX 4740: Evans, Tr. (Telex) 3961-62; see also Cary, Tr. 101394-95; PX 4324; PX 4421, p. 2; PX 3256B, pp. 1-2.
141. PX 4505.

142. DX 1639; DX 1640.
143. Case, Tr. 73749-51.
144. PX 2388, p. 117.
145. PX 2388, p. 121; see pp. 125-28.
146. PX 2388, pp. 48, 68.
147. PX 2399, p. 3; see also DX 14201, p. 2; PX 2502B, p. 2.
148. DX 14201, p. 2; see PX 2388, pp. 119-20.
149. DX 14201, p. 4.
150. DX 14479.
151. PX 2468A, p. 2; PX 2502B, p. 2; PX 2558B, p. R21; PX 4233.
152. See PX 4505, pp. 3, 5-6.
153. PX 2399, p. 4.
154. Ibid.; DX 14201, pp. 2-3.
155. PX 2399, p. 4; PX 3256C, p. 2.
156. PX 2399, p. 4; PX 4505, p. 3.
157. PX 3256C, p. 2; PX 4505, p. 1.
158. DX 13521, p. 2.

CHAPTER 12

1. See, e.g., Department of Justice submission to Federal Communications Commission's Computer Inquiry I (Docket no. 16979), Plaintiff's Admissions, set II, paras. 312.5-.7; Plaintiff's Admissions, set IV, para. 231.0; PX 353, p. 18; DX 438, p. 1; DX 1553A, p. 2; DX 9110, p. 1.
2. DX 7568, pp. 13-14.
3. DX 14310, p. 35F-15.
4. DX 3811; DX 8224.
5. DX 5504, p. 8; see also DX 5476, pp. 6-7 and the references in note 1 above.
6. PX 4829, p. 8.
7. Ibid.
8. PX 4830, p. 8.
9. PX 4832, p. 8.
10. PX 4832, p. 6.
11. PX 4833, p. 10; PX 4834, p. 14.
12. See, e.g., Macdonald, Tr. 6926-30; PX 353, pp. 18, 54.
13. DX 3753 (Tr. 80198).
14. DX 4355, p. 6; see also DX 7566, pp. 10, 16; Plaintiff's Admissions, set IV, paras. 206.0, 221.0.
15. DX 923, pp. 11-17; DX 924, pp. 2, 596-97; DX 7568, pp. 13-14.
16. See Plaintiff's Admissions, set II, paras. 312.8-.10.
17. Knaplund, Tr. 90613, 90620-22.
18. Hurd, Tr. 86347-50; see also Hart, Tr. 80221-22.

19. Plaintiff's Admissions, set IV, para. 205.0; see also DX 44, p. 5.
20. PX 4829, p. 9.
21. See, e.g., J. Jones, Tr. 78954-56; PX 4830, p. 10; DX 5416: Francis dep., pp. 7-8.
22. PX 320, pp. 9-10.
23. Plaintiff's Admissions, set II, para. 312.24.
24. Plaintiff's Admissions, set II, para. 312.23; see also PX 4830, p. 14.
25. Plaintiff's Admissions, set II, paras. 312.11-.12.
26. DX 5377, pp. 1-2.
27. Perlis, Tr. 1830-31; see also DX 3753 (Tr. 80193).
28. PX 4830, p. 9.
29. PX 4833, p. 10; see also PX 4832, p. 8.
30. PX 4830, pp. 9-10; PX 4832, pp. 10-11; PX 4833, pp. 27-28; DX 9110, p. 3.
31. DX 3753 (Tr. 80191).
32. DX 4755.
33. DX 1402, p. 11; DX 911, p. 5.
34. DX 1402, p. 3; DX 911, p. 6.
35. DX 3554D.
36. Ibid.
37. Tr. 94860-61; JX 38, pp. 439-40; PX 6072.
38. Case, Tr. 72650-55; JX 38, pp. 840-41; PX 4526, p. 3; DX 3553B.
39. See, e.g., DX 4113: Terry, Tr. (Telex), pp. 3314-15.
40. Perlis, Tr. 1993.
41. DX 3753 (Tr. 80187-88); see also DX 5154: Heinzman, Tr. (Telex), 3387-88.
42. Withington, Tr. 57678.
43. Withington, Tr. 57680-81.
44. Macdonald, Tr. 6914; J. Jones, Tr. 78771-72, 78868-69, 78877-78, 79689-90; DX 3753 (Tr. 80192-93).
45. DX 3753 (Tr. 80192).
46. DX 3420A (classified), paras. 18-25, 29-55, 60-98, 267-455.
47. Weil, Tr. 7044; Crago, Tr. 85975.
48. DX 5421: Davis dep., p. 214; DX 13455, p. 3.
49. DX 7530: Kraft dep., pp. 48-49A; DX 7578, p. 2.
50. DX 331, p. 9.
51. Plaintiff's Admissions, set IV, para. 204.0; DX 10283, pp. 6-7.
52. Weil, Tr. 7044; see also DX 5313, pp. 14-15; DX 5654: Webster dep., pp. 360-62.

53. DX 4355, pp. 6, 11; DX 7567, p. 9; DX 13455, p. 1; Plaintiff's Admissions, set II, para. 312.8.

54. DX 4355, p. 6; see also DX 923, pp. 1, 7, 10-12, 17-23; DX 924, pp. 2-19, 595-97; DX 4589, pp. 5-16, 297; DX 7566, p. 16; Plaintiff's Admissions, set IV, para. 221.0.

55. Plaintiff's Admissions, set II, para. 354.1; PX 481; DX 1783, p. 13; DX 5703, pp. 11 ff.

56. DX 4355, p. 14.

57. DX 4355, pp. 15-16.

58. DX 4321, p. 1; DX 5212, p. 1; DX 9071: Crone dep., pp. 101, 759-61, 782-90, 960-61, 975-76.

59. See DX 9071: Crone dep., pp. 50-52.

60. DX 9071: Crone dep., p. 44; Plaintiff's Admissions, set II, para. 357.9.

61. Plaintiff's Admissions, set II, para. 138.0.

62. DX 923, p. 19; see Plaintiff's Admissions, set IV, para. 215.4.

63. Plaintiff's Admissions, set II, para. 371.9.

64. Plaintiff's Admissions, set II, para. 371.10.

65. Plaintiff's Admissions, set II, paras. 371.0, 371.1, 371.11.

66. Plaintiff's Admissions, set II, paras. 539.0-.3; Plaintiff's Admissions, set IV, para. 228.1.

67. Plaintiff's Admissions, set II, para. 370.1.

68. DX 5714, p. 3; Plaintiff's Admissions, set II, para. 370.2.

69. Plaintiff's Admissions, set II, para. 370.4; DX 5654: Webster dep., pp. 129-31; DX 5834: Hiniker dep., pp. 4-5; DX 7528: Mahoney dep., pp. 109-10; see also DX 6257: Gold dep., pp. 17-18; DX 9071: Crone dep., pp. 20-21.

70. See DX 4355, p. 15; Plaintiff's Admissions, set II, para. 370.9.

71. DX 5188, p. 2; Plaintiff's Admissions, set II, para. 364.1.

72. See, e.g., Plaintiff's Admissions, set II, para. 357.8.

73. Plaintiff's Admissions, set II, para. 368.2; see paras. 369.0-.18 for specific examples; see also DX 5654: Webster dep., pp. 67-69, 106-07.

74. Plaintiff's Admissions, set II, paras. 354.5, 364.3-.4.

75. Plaintiff's Admissions, set II, para. 366.0.

76. See O'Neill, Tr. 76243; PX 4829, p. 34; DX 5654: Webster dep., pp. 251-52.

77. See Withington, Tr. 56170-71; J. Jones, Tr. 78714.

78. Withington, Tr. 56174.

79. Withington, Tr. 58270-71.

80. See J. Jones, Tr. 78980-83 (Southern Railway's selection of IBM 7040/44); Plaintiff's Admissions, set IV, paras. 66.0-.2 (Knolls' and Bettis' selection of Philco 2000 Models 211/212).

81. See, e.g., Withington, Tr. 56174-75, 58229-30; DX 2583.

82. O'Neill, Tr. 76244-45, 76248.

83. O'Neill, Tr. 76249; see also Withington, Tr. 56026-27, 56189-90; J. Jones, Tr. 79036-39, 79044-49, 79622-24, 79880; Akers, Tr. 96667-70.

84. Wright, Tr. 13554-57; DX 862.

85. Wright, Tr. 13557.

86. DX 8224.

87. DX 3811.

88. Ibid.; DX 8224.

89. PX 353, p. 23; see also Oelman, Tr. 6129-30; Hindle, Tr. 7448-49; R. Bloch, Tr. 7761-62; R. Jones, Tr. 8865-67; McCollister, Tr. 9697; Hangen, Tr. 10415, 10423-24; Butters, Tr. 46654; Withington, Tr. 56556-58, 56580, 58571-72; PX 376, p. 19; PX 1077; DX 193, pp. 2-3; DX 1406; DX 3132, p. 2; DX 4321; DX 4806; DX 6257: Gold dep., pp. 96-97; DX 7523: Farrar dep., pp. 56-57; DX 7527: Slaughter dep., pp. 109-10; DX 7528: Mahoney dep., pp. 17-18; DX 9067: Higgins dep., pp. 104-05.

CHAPTER 13

1. DX 3811; DX 8224. The Census II count of EDP competitors was 420 in 1968, 617 in 1972.

2. McDonald, Tr. 2896; Spangle, Tr. 5087.

3. PX 5767, p. 5.

4. Guzy, Tr. 32537; Butters, Tr. 43719-20; Brown, Tr. 53169-70; Powers, Tr. 95413.

5. DX 4381; DX 4567; DX 5212.

6. PX 2463A, p. 2; PX 2474B, p. 1; Akers, Tr. 101360-62.

7. IBM's "net sales record increase," an internal measure based on "point" value, was negative in 1971, meaning that the volume, in points of monthly rental

dollars, of equipment being returned to IBM was greater than the point value of orders for new equipment – despite the introduction of System/370. PX 2896, p. 3; Akers, Tr. 101462-65.

8. PX 4505; DX 912A, p. 4; JX 38, p. 32. The prices compared are the purchase prices of each processor with the amount of main memory indicated, along with any console of features necessary for the CPU to operate. These and subsequent similar comparisons do not take into account the fact that the purchasing power of the dollar dropped significantly between 1964-65 and 1970-72.

9. PX 4505; JX 38, pp. 393-94.

10. DX 7858. The analysis mentioned Burroughs, CDC, DEC, GE, Honeywell, NCR, RCA, SDS, Univac, Century Data Systems/CalComp, Data Recording Instruments, Friden, GE, Hitachi, ISS, Linnel, Marshall, Memorex, Potter, Tracor-PGI, ICL, Talcott Leasing, Greyhound, Telex, Bryant, and MAI.

11. DX 1437, p. 1; DX 4106, pp. 78-80; JX 38, pp. 971-74.

12. Rooney, Tr. 12048-49.

13. DX 1437.

14. PX 4527; DX 912A; JX 38, p. 32.

15. PX 4527; DX 4742, pp. 522-24.

16. DX 4740: Evans, Tr. (Telex) 4010-11.

17. PX 4527; Haughton, Tr. 95021-22.

18. DX 4756A; JX 38, pp. 981-83.

19. DX 2137; DX 4253; DX 5155; DX 7169: Winger, Tr. (Telex) 5696-5718.

20. JX 38, pp. 988-92.

21. PX 3147.

22. PX 4528; JX 38, pp. 32, 79.

23. DX 4355; DX 4381; Powers, Tr. 95420.

24. Powers, Tr. 95824-26, 96041-42; PX 3158A; PX 3692A.

25. PX 4592; PX 6401; DX 4551.

26. Powers, Tr. 95424.

27. PX 4593.

28. JX 38, pp. 1049-57; PX 4529.

29. PX 3764, p. 28; Withington, Tr. 58563.

30. JX 38, pp. 1049-51.

31. PX 4505; PX 4531; DX 4740: Evans, Tr. (Telex) 4029-30.

32. DX 4740: Evans, Tr. (Telex) 3967-80.

33. DX 1976, p. 12.

34. DX 4740: Evans, Tr. (Telex) 3942-46.

35. JX 38, p. 1072; PX 4533.

36. Case, Tr. 74101-25.

37. PX 4534; PX 4537; JX 38, pp. 694-705, 1076.

38. *Transamerica Computer Company* v. *IBM*, 481 F. Supp. 965, 1007-08 (1979).

39. DX 14138.

40. The recording method was known as Group Code Recording (GCR). JX 38, pp. 1104-05.

41. PX 4538; Haughton, Tr. 94917-25.

42. PX 4539; Haughton, Tr. 94993-95.

43. DX 13962.

44. DX 12604, p. 10; DX 341, p. 3.

45. DX 8073, pp. 27-30.

46. PX 4536.

47. JX 39; Aweida, Tr. 49711-13.

48. PX 4762, pp. 193-214.

49. Aweida, Tr. 49698.

50. PX 5585; PX 5586; PX 5587; DX 14361.

51. CDC vs. IBM, filed in U.S. District Court for the District of Minnesota, Third Division, Civ. no. 3-68-312, dated December 11, 1968.

52. "Stipulation of Dismissal" (D. Minn. 3rd Div.) dated January 12, 1973.

53. "Agreement of Purchase," signed by William C. Norris and Frank T. Cary, dated January 12, 1973.

54. *Greyhound Computer* v. *IBM* filed in the Circuit Court for the 16th Judicial Circuit, Kane County, Illinois, Civ. no. 69-CI-9852, dated October 28, 1969.

55. *The Telex Corporation* v. *IBM* filed in the U.S. District Court for the Northern District of Oklahoma, Civ. no. 72-C-18, dated January 21, 1972.

56. *California Computer Products* v. *IBM*, filed in the U.S. District Court for the Central District of Calif., Civ. no. 73-2331-F, dated October 3, 1973.

57. *Hudson General Corporation* v. *IBM*, filed in the U.S. District Court for the Central District of California, Civ. no. 73-27960 JWC, dated Nov. 30, 1973.

58. *Marshall Industries* v. *IBM*, filed in the U.S. District Court for the Central District of Calif., Civ. no. C-73-3043, dated December 26, 1973.

59. *Memorex Corp.* v. *IBM*, filed in the U.S. District Court for the Northern District of California, Civ. no. C-73-2239-SC, dated December 14, 1973.

60. *Transamerica Corp.* v. *IBM*, filed in the U.S. District Court for the Northern

District of Calif., Civ. no. C-73-8132-WTS, dated October 15, 1973.

61. *Forro Precision Inc.* v. *IBM*, filed in the U.S. District Court for the Northern District of California, Civ. no. C-74-1653, dated August 6, 1974.

62. *Memory Technology Inc.* v. *IBM*, filed in the U.S. District Court for the District of Massachusetts, Civ. no. 74-5051-S, dated November 4, 1974.

63. *Sanders Associates Inc.* v. *IBM*, filed in the U.S. District Court for the District of New Hampshire, Civ. no. 75-14, dated January 7, 1975.

64. *U.S.* v. *IBM*, filed in U.S. District Court for the Southern District of New York, Civ. no. 69-200, dated January 17, 1969.

CHAPTER 14

1. PX 2606, p. 166; DX 10716.
2. PX 4537; PX 4966; DX 10265, pp. 18, 20.
3. Macdonald, Tr. 6914, 6892-93.
4. DX 3269; DX 10265, p. 22.
5. DX 10716, p. 13.
6. Jones, Tr. 79062-63.
7. DX 3292A; DX 10265.
8. PX 355, p. 37; DX 306; Norris, Tr. 5893.
9. PX 355, p. 38. Norris, CDC's chief executive officer, testified that a substantial portion of the Cybers delivered in 1972 and thereafter went to new customers who had previously used the EDP equipment of other manufacturers. Tr. 6076-77; JX 24.
10. PX 4839, p. 24; DX 297; Norris, Tr. 6021.
11. Brown, Tr. 51008-09, 51486-89.
12. Brown, Tr. 52598.
13. PX 4753; Brown, Tr. 51003, 51083-84.
14. Brown, Tr. 51009, 52616-23.
15. Brown, Tr. 51003, 51456-58, 52048-62, 52084-89.
16. DX 306; DX 435.
17. DX 510; DX 511; DX 512.
18. PX 377A; Hindle, Tr. 7430, 7354-55. DEC's 1973 Annual Report stated, "The PDP-11/45 has proven popular with end-users as an alternative to large-scale computers." DX 510, p. 6.
19. Hindle, Tr. 7332.

20. DX 9406, p. 4.
21. DX 514; DX 9406; Hindle, Tr. 7360, 7419-21.
22. DX 514, p. 6; DX 8224, p. 142.
23. DX 122, p. 33.
24. DX 122, p. 6.
25. DX 163, p. 34; see also DX 10031, p. 32; DX 14409.
26. DX 127.
27. DX 10031, p. 32.
28. DX 165, p. 15.
29. DX 341, p. 2; DX 373, pp. 3, 4.
30. DX 339.
31. DX 354, p. 3.
32. DX 340A; DX 341, p. 17; DX 398, pp. 5, 13.
33. Oelman, Tr. 6163; see also DX 398, p. 4.
34. DX 341; DX 375; DX 398; DX 409; DX 425A.
35. DX 341, p. 3.
36. DX 341, p. 3; DX 354, p. 7.
37. DX 354, p. 7.
38. DX 8060, p. 1.
39. DX 9, p. 1. Emphasis in original.
40. DX 14225; DX 14226; DX 14227; DX 14283; DX 14382.
41. PX 406; DX 63.
42. DX 68, p. 12; McDonald, Tr. 4045-46.
43. DX 86A; McDonald, Tr. 4056-64.
44. DX 3292A.
45. DX 12288, p. 15.
46. DX 12291.
47. DX 12287; DX 12288.
48. DX 14233.
49. DX 12290, p. 9.
50. DX 12291; DX 14235.
51. DX 306; DX 12304.
52. DX 12597; DX 12304.
53. Control Data in 1977 made peripherals for all of the 25 largest "minicomputer" companies in the United States, among others. DX 12303.
54. DX 12597; Norris, Tr. 5655-57.
55. DX 11342; DX 11365; DX 13210; Brown, Tr. 51267-69, 51433-37, 51456-58, 51601-03, 51662-63. CDC's answer to IBM's 3850 mass storage system was mentioned above. Versions of most of these plug-compatible devices were also used on CDC's own systems and were marketed on an OEM basis to other manufacturers.
56. DX 12302, p. 9.
57. DX 3103A. The CYBER 170 was partly funded and developed in Canada as a

cooperative program with the Canadian government.

58. DX 2435, p. 5.
59. DX 2597, p. 2.
60. DX 14104.
61. DX 510; DX 14125; DX 15126; DX 14127. In 1973 IBM lost a System/370 bid for a reservation system for Ramada Inns to the DECsystem 10. Akers, Tr. 96730.
62. DX 13285. See also Hindle, Tr. 7440.
63. DX 2861A; DX 13289.
64. DX 509A, p. 7.
65. DX 3524; DX 2750; DX 12321; DX 13297; DX 14393.
66. DX 14108; DX 14109.
67. Hindle, Tr. 7444-45; DX 510.
68. DX 165, p. 14; DX 12342, p. 3.
69. DX 12339; DX 12340; DX 12341; DX 12342. MOX/LSI stands for Metal Oxide Semiconductor/Large-Scale Integration.
70. DX 3355A, p. 14; DX 12340; DX 12342; DX 14198.
71. DX 14111.
72. DX 14252.
73. DX 14128.
74. DX 368, p. 19; DX 14088, pp. 3, 25.
75. DX 2780, p. 9.
76. DX 14086; DX 14087.
77. DX 14088; DX 12259.
78. DX 14093.
79. DX 14122; DX 13786.
80. DX 14122.
81. DX 13786.
82. DX 12384; DX 14420.
83. DX 14129.
84. DX 62, p. 10; DX 12381, p. 15.
85. DX 12381, p. 15; DX 13021, p. 9.
86. By the end of 1974 Sperry had realized $61 million from bookings of Univac computers to RCA equipment users, $27 million from Univac disk and tape products marketed to RCA users, and cumulative revenues – in sales, rentals, and maintenance – of $370 million from RCA's installed equipment. DX 68, pp. 11-12; McDonald, Tr. 3900-03, 3908-09.
87. DX 12381; DX 13022; DX 13020.
88. Xerox acquired SDS in a stock-for-stock, pooling-of-interest transaction. Xerox exchanged nearly 10 million shares of its stock, then valued at approximately $980 million. That represented nearly 100 times

SDS's 1968 earnings and eight times the book value of its assets at the time of the acquisition. DX 45, pp. 2-3.
89. PX 5009, p. 16; DX 13400, p. 34.
90. According to witnesses from XDS: Currie, Tr. 15377-83; DX 1000. The phrase "tired iron" was used to describe the XDS line in 1971: its price/performance was no longer competitive. Cohen, Tr. 14580-84.
91. Currie, Tr. 15377-84.
92. Currie, Tr. 15371-72; DX 7929, p. 5.
93. DX 7929, p. 5; see also Currie, Tr. 15371-72.
94. Currie, Tr. 15330-32, 15304-06. This reorganization was similar to the way in which Sperry Rand had organized itself during 1959-64 – and produced similar results.
95. PX 5008, pp. 10-11; see also DX 13405, p. 8.
96. PX 5029, p. 31.
97. Ibid.; DX 13945, p. 7.
98. DX 12089.
99. DX 13402, pp. 34-35; DX 13405, p. 12; DX 13407, pp. 10, 32; DX 13409, p. 9.
100. DX 12090; see also DX 13408.
101. DX 13408; DX 13409.

CHAPTER 15

1. DX 1699; DX 1780; DX 4242, p. 8; DX 5155, pp. 44-45.
2. PX 5602; DX 4240.
3. DX 4242, p. 6 (paraphrased).
4. DX 1926; DX 4192; DX 4739: Wilmer, Tr. (Telex) 4266, 4292-93.
5. DX 1532; DX 1720; DX 1758; DX 4181; DX 4240; James, Tr. 35092-98; Navas, Tr. 40243.
6. The financial data from 1970 and 1971 included "front-loading" of income that accounting experts then found improper under generally accepted accounting principles. In 1971 and 1972 Telex began to change its accounting methods; had it used appropriate accounting methods to begin with, its reversals beginning in 1971 would not have appeared so precipitous. Briloff, Tr. 80723-24, 80992-99, 81197-202; Davidson, Tr. 98713-29.
7. DX 4250; DX 4242; DX 5602; DX 5603.
8. DX 1748A.

9. DX 1765. See also DX 1884; DX 1736; DX 1948; DX 1949; DX 4742, p. 115.

10. DX 1732; DX 4279.

11. PX 5605, p. 4; see also PX 5604; DX 13690, p. 18.

12. DX 1690, p. 6.

13. DX 13689; DX 13690.

14. DX 13689, p. 5.

15. PX 4705; PX 4708A, pp. 8, 15-18; Aweida, Tr. 49099-100.

16. PX 4699; DX 2191, p. 17; Aweida, Tr. 49781-83.

17. PX 4699; PX 4700; PX 4701; PX 4703.

18. PX 4700; PX 4701; PX 4539; DX 1437; DX 10647.

19. DX 12607; DX 12608.

20. DX 12607. p. 24; PX 4704.

21. PX 4704; DX 12608, p. 19.

22. DX 12607, p. 22; DX 12608, p. 7.

23. PX 3698; DX 1636; Spitters, Tr. 42901-02; Saalfeld, Tr. 44764-69.

24. DX 1526.

25. DX 1269; DX 1270; DX 1271; Spitters, Tr. 43095-96, 43106-07.

26. DX 1269; Spitters, Tr. 55223-26, 54295-98, 54316-26.

27. DX 1282; Spitters, Tr. 55316-20.

28. DX 1461; DX 1465; DX 1470; DX 1481.

29. DX 1271; DX 1272; DX 2560; Spitters, Tr. 55090-98, 55181-86, 55328-30.

30. DX 1319; DX 3063A; DX 1696A; DX 2469; DX 1629; DX 1272; DX 2504A.

31. Saalfeld, Tr. 44674-76; Rice, Tr. 45281-86.

32. DX 13945, p. 15.

33. DX 1273; DX 1274.

34. DX 1635; DX 2351. Winchester disk drives were replaceable units that were fully enclosed, having permanent read/write heads included with the disks.

35. DX 1635, p. 8.

36. DX 13397; DX 13681.

37. *Datamation*, June 1981, p. 10. The Business Systems Division was dropped in 1980.

38. AMS obtained $500,000 in start-up private financing from the Diebold Technology Venture Fund, Inc., and Value Line Development Capital Corporation. The management and sales force at AMS included many former IBM employees. DX 1964,

pp. 5, 10-11; Andreini, Tr. 46894.

39. DX 1965; DX 1966; DX 1967. AMS had announced its first memory product in December 1969. It was a very high-speed memory intended for functions such as buffering, main memory, high-speed control, and register replacements. DX 1964, pp. 7-9.

40. DX 1965; DX 1966; DX 1967; DX 1968.

41. DX 1969; DX 1971A; Andreini, Tr. 48822-32.

42. DX 1971A; DX 14083, pp. 1, 6.

43. PX 4504; DX 1911; DX 9416A.

44. PX 2685, pp. 49, 57; JX 3; Jakes, Tr. 50193-96.

45. DX 14363; Enfield, Tr. 20136-37, 20148-49, 20167-69, 20186-87.

46. DX 14048; DX 2646A; JX 3; JX 38, pp. 971-74; Enfield, Tr. 20800-08; Friedman, Tr. 50434-36.

47. As demonstrated by IBM's Significant Wins and Losses Reports for 1974 and 1975. PX 6467, vols. 1 and 2.

48. Briloff, Tr. 80724.

49. DX 9416A; Spain, Tr. 88767-68.

50. Write-offs were especially heavy in 1972-73. For example, Diebold wrote off more than $46 million; Boothe, more than $50 million. DX 9436.

51. DX 9416A, pp. 3, 5.

52. Chemical Bank received 12 proposals from leasing companies in 1977 for a single 3032 acquisition, for terms of three, four, and seven years. Welch, Tr. 75270-73.

53. DX 9099; DX 14211; DX 14396; DX 14398; Rice, Tr. 45246-47.

54. DX 14340; DX 14397; DX 14389. Comdisco's revenues increased from $1 million in 1970 to $225 million in 1979. DX 12295.

CHAPTER 16

1. One example was Four Phase, a terminal manufacturer that was one of the first to put processing capability in the terminal itself. DX 11493. EDP terminals, including many for special kinds of applications as well as for data display and intelligent interactive processing, were offered by many more suppliers and in more varieties than we can catalog here. Only a sample of the notable new terminal offerings is given

in this chapter.

2. DX 13886; DX 14215; DX 14419
3. DX 13886; DX 14215.
4. DX 13886.
5. DX 12308; DX 3527.
6. DX 11398; DX 12309; DX 12310; DX 14223A.
7. DX 13945; DX 14708.
8. DX 6926, p. 20; see also DX 11610.
9. DX 14708; DX 11609; DX 12938, p. 19.
10. DX 6926, p. 20. In the early 1970s Hewlett-Packard had acquired 2314-type disk drives from ISS.
11. DX 12935, pp. 9-12.
12. DX 3704, pp. 2, 40-43; McGrew, Tr. 76413 ff.
13. DX 14219, pp. 6, 37.
14. DX 14219, pp. 3, 36-39.
15. DX 12998, pp. 2-14.
16. DX 12997; DX 12999. In March 1980 Prime reported that about half of its installed computers were used in scientific/ engineering computation, and the remainder for interactive business data processing. DX 14219.
17. DX 14228. These were Prime's own marketing claims.
18. DX 11907; DX 14272; see also DX 9407 for IBM's view.
19. DX 12367; DX 12369; DX 12371; DX 12372.
20. DX 12996, p. 16.
21. DX 12368, pp. 12-13.
22. DX 12993, p. 8.
23. DX 11886; DX 12372.
24. DX 3899; DX 3993; DX 4909; DX 14217.
25. DX 12333, p. 6.
26. This claim is from Harris's announcement: DX 12923, p. 2.
27. DX 12333; DX 12910.
28. DX 8224; DX 12405; DX 13945. Wang Laboratories is not to be confused with Wangco, acquired by Perkin-Elmer in 1976.
29. DX 12403; DX 12405, p. 16; DX 12075.
30. DX 12405, pp. 18-19.
31. DX 12395, p. 31.
32. DX 12395, p. 5.
33. DX 13918, pp. 15-16; DX 12395, pp. 5, 12; DX 13030, p. 7.
34. DX 12312; DX 12313; DX 12905.
35. DX 12495.

36. DX 12311; DX 12314.
37. DX 4354.
38. DX 3525; DX 4354.
39. DX 12268, p. 4; DX 3525; DX 9410; DX 13076; DX 14344.
40. DX 12268, p. 9.
41. DX 14117.
42. DX 14118.
43. DX 2269, p. 1.
44. DX 14348.
45. DX 13721; DX 14366.
46. DX 14404; DX 13249.
47. DX 11819; DX 14383; DX 14405.
48. DX 14354.
49. DX 13895; DX 13896.
50. DX 12030; DX 12032; DX 12036.
51. DX 12344, p. 21; DX 14255; DX 14256; DX 14257; DX 14258; DX 14259.
52. DX 12343; DX 12602; DX 3303A.
53. DX 11720; DX 11721.
54. Brueck, Tr. 22050-56; DX 12626.
55. DX 12365, p. 15.
56. DX 12364, p. 17; DX 12365, p. 3; DX 12366, p. 16; DX 13682, p. 13.
57. DX 11827; DX 14117; DX 13751.
58. PX 6467, vol. 5, January, p. 14. IBM's loss of this business represented a potential of about $1.2 million per month in rentals.
59. DX 13107; Akers, Tr. 97040.
60. DX 12273, pp. 13-14.
61. Based on a report in *Datamation*, DX 13101. See also DX 12275.
62. DX 11165.
63. DX 13894.
64. DX 14443, p. 13.
65. DX 14443; DX 13894.
66. DX 14443; DX 13894.
67. DX 14443, p. 16.
68. DX 14248.
69. DX 14443, p. 16.
70. DX 12702 (FCC decision), p. 38.
71. DX 12702, pp. 39-40.
72. DX 12702, p. 68.
73. DX 12702, p. 117-23.
74. DX 13662, pp. 21, 28.
75. Welke, Tr. 17167-68, 17176-81, 17400.
76. Enfield, Tr. 20167.
77. DX 1072, pp. 8, 23; DX 11706; DX 14237.
78. DX 12771; DX 12772.
79. DX 2642A.
80. DX 12644, pp. 5-9.
81. DX 12641, p. 90.

ABOUT THE AUTHORS

FRANKLIN M. FISHER is Professor of Economics at Massachusetts Institute of Technology.

Professor Fisher has published extensively in economics, specializing in economic theory, econometrics and industrial organization. He is the author or co-author of eight other books, including *Folded, Spindled, and Mutilated: Economic Analysis and U.S. v. IBM.*

RICHARD B. MANCKE is Professor of International Economic Affairs at The Fletcher School of Law and Diplomacy, Tufts University.

Professor Mancke is the author of four books as well as of articles appearing in several professional journals. He specializes in industrial organization and energy economics and has served as a consultant to governmental and private organizations.

JAMES W. McKIE has been Professor of Economics at the University of Texas at Austin since 1971. He had previously served on the faculties of Vanderbilt University, Harvard University, and Williams College.

Professor McKie is a specialist in industrial economics and the economics of resources. His publications include articles and reports on industrial organization and antitrust policy. He has been consultant to private industry and research organizations, and to Federal and State government agencies and commissions.